W9-DBY-741

Muhlenberg College - Library
2400 Chew Street
Allentown, PA 18104-5586   65650

Equity and Efficiency in Economic Development

Muhlenberg College Library
2400 Chew Street
Allentown, PA 18104-5586

WITHDRAWN

Equity and Efficiency in Economic Development

*Essays in Honour of
Benjamin Higgins*

EDITED BY
DONALD J. SAVOIE
AND
IRVING BRECHER

McGill-Queen's University Press
Montreal & Kingston • London • Buffalo

© McGill-Queen's University Press 1992
ISBN 0-7735-0847-3

Legal deposit third quarter 1992
Bibliothèque nationale du Québec

Printed in the United States on acid-free paper

This book has been published with the help of a grant from
the Institut canadien de recherche sur le développement
régional

Canadian Cataloguing in Publication Data

Main entry under title:
   Equity and efficiency in economic development:
   essays in honour of Benjamin Higgins
   ISBN 0-7735-0847-3
   1. Economic development. 2. Economic policy.
   I. Savoie, Donald J., 1947– . II. Brecher,
   Irving, 1923– . III. Higgins, Benjamin,
   1912– .
   HD82.E68 1993   338.9   C92-090375-4

Published simultaneously in the United Kingdom
by Intermediate Technology Publications.

Composition in Times Roman by
Acappella, Sebright, Ontario, Canada

Contents

Tables and Figures

FIGURES

Preface

Few things have given me more personal pleasure than seeing this book through to publication. Ben Higgins is a close friend. He has given me and the Canadian Institute for Research on Regional Development at the Université de Moncton a great deal. He has been and is a teacher, a writer, a colleague, a role model, a source of inspiration, and above all a deeply committed friend to me and to everyone at the institute. We know full well that we will never be able to repay him fully. Indeed, I can hardly imagine how we could begin to thank him for everything he has done for the institute. This book, then, is a small token of our deep appreciation for Ben Higgins, for his work, for his contribution to the institute, and for his friendship.

At the time he was awarded an honorary degree by McGill University, Ben Higgins was described as a "one of a kind. The economics profession has never produced his likeness before, and one can safely predict that no way will be found to clone him in the years and decades ahead."

The accomplishments of Ben Higgins the economist are well known. He was nominated for the Nobel prize and is the author of twenty books, two dozen major reports, and over one hundred articles. His widely read magnum opus *Economic Development: Problems, Principles and Policies* is a standard work in the field. Still, Ben Higgins has never been content simply to sit back and rest on his laurels and past successes. Nor, for that matter, has Ben been content to walk away from the fray and only write books and scholarly papers. He has been an adviser to the Canadian government on numerous occasions and has been called upon to work on economic development plans in over forty developed and less-developed countries.

Ben is equally well known as a teacher. He has taught economics in some of the leading English- and French-language universities in North America – notably Harvard, Yale, the Massachusetts Institute of Technology, Texas, California-Berkeley, Minnesota, McGill, Université de Montréal, and Université d'Ottawa. Among his students have been leading figures in politics, the public service, private enterprise, and the academic world, including President John F. Kennedy and his brother Robert, US attorney-general; Abdel Meguid, past deputy prime minister of Egypt; Edward van Roy, head of the social development division of the United Nations Economic and Social Commission for Asia and the Pacific; Beni Widjojo, director of the multinational corporations division of the United Nations; Sylvia Ostry, chairman of the Economic Council of Canada and director of the economic division of the Organization for Economic Co-operation and Development; Angus Maddison, who held the same position with the OECD; Helen Hughes, former director of research in the World Bank and now director of the National Centre for Development Studies at the Australian National University; Eric Kierans, Canadian minister of communications and postmaster general; Tom Asimikopulos, Irving Brecher, and Jack Weldon, all professors of economics at McGill; Robert McIntosh, executive vice-president of the Bank of Nova Scotia; and John Chipman, professor of economics at the University of Minnesota.

Ben has also been associated with leading thinkers of this century. Among his mentors were Lionel Robbins and Friedrich von Hayek at the London School of Economics, and Alvin Hansen and Joseph Schumpeter at Harvard. Among his acquaintances were John Maynard Keynes and Bertrand Russell; among his close friends were Gunnar and Alva Myrdal and John Kenneth Galbraith. A list of fellow students at LSE, Harvard, and Minnesota reads like a Who's Who of contemporary economists. Some of them are contributors to this volume. Others, whose prior commitments prevented them from taking part, are Paul Samuelson, Robert Solow, and Evsey Domar. All the authors in this book are internationally renowned scholars, and all responded quickly and positively when asked if they would be interested in contributing a paper to honour Ben.

This did not surprise me. No one remains indifferent to Ben's lust for life, his wit, his charm, and his genuine hand of friendship. Irving Brecher once wrote of the "lighter side of the Higgins legend." It is this aspect of Ben that has made him a friend to so many in so many places throughout the world. His love of knowledge and of people and their distinguishing characteristics is contagious.

We also have come to know, at the institute that Ben is completely unpretentious and remains totally unimpressed by the material world. Every year he spends several months at the institute as a visiting fellow. Every year he happily accepts the most modest of university or private lodgings. Every year he sets out to visit isolated communities in Atlantic Canada, and every time he comes back with spell-binding stories about the people he has met and the landscape he has admired.

Yet when it comes to ideas, though he is always courteous, Ben never hesitates to disagree strongly whenever he feels the need. He has had plenty to disagree with of late. As his chapter in this book makes clear, he never jumped on the neoclassical bandwagon. For him, government must continue to play an important role, not just to lessen the sting of economic misfortune but also to nudge along the pace and place of economic activity. Ben is also willing to take a firm and decisive position when necessary. A few years ago, the publisher of a manuscript he and I had put together wrote to say that he had some serious problems with my preface and suggested that it be dropped altogether. I felt rather strongly about the preface because in it I had written about the home of my ancestors – the conference that gave rise to the book had been held overlooking the Grand Pré area from which the Acadians had been deported over two hundred years before. I sent a copy of the publisher's letter to Ben in Australia. A week or so later, I received a copy of his answer to the publisher. It read simply: "Dear Sir – No preface, no book – Ben Higgins." Nothing else was needed and the preface stayed.

Ben Higgins has steadfastly refused to retire. He has held several academic positions since he left the Université d'Ottawa as professor emeritus in 1979. In 1981 he was appointed director of the Centre for Applied Studies in Development at the University of the South Pacific, in Fiji. In 1984 he was appointed fellow of the Canadian Institute for Research on Regional Development at the Université de Moncton, a position he still retains.

What, one may well ask, motivates Ben Higgins to continue participating fully in the intellectual life of his profession? His love of life and of ideas is one answer. But there is more. You need not spend much time with Ben before you notice his deep commitment to public service. For example, in the 1960s he left the prestigious and lucrative Ashbel Smith Professorship of Economics at the University of Texas – a large world-class and well-endowed university – for a position at the French-language Université de Montréal because he sensed that the unity of his own country was on shaky ground and that Canada was about to enter a very turbulent period. History, of course, now tells us that he was right. He felt a deep need to do his bit to keep the country united. He did so in many varied ways, including as a contributor to the Royal Commission on Bilingualism and Biculturalism, as a key author of an economic development plan for Quebec, and as an adviser to Canadian governments. His return to Canada in 1967 was due in large measure to his conviction that regional tensions were on the increase and were perilously close to debilitating the country. This time he fears that the growing problem of regional economic disparities and our apparent inability to deal with the matter not only threaten national unity itself but also constitute a crippling stumbling block to a sense of national Canadian identity. History, I fear, will once again prove him correct.

Ben worries deeply about Canada's unity, the plight of less-developed countries, and difficult economic issues facing Western industrialized countries. He has contributed more than his share to a clearer understanding of many of these complex issues. He still asks nothing more than an opportunity to continue to contribute. He believes that he was given a special intellectual gift, and he is deeply committed to assisting humanity.

Spring is always a welcome season at the Canadian Institute for Research on Regional Development. This is true not simply because the harsh Canadian winter has once again come to an end but because we know that Ben Higgins will be with us for several months. The pleasure is greater still because Jean, his wife, now accompanies him for his full stay at the institute. Everyone here cherishes the pleasure of their company every spring and summer and, in particular, at the annual lobster dinner we always organize in their honour. Jean is a delightful person, as charming as Ben, and a powerful intellect in her own right. I have no doubt that Ben could not have contributed as much to his profession as he has done over the years without Jean at his side. And so, in preparing this book to honour Ben, we never lost sight of Jean's presence and support.

Donald J. Savoie
Université de Moncton

Equity and Efficiency in Economic Development

Introduction

DONALD J. SAVOIE and
IRVING BRECHER

Economists have often lamented that they are unable to conduct controlled experiments in the way that natural scientists do. Yet the twentieth century will surely go down in economic annals as a century of unprecedented economic and social experimentation. Today, economists can look back at a series of extraordinary experiments that, if not exactly controlled, are nonetheless highly revealing. The first half of the century saw the launching of the Soviet experiment with communism, the brief and disastrous experiment with fascism and the corporate state in Italy and Germany, and the well-intentioned but ill-fated experiment with the League of Nations. After the Second World War, the international community once again experimented with a supranational body in the form of the United Nations, and the liberation of a host of Third World countries resulted in a virtual global laboratory as the emerging countries experimented with different blends of socialism, with capitalism and the free market, and with elements of their traditional cultures. The industrialized countries helped them, experimenting with bilateral aid in conjunction with eager promotion of their own paradigms and suggestions for development strategies. Meanwhile, throughout the century, the countries of the Western world have continued their unceasing, restless search for just the right blend of free market and management in their own mixed economies.

Ironically, when the collapses or near-collapses of the economies in the Soviet Union and Eastern Europe enhanced the allure of Western systems, the Western economies were, in fact, in critical disarray. There had been a swing to the right in these countries well before the fall of socialism, but recent experiences in countries with mixed economies, such as the United States, the United Kingdom, Argentina, Australia, Canada, and New Zealand, have shown that the transition from a regulated welfare economy to a free-market economy is neither simple nor painless. Small wonder that socialist countries find their transition even more difficult. To borrow a phrase from Ben Higgins, the way to a free-market economy is a "road paved with vicious circles."

Never in human history have various economic *systems* been so visibly, vocally, and audibly on trial as in the present era. We are also learning that large and unified nation-states may not be the "climax" condition of *political* development after all. All over the world – in Africa, in Canada, in Cyprus, in Eastern Europe, in Spain, in Sri Lanka – particular ethnic, linguistic, and religious groups are clamouring for independence. The USSR has collapsed. In addition to the experimentation with economic systems, we may be on the verge of an era of breakup of nation-states as well.

In choosing a theme for this volume, drafting an outline of its contents, and selecting contributors, the editors had in mind the cataclysmic state of the world and the related uncertainties in the discipline of economics. We wanted a theme that would allow the contributors enough rein to express their own views on the current soul-searching about scope and method, shifts in direction, conflicts on basic policy issues, and the increased willingness to experiment and the related confusion that the extraordinary state of the world has injected into the economics discipline at the present time. We wanted a subject broad enough to encompass the whole wide range of Ben Higgins's interests in the course of his long and varied career. We also wanted the contributors to include all major schools of economic thought – right, left, and "extreme centre" (to use André Gunder Frank's felicitous phrase). Finally, we wanted contributors who were not only friends and either former colleagues or former students of Ben Higgins, leaders in their special fields, and interested in policy issues, but who were also genuinely interested in human welfare, as distinct from science for science's sake.

The balance between "pure science" and moral philosophy varies from essay to essay, but both are present in each. It is also of interest that while "development " is one of the key words in the book's title, *not a single one* of the authors interpreted "economic development" to mean an exclusive concern for the problems of the less-developed countries. The field of "development economics" is at last returning to what it was in the works of such scholars as Schumpeter, Ayres, Veblen, and the classical school: a general interest in what makes economies grow or progress, stagnate or decline. With the global economy and the economics discipline both in such a yeasty state, it is not to be expected that the essays will display a high degree of ideological unanimity. On the contrary, ideological rifts are apparent. Indeed, given the breadth of the spectrum of basic political views held by the authors, it is remarkable that there is so much agreement on the fundamental issues raised by this volume.

Let us now briefly summarize the main points made in each of the essays. The reader can then more conveniently draw comparisons and contrasts among them. But such short summaries are likely to satisfy no one, and least of all the authors. They are in no sense a substitute for reading the chapters themselves.

HIGGINS

In his introductory essay, Benjamin Higgins makes the point that neoclassical economics, which is often presented as free from value judgments, is in fact full of them, although they are often unexpressed. The case for the superior efficiency of the market economy, for example, rests on the staggering value judgment that "a good society" is one that allows individuals to do what they want to do, including buying the goods and services they want, within constraints imposed by limited resources and the wishes of other individuals to do and buy what they want. He agrees that competitive markets limit the scope for gross misuse of resources, and would leave most routine decisions about allocation of resources among various goods and services to the market. He also agrees with Robin Marris that the desire of managers to see their enterprises grow curtails damaging use of monopoly power. He denies, however, that "the market" guarantees the achievement of any "maximum" or "optimum" that is truly significant in terms of human welfare. He itemizes important factors for human welfare that the market leaves out, and maintains that the most important factors for welfare – and thus for "development" defined as improvements in human welfare – are efficient collective (public) choices, rapid and efficient adjustment to change, innovative technological progress, and Schumpeterian entrepreneurship. He considers management of private enterprises to be deficient in all these respects, especially in less-developed countries (LDCs), and insists on the need for the injection of the requisite range of expertise into the decision-making process.

BOULDING

Kenneth Boulding starts by asking if the world will be better off in the year 2000 or 2050 than it is now, and suggests that we have no way of knowing. Selfishness (which is the basis of the supposed "efficiency" of the market economy) is merely the zero point on the scale from benevolence to malevolence, and all three exist. One may think of equality, equity, and a minimum standard as three alternative goals. The minimum standard has existed since the Elizabethan poor laws and is attractive as a social objective. Certainly, the abolition of poverty is a condition for "a better world." But how to get rid of poverty?

There are two broad alternatives: redistribute income and wealth, or develop poor countries, regions, sectors, and societies. Poverty is the result of low productivity rather than exploitation, so the development alternative is more effective. But what kind of development? The non-imperialist countries (Sweden, Switzerland) have actually done better than the imperialist ones. Britain and France (and one could add Holland, Spain, and Portugal) have developed more rapidly since giving up their empires. Countries such as Japan that have stressed education have done well. Development is not likely to take place where wealth is concentrated in the hands of a small landlord class and education is controlled by an authoritarian church. Socialist ideology has not turned out very well; nor has military capitalism. Centrally planned economies of left or right are the enemy of liberation; self-pity and envy are the enemy of development.

There is no such thing as a "Third World"; every country, even every region within each country, is different. "It is easy to mess up an eco- system by distorting the price structure, which governments seem to like to do." Poverty or affluence is more a matter of capital than of income; the feedback system in which capital produces income which produces more capital which produces more income is a prime source of inequality. But human capital – body and mind – is a vital part of the total stock of capital. But except in the case of slavery, human capital cannot be redistributed. The solution lies in developing human capital; development is largely a matter of learning. Agents are the poor people themselves, the multinationals, and international organizations such as the United Nations (although the history of UNESCO is depressing). Most effective may be the non-government organizations.

ROSTOW

Walt Rostow's essay has tremendous sweep, covering both events and ideas since the late eighteenth century. Consequently, it is a particularly difficult piece to summarize. He begins with the "founding fathers," David Hume and Adam Smith. Both were deeply troubled by gross inequality of income distri- bution and both were committed to justice. Yet both also believed in more competition and less bureaucracy. How can the two be reconciled? In their efforts to do so, they "found a substantial legitimate role for government."

The increasing domination of economics by the neoclassical school after 1870 actually coincided with the growth of social expenditures. Even Walras, perhaps the purest of the first generation of neoclassical economists, advo- cated social and economic reform. Rostow quotes John H. Williams, a lead- ing neoclassical economist of the interwar generation, with approval. "The classical theory assumes as fixed, for purposes of reasoning, the very things which, in my view, should be chief objects of study." Williams's remark could be said of mainstream economics as a whole in the wake of the revol- ution of 1870 and after. Yet economists "did not abandon the right to hold strong personal views on issues of policy and social justice." Pigou conducted a "strongly felt but well mannered crusade" for social reform, and poverty was Marshall's chief concern. The growth of social expenditures after the Second World War proceeded quite independently of the theoretical refinement of welfare economics during the same period. In the 1970s and 1980s socialism lost ground because, while capitalism's performance was not "particularly glamorous," that of socialism was "markedly worse" (a point which André Gunder Frank makes equally strongly).

Rostow maintains that there are three links between welfare *economies* (as distinct from welfare economics) and development analysis and policy. First, economists like Gunnar Myrdal, who promoted the welfare state in industrialized countries, also insisted on the need to improve the lot of poor people in poor countries. Second, towards the end of the 1960s there came a revolt against orthodox development economics in the form of the basic-needs strategy. Third was the thrust for a new international economic order and the related "structuralist" approach. The "revolt from the left" was sometimes a bit fuzzy and provided neoclassicists with "a splendid gallery" of figures to caricature, but "those who argued that there was an important role for public policy in the early phases of development operated from premises rooted in Hume and Smith, Marshall and Pigou, and their case was made with some precision." Rosenstein-Rodan's theory of the "Big Push" is a case in point. Development economists as a whole have been against *dirigisme*. "The bloated public sectors, which have been a legitimate target of critics – neoclassical and otherwise – must be viewed as the outcome of an historical process rather than misguided development theories." Politics are more important than economics in LDCs. Many measures for equity (educating children of the poor) promote efficiency as well. "Behind it all was an acute awareness of the brutal human consequences of poverty, and of the more civil and freer life of widened choices economic development could bring." The next phase of development "will require, on a global scale, the maximum expression of the quality David Hume and Adam Smith called sympathy."

SPULBER

And what of the other side of the coin: equity, efficiency, and development under socialism? Nicolas Spulber answers this question in terms of the experience of the now-defunct Soviet Union. According to Marxists, capitalism is a system of inequality and exploitation. With socialism, exploitation ceases; but, Spulber points out, Marx never argued that socialism would bring equality. Income received is proportional to labour supplied, with due allowance for differences in quality of labour. The "right" of equal exchange is in reality "an unequal right for unequal labour." Soviet leaders claimed that socialism was "completed" in the USSR in 1937 and that the Soviet

Union was in "the prolonged stage of developed socialism," which retains the "fundamental socialist principle" of "unequal right for unequal labour."

Under Stalin the command economy was extended to all economic sectors, and this system continued until March 1985, when Gorbachev launched his program of "restructuring." Structural change that occurred in the USSR between 1940 and 1985 was of the same sort that took place earlier in the industrialized capitalist countries (ICCs), but employment was still relatively high in agriculture and relatively low in services. The Soviet Union still lagged technologically, equipment was obsolete, there was much disguised unemployment, and productivity was declining. There was "retooling" on a massive scale, with consequent technological unemployment. Income differences were increasing. There was a heavy burden of party bureaucrats, which Gorbachev wanted to reduce. The inequalities in income bore little relationship to productivity. Within job categories, however, wages were relatively equal. Gorbachev wanted to increase margins to provide incentives. There were still serious lags in agriculture and housing. "The shattered illusions about growth, efficiency, and full employment have fallen to the ground, along with the dashed hopes about 'socialism with a human face,' socialist abundance, socialist 'equitable' (meaning egalitarian) distribution of income, and idyllic 'social justice.' "

ADELMAN

What does the record show regarding equity and development? Irma Adelman tackles this question once again in her essay. She begins with a reference to "Kuznets optimism," the thesis that as development takes place, equality first diminishes but then increases, following a U-shaped curve. This optimism was shattered by the discovery by the International Labour Organization (ILO) that rapid industrialization and growth bring alarming increases in unemployment. The Adelman-Morris study of 1971 confirmed the U-hypothesis, but the U was rather flat.

The present essay indicates that "for an average non-Communist developing country, there was a steady increase in within-country inequality over two decades (1960–80)." For 1970–80, faster growth brought a declining share to the poorest 20 percent, the poorest 40 percent, and the middle 40 to 80 percent. The shares of the richest 20, 10, 5, and 1 percent all rose steadily with faster growth of per capita gross national product (GNP) in 1960–80. For 1970–80, the results were "less stark."

There is a positive relationship between the level of development and the rate of growth. The effect of increasing national indebtedness on the share of rich and poor "depends on the projects and policies the new debt finances." Neglect of agriculture reduces the share of the poor and increases the share of the rich; industrialization does the same. Increased literacy and primary education favour the poor, expansion of secondary education favours the rich. As means to offset the negative impact of accelerated development on the share of the poor, hope seems in lie in rural development and a "big push" in primary education.

MUSGRAVE

Richard Musgrave observes that equity in fiscal policy is more important in poor countries than in rich ones, but so is the need to avoid the growth-deterring effects of equity-based policies. There are two concepts of equity in taxation: that tax burdens should equal benefits received; and that tax burdens should reflect ability to pay. The first fits the basic philosophy of the market, the second is more closely related to the "concern of this chapter [Musgrave's]" (and of the book). Following the utilitarian tradition, equity has been taken to call for the tax burden to be distributed so as to minimize the aggregate welfare loss, as measured by a stipulated social welfare function. Given that the social marginal income utility is taken to fall as income rises, this calls for a progressive tax, especially so in the case of LDCs, where income distribution typically is highly unequal. If national income is unaffected by the tax structure, progressive taxation yields a higher gain the poorer the country. Among countries of equal income, more progressive taxation yields the larger gain to countries with the less equal distribution.

Equity gains from progressive income taxation may be offset, however, by detrimental effects on saving and investment. Ideally, this potential conflict between equity and growth could be avoided or reduced by a personalized and progressive tax on expenditures rather than on income. However, such an approach, though feasible in industrialized countries, encounters severe institutional and administrative difficulties in most LDCs. A more feasible, if second-best solution, is provided by selective excise taxes on items of high-income consumption. Property taxation as well offers a promising approach, but problems of assessment typically interfere with effective use thereof. Here, as elsewhere, the options for tax policy in LDCs are limited by a lack of tax handles and administrative capacity.

With regard to the expenditure side of the budget, transfers may serve to reduce excessive inequality at the lower end of the scale and public capital may make an important contribution to economic growth. Human investment in health and education in particular may serve to combine equity and growth objectives, thus overcoming the conflict inherent in a tax-based approach. Other concerns dealt with in the essay address the issue of tax versus loan finance and its implications for intergeneration equity. Finally, consideration is given to the international aspects of tax policy, the threat of capital flight as a limiting factor in equity-oriented tax measures, and the need for international coordination.

BRETON

Albert Breton applies neoclassical analysis to regional development, but in terms of political rather than economic problems. He begins by asking, "Why does virtually every government in the world pursue regional development policies when economists keep telling them that they should be encouraging mobility of people and non-sunk capital instead? Could there be some rational political purpose that offsets the economic inefficiency of regional policies?" He concentrates on cases of "competitive federalism" in which the various governments within a federation compete for resources. He proceeds "to demonstrate that because of the presence in governmental bodies of certain structural features, competition between units located at the same jurisdictional level – for example, governments at the provincial or municipal level – is inherently unstable." Governments compete in a manner much like business firms with respect to prices, policies, and innovations. Problems caused by economies of scale could be solved in a pure market framework by bankruptcy of smaller units, or by the abandonment of certain of their functions. But "governments are not allowed to consolidate through an insolvency process, and ... centralization is kept in check" by devolution of powers. "Intergovernmental competition ... is inherently unstable."

Central governments respond to this situation with regional policy. In the United States, regional policy consists of defence expenditures, and if Canada's regional policy is struck down by the Canada-US Free Trade Agreement (FTA), Canada may have to resort to defence expenditures to maintain intergovernmental stability as well. No matter what the economic impact, therefore, "if regional development policies prevent urban and provincial crises by stabilizing horizontal competition between governments, they are efficient."

HANSEN

Niles Hansen also raises the issue of misallocation of resources and retardation of national development through policies intended to improve equity among regions, but he approaches it in a more purely economic manner and in a West European rather than North American context. He argues that (a) economic "losers" may be prepared to pay for their loss out of a sense of fairness, so that they are not really losers after all, and (b) regional policies do not necessarily impede efficiency of the national economy.

To support (a), he presents survey data from nine European countries which show that a plurality of people feel their strongest sense of belonging is to their city locality, and only secondarily their nation. Region or province, world, and Europe fall well behind. Nonetheless, an overwhelming majority feel that part of their taxes should be spent on development of the most disadvantaged regions of their own country, and one-third feel that some of their taxes should be spent on the most disadvantaged regions of the European community. Hansen concludes that concern for fairness is a significant part of the social welfare function.

With regard to (*b*), Hansen cites a study of Mexico which shows that the country need not accept a lower rate of national growth in order to lessen regional disparities. Rather, the results suggest that if economic infrastructure is concentrated in intermediate regions and social infrastructure in lagging regions, the implicit trade-off between growth and equity need not exist. Studies in the United States suggest that economic-infrastructure expenditures are more effective in intermediate than in lagging regions, but studies in France find no relationship between overall development and amounts of infrastructure. He concludes that considerations of fairness in regional policy are not irrational, and that if properly designed to fit the conditions of the country, regional policies to reduce inequities do not have to sacrifice national development objectives. Canada is lacking in evidence that a sense of fairness plays a significant role in regional policy.

MARRIS

Robin Marris signals his basic antagonism to the neoclassical theory of the firm with the quotation from scientist Francis Crick that begins his essay. Marris has his own "managerial" theory of the firm, which "sees the firm as a financially autonomous administrative organization subject to almost no constraints on its ultimate size, but subject to determinate constraints on its rate of growth." He adds, "The peculiar feature of the corporate constitution – namely, the existence of a body of shareholders with no collective rights and with individual rights strictly confined to equitable voting and equitable shares in distributed profits – is an essential element in the theory." He also insists that "the institution is inherently set up to grow, to be able to grow, and often to be forced to grow." The helplessness of managers to resist their own fundamental drives is reminiscent of Marx; but growth of the enterprise, not accumulation of capital in the hands of the capitalist, is the overwhelming objective. Just enough attention is paid to stockholders' interests to avoid stockholders' revolts or take-overs. "We can thus find a growth rate that maximizes the shareholders' utility and we can find another that maximizes managerial utility, that is, represents the policy that will actually be pursued."

After a skeletal presentation of his theory, Marris turns to Arrow-Debreu and the "agency problem." The difference between Arrow-Debreu and the "managerial" paradigm is that the latter is non-idealistic. It consequently lacks an ideological constituency, which explains some of the resistance to it within the economics profession. "Them that do, decide," and "the agency problem is inherently insoluble." The "take-over factor" requires "a sociology of management outlook" to be fully understood, as does the attitude of managers towards co-workers on the one hand, and stockholders on the other. But where managers minimize their concern for shareholders, growth will be faster, and economies with this kind of management will grow faster than others. He compares the nature of management and growth in such successes as Japan and in such failures as Argentina, Brazil, Mexico, Spain, Portugal, and Ireland. In conclusion, he reminds us that Alfred Marshall thought joint-stock companies were bad at growing: his extremely "strong economic intuition already told him that the success of joint-stock companies would be quite fatal to neoclassical economics. More precisely, they are quite fatal to the *validity* of neoclassical economics."

It may be worth pointing out that Marris's violent attack on neoclassical *theory* reflects no left-wing ideology. On the contrary, he seems quite happy with the giant corporations and their management; equity, efficiency, and development are all at higher levels with them than without them.

STREETEN

Paul Streeten deals with equity, efficiency, and development in the most basic imaginable terms: the need for food. "People must eat," he says, "even if they drink unsafe water, are illiterate, and are not inoculated or vaccinated against diseases." Poor people spend 70 to 80 percent of their incomes, and 50 percent of increases in incomes, on food. Inadequate food not only makes people less able to enjoy life, but reduces their ability and willingness to work productively, makes them more susceptible to disease, and affects both physical and mental capacity. There are 340 million people who are malnourished to the degree of threatening their health; 760 million have not enough calories for an active working life.

Hunger is not mainly the result of a shortage of food, although world production of food per capita has fallen since 1984. The problem is more one of distribution than of production. "It is the fact that hunger today is unnecessary that makes its continued existence so shocking." Hunger is largely a problem of poverty, and greater production of the foods poor people eat would help. Safe water and prevention of intestinal diseases would increase the nutritional value of the same amount of food. But the eradication of hunger is ultimately a question of the political power of the poor. "The market" cannot provide access to the labour force for people who are at too low a level of nutrition to be able to work. "It is access to political power of the poor themselves that alone can guarantee adequate food supplies to all."

To combat hunger there must be a multi-pronged attack. There is no necessary conflict between food production and production of agricultural exports, especially in Africa. An important issue is distribution of food *within* the family. Food aid *can* be helpful. More research on the production of subsistence crops would also help. Ecologically sound techniques are particularly suitable to small farmers.

BLAUG

During the later 1950s and 1960s, there was an explosion of interest in, and literature about, the economics of education. UNESCO, the OECD, other institutions, and individuals argued that education and training in all their aspects were a panacea for development. Many economists – including Ben Higgins – climbed onto this glittering new bandwagon at that time. Mark Blaug is one of the few who stayed on it, sadly watching its paint fade and peel and its wheels begin to wobble. In his essay here, he forcefully expresses the disillusionment of many interested in the relationship of education to equity, efficiency, and development. "We *cannot* say that education, however measured, is either a sufficient or even a necessary condition for economic growth and hence that any poor country is well advised to spend as much as possible on providing additional schooling for its people." Blaug writes "Just as there are many countries that seem to have overspent on education without generating any discernible economic benefits, so there are also many countries that have had remarkable achievements in economic growth without having paid conspicuous attention to education." Manpower planning turned out to be "notoriously unreliable and not much better than pure guesswork." Educated individuals may have higher incomes, but this fact does not mean that education makes them more productive; education may merely "select those who are more able and more achievement motivated by virtue of birth and family upbringing." The "optimism about the equalizing effects of greater access to educational opportunities" has given way to a "profound pessimism."

Blaug is particularly critical of the overspending on tertiary education in the Third World: "One of the things we can say is that higher education in the Third World is probably, nay, almost certainly, overexpanded and that it must be cut back." Successful countries like Japan and the Soviet Union allowed the educational pyramid to grow at the base, and only later allowed it to grow in the middle and at the apex. In the Third World since the Second World War, this sequence has been reversed. Moreover, in most of the Third World the cost of educating one university student would be enough to educate 50 to 100 primary school pupils. University education is also highly subsidized, despite the fact that both private and social returns are higher in secondary, and much higher in primary, education. But even the returns from primary education are suspect; for example, the industrialization of both the First and Second worlds took place with an essentially illiterate workforce.

Education may enhance political stability, which is necessary for development, but existing educational systems may well generate greater inequity, and "no tax system in the world, and certainly no tax system in the Third World, is so progressive that graduates ever pay back to society the full costs of their higher education." Higher education should be financed from fees and repayable loans, and the funds thus released redirected towards primary education.

BRECHER

Irving Brecher focuses on major issues in foreign-aid policy, with special reference to Canada. He views official development assistance (ODA) as standing, "above all, for the general proposition that substantial government intervention in the marketplace is a necessary condition for maximizing welfare." He also envisions an expanded equity goal: "Equity embraces protecting and promoting socio-economic needs as a matter of right – and giving parallel recognition to equal treatment before the law in a free society." The philosophical end-result follows: "Civil-political rights *and* democratic change can be logically viewed [alongside economic growth and social justice] as the third pillar of the conceptual structure housing Third World development." In this context, Brecher analyses the landmark report on Canadian aid by the parliamentary Winegard committee, considers the federal government's response to the committee's recommendations, and assesses the prospects for basic reform of Canada's foreign-aid program.

Although critical of the Winegard report for ambiguity on human-rights issues and timidity on mixed-credit distortions, he gives it "high marks" for stressing the virtues of basic human needs, untied aid, decentralized aid delivery, aid conditionality with respect to human-rights performance, and increased openness and public scrutiny in Canadian aid giving. The government, for its part, is commended for accepting a "Development Assistance Charter," embarking on a program of decentralization in aid delivery, and establishing the International Centre for Human Rights and Democratic Development. On the other hand, Ottawa is faulted on a number of major fronts: for pledging only a modest reduction in Canada's extensively tied aid; for being "unwilling or unable to [acknowledge] that [mixed credits] should be phased out and replaced with more efficient measures that promote Canada's exports without compromising development objectives"; for repeatedly falling short of, and resetting, the internationally recognized ODA/GNP target of 0.7 percent; for "an unwillingness to adopt any specific criteria for conditioning aid on human-rights performance"; and for a continuing, pervasive secrecy in basic decision making on Canadian ODA.

Brecher concludes that, on balance, one cannot yet speak of "new directions" in Canada's aid program. "The gap between Winegard proposals and government 'acceptance' turns out to have been a wide one." And there is "a great deal of room for scepticism about the likelihood of early policy reversals that will significantly narrow this gap."

KEMP

Murray Kemp's essay on foreign aid differs sharply from Brecher's. It provides us with a fine specimen of the mathematical branch of neoclassical economics. At the outset, he states clearly the limits of his analysis: it is static, with no consideration of the optimal timing of aid; it ignores questions of absorptive capacity; it says nothing about the role of aid in promoting research on development problems or in training government officials and others; and it retains the assumption of complete and competitive markets. His analysis does, however, challenge the conventional wisdom that aid is always a loss to the donor and a gain to the recipient. It shows, for example, that in some circumstances a particular country may not be able to help another by transfer of goods. Transfers of goods change the price structure in ways that may harm either the recipient or the donor. Samuelson's proposition that transfers raise wages in the recipient country and lower them in the donor country is substantiated for the case of two countries with a dynamically stable trading relationship. But Samuelson's assumptions are highly restrictive: two countries, two commodities, two factors of production, pure competition, and neutral finance. His proposition does not survive outside this context. There are cases where the donor (Don) may be able to help the beneficiary (Ben) by giving aid indirectly but not by giving aid directly. It may be impossible for Don to help Ben at all. Where there is more than one Don and more than one Ben, both Bens may be made better off with a *smaller* total outlay on aid by Don.

Kemp next considers the transfer of information (technical assistance). It may impoverish the donor. The analysis becomes even more complex: the outcome depends on preferences. The general conclusion? "It depends." Kemp closes by reminding his readers of the limitations of the analysis. His final sentence is, "There is plenty of useful work to be done."

CHIPMAN

John Chipman discusses the effects of technological change and trade restrictions on the international distribution of welfare, and in particular the relative merits of trade restrictions and foreign aid in improving a country's welfare or mitigating a welfare loss. In the first section of his essay, he extends the Hicksian concepts of compensating and equivalent variation from individuals to countries, using the countries' indirect trade-utility functions in place of individual indirect utility functions. He notes that, unlike the case of individuals, it cannot be assumed that if countries receive payment to compensate for a welfare loss, the prices they face will remain unchanged; on the contrary, a transfer will generally change a country's terms of trade. Thus, the measurement of countries' welfare along Hicksian lines must take account of the transfer problem.

Chipman goes on to take up the question posed by Hicks in the 1950s concerning whether a technical improvement in one country will benefit or harm other countries; he does this in the context of the traditional two-commodity/two-factor model with no non-tradable goods as well as in the context of a model in which each country specializes in a tradable and a non-tradable good. In the first case – in which a transfer is unlikely to have any effect on a receiving country's terms of trade – he obtains the result that a rise in the efficiency of the factor used relatively intensively in a "progressive" country's import-competing industry will improve its terms of trade, while a rise in the efficiency of the factor used relatively intensively in its export industry will worsen its terms of trade; a uniform factor-augmenting improvement will worsen the country's terms of trade. In the second case – in which a transfer will generally improve the receiving country's terms of trade – a rise in the efficiency of the factor used relatively intensively in the progressive country's export industry will worsen its terms of trade, whereas a rise in the efficiency of the factor used relatively intensively in the non-tradable sector may, but need not, improve its terms of trade; a uniform factor-augmenting technical improvement will – if the country's trade is balanced – lead to a worsening of its terms of trade. Thus, in this second model, it is less likely than in the first one for technical progress in a country to worsen the foreign country's terms of trade; even when it does, a smaller transfer payment to the foreign country will compensate it for its loss.

Chipman then takes up a question raised by Kahn in 1950: Is a country better off receiving foreign aid or imposing tariffs yielding the same amount of revenues? From the global point of view, it is clear that, to the extent that they are possible, lump-sum transfers from rich to poor countries are preferable to trade restrictions imposed by the poor countries to improve their terms of trade, since the latter result in global dead-weight loss. Chipman shows, however, that under certain plausible conditions this superiority of foreign aid to trade restrictions holds also for an individual country. The conditions are that (1) a transfer to the poor country should improve or at least not worsen its terms of trade, and (2) a tariff imposed by the poor country should be protective, that is, should result in a higher domestic price for its import good relative to its export good. The first condition is the so-called orthodox effect of a transfer; the second, the absence of the "Metzler paradox." The reasoning is quite simple: under the given assumptions, a transfer to the poor country causes the domestic price of its import good to fall or remain the same (relative to the export price), whereas a tariff causes the domestic price of its import good to rise or remain the same (relative to the export price). Since the country's trade utility is an increasing function of both the domestic price of its export good and the deficit in its balance of trade (reckoned in domestic prices) and a decreasing function of the domestic price of its import good, the result follows, since in both cases the trade deficit denominated in domestic prices is the same – in the one case it corresponds to the foreign aid and in the other to the tariff revenues.

FRANK AND FUENTES

The autobiographical essay by André Gunder Frank and Marta Fuentes Frank weaves together the story of the international development effort since the Second World War, the evolution of thinking about development in the same period (left, right, and "extreme centre"), and an account of their own participation in both. With so broad a scope, this contribution touches on many of the issues discussed throughout this volume, and indeed is almost a summary of it.

The authors begin by dividing development economics, and economics in general, into three strands: neoclassical (right), Keynesian (centre), and Marxist (left). They report the general feeling among the 1,000 delegates at the 1988 meeting of the Society for International Development that development is in crisis and development economics bankrupt. The socialist countries are in crisis no less than the capitalist ones. In the South and East, not development but crisis management has become the order of the day. They ask what "equity" can mean in a world of inequalities – equity for whom? efficiency for whom? development for whom? They speak of their "passion for justice and equity" and of their "agonizing reappraisals" of socialism: "We shared them [socialist illusions about equity and efficiency] with many in the 1960s, agonized over them in the 1970s, and had to leave them by the wayside of our long and not yet ending road in the 1980s."

Much like Rostow, in tracing the evolution of thought about economic development, the authors begin with the classical political economists, treat the period 1870–1936 as an aberration, and state that "it took another Kondratieff B-phase crisis in the world economy and the Keynesian revolution to put economists back on track." But in their view, economists did not stay on track. "If anthropology was the child of imperialism and colonialism, then the new development thinking [of the postwar era] was the child of neo-imperialism and neocolonialism." They cite the MIT Center for International Studies (in our view a bit unfairly) as a prime example of the reactionary tendencies of the new development economics. They reiterate Gunder Frank's well-known antagonism to all theories of dualism and report their conclusions as of the mid-1960s that development of the LDCs would be impossible without de-linking from the capitalist system. They then relate the story of the evolution and spread of dependency theory and offer a telling critique of that theory, with which the name of Frank, in particular, is so much associated. They present, as well, an evaluation of the Allende regime in Chile, with which they were also associated.

With the end of that regime and the advent of "the Chicago Boys" in Chile, dependency theory was dead in that country. The industrialized socialist countries (ISC)s were reincorporated into the world capitalist system, and the "basic needs" approach shoved other paradigms off the development stage. The New International Economic Order gave governments of LDCs another scenario besides dependency and de-linking, and the debt crisis weakened the bargaining position of both LDCs and ISCs. The socialist countries were in trouble. Attempts at de-linking, too, had failed. The authors now believe, with Gorbachev, that a policy of de-linking from the global economy is unrealistic.

They also now believe that a form of dualism may be developing after all through the the marginalization of some societies. There is a lack of democracy everywhere. "The political crisis of military and authoritarian rule in the Third World and the crisis of socialism (and Marxism) in the East increasingly opened people's eyes." They end on a note not very different from Jan Boeke's plea for de-linking of traditional societies, deriving some comfort from the fact that "all around the globe, regional, local, peasant, native, tribal, and other environmental movements are mobilizing to protect their own sources of livelihood."

SUMMING UP

This book illustrates very well the current yeasty state of the economics profession. No school of economic thought – not even the mainstream neoclassical school – displays today the same lofty confidence in the accuracy of their conclusions that both neoclassicists and Marxists did in the 1920s or that Keynesians did in the 1940s and early 1950s. Moreover, the borderlines between these schools, and between right, left, and "extreme centre," are becoming blurred. An amusing game for you, the reader, to play would be as follows: Suppose the chapters in this volume were all that you ever read of each author; then consider where you would place him or her in terms of these six categories.

In a strange way, the events of the last decade, and particularly of the last few years, despite quarrels among economists regarding their interpretation, have brought about a certain convergence of thought. There is at least widespread agreement that no economy in the world today is performing in a completely satisfactory manner. For those who can remember it, or who have read enough to have a sense of it, today's controversy among economists, reflected in this volume, is reminiscent of the controversy of the 1930s. The groping for a new theoretical framework, one that will better serve as a guide to policies to solve today's problems, may foreshadow the first major breakthrough since the Keynesian revolution. A new and better paradigm may be just around the corner. Donald Savoie and Ben Higgins will have more to say on this theme in the final chapter of the book.

PART ONE

Concepts

1 Equity and Efficiency in Development: Basic Concepts

BENJAMIN HIGGINS

This symposium is concerned with three basic concepts and their interactions: equity, efficiency, and development. In this chapter, I would like to suggest working definitions of the three concepts and then to express briefly my own views on the manner in which they interact. I shall deal with the concepts in the reverse order of the sequence in the title. Within the framework of my own analysis, at any rate, logic requires a clear definition of "development" before "efficiency" can be sensibly discussed; and one must know what is meant by "efficiency" before one can say anything meaningful about equity.

DEVELOPMENT: AN "IS" AN "OUGHT," OR AN "OUGHT NOT"?

As more and more people from more and more disciplines are brought into the development field; as the number of persons gaining their livelihood from full-time occupation with the subject mounts; as the literature strains the storage capacity of the world's libraries, and as development policy and planning absorb more and more of the time and energy of individual governments and international bodies, it seems that we have become more expert in promoting and accelerating development in particular countries, but more and more confused about just what "development" is. John P. Schlegel, a political scientist at the University of Santa Clara and one of the editors of the OECD volume *Towards a Redefinition of Development*, laments in his preface to the English edition of that volume:

It appears that out of the one-time certainty of knowing what development needs were and, indeed, what development itself was, there has emerged both doubt and confusion. Did we, in fact, have a proper understanding and an adequate definition for development, which could provide the basis for theorizing and acting? Certainly much theorizing and even more activity have marked the whole of development since 1945, but this is not to say that either the theory or its implementation has been successful or adequate ... As Paul Marc Henry noted in his presentation of this project, "The word 'development' delineates a vast arena but does not specify what play is being enacted."

This 1977 OECD volume still provides the most elaborate examination of the concept of development that I know, and offers a convenient peg from which to hang my own analysis of the concept. The book in question reports the results of an exercise that involved some sixty of the world's most distinguished participants in the global development effort. These men and women, from a wide range of disciplines and countries, were asked to respond to a questionnaire concerning the redefinition of development, and to contribute essays under the general heading "Development in a Global Perspective." The book makes interesting reading. The essays are profound, the debate lively, but it cannot be said that the participants achieved solidarity among themselves regarding the concept, content, essence, or nature of development. A large part of this lack of unity can be explained by the fact that each contributor started with his or her own schema for a play in this vast arena, his or her own precept, even prejudice, about the meaning of development, seldom put forth in formal terms and sometimes, perhaps, even unconscious; and then judged "development" to be good, bad, or indifferent on the basis of this unstated definition.

At one point or another in the OECD book, we can find the following views, presented with equal authority and plausibility:

1 There is a development process within all societies (unless interfered with) that is both natural and good and that should therefore be encouraged (and any obstacles removed or overcome).
2 There is a development process under way that has terrible force, that is destructive and bad, that should be stopped if possible, and, if not possible, that at least should be slowed down, offset, guarded against, counterbalanced.
3 There is a natural development process that cannot be altogether stopped, but it can be directed, controlled, managed, so that the goals of the society in which it takes place can be achieved, and harmful side-effects avoided.
4 The development process is simply the result of interacting decisions of individuals and groups, and so reflects the aspirations, and the degree of

knowledge of how to achieve them, of human beings. If in any society there is a high degree of consensus over goals and sufficient knowledge of how both the physical environment and the socio-economic system work, then in the course of time all these goals can be achieved.

5 There is no such thing as "the goals of society." There are only the aims and ambitions of particular social groups or classes. The goals of each group or class conflict with those of all the other groups or classes. Some groups have much more power than others, so only their goals will be achieved and the other groups will be exploited. For the masses to achieve their aims and ambitions, power, including ownership of the means of production, must be in their hands.

6 There is no process of development that is "natural" to all societies. When we observe human experience throughout recorded history, we see long periods of stagnation, some centuries long, interrupted by brief spurts of rapid change bringing marked improvement in the human lot in economic, social, and political terms. One of these periods, sometimes referred to as "the great ascent" or "the great transformation," occurred roughly between 1700 and 1929. Another period, involving much more rapid change, appeared after 1950. But not all countries shared in either of these "great ascents," and even within those that did, not all groups in society shared in the benefits. Moreover, there is no assurance that the recent rapid change will not be followed by another centuries-long "Dark Ages," marked by stagnation or even regression. Development is something that human beings *make happen*, as individuals and as members of groups of various kinds. Some socio-cultural political and physical environments are more favourable than others to the right decisions and actions. The task, therefore, is first to determine what conditions are most conducive to people, individually and in groups, taking the decisions and actions that will *make* development happen, and then to establish those conditions.

How can reasonable people reach such diverse conclusions? True, development is an extremely complex concept and an even more complex process. Differences in viewpoint are to be expected. But it is clear that the wide discrepancies in attitude towards development listed above arise because the people who express them are really talking about different things. They are *defining* development in different ways. It is not that they hold widely differing values; they do not. Nor do they have vastly different pictures of the world as it is. They express a wide range of optimism or pessimism about the future, but all are worried about it and feel that something must be done – and soon. Let us look more closely at the reasons for these different interpretations of the nature of development.

Let us note to begin with that the participants in the OECD symposium were in agreement on two fundamental points, which did not prevent them from arriving at diametrically opposed views of "development."

1 The global economy, and perhaps still more the global society, is in a distressingly bad condition. There is no country in the world where the social, economic, and political situation can be considered satisfactory on any reasonable set of criteria.
2 From the seventeenth century on, but increasingly today, science and technology (together with the capital accumulation and the structural change that are the vehicles for their application) comprise the "driving force" in development. This statement holds whether development is defined as an "is" or an "ought."

Agreement on the state of the world economy and society, however, leads directly to violent disagreement about whether "development" is "good" or "bad" because of differing definitions, usually unstated, of development. Some contributors are evidently thinking of development as an "is," that is, as an aggregation of "developments" – social, economic, political, scientific, and technological. Development is the equivalent of the evolution or history of human society in all its aspects. Since these contributors don't like what is happening, at least currently, to human society, "development" is seen as bad, as something that should be stopped or somehow made to change its character or direction. Others, however, define development as an "ought," as tantamount to social and economic (and perhaps political) progress. The introduction to *Towards a Redefinition of Development* gives three alternative definitions of this sort: the improvement of the economic and social conditions of peoples; the advance of societies and their efforts at organization as a result of the action potential created by the continued growth of applied science and productive technologies; and the transition of some of the earth's populations from a less human to a more human phase. Thus defined, development is not merely "good" but something devoutly to be wished. But at the same time, this definition gives no clue about whether or not development is going to happen or what is required to make it happen.

Much confusion arises from the use of the same word for two fundamentally different concepts. We need two words, not one. If the first definition is used, development can be bad. It is also possible to speak, as Johan Galtung does, of "overdevelopment," just as one might maintain that weight-lifting leads to "overdevelopment" of some muscles, and argue that swimming or gymnastics leads to a more harmonious development. But if the second definition is used, there can be no "over"development, by definition, and development can never be bad, because it is defined as the aggregation of all that is good for human society.

Arguments can be made in favour of both definitions. Many books and articles on development use the term as an "is," and are concerned with analysing the process of evolution of human society, good or bad. The word is also frequently used in this sense in common parlance. On the other hand, the host of government departments and ministries throughout the world that have the word "development" in their titles, the numerous international agencies devoted to "development," the Society for International Development – the whole vast and complex apparatus of the international development effort, as well as the institutes and centres for development scattered throughout the world – are obviously using the term in the second sense, as an "ought." It doesn't matter very much which choice is made provided we have two separate and clear terms for each concept and use them consistently. We shall return to the question of this choice below.

When it comes to deciding whether science and technology, with the related capital accumulation and structural change, are good things or bad things, the same differences of interpretation appear. Those who define development as a process that is actually taking place tend to be fearful of science and technology and its impact on human society. They speak as though science and technology had an independent life and evolutionary force of their own, essentially uncontrollable, leading to exhaustion of resources, ruination of the environment, exploitation of some nations and some social groups by others, violence and destruction. Those who think of development as an "ought," and an attainable "ought," tend to think of science, technology, capital accumulation, and structural change as mere tools in the hands of rational human beings; it is only a matter of deciding which tools are most effective for achieving the aspirations of humankind and how best to use them. Thus, the organizers of the symposium (the editors of the volume) in posing the first question of the questionnaire (Is technical and industrial evolution irreversible or not?) wrote: "It is as if some 'gigantic machine' were in motion above our heads which nothing seems able to stop. Just when man thought he had gained control over nature and no longer had to submit to it, he built a form of second nature with a whole network of *technical structures* which he installed (in the driving-seat, one might say)."[2]

Leopoldo Zea of Mexico wrote in response to another question: "The development achieved so far, and which has only served to provide so-called happiness for some and misery for others, must be restrained. The development which has been achieved so far has not benefited mankind as a whole but only a privileged group. However, it is now, in the name of humankind, of all mankind, that we must call for limits to this growth."[3]

Most of the respondents felt that the application of science and technology could be controlled for the benefit of humankind, at least in developing countries, where the "machine" has not yet become so "gigantic." In their conclusions to Part 1, the editors admit that the majority view was that technology, science, and industry are tools, rather than masters, of humankind, but they return to the attack themselves, insisting that "time and human evolution itself are irreversible," that "there is something irrevocable in mankind as it now exists," that science "contains a principle of violence," and that human nature is "violence talking reason."[4]

It is important to note that the conclusion (reached from careful analysis) that it is very difficult to gain control over science and technology so as to assure their use for the benefit of humankind, would not invalidate the *definition* of development as social and economic progress. While it may seem inconvenient to define development in such a way that it is in fact unattainable, such a definition may nevertheless be useful. Perhaps "perfect love" is unattainable this side of heaven, but it may nonetheless be convenient to have a precise definition of it and to strive to attain it as nearly as possible.

Marshall Wolfe provides an excellent statement about the "is" and "ought" concepts of development:

In the quest for more adequate conceptions of what development is and why it is wanted, it seems essential to insist on the making of a clear distinction between two legitimate uses of the term "development," but also to keep the interpretations deriving from these two uses in continual contact with each other.

According to the first interpretation: "Development" consists of systematically inter-related growth and change processes in human societies, delimited by the boundaries of national state, but also highly interdependent on a world scale ...

According to the second interpretation: "Development" expresses an aspiration towards a better society. In this sense, it implies choices derived from value judgements concerning the content and characteristics of a better society.

It also implies value judgements concerning the right of the existing society, through general consensus or through agents claiming to represent the best interests of the society, to make such choices and enforce them through developmental policies ...

In this sense also, development is societal and constitutes a system of interactions, but the content of the system is determined by the values and preferences of the dominant forces in the society.[5]

DEVELOPMENT IS AN "OUGHT"

We must now make up our minds. Should we define development so that it is an "is," an "ought," or an "ought not"?

With so many well-intentioned people devoting their lives to promoting one or another aspect of a process that they think of as development, I have concluded that I cannot, for myself, make any other choice but to define development as an "ought." I will therefore define it in the simplest terms as a process of economic, social, and technological change by which human welfare is improved. Thus, development is "good" by definition. With this definition, we are able to deal with "oughts" and "ought nots" simultaneously. Anything that raises the level of human welfare contributes to development; anything that reduces welfare is anti-developmental, a subtraction from development. Thus, damage to the environment, exhaustion of non-renewable resources, deterioration of the quality of life, destruction of traditional cultural values, increasing inequalities, and loss of freedom that may appear as side-effects of certain strategies to promote development reduce the amount of development that is actually achieved.[6]

We will need to elaborate this definition, make it more precise, and provide a method of quantifying and measuring it. Before we do so, however, let us first deal with the problem of finding another term for development as an "is" that could be either good or bad. A society is an organism, and in any society there are powerful economic, social, and technological tendencies that impel it towards growth or towards stagnation or decay; towards greater justice and equality or towards curtailment of liberty; towards modernization or towards preservation of traditional values and institutions; towards diffusion of power or towards greater concentration of power; and so on. These forces are there with or without conscious intervention in the process in the name of development, by government or some other powerful group. It was this constellation of forces and the outcome of their interactions that Joseph Schumpeter and some other economists have called "development." Most of them considered this process to be *on balance* "good" despite negative side-effects. It is this definition of development that I have just rejected; but there is no doubt that the process exists, and we need a word for it.

I have been unable to find a better term for this process, and for the path through time of human welfare that emerges, than "social evolution." Evolution is not necessarily good. Darwinian evolution has been adjudged to be good *on balance* by many scientists, philosophers, and just plain people. But the process is a harsh one, and for particular species for which evolution means stagnation, decline, and destruction, it is catastrophic. In the process of social evolution, a particular society, like a particular species in biological evolution, may stagnate, decline, and disappear. Or it may survive but suffer severe maladies in the meantime. (The survival of the fittest is only the survival of the species or society most fit to survive in the given environment; philosophically, there is nothing intrinsically "good" in the survival or extinction of a particular species or a particular society.)

The task of the person professionally concerned with development, as we have defined it, is to steer the evolutionary process onto the path to development and keep it there. *Homo sapiens* may be doomed to extinction in the long run, but there are many people with various kinds of professional training – scientists, engineers, economists, other social scientists, ecologists, the medical profession – who are devoted to preventing or postponing that extinction and to making particular individuals, groups, communities, and societies as healthy and happy as possible for as long as possible. Given the evolutionary forces that exist, some of which are extremely destructive, what are the chances of producing development instead? Tackling this question is the task of the development theorist. Given a workable theory, the formulator of development policy can set to work striving to find policies and actions that will make "social evolution" and "development" converge. Finally, the political process, whatever it is, will determine what policies and plans are actually implemented in each society. As for the "workable theory," my own version of it will be briefly outlined in the final chapter.

GROWTH VERSUS DEVELOPMENT?

The reaction against development strategy in the form of maximizing growth of national income (or of per capita income) has now gone so far that some writers speak as though growth were the enemy of development, or at least of "true" development. It is certainly true that a strategy of maximizing growth of national income could lead to undesirable side-effects. It might, in some countries at certain periods, lead to greater inequality in the distribution of income and wealth; it might lead to exhaustion of non-renewable resources and other damage to the environment (leading to lower rates of growth in the long run); it might conceivably, for a limited period, result in less expenditure on health and education. It might implant false values, increase conflict, and bring an inferior "style" of development and quality of life.

Nonetheless, there are two senses in which growth is a part of development, rather than something opposed to it. First, it is extremely difficult to improve the welfare of all members of society at once without growth of national income. Indeed, in the poorer countries, it is virtually impossible to eliminate absolute poverty of the masses of the population without raising national income. Rising national income provides all sorts of *opportunities* for improving living conditions – and the quality of life – that are not present when national income is stagnant or declining. If growth cannot be achieved without negative side-effects, then these must be weighed against the benefits that higher national income brings.

Second, growth *theory* is a significant part of development *theory*. Consider the variables that appear most frequently in growth theory: savings, investment, technological change, structure of capital, consumption. Few development theories exclude these variables. One cannot know what is happening or will happen in any society without knowing what is happening or will happen to these variables.

At the same time, there are enormous differences between growth theory and development theory. As a rule, growth theory does not look beyond or behind factors that lead to rising national income. It doesn't ask whether rising national income is necessarily a "good thing." It takes that for granted and proceeds to determine what the "optimal" conditions for growth are. "Optimal" is usually defined as the maximum rate of growth over a stipulated period (turnpike theorems) or as "steady" growth, or dynamic equilibrium, usually incorporating full employment without inflation. It is concerned with *balance* among variables. Also, whereas development theory is much concerned with the causes of innovation and the choice of technology, growth theory as a rule simply assumes some rate of technological change, as well as the nature of it (labour saving, capital saving, neutral).

Similarly, development theory is concerned with basic changes in behaviour that will raise the ratio of savings and investment to national income. Growth theory takes savings *functions*, investment *functions*, and consumption *functions* as given. Policy recommendations arising out of growth models – on the rare occasions when these models are realistic enough to permit application to policy – do not seek to change the functions themselves but rather to operate upon them. The task is not seen to be one of changing human behaviour, but rather, from a knowledge of basic human behaviour, one of providing incentives and disincentives that will induce marginal changes in choices made. For example, the adviser to the treasurer or minister of finance, on the basis of his or her growth model, might recommend an expenditure tax to reduce consumption and increase savings. But a development planner, especially one of the *animation sociale* persuasion, might conduct a campaign at the village level to alter basic behaviour patterns in such a way that, with no change in external incentives or disincentives, the peasant would spend less on current consumption and instead buy improved seed, fertilizer, tools, and equipment. The University College of Cape Breton has a number of programs designed to *promote*, not just to study, entrepreneurship in this retarded region of Canada.[7] Again, growth models provide no hint of how to get more output from a given bundle of resources, but that aim is the essence of development policy.

Development theory not only asks why entrepreneurship appears and what kind of innovations are made, why there is resistance to technological change among peasants and how the resistence can be overcome, why some people are willing to migrate long distances to better jobs and others not, and so on. Development theory also looks at the *results* of various decisions and actions in terms of other variables, such as nutrition and health, birth rates and death rates, education and training, and productive efficiency. These "results" are at the same time inputs into the development process. Thus, the broader scope of development theory, as compared to growth theory, leads inevitably to the discovery of loops and feedbacks. Such discoveries lead in turn to a different sort of methodology from that of growth theory, with less emphasis on the distinction between dependent and independent variables, between ends and means, between policy variables and active variables, and more emphasis on systems analysis, decision theory, conflict resolution, cybernetics, and the like. It also leads to the selection of different agents as the principal actors in the play being staged in the "vast arena."

Of course, use of growth *models* does not commit anyone to a *policy* of achieving maximum growth or steady growth. Knowledge of what makes a machine go fast can also be used to slow it down, stop it, or reverse it. There are some who argue that if the world economy had continued to grow at the rapid pace of the 1950s and 1960s, it would have exploded or smashed itself to bits. On the other hand, some machines are so designed that they are difficult to stop or reverse at high speed without serious damage to the machine itself. *The New Yorker* cites Mr Ferrari as saying to one of his racing drivers, who complained that his brakes were defective, "My cars are built to go, not to stop." There is evidence that an economic system, whether capitalist or socialist, is a machine with a design similar to a Ferrari when it comes to stopping it quickly or reversing it in the midst of high-speed performance. Whatever the true facts about the relationship between growth and development are, Marshall Wolfe is surely right in insisting that one must know the laws of *evolution* of any society in order to prescribe effective policies for its *development*.

FORMALIZATION, QUANTIFICATION, MEASUREMENT

Let us now elaborate our definition of development, formalize it, and suggest ways of quantifying and measuring development. According to the definition, the overall objective is to provide the highest possible level of social welfare to the societies for which development strategy and policy are being formulated. Development is a matter of eliminating disparities between the current state of the society and various norms of social welfare.

In the Lower Uva region of Sri Lanka, an experiment was performed, utilizing a concept of "social health" as a measure of welfare, that with some refinement offers a means of greatly improving the process of development policy formulation.

To formalize the approach, we shall use the following symbols:

W = social welfare
$w_1 ... w_n$ = weights attached to norms of social welfare
$N_1 ... N_n$ = norms of social health (welfare)
$S_1 ... S_n$ = current status of the regional society with respect to each norm
G = gaps between norms and current status, weighted according to importance for social health (welfare)
That is, $G_1 = w_1 (N_1 - S_1)$ etc.
D = development = ΔW

We then have $W = \dfrac{1}{w_1\,(N_1 - S_1) + w_2\,(N_2 - S_2) + \ldots w_n\,(N_n - S_n)}$

$$W = \frac{1}{\Sigma\,(G_1 \ldots G_n)}$$

$$D = \vartriangle W = \vartriangle \left\{ \frac{1}{\Sigma\,(G_1 \ldots G_n)} \right\}$$

This equation is not really a mathematical expression to be rigorously maximized over a planning period; it says simply that the objective of the development plan is to eliminate as rapidly as possible maladies in the economy and society. The weighting of norms is also a matter of discussion among the target population, the planning team, and the ultimate decision makers who control budgets, tax policy, trade policy, monetary policy, and the like. In practice, the weighting may be done implicitly in the course of evaluating projects.

Thus, development is defined as a movement towards a state of maximum welfare in this sense, on the basis of selected and appropriately weighted norms. It consists in a reduction of deviations from a state of maximum welfare. Welfare is, of course, maximized when the sum of the variances or deviations is zero; social welfare is then infinite, and the society is "fully developed." Most societies, however, will modify at least some norms as conditions improve and standards are raised. The signs of the deviations are ignored. There are, of course, major questions relating to how norms are chosen and weighted in the course of planning and policy making. But most societies would, and most governments of developing countries do, include in their norms some standards of health, nutrition, education, housing, environmental protection, employment/unemployment, price stability, distribution of income among regions and social groups, growth of income, output per hectare and per man-hour, participation, and responsible government.

In actual planning operations, the task of "maximizing" the final equations could not be taken altogether seriously, any more than medical practice could be guided by an effort to "maximize" a similar equation for the health of an individual or community. Professional judgment has to be brought to bear as well as measurement. This definition of development does require that all projects be evaluated in terms of their contribution to achievement of the norms chosen, as was done in the Lower Uva project in Sri Lanka.

One of the important advantages of this pragmatic concept of welfare is that it conforms much more closely to the meaning of the same word in common parlance. More important still, it relieves economists of the need to derive tests for determining whether or not a certain policy improves welfare from the same models used to analyse how an economy behaves. Models to explain the functioning of an economy can be constructed on the basis of the actual behaviour of the principal actors within it. How *well* the economy is functioning is determined not in terms of these models – that is, not in terms of the degree to which *individuals* are getting what they want, as indicated by choices made in the market – but in terms of how close the collective aims come to being achieved. The analytical models do not determine what is "good" for society; they only provide guidance about how the society can best move towards goals determined by a different process than market choices. However, the knowledge of how the economy functions is still necessary to determine what policies and plans will be most effective in moving the society towards its goals, thus raising the level of social welfare.

EFFICIENCY

With these definitions, the "efficient" economy maximizes the rate of development; that is, it maximizes the rate at which gaps between the norms of welfare accepted in a particular society and the *status quo* are reduced. "Efficiency" of an industry or firm, or of a government department, means maximizing its contribution to development, or to the increase in welfare, in this same sense. This concept of efficiency retains much of the neoclassical concept of efficiency. It involves minimizing opportunity costs and getting the maximum amount of physical output of the product-mix of any enterprise or any economy from a given bundle of resources. The logic behind "the rule" (marginal cost equals price) still holds. It is more efficient to produce things people want than things they don't want. But my concept of efficiency also recognizes that many of the things people want (environmental protection, national security) have no market price, and that many of the actual market prices are an imperfect measure of the relative degree of satisfaction people gain from the various things bought and sold.

What must we do to assure efficiency? What *system* should we choose? Writing early in 1991, I would say there is no need to elaborate the reasons for not choosing a system of centralized planning. So we are back to some sort of market system, if somewhat regretfully. I find myself thinking of Winston Churchill's famous evaluation of democracy as a political system. After enumerating its faults, he remarked, "Too bad we have nothing better." One might say the same of the market economy. Considering the present disarray in many market economies, as well as in the former socialist economies, to what system do we turn? Obviously, it must be some kind of mixture. But what kind?

There are still some mainstream neoclassical economists who maintain that a pure market economy, with government intervention kept to an absolute minimum, is still the system that will give the best results, always and everywhere. They attribute imperfections in the performance of actual market economies to excessive government intervention or to misguided attempts to introduce elements of "planning," or at least "management," into the market system. This view makes a good starting point for discussion of various alternatives. It is at one end of the ideological spectrum and still has supporters. The other end of the spectrum – centralized planning unadulterated by market influences – is now generally regarded as discredited and discarded. The pure market system is therefore the best measuring rod for comparing other systems worthy of consideration. What then is the foundation of the argument for the free market, and how solid is it? Answering this question requires consideration of a crucial debate about how the market actually functions in the real world, as well as a quick look at the neoclassical welfare economics with which the argument for a free market is inextricably intertwined.

HOW EFFICIENT IS THE MARKET?

A part of "the magic of the market" is that it is supposed to generate forces that will bring the economic system into "equilibrium" or return the system to equilibrium if it is temporarily disturbed. Obviously, a very important question to ask in evaluating the market system is, "Is this characterization of the market system realistic or not?" There are economists at the very core of the establishment, including some Nobel Prize winners, who argue emphatically that it is not. The theory of circular or cumulative causation, associated mainly with Gunnar Myrdal, maintains that movements of the market in any direction tend to become cumulative, taking the system further and further from equilibrium. The "knife-edge theorem," first formulated by Roy Harrod and Evsey Domar, says that not only is there a tendency for cumulative movement away from equilibrium, but that equilibrium, and particularly equilibrium with full employment and no inflation, is an extremely delicate balance, leaving the economy poised on a knife edge, so that the slightest disturbance will result in its falling off the knife edge in one direction or the other. Steady growth, with unemployment and without inflation, is virtually impossible and is likely to occur only by accident.[8] Which of the two contrasting views is correct is a question of fact, not of pure theory. I have suggested elsewhere that both are correct. In certain periods, the market pulls the economic system towards equilibrium. In other periods, it pushes the system away from equilibrium. Theories of economic fluctuations depend on such alternations. In any case, there is little evidence that a pure market economy tends always to stay in equilibrium if it is already there, and tends always to return quickly to equilibrium when it is disturbed.

Neoclassical welfare economics originated in the marginal revolution of the 1870s. It was then that economists started trying to convert the discipline into a pure science. The importance attached to *Wertfreiheit* (freedom from value judgments) was a byproduct of this effort. For economics to be a pure science and still have something to say about policy, there had to be a way to get from impartial, value-free observations to a determination of what is good for society. The neoclassical economists found this bridge in the theory of marginal utility, which, they thought, allowed them to identify relative prices with relative marginal utilities and thus with relative values for everybody. The way was open to a "scientific" welfare economics.[9]

Underlying this analysis, however, are in fact some colossal, and philosophically untenable, value judgments:

1 Market choices provide information about individual welfare. People know what is "good for them," or at least what they "want," and behave accordingly in spending their incomes, choosing their jobs, etc.
2 Social welfare is therefore maximized when individuals are free to go as far as possible in choosing things they want without depriving other individuals of choices of things they want.
3 The maximum welfare position can therefore be determined in a rigorous scientific fashion by observing choices and the conditions in which they are made.
4 Maximizing welfare in this sense is "a good thing" for society.

Let us take these value judgments in reverse order. The last of them, of course, begs the question of income distribution – of equity, in other words. Under ideal market conditions, every individual draws from national income what he or she contributes to it, either by providing labour or by providing land or capital he or she owns. It would be possible to make a separate value judgment to the effect that such an income distribution is "just" and "equitable," but few neoclassical economists are prepared to go that far; most would favour some sort of incomes policy to relieve the absolute poverty and gross inequity that such an income distribution would entail in most societies. The trouble is that if the market is to continue to function "efficiently" on neoclassical criteria, any redistribution of income undertaken on grounds of equity must leave the allocation of resources unchanged, and that may turn out to be impossible.

The other flaw in the fourth value judgment is that the maximization of the society's welfare or satisfaction requires equalization of marginal satisfaction of all individuals, and that requires redistribution of income away from those with limited capacity for enjoyment to the super-enjoyers. To those who have shall be given and from those who have not shall be taken away even that which they have. Despite the biblical support, few people today would argue in favour of such a system of ethics. The fact is that "maximization of satisfaction" of society on the basis of "revealed preferences" of individuals makes no philosophical sense. There are very few individuals, apart from a few economists, who would derive satisfaction from the news that *marginal* satisfactions had been equalized the world over; a situation that satisfies almost no one cannot be an optimal situation for society as a whole. For any situation to be accepted as "optimal" for a particular society, there must be some degree of consensus among its members that it really is the best that can be attained. And what society, by the way? Village, province or state, nation-state, global?

The third statement, of course, depends on the validity of the first two. In addition, it has flaws of its own. The neoclassical economists, as a rule, do not try to find out how much satisfaction individuals get from the choices they make or whether they could get more satisfaction from a different set of choices. In principle, neoclassical economists determine how far market conditions vary, as a result of "market failure" or "government failure," from those that would permit maximization of satisfaction. In truth, there is no precise or "scientific" way of performing that task. Neither marginal cost nor minimum average cost is revealed in any market. To determine how far prices diverge from marginal costs and how far average costs are from the minimum would be a monumental undertaking; instead, economists try to get some idea of how much imperfection there is in various markets. However, as Robert Solow pointed out in his presidential address to the American Economic Association a few years ago, there is scarcely a subject on which there is so much difference of opinion among economists as the degree of market failure. And to appraise the degree to which government policy is making the market work better or worse, one must have an idea of how well the market works on its own.[10]

The second value judgment is essentially the Pareto optimum. There is nothing wrong with it as far as it goes. If any individual can increase his or her satisfaction without reducing the satisfaction of anyone else, there is no reason to prevent him or her from doing so. But the Pareto optimum is consistent with any income distribution whatsoever and thus with widely varying levels of true social welfare. As I argued in one of my earlier papers:

It should be obvious that a society which does no more for its members than to provide a mechanism for exchange in which everyone can continue to make choices which add to his satisfaction, up to the point where further such choices would diminish the satisfaction of someone else, falls far short of the "good society." A good society must, and most societies do, go well beyond a Pareto optimum in making common-sense but generally accepted interpersonal and intergroup comparisons of utility, in order to discriminate in favor of the sick and disabled, the very young and the very old, the unemployed, the weak in bargaining power, the residents of retarded regions, the victims of catastrophe, and so on.[11]

Still, a society can take steps to protect the underprivileged and nonetheless utilize the market mechanism for most of the task of resource allocation.[12]

It is the first proposition that is the crux of the neoclassical concept of efficiency. An economy is efficient if its market functions in such a way that a Pareto optimum can be achieved. There is an element of circular reasoning in this proposition: efficiency is defined in terms of the functioning of the market (Pareto optimum, marginal cost equals price, average cost minimized), and an economy is considered efficient if its market functions in this way. Any departure from this pattern is inefficient, and any policy that causes such a departure is bad policy.

This concept of efficiency has been attacked on various grounds that have long since become familiar: imperfect knowledge and foresight, incomplete information, misleading advertising, externalities, inapplicability to public goods. Virtually all societies impose some limitations on freedom of choice in the market to prevent people from harming themselves or other people through ignorance or perverseness: controls on purchase and sale of drugs, firearms, alcohol, securities, and so on. Once a society starts along this road, it finds it hard to tell where to stop. As knowledge grows, more and more goods and services are recognized as being harmful to their users or to society as a whole: tobacco, various carcinogens, aerosol bombs, prostitution (aids), leaded gasoline. In least-developed countries, where malnutrition is a barrier to breaking out of the vicious circle of poverty, it is a question of whether people should be free to produce, sell, and buy foodstuffs that are less nutritious than others that could be produced with the same resources.

Beyond all that, however, is the absurdity of the claim that defining the good (efficient) society as one that maximizes opportunities for people to buy what they want is value free. One can, of course, make such a value judgment, and even defend it on eighteenth- and nineteenth-century liberal grounds; people should be free to choose even if they are ignorant, ill informed, and have atrocious taste, and their choices consequently harmful to themselves and offensive to their neighbours.[13] But it must be recognized that others have the right to reject this value judgment and can make a strong case for doing so. The concept of efficiency must include some standard for improvement, growth, and development, as well as standards for resource allocation at a point in time. It must include some standards regarding distribution of income among nations, regions, social groups, and individuals. And it must include targets or norms for public goods such as health, education, nutrition, and the like.[14]

Some economists, working essentially in the neoclassical tradition but aware of the defects of neoclassical welfare economics, retreat to the position of saying that it is for democratically elected governments to lay down the welfare function for a society; the economist's job is merely to tell government how to achieve it. In this manner, *Wertfreiheit* is thought to be preserved, since the economist expresses no value judgments of his or her own. But, of course, this whole approach involves a colossal value judgment: that duly elected governments know what people want, or even what is "good" for society. My own appraisal is that governments are even clumsier instruments for finding out what people want and giving it to them than markets. It is for this reason that I prefer a system that maximizes decision making by the target populations themselves, in consultation with whatever "experts" may be required to ensure well-informed decisions, and that keeps government *out* of the decision making to the greatest degree possible. A family consulting a doctor, lawyer, or architect provides an analogy of the desired process.

Much of the growing literature on public goods and collective choice is directed towards finding means of making public choice approximate individual choices in a market; the underlying concept of efficiency remains the same, and the analysis is subject to the same structures, as in the case of neoclassical welfare economics. The literature on conflict resolution is in another category and is closer to my own line of thought. This kind of analysis does not rely on a basic harmony of interests and the "invisible hand" to promote efficiency, equity, and development, and it recognizes that the capacity to resolve conflicts is part of what makes any society and any economy efficient. Without some degree of consensus – conscious and articulate consensus – significant movements to close gaps between norms and the current state of affairs cannot be achieved.

When welfare functions are defined by government, efficiency is presumably measured by the degree to which the objectives laid down are actually achieved. In that respect, the concept of efficiency with this approach is similar to my own. However, there is one fundamental difference between my approach and this one. Instead of relying on governments alone to determine welfare functions, I would avoid governments, and especially central governments, as much as possible. Churchill's comments on democracy are apt. The way our parliamentary systems work pushes central governments towards more intervention and more spending, even when their announced policies are budget restraint, deregulation, and privatization. At the same time, central governments do not respond accurately or sensitively to the wishes of people at the local or regional level.[15] Needless to say, when a government engages in centralized decision making without being responsible and accountable to an electorate, as in China and in the recently deposed socialist governments in the USSR and Eastern Europe the results are even worse.

EQUITY

And so at last we come to equity. It is a concept that cannot be formulated precisely. The closest to precision that one could come would be to define equity as equality. But even "equality" is not really a very precise term, and no society in the world is seriously striving for absolute equality. As the term "equity" is normally used, it is akin to social justice or, for example, to the unwritten social contract in Australia: everyone should have "a fair go," all Australians should be protected against exploitation by any non-Australians, and every social group in Australia should be protected against exploitation by any other social group in Australia. I have a friend who defines "racism" as disliking some racial or ethnic group more than one should. Similarly, "equity" means not permitting greater inequalities of income, wealth, power, privilege, and social status than a good society should. To some degree such a concept of equity can be written into law, as it is in Australia, through the arbitration commission, the grants commission, the loans council, and the system of protection.

Any society's concept of equity will be reflected in the welfare function that also defines "development" and "efficiency." My own value judgment is that no society should tolerate absolute poverty, unemployment, malnutrition, bad housing, exclusion from access to health facilities, or exclusion from as much education as each individual wants and can effectively use. These injustices exist even in the richest countries, and in them they are a disgrace. Some countries, of course, are too poor to eliminate all these deficiencies at once,; but even in poor countries they should not be accepted with resignation. On the other hand, inequities among the "capitalist class," "middle class," and "working class" in countries like Australia, Canada, and the United States do not bother me very much. It does not matter much if some people are very rich if no one is poor and there is opportunity for upward mobility.

And so we come to a basic "contradiction" in the mixed-and-managed economy. Given the normal tendency to risk aversion and reluctance to venture into the unknown, in both the private and the public sector, the redistributive aspects of equity measures are likely to dilute incentives, diminish risk taking, retard innovation, and slow down growth until the rate of development is reduced, possibly to the point where even the very level of welfare of the underdog, which the equity measures are designed to help, is lowered instead. Again, we have here a question of facts, and of facts not easily come by, but the policy makers and their advisers must do their utmost to pin them down, lest ill-construed measures to promote equity destroy efficiency, slow down development, and lower welfare all around, as they often have, notably in the "failed industrialized countries" of Argentina, Chile, Uruguay, Venezuela, Ireland, New Zealand, Spain, and Portugal. There have been suggestions that Australia is on the same path, and Canada, the United Kingdom, and even the United States show symptoms of inefficiency in this sense.[16] Efficiency seems to have been destroyed in socialist countries as well, although in their case there are now doubts even about the sincerity of the efforts to promote equity.

EQUITY AND EFFICIENCY IN SPACE

In Canada the debate has been especially keen with regard to equity and the efficiency of allocation of resources in space. In the simplest terms, it is argued that the combination of policies to develop lagging regions and to provide unemployment benefits and establish of minimum wages in all regions is retarding "adjustment," misallocating resources, lowering gross domestic product (GDP), and delaying the solution of the problem of regional disparities. To establish definitively whether or not this argument is in fact correct would be a daunting task. Here let us be content with some conceptual clarifications within the framework outlined above.

The first point that must be made is that, within that framework, the impact of regional and related policies on GDP cannot by itself determine whether or not these policies are "efficient." One would have to consider their impact on the welfare of both gainers and losers. If people want to stay where they are and productive employment can be found for them there, social welfare may be enhanced thereby. But no one has an inherent right to enjoy, say, living in the Atlantic provinces, which he or she loves, and also enjoy the same monetary income that people in the same occupation earn in Ontario, which the Maritimer hates.[17] In other words, in promoting equity in space, the governmental effort should be directed towards creating equality of opportunity and full utilization of human and natural resources, rather than towards equalizing wage rates or per capita monetary income. The latter objective should be sought only if the people of the richer regions have strongly held convictions that the good society should provide such equality, which many people do in Australia and Western Europe (see Niles Hansen's chapter in this volume) and which some do even in Canada and the United States.

As I pointed out in my essay for the volume in honour of François Perroux,[18] when it comes to equity in space, many values that should be taken into account are not accurately and overtly priced in any market. I listed twelve of these. Here, let me mention only four:

1 The contribution to welfare of people in disadvantaged areas of being able to earn a satisfactory living where they are, rather than emigrating
2 The contribution to welfare of other Canadians of having people in the disadvantaged regions stay where they are, rather than emigrating and competing in other areas for jobs, housing, public transport, public utilities, etc.[19]
3 The loss of infrastructure in the form of housing, public utilities, transport, schools, and hospitals in regions where net emigration takes place, including the impact of the tendency of such emigration to become cumulative, once started
4 The cost to those who remain in disadvantaged regions of emigration of young, well-trained, ambitious, high-need-achievement people of their

community, leaving behind a distorted age and social structure and broken families

While the market provides no direct estimate of such costs and benefits, they can be estimated as part of a regional planning exercise.

INDIVIDUAL CHOICE, COLLECTIVE CHOICE, AND EXPERTISE

Have I not painted myself into a corner? I am opposed to leaving everything to the market, and I am opposed to leaving everything to government. So how do I solve this dilemma? What do we do, what kind of system do we create?

To begin with, we should leave everything possible to individual choice, to the market, to the polls, and to other avenues of individual choice. We should rid ourselves of Brobignanian government structures, where they exist, to create effective minimal management limited to routine activities that private enterprise cannot deal with. When a special policy is embarked upon, a government can assemble a small, carefully selected team of experts to handle it, as in the case of freeing the market. After a century or more of "government failure" in the form of protectionism and ill-founded intervention of various kinds, sudden freeing of the market can bring painful disruption without much "adjustment," as we are seeing in Australia and New Zealand. Adjustment without pain or waste of resources needs astute management. More generally, the degree of efficiency – the pace of development – in a market economy can be significantly augmented by assuring that the requisite expertise is brought to bear on the decision-making process.

Injection of the requisite expertise is needed at all stages and for all aspects of the development process if it is to take place in an optimal manner. In many situations, of course, the management of private enterprises has within it the expertise needed for good choices to be made about what to produce and how to produce it in response to market signals. Surprisingly often, however, neither individual consumers nor the individuals comprising management of private enterprise have the expertise that good choices would require. Moreover, in many cases they are unable to acquire this expertise, cannot afford it, don't recognize the need for it, don't know quite what kind of expertise is needed, nor where to find it even if they do. When it comes to collective choice, the expertise is even more frequently missing, and in those cases, there must be some mechanism for providing it collectively. It is often of a sort that is not normally engaged by private enterprise in its regular production of goods and services, or by government in its routine, bureaucratic operations. It must be recruited and organized through other channels: private consulting firms, various blends of governmental and private nongovernmental organizations (including not only the officially recognized

NGOs but a lot of other organizations outside government and private enterprise as well), international organizations, and mixtures of all of these.

Organizations outside government and private enterprise are playing an increasing role in the international development effort and in domestic development as well. They include the established foundations, like Ford, Rockefeller, Carnegie, and many others; hundreds of church groups; royal commissions and congressional committees; and United Nations specialized agencies. Increasingly, universities are injecting their knowledge and skills directly into the development process, rather than confining their activities to basic research that may be the source of innovation by entrepreneurs outside the academic community. Universities even supply venture capital to commercialize their own scientific discoveries. In the United States, examples are the University of Texas's 475-acre Balcones Research Centre, the Stanford Research Park, the Triangle Research Park in North Carolina, and the Pittsburg-Carnegie-Mellon "Pittsburgh Enterprise Corporation."

A common feature of all these organizations – let us call them OGs, (organizations outside government) to distinguish them from the official NGOs – is a certain freedom from bureaucratic control over the activities and decisions of the experts involved. Even in the case of a United Nations expert, there is a good deal of independence from the headquarters of the specialized agency involved, and considerable insulation from the politics of both donor and recipient countries. In the case of my UN mission as monetary and fiscal adviser to the Indonesian government, UN headquarters made no attempt to influence the advice I gave, and nearly all of it was accepted sooner or later, once the political situation in Indonesia was propitious. In the case of missions undertaken for the Commonwealth secretariat, for example, there is still more freedom, insulation, and independence. Such independence is more difficult in a government setting, but Canada has some interesting examples.

POTENT MIXTURES

Atlantic Canada provides a number of examples of successful mixtures of government action, private enterprise, and independent private expertise in regional development. Among these are the cooperative efforts to rehabilitate Moncton, New Brunswick, and Halifax, Nova Scotia. In the early 1970s, the Department of Regional Economic Expansion (DREE), as part of its broad effort to put the Atlantic provinces on their feet, let a contract for a Moncton regional plan to a private consulting firm, which invited me to join the team. Moncton was then a moribund and grimy town, with its decaying and deserted main street, apparently surviving only as a railway junction and site of the Canadian National Railways (CNR) shop. It was enough to daunt the boldest of planners. But the team realized that the city had some assets, notably the thriving francophone Université de Moncton, other francophone institutions, budding francophone entrepreneurs, and some anglophone enterprise as well. Around these we could build a plan that DREE generously supported.

By great good fortune, Public Works Canada (PWC) had at the time a brilliant and imaginative assistant deputy minister for planning and corporate affairs, Douglas Hartt, who had the support of both his minister and his deputy minister. Hartt assembled one of the brightest and most competent teams in the whole federal government. It consisted of some staff members, some independent consultants like myself, and a small private consulting firm (David Hamilton and Associates). The team was relatively young and highly interdisciplinary.

Hartt and his team saw the potential of the Moncton plan and persuaded Hartt's minister and deputy that PWC should give it strong support. They realized that development of the sort that could rescue Moncton cannot take place unless it includes an urban centre that has critical mass and is both lively and attractive. High-tech industries and sophisticated services require highly trained and innovative entrepreneurs, managers, scientists, engineers, and technicians; such people want a sophisticated urban environment. One of the things PWC did was to transform Main Street. Small side streets were shut off to make inviting parks, sidewalks were repaved with tiles set in attractive patterns, trees were planted, huge tubs of flowers were placed on the sidewalks, and charming streetlamps and benches were added. From a place to be avoided, Main Street became the ideal setting for elegant shops and office buildings, first-class hotels and restaurants; pleasure-seeking pedestrians day and night sought out this beautiful and bustling boulevard. Moncton, as a whole, has been converted into an attractive city, the most dynamic in the province, with rapid growth based on high-tech industry and sophisticated services. As foreseen, both the university and private entrepreneurship have played a major role in this growth.

Halifax is a similar story. Doug Hartt and his team saw the possibilities inherent in PWC, Nova Scotia, the City of Halifax, and private enterprise all owning property on the city's decaying waterfront. Using PWC's leverage, a plan was drafted and land assembled to make the total rehabilitation of the waterfront possible, so that today the area is a major attraction for tourists and residents alike. The restoration of the waterfront made a major contribution to the conversion of Halifax into the dynamic city that it is today.

WORKING WITH TARGET POPULATIONS

The ideal situation for injecting expertise is where opportunities are offered for the experts to work directly with the target population whose benefit is sought. Such an opportunity existed in Libya in 1952. The shortage of requisite skills was very apparent and the impact of injecting them highly visible. When the United Nations assembled a team to prepare the first Six Year Plan for the development of Libya, the country was one of the poorest in the world. Its population consisted mainly of peasants, nomadic graziers, and fishermen. (Oil had not yet been discovered, and it seemed then that there was little prospect that it would be.) The team quickly decided that there was little scope for drastic structural change and that development would have to be largely a matter of doing better what Libyans were already doing. Accordingly, the team did not limit itself to telling the government what to do. They told the *people*, and then they *showed* the people what to do. Experts on the team began introducing improvements in technology before the plan was even completed. For example, the Scottish wool expert greatly enhanced the income of the graziers by teaching them how to shear, scour, sort, and package their wool for the Rome market. The leather expert taught them how to flay cattle without making holes in the hide. Our Greek fisheries expert found that the fishermen could increase their catch substantially by going a bit further out to sea.

In similar fashion, the Canadian International Development Agency (CIDA) team in Haiti doubled the net income of peasants in its region just by getting rid of the rats. With the CIDA team in the Lower Uva region of Sri Lanka, we move quite a way up the technology scale. The plan included two sugar refineries that were profitable for private investment. In addition, the industrial engineer, the industrial economist, and the foresters together identified an opportunity for profitable private investment in a biomass plant, based on 10,000 hectares of permanent-yield forest, that could replace 25 percent of Sri Lanka's imports of petroleum products.

Sometimes the needed expertise is not provided through normal private enterprise channels because it is not desirable that it should be. The planning of the Malaysian region of Pehang Tenggara would have been profitable for a multinational, multiproduct corporation if it bought up and developed the whole region, thus making the entire present and future population (presently about 300,000 people and still growing) dependent on it. The social and political disadvantages of creating such a "company town" – or feudal fiefdom – are too obvious to need elaboration. At the time, there was no collection of small private enterprises capable of raising the capital and assembling the expertise to do the job and the Malaysian government could not have afforded it either. Instead, a CIDA team of fifty experts was assembled to do a complete soil analysis and a complete forest inventory, as well as hydrological and rainfall studies, topological studies, and market surveys for various possible products. When the team's work was done, the private investors, who would be responsible for most of the implementation of the scheme, could make their decisions knowing just which products were likely to be most successful on each bit of land in the region. The plan was prepared by a consortium of private consulting firms; much of what is called "development planning" is done *by* private enterprise *for* private enterprise. Such planning raises profits and reduces risk for private investors. That plan cost $4 million but required an estimated $1 billion of investment, public and private, to implement. If the $4 million spent on the plan improved returns on this investment by even 1 percent, the returns to the *planning* exercise would be enormous. In this case, because all the development projects were in the modern sector, the knowledge and skills involved were at a high level of technology.

It is worth noting that all of these CIDA teams were composed of private Canadian consulting firms and individual experts recruited by them; the firms were under contract to CIDA. The money came from government but the expertise came from the private sector and the job was done by private enterprise. Such mixtures of government and private enterprise can occasionally produce very good results.

COLLECTIVE CHOICES

It is in collective choices that the injection of the requisite expertise is most badly needed and is most often lacking. Whatever the mechanism for collective choice – town meetings, village councils, referenda, parliamentary elections, and cabinet decisions – the expertise is needed. To revert to an example where the level of technology involved in collective choice was relatively simple, we might look at the Inter-American Development Bank feeder road project in Haiti. Here, the villagers were consulted on their preferences regarding the traces of the roads. For the most part, they were interested in better access to sources of water, to markets, to schools, and to clinics and hospitals. To the extent possible, the roads were to be constructed by the villagers, but the compacting would be done by heavy machinery and, where necessary, blasting would be done by dynamite. Thus, while the wishes of the villagers concerning the trace of each road were respected, the engineers had to have their say regarding the technical problems and the costs involved in the various routes. In a simple case like this one, the need for an appropriate blend of collective choice and individual expertise is fairly obvious; though not as obvious, this need also exists when it comes to making such horrendously complex decisions as those concerning the design of a public health or education system, or the optimal mix of export-promotion and import-replacement strategies. The simple maxim "Oh, just leave it to the market" will not do in such cases. Nor is there any simple set of rules to instruct a society on how best the market can be bolstered or supplemented in such cases. The answer will vary from case to case, and there is no escape from studying each case on its own if the best results are to be achieved. And the studies of various aspects of each case must be made by people with the required expertise.

NOTES

1 Alain Birou, Paul-Marc Henry, and John P. Schlegel, eds., *Towards a Redefinition of Development: Essays and Discussion on the Nature of Development in an International Perspective* (Paris: Pergamon for the OECD, 1977).
2 Ibid., 2.
3 Ibid.
4 Ibid., 135.
5 Marshall Wolfe, *Elusive Development* (Geneva: United Nations Institute for Research on Social Development, 1981).
6 Ian Little begins his book *Economic Development* by referring to Dudley Seers's well-known article in the *International Development Review*, "The Meaning of Development." He then goes on to present his own view: an index of development certainly has welfare implications because "development is a word that undoubtedly carries value overtones, just as do words like 'welfare' and 'optimum.' If the above were false, Seers would not repeatedly write about the meaning of 'development,' which he rightly recognizes to be a normative word ... My discussion of value judgments implies that there can be no objective definition of development and therefore no universally acceptable indicator. The best one might hope for would be to get some rough consensus on objectives and hence on how progress towards these objectives can be measured ... There is a definition that I believe to be acceptable to most liberal economists. It integrates economic development with welfare economics."
   Up to this point Little and myself are in complete agreement. However, he loses me in his next sentence: "Economic development occurs if there is a rise in the present value of average (weighted) consumption per head." In my definition, per capita consumption is only one indicator of development, and specific (weighted) public goods must be added to the welfare function as targets. (Ian Little, *Economic Development: Theory, Policy, and International Relations* [New York: Basic Books, for the Twentieth Century Fund, 1982], 3–4, 6.)
7 Benjamin Higgins, *Cape Breton and Its University: Symbiotic Development* (Moncton: Canadian Institute for Research on Regional Development, forthcoming).
8 Evsey D. Domar, *Essays in the Theory of Economic Growth* (New York: Oxford University Press, 1957), especially chapters 3 and 4; R.F. Harrod, *Towards a Dynamic Economics* (London: Macmillan & Co., 1984); Gunnar Myrdal, *Economic Theory and Underdeveloped Regions* (London: Duckworth, 1957).
9 I do not claim any high degree of originality in my critique of neoclassical economics, and especially its welfare economics. Indeed, there is considerable overlapping of the points I am making and those made by the authors cited in these notes and in my bibliography. I might mention particularly Arrow, Bell and Kristol, Bensusan-Butt, De Gregori and Pi-Sunyer, Hahn and Hollis, Hollis

and Nell, Kornai, Lekachman, Lutz and Lux, Myrdal, Perroux, Phelps, Sen, Simon, Sugden, and Rosley and Peacock.

10   Hollis and Nell specify "four objections to neo-classicism": (1) in the model of perfect competition no bearer (of a variable) could possibly be both rational and possessed of complete market and technical information; (2) there is a contradiction in the notion that investment is governed by considerations of marginal productivity; (3) there is a contradiction between the assumptions of perfect mobility and perfect information; and (4) the assumptions of perfect mobility and rationality conflict. They claim that "the four objections are powerful." (Martin Hollis and Edward J. Nell, eds., *Rational Economic Man: A Philosophical Critique of Neo-Classical Economics* [Cambridge: Cambridge University Press, 1977], 217–30.)

11   Benjamin Higgins, "Economics and Ethics in the New Approach to Development," *Philosophy in Context* 7 (1978): 7–29.

12   *The Pareto Optimum.* The concept of the Pareto optimum has recently come under increasing attack. Robert Sugden maintains that the very term is misleading; we should speak only of "Pareto-efficient" end states. "Every Paretian will agree that the best feasible end state is one of the set of Pareto-efficient end states. This does not mean that every Paretian believes that every Pareto-efficient point is a good one." He goes on to argue that many Paretian propositions are "so circular as to make the Paretian approach practically empty." He recognizes that the Paretian approach is based on "recognizably liberal principles, but not principles that everyone accepts." Kenneth Arrow, in his famous "impossibility theorem," raises doubts as to whether the implications of the Pareto principle are necessarily all that liberal. He demonstrates that "there can be no constitution simultaneously satisfying the conditions of collective rationality, the Pareto principle, the independence of irrelevant alternatives, and non-dictatorship" ("Values and Collective Decision Making," in Frank Hahn and Martin Hollis, eds., *Philosophy and Economic Theory* [Oxford: Oxford University Press, 1979]). Amartya Sen presents his own case of conflict between liberal and Paretian principles: "The dilemma posed here may appear to be somewhat disturbing ... The ultimate guarantee of individual liberty may rest not on rules for social choice but on developing individual values that respect each other's personal choices. The conflict posed here is concerned with those societies where such a condition does not hold and where pairwise choice based on liberal values may conflict with those based on the Pareto principle" ("The Impossibility of a Paretian Liberal," in Hahn and Hollis, *Philosophy and Economic Theory*, 131). Similarly, Rowley and Peacock: "We charge those who deal in Paretian welfare economics with being implicated, in greater or lesser degree, knowingly or in ignorance, in a professional disdemeanor which forms the basis for the established dictatorship. In its most serious form, the misdemeanor amounts to a policy of presenting a value-based dogma as value-free, immutable and incontestable" (Charles

Rowley and Alan T. Peacock, *Liberalist Welfare Economics* [London: Martin Robertson, 1975], 1).

13   *On Value Judgments*. A good many economists working essentially in the neoclassical tradition admit the need for value judgments in making recommendations for policy. Vickrey, for example, is quite blunt about it: "Whether he consciously admits it or not, the economist who goes far towards using his discipline as a means for recommendations, or who even steps beyond the stage of building abstract logical structures in a vacuum, must develop some scheme of ultimate values as a criterion for his judgments" (W.S. Vickrey, "An Exchange of Questions between Economics and Philosophy," in E.S. Phelps, ed., *Economic Justice* [London: Penguin, 1973], 36). Much of Arrow's work is concerned with little else than value judgments ("Values and Collective Decision-Making," in Phelps, *Economic Justice*, 117). Sugden maintains that the economists can't really do their job without some concern for value judgments: "An economist who refuses to think about value judgments at all is helpless in the face of the sheer volume of facts to his disposal" (Robert Sugden, *The Political Economy of Public Choice: An Introduction to Welfare Economics* [Oxford: Martin Robertson, 1981], 2). Little agrees that "anyone who writes that such-and-such a policy would further economic development is making a value judgment," but he also argues – quite rightly – that analysis of the operation of an economy – measuring the elasticity of supply of tea from Assam – need involve no value judgments at all (Little, *Economic Development*, 5–6).

14   Neoclassical welfare economics is closely associated with liberalism in the sense of individualism. As W.S. Vickrey points out, one consequence of this association is that individual choices are treated as sacrosanct: "Here (in modern Western economics) we find that the satisfaction of desires and preferences of individuals comes close to being considered a final value." Vickrey considers this position untenable when it comes to policy recommendations: "Thus even the most individualistic economist is compelled to be beyond the mere preferences of each individual in society if he is to make any but the most restricted recommendations as to policy, either individual or social" (Vickrey, "An Exchange of Questions," 37, 43).

15   Savoie, Donald J., *The Politics of Public Spending in Canada* (Toronto: University of Toronto Press, 1990).

16   Lawrence Krause, *The Australian Economy: A View from the North* (Washington D.C.: Brookings Institution, 1984).

17   Thomas J. Courchene and James R. Melvin, "A Neoclassical Approach to Regional Economics," in Benjamin Higgins and D.J. Savoie, eds., *Regional Development: Essays in Honour of François Perroux* (Boston and London: Unwin Hyman, 1988), 169–92.

18   Higgins and Savoie, eds., *Regional Development*.

19   *Psychology and Economics*. Few aspects of economic analysis have been more

keenly debated over the last fifty years than the relationship of the behavioural assumptions of economics to psychology as a professional discipline. I wrote my MSc thesis on this subject, under the supervision of Lionel Robbins, and my first article in a professional journal was based on that thesis. Being much under Robbins's influence, I then regarded ''the de-psycholization of economic theory,'' leaving economics immune to attacks from the psychologists, as a major triumph of economic science (*Manchester School*, 1935). Robbins seems to have clung to this view throughout his career. In his article ''The Nature of Economic Generalizations,'' he writes: ''The borderlands of Economics are the happy hunting-ground of minds averse to the effort of exact thought, and, in these ambiguous regions, endless time has been devoted to attacks on the alleged psychological assumptions of Economic Science. Psychology, it is said, advances very rapidly. If, therefore, Economics rests upon particular psychological doctrines ... (and) psychology has changed its fashion, Economics needs 'rewriting from the grounds upwards' ... Professional economists, absorbed in the exciting task of discovering new truth, have usually disdained to reply'' (Hahn and Hollis, *Philosophy and Economic Theory*, 40). Milton Friedman goes Robbins one better, arguing that the behavioural assumptions of economics *ought not* to be realistic: ''Truly important and significant hypotheses will be found to have assumptions that are widely inaccurate descriptions of reality, and, in general, the more significant the theory, the more unrealistic the assumptions (in this sense) ... Such a theory cannot be tested by comparing 'assumptions' directly with 'reality' '' (''The Methodology of Positive Economics,'' in Hahn and Hollis, *Philosophy and Economic Theory*, 26, 28).

This view has not gone unchallenged. Nobel laureate Herbert Simon, who is known as a psychologist as well as an economist, writes: ''Economics will progress as we deepen our understanding of human thought processes; and economics will change as human individuals and human societies use progressively sharpened tools of thought in making their decisions and designing their institutions ... In this paper, I have contrasted the concept of substantive rationality, which has dominated classical economics and provided it with its programme of structural determinism, with the concept of procedural rationality, which has prevailed in psychology. I have described also some of the concerns of economics that have forced the discipline to begin to concern itself with procedural rationality – with the actual processes of cognition, and with the limits on the human organism that give those processes their peculiar character'' (''From Substantive to Procedural Rationality,'' in Hahn and Hollis, *Philosophy and Economic Theory*, 83–4).

Mark Lutz and Kenneth Lux – the first, an economist, and the second, a clinical psychologist – in the opening chapter of their book, reject the ''physics model'' as a basis for economic analysis, reject also Friedman's positivism and determinism, and opt instead for Maslov humanistic psychology, with a hierarchy of needs rather than a uniform utility.

David Bensusan-Butt admits that models must be to some degree unrealistic; "a theoretical model in any of the social sciences must be that (unrealistic) to some extent because the complexities of human nature defy description." The trouble is that the behavioural assumptions of neoclassical economics are not really simplifying assumptions: "Economic man is not a manageable simplification, a starting point for theorising, a possible candidate for selection as the best of all possible starting points. So far from being a simplification, he is a psychological complication of appalling magnitude ... The simplifications involved in the definition of this (model) are not only too numerous and important, but they do not succeed in yielding an end product that is, in psychological terms, simple at all." He insists on the need for economists to study psychology directly: "Both for positive and normative purposes econometric conclusions have to be interpreted in terms of the conscious psychology of the agent concerned ... Any mythical 'as if' psychology that was useful to econometricians must be consistent in its predictions with an empirically observed psychology of the determination of the same events: and why use fairy tales in a social science when truth is at all accessible?" (D.M. Bensusan-Butt, *On Economic Man: An Essay on the Elements of Economic Theory* [Canberra: Australian National University Press, 1978], 115, 175, 177). In a later publication, he adds: "I conclude that, if it is to remain in contact with reality, the theoretical foundations of economics should be rooted in generalizations about the conscious behaviour of economic agents" (Bensusan-Butt, *On Economic Knowledge: Some New Measurements* [Canberra, ANU Press, 1980], section III).

Pattanaik makes the same point as Bensusan-Butt with regard to simplicity and truth: "But as Arrow himself recognizes, one of the tests for judging among alternative scientific hypotheses is that of simplicity. If two hypotheses serve equally well to explain, it is scientific practice to accept the simpler of the two and reject the other" ("Alternative Conceptions of Justice," in Phelps, *Economic Justice*, 315). My own current stand on this issue is that while economists can learn something useful from the literature of both psychology and anthropology to arrive at useful behavioural assumptions, it is necessary for economists themselves to observe the behaviour of members of particular societies in relation to their environment, on the spot and over time, in a *semi* anthropological manner. A similar view is expressed by De Gregori (economist) and Orio Pi-Sunyer (anthropologist), especially on pages 38 and 51 (Thomas R. De Gregori and Orio Pi-Sunyer, *Economic Development: The Cultural Impact* [New York: John Wiley, 1969]). I return to this question in the final chapter of this volume.

BIBLIOGRAPHY

Afriat, Sydney. *Logic of Choice and Economic Theory.* Cambridge: Cambridge University Press, 1987.

Bell, Daniel, and Irving Kristol, eds. *The Crisis in Economic Theory*. New York: Basic Books, 1982.

Friedman, Milton, and Rose Friedman. *Free to Choose: A Personal Statement*. London: Secker and Warburg, 1980.

Higgins, Benjamin. "Regional Development and Efficiency in the National Economy." In Higgins and Savoie, *Canadians and Regional Development*, 193–223.

– *Towards Growth and Stability in Construction*. Ottawa: Public Works Canada, 1978.

– "Trade-off Curves, Trends and Regional Disparities: The Case of Quebec." *Économie Appliquée* 28, nos. 2–3 (1978): 331–60.

– "Welfare Economics and the Unified Approach to Development Planning." In Antoni Kuklinski, ed., *Social Issues in Regional Policy and Regional Planning*, 91–114. The Hague: Mouton, 1977.

Higgins, Benjamin, and Donald J. Savoie, eds. *Canadians and Regional Development at Home and in the Third World*. Moncton: Canadian Institute for Research on Regional Development, 1988.

Kornai, Janos. *Anti Equilibrium: On Economic Systems Theory and the Tasks of Research*. Amsterdam and London: North Holland, 1971.

Lekachman, Robert. *Economists at Bay: Why the Experts Will Never Solve Your Problems*. New York: McGraw-Hill, 1978.

Lutz, Mark, and Kenneth Lux. *The Challenge of Humanistic Economics*. Menlo Park, Calif.: Benjamin Cummings, 1979.

Pattanaik, P.K. "Rist, Impersonality and the Social Welfare Function." In Phelps, *Economic Justice*, 298–318 (see note 13).

Perroux, François. "Au-delà du welfare state: une société pleinement économique." *Économie Appliquée* 37, no. 1 (March 1984).

– "The Pole of Development's New Place in a General Theory of Economic Activity." In Higgins and Savoie, *Regional Development*, 48–76 (see note 17).

2 Development, Equity, and Liberation

KENNETH BOULDING

WHAT IS A "BETTER WORLD"?

Will the state of the world be better or worse next year, or by the year 2000, or 2050? This is the sort of question that cannot elicit an exact answer, but it is still a very important one. It is a matter of human valuation, and the valuations of different people will differ. Nevertheless, there is more consensus in human valuations than is often recognized. Nearly everyone will agree that if we have a major nuclear war at some time in the future, the world will be very much worse off. If the health of the human race declines – if there is an increase in infant mortality, for instance, or a decline in the average life expectancy, or an increase in the proportion of time that humans are incapacitated by sickness – there will be wide agreement that this is a movement for the worse. Most people would also agree that if the world gets distinctly poorer, especially on a per capita basis, it is becoming worse off.

THE PROBLEM OF POVERTY

There may be more disagreement when it comes to the distribution of riches and poverty – for instance, if some people get poorer and some people get richer. Economists have always shied away from this problem, though even they have suggested that a given increase in riches is less significant if it goes to a rich person than if the same increase goes to a poor person. This is the famous principle of the diminishing marginal utility of income or wealth. Even economists can hardly deny that there is benevolence and malevolence and that indeed selfishness is merely the zero point on this scale. In contemplating the state of our own country or of the world, we may also feel various levels of pride and shame. This, I argue, should be a very important element not only in the evaluation of the total system but also in the evaluation of public goods.[1]

In regard to poverty and riches, especially in regard to their distribution, there are three related concepts that are significant in evaluating the total state of the world: equality, equity, and a minimal standard. About equality, there is a good deal of variety and perhaps even inconsistency of opinion. Certainly a world in which only one person was rich and everybody else was poor would be unacceptable. On the other hand, complete equality in economic terms not only seems to be virtually impossible to achieve, but is a real question of whether people would want it. If you ask people, Would you rather live in a society in which there is some chance of getting rich or no chance? they might well prefer the former. This would imply acceptance of inequality. Every purchase of a lottery ticket indeed represents a demand for economic inequality.

There may be a real conflict between equality and equity if equity means that people should get what they deserve. This is part of the extremely complex and difficult concept of justice. On the other hand, if you ask people, Would you want to live in a society in which everything bad that happened to you was your own fault? I am not sure they would answer yes. The tempering of justice with mercy is often the only thing that makes it tolerable. Without some forgiveness society falls apart, as we see in Ulster, Northern Ireland, and Lebanon, and as we may see in South Africa.

The concept of a minimal standard (i.e., a level of economic welfare below which society regards the level of poverty as unacceptable) has been around in principle for quite a long time, certainly going back to the Elizabethan poor laws in England. Just as it would be considered inadmissable on the part of two parents to starve one of their children to benefit the others, so, too, if we think of ourselves as belonging to the human race, we will feel shame at contemplating a world in which a significant proportion of people are below what is considered a minimal acceptable level. Certainly in the world as we see it today, at least 20 or 25 percent of the human population are at an economic level where a "good life" is almost impossible, and it is reasonable to believe that one of the necessary conditions of the "better world" of the future is that poverty below some minimal level should be abolished.

Exactly where the minimal level should be defined, of course, is a difficult question. By current American standards, my own grandfather and his family would have been considered to be well below the minimal level. He was a blacksmith in the west of England who could not even afford a bicycle. On the other hand, he was a Methodist lay preacher, he was much respected, he had great self-respect, and if anybody had called him poor, he would have been insulted. Poor people were people who drank and went to the Salvation Army. I think he also had very little envy. Rich people were of another world, with which he never interacted, and they did not concern him very much. I suspect he thought they might have difficulty, in the biblical sense, in being saved.

Wherever we put the minimal level, however, it is pretty clear that we will find a lot of people below it. As we go down the scale from riches to poverty, we find increasingly that the potential for the "good life" is not realized. Every fertilized egg – and certainly every baby – has a potential for physical growth, for health and activity, and for learning. Beyond a certain point, whatever prevents the realization of this potential is a form of poverty. Even rich children, of course, may grow up in an environment that prevents the realization of their potential as human beings. They may be starved of love, they may become "rakes," they may even commit suicide. For the children of the poor, however, the chance of realizing the implicit potential is much diminished. They are likely to suffer from malnutrition, which will prevent their physical development; they will also be subject to preventable disease. Most of all, they will be deprived of learning opportunities which would help to fulfil the enormous potential of their minds. Because the potential implied in our genetic structure is so enormous, no human being ever fulfils it completely. Nobody can do everything that they might have done. There are, of course, differences in genetic potential and there are people with genetic defects. Even for those individuals with genetic defects, however, environmental limitations are still of great importance and may prevent the realization of what potential they do have.

How, then, do we get rid of poverty? This is a question with a great diversity of answers, none of which seem very satisfactory. At one end of the scale, we have the liberationists and revolutionaries who see the problem primarily in terms of redistribution. They would end poverty by taking from the rich and giving to the poor. The question arises, Who is to take from the rich, and how? This relates to the question of the nature of the power structure in society. I argue that there are three forms of power. The first is *threat power*, which is what the bank robber, the tax collector, the terrorist, the commander-in-chief, and also, one should add, the nonviolent resister, may have. The second is *economic power* itself, which is the power to produce, to exchange, and to accumulate. The third is *integrative power*, which is the power that goes with legitimacy and respect, affection, identification, love, and so on. Over all three forms lies the power to *learn*.

THREAT POWER

The overall magnitude of power is a very complex function of all three types. A naked threat is a very ineffective one, as in the case of the bandit and the terrorist. The legitimated threat of the tax collector is much more powerful. Threat power without economic power is very ineffective. It is economic power that produces the means of threatening. On the other hand, producing the means of threatening destroys the economic power that produced the means. Concentration on the war industry, for instance, tends to destroy the economic power that produced it in the first place, as we see happening today in the United States. Threat very often perpetuates the system it tries to overthrow: the French Revolution produced Napoleon, the Russian Revolution produced Stalin. Liberation movements easily enslave the liberated by creating even greater concentrations of political power than existed before. Nevertheless, the distribution of property is a significant element in the inequality of riches, and titles to property often go back to some form of theft, as in the case of William the Conqueror in England or the European invaders of the Americas.

ECONOMIC POWER

At the other end of the scale, we have what might be called the "developers," people who see the abolition of poverty as a result of the process by which everybody gets richer. Thus, in the United States the proportion of the population in poverty (by almost any standard we wish to select) more than halved between 1950 and about 1975, but has been rising a little since then. This happened, however, with virtually no redistribution of income. The proportional distribution of income is astonishingly stable. A critical question here is, How much poverty is a result of exploitation (i.e., do the poor produce something that the rich take away from them) and how much is a result of low productivity? Exploitation certainly cannot be entirely ruled out, but if we look at world income as it is distributed between the rich countries and the poor countries, it is pretty clear that exploitation as such plays a very minor role. The rich countries are not rich and the poor countries poor because the poor countries produce a lot and the rich take it away from them. The rich countries are rich because they produce a lot and the poor countries are poor because they do not produce very much.

THE DYNAMICS OF RICHES AND POVERTY

If we look at the problem dynamically, the rich countries are rich because they have been getting rich at a faster rate for a longer time than the poor countries. It could be argued that the rich countries by their imperialist domination and so forth prevented the poor countries from getting richer, but given the total picture, even this proposition becomes dubious. It is very clear now that the imperialist countries, like Britain, France, and Russia, actually hampered their own development by devoting resources to the conquest and exploitation of empire. From the middle of the nineteenth century on, certainly those European countries that stayed home and minded their own business, like Sweden and Denmark, did much better economically than Britain and France and, of course, very much better than Russia. Furthermore, since giving up their empires, Britain and France substantially increased their own rates of development. Japan is an even more striking example. Conquering Korea cost Japan something like ten years of development, and its military defeat in 1945 was followed by an unprecedented generation of economic growth. West Germany is a similar example. Here again, military defeat led into a period of very remarkable economic development.

On the other hand, there are a variety of reasons why some countries have failed to develop. Some of these are connected to the internal distribution of power and property. The nature of religious and educational institutions may also play an important role. One suspects that where property is heavily concentrated in the hands of a small land-owning class, and also where the learning and educational processes of a society are concentrated very heavily in a uniform and authoritarian religious body, development is hard to get off the ground. One thinks of Islam after the 1400s as an example; here a civilization that previously had exhibited substantial scientific and technical development seemed to freeze with the Turkish conquests, though it was also damaged earlier by the Mongol conquests. Other examples would be Latin America and, indeed, Spain itself. Here again the concentration of property in large landholdings on the one hand and the dominance of a single church on the other may well have been important limiting factors in general development. By contrast, in northern Europe and also in the United States and Canada, the diversity of sects, and especially the development of sects that put a high value on the learning process, and the undermining of the monopoly of landlords by rising financial and business institutions had something to do with the much more rapid rate of change and economic growth.

If we are to resolve the dilemmas presented by these different points of view and increase our knowledge of the very complex and diverse reality of economic power, we must look more closely at the nature of riches and poverty and the factors that limit both development and distribution. One key to the problem, only rarely turned, is the relationship between the capital and income components of economic welfare.

CAPITAL AND INCOME

Capital is a flashlight photograph. Income consists of those events that happen between one flashlight photograph and the next. When events are regular over time, like the flow of a river or the weekly appearance of paycheques, we think of income as a flow and of capital as a stock, but this can be a little misleading when events are not very regular.

Both capital and income, the existing populations of people and goods, and the events that change them are significant in the overall evaluation of economic welfare. Economists have concentrated far too much on income as a measure of economic welfare, whereas in many ways the capital aspects are more significant. We see this, for instance, in the concept of consumption. Economists have tended to identify household purchases with consumption, which is absurd. Household purchases are exchange. A household pays money to the store and receives in return food, clothing, furniture, automobiles, or books, which are initially part of the capital stock of the household. Like all capital stocks, these will usually depreciate, as clothes, furniture, automobiles, and so on wear out. These capital stocks may also be consumed in producing something else. Food, for instance, is consumed, is digested, and is transformed into bodily materials and energy. These, however, depreciate as breakfast depreciates and has to be replaced by lunch. Income allows us to replace and expand our capital stock. When we work for somebody, this increases our capital stock first by the wage claim. When the wage claim is exchanged for money, then we can use the money to repair, to replace, or to expand our capital stock, including our human capital through investments in learning.

It is very important that we include some valuation of our own body and mind in our total capital stock and net worth. This is closely related to our earning capacity over our lifetime, that is, the gross additions that we make to our capital stock either through producing things ourselves or by working for wages or salaries and producing things for an employer. It is only in a slave society that human capital is actually reflected in the marketplace directly. In a non-slave society we are each the owners of our own body and mind, but it is still important to put a value on this property. Moreover, non-human capital assets in the form of land, buildings, and machinery can be taken from their owners. Human capital, unless we go back to slavery, cannot be taken from the individual owner. This value of human capital grows from birth; the body grows and the mind learns and grows to some kind of maturity, after which it may decline in old age until death, when it becomes zero.

Our "riches," or economic welfare, are a function mainly of the capital stock. The income flow, however, is also significant, partly because it replaces depreciated stock and also because some consumption, like eating, is valued for its own sake. We get most of our satisfaction in the utilization of the capital stock that surrounds us, including our own bodies and minds. It is because this utilization involves depreciation that we have to have income to replace the depreciation. On the other hand, we like variety and new things, and we get satisfaction out of destroying some things, as when we eat food. Our total economic welfare is a complex function of our capital stock and the throughput through it in terms of income. There are also good evolutionary reasons why we like eating as well as being well fed, which is the corresponding capital stock. This idea, however, that our satisfaction all comes from consumption is nonsense.

The relations between capital and income have their own dynamics. Certain forms of capital actually appreciate over time: some because of changes in the assigned value, as when something old-fashioned becomes an antique; some because of changes in the market price, like stocks or real estate that rise in value. Moreover, quite apart from changes in market price, the value of a bond increases as interest accrues; then as interest is paid, we exchange this accrual for cash. Similarly, real estate may rent for an annual sum that is greater than its depreciation. A very fundamental relationship here is that income is the gross addition to our net capital stock or net worth, while consumption is the subtraction from it. If, therefore, income exceeds consumption, our capital stock will grow; if consumption exceeds income, it will decline.

POSITIVE AND NEGATIVE FEEDBACK PROCESSES

There is a further relationship between capital and income. Not only does an excess of income over consumption increase capital, but an increase in capital has a strong tendency to increase income. We see this, of course, in such investments as land, equipment, and fertilizer for the farmer and better equipment for the artisan or the factory. We see it also in financial instruments, for example, in the acquisition of stocks and bonds and promissory notes bearing positive interest and profit rates. What we see here is a "positive feedback process" – the more income, the easier it is to increase capital; the more capital, the more income. This is indeed a prime source of inequality. It is a process that has become known as the "Matthew Principle;" as the verses in the Gospel of St. Matthew say, "To him that hath shall be given, and to him that hath not shall be taken away even that he hath."[2] If a society started off with an absolutely equal distribution of overall capital and income, random forces would make some people a little richer than others. The ones that became richer would find it easier to get still richer. The ones that became poorer would find it harder to get richer. It is not surprising, therefore, that inequality develops.

This tendency towards inequality is recognized, oddly enough, in the Old Testament. In the "Year of Jubilee," the Israelites were supposed to forgive all debts and restore lands to their previous owners every fifty years.[3] It is very doubtful that this was ever done. We seem to come closest to this in times of revolution: the French Revolution deposed and killed off the old landlords; and the Russian Revolution went even further in the First Collectivization and killed off the good farmers and then created a famine. A much more benign method of preventing unacceptable inequality, which at least saves human capital, is progressive income taxation and inheritance taxation. This we seem to be backing away from, unfortunately.

OFFSETS TO RISING INEQUALITY

Other offsets to rising inequality are independent of government action. There is, for instance, a certain tendency of the rich to lose their money. This happens partly because of the "shirtsleeves to shirtsleeves in three generations" principle, as in *The Rake's Progress*, which is by no means unknown, although I know of no studies that show how common it is. Another offset is the tendency of the rich not to have children, noted even by Adam Smith. Galton explained the disappearance of old families in England on the grounds that the wealthy young men from these families tended to marry heiresses, and an heiress would not be an heiress if she had come from a fertile family. How valid this is, again I do not know. A third offsetting factor is the tendency of the rich to enter speculative markets in which there is a constant redistribution of assets between those who are holding assets that are rising in value and those holding assets that are falling in relative value. If the total of assets were constant, these would be exactly equal and every gain in the market would be balanced by somebody's loss. On the other hand, there are examples of old families that stay rich for several generations, which suggests that the offsetting factors are by no means wholly effective. One reason for such families' continued success would surely be the continuing reinforcement of their human capital.

THE POPULATION PROBLEM

In looking at the dynamics of poverty and riches, one should not overlook the impact of both the absolute size and the rate of growth of population. Absolute size is the classic Malthusian problem: high population density combined with low productivity certainly implies poverty. Rapid population growth also makes for poverty, as we now see in many parts of the Tropics. The population explosion all over the Tropics complicates the picture. This is largely the result of the introduction of a little bit of the modern world, resulting in a reduction in infant mortality without the corresponding realization that births had to be cut down. A country that doubles in population every generation, like Kenya, has to build a whole new country every generation in order to stay where it is. So far, world food production has roughly kept pace with the population increase, at least until the 1980s, but how long this can go on is a very worrying question. Many of the African countries, especially, seem to be heading for a disaster that will make the Irish famine of the 1940s look small. We cannot predict, of course, what the "green gene" revolution of human intervention in genetic material will do. The future is full of profound uncertainty.

DEVELOPMENT AS A LEARNING PROCESS

Economic development is fundamentally a learning process and very little else. Natural resources are almost irrelevant to it. Indeed, they may even be a handicap. They may divert attention from the real problem, as we see in many of the resource-rich countries. Japan is perhaps the country that best demonstrates the unimportance of natural resources and the tremendous importance of human capital in the development of a *learning society*. We could modify this by saying that people get rich either by luck or by learning, but of these, learning is the only sure thing. The countries that are rich today got so not so much by exploiting the poor (though there may have been a little of that), but by developing systems of education and research that increased the total stock of useful human knowledge. Human learning, of course, does not depend entirely on formal institutions. A lot of learning takes place in the field and through personal experience. Whether the overall pattern of a society encourages or discourages such learning can be very important. Societies that think they know everything already, as may happen when a particular ideology becomes dominant, are apt to be pretty poor at learning.

Our problem is that practical learning is frequently – and sometimes quite rightly – a highly local phenomenon, while the organized institutions of learning tend to be worldwide and large scale. Bringing these two forms of learning together and integrating them is difficult. This problem is particularly important in agriculture. The world's atmosphere – and to a lesser extent, the oceans – may be a single system, but the land is a great mosaic of very different systems of soil, rainfall, climate, and so on that the large structures of organized knowledge, for instance, in universities and in the scientific community, cannot readily penetrate. A group that has occupied one place for a long time gets a certain amount of traditional wisdom about it that outside developers may easily overlook. It is particularly easy for male developers to overlook the knowledge of women, who often have more of a learning culture than the men. Here the skills of the anthropologist in studying the knowledge and the culture of particular communities can be extremely important in mediating between the often harsh and overriding impact of the world scientific and technological culture and the folk knowledge of local people.

At the national level there is also a great deal more to learn. In a world of more than a hundred new nations, national political competence is, unfortunately, an important part of the general picture, and here we find enormous variety. I have sometimes said that there is no such thing as the "Third World." It is 3.01, 3.02, 3.03, and so on, with every country, and sometimes regions within countries, very different from the others. Economics and ecology are significant here; unwise intervention, for example, in the ecosystem can easily cause economic disaster. It is easy to mess up an ecosystem by distorting the relative price structure, which governments seem to like to do, particularly in the Tropics, where ecosystems are rather fragile. Ideology does not seem to be much help when it comes to competence. Socialist ideology certainly has not turned out very well in the Third World – Mozambique, Angola, Guinea, Ethiopia, and even Tanzania are examples of its destructive effects. At the other end of the scale, the ideologies of what might be called "militarist capitalism" have also been disastrous, for instance, in Argentina, Uruguay, and Chile.

LIBERATION: DISTRIBUTION OF POWER

It is clear that the existing institutions of the world, whether socialist or free-market, are not adequate to deal with the problem of getting rid of poverty. Liberation in one sense describes what we are trying to do, but it does not tell us how to do it. Liberation refers essentially to the distribution of power. The emancipation of the slaves was very clearly liberation. It distributed the ownership of human capital from the slave owner to the former slave. Now, with very few exceptions, every person on the planet is his or her own slave, though this does not quite deal with the status of children, conscripts who are temporary slaves, prisoners, people in concentration camps, and the infirm and incompetent. We cannot, however, as we have seen, redistribute human capital, which is an inalienable property of the person owning it, except through the redistribution of education and other processes that increase the value of human capital. Redistribution of non-human capital may certainly be on the agenda, but if redistribution is done in a way that destroys the organization of the capital itself, it is useless. Decisions that lead to an increase in private capital are strongly affected by the degree of uncertainty in the system. The greater the uncertainty, the greater the reward in the shape of profit must be in order to persuade people to invest. High rates of profit in poor countries very often reflect the political uncertainties of these societies, which means also that there is not very much investment in them. A political regime may be almost absurd, like that of Hong Kong, but if it has the integrative power to create stability, capital will grow and enrichment will take place.

The distribution of power is in many ways more important than the distribution of wealth, which is only one form of power. Centrally planned economies, to date, have been the enemy of individual liberation and have resulted in the concentration of power, not in its wider distribution. They have produced societies in which most people are the victims of decisions they are powerless to alter. A centrally planned economy is a one-firm state. Under what might be called "social capitalism," however, power is at least divided among firms and government and is much more widely distributed.

Perhaps a liberation movement's greatest contribution is to liberate the latent power in people themselves. One of the most fruitful aspects of the liberation theology of Latin America has been the success of the church in integrating little economic communities of people who have released some of the power that was latent in themselves.

SELF-PITY AND ENVY

One of the great obstacles to development in many parts of the world is an ideology of self-pity, which decreases human capital. If we think that what is wrong with us is always somebody else's fault, we are not going to do very well at releasing the latent power that lies within us. Economic development is very closely associated with cultures that have cast aside self-pity, that develop a strong sense of self-identity, and that assume if there is something wrong, it is probably their fault rather than somebody else's. This leads into the release of latent power and an increase in the value of human capital.

An important source of self-pity is envy, which can inhibit the release of latent power. There are those who argue that all that matters is relative poverty, that if everybody gets richer together nobody is any happier because somebody is always richer than he or she is. This seems to me a very destructive philosophy. It is the absolute level of poverty that denies the realization of human potential. This is what we need to get rid of even if, under some circumstances though not all, the easiest way to get rid of it is to make everybody richer.

WHICH INSTITUTIONS DIMINISH POVERTY?

This still leaves us with the question, Which institutions, especially on a world scale, will increase the value of human capital, especially of the poorest quarter of the human race? This is the really critical question. If we increase the value of human capital with the development of learning experiences, often of many different kinds, non-human capital tends to take care of itself, given that we learn what we have to do in order to increase it. Much of what has to be done to eradicate poverty will have to be done at the local level and by poor people themselves. If they don't have a vision of a better world for themselves, nothing much will happen. Nevertheless, the organizations that belong to the larger world can have a role in this much hoped-for process.

Four general groups of organizations are the most likely candidates:

1 Multinational corporations already form a worldwide network, which includes human learning and human capital as well as physical capital. The variety among the multinationals is about as great as it is among the

Third World countries themselves. It is very hard to generalize about them. Their character and influence often depend on what field they are in. It is very hard to estimate their influence on poverty. Sometimes their influence may be ineffective or adverse if they concentrate on the richer sectors of poor societies or if they develop enclaves, like plantations or mines, which have little spillover into the rest of the economy and hence do not contribute significantly to the general learning process. Many of them, on the other hand, like those involved in retailing, in local manufacturing, and in producing more efficiently the goods most likely purchased by the poor, can have a real effect in diminishing poverty. They may be more successful in doing this for the richer sectors of the human population than for the poorer sectors, for whom large-scale operations are often not very effective. The multinationals are most likely to be effective in diminishing poverty in societies that are themselves fairly well organized and can handle worldwide organizations on fairly equal terms. This is less likely to be the case, of course, for the poorest countries.

2   The role of small businesses should also not be overlooked. In the United States, for instance, the diminution in poverty and the expansion of the labour market in recent decades have probably been more the result of the spread of new businesses that have new ideas and take advantage of new opportunities, than the result of the activities of the old, established, and rather unimaginative large corporations. This has been true in many different industries. Part of the difficulty of diminishing the poverty of the poor countries is the absence of an intermediate layer of small and innovative businesses between the multinationals and the poorer people.

3   Another level of world interaction is that of the international government organizations, most of which are affiliated with the United Nations. It may be that what we need is a greatly expanded UNESCO that could send carefully trained teachers into all the poorer parts of the world, drawn mainly, of course, from these parts themselves. Such teachers would be able to awaken the learning capacity that is latent even in the poorest of human beings and so build up both the human capital and the other forms of capital necessary to a noticeable movement out of poverty. Again, it may be that governmental organizations like UNESCO cannot do the trick; certainly UNESCO's history has been depressing in recent years.

4   A fourth category of world culture is the NGOs, the non-governmental organizations. These may well turn out to be the most effective levers to move people out of poverty. They tend to be closer to the people themselves than are the corporations or the government organizations. To some extent, they are having an impact already, both on the religious and the secular sides. A great expansion of these activities will be needed, however, if the problem of poverty is really to be solved.

NOTES

1 K.E. Boulding, "The Economics of Pride and Shame," *Atlantic Economic Journal* 15, no. 1 (March 1987): 10–19.
2 Matt. 13:12, 25:29.
3 Lev. 25:8–19.

PART TWO

Facts

3 Development, Efficiency, and Equity in Historical Perspective

W.W. ROSTOW

INTRODUCTION

In responding to my assigned task, captured in the title, I shall proceed in five steps as follows:

- by defining the eighteenth-century roots of development and welfare policy;
- by tracing schematically the evolution of thought and policy from 1776, when Hume died and *The Wealth of Nations* was published, to the marginalist revolution round about 1870;
- by tracing similarly the rise of welfare economics and the welfare state over the subsequent century;
- by commenting on the debate about development, efficiency, and equity in post-1945 development theory and practice; and
- by making a few final observations on future tasks.

FOUNDING FATHERS: DAVID HUME AND ADAM SMITH

Modern political economy was created as part of a much larger venture: the shifting of the Heavenly City of medieval Christianity "to earthly foundations."[1] This secular redefinition of the good life and the good society forced the leaders of the Enlightenment back to first principles and led them into philosophy, psychology, politics, sociology, and culture, as well as economics. David Hume, in fact, began with psychology, as this quotation from his youthful *Treatise of Human Nature* suggests: "These principles of human nature you'll say, are contradictory. But what is man but a heap of contradictions."[2] The founding fathers of modern economics were under no illusion that human beings were maximizers.

Hume's view of the human condition is directly in the line from Plato to Freud. In a powerful simplification, Plato analysed the problem of keeping the "spirited" side of human beings, "appetite," and "reason" in balance The roughly analogous elements for Freud were, of course, the id, ego, and superego. In a graceful move from micro- to macro-analysis, which economists have never been able to emulate, Plato linked politics and psychology by regarding his tripartite view of the individual as "the state within us" on which public life is built. Freud made a similar linkage of the two domains in *Civilization and Its Discontents*.

Hume's tripartite simplification consisted of "action," "pleasure," and "sympathy." (He also included "indolence" as a requirement of respite from the sustained pursuit of action and pleasure, to which diminishing relative marginal utility evidently applied.) He used his system as the basis for some propositions of considerable substance.

He identified action as well as pleasure as "causes of labour," action constituting the exercise of physical, mental, or artistic talent in a setting of challenge for some practical purpose. In this, Hume evokes Keynes's later dictum: "If human nature felt no temptation to take a chance, no satisfaction (profit apart) in constructing a factory, a railway, a mine or a farm, there might not be much investment merely as a result of cold calculation."[3]

Hume saw, quite particularly, that the rise of urban life, as increasing commerce expanded the cities, would bring human beings together in more closely knit, interdependent societies and heighten the power of sympathy, on which civilized life ultimately depended. More generally, he argued that the expansion and diversification of manufactures and the increase in productivity brought about by the expansion of commerce and exploitation of comparative advantage not only enriched private life, by expanding the range of choices open for the pursuit of action and pleasure, but also had wide-ranging, benign social consequences for the non-economic dimensions of society, including provision of the foundation for human liberty and "mild" if not wholly democratic government. Thus, Hume saw economic change as fundamental to social and political change; but he also saw economic change as dependent rather more on non-economic than on economic motives.

Hume also enunciated clearly one of the most powerful of all propositions in welfare economics, one that, again, flowed directly from his perception of people: "Every person, if possible, ought to enjoy the fruits of his labour, in a full possession of all the necessaries, and many of the conveniences of life. No one can doubt, but such an equality is most suitable to human nature, and diminishes much less from the happiness of the rich than it adds to that of the poor."[4] This perception later converged with a realization of the inherently psychological and social forces that determined the subsistence wage, leading Ricardo, for example, to argue: "The friends of humanity cannot but wish that in all countries the labouring classes should have a taste for comforts and enjoyments, and they should be stimulated by all legal means to procure them. There cannot be a better security against a superabundant population."[5]

Adam Smith derived much from Hume, and in many ways both were pre-Bentham utilitarians.[6] They both were deeply troubled by gross inequality of income distribution. Indeed, *The Wealth of Nations* refers on its second page to the fact that "a great number of people do not labour at all, many of whom consume the product of ten times, frequently of a hundred times more labour than the greater part of those who do work." But they were puzzled about how a more just system could be reconciled with the need for competition. After all, they were at war against excessive bureaucracy and battled for a greater degree of privatization. They saw competition as the most efficient way to tame the evil, monopolizing instinct of entrepreneurs; with some reluctance, they accepted the inequality that competition yielded but groped for ways to mitigate it. There was also a strong, untamed non-utilitarian strand in Smith. The opening sentence of his *Theory of Moral Sentiments* was, "How selfish soever man may be supposed, there are evidently some principles in his nature, which interest him in the fortune of others, and render their happiness necessary to him, though he derives nothing from it, except the pleasure of seeing it." Istvan Hont and Michael Ignatieff have been correct in reminding us that Hume and Smith were committed to justice – albeit in a world of human beings moved by conflicting impulses and consequently confronting forces that often did not converge.[7]

On utilitarian grounds both Hume and Smith found a substantial legitimate role for government. As early as 1739, in his *Treatise of Human Nature*, Hume set out the case for the public role in a substantial array of enterprises as well as it has ever been done: bridges, harbours, ramparts, canals, fleets, armies.[8] All this was crystallized in Smith's famous tripartite description of the three legitimate functions of government under a system of natural liberty: national defence; the provision of justice, and erecting and maintaining public works and institutions needed by and profitable for "a great society" but unprofitable for private enterprise.[9] The third category included strong support for popular education; here, once again, Smith embraces but goes beyond the utilitarian argument: "Though the state were to derive no advantage from the instruction of the inferior ranks of people, it would still deserve its attention that they should not be altogether uninstructed. The state, however, derives no inconsiderable advantage from their instruction"[10] – an advantage he proceeds to specify. In fact, welfare economics for two and a half centuries has had a dual character. Economists have argued that providing for equality of opportunity and otherwise struggling against poverty are good for society – a profitable investment – but they have also argued, as did Adam Smith on education, that such endeavours are morally right and necessary for a decent, civilized society held together ultimately by mutual sympathy.

The classical tradition in political economy emerged from the Enlightenment and all that had preceded it. It included strands from Greece and Rome and strands from Christianity that were slipped in through the back door; it reflected inspiration from the Scientific Revolution and lessons learned from the brutal seventeenth-century struggles from Britain to Bohemia. It thus created canons of private and public ethics that remain to the present day in the Atlantic community, but with influence far beyond.

That tradition was rooted in Hume's sense of the almost impenetrable complexity and diversity of individuals and the respect society ought to accord that uniqueness within the limits permitted by the minimum imperatives of social organization. From those propositions flowed a claim for mild and permissive government, but they also led to a bias against monopolistic power and to reliance on the discipline of competition – where competition was possible. In this bias, efficiency and virtue seemed to converge but with acknowledged and troubling costs in equity. As for development, the classical tradition unashamedly reversed the view that the good, uncorrupt society must be spartan. It argued that commerce in luxuries was essential to expanding the wealth of nations, and that expanded wealth was necessary for human freedom, mild government, and an increasingly civilized life based on enlarged sympathy for one another among the citizenry. Embedded in this panoramic view of the individual in relation to society was a theory of economic growth.

In Hume's case, his quite recognizable production function emerges from his series of short, often polemical, policy essays which incorporate most of his contribution to economics. Output in Hume's system is a function of labour, land, and manufactures; the productivity of labour and of land is determined by the scale of manufactures; and the scale of manufactures is determined by the scale of trade, foreign and domestic, and the productivity increases provided by the exploitation of comparative advantage. The productivity increases reflect the increased human effort induced, in the first instance, by the availability of a widened range of "luxuries" and, then, by the cumulative experience of merchant, worker, farmer, and manufacturer operating within a progressively more diversified economy. This diversified economy offered both heightened challenges and rewards which, in Hume's view, were the optimum setting within which people stretched their capacities to the limit and came to prefer frugality and gain to the immediacy of pleasure.

As for capital and technology, Hume argued that it is the general prosperity of a country, not the money supply, that yields low rates of interest; that rates of interest are a product of demand and supply; and that in generating the necessary supply of savings, once again the merchant emerges as hero, this time as miser rather than as exploiter of comparative advantage:

There is no craving or demand of the human mind more constant and insatiable than that for exercise and employment; and this desire seems the foundation of most of our passions and pursuits ... But if the employment you give him be lucrative, especially if the profit be attached to every particular exertion of industry, he has gain so often in his eye, that he acquires, by degrees, a passion for it, and knows no such pleasure as that of seeing the daily encrease of his fortune.[11] And this is the reason why trade encreases frugality, and why, among merchants, there is the same overplus of misers above prodigals, as, among the possessors of land, there is the contrary.[12]

Hume assumed that, in stimulating diversified manufactures by the exploitation of comparative advantage, the "mechanic arts" would flourish and even his normally prodigal proprietors of land would divert some of their surplus from consumption to investment and "study agriculture as a science, and redouble their industry and attention." One fundamental and abiding proposition relating to technology was enunciated by Hume with clarity: "Necessity ... is the great spur to industry and invention."[13]

Smith's growth theory, incorporated in a large treatise, is more explicit and extensive. It has lent itself to a good deal of formal modelling.[14] Labour, land, and capital are unambiguously his three factors of production. The system is driven forward, as in Hume, by the savings of the frugal merchants and manufacturers who are assumed to invest all savings, without leakage. Leakage occurs when the rich – notably, rich landlords – and government indulge in expenditures that employ "unproductive" labour. Capital permits the widening of the market and, thereby, the division of labour. Capital is mainly envisaged as working capital supplying labour with necessaries, raw materials, and simple tools. "Machines" appear somewhat more explicitly in Smith than in Hume, but they come to much the same thing as Hume's "mechanic arts." In explaining how the division of labor increases productivity, Smith identified three forces: the worker's increase in dexterity; the saving of the worker's time as he concentrates on a single task rather than moving from one task to another; and "the invention of a great number of machines which facilitate and abridge labour, and enable one man to do the work of many."[15] Smith distinguishes these significant refinements of familiar technologies from occasional, rare, major technological breakthroughs accomplished by "philosophers" (scientists) – an important quasi-Schumpeterian distinction to the best of my knowledge not to be found earlier in the literature of economics.

Both Hume and Smith had a good deal to say in dynamic terms about the rich country/poor country problem – that is, the effect on a more-advanced country of an effort by a less-advanced country to close the gap in per capita income and technological competence.[16] They urged the more-advanced country, in Hume's phrase, to be "civilized and industrious," that is, to enjoy the expansion in exports and income per capita to be derived from the rise of the less-developed country and to compensate for the inevitably increased low-priced imports from that country by shifting rapidly to production and export of technologically more sophisticated-products and otherwise exploiting the assets developed during its period of unchallenged primacy.

The Smithian model asserted, in effect, that a society could expand for a time, its output, and, for a shorter time, its real income per capita, but that in the end a limit was reached at its "full complement of riches." A limit to growth was reached for three reasons: technological progress was constrained by geographical or other limitations on the expansion of the market (and thus on incremental technological change) and by the fact that major technological change is judged to be an occasional once-over event; the rise in real income per capita was constrained by the rise in population that resulted, after a lag, from an initial rise in the real wage; and diminishing returns (in different degree) constrained the expansion of production of basic commodities.

1776–1870: THE ELABORATION OF THE CLASSIC TRADITION

As welfare economists, Hume and Smith inveighed, above all, against the domestic and international aspects of mercantilism. Their enemies were monopoly, war, and (in Smith's case) empire. In welfare terms, their hope for all humanity was in Hume's good phrase, "liberty, industry, and good government." They wished to see all nations achieve their "full complement of riches" in peace.

But that ceiling – based on technological, population, and resource constraints – began to lift less than a decade after the publication of *The Wealth of Nations*. In the 1780s, after a generation's inventive ferment, major innovations began to unfold as a flow, starting with the convergence of the new textile machinery, Watt's more efficient steam engine, and Cort's method for fabricating iron. British patents sealed averaged 29 per annum in the 1770s. They moved up as follows in the next four decades: 48, 65, 92, and 101. By the 1840s the annual average was 458. Invention and innovation had become a substantial if erratic flow, which had never happened before in human history.

Then, in 1812, a second constraint was broken: the price of wheat fell from its peak of 152*s*. (per quarter) in August 1812 – the Napoleonic Wars peak – to 75*s*. in December 1813. It proceeded erratically to a further trough in 1822, when it levelled off as a matter of trend until the price explosion of 1852–54. The post-1812 decline combined with the gradual emergence of the

United States and other major overseas suppliers of food and raw materials and an awareness that British population growth was decelerating. These developments ended, for a time, the concern with population and the food supply, which had understandably obsessed Malthus and Ricardo down to 1812. Their post-1815 writing and debate were, in one sense, neither Malthusian nor Ricardian: they argued over the character of the postwar malaise and the impact of machinery on employment. But the stationary state (or worse) that had haunted them in the most acute period of wartime pressure of population on the food supply was pushed far down the road. If not quite ebullient over the human prospect, they ceased to be dismal scientists.

This late phase in the work of Malthus and Ricardo constitutes a significant transition, for a generation later, John Stuart Mill and Karl Marx, from quite different perspectives, accepted invention and innovation as an ongoing, almost automatic process. Marx assumed that it was possible to defeat the power of diminishing returns in agriculture indefinitely; Mill, that there was time to bring population and growth under control before diminishing returns forced a stationary state on the world economy. They both focused on a quite different welfare problem: that is, how best to ameliorate the evident harshnesses of the industrial society emerging in their time on the continent and in the United States as well as in the more-advanced Britain. Like Smith and Hume and pre-1813 Malthus and Ricardo, Mill and Marx believed there were (or should be) limits to growth. But their limits arose not from diminishing returns but from diminishing relative marginal utility for real income itself, conventionally defined. Mill looked to a time when birth control would render labour rather than land the scarce factor of production and when real wages (rather than rent) would rise to a point where men and women could choose an affluent but essentially static real income in a physical environment unstrained by excessive population or excessive industrialization. Marx's equally romantic notion of communism envisaged a time when all material wants were satisfied and work itself had become a psychological necessity.

But Mill was not merely the first no-growth environmentalist, but also an early articulater of major aspects of what was to become the welfare state. While retaining a fierce loyalty to individual human liberty and the disciplining virtues of competition, he set out the legitimate welfare functions of government in much greater detail than his major predecessors:

- Cases in which the consumer is an incompetent judge of the commodity, of which education is the major example cited
- Cases of persons exercising power over others, notably the protection of young persons and the insane
- Cases of contracts in perpetuity in which an individual is not in a position to judge his or her interest at some future and distant time

- Cases of delegated management where public surveillance and limited powers over joint-stock companies are judged legitimate to assure that inherently monopoly powers are not abused. Mill judged public ownership and operation of economic units to be inefficient; but he thought private joint-stock companies were little better, if better at all.
- Cases where public intervention is required to achieve a broadly agreed objective: for example, the reduction of hours of work, which, if not accomplished by law, could be disrupted by a minority of workers or factory owners. Mill also cited the control over the disposition of land in land-rich, population-poor colonial areas.
- Poor laws, where it is necessary to reconcile the need to aid the destitute with the need to avoid generating habitual reliance on such aid
- Colonization, where it is necessary to reconcile the legitimate private interests of those planting or developing colonies with "a deliberate regard to permanent welfare of the nations afterwards to arise from these small beginnings"[17]
- Finally, the Hume-Smith category: support for enterprises, installations, or institutions clearly in the public interest but not capable of generating adequate private support (e.g., voyages of discovery, lighthouses, scientific research in universities, etc.) and for similar public activities in areas where private agencies "would be more suitable" but where the society has not developed the experience and habits of private cooperative action (e.g., roads, docks, harbours, canals, etc.)

In the meanwhile, a whole array of ameliorative actions were, in fact, generated as modern industrialism diffused. Welfare policy, in the widest sense, became increasingly important if not yet as central to politics in the Atlantic world as it was to become in the century after 1870. Nevertheless, the political, legal, and intellectual foundations of the welfare state were being laid in the more-advanced industrial countries before 1870.

This is the case because those foundations lay in universal male suffrage, a recognition of the legitimacy of labour unions, and mass public education. None of these conditions were fully achieved before 1870. And movement in these directions after 1870 among Britain, France, Germany, and the United States was certainly not uniform. The pace was much affected by the degree of industrialization and urbanization. France, for example, with its continued rural majority tended systematically to lag, and, in the United States, the states, which assumed primary responsibility for welfare policy, moved fairly consistently in the order of their industrial experience (e.g., Massachusetts, New York, Pennsylvania, etc.).

By 1870, or thereabouts, universal male suffrage was more or less accepted as a principle, although there was hedging in various ways (e.g., inhibitions on black voting in the South and the continued control of the budget by the German executive rather than parliament). And, of course, the vote for women was several generations away.

Similarly, after initial legal inhibitions on the formation of labour unions, they had established what might be called inhibited legitimacy by 1870, with chronic challenge or harassment by the courts, the executive authorities, or both.

In terms of the British urban worker's round of life, the limitation of hours of work was the most substantial achievement, a parliamentary effort begun in 1802 that reached its climax with the quite well policed Ten-Hours Bill of 1847. In the United States, the federal government symbolically led the way with a ten-hour limitation in the navy yards; however, not only were the arrangements in the different states varied, but the laws, where put on the books, were not well enforced. Except in Britain, the issue was placed on the agenda of politics but awaited further industrialization, urbanization, and agitation before it was resolved.

The most fundamental issue in welfare economics of this era, however, was the debate over socialism: that is, the comparative merits and demerits of socialism and capitalism for the long pull. Marx was formed and Mill was strongly influenced by the ferment generated by socialist literature that emerged on both sides of the channel, notably in the 1840s. This is not an occasion to reiterate the fine-grained balance sheet drawn up by Mill, an assessment heightened by Harriet Taylor's sympathetic view of socialism.

Essentially, Mill took the view that despite the likelihood of inefficient enterprises under socialism, the balance, when set against the capitalism of his time, tipped to socialism because of capitalism's gross inequity and harshness. However, he judged that capitalist societies, over time, would reduce these blemishes, and believed besides that the disciplining virtues of competition were required. His verdict – "If a conjecture be hazarded, the decision will probably depend mainly on one consideration, viz, which of the two systems is consistent with the greatest amount of human liberty and spontaneity."[18] And so, it was in arguing for a reduction in the blemishes of capitalism – including a battle for women's voting rights – that J.S. Mill became one of the founding fathers of the democratic welfare state.

1870–1975: THE AGE OF SOCIAL WELFARE

In historical restrospect, the century that began with Bismarck's pioneering social legislation of 1871 (accident insurance) and ended with the levelling off of transfer payments as a proportion of gross national product (GNP) in most advanced industrial countries in the mid-1970s might well be called, in one of its dimensions, the Age of Social Welfare. Table 3.1 provides some indication of the timing and scale of this massive phenomenon.

TABLE 3.1
Approximate Social Service Expenditures: Advanced Industrial Countries, 1890–1981
(all levels of government: percentage of GNP [or GDP])

	United States	United Kingdom	Germany	Seven Major OECD Countries
1890	1.8	1.9	n/a	–
1913	2.1	4.1	5.1	–
1929	3.2 (1927)	9.5	19.3	–
1940	6.9	11.3	–	–
1950	6.2 (1948)	18.0	24.2	–
1960	[10.9]	[13.9]	[20.5]	[14.3]
1970	–	–	–	[19.5]
1975	–	–	–	[22.0]
1981	[21.0]	[24.9]	[31.5]	[24.0]

Sources: Unless otherwise indicated in note below, data are from Richard A. Musgrave, *Fiscal Systems* (New Haven: Yale University Press, 1969), 94-5 (Table 4-1).
Note: Social services include education, welfare programs, and housing as well as social insurance. There are no estimates for total German social expenditures for 1890 and 1913. The more narrow category of social insurance expenditures appears to have increased as follows as a proportion of GNP: 1891, 0.7%; 1901, 1.3%; 1912, 1.8% (calculated from Supan Andic and Jindrich Veverka, "The Growth of Government Expenditure in Germany Since the Unification," *Finanzarchiv* 23, no. 2 [January 1964]: 199–200 [per capita total budget expenditures in constant (1900) prices and per capita social insurance as % of total expenditure; p. 238 (population); and p. 241 (GNP at 1900 prices). Bracketted figures are from an OECD study summarized in "Social Expenditure: Erosion or Evolution?," *OECD Observer*, no. 126 (January 1984): 3–6. These figures include expenditures for: education, health, pensions, unemployment insurance, family allowances and other programs. They are related to GDP rather than GNP.

The figures in Table 3.1 rise until the mid-1970s under a sequence of quite dissimilar impulses:

- in response to political pressure from urban constituencies as the relative rise in food and basic commodity prices decreased or limited the rise in real wages from the mid-1890s to 1914;
- in a typical postwar surge in social outlays during the 1920s as if in compensation for hardships endured;
- in response to the depth and severity of the Depression of the 1930s;
- in another postwar surge in social outlays after 1945; and
- finally, as a result of the unexampled boom (producing a majestic expansion) of the 1950s and 1960s in which the citizens of advanced industrial societies chose more or less consciously to take a substantial proportion of their rise in real incomes in the form of enlarged social services.

The sequence ends with the pressure on real wages of the oil price and other shocks of the 1970s, in response to which the citizenry tried to protect their real incomes, accepted a halt in the expansion of social services, but resisted a drastic reduction in their proportionate share in total output. The post-1975 deceleration is captured in Table 3.2.

TABLE 3.2
Social Expenditure by Country, 1960–81

	Social Expenditure As a Percentage of GDP		Annual Growth Rate of Real GDP		Annual Growth Rate of Real Social Expenditure	
	1960	1981^a	1960–75	1975–81^a	1960–75	1975–81^a
United States	10.9	21.0	3.4	3.2	7.7	2.9
Japan	8.0	17.5	8.6	5.1	9.7	8.9
Germany	20.5	31.5	3.8	3.0	6.7	1.9
Canada	12.1	21.7	5.1	3.3	9.5	2.9
France^b	13.4	23.8	5.0	2.8	7.4	7.6
Italy	16.5	29.1	4.6	3.2	7.4	3.1
United Kingdom	13.9	24.9	2.6	1.0	5.6	3.3
Australia	10.2	18.6	5.2	2.4	8.6	2.4
Austria	17.9	27.9	4.5	2.9	6.0	4.6
Belgium	17.0	38.0	4.5	3.0	9.1	4.6
Denmark	10.2	29.0	3.7	2.2	9.3	4.4
Finland	13.2	n/a	4.5	2.9	7.3	n/a
Greece	8.7	12.8	6.8	3.5	7.8	2.3
Iceland	11.7	27.1	4.3	3.5	8.2	5.2
Norway	11.7	27.1	4.3	4.1	9.5	5.6
Netherlands	16.3	36.1	4.5	2.0	9.2	1.4
New Zealand	13.0	19.6	4.0	0.4	4.4	3.7
Sweden	14.5	33.5	4.0	1.0	8.4	4.0
Switzerland	7.7	14.9	3.4	1.8	6.9	2.5

Source: OECD, as in Table 3.1.
Notes: ^{a} Or latest available year
^{b} Excluding education expenditure
n/a) = not available

Evidently nations have differed in the proportion of their resources they have chosen to allocate to social services. For example, in 1977 transfer payments were 15.4 percent of GDP for the United States, at the bottom of the league, and 39.3 percent for the Netherlands, at the top.[19] And differences extended to the various components that make up social services. But the sustained high priority for outlays of this kind in the advanced industrial countries is, evidently, one of the most remarkable aspects of political and economic history over the past century, as seen, for example, in the tendency of this proportion to level off in the course of the 1970s. The power of the thrust for expanded social welfare services during the great OECD boom of the 1950s and 1960s is captured in Table 3.3, which exhibits the income elasticity of government spending for thirteen countries.[20] The average elasticity of almost 3 for transfer payments whose movements are dominated by changes in social welfare outlays is an extraordinary figure, which evidently could not persist for long.

TABLE 3.3
Income Elasticity of Government Spending in Constant Prices, 1950–77

	Total[a]	Consumption[b]	Transfers[c]
Austria	1.80	0.54	3.23
Canada	1.96	1.17	2.90
Denmark	2.25	1.54	3.09
Finland	1.70	1.20	2.30
France	1.61	.60	2.54
Germany	1.46	.92	2.06
Greece	1.27	.68	2.11
Ireland	2.47	1.21	4.33
Netherlands	2.46	.63	4.38
Sweden	2.70	1.42	4.43
Switzerland	1.89	.79	3.41
United Kingdom	1.37	.77	2.07
United States	1.74	1.18	2.59
Median	1.80	.92	2.90

Source: United Nations, *Yearbook of National Accounts Statistics*, 1977 and 1964;
and replies to questionnaire for 1978 yearbook (unpublished).
[a] Total current disbursements of general government
[b] Government final consumption expenditure
[c] Transfer outlays of general government

When we examine this climactic surge more closely, we find it was rooted in an intellectual and policy revolution with a clearly marked turning-point in about 1870. This turning-point had two not necessarily convergent dimensions, although Alfred Marshall captured both: a new and more formal emphasis on the optimum allocation of resources and the conditions for equilibrium, set out in terms of marginal analysis; and a heightened concern with issues of social welfare. The year 1870 comes close to the time when Jevons (1871), Menger (1871), and Walras (1874) published their respective formulations of marginal analysis, although Jevons's "coefficient of utility" dates back to 1862. In addition, the date approximates 1867, when the first volume of *Capital* appeared and Marshall began his serious study of economics; it is close enough to 1871 when the seventh edition of Mill's *Principles*, the last edited by the author, was published. As turning-points go, then, 1870 is a reasonable if somewhat arbitrary symbol.

It is also the time when the advanced industrial societies of that era seriously began to come to grips with problems of welfare, income distribution, monopoly power, and other contentious matters that forced themselves to the centre of the political stage. Operationally, these issues were posed by the rise of new political forces often linked to an extension of the ballot: the Populists, Grangers, and Progressives in the United States; the Labour Party and the invigorated Liberals in Britain; the Socialists on the Continent; the labour unions everywhere; and, down to the mid-1890s, the embattled American farmers.

The relation of mainstream economics to this essentially political process was complex. The demonstration that differential calculus was a viable tool in economics had a powerful impact. It proved capable of expressing with precision certain fundamental economic propositions and, especially, defining, under strict limiting assumptions, conditions of stable equilibrium in both specific markets and for an economy as a whole. The major economic figures – in Britain, on the Continent, and in the United States – became caught up in the authentic adventure of refining market analysis for both final output and factors of production under what came to be known as Marshallian short-period assumptions – excluding the dynamic supply forces, as well as changing incomes and tastes, at work in the process of economic growth. Without these complications, pure theories of production and distribution could be brought together in splendid symmetry, but political economy gave way to economics. The discipline focused on evolving methods of analysis, not on the great problems demanding solution in the active world, and the increasingly refined methods of analysis led, in most – not all – cases, away from, rather than towards, the issues of political economy in active contention. What John Williams had to say after an exhaustive test of the classical theory of foreign trade could be said of mainstream economics as a whole in the wake of the revolution of 1870 and after: "The classical theory assumes as fixed, for purposes of reasoning, the very things which, in my view, should be chief objects of study."[21]

Moral and ethical issues did not, of course, disappear from economics, and economists certainly did not abandon the right to hold strong personal views on issues of policy and social justice. Even Leon Walras was an advocate of wide-ranging economic and social reform, but this stance was clearly divorced from his work as an economist. While economists did not become less concerned with the fate of their societies, the linkage of theoretical formulation to problems of policy was attenuated by the seductive elegance of the new concepts and methods of analysis. There is an important sense, in fact, in which the intellectual underpinnings of the movement for what we might broadly call welfare reform were quite precisely related to the gaps between the formal assumptions underlying post-1870 mainstream economics and reality.

The central propositions of mainstream economic theory assumed perfect competition and steady full employment; the dissidents dramatized the reality of monopolies and severe cyclical unemployment. Formal theory linked income distribution to the net marginal value product of the economic functions performed by individuals; the dissidents dramatized (as had Mill) the institutions, patterns of landownership, inheritance law, relative access to education, and other non-economic determinants of income distribution emerging from the history of particular societies.

Among the inequities the dissidents identified was the asymmetry in the labour market represented by the power of the individual worker vis-à-vis the more concentrated power of the employer, operating individually or collectively. The market-oriented theory of distribution in its pure form was silent on such vicissitudes as accidents at the workplace, health facilities and educational opportunity for the poor, and old age insurance. By one form of argument or another, the dissidents dragged these issues towards the centre of the political arena. The examples could go on to embrace Henry George's powerful polemic built on an interpretation of the Malthus-Ricardo theory of rent; Thorstein Veblen on conspicuous consumption, the monopolistic corporation, and technology; Upton Sinclair on the Chicago slaughterhouses; the American institutionalists, the Fabians, including Shaw; and the German and British historical schools, including R.H. Tawney. And then – sometimes overlapping these examples and categories – there were various kinds of socialists, including those who wrote and argued in the tradition of Marx as they chose to interpret him.

I would emphasize again that the mainstream economists did not universally and systematically oppose the measures that arose from these heterodox sources. Some, in fact, supported them. But the formal constructs of mainstream economics were a poor basis for crusading zeal. The social welfare movement, which progressively gathered momentum down to the First World War, was, in fact, nourished mainly by an array of iconoclasts who were crusading not only on behalf of the less advantaged but also against the inadequacies they thought they perceived in mainstream economics.

It does not follow that the quiet acknowledgment of the inhumanities of capitalism, the exploration of possible remedies, and the authentic concern for the less advantaged that motivated Mill, Marshall, Pigou, and others in that non-polemical tradition were unimportant in democratic societies. While these factors did not provide the banners and rhetoric for the ardent reformers, they helped persuade the critically important "moderate, decent, conservative margin" in the middle of the political spectrum that major reforms were legitimate and necessary.[22] And, indeed, when Pigou came to formalize welfare economics, a good deal of the machinery of marginal analysis – including the distinction between marginal net social products and private products – could be mobilized for a strongly felt but well-mannered crusade.

Alfred Marshall (1842–1924) holds a special place in this story. He is, clearly, the founder of modern welfare economics, although quite consciously in the classical tradition. Moving on proximately from J.S. Mill, he took problems of welfare very seriously indeed. His contribution to theory is generally reckoned primarily in the field of partial equilibrium analysis. But he came to economics by a route that led him from mathematics to metaphysics to ethics, and, finally, without enthusiasm, to political economy. The heart of his commitment lay in a deeply rooted desire to lift from the working classes the burden of poverty – the psychological, social, political, and cultural burden, not merely the economic. Thus, in the first edition of *The Principles* (1890), he wrote that "the study of the causes of poverty is the study of the causes of the degradation of a large part of mankind."[23] Writing late in life about his transition to economics, Marshall recalled: "I had doubts about the propriety of inequalities of *opportunity*, rather than material comfort. Then, in my vacations I visited the poorest quarters of several cities and walked through one street after another looking at the faces of the poorest people."[24]

In his studies rooted in this concern, Marshall asserted a good many propositions of substance; for example:

There is no extravagance more prejudicial to the growth of national wealth than that wasteful negligence which allows genius that happens to be born of lowly parentage to expend itself in lowly work. No change would conduce so much to a rapid increase of material wealth as an improvement in our schools, and especially those of the middle grades, provided it be combined with an extensive system of scholarships, which will enable the clever son of a working man to rise gradually from school to school till he has the best theoretical and practical education which the age can give.[25]

He systematically explored the implications of perhaps the most fundamental proposition in welfare economics – already present in Hume: "The same sum of money measures a greater pleasure for the poor than the rich."[26] All this built up to one of the boldest calculations in the history of welfare economics:

It is a common saying that we have more reason to be proud of our ways of making wealth than of our ways of using it ...

Opinions are not likely to agree as to the amount of private expenditures which is to be regarded as socially wasteful from this point of view. Some may put it as high as four or even five hundred millions a year. But it is sufficient for the present that there is a margin of at least one or two hundred million which might be diverted to social uses without causing any great distress to those from whom it was taken; provided their neighbours were in a like position, and not able to make disagreeable remarks on the absence of luxuries and of conventional "necessaries for social propriety" which are of little solid advantage.[27]

By Marshall's calculation UK annual income was £1.7 billion. His proposed additional social allocation would, therefore, be 5.9 to 11.8 percent of national income – by no means a trivial proportion.

But it was certainly through his pupils (and their pupils) that Marshall's influence was carried forward: A.C. Pigou, D.H. Robertson, and Keynes above all, but also, less directly, Bickerdike, Colin Clark, and many others. It was, in fact, an issue in welfare economics – income distribution – that forced the pace of national income accounting on both sides of the Atlantic.[28] But, of course, chronic high unemployment in Britain and most of Western Europe in the 1920s and then the Great Depression of the 1930s came to dominate the welfare concerns of both orthodox and unorthodox economists. Here Marshall's three great pupils at Cambridge played a central role, moving on from Marshall's incomplete monetary theory to grapple with the business cycle and chronic high unemployment in real as well as monetary terms; however, Swedish, Continental, and American economists, of different or more diversified lineage, made significant contributions to an increasingly international effort that climaxed in 1936 with the publication of Keynes's *General Theory*.

Meanwhile, the debate on the relative merits of socialism versus capitalism, now just about a century old, was heightened during the interwar years by the existence of a socialist state and economy in the Soviet Union and by the extraordinary disarray of the capitalist world, which evidently played a substantial role in bringing on the Second World War.

In the wake of that war, as we have already noted, there was an immediate expansion of social services in Britain and the United States, followed, as the boom of the 1950s and 1960s took hold, by a generation-long surge in welfare outlays throughout the advanced industrial world.

Table 3.4 captures the average composition of welfare outlays in 1960 and 1975, for seven major OECD countries, with some indication of the factors determining changes between those two years. The unexpected, sustained vitality of the economies of Western Europe, Japan, and the United States permitted this rounding out of the welfare state, one of whose most striking characteristics was a revolutionary extension of higher education that moved the advanced industrial societies a good deal closer to the criterion that no young man or woman capable of and interested in acquiring a higher education should be denied that experience. Table 3.5 suggests the scale of the expansion and, in most cases – with Japan a notable exception – the deceleration or levelling off after 1975.

The post-1945 years also saw a great deal of theoretical refinement in the field of welfare economics, on which Ben Higgins and others in this volume have commented. I would only note here that the massive expansion in welfare outlays in, say, the quarter-century 1950–75 was, as nearly as one can perceive, quite independent of this intellectual development. The expansion appears to have been a quite pure product of the income elasticity of demand expressing itself through the democratic political process. But woven into that process was a strand of Hume and Adam Smith's "sympathy": that is, a willingness of citizens to see a margin of the increment to their real incomes, at a time of rapid increase, diverted to the less advantaged without expectation of direct or indirect private advantage.

TABLE 3.4

Growth Rate of Social Expenditure, 1960–81: Averages for the Seven Major OECD Countries

	For Reference: Social Expenditure As a Per-cent of GDP	Of which: Growth of Social Expenditure at Current Prices	Change in Overall Price Level	Change in Relative Cost of Welfare Benefits	Increase in Real Social Expenditure	Due to: Change in Demographic Pattern	Change in Coverage	Change in Real Benefit Levels
		1960			Annual Change 1960–75 (%)			
Education	4.2	14.7	5.4	2.57	6.1	0.29	1.90	3.83
Health	2.7	17.1	5.4	1.35	9.6	1.03	0.60	7.83
Pensions	4.5	14.3	5.4	0	8.4	2.23	1.62	4.35
Unemployment insurance	0.4	18.0	5.4	0	12.0	5.08	0	6.60
Family allowances and other programs	2.5	14.0	5.4	0	8.2	n/a	n/a	n/a
Total social expenditure	14.3	15.0	5.4	1.0	8.0	1.36	1.43	5.03
		1975			Annual Change 1975–81 (%)			
Education	5.1	12.9	9.65	1.14	1.8	-1.74	0.20	3.40
Health	5.1	14.2	9.65	1.02	3.1	0.26	0	3.10
Pensions	7.3	16.9	9.65	0	6.6	1.77	0.78	3.94
Unemployment insurance	1.1	16.7	9.65	0	6.4	7.84	-2.30	1.00
Family allowances and other programs	3.4	13.4	9.65	0	3.4	n/a	n/a	n/a
Total social expenditure	22.0	14.8	9.65	0.50	4.2	0.75	0.22	3.20

Source: OECD Observer, February 1984.

TABLE 3.5
Industrial Market Economies: Number Enrolled in Higher Education As Percentage of Relevant
Age Group

	1960	1965	1975	1984
Industrialized countries (average)	16	21	34	38
Spain	4	6	21	26
Ireland	9	12	16	22
Italy	7	11	25	26
New Zealand	13	15	27	29
Belgium	9	15	22	31
United Kingdom	9	12	17	20
Austria	10	9	25	26
Netherlands	13	17	26	31
France	8	18	24	27
Australia	13	16	23	27
Finland	8	11	19	31
Germany, Fed. Rep.	6	9	20	29
Denmark	10	14	30	29
Japan	9	13	17	30
Sweden	9	13	28	38
Canada	16	26	39	44
Norway	7	11	22	29
Switzerland	7	8	14	21
United States	32	40	58	57

Source: *World Development Report 1979*, 111; *World Development Report 1987*, 263.

From the turbulent mid-1970s, however, a Proposition 13 mentality began to prevail. As the OECD study cited earlier observed: ''Some slowing down of this rapid growth [in social expenditure] was to be expected, but what could have been an acceptable evolution instead assumed aspects of a financial crisis. Economic circumstances have forced an earlier, more severe, and more urgent re-examination of social policies than would have been the case if high rates of economic growth had persisted and inflation been avoided.''

As for that part of the welfare economics debate concerned with the relative virtues of capitalism versus socialism, socialism continued to lose ground, not because capitalism's performance in the 1970s and 1980s was particularly glamorous, but because the performance of the socialist economies was markedly worse. The candid acknowledgment of socialism's failure in China and the struggle there to acquire the benefits of competitive markets were particularly influential in shifting the climate of opinion in the developing regions of the world economy. For reasons we shall shortly consider, the common enemy in an astonishing array of countries became the ''state bourgeoisie'' rather than the capitalist bourgeoisie.[29]

Economic growth theory came back into intellectual fashion for the first time since 1870 in the period, roughly, 1949 (when the United Nations and the United States launched technical assistance programs) to 1973 (when the great postwar boom was distorted by the explosion of grain and oil prices). Work on growth took the form of a kind of three-ring circus, with some, but relatively limited, communication among the rings: Harrod-Domar and the neoclassical growth models; statistical analyses of the morphology of growth pioneered by Colin Clark carried forward after the war by Simon Kuznets; and analyses addressed directly to the aspirations and problems confronted in Latin America, Africa, the Middle East, and Asia as governments and peoples sought to move forward in the complex, many-sided process of development.

THE DEVELOPMENT RING OF THE POSTWAR GROWTH CIRCUS

Here I shall only consider the development ring of the postwar growth circus. In particular, I shall examine three quite different links between welfare economies and development analysis and policy and draw a broad conclusion.

First, there is the link between welfare economics in advanced industrial countries and development economics. The link was strong because, for most major figures in the field, development economics was a kind of second marriage and a good many were permanently marked by their experiences in wrestling with the severe economic and social problems of the 1930s and of the immediate postwar years in Europe.

Among the ten "pioneers in development" who contributed essays to the first volume on that theme organized by the World Bank, seven cited the formative role of such linkages.[30] Typically, Gunnar Myrdal was most explicit in articulating the somewhat Marshallian value premise that underlay both his rationale for the Swedish welfare state and his approach to development:

In the 1920s and 1930s, when my research and policy work had focused on conditions in Sweden, I held the view that an equalization in favor of the lower-income strata was also a productive investment in the quality of people and their productivity. And I found support for this opinion in comparisons of different rich nations' growth statistics. It seemed clear that income equalization would have an even greater effect in this direction for underdeveloped countries, where the masses of people are suffering from very severe consumption deficiencies in regard to nutrition, housing, and everything else. *The productivity of higher consumption levels stands for me as a major motivation for the direction of development policy in underdeveloped countries. Higher consumption levels are a condition for a more rapid and stable growth.*

In underdeveloped countries such a redistribution of income cannot, however, be carried out by taxing the rich and transferring money to the poor via social security schemes and other such measures to raise their levels of living. The poor are so overwhelmingly many, and the wealthy so relatively few – and tax evasion among them so common. What is needed in order to raise the miserable living levels of the poor masses is instead radical institutional reforms. These would serve the double purpose of greater equality and economic growth. The two goals are inextricably joined. This implies a fundamental difference from developed countries, where the two goals can be, and often are, pursued separately.[31]

This is not an appropriate occasion to explore all the explicit and implicit linkages between welfare economics in advanced industrial countries and development economics as it emerged in the 1950s and 1960s. It is, however, worth noting one respect in which development economists were directly in the line of welfare economists reaching back to Adam Smith: they sought (like Myrdal in the quotation above) to demonstrate that what was morally right was also good for the economy. But, again like their predecessors, there was a quite independent strand of moral or religious commitment – of pure sympathy – to assist the less advantaged, heightened by what might be called historical excitement at the drama of intensified efforts at modernization that began to unfold in Asia, the Middle East, Latin America, and Africa.

By the end of the 1960s, a second, quite different, linkage between development and welfare economics emerged. It began with an intellectual revolt against what might be called the orthodox development position of the 1960s, and took the form of the "basic human needs" strategy. This strategy arose, in turn, from two sources. First, and most important, in a good many countries, high, overall real growth rates were accompanied by considerable mass poverty, unemployment and partial unemployment, and other social ills. Second, within the basic-needs movement, there was a strand of a limits-to-growth doctrine, according to which, in order to preserve the human habitat, growth must stop, income must be redistributed, and real income must be stabilized at a level that would provide for basic human needs. There was also sometimes a touch of romanticism about Mao's China and Castro's Cuba in the exposition of this doctrine.

One of the best and most lucid articulations of the basic-needs doctrine came in response to the report of the Pearson Commission, *Partners in Development: Report of the Commission on International Development* (1969). That report, financed by the World Bank, was an effort to dramatize the need for continuing and even enlarged development assistance at a time when political support in the advanced industrial countries was weakening.

The Pearson Commission recommended that an average growth target for the developing countries of 6 percent be set for the 1970s; that official development assistance (ODA) be targeted at 0.7 percent of GNP for the advanced industrial countries with 20 percent allocated through multilateral agencies; and that the terms of ODA be limited to 2 percent interest (with 25–40 year maturity). The quantitative target percentage of GNP was twice the current level. In that sense, the Pearson Commission report was ambitious.

The report was reviewed at an international conference organized by Columbia University and held at Williamsburg and New York, 15–21 February 1970. These gatherings yielded a document called the Columbia Declaration, which captures well the themes and mood of the basic-needs doctrine:

In incomes, living standards, economic and political power, one-third of the world has in recent decades been pulling steadily ahead, leaving the remainder of mankind in relative poverty, in many cases to live without clean water, education, basic medical facilities or adequate housing. Yet with modern technology and existing productive capacity, none of this need continue if mankind would develop the will and organization to use the resources at hand ... New objective criteria for effective development assistance are required. An over-all minimum growth rate for all countries is, no doubt, a desirable objective. But it is essential also to develop targets designed to achieve a minimum average per capita income of $400 to be reached by all countries not later than the end of the century. Criteria are also needed which focus on the living standards of the bottom quarter of each country's population. We also suggest setting up of a special fund devoted specifically to the fulfillment of social objectives in the areas of education, health, family planning, rural and urban works housing and other related programs.

... There is an urgent need to strengthen the multilateral international framework in the fields of trade, aid, and relations between rich and poor nations ... Such strengthening necessarily involves the channeling of increased and independent finance and moves toward compulsory contributions by member countries. International power must increasingly be shared democratically; and this objective can only be attained by strengthening the role of institutions in which the developing economies have a representative vote.[32]

This doctrine was not wholly ignored in the 1970s. The World Bank, for example, under Robert McNamara's direction, allocated increased resources for social purposes and conducted sophisticated analyses of the relationship of poverty and excessively skewed income distribution to aggregate and sectoral growth rates. A great deal of both poverty and abnormally skewed income distribution was, in fact, linked to excessive rates of population increase and inadequate attention of government to agriculture and to the modernization of rural life. Inadequate tax collection and the diversion of government funds to a variety of dubious subsidies (thus constraining allocations for health, education, and other important social purposes) also played a role. Where birth rates were rapidly declining and agricultural productivity and the modernization of rural life taken seriously, the lowest 20 percent of the population received proportions of total income comparable to distribution patterns in advanced industrial countries (e.g., South Korea and Taiwan). Despite these deeper forces, which largely determined the social outcome in developing nations, the rise of the basic-needs doctrine undoubtedly led to some reallocation of national and international development resources and, perhaps equally important, to intensified analyses of the anatomy of poverty in developing countries.

What was not accepted was the doctrine that the resources of the rich countries should come to some significant degree under the political control of bodies substantially controlled by poor countries. This was a fundamental principle of the New International Economic Order expounded year after year in United Nations bodies. It constituted an extension to an international community of the principle of declining relative marginal utility, more or less recognized within national societies. But the international community of the 1970s and 1980s was still rooted in jealously guarded sovereignties; on the whole, the asymmetrical assertion of rights and duties asserted under the banner of the New International Economic Order proved unproductive or worse.

The basic-needs doctrine and the thrust for a new economic order – related in fact but not necessarily in logic – can be regarded as an attack from the left. The neoclassical assault on the "structuralists" can be regarded as a sortie from the right. Ian Little reduced the neoclassical case to elemental terms as follows: "Until fairly recently I see the story as one of the battle between structuralists who see the world as bounded and flat, and consisting of stick-in-the-muds, who have to be drilled – and neo-classicists who see it as round and full of enterprising people who will recognize themselves in a fairly effective manner."[33]

The neoclassicist – Peter Bauer, for example – can find a splendid gallery of figures to caricature if from no other source than United Nations debates. But in an essay on development, efficiency, and equity, there is a bit more to be said.

First, those who argued that there was an important role for public policy in the early phases of development operated from premises rooted in Hume and Smith, Marshall and Pigou, and their case was made with some precision. Paul Rosenstein-Rodan, for example, isolated four issues arising from possible flaws in the working of private markets: disguised unemployment (or excess population) in the countryside; Marshall's "pecuniary" external economies, yielding economies of scale; the indispensable role of large blocks of infrastructure investment as a necessary foundation for profitable industrialization; and the importance of "technological external economies," notably public investment in education and training.

Taken all together, the reality of these forms of market failure constituted Rodan's case for planning the kind of "Big Push" he envisaged as necessary to lift a relatively stagnant underdeveloped country into sustained growth:

The market mechanism does not realize the "optimum" either in one nation or between nations because it relies on such unrealistic assumptions as a linear homogeneous production function, no increasing returns or economies of scale or of agglomeration, and no phenomenon of minimum quantum or threshold. This obscures the nature of the development process and the risks involved. Nothing in theology or technology ordains that God created the world convex downwards.[34]

Rodan's fourth public function should, in my view, be widened beyond education in the narrow sense to include all the dimensions of the expansion in technological absorptive capacity: institutions, tax and other incentives, and the encouragement of entrepreneurs capable of and willing to risk the introduction of new production functions.

This suggests a second point neoclassicists do not regularly address: that is, the appropriate framework for policy making in a developing country depends intimately on time and its stage of growth. For example, on a visit to Thailand in 1961, I found, as in much of Southeast Asia, modern entrepreneurship overwhelmingly in the hands of overseas Chinese who were sometimes "married" – for protection – to Thai military officers. Twenty-two years later, modern entrepreneurship was much more widely spread and Thai planners could focus substantially on creating a benign macroeconomic framework for a vital private enterprise system.

If we accept, for a moment, Ian Little's definition of the dividing line among development economists as that between structuralists and neo-classicists, the distinction becomes highly sensitive to time and the historical stage of the economy or economies one has in mind. A country in what I call the preconditions-for-take-off stage (say, Indonesia as of the 1960s) not only may lack, as did Thailand, an indigenous cadre of entrepreneurs, but may also have a low level of literacy; a grossly inadequate secondary and higher educational system, a traditional agriculture essentially untouched by the productive methods available to modern labour-intensive farming, an infrastructure incapable of underpinning an efficient national market or a vital place in the international economy, a feeble if not obstructive and corrupt bureaucracy, and a flow of public revenues incapable of supporting the minimum irreducible functions of government, as defined, say, by Adam Smith. The net investment rate may be 5 percent or less and concentrated in enclaves developed by foreign investors to expand raw material exports.

I cite this familiar array of underdevelopment characteristics to specify what I mean by "structural" problems, a term often used ambiguously. The first and obvious point to be made – somehow lost in Little's structuralist versus neoclassical paradigm – is that a sensible policy prescription for a country will vary greatly with its stage of growth: where it stands in the preconditions-for-take-off stage, in take-off (which is always a phenomenon limited by sectors and, often, by regions), or in the drive to technological maturity beyond take-off, also a dynamic process which takes time. The role of the state is bound to be greater relative to the private sector in the precon-ditions-for-take-off stage than in, say, the drive to technological maturity. After all, the proportion of investment allocated to infrastructure (excluding housing) is normally above 30 percent in all societies. The development theorists of the 1950s and the 1960s were visiting, staring at, prescribing for societies primarily at the lower end of the growth spectrum. Put another way, economies moving along well in the drive to technological maturity can, increasingly, be analysed and prescribed for with the same techniques as those applied to more-advanced industrial countries, though I would certainly not qualify neoclassical economics as adequate to either task.

Take, for example, the following description of the situation in one developing country:

The Egyptian economy bears the legacy of economic policies dating from the 1950s which were motivated by concern for equity and assistance to the poor. These policies were characterized by price regulation, subsidization of consumer goods, a dominant public sector and state control. Subsequently the government has tried to insulate the average citizen from many of the shocks in the international economy and has not adjusted prices over the years ... consumers have not faced world prices for energy or many basic commodities. Both prices and wages of government workers in particular have been held down significantly. As the gap between the market and the adminis-tered prices has grown, it has become more and more difficult and costly to maintain the current system.[35]

This passage applies, of course, to a good many developing economies in Asia and Latin America as well as the Middle East.

The bloated public sectors that have been a legitimate target of critics – neoclassical and otherwise – must be viewed as the outcome of a historic process rather than of misguided development theories. They resulted from the convergence of what might be called technical, economic, and political forces and certain strongly held attitudes in the developing countries of the 1950s.

On the economic side, there was the inability to earn or borrow, at toler-able rates, sufficient foreign exchange to avoid highly protectionist import substitution policies. These projectionist policies led directly to insufficient competition in domestic markets, damping the entrepreneurial quality of both the private and public sectors. Foreign-exchange rationing was also a policy that required large powerful bureaucracies to decide what should be imported. In many countries, that process was the heart of what passed for planning. On the political side, there was the fear of explosions in the volatile cities and a decision, in effect, to exploit the farmer on behalf of the urban population. This was generally done by enforced low prices for agricultural products and subsidized selling prices in the cities. This had, of course, the effect of reducing incentives in the agricultural sector and slowing the rate of increase of agricultural production, forcing increased grain imports at the expense of capital goods for industry and transport.

With respect to attitudes, in the 1950s capitalism was an unpopular word and socialism a popular one in the developing regions. Capitalism was associated with colonial or quasi-colonial status; it was systematically represented as an intrusive external power and was denigrated by political leaders over a wide range. Socialism, on the other hand, had considerable sentimental appeal at this time: some of the European social democratic governments were doing quite well; Mao's Great Leap Forward and Chinese Communist policy in general found considerable favour among those who did not investigate it too deeply; and even Khruschev's boast that the USSR would soon outstrip the US in total output had a certain credibility in the late 1950s. To all this one can add that many of the emerging political leaders were often intellectuals or soldiers, both types inherently suspicious of the market process and inclined, for different reasons, to have excessive faith in the powers of government administration.

In the present narrow context, it is fair to ask to what extent, if any, structuralist development economists bear some responsibility for this outcome. Stripped of rhetoric, the charges can be reduced to three:

• postwar "export pessimism" and excessive reliance on import substitution;
• inadequate incentives and support for agriculture combined with excessive subsidies to maintain low prices for "basic needs" in the cities; and
• excessive reliance on government ownership and control of industry, as well as inadequate encouragement of domestic competition and foreign private investment.

With respect to the first charge, it should be recalled that import substitution policies – if not traced back to Alexander Hamilton – were the product of a condition not a theory, that is, a product of the Great Depression of the 1930s. Prebisch, trained as a classical economist, supported such policies on pragmatic grounds in the face of the overwhelming balance-of-payments crisis that confronted Argentina and a great many other developing countries of the period. The later homilies of, say, Jacob Viner or Peter Bauer would have sounded hollow indeed in Latin America of the 1930s. Economic Commission for Latin America (ECLA) doctrine, which, in a familiar pattern, turned out to be fighting the last war, came later.

Export pessimism in the early postwar years was in part the result of a general expectation that a depression in the world economy was likely to recur after a brief restocking boom. There was, moreover, a universal failure among economists to anticipate the pace of the global boom of the 1950s and 1960s: GDP per capita in the advanced industrial countries in the period 1950–73 increased at an annual rate (3.8 percent) almost three times the highest previous sustained rate (1.4 percent, 1870–1913). Export pessimism suffused the view of prospects for certain advanced industrial countries (e.g., Italy, France, Japan), as well as for the developing regions in the early postwar years.

As for the tilt of policy towards the cities at the expense of agriculture and rural life, development economists bear little or no blame. They did, of course, vary in the strength of their protests against these distortions, and Peter Bauer can argue legitimately that he should have been more strongly supported by his colleagues in protesting the damage to agriculture wrought by the African marketing boards. Moreover, most development economists did not fully appreciate the corrosive (as well as positive) consequences of US agricultural products supplied under Public Law 480. But the relative neglect of agriculture and increasingly onerous subsidies to urban populations surely arose not from the propositions and prescriptions of development economists, but primarily from the political life of the developing regions and irrational reactions against real or believed distortions of the colonial (or quasi-colonial) past.

In short, politics was generally more important than economics in the developing world, and the critical political issues were substantially different than those of the advanced industrial countries. Here, I believe, is the reason for the inadequacy of, say, Bauer's plea that aid only be granted to those governments that rely on the market and thus move towards democracy or, say, Myrdal's and Singer's easy transfer of the canons of the post-1945 social democratic welfare state in northwestern Europe to the developing world. In fact, seven of the nine World Bank pioneers I have evoked for present purposes ended up in puzzlement or disappointment at the extent to which politics frustrated the economic development outcomes they envisaged or hoped for.

SOME CONCLUSIONS AND COMMENTS ON THE FUTURE

By the time Adam Smith's *Wealth of Nations* was published, certain propositions, after several generations of thought and intense debate about the political economy of growth, were established that bear directly on the subject matter of this book.

- Economic development was conceived as an essential part of a process of building morally good and civilized domestic societies and a peaceful and decent international society. Living in a mercantilist world in which, for example, Britain was at war for some forty years of the eighteenth century, a world in which the intrusions of government were often inefficient and driven by narrow special interests, those who created modern political economy saw in enlarged domestic and international competitive commerce not only a way to discipline and harness the self-seeking propensities of human beings and governments, but also a way to strengthen within and across international boundaries the healing quality of "sympathy." They looked to governments with reduced but still substantial functions in a society that, to the maximum consistent with the security of others, respected the freedom of unique individuals.

- As for efficiency and equity, these economists found a good deal of potential convergence, but they also found some painful choices whose consequences might require mitigation on moral grounds. Efficiency, for example, required an acceptance of an unequal distribution of income and wealth, but it was in the name of efficiency that the children of the poor should be educated, and it was considered morally right to temper inequity further by recognizing Hume's dictum: "No one can doubt, but such an equality is most suitable to human nature, and diminishes much less from the happiness of the rich than it adds to that of the poor."

Efficiency required specialization of function, but that process, in Smith's view, could narrow the range of human experience and sensibility. It was right to try to mitigate this cost with public education.

Behind it all was an acute awareness of the brutal human consequences of poverty, and of the more civil and freer life of widened choices economic development could bring.

The world of Hume and Smith was one in which thoughtful observers were also conscious of societies at different levels of real income per capita: they recalled that England itself was, a few centuries back, a rather primitive upstart compared, say, to the Hapsburg-dominated continent; and they compared the North American to the Latin American colonies, the Dutch to all others in Europe, the still vital Chinese economy to decaying Bengal, and, indeed, England to Scotland, the latter progressing but in line astern. Thus, speculation on the dynamics of narrowing the gap between relatively rich and poor countries and attempts to define an appropriate, efficient, and equitable policy of the rich towards the upwardly mobile poor were actively on the agenda of the third quarter of the eighteenth century. And the issue of growth in relation to the good society remained central to political economy through J.S. Mill and Marx down to Marshall, who uniquely belonged to both the pre-1870 and post-1870 worlds.

But, putting Marshall aside, there were few who took development in its full classic sense seriously between 1870 and the post-1945 era. Indeed, there were not many who studied economic growth, in its narrower sense. Economic growth was assumed as virtually automatic in the advanced industrial world. It entered into analyses of the business cycle in one way or another and, occasionally, the terms of trade. However, except for Schumpeter, the young Kuznets, Walther Hoffmann, and a handful of others, interest in it moved to the periphery for about eighty years. And when Harrod produced a growth model in the 1930s, it was to demonstrate the likelihood, if not certainty, of short-run instability in a capitalist economy.

When the concern for development moved onto the global agenda after the Second World War, few picked up where the classicists left off – Arthur Lewis being a notable exception. For practitioners of development, including politicians in the developing regions, all the great classical issues were, in fact, alive: What kind of society should we try to build? How should we exploit convergences between efficiency and equity and what do we do when they don't converge? What priority should development be given over the other imperatives of politics? How should poor and rich countries relate to each other? What is the correct role for competitive markets relative to that of government? Development economics inevitably was caught up in these problems because it became a field for practitioners as much as for theorists. But there was no common base, no agreed upon political economy of development. The debates over basic needs, over the right of poor countries to appropriate the income of rich countries, and over market-versus-government planning provided, it's fair to say, little illumination. Behind it all was an almost automatic carry- over of debates in the advanced industrial countries of the 1930s – right, centre, and left – to often irrelevant settings.

The line of argument set out in this paper suggests that the next generation ought to try to build a fresh political economy of development, reaching back for inspiration, if not for definitive answers, to the spacious architecture of the eighteenth-century founding fathers. I suggest this course because the problems evidently on the agenda require a kind of treatment not provided by conventional growth theory or by neoclassical economics or by Marxism in its various versions. I believe there are five great problems ahead.

- The foreseeable arrival at technological maturity of what I call the Fourth Graduating Class (Figure 3.1), embracing *inter alia* China and India, Brazil and Mexico. Their peaceful absorption into the world economy and world polity without the violence and tragedy that accompanied the absorption of Germany and Japan is a central challenge for the next half-century and more – indeed, an imperative for survival in a nuclear age.
- The continued improvement of relations between the industrialized capitalist countries and the countries of the former Soviet bloc, and the reconstruction of the economies and societies of the latter
- The maintenance of economic vitality and a high degree of cooperation in and among the countries of Western Europe, Japan, and the United States – a condition for successful management of the first two tasks. The outcome will depend greatly on the pace at which the present round of new technologies is elaborated and efficiently applied in the advanced industrial world.

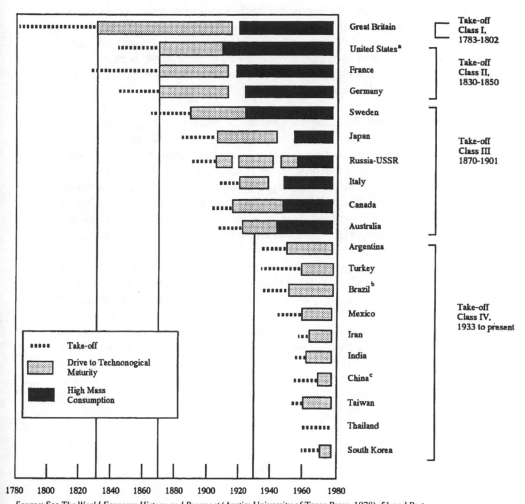

1780	1800	1820	1840	1860	1880	1900	1920	1940	1960	1980

Source: See *The World Economy History and Prospect* (Austin: University of Texas Press, 1978), 51 and Part 5.

[a] New England regional take-off, 1815–30.

[b] Sao Paulo regional take-off, 1900–20.

[c] Manchuria regional take-off, 1930–41.

Figure 3.1
Four Graduating Classes into Take-off: Stages of Economic Growth, Twenty Countries

- Intense international cooperation to cope with the mounting pressures on the physical environment exerted by the movement to full industrialization of, say, 80 percent of a global population, which could reach 11 billion by the middle of the next century

- Patient assistance, where possible, to the nations that have found development particularly difficult: for example, Africa south of the Sahara, Bangladesh, Haiti, Yemen, Afghanistan, Burma, and some of the Pacific Islands. These nations contain perhaps 20 percent of the human population and are an inescapable welfare charge on the more fortunate early-comers to modernization.

The old debate about the state versus the market is being settled by the movement beyond take-off into the drive to technological maturity of most developing countries combined with a belated recognition that an efficient agriculture not only is essential for an industrial society but requires strong private incentives, including fair prices for the farmer. The increasingly sophisticated and diversified technologies of the drive to technological maturity simply do not lend themselves to state management, notably at a time when a powerful technological revolution imposes a vertiginous pace of obsolescence year after year.

Moreover, it may well be that the human impulse to exercise increased control over one's destiny as modernization proceeds is pushing political communities increasingly towards one serious version of democracy or another. The passage of time in an environment of development – erratic, uneven, and ungainly as development has been – may be settling some of the old debates. But a fairly clear-cut triumph of private markets and democracy will not clear the development agenda, nor, indeed, in itself guarantee peace and a viable world economy. Above all, I suspect, the next phase will require, on a global scale, the maximum expression of the quality David Hume and Adam Smith called sympathy and regarded as the essential bond among human beings in a civilized society.

NOTES

1 Carl Becker, *The Heavenly City of the Eighteenth Century Philosophers* (New Haven: Yale University Press, 1932).

2 David Hume, *Philosophical Works*, edited by T.H. Green and T.H. Grose (London: Longman Green, 1912), 3:238.

3 J.M. Keynes, *The General Theory of Interest, Employment, and Money* (London: Macmillan, 1936), 150.

4 David Hume, *Writings on Economics*, edited and with an introduction by Eugene Rotwein (Madison: University of Wisconsin Press, 1955), 15, 21–32.

5 Piero Sraffa, ed., with the assistance of Maurice Dobb, *The Works and Correspondence of David Ricardo* (Cambridge: Cambridge University Press, 1951), 1:96–7.

6 For Hume's priority in utilitarianism, his great influence on the subsequent

tradition among economists, and Adam Smith's distinctive characteristics in this field, see Lionel Robbins, *The Theory of Economic Policy* (New York: St Martin's Press, 1952), especially 176–8.

7   Istvan Hont and Michael Ignatieff, eds., *Wealth and Virtue: The Shaping of Political Economy in the Scottish Enlightenment* (Cambridge: Cambridge University Press, 1983), 7.

8   David Hume, *Philosophical Works*, 2:304.

9   Adam Smith, *The Wealth of Nations*, edited by Edwin Cannan, with introduction by Max Lerner (New York: Random House, Modern Library, 1937), 651.

10   Ibid., 740.

11   See in Sraffa and Dobb, *Works and Correspondence*, 10:90, the contrast between Nathan Rothschild's Humeian passion for business and Ricardo's temperance.

12   Hume, *Writings on Economics*, 52–3.

13   Ibid., 17–18.

14   My *Theorists of Economic Growth from David Hume to the Present* (New York: Oxford University Press, 1990) discusses at some length the formal characteristics of Adam Smith's growth theory and presents in a mathematical appendix (done with Michael Kennedy) one-sector and three-sector Smithian growth models.

15   Smith, *Wealth of Nations*, 7.

16   See, especially, the extensive treatment of this issue in Hont and Ignatieff, *Wealth and Virtue*. The mathematical appendix referred to in note 14 also contains a model of the rich country/poor country problem.

17   J.S. Mill, *Principles of Political Economy*, edited by V.W. Bladen and J.M. Robson (Toronto: University of Toronto Press, 1965), 963.

18   Ibid., 208–9.

19   Morris Beck, "The Public Sector and Economic Stability," in *The Business Cycle and Public Policy*, a compendium of papers submitted to the Joint Economic Committee, 23 November 1980 (Washington, D.C.: Government Printing Office, 1980), 129.

20   Ibid., 113.

21   John Williams, "The Theory of International Trade Reconsidered," *Economic Journal* 39 (1929): 195–209.

22   The adjectives set off by quotation marks are from John F. Kennedy's often repeated definition of the group that had to be won over by a victorious candidate in an American presidential election. For context, see my *Diffusion of Power* (New York: Macmillan, 1972), 129.

23   Quoted in J.M. Keynes, "Alfred Marshall, 1842–1924," in A.C. Pigou, ed., *Memorials of Alfred Marshall* (London: Macmillan, 1925), 9–11.

24   Ibid., 9.

25   Alfred Marshall, *Principles of Economics*, 8th ed. (London: Macmillan, 1930), 212.

26 Pigou, ed., *Memorials of Alfred Marshall*, 11.

27 Ibid., 323.

28 On British pioneering, see J.C. Stamp, *British Incomes and Property* (London: P.S. King, 1916); A.L. Bowley, *Wages and Income Since 1860* (Cambridge: Cambridge University Press, 1937); and Colin Clark's reminiscence in his "Development Economics: The Early Years," in Gerald Meier and Dudley Seers, eds., *Pioneers in Development* (New York: Oxford Press for the World Bank, 1984). On the American side, the story centres on a debate about income distribution that led to the creation of the National Bureau of Economic Research well described in Solomon Fabricant, *Toward a Firmer Basis of Economic Policy: The Founding of the National Bureau of Economic Research* (Cambridge, Mass.: NBER, 1983). See also Carol S. Carson, "The History of the United States National Income and Product Accounts: The Development of an Analytic Tool," *Review of Income and Wealth*, series 21, no. 2 (June 1975).

29 The phrase "state bourgeoisie" emerged from the debate on the appropriate relative role of public and private sectors in Latin America. It is referred to in William Glade, "Economic Policy-making and the Structures of Corporations in Latin America," offprint ser. no. 208 (Austin: Institute of Latin American Studies, University of Texas at Austin, 1981).

30 Meier and Seers, eds., *Pioneers*. The following "pioneers" explicitly linked their views on development to one aspect or another of their earlier professional and policy concerns: Colin Clark, Albert O. Hirschman, Gunnar Myrdal, Raul Prebish, Paul N. Rosenstein-Rodan, Hans Singer, and Jan Tinbergen. P.T. Bauer's contribution (first professional work) was on Southeast Asia and West Africa; Arthur Lewis's, on Jamaica and the Caribbean; mine, on economic history.

31 Ibid., 154. Myrdal also notes that he applied the method of his *An American Dilemma* to his *Asian Drama*, which, in method, he described as a kind of "replica of *An American Dilemma*" (153).

32 Barbara Ward, J.D. Runnalls, and Lenore d'Anjou, eds., *The Widening Gap: Development in the 1970s* (New York: Columbia University Press, 1971), 11–13.

33 Little's statement comes from a letter to Paul Streeten quoted in his "Postscript: Development Dichotomies," in Meier and Seers, eds., *Pioneers*, 345. Little's full critique of the structuralists is incorporated in his *Economic Development: Theory, Policy, and International Relations* (New York: Basic Books, 1982).

34 Meier and Seers, eds., *Pioneers*, 209.

35 This passage comes from an unclassified US government document written by an anonymous US public servant. I quoted it in a lecture at the National Bank of Egypt in November 1983 "Prospects for the World Economy."

4 Equity and Efficiency in the "Mature" Socialist Society, the USSR

NICOLAS SPULBER

The oldest, the strongest, and industrially the most advanced socialist society, the USSR, collapsed in 1991. How did that society handle the key issues of equity and efficiency? To what extent and in which ways were these issues interrelated with the collapse of the entire Soviet system? Certainly questions concerning the "social justice" of institutions and policies involve complex and intertwined economic, social, and political issues. Even in a narrow economic sense, the problems raised are numerous and intricate. Equity considerations may arise in the following areas: (*a*) apportionment of incomes among factors of production, (*b*) allocation of income across individuals, (*c*) division of income between consumption and investment, (*d*) distribution of wealth and the access to certain jobs, (*e*) the impacts of unemployment and of technological change, and finally (*f*) the variety of causes that may account for the existence and persistence of poverty in the society.

According to the neoclassical economists, given the initial distribution of endowments, incomes and prices are the simultaneous outcomes of market processes. The market yields an efficient distribution of wages and salaries, rents and profits. Beyond this, there may be attempts to correct certain undesired market outcomes via progressive taxation or other measures.

According to Karl Marx, in contrast, distribution of income and of the means of consumption is automatically determined by the *mode of production* and by its underpinning *ownership relations* (feudal, capitalist, or socialist). No matter what the capitalists think or do, Marxists believe that "fairness" eludes them: theirs is a system of inequality and of "exploitation." Yet the reversal of this system *does not* engender "equality" in the sense of reduction in income dispersion, although "exploitation" is said to cease when the form of property changes. Marx asserts in his famous "Critique of the Gotha Program," that in the cooperative society based on the common ownership of the means of production, which emerges "after prolonged birth pangs from capitalist society," the "bourgeois right" concerning the equivalent exchange of commodities continues to reign. Accordingly, in that society "a given amount of labour in one form is exchanged for an equal amount of labour in another form." This right cannot supersede the economic structure and the cultural developments it conditions. The income received by each producer (i.e., by each worker, since there are no longer private owners of land and capital) remains *proportional* to the labour each one supplies. "Equality," then, consists only in that "the measurement [of this supply] is made with an *equal standard*, labour."

Since people's natural endowments and needs are unequal, the "right" of equal exchange is in *reality* "an unequal right for unequal labour." And Marx adds that this "right of inequality" will be surmounted only "in a higher phase of communist society." This higher phase will emerge when the division of labour has been overcome, when the antithesis between mental and physical labour has vanished, when labour becomes "life's prime want," and when the productive forces "flow more abundantly." Only then will the "bourgeois right" of each producer to receive back from society "exactly what he gives to it" (after various deductions for replacement of the means of production, expansion, reserves and the costs of administration) be superseded by an entirely new principle. The new "right" would be "from each according to his ability, to each according to his needs," that is, the "right to a truly *egalitarian* distribution, different from that conditioned by the *equivalent* exchanges of goods for the quantity of labour delivered to the society.[1]

The Soviet leaders and the Soviet economists used to claim that socialism was "completed" in the USSR in 1937. Marx's idea that under socialism – that is, during the transitional phase from capitalism to communism – income will continue to be distributed as under capitalism (proportionally to the work supplied by everyone) was exalted from Stalin to Gorbachev as "the most fundamental socialist principle," indeed as its "principle of social justice."[2] In other words, the "bourgeois right" – that is, the "unequal right for unequal labour" – was stated to remain the supreme principle of Soviet socialism.

Does that mean that the Soviet income distribution did always conform to that principle? That the Soviet leaders did not take into account status and position in the party and state hierarchies, or, conversely, the questions of equity and poverty, and finally, the critical importance of efficiency and of incentives? That they did not reshuffle wage policies with these and other objectives in mind? Of course not. In the Soviet economic system, wages and labour policies in general were traditionally viewed by the leadership as "the most important and the most complicated elements of the guidance of the economy," the locus of "the social-economic policy of the party and of the state."[3] To understand the Soviet leadership's approach to these "most important and most complicated elements" of the Soviet economic steering system, let us recall briefly the basic framework within which this approach unfolded.

The Soviet economic system that eventually emerged from the Russian Revolution of October 1917 exhibited the following key characteristics: (a) integration of the summits of the Communist Party, the state's administration, the economy's management under the party's direction, and control by the party of the administration and management at all levels; (b) socialization (nationalization) of the economy's "commanding heights" (in industry, banking, transport, wholesale trade); (c) centralized, directive planning concerning inputs, outputs, the distribution of scarce goods, and the reduction of market mechanisms to subsidiary roles; and (d) assertion of the primacy of society over the individual and of the primacy of production over consumption.

Under Stalin's leadership (1928–53) the party's command and control functions were expanded so as to encompass *all* the activities of the society; socialization was extended to *all* the economic sectors, including agriculture (in combination there with the collectivization of peasants) and retail trade; central directive planning superseded the use of most market mechanisms; and the primacy of production over consumption was inflexibly imposed. Except for various revisions in its working arrangements, the system forged by Stalin continued under his successors until March 1985. At that time, the new secretary general of the party, Mikhail S. Gorbachev, launched a comprehensive program of both political and economic *restructuring (perestroika),* aiming to modify the Stalinist system in a *series of successive stages* that would follow over the balance of the century and possibly beyond.

The four basic characteristics of the system as they had evolved under Stalin had been modified in various ways even before the launching of the *perestroika.* The functions of the party and of the state administration had been redefined in a number of ways. Below its upper levels, the party had ceased its day-to-day control over the administration, while in turn, the latter had ended its day-to-day management of the economy. More specifically, when Gorbachev took power,

- the party's top leadership continued to determine only the broad directions and prospects of the country's development, while the party's staff and vast organization below the top leadership started to be cut drastically, with real power flowing increasingly towards the *state's government bureaucracy* via expansion of its tasks and the responsibilities of its hierarchy of local, regional, and supreme Soviets (councils);

- socialization (nationalization) had ceased to be all-encompassing below the "commanding heights," but private enterprise and initiative were only reluctantly encouraged to develop;
- central planning started to be confined to the setting of basic proportions among sectors and branches and to the broad division of the national income between investment and consumption – concomitantly, more meaningful *contractual relations* began to develop among the enterprises; and
- in the long-run perspective, attention was to be paid to the consumer's rather than the planner's preferences for goods and services.

In the following section, I shall sketch in broad outline the transformations that occurred in the USSR since 1928 in the growth and distribution of the *gainfully employed* and in the evolution of the balance among sectors.

I shall then raise the question of *equity and efficiency* both before and after Gorbachev's accession to power and point to the built-in mechanisms that have systematically accentuated the disparity of incomes between the administrative-professional personnel on one hand and the workers and farmers on the other. I shall focus on the special position of the *executive personnel*, on its hierarchical structure and ranking, and on its social weight and its privileges with regard to access to goods, housing, and travel. I shall show how and to what extent some of Gorbachev's measures tended to limit the size of the *nomenklatura*, that is, the holders of administrative, management, and professional positions.

Next, I shall consider the situation of the *workers*: the wage scales; the discrepancy of labour rewards among branches, sectors, and geographic areas; the difference between the average and minimum pay; and the average-pay differences between engineering-technical personnel, industrial workers, and people employed in agriculture. After examining the changes in wage policies until the advent of Gorbachev, I shall discuss the eventual impact of his ideas of reform on wages, incentives, equity, and efficiency.

Finally, I shall present some concluding remarks concerning the Soviet critique of the Western approaches to the issues of income distribution, inequality, divergence of interests, incentives, and the role of "economic laws" under different economic systems.

FROM GROWTH TO STAGNATION AND "RESTRUCTURING"

From the late 1920s on, a high degree of centralization, directive planning, and priority of production over consumption, of heavy industry over light industry, and of the machine-tools branches over all other branches, seemed to allow the fully socialized Soviet economy to reach ever-higher levels of industrialization and of capital, labour, and technology. The Soviet strategy for economic growth clearly enshrined the preferential allocation of investments to industry, and within industry, to the heavy industrial branches, the systematic growth of fixed production assets, the rapid growth of the labour force in the national economy (i.e., excluding the peasant economy), and the vast increase of the "industrial proletariat."

According to the official Soviet data, the number of gainfully employed in the nationalized economy grew from 10.8 million in 1928 to 32.6 million in 1940, thereafter almost doubling by 1960 and again almost doubling by 1985. Employment in manufacturing grew at an even faster pace between 1928 and 1940, namely from 3.7 million in 1928 to 13.0 million in 1940.[4] By 1985 manufacturing employment was nearly three times as large as that of 1940. The share of manufacturing in total employment rose from some 21 percent in 1940 to some 27 percent in 1960 and to around 29 percent from 1970 on. Employment in agriculture fell from over 32 million in 1940 to less than 30 million in 1960 and to around 25 million from the 1970s on into the 1980s. The crossover from predominantly agricultural employment to predominantly non-agricultural employment occurred in the 1940s. The crossover from a higher employment in agriculture than in manufacturing to the reverse situation took place only in the late 1960s (see Table 4.1). In total employment, the share of agriculture fell from over half in 1940, to around 35 percent in 1960, and then to around 25 percent from the 1970s on, when massive flights from the villages were spurred by a disastrous program of reorganization of the countryside into a number of "central" settlements.

Planned, massive growth both in capital assets and gainful employment, particularly in manufacturing and in the other non-agricultural material branches, as well as a significant increase in the proportion of the manpower with educational degrees did not, however, yield the hoped-for results. By 1985, the new Soviet leadership headed by Mikhail Gorbachev asserted candidly that a significant part of the fixed assets of production was old and run down, that already "at the designing stage some newly created equipment turned out to be obsolete and lagging behind the best models in its reliability, work capacity and efficiency," that "on the whole" the economy was in many respects wasteful, and that the quality and technical level of the goods produced represented "one of the most vulnerable areas of our economy and a source of many difficulties and problems."[5] The impressive expansion in gainful employment was due, and increasingly so, to declines in the productivity of labour, to the inordinate growth in new construction, and also, and in no mean measure, to the widespread system of labour "loading" in order to cope with the exigencies of input deliveries and plan requirements. Indeed, as pointed out in 1986 by the economist E. Manevich, "a large percentage of enterprises and institutions" were known to maintain many surplus workers, engineers, and employees" striving to acquire "the largest number of person-

TABLE 4.1
Gainfully Employed in the Soviet Economy, Selected Years, 1940–85 (in millions)

Employment	1940	1960	1970	1980	1985
Labour force	62.9	83.8	106.8	125.6	130.3
(M) Manufacturing	13	22.6	31.6	36.9	38.2
(A) Agriculture	32.3	29.2	25.6	24.9	27.7
(O) Other material product	6	13.3	18.2	23.1	23.8
(S) Services	11.6	18.7	31.4	40.7	43.6

Source: SSSR v tsifrakh v 1986 godu, Kratkii statistickeskii slovar (The USSR in figures in 1986, Small Statistical Handbook) (Moscow: Finansy i statistika, 1987), 141, 144, 171–5; and Narodnoe khoziaistvo SSSR za 70 let, Iubileinyi statistickeskii ezhegodnik (The National Economy of the USSR for seventy years, Jubilee issue of a statistical yearly) (Moscow: Finansy i statistika, 1987), 411.

nel ... maintained entirely at state expense.'' Now this surplus was badly needed in order to cope with the disruptions caused by the vagaries of supplies or with the pressure to fulfil certain plan indices at the appointed dates.[6] Moreover, as Gorbachev himself had confessed in 1985, no less than 50 million workers were still engaged in *manual labour*, that is, ''approximately one third of industrial workers, more than half of construction workers, and three-fourths of agricultural workers.''[7]

The slowdown in economic growth during and after the eighth Five Year Plan (FYP) became increasingly obvious from one period to the next. According to official Soviet figures, the annual rate of growth of the net material product fell from 7.8 percent during the eighth quinquennial period (1966–70) to 3.6 percent during the eleventh (1981–85). Productivity decreased in each economic sector and total productivity fell to all-time lows (see Table 4.2). According to Western computation, the declines were much more significant than the official data implied. Capital productivity and total productivity had declined drastically to –4.5 percent and –1.4 percent per year by 1985.[8]

It is these sharp declines that helped bring Gorbachev to power. The new general secretary decided to break openly and publicly with certain past habits and methods and to put forward new solutions. Gorbachev came out forcefully against the former policy makers' and planners' ''subjectivist approaches'' and ''voluntaristic attitudes'' in regard to economic realities; he publicly chastised the entire party and state hierarchies, saying they had complacently glorified ''achievements based on disregard of laws, report-padding, bribe taking and encouragement of toadyism and adulation,''[9] and he outlined a series of demanding tasks for pulling the economy out of the doldrums. Besides the basic measures concerning the relations between the planning centre and the enterprises to which we have referred in the preceding section, he emphasized the need to increase economic efficiency by retooling the entire economy, to trim and reshuffle the top-heavy managerial levels, and to stimulate labour productivity.

TABLE 4.2
Net Material Product (NMP) and Productivity, Annual Rates of Growth, Quinquennial Periods,
1961–85

Periods	NMP	Total	Productivity Manufacture	Agriculture	Construction
7th FYP (1961–65)	6.5	6.1	4.6	4.8	5.3
8th FYP (1966–70)	7.8	6.8	5.8	5.4	4.1
9th FYP (1971–75)	5.7	4.5	6.0	4.0	5.2
10th FYP (1976–80)	4.3	3.3	3.2	2.6	2.1
11th FYP (1981–85)	3.6	3.1	3.1	1.5	2.6

Source: *Narodnoe khoziaistvo SSSR za 70 let*, 51, 107.

The goals set for the rate of growth during the twelfth FYP (1986–90) and in the projections for the balance of the century were brought into line with the performance of Brezhnev's "years of decline" rather than with what allegedly preceded it. Thus, for instance, the planned *quinquennial* rates for the growth of the net material product for the twelfth FYP were set at from 19.3 to 22.2 percent as compared to the officially claimed increases of 41 percent for 1966–70 and of 28 percent for 1971–75. Increments for labour productivity were set at from 19.9 to 22.8 percent as compared to rises of 39 and 25 percent claimed for 1966–70 and 1971–75.[10]

"Retooling" on a scale not witnessed since 1928 was alleged to be the indispensable means for eliminating widespread obsolescence, lagging technology, outputs of unwanted and unsalable goods, superfluous jobs, and flagging productivity. While in 1928 Stalin had set his sights on the forced creation of a large-scale industrial complex and a powerful army based on the smoke-stack technology of the first decade of the century, in 1985 Gorbachev set his sights far higher – not only on the rejuvenation of that obsolete machine, but also on the mass-scale introduction of electronics and computers. He stressed the need to restructure the entire machine-tools industry and to increase for this purpose the production of modern machine tools, forges and presses, and foundry, welding and other equipment. For good measure, he also emphasized the need to develop at a rapid pace microelectronics, computer equipment, instrument building and the whole information industry, as catalysts of technical progress.[11]

Emphasis on "quality of output and work," with penalties for administrators, managers, and professionals as well for the ordinary labour rank and file, was said to be the order of day. Technological upgrading was supposed to lead in time to a weakening of the demand for labour and, in combination with factory amalgamations and eventual closures, to the spreading of the allegedly "capitalist disease" of unemployment. More important perhaps, the new emphasis on rewards, based on "quality of output and work," was to accentuate wage differentials and increase the rewards going to a new strata of privileged *neo-Stakhanovites* in comparison to those left to the rest of the workers.[12] We turn to these issues in sections below.

THE ADMINISTRATIVE-MANAGERIAL-PROFESSIONAL CLASS

Since the beginning of the Soviet regime, power had been vested in the integrated summit of three hierarchies – *"apparats"* as the Russians call them – including the leaders of the party, of the state administration, and of the economy's management. Since Stalin's time, appointments in the leading positions of the party, the state, and the economy were made by *co-optation* rather than by election, competition, training, or merit. The selections and the assignments of "cadres" (*podbor i rastanovka kadrov*), starting from the locus of supreme power, the Secretariat of the party, down through the various echelons of the party and its satellite organizations, the state's administration, and the economy, were carried out as a *gift* from the party. Anybody could be dismissed and replaced by the appropriate party committee if the party withdrew its confidence. Because of this, the Soviet civil service became in practice "an extension of the party in composition and training."

The *hierarchical system of positions* within the party-state and the economy (and by extension, the *holders of these positions*), shrouded in secrecy, formed the so-called *nomenklatura*, the Soviet Union's commanding core.[13] After his rise to power, Mikhail Gorbachev decided reluctantly, to trim the party, state, and management hierarchies and, up to a point, to let training, merit, and ability count in the selection and promotion of cadres.

How large was the *nomenklatura*? What exactly happened to its structure after 1985? What claims does it still have in regard to the distribution of income and goods? To start with, even after the official dismemberment of the USSR primary party organizations still function even though "unofficially" in all the enterprises of state and collective farms, in the units of the armed forces, and in all forms of organizations, as well as in ministries, economic institutions, and departments where they still control, below newly appointed leaders, the *selection, placement*, and *education* of the rest of employees. In the army, even such political organs as the Chief Political Administration of the Soviet Army and Navy have not been officially liquidated.[14]

By the end of the 1980s, the *nomenklatura* of the state administration and of the economy comprised a total of no less than 18 million. In a speech in Murmansk in October 1987, Gorbachev referred directly to this enormously bloated apparatus: "In our country, about 18 million people are employed in the sphere of management, including 2.5 million in the apparatus of various administrative agencies and something like 15 million persons in the managerial staffs of associations, enterprises and organizations. All this comes to 15 percent of the country's labor resources. There is a manager for every six or seven people ... We should, naturally, give some careful thought to simplifying the inordinately bloated apparatus."[15]

Soviet data for 1980 and 1985 indicate that the executive state apparatus counted from 2.2 to 2.3 million persons, that is, less than 2 percent of the labour force (the structure of this top layer is detailed in Table 4.3). On the other hand, as indicated in the official *Unified List of Employees Positions (Edinaia nomenklatura dolzhnostei sluzhashchikn – ENDS)* and in the *Handbook of Employees Jobs Descriptions (Kvalifikatsionnyi spravochnik dolzhnostei sluzhashchikh – KSDS)*, the economic *nomenklatura* counted thirty grades (or echelons),[16] grades that were likely also standard in all branches of the state apparatus.

According to Soviet statistics, the average monthly pay of a member of the state apparat in 1986 was 170.5 rubles, as compared to 195 rubles for the average gainfully employed, and 216.5 for a worker.[17] However, these figures are misleading. The *nomenklatura* enjoyed various perquisites – decreasing from rank to rank as one went down the hierarchy. In February 1989, the Soviet people were told that Mikhail Gorbachev's salary was 1,500 rubles a month "plus a house and a car." But in fact, the top layers of the *nomemklatura* enjoyed extraordinary privileges, carefully hidden from the *vulgum pecus*. These involved access to all types of goods at special prices and in special stores closed to the rest of the population, as well as gratuities, including luxuriously appointed houses with rich furniture and works of art, summer homes, resorts, sanatoria, special hospitals and special care, entertainment, automobiles, and domestic and foreign travel. Many of these perks were administered and handed out directly from the so-called party household economy.

As far as the fixed assets were concerned, the nomenklaturist had, however, only the *usufruct* that can be enjoyed for as long as he or she had the party's confidence: the privileges were indeed withdrawn if the party withdrew its confidence and the nomenklaturist fell from grace. As far as the nomenklaturist's pay is concerned, the rubles were of a special kind, since they could buy an assortment of quality goods unavailable to the holders of "ordinary" rubles. All rubles looked alike, but some rubles were worth more than others – depending on who held them.[18]

The real claims of the *nomenklatura* on income distribution thus cannot be accurately evaluated. Comprehensive data on the relation between the social-professional classification of families and their income levels are absent. Illustrative data for the city of Taganrog, for instance, indicate that in the mid-1970s low-, middle-, and high-income levels could be found among all the strata of the society. Detailed data show, however, that the highest proportions of families with high-income levels were to be found, in decreasing order, among the executives, the teachers and doctors, the engineering-technical personnel, and the skilled workers (with extra jobs).

TABLE 4.3
Top Layers of the "Apparat" of the State and the Economy's Executive Organs, 1980 and 1985
(in thousands)

	1980	1985
Total personnel of the executive organs of the state and the economy, the cooperatives and mass organizations	2,231	2,376
of which:		
Executive organs of ministers and departments	1,531	1,623
of which:		
– all union apparat	104	107
– republics' apparat	134	140
– ministers of autonomous republics, and territories and districts	251	280
– regions and towns apparat	413	450
– agriculture	629	646
– presidia of Soviets and officials	297	312
– judicial system	84	92
– executive organs of cooperatives and of mass organizations	319	349

Source: Narodnoe khoziaistvo sssr za 70 let., 120.

In the process of purging his adversaries, reshuffling the central positions, and demoting various executives, Gorbachev sent a message that reverberated with increasing intensity throughout this "bloated apparatus."[19] But on the other hand, Gorbachev in no way challenged the *nomenklatura* system and its access to all kinds of covert privileges. "At a serious Moscow meeting" – as reported to *Izvestia* by special correspondent A. Plutnik – "someone spoke the words: break open the *nomenklatura* circle ... Let us think about it: Can the new management mechanism function if the old principle of personnel growth and advancement is left inviolable?"[20] Up to the beginning of the 1990s, Gorbachev has neither raised this question nor provided an answer to it. He challenged specific individuals of the *nomenklatura* and went as far as withdrawing certain privileges (e.g., chauffeur-driven cars) from the lower echelons of the hierarchy. But he did not challenge the structure of the system. The proclamations of independence of the Soviet republics has not brought about the complete liquidation of their respective nomenklatura. In fact many of the "new" leaders of the newly independent republic held also the top positions in the old Soviet system.

INCOME DISTRIBUTION "ACCORDING TO WORK"

In theory, the most important principle of socialism, its principle of social justice (namely, distribution of income *proportional to the work supplied by everyone*), reigned supreme *below the nomenklatura*. Here too, however, a variety of correctives were called into play. Traditionally, not only did wages differ in regard to sex, training, skills, and hardship or intensity of work, but they differed also between branches and sectors (according to policy makers' objectives) as well as among republics, regions, districts, and other areas and, finally, within the enterprises themselves, depending on premia, bonuses, and other supplements added to the base pay as a result of a variety of managerial considerations or trade union pressure. The Soviet policy makers and planners always saw in wage policies and in the population's balances of income and spending, of wages and consumption, crucial levers for further-ing planned objectives and work stimulation.

As might be expected, the ratio of the "social surplus" (i.e., profits) to the "wage fund" tended to fall through the 1970s and early 1980s, as did the rate of return to total outlays on raw materials and on the use of machinery (in Marxian terms "surplus" related to material inputs plus wages, $m/c + v$); see Table 4.4). This became one of the main preoccupations of the Gorbachev leadership, as we shall see immediately. Throughout the entire planning period, two tendencies interacted in the setting of wage rates. One tendency pushed towards higher wages via upgrading and the increase in pay rates for various categories of workers (depending on the ways managers perceived their needs for manpower and on whether the unions were either complacent or felt forced to show "activism") and, in certain conditions, also via an increase in the dismally low pay of the lowest-paid workers and farmers. Another tendency pushed in the opposite direction, namely towards larger wage differentials in order to increase incentives and productivity. Wage differentials increased sharply in the critical planning years 1931–33, when Stalin stepped up the pace of industrialization.[21] The wage span then decreased somewhat, until 1937, due to increases in the lowest wages in relation to the average wage. After 1937, and in the early postwar years, the spread between the unskilled and the skilled increased, ranging from 1:3.5 and even up to 1:4 or 1:8 in certain key industries, still less wide, however, than in the early 1930s. Towards the second half of the 1950s, the ratio decreased from 1:3.5 to 1:2. The process of wage readjustment in favour of the lowest-paid workers and towards decreasing wage differentials continued during the 1960s until the mid-1980s. Before its increases in 1955, the minimum wage was at the abysmal low level of 20 to 22 rubles per month, that is, on the order of 28 to 30 percent of the average wage (71.8 rubles). By 1977 the minimum rose to 45 percent of the average (70 rubles as against 155.2 rubles). Interesting changes occurred in the average pay itself among categories of gainfully employed in various branches. The wage differentials between the engineering-technical personnel and the workers' average pay tended to decrease. Sectoral pay differences between the engineering-technical personnel in industry and in agriculture narrowed sharply, as have the pay differentials (but to a lesser extent) among the workers in these two sectors. Finally, increases in the collective farmers' pay from the 1970s on increased significantly in relation to the agricultural workers' pay (see Figure 4.1 and Table 4.5).

TABLE 4.4
Growth and Change in the Soviet NMP by Factor Shares and Plan Ratios, Current Prices, 1960–85

Items	Billion Rubles at Current Prices			
	1960	1970	1980	1985
Social product (SP)	303.8	643.5	1,078.5	1,382.5
Net material product (NMP)	145.0	289.9	462.2	577.7
Wage fund (v)	69.4	147.6	272.6	322.4
Social surplus (m)	75.6	142.3	189.6	255.3
Ratios				
Exploitation rate: $\dfrac{m}{v}$	1.08	0.9	0.7	0.8
Organic composition of capital: $\dfrac{c}{v}$	2.3	2.4	2.3	2.5
Rate of profit: $\dfrac{m}{c+v}$ 33.1	28.3	21.3	22.6	

Sources: Computed from *Narodnoe khoziaistvo SSSR v 1983* (The National Economy of the USSR in 1983) (Moscow: Finansyi statistika, 1984), 47, 385, 393; *Narodnoe khoziaistvo SSSR v 1985*, 45; and *SSSR v tsifrakh v 1986 godu*, 179. Compare to L.E. Kunelskii, *Zarabotnaia plata i stimulirovanie truda* (Wages and work incentives) (Moscow, Ekonomika, 1981), 62, 67 (the wage fund as calculated in this table includes the payment of collective farmers from the collective fund).

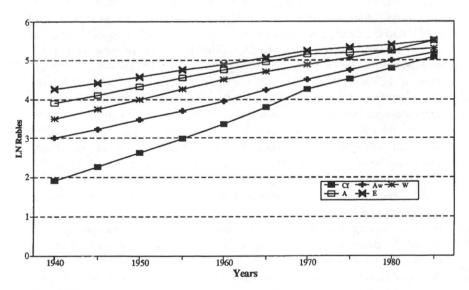

Figure 4.1
Logs of Average Monthly Pay in Ruble Main Branches, 1940–85

TABLE 4.5

Average Monthly Pay in the Main Branches of the Economy in Rubles and Percentages, 1940–85

	Rubles				
	1940	*1960*	*1970*	*1980*	*1985*
Industry					
Engineering-technical personnel	69.5	135.7	178.0	212.5	232.2
Workers	32.4	89.9	130.6	185.5	211.7
Agriculture (State farms and state entr.)					
Agronomists, zootechnicians and engineering-technical personnel	50.4	115.5	164.3	185.5	243.4
Workers	20.7	51.9	98.5	148.5	179.7
Collective Farmers (pays from collective fund)	6.6*	28.3	74.9	118.5	153.4
Row 2 as percent of 1	46.4	66.2	73.4	87.3	91.2
Row 3 as percent of 1	72.4	85.1	92.3	87.3	104.8
Row 4 as percent of 2	63.9	57.7	75.4	80.0	84.9
Row 5 as percent of 4	31.8	54.5	76.0	79.8	85.3

Source: sssr v tsifrakh v 1986 godu, 143, 179; Kunelskii, Zarabotnoia plata, 108, 122; and Narodnoe khoziaistvo sssr za 70 let, Iubileinyi statisticheskii ezhegodnik, 431.

* Estimate; percentages computed.

In the wage scale prevailing in the early 1980s, the step increases within each branch varied between 1:1.58 and 1:1.86, from agriculture-foodstuffs-clothing to lumber-oil extraction and underground coal work. The spread between the lowest pay (74.9 rubles per month in agriculture-foodstuffs-clothing and construction) and the highest pay (241.3 rubles per month in underground coal work) was 1:3.2 (see Figure 4.2). Under Gorbachev, in the late 1980s the salaries of shop and department chiefs increased officially by up to 90 percent above the rates of workers in the highest wage-skill grades, while the salaries of managers rose to between 400 and 470 rubles in heavy industry and between 275 and 350 in light industry.[22] One should not forget, however, that bonuses, premia, and arbitrary classification upgradings of all kinds were intertwined with the centrally fixed wage scale, often tending to jack up or decrease the differential within and between branches.

In the early 1930s, when Stalin wanted to step up the industrialization drive and break up the old work habits as well as the prevailing work norms, he denounced "wage equalization" in the following terms: "In order to put an end to this evil we must draw up wage scales that will take into account the difference between skilled and unskilled labor, between heavy and light work ... Marx and Lenin said that the difference between skilled and unskilled labor would exist even under socialism, even after classes had been abolished ... consequently, even under socialism, 'wages' must be paid according to work performed and not according to needs ... But the equalitarians

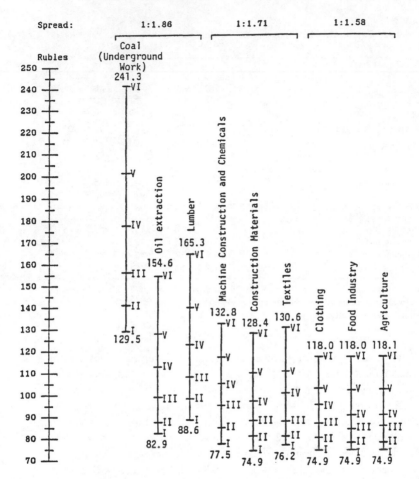

Source: Kunelskii, *Zarabotnaia plata i stimulirovanie truda*, 148.

Figure 4.2
Wage Scale, Monthly Payments in Rubles, 1980

among our business executives and trade-union officials do not agree with this ... Who is right? Marx and Lenin, or the equalitarians. It must be supposed that it is Marx and Lenin who are right."[23]

Gorbachev, whose stated aims were the liquidation of "parasitic confidence in guaranteed work" and of "warped" attitudes towards work (i.e., laziness, drunkenness, and irresponsibility), attacked wage equalization and past practices as follows: "Large, unjustified bonuses and fringe benefits were paid and figure-padding for profit took place. Parasitic sentiments grew stronger and the mentality of wage levelling began to take hold. All that hit those workers who could and wanted to work better, while making life easier for the lazy ones."[24] And, in a speech at the Congress of the Trade Unions, he added for good measure: "You know even better than I do that certain enterprises are still reluctant to part with wage levelling. Their managements are reluctant because it is a bothersome matter, [and] the trade union locals ... often want to go on living with this kind of 'timidity.' Some people – the slacker, the drunkard, and the idler – have got to have their toes stepped on ... At the same time, we will elevate – both materially and morally – the diligent and conscientious worker."[25]

However, as some pro-Gorbachev economists stressed at the time, the *increases* in wages were also to be kept under watch. E. Kasimovskii, for instance, noted that "the principle of social justice in labor remuneration" was allegedly operative "when the latter grows at a slower rate than labor productivity." In the 1970s and early 1980s, however, the growth of labour productivity declined and the remuneration of labour increased considerably faster than productivity. "This violated the principle of social justice in labour remuneration."[26] Be that as it may, Tat'iana Zaslavskaia also asserted that Gorbachev's reforms had left in place "many deformations" of the wage system that partial measures cannot eradicate.[27] Other writers asserted more or less cynically that the spectre of unemployment was "not bad medicine for laziness, drunkenness, and irresponsibility."[28]

While all this did sound menacing for the stragglers, it did not encourage the "diligent" to produce more and better. What really matters above all is what one can finally buy with the increased pay. For the public at large, this in turn depends on a number of factors: first, on the question of the *prices* at which goods and services are available, and then on the impact of governmental measures on the overall availability of food supplies, the extent of access to and the schedule of delivery for durable and non-durable goods of mass consumption, the appearance, assortment, and quality of such goods, the nature and effectiveness of retail trade and of repair and personal-care services, and the availability and possibility of acquiring decent living conditions.

Consider first the question of prices and their interrelations with wages. Much effort had been spent, until the turn of the 1990s, on calculating the *planned prices* that were supposed to serve in all inter-firm transactions and in the state retail trade, where some of the goods available to the population are sold and bought. This was a very complex affair, carried out over long time intervals. Up to the beginning of the 1990s, the building blocks of Soviet prices remained the so-called *prices of production*. These were the average, prices of an association of enterprises, or of an industrial branch, for each and every type of product each produces – average, since costs and technologies differ among the enterprises in question. These prices consisted of total outlays (inputs of materials and depreciation – in Marxian notation c plus wages v) plus a planned "surplus" calculated in relation to total outlays in the association and the branch plus other markups related to total outlays in the economy as a whole, including the upkeep of the state administration and of the army. Goods were brought to the wholesale distributing system (the Material Technical Supply) at the prices of production. In turn, as was usual, the latter slapped on top of them its own markups: a sales tax (so-called turnover tax) that varied, according to the category of goods, plus charges for handling these goods and a planned profit. These so-called *wholesale prices of industry* continued to be the prices used in inter-firm transactions until 1990, when the collapse of the planning system freed all the prices, including most state *retail prices* (that is the wholesale prices of industry augmented by charges added by the state retail network for handling the goods, plus a planned profit).

Wages were, of course, a crucial element in all these calculations. The planners aimed to keep this key element *as low as possible,* with careful attention paid not only to each branch but also to the economy as a whole. As of the end of the 1970s and the beginning of the 1980s, wages accounted for less than 15 percent of total costs – higher in the machine-tools and metal-working industries and lower in the light industries (see Table 4.6). Simultaneously with the increase in wage differentials and the general lowering of the wage bill – through firing on an unknown scale until now, various efforts have been made to eliminate from the retail prices the heavy subsidies that have prevailed for basic goods, namely for meat, butter, vegetables, and potatoes. The Gorbachev *perestroika*, similar to Stalin's industrialization drive, aimed, but without success, at systematically lowering the total wage bill. Finally, the 1991 collapse of the economy brought also the virtual disintegration of the entire price-wage structure, both at the centre and in the republics.

An often insuperable problem in the Soviet framework, involved not only the unwieldy structure of prices, but also the incessant, time-consuming hunt for the needed goods.[29] The ordinary Soviet consumer always had to spend an enormous amount of time fighting the near-paralysis of the system of supply and distribution of goods. Goods in short supply (*defitsitnye tovary*) could sometimes be purchased (but at a price) in the state stores but from under the counter (*pod prilavkom*), thanks to the paid complicity of salespeople, or more often on the all-pervasive black or shadow market (*tenevoi rynok*). Why the shortages? The answer lay in the interplay of a vast number of factors – to start with, the diversion of goods towards the privileged and the innumerable failures of the producing enterprises and of the trade network as far as deliveries are concerned; the shoddy quality and poor assortment of goods put on sale, along with the complete disregard for state property; the vastly ramified and corrupting influences throughout the society (a deeply ingrained disease which *perestroika* could not even begin to affect). The breakdown of the social, political, and ethnic ties among the components of the former USSR, further aggravated the terrible plight of the consumer.

TABLE 4.6
Structure of Costs in Manufacturing, in Percentages, 1980

	Total	Raw Materials	Other Materials	Fuel	Electric Power	Depreciation	Other Expenditures	Wages
Total manufacturing	100	63.0	4.3	3.5	2.5	7.0	4.8	14.9
Machine tools and metal working	100	58.0	3.8	1.2	2.0	6.2	5.7	23.1
Light industry	100	85.0	2.6	0.3	0.7	1.5	0.8	8.5

Source: Anatolii N. Ezhov, *Ekonomicheskii mechanizm plannovogo upravleniia tsenami pri sotsializme* (The Economic Mechanism of the Planned Guidance of Prices under Socialism) (Moscow: Vyschaia shkola, 1981), 196.

Western writers have rightly pointed out long before the breakdown of the USSR, that innumerable threads connected the stagnant surface economy with its teeming "shadows," the barter and/or the black market economy – the first chasing after an often elusive double coincidence of opposite wants, the second brimming with stolen state property, clandestine private production, and all kinds of illicit diversions of public goods.[30] Some Soviet writers still pretended in the early 1980s that "speculative prices and incomes, graft, and embezzlement of socialist property ... are anti-social phenomena that contradict the very essence of socialism,"[31] instead of recognizing that these "anti-social phenomena" flew in fact from this very "essence" itself.

The "food problem," which was supposed to be solved in the early 1980s, became severe even before the complete collapse of 1991. The performance of Soviet agriculture remained disastrous not only in terms of planned output levels, but also in terms of harvesting, storing, transporting, and processing what it actually produced.[32] The performance of both the food-processing branches of the "agroindustrial complex" and of the light industries (mainly textile, clothing and footwear) was adversely affected. The production of durables (except perhaps for automobiles) was organized haphazardly, and efforts of coordination and standardization were never successful.[33] Obtaining decent housing remained an elusive goal for a large part of the urban population, while investment in housing had, in relative terms, tended to steadily decrease from the 1960s on. On the other hand, the system of allocation of the scarcest goods and services, such as housing and educational and health-care services, free of charge or at nominal prices, led to the paradoxical result that "a well-paid worker can buy furniture, a refrigerator and television set, but must wait years to get an apartment to put them in."[34]

Soviet economists and statisticians used to emphasize, with great pride, the continuous increase in the total and per capita public consumption funds, and to stress the various contributions of these funds in the form of pensions, grants, supplements to wages, and gratuities or subsidies for education, health care, housing, and communal services.[35] As L.E. Kunelskii put it, "In our country payments for dwellings and communal services are low ... accounting for less than 3 percent of the outlays of workers and employees," and as Professor A.D. Smirnov and others noted, "The low rent fixed by government, and the stability of prices for the basic, mass consumer goods, provide a firm basis for an increase in the material welfare of all the working people."[36]

But since the mid-1980s, these contentions have proven shallow. Subsidies in general were no longer regarded as a way of increasing material welfare, but as some of the principal contributors to the distortions of the price system. As for dwellings, it became increasingly evident that the distribution at a nominal price of the scarcest goods actually favoured the high- rather than the low-income groups. Instead of expanding for a fee the sphere of housing, including the raising of rents and the just differentiation between them with regard to the quality and location of apartments, the system encouraged speculation in state housing, subletting at high surcharges, and other shady deals in apartment swapping. The intended contribution of social consumption funds, both "to supplement the distribution according to one's labor to a certain degree" and "to equalize its injustice that is imposed on those who despite their desire are not able to work effectively," had thus been completely thwarted.[37]

CONCLUDING COMMENTS

Until 1985 the dominant Soviet view with respect to management and planning was that the Soviet economy constituted a single national complex (*edinyi narodnokhoziaistvennyi kompleks*) that could be entirely manipulated from the directive centre as a single servo-mechanism.[38] A different approach had already been proposed in the early 1960s, notably by academician Vasilii S. Nemchinov, whose ideas were adopted by Gorbachev a quarter of a century later. Nemchinov noted that the national economy was not identical to a single sum of its elements and primary units. The economy, he stated, is comprised of a number of smaller economic units – branches, regions, associations – which, in turn, break down into firms and consuming units (families). "A primitive view of the interrelations between large and small economic systems can only create the type of ossified, mechanistic system in which all the parameters of operation are set in advance and the whole system runs by quotas from top to bottom for every given moment on every given point." The alternative suggested by Nemchinov was that the basic inter-sector, inter-branch economic proportions and balances chosen by the centre be upheld by letting the enterprises function on the basis of cost accounting and a more liberal use of their own funds. He further proposed that the centre distribute sufficiently profitable contracts for the products included in the national economic plan "among the enterprises that propose conditions that are most advantageous to the national economy as a whole."[39]

Clearly, at its inception, the Gorbachev *perestroika* was related in many ways to Nemchinov's ideas and also reflected kaleidoscopically almost all of the actual or intended east European "experiments" carried out in Yugoslavia, Poland, and Hungary before 1989. But there was also something entirely new and dramatic in the unsuccessful Soviet drives for change, more dramatic even than the collapse of communism in the whole of Eastern Europe. For the first time in history, the very model of Marxism-Leninism in power – the "mature" socialist society that had been emulated not only in Eastern Europe but also in many less-developed countries and that was supposed "to catch up with and surpass the highest indices of capitalism," started to unravel, torn apart spasmodically and unstopably by the "contradictions" it had claimed to have eliminated forever. Official criticism now acknowledges without qualms that the "Soviet economic mechanism" had not been able to formulate and implement coherent and efficient plans, had not been capable of satisfactorily apportioning incomes among its population, had failed to achieve either efficiency or equity, and had not succeeded in sustaining high rates of economic growth – higher than those of advanced capitalism as the Soviet textbooks used to claim. Indeed, it could no longer properly feed its own people. The attempts at restructuring that technologically obsolete and poorly held together "economic mechanism" have first brought about a further slowdown in output and large unemployment – instead of the vaunted socialist efficiency, unequalled technology, and permanent full employment – and then led to utter collapse. The shattered illusions about planning, growth, efficiency, and full employment have fallen to the ground, along with the dashed hopes about "socialism with a human face," socialist abundance, socialist "equitable" (meaning equalitarian) distribution of income, and idyllic "social justice."

NOTES

Author's note: I wish to thank Robert Becker, Roy Gardner, and Scott H. Gordon for their useful comments. Any remaining errors are my responsibility.

1   Karl Marx, "Critique of the Gotha Program" (1875), in Robert C. Tucker, ed., *The Marx-Engels Reader*, 2d ed. (New York: W.W. Norton, 1978), 525 ff. See also A.D. Smirnov et al., eds., *The Teaching of Political Economy*, a critique of non-Marxian theories (Moscow: Progress Publishers, 1984), 68–9.
2   Mikhail Gorbachev, *Reorganization and the Party's Personnel Policy*, report at the plenary meeting of the CPSU Central Committee, 27–8 January 1987 (Moscow: Novosti Press Agency Publishing House), 13. "The main source of in-

come in the Soviet Union," according to Ivan Gladky, the then chairman of the State Committee of the USSR on Labour and Social Issues, "is pay received according to the results of one's effort. This is the essence of the principle of social justice and the fundamental law governing the distribution of material benefits under socialism." Gladky thus stressed that what mattered was not simply *labour input* but rather the *productivity* of labour. See Ivan Gladky, *Social Programmes Benefit from Economic Restructuring* (Moscow: Novosti Press Agency Publishing House, 1987), 21. See also E. Kazimovskii, "Sotsial'naia spravedlivost' i sovershenstvovanie raspredelitel'nykh otnoshenii v SSSR," *Ekonomicheskie Nauki*, 1986, no. 12, "Social Justice and the Improvement of Distribution Relations in the USSR," trans. in *Problems of Economics* 30, no. 5 (September 1987): 64.

3 E.M. Trenenkov, *Organizatsia oplaty truda rabochikh i sluzhashchikh* (The Organization of the Work Remuneration of Workers and Employees) (Moscow: Profizdat, 1986), 3.

4 Data for 1928 from *Narodnoe khoziaistvo SSSR v 1959 godu* (The National Economy of the USSR in 1959) (Moscow: Gostatizdat, 1980), 588–9. For the other years, see Table 4.2.

5 See Mikhail Gorbachev's reports to the Plenum of the Central Committee of the Communist Party of the USSR, 25 June 1987, "O zadachiakh partii po korennoi perestroike upravleniia ekonomikoi" (On the Tasks of the Party on the Basic Restructuring of the Guidance of the Economy), *Kommunist*, no. 10, 1987, 5ff, and Mikhail Gorbachev, "Fundamental Issues of the Party's Economic Policy," *Kommunist*, no. 9, June 1985, trans. in *Daily Report Soviet Union*, FBIS (Foreign Broadcasting Information Service) 3, no. 142, Annex no. 062 (24 July 1985): 6, 11.

6 E. Manevich, "Puti perestroiki knoziaistvennogo mekhanizma," *Voprosy ekonomiki*, 1986, no. 11 (Means of Restructuring the Economic Mechanism), trans. in *Problems of Economics* 30, no. 1 (May 1987): 82.

7 Gorbachev, "Fundamental Issues."

8 See also Guy Ofer "Soviet Economic Growth 1928–1985, *Journal of Economic Literature* 25, no. 4 (December 1987): 1778–9.

9 See Gorbachev, *Reorganization and the Party's Personnel Policy*, 10, 11, 12, 14, 16.

10 *Guidelines for the Economic and Social Development of the USSR for 1986–1990 and for the Period Ending in 2000*, report by Nikolai Ryzhkov, 3 March 1986 (Moscow: Novosti Press Agency Publishing House, 1986), and G. Sorokin, "Tempy rosta sovetskoi ekonomiki," *Voprosy ekonomikii*, 1986, no. 2, 11ff. Many economists viewed these projections as unrealistic. L.I. Abalkin, for instance, pointed out that the simultaneous goals of quantitative growth and of qualitative transformations set for the twelfth Five Year Plan (1986–90) were "from a scientific point of view, incompatible." And R.R. Simonyan stressed that "the growth rates of the basic branches of production *must* be decreased." See L.I. Abalkin, "Socialism Has No Ready-Made Patterns,"

Pravada, 30 June, 3–4, trans. in *Current Digest of the Soviet Press* 40, no. 27 (1988): 7, and R.R. Simonyan, "Where We Stand," *Izvestia*, 8 July, 3, trans. in ibid., 15.

11 See Gorbachev, "Fundamental Issues," 6, 8, 9.

12 In the 1930s, Stalin wanted to change rapidly and extensively the prevailing work norms and worker rewards. Stakhanov, a coal miner coached by the party, became the national symbol of the breaker of old norms, that is, the achiever of higher output levels which the rest of the workers were eventually coaxed to match under the penalty of lower rewards and, in certain cases, of deportation to labour camps. Under Gorbachev the Stakhanov myth has been put to rest: it has been recognized as a pure fabrication of Stalin and his henchmen.

13 See Helene Carrere d'Encausse, *Confiscated Power, How Soviet Russia Really Works*, trans. by George Holoch (New York: Harper & Row, 1980), 139ff. See also Michael Voslensky, *La Nomenklatura, les privilégiés en URSS* (Paris: Belfond, 1980), 90.

14 See Graeme Gill, *The Rules of the Communist Party of the Soviet Union* (Armonk, NY: M.E. Sharpe, 1988), 79–81, 236, 247.

15 "Perestroika, priamoe prodolzhenie Oktiabria," Rechi tovarishchia Gorbachev, M.S. (Restructuring, a direct continuation of October [revolution], Speech of comrade M.S. Gorbachev), *Ekonomicheskaia gazeta*, no. 41 (October 1987): 3.

16 L.S. Bogatyrenko, eds., *Trud i zarabotnaia plata v SSR*, Slovar' Spravochnik (Labour and Wages in the USSR – A Handbook) (Moscow: Ekononika, 1984), 101, 119–20.

17 See *SSSR v tsifrakh v 1986 godu*, 179–81.

18 As Tat'iana Zaslavskaia rightly put it: "But the fact that different social groups have unequal access to different channels of trade creates a specific form of social inequality, and essentially means the formation of consumer markets in which the ruble has varying purchase power. However, the 'equality of all rubles' as the measure of consumption is the basic premise of the wage system" (Tat'iana Zaslavskaia, "Chelovecheskii faktor razvitiia ekonomiki i sotsial'naia spravedlivost,'" *Kommunist*, no. 13, 1986, trans. as "Social Justice and the Human Factor in Economic Development," *Problems of Economics* 30, no. 1 (May 1987): 24.

19 According to a statement of Gorbachev of 8 May 1988, as many as 66 percent of all ministers were recently appointed, as were 61 percent of all first secretaries of province party committees and 63 percent of all the first secretaries of city and district party committees. See "Meeting in the CPSU Central Committee," *Pravda*, 8 May 1988, trans. in *The Current Digest of the Soviet Press* 40, no. 19 (8 June 1988): 3.

20 A. Plutnik, "The Man Who Replaced Me," *Izvestia*, 13 January, 3, trans. in *The Current Digest of the Soviet Press* 39, no. 3 (1987): 7.

21 For a more extensive discussion of the wage policies, see Trenonkov, *Organizatsia oplaty truda*, 22–4.

22   See V.I. Shcherbakov, "Kardinal'naia perestroika oplata truda" (The Whole-sale Restructuring of Wages), *Ekonomika i organizatsiia promyshlenogo proiz-vodstva*, 1987, no. 1, trans. in *Problems of Economics* 30, no. 6 (October 1987): 72ff.

23   I.V. Stalin, *Sochinenia* (Works) (Moscow: Ogiz – Foreign Languages Publish-ing House, 1955), 13 (July 1930–January 1934): 59.

24   Gorbachev, *Reorganization and the Party's Personnel Policy*, 13.

25   Mikhail Gorbachev, *Restructuring – A Vital Concern of the People*, speech at the 18th Congress of the Trade Unions of the USSR, 25 February 1987 (Mos-cow: Novosti Press Agency Publishing House, 1987), 21–2.

26   E. Kasimovskii, "Sotsial'naia spravedlwost' i soversherstoovaine raspredeli-tel'nykh otnoshenii v SSSR" (Social Justice and the Improvement of Distribu-tion Relations in the USSR), *Ekonomicheskie nauki*, 1986, no. 12, trans. in *Problems of Economics* 30, no. 5 (September 1987): 65.

27   See Zaslavskaia, "Social Justice," 22.

28   See Nikolai Shmelev, "Avansy i dolgi" (Advances and Debts), *Novyi Mir*, June 1987.

29   As an astute reporter put it: "The key economic reality for most Soviet citizens is not how much they make, but what type of money they make and what kind of access they have to people and organizations that can provide scarce goods and services" (Philip Taubman, "In Soviet-Shopping: Rubles, Coupons and 'Real' Money," *New York Times*, 22 July 1987).

30   See Basile Kenblay and Marie Lavigne, *Les Soviétiques des années 80* (Paris: Armand Colin, 1985), 124–5. See also Patrick Meney, *La Kleptocratie, La délinquence en URSS* (Paris: La Table Ronde, 1982), 196–8, and *passim*.

31   A.D. Smirnov et al., eds., *The Teaching of Political Economy: A Critique of Non-Marxian Theories*, trans. H. Campbell (Moscow: Progress Publishers, 1984), 260.

32   Gorbachev, "Fundamental Issues," 8.

33   Gertrude E. Schroeder, "Soviet Living Standards: Achievements and Pros-pects," in *Soviet Economy in the 1980: Problems and Prospects*, selected papers, Joint Economic Committee, 97th Congress, Second Session, (Washington, DC, GPO, 31 December 1982), part 2, 367ff.

34   Zaslavskaia, "Social Justice," 25.

35   For 1940–1985 detailed data, see *Narodnoe Khoziaistvo SSSR v 1985*, 412–13.

36   Kunelskii, *Zarabotnaia plata*, 62–3; Smirnov et al., eds., *The Teaching of Political Economy*, 265; and also Gladky, *Social Programs*, 8, 21–2.

37   Zaslavskaia, "Social Justice," 25.

38   See Smirnov et al., eds., *Teaching of Political Economy*, 263 and *passim*.

39   Vasilii S. Nemchinov, "Economic Theory and Practice: Socialist Economic Management," *Kommunist*, 1964, no. 5, trans. in *Current Digest of the Soviet Press* 16, no. 18 (1964): 3–4.

5 What Is the Evidence on Income Inequality and Development?

IRMA ADELMAN

INTRODUCTION

The long-term relationship between income distribution and development has been one of the most closely investigated issues in development economics. In his path-breaking article "Economic Growth and Income Inequality," Kuznets[1] formulated the hypothesis that early economic growth increases inequality, while later economic development narrows it. He based this hypothesis on an analytic model, on data for developed countries since the 1930s that showed a narrowing of inequality, and on cross-country comparisons between inequality in developed countries and inequality in two developing countries, comparisons that showed considerably greater inequality in the latter. This paper formulated the U-hypothesis and posed the research agenda for subsequent studies of the relationship between income distribution and development.

Nevertheless, the first twenty years of economic development immediately following the Second World War proceeded on the basis of an optimistic view of the relationship between economic development and inequality. In the design of development policy and of foreign assistance, it was assumed that the growth of the modern sector, if sustained, would eventually spread the benefits of economic growth to all, including the poorest. Economic growth and industrialization were proceeding at an unprecedented rate. The benefits to newly prosperous urban groups, to the workers in the modern sector, and to an expanding middle class of merchants, professionals, and civil servants were easily apparent, while data on unemployment, poverty, and income distribution were not available to cast doubt on the rosy picture of the effects of development. The U-hypothesis was ignored by all but a few radical critics, such as Baran[2] and Myrdal.[3]

The first identification of development failures by mainstream Western economists came in the late 1960s, when, as a result of the work of the International Labour Organization (ILO), it was realized that despite rapid industrialization and increasing gross national product (GNP), unemployment was rising to alarming proportions of the urban labour force. Slow labour absorption in the modern sector, rapid population growth, an education explosion, and the exploitation of agriculture had combined to transform disguised rural unemployment into disguised urban unemployment in the informal sector and increased open unemployment of recent secondary and university graduates. The realization of these trends revived interest in the Kuznets U-hypothesis. Distributional and poverty issues came to the centre of the development agenda.

In the early 1970s, initiatives were taken to conduct research on the distribution of benefits of growth in developing countries. Data on income distribution in developing countries, however, were (and remain) scant. The first major study of the relationship between income distribution and economic development was by Adelman and Morris.[4] Completed in 1971 as a report to the Agency for International Development and based on unpublished income-distribution studies in forty-four developing countries, their study confirmed the increase in inequality inherent in the Kuznets U-hypothesis while indicating that the subsequent decrease in inequality with continued development was dependent on specific policy choices made in the course of the development process. With policies stressing the reduction of economic dualism and increases in primary and secondary education, the later stages of development would reduce inequality; with a continuation of dualistic growth involving neglect of the agricultural sector and a narrow educational pyramid, inequality would not decrease, even at the latest stages of development. The Adelman-Morris study did not use regression analysis to establish the relationships between income distribution and development. The authors argued that the heterogeneity of the data and the state of ignorance about the appropriate functional form made the use of regression analysis a dangerous research tool. Instead they relied on the use of analysis of variance (the analysis of hierarchic interactions), which was relatively robust to data quality and did not require the prior specification of functional forms.

Following their analysis, a large number of investigators used cross-section regressions to study the relationship between inequality and development.[5] These studies generally used a functional form that is quadratic in the log of per capita GNP. They also added some conditioning or policy variables to the regressions, such as education, population, or a socialism dummy. The samples of countries varied, sometimes including and sometimes excluding developed and Communist countries. The regressions all confirmed the existence of the Kuznets curve. Anand and Kanbur,[6] however, argue that the location of the minimum point of the U is sensitive to sample composition and to the specific functional form. Such sensitivity is to be expected if, as claimed by Adelman and Morris,[7] the underlying relationship is either U-shaped or J-shaped, depending on policy choices made at higher levels of development for developing countries. Papanek and Kyn[8] contradict the Anand and Kanbur contention, and find the relationship to be stable and insensitive to the inclusion or exclusion of specific countries. The conditioning variables they include, however, capture the very policy choices that affect whether the relationship is U- or J-shaped. They also find the Kuznets curve to be quite flat.

In this chapter, we investigate the issue of whether there is a trade-off between inequality and economic growth, using changes over time in the shares of income accruing to the poor and rich deciles as dependent variables and the rate of growth of per capita GNP together with conditioning variables as independent variables. Our procedure provides a more direct test than previous studies of the policy issues raised by the Kuznets curve.

THE STATISTICAL ANALYSIS

The estimation of trends in the size distribution of income within countries requires a consistent series of calculations of income distribution within countries over time. Unfortunately, there are very few countries with more than a single estimate of the size distribution of income. Of those for which estimates of the size distribution of income are available for more than one point of time, differences in coverage and differences in the definition of the basic income-recipient units make for lack of comparability of income shares over time. In addition, cross-country comparisons of income-share changes require comparability across countries as well. To mitigate these difficulties, we adopt a three-step estimation procedure.

In the first step, we use cross-country regressions to estimate how the within-country distribution of income varies in response to changes in a set of independent variables. In the second step, we use these regressions together with data on the independent variables to estimate decile income shares for all non-Communist developing countries with populations of more than two million in 1960. In the third step, we regress the changes in the estimated shares between 1960 and 1970 and 1970 and 1980 on the rates of growth of per capita gross domestic product (GDP) and other conditioning variables to see whether the Kuznets U-hypothesis holds over time. Conceptually, this three-step approach is the equivalent of two-stage least squares. The primary statistical differences between the present approach and classical two-stage least squares are that (1) the sample coverages for the two stages of the estimation procedure are different and (2) the regressions in both stages are non-linear.

The advantages of this approach are twofold: it provides for consistent estimates of income distribution over time and across countries, and it enables the use of a large sample. Generally, the data sources for the estimation of income distribution are consumer household budget surveys, blown up to mimic national coverage. In these surveys, the definitions of response units, the income concepts, and the procedures used to blow up the sample surveys to national coverage vary across countries. Because our approach to estimating income distributions involves using regressions, this study's basic response unit, income concept, and blow-up procedures are "standardized averages" of a constant and consistent, but undefined, nature. The procedure used enabled us to extend the sample of countries from about thirty to about seventy.

ESTIMATING INCOME DISTRIBUTIONS WITHIN COUNTRIES

To estimate the decile distributions of income, we must first assume a one- or two-parameter distribution function for incomes. We experimented with two alternatives, the log normal distribution and the Pareto distribution, and found that the latter gave closer overall fits. We decomposed the economy into two sectors, rural and urban, and assumed that each sector has its own Pareto distribution. The Pareto distribution used in this study is a one-parameter function of the form $Y = X^\alpha$ where Y is the relative frequency of people having income greater or equal to X and α is a parameter indicating the degree of inequality of the distribution of income. (Other forms of the Pareto distribution exist.) The dependent variables in our cross-country regressions are the exponents α for income inequality in each country's rural and urban sectors. To estimate α, we fitted the Pareto distribution to the decile distributions for the rural and urban sectors of those countries for which we had data.

The next step involved estimating polynomial regression functions relating α to set of independent variables that were deemed on *a priori* grounds to be potentially relevant to within-sector inequality. Since the ultimate purpose of the regressions is projection, we limited ourselves to candidate variables for which time series are available from international statistical compendia, such as the World Bank's World Tables. The variables were in logs and entered in polynomial form. Whether sectoral inequality increases or decreases with an increase in the level of a particular variable therefore varies with the level of the variable. The regressions are summarized in Table 5.1. The column labelled "Power" in the table indicates the degree of the polynomial.

For the rural sector, the statistically significant variables were the share of agricultural exports in agricultural gross domestic product, the agricultural terms of trade, and the school enrolment ratio. R-squared for the regression

TABLE 5.1
Pareto Coefficient Regression Equations

RURAL PARETO COEFFICIENT

R² = .578; degrees of freedom = 28	Power	Coefficient	Standard Error
Intercept		1.943	
Independent variables (log)			
Share of agricultural exports in agricultural output	1	1.054	.355
	2	1.656	.644
	3	1.151	.480
	4	.365	.155
	5	.425	.018
Agricultural terms of trade	1	−.297	.126
School enrolment ratio	2	−.246	.113
	3	.040	.019

URBAN PARETO COEFFICIENT

R² = .561; degrees of freedom = 30	Power	Coefficient	Standard Error
Intercept		-318.512	
Independent variables (log)			
School enrolment ratio	1	277.886	143.520
	2	−111.254	56.234
	3	19.681	9.754
	4	−1.29	8.632
GDP per capita	1	42.634	17.645
	2	−11.245	4.644
	3	1.304	.539
	4	−.056	.023
Share of non-agricultural exports in non-agricultural output	1	−.226	.123
	2	−.071	.041
	3	−.006	.004
Ratio of productivity in non-agricultural activity to productivity in agriculture	1	−.029	.019

was .59. The estimated relationship indicates that a larger share of agricultural exports increases rural inequality, presumably because agricultural exports are produced mostly in large commercial farms and plantations. It suggests that higher agricultural terms of trade reduce rural inequality, probably because they increase the employment of landless labour and raise the marketed surplus and off-farm employment of small, semi-commercial farmers. The estimated regression suggests that the impact on inequality of increases in the national school enrolment ratio varies with the school enrolment ratio, but is mostly negative; it is usually only at quite high levels of national schooling that mass education spreads to rural areas.

For the urban sector, the statistically significant explanatory variables were per capita GDP, non-primary exports as a ratio to non-primary GDP, and the ratio of the productivity in agriculture to productivity in the primary sector. R-squared for the regression was .56. Both school enrolment and per capita GDP have a U-shaped effect on urban inequality, increasing it at low levels of education and GDP and then reducing it. Increases in the share of non-agricultural exports in non-agricultural output unambiguously reduce urban inequality, presumably because manufacturing exports from less-developed countries (LDCs) tend to be labour intensive. Similarly, when the ratio of productivity in non-agricultural activities to productivity in agriculture increases, urban (but not, as we shall see below, national) inequality is reduced.

These estimated regression functions were used in conjunction with time series for the independent variables in the regressions to derive sectoral-size distributions of income for each non-Communist developing country in each of three years: 1960, 1970, and 1980. For each year, the sectoral distributions were then aggregated numerically in each country to derive within-country decile distributions of income. These deciles formed the basis for our subsequent exploration of the Kuznets hypothesis.

The results of these computations were used to estimate the changes in the average decile distributions within developing countries. Table 5.2 indicates that, for an average non-Communist developing country, there was a steady increase in within-country inequality over two decades. The share of income of the poorest 20 percent fell from 7.3 percent in 1960 to 6.8 percent in 1970 and to 6.7 percent in 1980, while the share of the richest 5 percent rose from 37.5 percent in 1960 to 39.4 percent in 1970 and to 40.1 percent in 1980. The most substantial increases in inequality occurred between 1960 and 1970, as might be expected from the Kuznets hypothesis.

The decline in income share of the poorest over the first quarter century of development is also consistent with the historical experience of currently developed countries. Typically, the historical increase in inequality in currently developed countries during the early stages of their industrialization lasted about half a century or more. Lindert and Williamson[9] display evidence for income inequality rising steadily during the Industrial Revolution in Great Britain and levelling in the last quarter of the nineteenth century. Morris and Adelman[10] find that Belgium, France, Germany, Great Britain, and Switzerland all underwent an industrialization process that followed the Kuznets curve: the numbers in extreme poverty increased early in the nineteenth century in all but Great Britain, where the increase occurred earlier; and in the latter half of the nineteenth century, widely based economic growth and industrialization resulted in reductions in poverty, labour absorption, and

TABLE 5.2
Mean Income Shares for 1960, 1970, and 1980, Non-Communist LDCs

Group	1960	1970	1980
Poorest 20%	7.3	6.8	6.7
Poorest 40%	15.8	14.9	14.7
Poorest 60%	26.4	25.1	24.7
Middle 40%*	25.6	24.4	24.4
Top 20%	58.6	60.3	60.9
Top 10%	46.8	48.7	49.4
Top 5%	37.5	39.4	40.1
Top 1%	22.8	24.4	25.0

Source: Estimated, see text.
* The middle 40 percent group is the fifth through eighth deciles, inclusive.

steadily rising average wages. Denmark, Norway, and Sweden also displayed a Kuznets curve, but the dynamics of the curve were somewhat different: increases in extreme poverty occurred during the first half of the nineteenth century, especially among the landless, as a result of surges in population growth and negligible industrialization; and the subsequent reductions in poverty occurred in the second half of the century as a result of major emigration of surplus agricultural population and the expansion of specialized agriculture and small-scale industrialization.

We now turn to an examination of the systematic connections between growth and inequality. This is a particularly important issue because it is relevant to development policy. In particular, the dynamic version of the Kuznets curve elucidates whether there is a policy trade-off between the speed of economic growth and the extent of inequality.

DOES FASTER GROWTH INCREASE INCOME INEQUALITY?

Most tests of the Kuznets hypothesis have been based on cross-section data. As indicated earlier, all these cross-section studies trace out a Kuznets curve, showing that income inequality first increases with development and then declines. But how is income inequality related to the process of transition from one development level to another? There is no time dimension to cross-sections. And special assumptions, amounting to acts of faith, are required to enable one to take the cross-section curve, which traces out average relationships among economic states, as indicative of processes of change between neighbouring economic states. For this, time series of change in individual countries are required.

There are two recent combined cross-section time-series analyses, both of which support the Kuznets hypothesis. Papanek and Kyn[11] used the income share of various income deciles as dependent variables, and the log of per capita income, its square, time, socio-political dummy variables, education, and the structure of exports as independent variables. They confirmed the Kuznets U-hypothesis in their regressions but found the Kuznets curve to be quite flat. They also investigated the hypothesis that faster growth is associated with a greater deterioration in the share of income accruing to the poorest deciles. They confirmed the hypothesis but again found that the deterioration in income share with more rapid growth is small.

In the present paper, we test the hypothesis that faster growth is negatively correlated with the share of income accruing to the poor more directly than has been done in previous studies. We take as our dependent variable not the income shares of the poor (and rich) deciles, but rather the changes in these shares over time. And we do not use per capita income as an explanatory variable, but rather the rate of growth of per capita income. Thus, our cross-section analysis is based on the dynamic variables that are directly related to the policy issue of whether there exists a trade-off between economic growth and the equality of the distribution of income.

The results of our analysis are summarized in tables 5.3 and 5.4, for 1960 to 1970, and in tables 5.5 and 5.6, for 1970 to 1980. In fitting the regressions, we started with a set of uniform independent variables and then omitted from the regression set for each period those variables that were not statistically significant, on the basis of either a t-test for individual significance or on an F-test for the specific subgroup, for any of the regressions for the particular period. As a result, the list of independent variables is larger for the 1970–80 period than for 1960–70. The values of R-squared for the regressions range from between about .4 and .5 for the 1960–70 period and between about .71 and .73 for 1970–80. These values of R-squared are very high when one considers that both our dependent variables and most of our independent variables are expressed in rates of change rather than in levels. The F-tests for the entire regression and for particular subgroups of variables are all high.

In selecting the list of candidate variables, we did not include variables that are directly related to the derivation of the national income shares from the sectoral distributions. For example, we did not include changes in the share of population in non-agricultural employment; rather, we included changes in the share of population in industry. We were also limited to variables for which time series exist for a large number of developing countries. Some candidate variables were not significant in any of our regressions and therefore do not appear in the summary of results. For example, we tested for the significance of regional dummies on all regions, for all classes of independent variables, and found that only a Latin America dummy for rates of growth of per capita GNP and an Asia dummy for the debt-service ratio

TABLE 5.3

Change in Income Shares of the Poorest Groups, 1960–70, Regression Results

Variable	Poorest 20%* Coefficient	t-value	Poorest 40%* Coefficient	t-value	Poorest 60%* Coefficient	t-value	Middle** 40%* Coefficient	t-value
1. Base income share	-3.94	-4.17	-1.84	-4.24	-1.1	-4.21	-1.09	-3.94
2. GDP per capita growth rate (G)	-0.857	-0.60	-0.849	-0.62	-0.765	-0.60	-0.490	-0.47
3. Square of G	-14.5	-1.08	-13.9	-1.07	-13.7	-1.13	-13.1	-1.33
$F_{(2,57)}$***		5.21		5.31		5.47		6.02
4. Lat. Am. dummy X G	-25.1	-4.16	-23.8	-4.10	-22.3	-4.09	-17.7	-3.98
5. Lat. Am. dummy X sq. of G	1050	4.75	992	4.69	931	4.67	737	4.54
$F_{(2,57)}$***		12.1		11.8		11.8		11.1
6. Change in share labour in ind.	-0.136	-2.02	-0.133	-2.03	-0.124	-2.02	-0.0964	-1.92
7. Constant	0.327	3.92	0.332	4.02	0.328	4.03	0.309	3.87
R-squared	0.495		0.495		0.496		0.484	
R-squared adjusted for degrees of freedom	0.442		0.442		0.443		0.429	
F on full regression (6,57)	9.32		9.32		9.34		8.90	

Note: See Table 5.7 for a description of variables and sources.

* The dependent variable is the ratio of the change in income share to the base income share.

** The middle 40 percent group is the fifth through eighth deciles, inclusive.

*** Joint F-statistic for variables and their squares. Values in parentheses are degrees of freedom in the numerator and denominator.

TABLE 5.4
Change in Income Shares of the Richest Groups, 1960–70, Regression Results

Variable	Top 20%* Coefficient	t-value	Top 10%* Coefficient	t-value	Top 5%* Coefficient	t-value	Top 1%* Coefficient	t-value
1. Base income share	-0.564	-4.44	-0.715	-4.26	-0.903	-4.06	-1.52	-3.55
2. GDP per capita growth rate (G)	0.628	0.72	0.896	0.68	1.17	0.64	1.69	0.51
3. Square of G	4.74	0.57	7.11	0.57	9.68	0.56	16.8	0.54
F(2,57)**		3.05		2.83		2.61		2.00
4. Lat. Am. dummy X G	12.2	3.27	17.8	3.16	23.9	3.05	40.2	2.83
5. Lat. Am. dummy X sq. of G	-497.0	-3.66	-726	-3.53	-967	-3.39	-1610	-3.12
F(2,57)**		6.98		6.48		5.95		5.00
6. Change in share labour in ind.	0.0581	1.38	0.0775	1.22	0.0955	1.08	0.123	0.77
7. Constant	0.325	4.43	0.331	4.17	0.339	3.85	0.366	3.11
R-squared	0.419		0.398		0.375		0.321	
R-squared adjusted for degrees of freedom	0.358		0.335		0.309		0.249	
F on full regression (6,57)	6.85		6.29		5.70		4.48	

Note: See Table 5.7 for a description of variables and sources.

* The dependent variable is the ratio of the change in income share to the base income share.

** Joint F-statistic for variables and their squares. Values in parentheses are degrees of freedom in the numerator and denominator.

TABLE 5.5 Change in Income Shares of the Poorest Groups, 1970–80, Regression Results

Variable	Poorest 20%* Coefficient	t-value	Poorest 40%* Coefficient	t-value	Poorest 60%* Coefficient	t-value	Middle*** 40%* Coefficient	t-value
1. Base income share	-6.15	-5.77	-2.79	-5.70	-1.64	-5.65	-1.64	-5.70
2. GDP per capita growth rate (G)	-2.00	-2.27	-1.87	-2.21	-1.74	-2.18	-1.31	-2.08
3. Square of G	53.8	2.76	50.4	2.68	47.5	2.69	36.9	2.65
$F_{(2,44)}$***		3.89		3.69		3.68		3.55
4. Lat. Am. dummy X G	2.46	0.87	2.27	0.83	2.18	0.85	1.92	0.94
5. Lat. Am. dummy X sq. of G	147	1.67	140	1.65	130	1.63	92	1.45
$F_{(2,44)}$***		9.44		9.05		9.02		8.42
6. Debt service/export ratio (D)	5.32	2.98	5.2	3.02	4.88	3.02	3.93	3.07
7. Square of D	-41.1	-2.81	-40.0	-2.84	-37.5	-2.83	-30.0	-2.86
8. Cube of D	89.2	02.7	86.6	02.7	80.8	02.7	64.3	02.7
$F_{(3,44)}$***		3.70		3.27		3.27		3.38
9. Asia dummy X D	3.37	0.67	2.98	0.61	2.80	0.61	2.17	0.60
10. Asia dummy X sq. of D	-17.3	-0.22	-13.5	-0.18	-12.8	-0.18	-10.3	-0.19
11. Asia dummy X cu. of D	32.4	0.12	21.4	0.08	20.7	0.08	18.7	0.09
$F_{(3,44)}$***		3.98		3.83		3.79		3.79
12. Change in Non-ag/AG inc. ratio	-0.248	-4.14	-.233	-4.03	-0.22	-4.05	-0.18	-4.19
13. Change in literacy rate	0.0173	1.65	0.0161	1.59	0.0152	1.60	0.012	1.61
14. Constant	0.174	1.78	0.178	1.85	0.185	1.98	0.221	2.64
R-squared	0.717		0.711		0.711		0.716	
R-squared adjusted for degrees of freedom	0.634		0.625		0.626		0.632	
F on full regression (13,44)	8.58		8.30		8.32		8.53	

Note: See Table 5.7 for a description of variables and sources.

* The dependent variable is the ratio of the change in income share to the base income share.

** The middle 40 percent group is the fifth through eighth deciles, inclusive.

*** Joint F-statistic for variables and their powers. Values in parentheses are degrees of freedom in the numerator and denominator.

TABLE 5.6 Change in Income Shares of the Richest Groups, 1970–80, Regression Results

Variable	Top 20%* Coefficient	t-value	Top 10%* Coefficient	t-value	Top 5%* Coefficient	t-value	Top 1%* Coefficient	t-value
1. Base Income Share	-0.554	-4.70	-0.686	-4.67	-0.850	-4.63	-1.39	-4.48
2. GDP per capita growth rate (G)	1.44	2.75	2.02	2.66	2.56	2.55	3.8	2.31
3. Square of G	-28.7	-2.68	-40.3	-2.60	-51.5	-2.50	-76.1	-2.27
$F(2,41)$**		4.16		3.91		3.61		2.96
4. Lat. Am. dummy X G	0.122	0.08	0.230	0.11	0.360	0.13	0.857	0.19
5. Lat. Am. dummy X sq. of G	-69.4	1.56	-96.5	-1.50	122	-1.43	-176	-1.27
$F(2,41)$**		3.65		3.26		2.86		2.05
6. Debt service/export ratio (D)	-3.17	-3.50	-4.68	-3.56	-6.31	-3.61	-10.5	-3.67
7. Square of D	25.1	3.41	37.0	3.46	49.6	3.49	82.2	3.53
8. Cube of D	-54.8	-3.3	-81.0	-3.3	-108.0	-3.3	-178.0	-3.4
$F(3,41)$**		4.27		4.41		4.51		4.65
9. Asia dummy X D	9.10	2.13	14.2	2.29	19.7	2.40	34.8	2.61
10. Asia dummy X sq. of D	-184	-2.39	-283	-2.55	-392	-2.66	-683	-2.85
11. Asia dummy X cu. of D	790	2.50	1220	2.66	1680	2.76	2930	2.96
$F(3,41)$**		2.58		2.81		2.94		3.26
12. Change in non-ag/AG inc. ratio	0.0939	3.06	0.133	2.98	0.172	2.90	0.265	2.73
13. Change in sec. educ. rate	0.0311	2.93	0.0462	3.00	0.0620	3.02	0.105	3.13
14. Constant	0.428	5.30	0.473	5.26	0.523	5.14	0.653	4.74
R-squared	0.732		0.732		0.729		0.721	
R-squared adjusted for degrees of freedom	0.648		0.647		0.643		0.633	
F on full regression (13,41)		8.63		8.62		8.49		8.16

Note: See Table 5.7 for a description of variables and sources.

* The dependent variable is the ratio of the change in income share to the base income share.

** Joint F-statistic for variables and their powers. Values in parentheses are degrees of freedom in the numerator and denominator.

TABLE 5.7
Description of Variables

Dependent Variable

1. Change in income share of poorest and richest groups – For group x and period $t1$–$t2$ this is

$$\frac{\text{Income share of group } x \text{ in } t2 - \text{ income share of group } x \text{ in } t1}{\text{income share of group } x \text{ in } t1}$$

Explanatory Variables

2. Base income share – Income share in 1960 for 1960–70 results and 1970 for 1970–80 results
3. GDP per capita growth rt (G) – Growth rate of per capita GDP from $t1$ to $t2$ in Kravis dollars for each period.
4. Debt service/export ratio (D) – Ratio of external public debt service to exports of goods and services, average of 1970 and 1980 values.
5. Change in non-ag/ag inc. ratio – For period $t1$–$t2$ this variable is

$$\frac{\text{NAR2-NAR1}}{\text{NAR1}}$$

where NAR# is the ratio of non-agricultural income per capita to agricultural income per capita in period #.
6. Change in literacy rate – For period $t1$–$t2$ this variable is

$$\frac{\text{LIT2-LIT1}}{\text{LIT1}}$$

where LIT# is the number of literate adults as a percentage of the population 15 years or older in period #.
7. Change in sec. educ. rate – For period $t1$–$t2$ this variable is

$$\frac{\text{SER2-SER1}}{\text{SER1}}$$

where SER# is the number enrolled in secondary school as a percentage of 12-17-years-olds.
8. Change in share of labour in ind. – For the period $t1$–$t2$ this variable is

$$\frac{\text{IND2-IND1}}{\text{IND1}}$$

where IND# is the share of labour in industry as a percentage of the total labour force in period #.

Sources: 1, 2, Estimated, see text; 3, 5–8, World Bank, *World Tables*, 3rd ed., 1983; Kravis conversions from Irving B. Kravis, *World Product and Income: International Comparison of Real Gross Domestic Product* (Baltimore: Johns Hopkins University Press, 1975); and 4, World Bank, *World Development Report*, various years.

survived the significance test. The rate of population growth was never statistically significant, confirming recent studies of other authors on the ambiguity of the effects of rapid population growth on poverty and income distribution.[?] Also, none of the purely political variables survived the significance test. A variable characterizing the extent of political participation[13] and a variable characterizing the extent of a country's foreign dependence[14] were found to be statistically insignificant for both time periods. Since we excluded Communist countries from the analysis, we could not use a socialism dummy, as in other studies.

VARIATIONS WITH THE RATE OF GROWTH OF PER CAPITA GNP

Results

For the 1960–70 period, our regressions indicate that faster GNP growth was associated with a steadily increasing deterioration in the shares of income of the poorest 20 percent, the poorest 40 percent, the poorest 60 percent, and the middle 40 to 80 percent of the population. In our regressions, on the average for all developing countries, both the rate of growth of per capita GNP and the square of the rate of growth are negatively associated with the shares of income accruing to the poorest deciles during this period. The regressions in Table 5.3 thus suggest that, on the average over all countries, the shares of the poor could increase but only with negative growth rates. By contrast, on the average for all developing countries, the shares of the richest 20, 10, 5, and 1 percent of the population all rose steadily with faster growth in per capita GNP for this period (Table 5.4). For the rich, the signs of the coefficients of the rate of growth of per capita GNP and its square were both positive in the regressions for this period. Thus, our results for 1960 to 1970 indicate that during this period, in an average LDC, the benefits of faster growth were distributed in a very skewed manner. The rich not only captured their proportional share of benefits from growth but also benefited from a trickle-up from the poorest 80 percent of the population.

Our regressions suggest that in Latin American countries in the 1960s, the trade-offs were not quite as stark as for the average LDC. The coefficients in our regression for the product of the Latin America dummy variables and the rate of economic growth indicate that in Latin American countries in the 1960s, the changes in the income shares of both poor and rich traced a U-shaped relationship with growth rates, as they do for all LDCs during the 1970s. In Latin America, the income shares of the poor first decline and then rise, with faster growth and the shares of the rich first rise and then decline. Our estimates suggest that the rate of growth of per capita income up to which the shares of the poor decline in Latin America is about the same as the rate up to which the shares of the rich rise – 2.5 percent. However, this rate was exceeded by only three Latin American countries in this period.

For the 1970–80 period, our results are less stark. As in Latin America of the 1960s, we now find a U-shaped relationship for changes in the income share of each decile with the rate of growth of per capita GNP for all developing countries, on the average. For the poor, on the average, the signs of the regression coefficients of the income shares are negative on the growth rate and positive on its square (Table 5.5). This suggests that, up to a point, the shares of the poor decline with increases in the growth rates and after that they rise with higher growth rates. Our regression estimates indicate that, on the average for all developing countries, the positive GNP growth rate at which no change in the income share of the poorest occurred in the 1970s was 4.2 percent per capita. At positive growth rates lower than 4.2 percent per capita, the shares of the poor declined with more rapid growth; at rates above 4.2 percent, they rose. Since the average rate of population growth in LDCs was about 2.2 percent, the constant-income-share growth rate of total GNP was about 6.5 percent. A similar U-shaped relationship held for the income shares of the rich (Table 5.6). The positive constant-income-share growth rate for the rich was about 6 percent. At slower growth rates, on the average for all LDCs, the income shares of the rich rose with faster growth; at more rapid growth rates, the income shares declined.

Taken together, the results of our regressions for both periods indicate that growth, up to a point, tends not to benefit the poor, in relative terms, except with a substantial delay, and then only if growth is quite rapid. These results support the notion of a trade-off between growth and distribution up to quite high growth rates posited in the Adelman-Morris 1973 study.

Discussion

Relating these results to the Kuznets hypothesis requires that there be a significant association between development levels and growth rates, since the Kuznets' hypothesis relates to systematic variations in income shares of the poor with *levels* of development. Our data indicate that there was a statistically significant correlation between development levels and growth rates in both periods. Fourteen out of 16 countries with growth rates of per capita GNP in Kravis dollars less than 1 percent were at the lowest level of development, by the Adelman-Morris index of level of socio-economic development,[15] in the 1960–70 period. The analogous number for 1970–80 was 12 out of 17. At the other extreme, of the non-oil–exporting countries that had growth rates exceeding 3 percent per capita in Kravis dollars, 8 out of 11 in 1960–70 and 9 out of 10 in 1970–80 were at high or intermediate levels of development. Our results, which associate declines in the shares of income of the poor with increasing growth rates up to quite high rates of economic growth followed by a turnaround, may therefore be taken as confirming a dynamic version of the Kuznets hypothesis. The U-shaped relationship posited by Kuznets between the share of income of the poor and development levels extends also to the speed of transition between levels of per capita GNP. Not only development levels, but also the speed of transition among levels of per capita GNP, exhibit a U-shaped relationship with rates of economic growth.

There are many *a priori* reasons why one might expect more rapid growth to be associated with decreases in the share of income accruing to the poor. More rapid growth requires higher rates of savings and investment. Therefore, if more rapid growth is to materialize, income must be shifted from low savers (the poor) to high savers (the rich). This hypothesis was first advanced by Kalecki[16] and later taken up by Kaldor[17] and the Latin American structuralist school. But this hypothesis offers a closed-economy argument that does not incorporate the possibility of foreign aid and foreign borrowing as sources of investment funds and assumes that the government is neutral in the mobilization of savings. It also imparts the major role in the mobilization of savings to transfers among classes of savers rather than, as in the Lewis model, to transfers of savings between sectors, especially between agriculture and industry. The latter is probably a more significant mechanism for mobilizing savings than the former.[18]

Intersectoral transfers of resources affect the relationship between the distribution of income and the rate of economic growth indirectly, through the structure of growth, rather than directly, through savings requirements. Many Kuznets U-generating models of the relationships between income distribution and development rely on intersectoral transfers of population and income to provide the income-inequality-generating mechanisms. The course of income inequality with development is then explained by the technological and income-distribution characteristics within sectors and by how the development strategy and the strategy for mobilizing savings affect the income and productivity gaps between sectors and their relative rates of growth. This was the mechanism on which Kuznets himself relied to generate the U-hypothesis. More mathematical exposition was given by Fields.[19]

Lewis's 1957 model of development through industrialization is also in this spirit. It also implies the generation of a U-shaped income distribution through intersectoral transfers. The acceleration of growth in the early stages of industrialization implies increasing the income (and productivity) gap between industry and agriculture by transferring savings (and hence investment) and labour from the low-productivity, even distribution, traditional sector to the high-productivity, unequal distribution modern sector. Up to a point, this process will generate an increase in inequality. The per capita income and productivity gaps between sectors will start closing in the Lewis model only when a rising wage rate is required to attract increased labour into the modern sector. Numerical simulations and individual-country studies suggest that, in a given country, the association of decreased inequality with further growth will start after more than half the labour force is employed in the modern sector.[20]

A more dynamic explanation of the relationship between inequality and the speed of growth points to the contrast in initial conditions faced by the poor and the rich when responding to the new economic opportunities inherent in economic growth.[21] Fundamentally, all processes of economic change give rise to both increased absorption of some individuals and displacement and marginalization of others. Those who own (or have access) to factors used disproportionately in the expanding sectors or in the new technologies, or to complementary factors, are enriched by the change. Those who own factors used in producing substitute commodities or less productive technologies lose relatively from the change. How more rapid growth affects different deciles depends on the net balance between the two forces for each decile. Those with assets – including not only financial capital and land but also human capital, information, and networks facilitating migration and access to high-productivity jobs – are better positioned to take immediate advantage of the opening up of any set of new economic opportunities. The poor are slower to respond to increased opportunities because they have less assets, in the more general sense. Furthermore, since the poor use traditional technologies and combine them with small amounts of low-productivity complementary factors, they are more likely to be marginalized by new technological opportunities, to which they require more time to adapt. Slower growth also allows more opportunity for social adaptation by the poor (through demographic change, migration, and schooling) and hence is likely to affect them less unfavourably. The contrast between the extent to which economic growth marginalized the poor in the nineteenth century in France, a slow-growing country, and the extent to which it marginalized the poor in Germany and Great Britain, fast-growing countries, illustrates this point. During the early stages of the Industrial Revolution, poverty increased faster with growth in Great Britain and Germany than in France.

These considerations suggest not only reasons for the dynamic version of the Kuznets curve but also for the contrast between our results for the 1960s and 1970s. The average picture sketched by the regression results for the 1960s associated continued declines in the income shares of the poor with more rapid growth at even the highest growth rates. It is only during the 1970s that we found that at growth rates exceeding 6.5 percent in total GDP, higher growth rates led to improvements in the shares of income of the poorest. Both the Lewis model[22] and the "initial conditions of poverty" explanation of the previous paragraph are consistent with these findings. The initial-conditions explanation suggests why, in the face of structural change, delays as long as a decade may occur before a high rate of economic growth would benefit the poor. Historically, during the Industrial Revolution, periods as long as two generations passed before economic growth benefited the poor.[23]

The Lewis[24] turning-point is consistent both with the delayed reaction to high growth rates and with the specific 6.5 percent growth rate of aggregate GDP for a turnaround to be attained. At a minimum, the turnaround requires that the growth rate of employment in the modern sector exceed the growth rate of supply of labour to the modern sector. The growth rate of supply is the sum of the rate of population growth in urban areas from urban fertility and from rural–urban migration. In the 1970s, this sum, which equals the rate of urbanization, averaged 5 percent per year. This is the rate of growth of industrial employment that would just match the rate of increase in labour supply. However, the rate of growth of industrial employment must also be sufficient to absorb existing urban unemployment, before industrialization can result in increases in wages. In the early 1970s, the World Employment Missions of the ILO put the urban unemployment rate at about 20 percent in many middle-income developing countries. A rate of growth of 1.5 percent, maintained over a decade, would therefore be required to mop up the initial urban unemployment of 20 percent of the urban labour force. The sum of the two rates – 6.5 percent – just equals our estimate of the minimum rate of growth of GDP before growth increases the income shares of the poorest. These rates were attained by only eleven countries in our sample. Fei and Ranis[25] estimated that Japan, Korea, and Taiwan had reached the Lewis turning-point by the 1970s.

Papanek and Kyn's[26] study indicated that the Kuznets curve was quite flat and so was the relationship of income shares to growth rates. Our results do not support this finding for this period. Figure 5.1 portrays the relationship between the income share of the poorest 40 percent and the growth rate of per capita GNP in Kravis dollars estimated by our regression. We find that, for the 1970–80 period, the share decreased from 0.19 percent at a growth rate of −2 percent to about 0.12 at 2 percent, and that a one percentage point change in growth rate around the minimum income share produces an 9.5 percent change in the income share of the poorest 40 percent.

VARIATION WITH THE DEBT-SERVICE RATIO

Results

The debt-service ratio became a serious constraint on economic growth only during the 1970s. After the first oil shock in 1973, developing countries shifted from trade-and-aid-led growth to debt-led growth. The average debt-service ratio to exports rose from 8.9 percent in 1970 to 13.7 percent in 1980. After the second oil shock in 1980, the debt-service problem became a debt crisis, affecting growth and income distribution in all developing countries. Our time period, however, covers only the debt-accumulation phase.

A large literature on the incidence of adjustment to the debt crisis points to the fact that the poor have borne the brunt of the cost of adjustment.[27] We find, in our regressions of Table 5.5, that the impact of debt accumulation on the share of national income accruing to the poor was non-linear. For the poorest groups, there is a positive coefficient on the debt share to exports, a negative coefficient on the square of the debt share, and a small positive co-

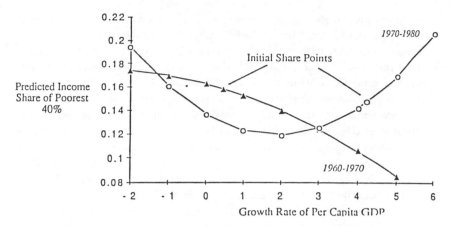

Source: Regressions, tables 5.3–5.6.

Figure 5.1
Income Shares versus Growth Rate, 1960–70 and 1970–80

efficient on the cube of the debt. For the rich (Table 5.6), the pattern of signs is the mirror image of that for the poor. The Asia dummy intensifies the quantitative impact of the basic pattern for both poor and rich deciles.

Discussion

The effects of debt accumulation on the poor and rich obviously depend on the projects and policies the new debt finances. If there is a correlation between the uses to which indebtedness is put and the relative size of the debt, changes in the share of debt to exports would have non-linear effects on the income shares of both poor and rich.

Higher debt ratios may benefit the poor when the debt is used to finance social programs and to subsidize consumption of food and public services by the poor, especially the urban poor. A large number of countries used foreign debt to maintain a dual price policy in agriculture, paying higher prices to rural producers than they charged to consumers. The dual price policy benefits the rural poor, especially agricultural workers and semi-commercial farmers, raising their marginal product. Also, after the food crisis of 1973, many developing countries borrowed for agricultural development projects. These investments decrease the productivity gap between sectors, thereby reducing overall inequality. Depending on the design of the agricultural projects (e.g., what types of irrigation were expanded and how the productivity-increasing measures were distributed between large commercial farms and small owner-operated farms), the investments could either increase or decrease income inequality within the agricultural sector.[28]

Alternatively, increased debt may reduce the income share of the poor. Countries that incurred foreign debt frequently used the proceeds to finance import-substitute industrialization, large-scale capital-intensive projects, industrial infrastructure, and armaments purchases. All of these investment patterns tend to have unequalizing effects on the distribution of income. Import substitution turns the terms of trade against agriculture, where the poor are concentrated. Capital-intensive industrialization is skill rather than labour intensive, and therefore does little to raise the employment of the poor while generating excess demand for the services of high-level manpower. It therefore makes the distribution of wages less equal, while reducing the share of wages in GNP. Armaments purchases have small domestic multipliers and indirect benefits that are concentrated among the rich.

Thus, debt accumulation may have quite disparate effects on income shares, depending on the different investment programs and policies that are financed by the debt. If social and agricultural programs predominate at both small and large levels of indebtedness while investments in import substitution, armaments, and heavy industry predominate at middling levels, one would expect to find the particular non-linear association between the income shares of the poor and debt accumulation that is present in our regression results.

VARIATIONS WITH OTHER ECONOMIC VARIABLES

Technological Dualism among Sectors

The rise and fall in sectoral imbalances in total-factor-productivity change may be expected to be a prime mover of income inequality. According to Kuznets[29] and the Chenery-Syrquin[30] studies, early development is characterized by an increase in the imbalance in productivity among sectors, followed by a levelling in productivity differentials, and finally by a movement towards more-balanced productivity growth, quite late in the development process. Even without population movement from the low-productivity to the high-productivity sector, the U-shaped movement in the productivity gap would by itself suffice to generate a Kuznets curve.

We experimented with several measures of changes in technological dualism: (1) changes in per capita income gaps between agriculture and non-agriculture (these also represent measures of productivity differentials between sectors); (2) total income gaps between the agricultural and non-agricultural sectors; and (3) relative changes in the composition of production. Of the three, the first measure was the most significant statistically. It also comes closest to the factor-productivity-differentials explanation of the Kuznets curve.

Our results indicate that the share of income of the poor decreases with greater relative neglect of agricultural productivity. Since the poor are concentrated in the agricultural sector, emphasis on industrial development at the expense of agricultural development decreases the share of the poorest 80 percent of the population. But the magnitude of the decrease becomes steadily smaller the higher the income of the poorest deciles, starting at an elasticity of –0.25 for the income share of the poorest 20 percent and decreasing to an elasticity of –0.18 for the share of the fourth to eighth deciles. By the same token, since the top 20 percent of the population derive their incomes from the non-agricultural sector, either as workers in modern industry or as owners of industrial enterprises, a decrease in the relative share of agriculture in total output benefits the upper-income groups. For the rich, a sectoral bias in development against agriculture is increasingly more beneficial the higher their income level, rising from an elasticity of 0.09 for the top two deciles to an elasticity of 0.27 for the richest 1 percent of the population.

The 1970s witnessed a renewed emphasis on agricultural development in many developing countries. Fuelled by the food crisis of 1973 and by the need to substitute for increasing imports of basic grains to feed the urban population, many semi-industrial LDCs and several low-income LDCs turned to agricultural development. Agricultural development has beneficial effects on the income share of the poorest[31] and on their food security[32] provided it is coupled with agricultural terms-of-trade policies that do not take away all the benefits of agricultural output increases from the farmers. Gaiha[33] finds a negative correlation between agricultural productivity and rural poverty in a cross-country analysis. Simulations by Adelman[34] of the income-distribution consequences of adopting an agricultural development strategy that combines increases in agricultural productivity on small- and medium-sized firms with increases in exports and in agricultural terms of trade in all developing countries[35] indicated that this strategy is likely to result in a substantial improvement in the distribution of income within LDCs, among all groups of LDCs except East Asia, among all non-Communist LDCs, and in the world as a whole. These agricultural development strategies also reduced worldwide absolute poverty by 30 percent relative to the base case.

Labour Absorption into the Modern Sector

Factor movements among markets with different pay structures are another potential major source of inequality. Even without changes in the relative magnitude of the productivity and income gaps among sectors in the course of development, transfer of labour from the low-paying sector with a low-income variance to the high-paying sector with a high-income variance would suffice to generate the Kuznets U.[36]

We could not use changes in the share of labour outside agriculture in our regressions, despite high correlations of income shares with this variable, because it comes too close to one of the variables we had used to derive national income shares from sectoral shares. Instead, we used the more restricted concept of changes in the share of the labour force employed in industry. This measure is indicative of labour absorption into the modern sector. We found that, during the 1960–70 period, increases in the share of labour force in industry reduced the share of the poor and raised the share of the rich. This finding is consistent with the early stages of the Lewis[37] model, when labour is transferred from the low-inequality to the high-inequality sector and the income gap between the sectors increases. In the 1970–80 period this variable was not statistically significant and therefore does not appear in the regressions despite its theoretical appeal.

The Distribution of Wealth

One would expect both land distribution and the distribution of physical capital to affect the distribution of income. Indeed, many revolutions (1848 in France and 1917 in Russia, in particular) have been based on this theory. Unfortunately, there are no time series we could construct to test this hypothesis. Also, as Lindert and Williamson point out,[38] major wealth redistributions such as land reform, slave emancipation, war, and losses from economic crises are too sporadic to offer a systematic explanation of the course of the Kuznets curve. They are likely to lead to important shifts in the Kuznets curve, however. Elsewhere, I have argued that land reform needs to be an important precursor to productivity improvement in agriculture, if technology change, such as the Green Revolution, is not to deteriorate the distribution of income rather than provide for egalitarian growth.[39]

What about the distribution of human capital? One policy prescription on which both conservative and progressive economists agree is that improving the educational attainments of the masses will make the distribution of income more equal. The "human capital" school[40] sees education as a means of improving the earnings capacity of individuals. The "redistribution with growth"[41] and the "redistribution before growth"[42] schools see the broadening of the educational pyramid as a redistribution of wealth. Chenery et al. argue for increasing the education of the poor as part of a strategy to redirect a larger share of investment towards increasing the assets of the poor. Adelman argues for increasing the education of the poor as part of a strategy to equalize the distribution of wealth of the major productive asset before its productivity is improved, as a means of setting the stage for more egalitarian subsequent growth. Previous regression studies all support the equalizing role of increases in primary education.[43]

We used two different educational variables to represent the educational continuum relevant for the particular income group – literacy for the poor and secondary schooling for the rich. We find (tables 5.5 and 5.6) that the elasticity of the income shares of the poor with respect to literacy is of the order of 0.02 and that the elasticity of the income shares of the rich with respect to the secondary schooling rate increases from 0.03 for the richest 20 percent to 0.10 for the top 1 percent. Our results thus indicate that the type of education that is improved has a bearing on income distribution. Increases in secondary (and presumably university) education will favour the rich and increase inequality, while increases in literacy (and presumably primary) education will decrease inequality.

SUMMARY AND CONCLUSION

Even in the absence of the debt crisis, the prospects for the poor in developing countries can hardly be considered satisfactory. For the 1960–70 period, our results indicate that the trade-off between the speed of economic growth and the share of income of the poor was unmitigated and that the deterioration in the share of income of the poor with growth was quite substantial. For the 1970–80 period, our results suggest the existence of an even stronger trade-off between the speed of growth and the equality of the distribution of income. At rates of growth less than 1 percent per capita, a levelling between 1 and 2 percent is followed by possibilities for a turnaround. However, our results also suggest that, in the typical LDC of the 1970s, the decline in the share of the poor with growth at low growth rates was sufficiently large to ensure that the poor would not recover their 1970 income share unless the LDC could attain quite high rates of growth for the period and reach at least moderate levels of development. These results hardly give much hope for attaining the goal of poverty eradication in LDCs through economic growth in the foreseeable future.

Our results do suggest policies that might mitigate the growth-equality trade-off somewhat. Foremost among those are rural development policies designed to close the agricultural/non-agricultural productivity and income gaps and massive primary education. I have advocated both approaches to the design of development strategies in earlier writings and found theoretical and empirical arguments to bolster these recommendations.[44]

In short, our findings support the view that the primary hope of the poor in the current low-growth world lies not in accelerating their country's growth rate, but rather in changing the structure of growth and the assets of the poor.

NOTES

1 S. Kuznets, "Economic Growth and Income Inequality," *American Economic Review* 45 (1955): 1–28.

2 P. Baran, *The Political Economy of Growth* (New York: Monthly Review Press, 1957).

3 G. Myrdal, *The Asian Drama* (New York: Pantheon Press, 1968).

4   I. Adelman and C. Taft Morris, *Economic Growth and Social Equity in Developing Countries* (Stanford, CA: Stanford University Press, 1973).

5   F. Paukert, "Income Distribution at Different Levels of Development: A Study of Evidence," *International Labor Review* 108 (1973): 97–125; H.S. Chenery et al., *Redistribution with Growth* (Oxford: Oxford University Press, 1974); M.S. Ahluwalia, "Inequality, Poverty and Development," *Journal of Development Economics* 6 (1976): 307–42; M.S. Ahluwalia, "Income Distribution and Development: Some Stylized Facts," *American Economic Review* 66 (1976): 128–35; J. Cronwell, "The Size Distribution of Income: An International Comparison," *Review of Income and Wealth* 23 (1977): 291–308; M.S. Ahluwalia, N.G. Carter, and H.B. Chenery, "Growth and Poverty in Developing Countries," *Journal of Development Economics* 6 (1979): 299–341; E. Bacha, "The Kuznets Curve and Beyond: Growth and Change in Inequalities," in E. Malinvaud ed., *Economic Growth and Resources* (New York: St Martin's Press, 1979), 52–73; and Papanek and Kyn 1986 (see note 8); Papanek and Kyn 1987 (see note 11).

6   S. Anand and S.M.R. Kanbur, "Inequality and Development: A Critique," paper presented to the 25th Anniversary Symposium, Yale Growth Center, 11–13 April 1986.

7   Adelman and Morris, *Economic Growth and Social Equity*.

8   G.S. Papanek and O. Kyn, "The Effect of Income Distribution on Development: The Growth Rate, and Economic Strategy," *Journal of Development Economics* 23 (1986): 55–66.

9   P.H. Lindert and J.G. Williamson, "Growth, Equality and History," *Explorations in Economic History* 22 (1985): 341–77.

10 C. Taft Morris and I. Adelman, *Comparative Patterns of Economic Development, 1850–1914* (Baltimore: Johns Hopkins University Press, 1988).

11 G.S. Papanek and O. Kyn, "Flattening the Kuznets Curve: The Consequences for Income Distribution of Development Strategy, Government Intervention, Income and the Rate of Growth," *Pakistan Development Review* 26 (1987): 1–54.

12 N. Birdsall and C.C. Griffin, "Fertility and Poverty in Developing Countries," *Journal of Policy Modelling* 10 (1988): 30–55; and C.Y.C. Chu, "The Dynamics of Population Growth," *American Economic Review* 77 (1987): 1054–6.

13 Adelman and Morris, *Economic Growth and Social Equity*.

14 I. Adelman, J.B. Lohmoller, and C. Taft Morris, "A Latent Variable Regression Model of Nineteenth Century Economic Development," Giannini Foundation Working Paper 439, University of California, Berkeley, 1988.

15 I. Adelman and C. Taft Morris, *Society, Politics, and Economic Development – A Quantitative Approach* (Stanford, CA: Stanford University Press, 1967).

16 M. Kalecki, *Studies in Economic Dynamics* (London: Allen and Unwin, 1943).

17 N. Kaldor, "Alternative Theories of Distribution," *Review of Economic Studies* 23 (1955): 83–100.

18 W.R. Cline, *Potential Effects of Income Redistribution on Economic Growth: Latin American Cases* (New York: Praeger, 1972); and I. Adelman and S. Robinson, "Macroeconomic Adjustment and Income Distribution in Two Economies: Alternative Models Applied to Two Economies," *Journal of Development Economics* 29 (1988): 23–44.

19 G.S. Fields, *Poverty, Inequality and Development* (New York: Cambridge University Press, 1980).

20 S. Robinson, "A Note on the U-hypothesis Relating Income Inequality and Economic Development," *American Economic Review* 66 (1976): 437–40; J.C. Fei and G. Ranis, *Development of the Surplus Labor Economy* (Homewood, IL: Irwin, 1964); and G. Ranis, "Equity and Growth in Taiwan: How 'Special' is the 'Special Case'?" *World Development* 6 (1978): 397–409.

21 Adelman and Morris, *Economic Growth and Social Equity*; C. Taft Morris and I. Adelman, "Institutional Influences on Poverty," *Journal of Economic History* 43 (1983): 43–55.

22 W.A. Lewis, "Reflections on Unlimited Labor," in L.E. Marco, ed., *International Economics and Economic Development* (New York: Academic Press, 1972).

23 Morris and Adelman, "Institutional Influences"; Lindert and Williamson, "Growth, Equality and History."

24 W.A. Lewis, "Economic Development with Unlimited Supplies of Labor," *Manchester School* 22 (1954): 139–91.

25 Fei and Ranis, *Development of the Surplus Labor Economy*.

26 Papanek and Kyn, "Flattening the Kuznets Curve."

27 P. Pinstrup-Anderson, "Macroeconomic Adjustment Policies and Human Nutrition: Available Evidence and Research Needs" (Washington, DC: International Food Research Institute, 1986); and L. Taylor, *Varieties of Stabilization Experience. WIDER Studies in Development* (Oxford: Clarendon, 1988).

28 I. Adelman, "Beyond Export Led Growth," *World Development* 12 (1984): 937–50; E. Yeldan, "Turkish Economy in Transition: A General Equilibrium Analysis of Export-Led versus Domestic Demand Led Strategies of Development," unpublished doctoral dissertation, University of Minnesota, Minnesota, 1988.

29 S. Kuznets, *Modern Economic Growth* (New Haven: Yale University Press, 1966).

30 H.B. Chenery and Syrquin, M. *Patterns of Development, 1950–1970* (London: Oxford University Press, 1975).

31 I. Adelman and S. Robinson, *Income Distribution Policy in Developing Countries: A Case Study of Korea* (Stanford, CA: Stanford University Press, 1978); I. Adelman, "Beyond Export Led Growth"; and Yeldan, "Turkish Economy in Transition."

32 I. Adelman and P. Berck, "Food Security in a Stochastic World," *Journal of Development Economics* 34 (1991): 25–55.

33 R. Gaiha, "Rural Poverty: Dimensions and Trends," Food and Agriculture Organization (FAO), Mimeo, 1987.

34 I. Adelman, "The World Distribution of Income," *Weltwirtschaftliches Archiv* 121 (1985): 110–20.

35 Ibid.

36 Robinson, "A Note on the U-hypothesis."

37 Lewis, "Reflections on Unlimited Labor."

38 Lindert and Williamson, "Growth, Equality and History."

39 I. Adelman, *Redistribution before Growth – A Strategy for Developing Countries* (The Hague: Martinus Nijhof, 1978).

40 T.W. Schultz, *Investment in Human Capital: The Role of Education and Research* (New York: Free Press, 1971); and G.S. Becker, *Human Capital and the Personal Distribution of Income: An Analytic Approach* (Ann Arbor, MI: Institute of Public Administration, 1967).

41 H.S. Chenery, M.S. Ahluwalia and C.G. Bell et al., *Redistribution with Growth* (Oxford: Oxford University Press, 1974).

42 Adelman, "Redistribution before Growth – A Strategy."

43 Adelman and Morris, *Economic Growth and Social Equity*; Ahluwalia, "Inequality, Poverty and Development"; Ahluwalia, "Income Distribution and Development"; and Papanek and Kyn, "Flattening the Kuznets Curve."

44 Adelman, "Beyond Export Led Growth"; and Adelman, "Redistribution before Growth – A Strategy."

PART THREE

Policy

6 Fiscal Equity and Economic Development

RICHARD MUSGRAVE

I have been given the assignment of examining the role of fiscal equity in the context of economic development. This is an appropriate theme for me. As I have seen the fiscal problem over the years, the equity dimension plays a central role; and as I have seen that of development, fiscal policies are again of key importance. But the equity-development axis is troublesome, as it has a circular logic: equity in fiscal affairs is more important the lower the level of economic development, but so is the need to avoid the deterring effects of equity-based policies on economic growth. The cost of equity is thus highest when and where it is most needed. The task is to design policies that will minimize conflict between the two targets and, where conflict remains, balance benefits and costs at the margin. Our theme then is a mutual cost-benefit analysis of fiscal equity and economic growth.

THE MEANING OF FISCAL EQUITY

The concept of fiscal equity and its role in economic development may be taken to mean different things. From Adam Smith on, if not earlier, a distinction has been drawn between two quite different criteria for judging the equity of the fiscal system. The one, directed at the combined tax-expenditure package, calls for a distribution of the tax burden in accordance with benefits received. The other, addressing taxation only, calls for a distribution of the burden in line with ability to pay.

Under the benefit rule, high-income people will be taxed more than low-income people, as they assign a higher monetary value to the same public services. How much higher depends on the income elasticity of demand for public services. With an elasticity of one, a proportional rate of tax will be called for, while regressive or progressive rates will be in order if income elasticity is below or above unity. Much will depend on the composition of public services and the weight of what may be considered necessities and luxury components. As development proceeds and public services expand, the benefit-based tax structure may be expected to become more progressive.

The benefit approach thus fits the philosophy of the market. Taxes are prices and people should pay for what they get. Viewed in the broader context of distributive justice, benefit taxes also fit the Lockean premise that persons are entitled to keep and to use what they earn in the marketplace.[1] Tax payments are budgetary purchases of public goods, substituting (necessary due to the nature of public goods) for market purchases of private goods. That public goods cannot be provided for through the market is too bad, but they should at least be paid for as if they were so provided.[2] Since, in the Lockean entitlement scheme, the market-determined distribution of income is just, so is benefit taxation. Moreover, if distribution by the market is efficient as well as just, so may benefit taxation claim both virtues. The Lockean approach, restated more recently by Robert Nozick, thus naturally falls in line with the benefit rule.[3] Government should charge for public services rendered in line with the payee's benefits and thus leave the fiscal process distributionally neutral. Thereby, the benefit approach excludes the very central concern of this paper, which is the role of fiscal equity in relation to distribution.

Before leaving the Lockean frame of distributive justice, we should note that Locke's justice by entitlement to earnings has an important exception: that land has been given to mankind "to be used in common." People have a right to the produce they extract from land "at least where there is enough and as good left in common for others" so that, as long as land is ample, the entire return is theirs. But as land becomes scarce, the "as good" proviso comes into play, which suggests that the rent of land should be viewed as common property. While Locke tries to escape this conclusion, he does so unconvincingly and thus lays the basis for a view held by subsequent authors – including above all Henry George, with his single-tax movement – that the rent of land is an especially appropriate source of taxation.

This view is valid as well with regard to economic efficiency. Dating back to David Ricardo, taxation of land has been seen as especially appropriate because it is inelastic in supply and thus does not distort resource use. This peculiar role of land is of particular interest in the context of economic development. Due to population pressure, land in less-developed countries (LDCs) typically weighs more heavily relative to capital as a source of income than it does in industrialized countries, and, most important perhaps, it cannot be shipped to tax havens in the Caribbean. Land is thus an especially appropriate source of potential revenue in LDCs, even though, depending upon the distribution of landownership, it is frequently undertaxed. More about this at a later point.

We now turn to a second tradition in fiscal theory, namely, that the tax burden should be distributed in line with ability to pay, an approach more appropriate to the concern of this paper. Taxation in line with ability to pay calls for a social evaluation of income distribution and with it a principle of entitlement other than that of claim to market earnings. As developed in the fiscal literature, two applications of this alternative principle have been identified. The first application ("horizontal equity") deals with the requirement that people with equal "ability to pay" (as measured by some index such as income) should be treated equally. The second ("vertical equity") deals with the more difficult problem of determining the proper distribution of the tax burden among people with different abilities to pay. The case for horizontal equity has been at the centre of the tax structure debate, involving choice of the proper index (income, consumption, property) and the best way to define each. The issue of vertical equity, on the other hand, remains highly controversial but nevertheless is of primary concern here.

Various interpretations of vertical equity were offered and expressed in the form of sacrifice rules. Thus, it has been argued that all taxpayers should incur an equal absolute, equal proportional, or equal marginal sacrifice.[4] Depending on the postulated slope of the income-utility function, various patterns of burden distribution follow under the various rules. Given that marginal income utility declines with rising income, the equal marginal rule becomes equivalent to calling for minimum total sacrifice and is thus in line with the welfare economists' goal of maximizing welfare. In that sense, it becomes an efficiency as well as equity rule.

So far so good, but implementation requires the further and crucial step of choosing a scale by which the marginal utility of successive units of income can be valued or measured. At earlier stages of discussion, up to the 1930s, it was assumed that marginal satisfaction could be observed and measured cardinally, that it would be declining as income rises, and that the same response would hold across individuals. Beginning with L. Robbins's challenge, these assumptions were discarded as unsupportable by empirical verification.[5] Initially this left the ability-to-pay approach without foundation, but before long the premise of measurability was replaced by that of a social welfare function. This function, which assigns social weights to the value of successive income units, is not seen as psychological data but as a normative judgment of distributive justice.

Once an ability-to-pay approach in its normative perspective is taken, it becomes inconsistent to limit the argument to tax taking so as to distribute the cost of public services fairly. The same reasoning extends to securing a fair distribution of disposable income remaining for private use. The fiscal function thereby reaches beyond fair payment for public services to cover a tax-transfer system by which a fair state of distribution can be established.

Our second concept of fiscal equity thus squarely derives from a norm of distributive justice, leaving the crucial question of how it should be defined.

On one end of the scale, it is taken to call for an egalitarian solution, as suggested by Rousseau[6] and Marx, whose dream of utopian communism called for a pattern of "from each according to his ability and to each according to his need."[7] Assuming that the social welfare function assigns declining weights to the utility derived from successive units of income the egalitarian solution also meets the dictum, first advanced by Bentham, that rational thought calls for total utility to be maximized.[8] But, as Bentham hastened to add, adverse effects of redistribution upon the available level of income must be allowed for, and this imposes a brake upon equalization. Allowing for such effects, John Rawls more recently proposed fairness to be defined as calling for a pattern of distribution that would maximize the welfare of the lowest position, implicitly assigning a zero social weight to the marginal utility of income above that level.[9] A less extreme position postulates a utility function that lets the social value of the marginal income unit decline more gradually, so as to preserve a higher degree of inequality than called for by the Rawlsian model.[10]

Notwithstanding these different formulations, Lockean entitlement to earnings and equity-based fairness need not be given exclusive reign. Intermediate positions may be taken. Thus, fair distribution may be interpreted as calling for raising the lower end of the scale so as to assure an "acceptable" minimum level, sufficient to meet what are considered basic requirements, while accepting an entitlement premise to income above that level. A further adjustment might be made also at the upper end of the scale, so as to avoid what is considered undue concentration of wealth, thereby allowing for the externalities as well as the own-utilities generated by various patterns of distribution.

Practically inclined readers, overwhelmed by the realities of fiscal politics, may find this normative discussion rather unrealistic. Far from following the strictures of just solutions, is not the outcome of fiscal affairs determined by the politics of class and group interests that dominate the "real world"? And, most appropriate in our context, is this aspect not of special importance in developing countries that do not enjoy the benefit of an established and well-functioning democratic process by which matters of justice may be resolved?[11] Quite possibly so. A "positive" approach to the problem of fiscal policy (as to that of the market) is important, but so are normative considerations, especially when it comes to fiscal equity. What is considered equitable or fair does (not only should) matter even in the positive course of events, and in the end may be more important than the political expediencies of the day.

EQUITY IN TAXATION: GAINS AND COSTS

We now place these thoughts into the context of economic development. If we take per capita income as its index and fiscal equity as calling for improving the lower end of the scale, what is the relationship between the two? In particular, how does the pay-off on equity vary with the level of income, and how is that level affected by equity-oriented policies?

Beginning with potential gains from redistribution, suppose first that the level of per capita income is unaffected. We also postulate a social welfare function under which the social weight that society places on the marginal utility of income falls at a decreasing rate as income rises. We now consider two countries that have the same degree of inequality as measured by, say, the Gini coefficient but differ in per capita income. Raising the tax burden on the top decile by a given amount will permit reducing it similarly at the bottom.[12] This swap then yields a larger gain in the lower-income country where the transfer will move along a steeper part of the social utility schedule.

Next we consider two countries with equal per capita incomes but differing degrees of inequality. The tax change will now yield the higher gain in the country where inequality is larger. Here the income spanned by the transfer will be wider and so will be the differential in marginal utilities. Since income inequality tends to be larger in low-income countries, this once more adds to the importance of equity-oriented policy in such settings. Following Kuznet's U-hypothesis, this conclusion is qualified somewhat, since inequality tends to increase in the early stages of development, as manufacturing centres emerge while poverty and labour surplus in the agricultural sector remain unaffected.[13] Nevertheless, there remains a presumption that the potential welfare gains from reducing inequality will be larger for low- than for high-income countries.

We now turn to the other side of the coin, the effects of equity-oriented policies on the level of income available for distribution. Such effects take various forms, the most important of which is their impact on the level of saving and capital formation. As was stated by Sir Arthur Lewis at the beginning of the debate, "the central problem in the theory of economic development is to understand the process by which a country which presently saves or invests 4 or 5 percent of its national income or less, converts itself into an economy where voluntary saving is running at about 12 to 15 percent."[14] Saving matters because it is necessary to capital formation, and because capital formation, including human investment, is essential to raising productivity and hence per capita income. Whereas in developed countries technological progress has become the major source of productivity gains, the key factors in LDCs remain capital formation and raising the capital-to-labour ratio. The fiscal system's immediate impact on welfare gains and losses out of an existing level of income, is important, but productivity growth is the key factor in the escape from poverty over the longer run.

Leaving foreign sources of capital for later consideration, we turn to a central problem for development policy: how to raise the domestic rate of saving or, when it comes to taxation, how not to reduce it. As reported by the World Bank for 1986, the gross domestic savings rate for low-income countries (excluding India and China) was 7 percent, as compared to 15 percent for lower-middle-income countries, 26 percent for upper-middle countries, and 21 percent for industrial market economies.[15] The lower the income, the lower is the rate of saving.

The resulting conflict with tax equity is evident. Considerations of equity, as we have seen, suggest a progressive pattern of taxation, especially where income is low and distributed unequally. But that pattern also tends to depress private sector saving most severely. Such is the case because the propensity to save rises with income, so that higher incomes are the primary source of household saving. This potential conflict, much highlighted in the tax debate of developed countries, applies even more strongly to LDCs.

Now it might be argued that this takes too short-sighted a view. Is not the conflict reduced or made to disappear once a longer perspective is taken? Suppose that a progressive tax system is replaced by one more favourable to saving and investment. Increased capital formation and a higher rate of growth will raise the level of income in future years. The poor will come to share in the outcome and should therefore oppose progressive taxation. Perhaps so, but they will reap a net benefit only to the extent that this gain (or more precisely, its present value) will exceed their current loss as the tax burden is shifted towards them. By the same token, an equity-oriented policy may yield a net gain to the lower-income groups even if growth is reduced thereby. While quantification is difficult, it has been estimated that for a group of Latin American countries increased income equalization, while reducing growth, would nevertheless increase incomes for the lower 80 percent of the population for a period of thirty to forty years.[16] The problem is indeed a complex one, the more so as its equity implications differ depending on whether the future benefits accrue early and are derived by the same generation or whether they will benefit future generations only. We will return to this aspect when dealing with loan finance.

So far we have focused on the impact of progressive income taxation. It remains to be seen whether the conflicting goals of equity and growth can be reconciled or narrowed by directing taxes at high-income *consumption*. Ideally, this would call for a personalized and progressive tax on a person's total consumption. Imposed at the personal level, the consumption or expenditure tax would permit the use of exemptions and progressive rates as under the income tax, and thus be equitable in relation to the distribution of consumption. But saving would not be discouraged, especially over the higher-income ranges where marginal rates are steeper. A progressive tax on expenditures would be the more desirable if, as is frequently the case in low-income countries, high-income households are also big spenders. Moreover, whereas progressive income taxation invites capital flight, as noted further below, this danger is reduced under the expenditure tax.

If feasible, such an arrangement would indeed be the ideal solution. Discussed widely in recent years as an alternative to income taxation in developed countries, an expenditure tax would be no more difficult and might indeed be easier to administer than the income tax. Major difficulties would be avoided, such as the treatment of depreciation, interest and capital gains, as well as inflation adjustments. But there are also new problems, and these would be especially severe for LDCs. Administration of a personalized expenditure tax calls for the recording of financial transactions, with the tax base determined as the excess of income over net investment and cash withdrawals. Given the rudimentary state of financial institutions in LDCs, tracking the tax base would thus be more difficult. Resort to a cash-flow tax at the business level, now much discussed for industrialized countries, would bypass some of these difficulties, but at the unacceptable cost of largely omitting capital income other than rent from the tax. Finally, it need also be noted that some form of profit taxation at the enterprise level would have to be retained even if personal taxation was shifted to an expenditure base. This would be necessary in order to permit the source country some share in the tax base provided by the earnings of foreign-owned capital. The vision of a comprehensive and progressive expenditure tax, ideal though it might be for the LDC setting, is thus a hardly obtainable goal. Instead, use has to be made of a system of excise taxes, providing for selective taxation of high-income items of consumption, a second best, but more accessible approach.

More generally, the design of direct tax systems in developing countries is subject to severe institutional constraints, more severe than those encountered in developed countries. The choice of "tax handles," as I noted in an earlier context, is limited.[17] This, and not so much concern over saving, explains why the ratio of direct to indirect taxes rises with per capita income. Thus, the income tax share in total revenue rises from 16.8 percent in low- to 20 percent in middle- and over 30 percent in high-income countries, while that of commodity taxes falls accordingly.[18]

Finally, there is the role of property taxation. In line with the Lockean proviso and the tradition of Henry George, the taxation of land and real estate should be expected to play a major role in the tax system of LDCs. Taxation of large landholdings can add a progressive element to the tax structure and may induce the fuller utilization of underutilized land. Taxation of urban residential property similarly offers a way to reach luxury consumption. Notwithstanding these advantages, property taxation in LDCs is typically inadequate, reflecting poor assessment systems and political constraints. Given the ever-present danger of capital flight, the proper balance between equity and growth is indeed difficult to achieve.

EQUITY ASPECTS OF EXPENDITURE POLICY

While the equity-growth axis of fiscal policy is debated mostly in relation to the revenue side of the budget, expenditures matter as well and need to be considered in this context. Beginning with current outlays, transfers – by their nature also to be viewed as negative taxes – enter most directly in their effect on distribution. Next in importance are welfare-oriented expenditures in kind. In both cases, however, we find the share of such outlays to be less in low- than in higher-income countries. Thus, transfers range from 20 percent in low-income countries to 25 percent in the lower-middle range and 32 percent in the upper-middle level. The percent of welfare-oriented real outlays in turn ranges from 10.9 percent at the bottom to 29.7 percent in lower-middle- income countries.[19] Limitations of fiscal capacity again restrict such outlays most where there is the greatest need.

Though transfer and welfare programs enter most directly, public invest- ment also matters. Investment in human resources, such as health and education, renders a major contribution to equity as well as growth, leaving both targets now in happy agreement. Rates of return to primary education in developing countries have been estimated to average at 26 percent, as compared to a 13 percent return on investment in physical capital.[20] Expendi- tures on infrastructure, including transportation, communication, gas, electricity, and water, similarly play key roles at early states of development. Since such expenditures are instrumental in drawing backward population groups into the development process, both objectives are again served.[21] By affecting the structure of economic development, public capital formation may thus exert a major effect on income positions – absolute as well as relative – at the lower end of the scale. Indirect effects follow that may well be more far-reaching than those accomplished by cash transfers or shifts in taxation.[22]

INTERGENERATION EQUITY

Our discussion of fiscal equity, so far, has related primarily to its impact on income positions within a given population. But development takes time, and policies undertaken now may impact across future generations. The problem of intergeneration equity must thus be considered.[23]

Consider first the case of tax finance and suppose that income is distrib- uted equally. In that simple case, is it equitable to tax current consumption to finance public capital formation? The result will be to reduce current con- sumption in order to increase future consumption. To the extent that current taxes and later benefits are shared by members of the same generation, this only means a change in the own-consumption paths of particular individuals. Thus, no issue of intergeneration equity arises. But such a problem does arise once the benefits accrue to a future generation. Does fiscal equity condone such a transfer?

The problem of distributive justice is now confronted with a new dimension. First, there is the question of whether it is meaningful to aggregate welfare across generations, or whether each generation is entitled to maximize its own welfare. Secondly, if maximizing across generations is held acceptable, what, if any, discount rate is to be applied? Using a discount rate makes sense if the present generation is entitled to apply *its* valuation to the gains of future generations, but discounting becomes inappropriate if the welfare judgment is made, not from a particular point in time, but by a timeless observer and over the sequence of generations as a whole. Similar problems arise regarding the rate at which the present generation is entitled to exhaust natural resources, thus leaving future generations in a worse position. Problems of population growth as well may be viewed in this context.

Matters are complicated further if we allow for effects on income distribution. Tax finance for capital formation may affect not only the average level of future income but also its distribution. In this case, should distributive justice call on current members of the bottom decile to undertake sacrifices because future benefits will accrue to future members of the same decile? Should there be a "decile-class solidarity" across generations? Or does the criteria of distributive justice hold only within each generation? As the shape of the social welfare function is extended to embrace these additional dimensions, new difficulties arise that as yet have been given little attention.

Turning now to loan finance, suppose first that the government borrows in the domestic market. Private capital formation will be reduced. If the funds are used for public consumption, the present generation benefits and a burden is imposed on the future. But if the funds are used to finance public capital formation, total capital is unaffected, with a diversion from private to public investment only. In this case, no problem of intergeneration equity arises.

These outcomes remain essentially the same if borrowing is from abroad, as is typically the case in developing countries. If used for current consumption, the future is again burdened. If used for investment, the capital stock is increased. The present generation will reap part of the gain in increased income and the future generation will benefit from the remainder. If, in line with rules of prudent finance, interest is paid and the debt is amortized as the real capital is used up, each generation will carry that part of the cost that matches its benefits. Once more there is no intergeneration transfer. At the same time, a net gain from foreign borrowing arises only to the extent that the interest on the debt falls short of the investment yield. Permitting such a difference to arise presumably is (or should be) the rationale underlying the lending to LDCs by institutions such as the World Bank. Unnecessary to say, such a happy ending assumes that the loan proceeds are invested profitably rather than wasted or diverted into consumption; it also assumes that the debt is repaid while the asset is used up. Otherwise the future generation will be left with an unjust burden.

INTERNATIONAL TAX ASPECTS

We conclude by briefly noticing issues of fiscal equity that arise in the context of open economies and that are of special import for developing countries.

With the increased importance of trade and capital flows across countries, problems of international tax adjustments have become a major issue of tax policy. Regarding product taxes, the dispute has been settled by agreement that the revenue from such taxes should accrue to the country of destination, the rule followed in the European Common Market and more generally among other countries. The question of how income taxes and the yield of the corporation tax should be dealt with has remained more controversial, but is of especially vital concern to developing countries.

The normal procedure for the capital-exporting country is to tax profits from foreign investment when repatriated. The guest country in turn will apply its corporation tax to profits of foreign capital in its borders, and this tax may then be credited by the home country upon repatriation. Just how these arrangements are made bears on the profitability of investment in developing countries and on the effectiveness of such tax preferences in attracting foreign capital. Once more, the issue of tax equity is broadened further by adding an international dimension.

It remains to conclude this discussion on a rather sobering note. Seeking equity is all good and well, but what is left but fun and games once resource mobility and the every-present danger of tax-base flight is taken into consideration? Income inequality in LDCs, even more so than in high-income countries, derives primarily from the unequal distribution of capital income and rents that accrue largely at the top. Moreover, capital is mobile, as are high-paid professionals. Low-income, ordinary labour, is not. All this places serious restrictions on progressive taxation in LDCs, except for the taxation of land, which cannot be moved.

With near-perfect mobility of capital and easy residential mobility for high-income earners, international low-tax competition can attract resources by down-bidding tax rates. This process may be viewed in different ways. Some see government as an ever-expanding Leviathan and welcome low-tax competition as a healthy corrective. Others, including this author, question this perspective and the appropriateness of tax competition as a remedy. Tax competition is then seen as depriving political units of their freedom to choose their own fiscal arrangements, including, in particular, measures to deal with excessive inequality. Whatever may be the case among industrialized countries, low-tax competition hardly offers a prescription for LDCs. International tax agreements, such as tax sparing and adequate withholding rates, may be of some help. More ambitiously, countries of origin might be permitted to share in the income tax revenue derived from their high-income migrants by the new country of residence.[24] But short of a truly international fiscal system, the implementation of fiscal equity in developing countries will remain severely limited by the escape hatch of capital flight. As I have argued all along, the "distribution function" cannot be met adequately in a highly decentralized fiscal structure.[25] This not only holds within countries, but also across nation-states, especially the LDCs.

NOTES

1 J. Locke, *Two Treatises on Government* (1989), ed. P. Laslett, rev. ed. (New York: Mentor Books, 1963).

2 By noting that public or social goods must be "provided for" through the fiscal system, we do not mean that they must be publicly produced. Streetlights may be purchased from private manufacturers, but they may be paid for through the budget and financed by taxation. Since they are available to all who pass through, no individual will be willing to offer voluntary payments. Thus, a compulsory mechanism, including policy determination by voting, is needed to secure preference revelation.

3 See R. Nozick, *Anarchy, State and Utopia* (New York: Basic Books, 1968).

4 A long literature on this extends from J.S. Mill over Y. Edgeworth to A.C. Pigou, *Public Finance* (London: Macmillan, 1927).

5 See L. Robbins, "Interpersonal Comparison of Utility," *Economic Journal* 48 (1938).

6 See J. Rousseau, *The First and Second Discourses of Rousseau* (1775), ed. R.D. Masters (New York: Saint Mary's Press, 1964).

7 See Karl Marx, "Critique of the Gotha Program" 1875, in P.C. Tucker, ed., *The Marx-Engels Reader* (New York, 1972), 388. Inconsistent with his role as utopian philosopher, Marx, the economist, takes a Lockean entitlement tack when viewing the assignment of profits to capital as an "exploitation" of labour.

8 See J. Bentham, *The Theory of Legislation* (1830), ed. C. Ogden (London: Kegan, 1931).

9 John Rawls, *A Theory of Justice* (Cambridge: Harvard University Press, 1971). More specifically, the Rawlsian construct does not assign a social welfare function to start with, but begins with the premise that individuals are to choose impartially among alternative distributions from behind a veil, not knowing their identity. On the basis of a high degree of risk aversion, they then prefer an equal distribution.

10 This somewhat old-fashioned way of describing the social welfare function differs from more recent formulations in terms of a coefficient of inequality aversion as used in the World Bank's recent study. See D. Newbury and N. Stern, *The Theory of Taxation for Developing Countries* (Washington, DC: World

Bank, 1887). The difference, however, is formal and computational only. The coefficient approach is convenient in offering an overall measure but less sensitive to changes in the rate of decline in social weights when moving up the income scale.

11   See R. Musgrave, "Theories of Fiscal Crises: An Essay in Fiscal Sociology," in H. Aaron and M. Boskin, eds., *The Economics of Taxation* (Washington, DC: The Brookings Institution, 1980).

12   This oversimplifies matters, as it overlooks the dead-weight loss the transaction imposes at both ends of the scale, losses that also need to be allowed for in arriving at an optimal solution. This aspect of the problem is given special focus in the "theory of optimal taxation" that underlies the World Bank's study (see note 10). However, the conclusions drawn here are likely to hold as well under that more sophisticated approach.

13   See S. Kuznet, "Economic Growth and Income Inequality," *American Economic Review*, 1955.

14   See W.A. Lewis, "Economic Development with Unlimited Labor Supply," *Manchester School* 12, no. 2 (1954).

15   World Bank, *World Development Report* (Washington, DC, 1988), 230.

16   See W.R. Cline, *Potential Effects of Income Redistribution in Economic Growth: Latin American Cases* (New York: Praeger, 1972).

17   See R. Musgrave, *Fiscal Systems* (New Haven: Yale University Press, 1969), 125. See also R. Musgrave, "Tax Reform in Developing Countries," in Newberry and Stern, eds., *The Theory of Taxation in Developing Countries*.

18   See World Bank, *World Development Report, 1988*, 23.

19   See World Bank, *World Development Report* (Washington, DC, 1987), 64.

20   See World Bank, *World Development Report, 1988*, 266.

21   The role of public investment as seen here refers to infrastructure and human investments which are in the nature of public goods, rather than to government-operated enterprises for production in the market.

22   For a broad-based and comprehensive approach, see Irma Adelman and Sherman Robinson, "Income Distribution and Development," in H. Chenery and T.N. Svinivasan, eds., *Handbook of Development Economics*, vol. 2 (Amsterdam: Elsevier, 1989).

23   See R.A. Musgrave, "Public Debt and Intergeneration Equity," in K. Arrow and N. Boskin, eds., *The Economics of Public Debt* (New York: Macmillan Press, 1988).

24   See J. Bhagwati and M. Partington, eds., *Taxing the Brain Drain I: A Proposal* (Amsterdam: Elsevier, 1975); and J. Bhagwati, ed., *The Brain Drain and Taxation II: Theory and Empirical Analysis* (Amsterdam: Elsevier, 1976).

25   See R.A. Musgrave, *The Theory of Public Finance* (New York: Macmillan Press, 1958), 181.

7 The Status and Efficiency of Regional Development Policies

ALBERT BRETON

INTRODUCTION

I am neither a development economist nor a student of regional economics. But I have, over the years, maintained an abiding interest in regional economic development *policies*. What has fascinated me most is how these policies could be justified within a conventional economic framework in which persons and families are not denied a geographical habitat, but in which priority is explictly given to the individual and only derivative value accorded to particular locations. Is it possible, I kept asking myself, that regional development policies, which are part and parcel of the policy portfolio of virtually every government in the world, are all aberrations reflecting a misunderstanding of what would raise the general well-being of citizens? Why is it that governments do not pay greater heed to the advice of a large number of economists who advocate allocating resources to the enhancement of the mobility of people and non-sunk capital instead of trying to develop the region?

To focus the discussion, I will concentrate my attention on regional development policies in federal states. More precisely, I will propose a hypothesis that will make it possible to rationalize why regional policies are implemented by the federal or central governments of federations. This hypothesis will, at the same time, provide a basis for determining the efficiency of these policies. This essay is, indeed, aimed at defending regional development policies on efficiency grounds. I disregard altogether any equity rationale they may possess in certain circumstances. Because I will be concerned with the place and role of regional policies in federal states, I could have called these policies provincial (or state, or cantonal) development policies. I will, however, defer to custom and retain the traditional label. I do so, not so much out of respect for tradition, as because the model applies to all the governments that are "higher up" in the hierarchy of multi-tier public sector structures. To put it differently, the model to be developed can be used to rationalize and evaluate not only the regional policies of central governments in the provinces, but also the regional policies of provincial governments in the municipalities within their boundaries and the regional policies of municipal governments in jurisdictions "under" them, when such exist.

To proceed, I need a model of federalism. I, therefore, devote the next section to the task of outlining the bare bones of a model of "competitive federalism,"[1] that is, a model of intergovernmental competition. In the section following, I seek to demonstrate that because of the presence in governmental systems of certain structural features – such as large disparities in population sizes, wealth levels, and, hence, political power – competition between the units located at a given jurisdictional level (e.g., the governments at the provincial or municipal level) will often lead to equilibrium outcomes that are unstable in that an external disturbance will produce even larger population, wealth, and power disparities. The last section is directed at analysing the role and efficiency of regional policies in generating the observed stability of many real-world federal states.

COMPETITIVE FEDERALISM

I simply assume that intergovernmental relations are competitive without presenting the empirical evidence that can be marshalled to document that they are.[2] I assume that governments, much like business firms, compete in a number of domains. To simplify and shorten the presentation, I reduce these to three: prices, production and provision of public policies,[3] and innovation. To put the matter differently, I limit intergovernmental competition to price competition, policy competition, and "innovational" (Schumpeterian) competition.

The prices that are the object of price competition embrace tax rates (therefore deductions, exemptions, credits, and the multiplicity of other factors that establish effective rates), subsidy rates (and, therefore, tax expenditures as well as "in kind" transfers), tariffs, non-tariff barriers, and exchange rate devaluations, which are obviously more important in international intergovernmental relations than in federalist relations. Price competition pertains also to the pricing of public utility output such as rail, air, and ground transportation (a zero price is a price!), electricity, and gas, as well as the user charges levied for many publicly supplied services, such as telephone communications and garbage disposal.

The analysis of policy competition began with Tiebout's[4] model of local public goods (local public policies); within that framework, policy competition has been systematically researched. After Oates's[5] path-breaking empirical study of the capitalization of public policies in land and housing prices, a number of empirical studies have shown that at the local level at least, governments compete with each other.

Governments also compete by innovating, that is, by introducing new policies, new institutions, new modes of doing things (i.e., new technologies), etc. Let me focus attention for a moment on a world in which governmental relations are in equilibrium in the sense that the bundle of policies supplied by each and every government remains unchanged over time. Now assume that one government introduces a new policy. A good example of such an innovation is the very significant deregulation of financial institutions pioneered by the government of Quebec a few years ago after a long period during which all the provinces had essentially maintained the *status quo* in this domain. By so doing, the innovating government changes its position vis-à-vis the other governments in the system; it becomes a Schumpeterian entrepreneur and, in the process, makes itself into a temporary monopolist. Describing the effect of an innovation in a competitive market setting, Samuelson[6] graphically portrays it as a "change in [the] *quality* of market structure and entrepreneurial power" (p. 314).

In the public sector, a policy innovation also changes the "quality" of the governmental structure and the distribution of political power between its constituent units. This disequilibrium – for in the Schumpeterian model,[7] that is what it is – will act as a spur on other governments to introduce similar policies or policies that are substitutes for the one introduced by the innovator. That is exactly what has happened in Canada in respect of the deregulation of financial institutions.

Because imitators will not all act at once, the path to a new equilibrium will most likely be "cyclical." To put it differently, the rate of adoption of the new policies, institutions, or technologies will graph as a cumulative frequency distribution that will be S-shaped, much like the cycle created by the innovations of entrepreneurs and the imitations of rivals in the Schumpeterian model. There is much empirical evidence that the actual rate of adoption of new policies can indeed be represented by an S-shaped curve.[8]

In federal and, indeed, in all multi-tier public sector structures, there are two different kinds of intergovernmental relations. One pertains to the relations of provincial governments with each other, which I call horizontal relations, and the other relates to federal-provincial relations, which I label vertical relations. Both kinds are competitive, though what drives the competition varies between the two: horizontal competition is, in this essay, limited to considerations of price, policy, and innovational competition, while vertical competition is restricted to rivalry over the division of powers

In the pages that follow I limit myself to horizontal competition because I wish to examine the role of federal or central government regional policies in ensuring that the equilibrium outcomes produced by that competition are stable and efficient. In other words, I take the division of constitutional powers between jurisdictional levels as given and unalterable, so that vertical competition is effectively suppressed. (I defend this assumption in the next section.)

THE STABILITY OF COMPETITION

Per dollar of expenditure, the quantity of some public policies increases and/or their quality improves as jurisdictions become larger, at least over some range of sizes. Put differently, for the same level of per capita spending on services such as education, health, recreation, roads, arts and culture, and others, the evidence, admittedly not systematic, is that the volume, diversity (scope), and quality of output available in larger jurisdictions exceed that available in smaller ones. The tendency appears to be the same as that observable with regard to such private goods as banking, legal, medical, informational, engineering, and other services for which quantity, diversity, and quality increase with size and concentration.

It is true, of course, that on the other side of the balance sheet, crime, pollution, noise, congestion, and other costs increase with size and with density, so that a constant volume and quality of law enforcement, sewage disposal, pollution control, and ease of movement require larger expenditures as size and density increase. There is no way of establishing, on *a priori* grounds, whether the ''aggregate'' average cost curve – the curve obtained by taking the (vertical) sum, as size varies, of the unit costs associated with each public policy supplied – will be monotone negative or positive, or whether it will be horizontal or U-shaped.

One's expectation, supported by the meagre available empirical evidence, is that the average cost curves associated with different policies have different shapes: some are flat, some are rising, others are falling, and others still are U-shaped. If all the curves were horizontal or rising, the outcomes of inter-governmental competition in respect of policy implementation, prices, and in-novational activity would be stable. (Stability also requires efficiently design-ed and enforced rules of the game or property rights so that all the costs and the benefits of policy actions of competing governments are borne by the resi-dents of the jurisdictions whose governments are implementing the policies. In other words, the ''export'' of cost burdens to out-of-province residents can cause unstable outcomes, that is, still larger cost spillovers. In the remainder of this chapter, I suppress this source of instability by assuming that costs and benefits are borne by the jurisdictions producing them. This means that the effects of interjurisdictional spillovers are eliminated either by intergovernmental grants as in Breton[9] or by "coordination" as in Breton and Scott.)[10]

Negatively sloped or even U-shaped cost curves pose a problem. The problem arises from the fact that jurisdictions vary greatly in size. In Canada, Prince Edward Island is just about 0.20 percent the size of Ontario, and in the United States, Delaware is even smaller relative to California. It is possible to imagine that jurisdictional boundaries could be altered, but it would certainly be most unrealistic to do so, at least for provincial or state boundaries.

To grasp the nature of the problem posed by economies of size, let us look at two outcomes of adjustments to external disturbances in a (imperfectly) competitive market context. Suppose, then, that as a result of, let us say, an overall reduction in demand for an industry's output, some firms that had hitherto earned their way can now only do so by selling at a higher price because the fall in demand pushes them up the downward portion of their cost curves, while others in the same industry can continue selling at the old price or even at a lower one because they had been producing on the horizontal or upward section of their cost curves. Over time, we should expect demand to shift towards the latter group of firms, making the situation for the first group even worse and eventually causing them to go bankrupt. Ruling out boundary changes effectively rules out bankruptcies and "insolvency" processes of adjustment. In other words, the effective suppression of units that bankruptcy generates is not a solution in a federal setting. The provinces are there to stay and so, therefore, are their governments.

Another way that competition deals with economies of size in a market context following an external shock is through what Stigler[11] has called "vertical disintegration" when market size or demand expands and "vertical integration" when it contracts. Vertical integration implies that a given firm "captures" the functions, processes, or activities that display economies of size, "forcing" other firms to "abandon" them. The corresponding mechanism in a federalist context is the reassignment of powers to a higher jurisdictional level so that provinces (say) are left with only those responsibilities that can be met at a scale consistent with sustainable competition.

I have ruled out changes in the division of powers and, therefore, also that particular "solution" to the problem. At this point the reader may well wonder if I have not created an issue simply by ruling out all modes of adjustment. To see that this is not the case, let me explain why I have chosen to assume a fixed or constant division of powers. It is a fact that, in some particular cases, a particular constitutional power can be assigned to a jurisdictional level, not *in toto*, but only in part. For example, responsibility for education could be assigned to the provincial level, but not to provinces Y and Z. This would be a case of what could be called "split power," since the power would be provincial for provinces A, B, C ..., but federal for Y and Z.

As a general practice, however, when powers are assigned to a particular level, they are assigned to *all* the governments at that level.

Given this assumption, if powers were to be reassigned to a higher level of jurisdiction every time some economies of scale or of size are not fully exploited because jurisdictions are too small, the division of powers would be determined by the smallest jurisdiction in the federation and would lead to a highly centralized structure. It would mean assigning to the central level responsibilities that medium-size and larger provincial units could efficiently discharge. I suspect that the secular centralization of municipal functions at the provincial level in virtually all countries is the result of the operation of a vertical integration process in governmental systems in which the division of powers is not constitutionally entrenched and is, therefore, easy to alter.

Because governments are not allowed to consolidate through an insolvency process, and because centralization is kept in check by keeping those powers at the provincial level that a vertical integration process would reassign upwards, intergovernmental competition, in the absence of the necessary institutional remedies, is inherently unstable. The situation is portrayed in Figure 7.1 for two jurisdictions – J_1 and J_2 – which, given their sizes, have unit costs of C_1 and C_2, respectively. Figure 7.1 is drawn on the assumption that the two jurisdictions face the same cost curve AC; it should be obvious that I have made this assumption only because it simplifies the diagram. It would be easy to draw two different cost curves and get the same result. I have also drawn the cost curve sloping downward through its whole length. That too is only a simplifying assumption, at least as long as the smaller jurisdiction operates at a unit cost that is higher than the minimum.

Under the conditions depicted in the diagram, J_1 will always lose out to J_2 in the competitive struggle for talent, capital, and technology, and as a consequence its relative position will worsen. Eventually, competition will drive J_1 to bankruptcy or lead it to transfer its constitutional powers to a hierarchically higher government. By ruling out these two "solutions," I have opened the door to regional development policies as a mode of intervention that can prevent competition from suppressing J_1. I turn to that question in the next section.

FEDERAL REGIONAL POLICIES

There are a set of functions which are intrinsically national because they are indivisible ... [Among them] one may cite ... the control of relationships among lower governmental levels.[12]

Although the outcomes of intergovernmental competition have, to my knowledge, seldom been explicitly called unstable,[13] a number of proposed solutions to federalist problems implicitly acknowledge the fact. Let me illustrate

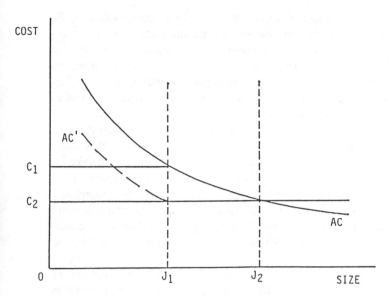

Figure 7.1
Competitive Adjustment of Jurisdictions

with two such "solutions." The first, already mentioned in the last section, is centralization or, more exactly, the *ceteris paribus* reassignment of a power to a higher-level government. Another is the design of institutions to promote cooperation or what is known as "cooperative federalism." Both solutions seek to deal, in different ways, with instability essentially by suppressing competition.

As an example of centralization and cooperation as solutions to instability, consider income redistribution in a federalist setting. A long list of scholars, including Buchanan,[14] Stigler,[15] Musgrave,[16] and Oates,[17] have argued that the (constitutional) power to redistribute income among individuals should be assigned to the national government – should be centralized – because if the power was given to the provinces or to the municipalities, no redistribution would take place. The reason is simple and well known. If a province taxes its higher-income population and transfers the proceeds to its lower-income citizens, the first will leave the province and lower-income people from elsewhere will be attracted to the province. To forestall an eventual bankruptcy and, also, to be in a position to offer its population the goods and services it desires, that province will refrain from income redistribution. Since all the provinces are in the same position vis-à-vis each other, only centralization – or an agreement by all provinces to adopt the same redistribution policies (a form of cooperation which is *de facto* equivalent to centralization) – will permit, it is argued, income redistribution to take place.

Notwithstanding what appears as complete unanimity among scholars, the notion that centralization and/or cooperation are the only solutions to the problem of instability with regard to income redistribution among individuals is mistaken. First, the fact that redistribution is implemented by governments at subnational levels in all federations is testimony to that; second, the fact that the form and mode of redistribution vary considerably between jurisdictions is a sign that cooperation is not what permits the redistribution to happen. This essay does not deal with income redistribution. It would, therefore, take me too far out of my way to analyse the institutions that allow competitive governments at the provincial and local levels to undertake income redistribution and to provide it in stable equilibrium volumes. I have mentioned this case and referred to some of the relevant literature to indicate that, in one area at least, the problem of instability is recognized and to warn the reader of the tendency to "solve" it by suggesting solutions – such as centralization and cooperation – that snuff out competition and, in effect, extinguish federalism.

In the area of provincial development policies, one also notices an unmistakable tendency, at least in the literature if less in the real world, to deal with competitive instability described in the discussion surrounding Figure 7.1 above through either centralization or cooperation solutions. The problem with these solutions is that virtually all the policies of provincial governments have a bearing on development. This is probably the case for income redistribution as well; while that fact has not been acknowledged in the literature,[18] it has been impossible to disregard it for development policies. Centralization and cooperation would reduce federalism to such a mirage that all, except those who decry federalism as a matter of principle, would hesitate to propose these as solutions.

How then do real-world federations deal with the instability that attaches to the pursuit by provincial governments of policies aimed at promoting the development of their province? The answer is provided by Stigler in the citation that I have placed at the beginning of this section – that is, by the federal government controlling "the relationships among lower governmental levels." Federal governments do this by implementing regional or, more precisely, provincial development policies of their own. These policies are put in place as a way of stabilizing horizontal intergovernmental competition, and it is on that basis that one must evaluate their efficiency.

Federal regional development policies include all the federal government policies that affect regional (provincial) development. These obviously include basic infrastructure policies related to railways, canals, airports and runways, communication networks, streets, roads and highway systems, water supply and water-storage reservoirs, port facilities, and many others. Most infrastructural projects are mechanical engineering undertakings that the provinces could very easily coordinate and implement by themselves. The reason why they are virtually always federal or federal-provincial enterprises is that in the absence of the federal government, the competition between the provinces would favour those whose costs were lower – generally the larger, more wealthy provinces that often benefit from economies of size to the detriment of the others.

Basic infrastructural undertakings are part of a much larger bundle of federal development policies implemented to ensure competitive viability of the various units of federations. Federal governments are also active in research and development for essentially the same reason. R&D activity involving experimental agricultural and forestry farms, as well as the operation of more conventional laboratories, are examples. In this connection, one should mention the role of military and defence R&D, which is additional to the production of military hardware. Over the last thirty or forty years, the federal government in the United States has progressively reduced its direct concern for regional issues to the point that at present regional matters seem totally absent from the agenda. I would like to suggest that this absence is an illusion: US regional policies are now embodied in defence expenditures. That fact makes it difficult to evaluate the efficiency of these regional policies or to identify the component of defence expenditure that is truly regional in character, but the task of stabilizing interstate competition is still accomplished. If defence expenditures play that role in the United States, they could come to play the same role in Canada. There is, indeed, evidence that they have recently begun to do so more than was hitherto the case. However that may be, if under the bilateral free trade agreement between Canada and the United States, the international monitoring panel determines that a significant part of Canada's regional policy arsenal is inconsistent with "free trade," one can confidently predict a substantial increase in defence expenditures in Canada as a conduit for regional policies. Interprovincial competition must be stabilized or else the federation will fragment.

In addition to infrastructural undertakings and to research and development activities, federal governments give subsidies, whether direct or indirect, in money or in kind, to labour, capital, and/or technology with the object of inducing them to locate in particular areas. There is no limit, it would seem, to the variety of forms the subsidies can take. They include loan guarantees, lower interest rates, lower tax rates, lower rents on federally owned land, in addition to capital grants and labour subsidies of various sorts.

On what basis should one appraise the efficiency of the regional policies implemented by the central governments of federal countries? The first point to note in addressing this question is that the answer depends on whether other policies also contribute to competitive stability. I have argued elsewhere that intergovernmental grants must be analysed as policy instruments aimed at competitive stability.[19] Consequently, if a grants system is in place and if it has been optimally designed to produce stability, federal regional policies would have to be seen as wasteful. If, however, the grants system is not optimal in the above sense, regional policies would have to be seen as complementary to the grants program.

The simplest case to look at is the one which obtains when there is no system of intergovernmental grants. That case does, indeed, provide us with all the elements we need to analyse the efficiency dimension of federal regional policies. In some federations, only a subset of all the constituent units compete with each other in certain policy areas. The literature on the diffusion of legislation and/or administrative measures clearly indicates this to be the case. However, if one considers development policies, broadly defined, it would seem reasonable to assume that all the constituent units partake in the competition. I thus will assume, without any loss of generality, that all the provinces, states, or cantons in a given country compete with each other. Furthermore, I will assume that the number of competing units is fixed – there is no exit and no entry, no bankruptcy and no new provinces. This last assumption reflects not a fact – though a fact it may be – but a constraint that the analysis must incorporate. Since instability, at the limit, would imply that some provincial governments would go bankrupt (would exit), the constraint is meaningful in that the analysis of efficiency would be vacuous without it.

The regional development policies of the federal government would be efficient if the unit costs of provincial development policies were equalized, as would happen if the average cost curve for J_1 in figure 7.1 was shifted, by policy, from AC to AC'. Three points should be emphasized about this efficiency property of development policy. First, efficient federal regional development policies are discriminatory – all provincial governments will not be treated in the same way. Some jurisdictions will be the target of significant attention by the central government, while others will receive very little. Second, virtually all governments in the system will be affected by federal regional development policy. Third, federal regional policies will reduce interjurisdictional mobility. Contrary to what could be inferred from figure 7.1, however, all mobility will not be eliminated. On the contrary, because jurisdictions will be competing on a more or less equal footing, the interjurisdictional mobility that will take place will be stable and productive.

One way to see this is to consider the problem at a different level in the political hierarchy. Local governments, just like provincial governments, compete with each other. That competition too can lead to unstable outcomes. In the absence of municipal development policies implemented by provincial governments or of substitutes for these policies, one is likely to observe what has been called the "urban crisis." That crisis, a phenomenon which well describes many cities in the United States, can indeed be interpreted as a manifestation of competitive instability. Bird and Slack,[20] in their analysis of the phenomenon, make the point that Canada is largely free of it; they attribute this to a number of factors, including, not unimportantly, what are in effect provincial regional (i.e., municipal) development policies.

The fact that there is no urban crisis in Canada – that inter-municipal competition is stabilized by a variety of means – does not imply that mobility has been suppressed. On the contrary, it simply means that mobility is efficient and productive. There is undeniably less inter-municipal mobility in Canada than in the United States, but that is not a sign of inefficient resource allocation, unless one also assumes that competitive relations are always stable. To put the matter differently, the existence of an urban crisis is a sign of excessive and inefficient interjurisdictional mobility. (The above should not be read to imply that there is sufficient local mobility in Canada.)

CONCLUSION

In this essay, I have, in effect, challenged the generally tacit assumption that competitive relations between governments at a given jurisdictional level always produce stable equilibrium outcomes. I have instead suggested that the stability we observe in the real world is a consequence of certain institutions and policies. I have suggested that regional development policies, which central governments in all federations pursue, can and do play that role. That is not to say that all regional development policies are always efficient, but it does dispose of the view, not uncommon today, that they are all inefficient and essentially a manifestation of rent seeking.

If regional development policies prevent urban and provincial crises by stabilizing horizontal competition between governments, they are efficient. They are also primarily allocational policies, although their implementation will have effects on the distribution of income that one may or may not want to decry.

NOTES

1 For a more detailed description of the model, see A. Breton, "Supplementary Report," in *Report of the Royal Commission on the Economic Union and Development Prospects for Canada* (Ottawa: Supply and Services, 1985), vol. 3, 486–526; reprinted as "Towards a Theory of Competitive Federalism," in *European Journal of Political Economy* 3, nos. 1 and 2 (1987): 263–329.

2 Some empirical evidence is summarized and analysed in A. Breton, "The Existence and Stability of Interjurisdictional Competition," in Daphne A. Kenyon and John Kincaid, eds., *Competition Among States and Local Governments* (Washington: Urban Institute Press, 1991): 37–56. See also D.A. Kenyon, "Interjurisdictional Tax and Policy Competition: Good or Bad for the Federal System" (Washington, 1989, Mimeo).

3 The set of actions that can be called public policies is defined in A. Breton, *The Economic Theory of Representative Government* (Chicago: Aldine, 1974),

chap. 2; and A. Breton and R. Wintrobe, *The Logic of Bureaucratic Conduct* (New York: Cambridge University Press, 1982), chap. 2.

4 C.M. Tiebout, "A Pure Theory of Local Expenditures," *Journal of Political Economy* 64, no. 5 (October 1956): 416–24.

5 W.E. Oates, "The Effects of Property Taxes and Local Spending on Property Values: An Empirical Study of Tax Capitalization and the Tiebout Hypothesis," *Journal of Political Economy* 77, no. 6 (November/December 1969): 957–71.

6 P.A. Samuelson, "Schumpeter As an Economic Theorist," in H. Frisch, ed., *Schumpeterian Economics* (London: Praeger, 1982); reprinted in K. Crowley, ed., *The Collected Scientific Papers of Paul A. Samuelson* (Cambridge: MIT Press, 1986), 5: 301–27.

7 The model suggested by J. Schumpeter in *The Theory of Economic Development* (New York: Oxford University Press, 1961).

8 Breton, "The Existence and Stability of Interjurisdictional Competition."

9 A. Breton, "A Theory of Government Grants," *Canadian Journal of Economics and Political Science* 31, no. 2 (May 1965): 175–87.

10 A. Breton and A. Scott, *The Economic Constitution of Federal States* (Toronto: University of Toronto Press, 1978).

11 G.J. Stigler, "The Division of Labor is Limited by the Extent of the Market," *Journal of Political Economy* 59, no. 3 (June 1951); reprinted in G.J. Stigler, *The Organization of Industry* (Chicago: University of Chicago Press, 1968), 129–41.

12 G.J. Stigler, "The Tenable Range of Functions of Local Government" in Joint Economic Committee, Subcommittee on Fiscal Policy, *Federal Expenditure Policy for Economic Growth and Stability* (Washington: US Printing Office, 1957), 213–19.

13 An exception is F.H. Mueller, "Area Development Expenditures and Economic Stability in Local Areas," in Joint Economic Committee, *Federal Expenditure Policy*, 803–4, who uses the word in the same sense as I do here.

14 J.M. Buchanan, "Federalism and Fiscal Equity," *American Economic Review* 40, no. 4 (September 1950); reprinted in R.A. Musgrave and C.S. Shoup, *Readings in the Economics of Taxation* (Homewood: Irwin, 1959), 93–109.

15 G.J. Stigler, "The Tenable Range of Functions of Local Government," in Joint Economic Committee, *Federal Expenditure Policy*, 218.

16 R. A. Musgrave, *Fiscal Systems* (New Haven: Yale University Press, 1969).

17 W.E. Oates, *Fiscal Federalism* (New York: Harcourt Brace Jovanovich, 1972).

18 An exception is Buchanan, "Federalism and Fiscal Equity."

19 Breton, "Supplementary Report."

20 R.M. Bird and N.E. Slack, *Urban Public Finance in Canada* (Toronto: Butterworths, 1983).

8 Regional Policies for Equity: Can They Be Justified?

NILES HANSEN

INTRODUCTION

Economists, and particularly those of neoclassical persuasion, typically maintain that regional policies to promote the development of lagging regions – thereby reducing interregional economic disparities – distort efficient resource allocation and impede national economic development. Regional policies clearly could have this effect. However, in a broadly socio-political-economic context, regional policies, whether or not they are strictly economically efficient from a national perspective, may lead to greater national coherence and solidarity, and such policies may be voluntarily supported by the economic "losers" in more-developed regions out of a sense of fairness.

This first part of this chapter considers the issue of fairness as a justification for regional policies with an equity orientation. In this regard, particular attention is given to survey data from Western Europe. The second part of the chapter deals with regional policy implementation. Here the focus is on equity and efficiency issues in the context of regional infrastructure investment policy. More specifically, it is argued that a regionally differentiated infrastructure approach could promote both equity and efficient national development. The conclusion considers some unresolved issues of equity and efficiency with respect to regional development policy.

REGIONAL IDENTITY AND PUBLIC SUPPORT FOR REGIONAL DEVELOPMENT POLICIES: SOME EVIDENCE FROM WESTERN EUROPE

In this section, consideration is given – within the context of the nine-nation European Community (EC) – to issues of geographical identity and to the question of whether people are willing to subsidize the development of economically lagging regions.

The data in Table 8.1 are derived from a survey of 9,000 persons in the nations of the European Community. The survey was carried out in 1978 by the central French regional planning agency, the Délégation de l'aménagement du territoire et à l'action régionale. For present purposes, it may be pointed out that, among all respondents, few expressed a feeling of belonging to the world as a whole (7 percent), or even to Europe as a whole (4 percent). The strongest geographic attachment of most people was to a subnational geographic entity, that is, to a particular locality or to a particular region; the proportion of respondents selecting these geographic entities was about twice that selecting the nation – 57 percent to 30 percent. As to differences among national respondents, it may be noted that 71 percent of the West Germans identified most closely with subnational geographic units, and only 20 percent identified most closely with the nation. Does this reflect a reaction to the nationalism of the Third Reich? Or does it reflect the historically late unification of Germany? Italy had a similar national experience, but the response pattern for Italians differs from that of the Germans. The Belgian response pattern is similar to that of West Germany, but in this case the relatively low degree of identification with the nation as a whole may well be attributable to cultural-linguistic differences between Flemish and Walloons. Clearly one could speculate at length concerning the differences among the various national response patterns. Yet whatever the differences in national histories, the fundamental fact remains that, whatever the country, more people are attached to a subnational geographic entity than to the nation as a whole.

Now consider the data in Table 8.2, which presents the results of a survey carried out in the late 1970s by the Commission of the European Communities. The essential survey questions were as follows: Would people agree to be taxed to support the development of disadvantaged regions in their own country, and, would they agree to be taxed to support the development of disadvantaged regions in the European Community, even if such regions are located in countries other than their own? The results indicate that 79 percent of all EC respondents would agree to be taxed to support the development of lagging regions in their own respective countries, and a third would be similarly disposed to contribute to the development of lagging EC regions even if they are in other countries. Again it is tempting to speculate on differences in response patterns among countries (particularly the relatively low propensity of West Germans to support their own nation's disadvantaged regions and their relatively high propensity to support lagging regions in other countries), but the main point seems clear.

In all countries, there is a pronounced willingness to be taxed to support others that cannot be explained in terms of the narrow economic self-interest of the respondents. I can think of only one caveat in this regard, which

TABLE 8.1

Responses, by Country, to the Question "Among the Following Geographic Entities, to Which One Do You Have the Strongest Feeling of Belonging?"

	France %	Belgium %	Denmark %	West Germany %	Ireland %	Italy %	Luxembourg %	Netherlands %	Great Britain %	European Community %
Nation	34	19	28	20	25	32	35	32	37	30
City, locality	32	57	55	60	60	34	29	45	37	43
Region, province	19	12	10	11	11	13	18	10	13	14
World	8	5	1	1	1	15	5	8	8	7
Europe	4	4	3	3	2	5	10	4	3	4
No response	3	3	5	5	1	1	3	1	2	2

Source: René Uhrich, *Pour une nouvelle politique de développement régional en Europe*, 2nd ed. (Paris: Economica, 1985), 237.

TABLE 8.2

Percent of Survey Respondents, by Country, Agreeing That Part of Their Taxes Should Be Devoted to the Development of the Most Disadvantaged Regions (a) of Their Country and (b) of the European Community

	Their Country %	European Community %
Belgium	74	25
Denmark	76	18
West Germany	65	45
France	85	29
Ireland	84	23
Italy	87	41
Luxembourg	93	41
Netherlands	83	48
Great Britain	80	17
Total of European Community	79	33

Source: René Uhrich, *Pour une nouvelle politique de développement régional en Europe*, 234.

involves population migration. If residents of more economically advanced regions feel that immigration from less-developed regions of their own country or of other countries creates economic or social problems, then they may, out of self-interest, prefer to subsidize economic and educational opportunities for residents in disadvantaged regions – either to stem migration or to make those persons who do migrate less liable to become a social burden in the receiving area. But this is a fairly subtle point. The evidence suggests that many people are in fact motivated by a voluntary sense of fairness. Despite the fact that most people identify most strongly with their own subnational community rather than with a broader national or international community, this does not preclude a widespread willingness to be taxed to help persons in other national regions or, even if to a lesser extent, in foreign disadvantaged regions. And, in fact, regional policies of the respective nations and of the European Community do involve such measures.

Fairness, Equity, and Regional Policies

Regional policies have been regarded by many economists as leading to sentimental distortions of efficient resource allocation, presumably because resources are redistributed from more efficient places to less efficient places. Does this mean that the survey responses shown in Table 8.2 reflect irrationality or illusion? Economists recognize that an individual's welfare can be evaluated only from his or her utility function, not from any direct valuation of the quantities of goods and services that flow to the individual. In other words, the economist does not question the likes and dislikes of the consumer. Yet, as Baumol points out, "we do not seem prepared to embrace all of what this viewpoint implies ... Just as there is nothing wrong with the choice of a consumer who prefers mango ice cream to strawberry, there is nothing pathological about a consumer who prefers a method of payment that actually costs him more but pleases him by making the price of his purchase *seem* lower."[1] Baumol further suggests that such considerations are relevant to superfairness analysis, with its reliance on the preferences of the persons affected by the circumstances whose fairness is to be evaluated. In Baumol's theory of superfairness, a distribution is fair if it involves no envy by any individual of any other.[2] A distribution is strictly superfair if each participant receives a bundle that is strictly preferred by that individual to the bundle received by anyone else, that is, if his or her holdings could be reduced without giving rise to envy. The voluntary spatial redistribution choices reflected in the data in Table 8.2 represent a *prima facie* example of superfairness.

Issues surrounding regional development policy in Canada are also pertinent in the present context. Savoie, for example, maintains that from the perspective of economic efficiency, critics of such policy can point to a variety of reasons why special regional development measures should be done away with: "However, an unrelenting pursuit of national efficiency is simply not acceptable in Canada. The cost in adjustment and in personal hardship would be prohibitive. Canada's interregional tensions could well become unmanageable."[3] In many respects, regional development policies have been as much a condition of Canada's social contract as building a railroad west was a condition for British Columbia to join the Confederation.

Or, as Savoie put the matter, "the sharing of prosperity among Canadians wherever they live has been part of the bargain of Confederation."[4]

It is appropriate to conclude these observations with a point that Baumol makes at the end of his study of superfairness: "The one broad pattern that seems to emerge from the formal analysis is the frequency with which fairness theory tends to support the equity judgments of non-economist observers. In cases where they have exhibited suspicion of the fairness of policy measures recommended by microeconomists such as myself, on grounds of economic efficiency, the fairness analysis often seems to confirm that there is something that does really merit suspicion."[5]

REGIONAL INFRASTRUCTURE POLICY: ARE NATIONAL DEVELOPMENT AND REGIONAL EQUITY CONFLICTING OBJECTIVES?

The Newly Developing Country Context

Consideration will now be given to equity and efficiency issues involved in regional policies intended to promote the development of less-developed regions. Of course, even where equity is the principal motive, public policy should nonetheless attempt to minimize the costs of achieving an exogenously determined profile of benefits. To illustrate some of the key issues, the discussion will deal with the regional distribution of infrastructure investments; because it most clearly illustrates the arguments, the context will be that of a newly developing country (NIC) where growth has been concentrated in a large primate city – certainly not an unusual situation.[6]

The primate city generates numerous external economies and diseconomies of agglomeration. It may be that external economies are such that the further growth of a primate city would be efficient from a national perspective, in which case a decentralization policy would have to be justified on equity grounds. On the other hand, detractors of primate cities argue, at least implicitly, that the net marginal social product (marginal benefits minus marginal costs, including externalities) associated with a given infrastructural project in such a place is negative, so that from a national efficiency point of view the project should be located elsewhere. However, even if the net social marginal product is positive in a primate city, it would still be more efficient to locate the investment in another area if the marginal net social product were even greater in the latter.

In a country with a primate city, it is not likely that the rest of the national territory is homogeneous from a development perspective. For example, there may be some places with an existing, if modest, industrial base, or others with growth potential in agriculture; however, many areas will have few evident development advantages. In contrast to the primate city, the latter type of region will be termed lagging, while the former will be termed intermediate.

A further distinction can be made between two types of infrastructure: economic (EI) and social (SI). The former consists of projects that are immediately necessary for the development of directly productive activities. Such projects involve transportation, communications, power, irrigation, and similar undertakings. In contrast, SI consists of projects involving training, education, and health activities that are oriented towards the development of human resources. While the latter investments are needed for long-run economic development, they are not immediately needed for directly productive activities in the same way as EI.

Ideally, investment outlays in a country should be allocated so that the marginal social product of investments in EI, SI, and directly productive activities is the same for the last outlay in each case. In practice this is a difficult outcome to achieve, not least because of the difficulty in measuring externalities. In any event, the following analysis of some key issues in the spatial allocation of infrastructure assumes that the aggregate national amounts of EI and SI are exogenously determined; both the total amount of infrastructure investment and its division between EI and SI are a result of political decision-making processes.

Assuming a regional policy that, for equity or efficiency motives, has decentralization from the primate city as an objective, it would not be efficient to scatter scarce resources for EI over the entire country. Instead, EI should be concentrated in intermediate regions so that, in combination with existing factors of production, it can generate significant external economies of agglomeration and induce directly productive activities in a manner that would not be possible in lagging regions. This is in fact the main rationale for a growth-pole regional development strategy. Whatever the many deficiencies of lagging regions, their greatest needs, in relation to other areas, are for improvements in health and education. Thus, in cost-benefit terms it would be most efficient to concentrate SI in lagging regions. This would also be consistent with the equity orientation of the basic-needs approach to development. Of course, intermediate regions will need some SI and lagging regions will need some EI. The issue is one of relative emphasis.

In the long run, the growth of directly productive activities in intermediate regions will generate the means for expanded SI, so that such regions can eventually enjoy more balanced growth. The emphasis on SI in lagging regions that do not have much immediate development potential may result in out-migration, preferably to intermediate regions with expanding employment opportunities. In any event, investment in human resources gives people choices that they would not otherwise have. However, in the long run, EI investments can be shifted towards lagging regions so that they too can eventually experience more-balanced growth.

The theses that EI will have its greatest economic impact in intermediate regions and that SI will have its greatest economic impact in lagging regions have been tested by Looney and Frederiksen in the context of the Philippines and Mexico. In the case of the Philippines, Manila was taken to be the primate city, and the remaining provinces were grouped into either the intermediate or the lagging category on the basis of a cluster analysis. Controlling for population size, the study revealed that the relationship between variation in paved-road density, considered to be EI, and variation in per capita provincial income was statistically significant for the intermediate group of provinces, but not for the lagging group.[7] Similarly, variation in the amount of electrification investment, another form of EI, was significantly related to variation in per capita income (controlling for population size and area) within the group of intermediate provinces, but not within the group of lagging provinces.[8]

In the case of Mexico, Looney and Frederiksen considered Mexico City (the Federal District) to be the primate city; a cluster analysis was used to group Mexican states into either the intermediate or lagging regional category.[9] With the use of multiple regression analysis, a production function was estimated for the intermediate and lagging groups, respectively. The results, after controlling for other variables, indicated that the coefficient of each of the EI measures was statistically significant in explaining the within-group variation of per capita gross regional product in the intermediate group of states. In contrast, none of the coefficients of the EI variables was statistically significant in explaining variation in per capita gross regional product within the lagging group of states. A test for causality suggested that EI was the initiating factor in the development process in the intermediate regions, rather than a passive or induced phenomenon. On the other hand, none of the SI measures used was statistically significant in explaining variation in per capita gross regional product among intermediate regions. But each SI measure was significant in explaining such variation within the set of lagging regions. The authors point out that their results indicate that Mexico need not necessarily accept a lower rate of national growth in order to lessen regional economic disparities. Rather, the results suggest that by concentrating EI in intermediate regions and SI in lagging regions, "the implicit trade-off between growth and minimizing differences in income need not exist,"[10] and that these results could at least be used as an initial screening device in the evaluation of competing public sector projects. It may also be added that, in light of the findings of Looney and Frederiksen, valuable insights for regional development policy may be gained by further research on the differing impacts of public investments, by category of project and by type of region.

The Relatively Developed Country Context

While the regional infrastructure paradigm discussed in the previous section may also be relevant to countries that are relatively advanced economically, the latter context tends to be more complex than that in newly developing countries. A recent empirical study of public investment and regional development in the United States suggests that EI will not strongly induce development in lagging regions and that such outlays may be most efficient when located in intermediate regions.[11] In contrast, an analysis of infrastructural and regional development in France found no relationship between the characteristics of regions and the amounts of their infrastructure. In many instances, the lesser-developed regions were relatively well endowed with respect to infrastructure, suggesting that these projects may not have been efficient from a developmental perspective, though it is also possible that the level of development attained would have been lower in the absence of abundant infrastructure.[12] The French study made a distinction between infrastructure with a point location (hospitals, schools) and infrastructure that involved a network (roads, canals) or that had both of these characteristics (telecommunications). It did not attempt to make EI/SI distinctions as such, but the point-location infrastructure tends to be SI, whereas the network infrastructure tends to be EI. To the extent that EI investments in lagging French regions were inefficient, this would be consistent with the arguments presented earlier concerning the need to be more spatially selective with respect to EI undertakings. However, the issue of SI investments in lagging regions of economically advanced countries merits further discussion.

The point that the objectives of national economic growth and of the reduction of regional income disparities through emphasis on SI in lagging regions can be mutually consistent "is particularly important because it is well known that interregional disparities in social indicators (such as social service facilities, e.g. hospital beds, schools) are much wider in developing countries than disparities in per capita income."[13] But such conditions are not limited to newly developing countries. They can also be found in the United States. For example, a recent study of the central Appalachian portion of Virginia found a "desperate situation" with respect to unemployment and poverty, a situation that also applies to the Appalachian parts of Kentucky and West Virginia.[14] Over twenty years ago, I stressed that Great Society regional development programs for Appalachia (and for other impoverished areas, e.g., Indian reservations, much of the rural South, and south Texas) should have emphasized SI rather than EI.[15] The major Appalachian regional development legislation passed in 1965 emphasized highway construction (EI) as the key to development, and most of the federally funded, development-oriented infrastructure outlays in the region have been devoted to highways.[16] The record of this approach is clear. While it has no doubt brought some benefits to Appalachia, it has not adequately addressed the most fundamental problems of the most poverty-stricken Appalachian areas. So, a generation later, it is being rediscovered that investments in human resources are the "most critical" need if these areas are to have a brighter future.[17]

The French case represents a significant contrast to that just discussed. In France, indices of SI development tend to be relatively high in southern regions, which in the past were considered to be less-developed areas. Such indices are relatively low in the long-industrialized regions of northern France – excluding the Paris region.[18] While the southern regions still have lower per capita incomes than the old industrial regions, in recent years the southern regions have been experiencing the most rapid development among all regions, whereas the old industrial regions have been stagnating or declining. The south's geographic amenities (mountains, sea, attractive landscapes) and its relatively high level of social development have been associated with a surge of development-inducing entrepreneurship. In light of these phenomena, there has been a shift in emphasis in French regional economic theory away from traditional firm-location theory in favour of theories concerning the development of an innovative milieu.[19] In this context it is not appropriate to make broadly regional generalizations with respect to the developmental and equity aspects of infrastructure investments. Account needs to be taken of a wide variety of local situations.

In the case of Canada, the wide differences in provincial public services that existed as recently as a generation ago have been virtually eliminated.[20] Nevertheless, the Atlantic provinces continue to be in a relatively unfavourable position in terms of per capita income and unemployment. It might be argued that because the developmental payoffs from SI investments are long term in nature, the Atlantic provinces have simply not had sufficient time for the equalization of public services to accelerate development, but in any event the EI/SI regional investment paradigm discussed earlier does not appear to be applicable to the current Canadian economy. Moreover, it is pertinent to point out that "a great number" of quality-of-life indicators "clearly favor the traditionally have-not regions."[21] This suggests that if account is taken of psychic income, the disparities among Canadian regions may well be less than would be implied by the usual economic indicators. Martin argues that seemingly disadvantaged residents of Canada's economically weaker regions who enjoy local non-economic amenities and refuse to migrate to more prosperous areas are in part stowaways. "In order not to be 'stowaways,' it would be required that these persons do as the Amish and Hutterites, who also attach value to their mode of life but do not demand subsidies for their local community enterprises."[22] It would indeed appear that the grounds for subsidies to the Atlantic provinces rest more on political factors than on those of an economic nature, unless they can, as they have not in the past, be utilized to assist these areas "in integrating their economies more successfully into the national economy and in supporting regional growth from within."[23]

CONCLUSIONS

Western European survey data indicate that even though the strongest geographic attachment of most people is to their own locality or region, there is nonetheless a pronounced willingness to be taxed to support regional development policies for economically lagging regions. Rather than regarding such choices as non-rational, if not irrational, it is argued here that they are consistent with fairness and superfairness theory, which tends to support the equity judgments of non-economist observers concerning many public preference patterns.

Moreover, regional policies do not necessarily have to sacrifice national development objectives to interregional equity objectives. For example, infrastructure development policy that emphasizes SI in lagging regions and EI in intermediate regions can be both equitable and efficient from a national perspective. The case in this regard is perhaps strongest in the newly developing country context, but this approach may also be relevant in some economically advanced countries, (e.g., the United States). In countries such as Canada, where infrastructural development is widely diffused and where the level of public services is virtually the same in all regions, it is more difficult to justify regional subsidies to lagging regions on economic grounds, especially when quality-of-life indicators (and presumably psychic income) are relatively high in these areas. Nevertheless, questions of fairness arise if alleviation of regional economic disparities is regarded by the general population as part of the social contract for national cohesion. But the extent to which fairness or superfairness exists depends on the attitudes towards regional development subsidies of those who do the subsidizing, and although such evidence is available for the European Community, it is lacking for Canada.

National efficiency normally implies the maximization of the gross national product. A more complete measure of national net economic welfare would need to adjust the GNP by adding in such items as the value of leisure and housewives' services and subtracting out such items as unmet costs of pollution, urban congestion, and the destruction of environmental amenities. However, whether one wishes to consider national efficiency in terms of the GNP or national net economic welfare, questions of interregional equity will still remain. If individuals in more-developed regions derive satisfaction from subsidizing less-developed regions out of a sense of fairness, then so far as these individuals are concerned, there need be no conflict between equity and efficiency. But not all individuals in the more-developed regions will wish to subsidize less-developed regions. Conflicts will remain that have no simple scientific resolution. The question of how much to pay for equity is one that must be decided through a political process. The tools of public economics have been improved by complementing sharp economic analysis with an equivalent input of social ethics. As Kolm has suggested, the next step is "to work out the consequences of a much richer and more truthful account of man's motives and capacities, along with an understanding and a consideration of institutions, both meaning psychology since it is how institutions enter into an individualistic social theory: through people's heads and hearts."[24]

NOTES

1 William J. Baumol, *Superfairness: Applications and Theory* (Cambridge: MIT Press, 1986), 205.

2 Envy of *B* by *A* is defined as $U^a (b) > + U^a (a)$, where *A* and *B* are, respectively, individuals assigned commodity bundles *a* and *b*, and U^a and U^b are their respective utility functions. It may be noted that this definition of envy involves no interpersonal comparisons of utility.

3 Donald J. Savoie, *Regional Economic Development: Canada's Search for Solutions* (Toronto: University of Toronto Press, 1986), 137.

4 Ibid., 139.

5 Baumol, *Superfairness*, 254.

6 The development via the regionally differentiated infrastructure paradigm outlined here was first presented in Niles Hansen, "The Structure and Determinants of Local Public Investment Expenditures," *Review of Economics and Statistics* 47, no. 2 (May 1965): 150–62; and idem, "Unbalanced Growth and Regional Development," *Western Economic Journal* 4, no. 1 (Fall 1965): 3–14.

7 Peter Frederiksen and Robert Looney, "Road Investment and Regional Economic Development: A Philippine Case Study," *International Journal of Transport Economics* 9, no. 3 (December 1982): 335–47.

8 Peter Frederiksen, "Electrification and Regional Economic Development in the Philippines," *Journal of Philippine Development* 12, no. 2 (1985): 409–17.

9 Robert Looney and Peter Frederiksen, "The Regional Impact of Infrastructure Investment in Mexico," *Regional Studies* 15, no. 4 (1981): 285–96.

10 Ibid., 295.

11 Jose da Silva Costa, Richard W. Ellson, and Randolph C. Martin, "Public Capital, Regional Output, and Development: Some Empirical Evidence," *Journal of Regional Science* 27, no. 3 (August 1987): 419–37.

12 Françoise Navarre and Rémy Prud'homme, "Le rôle des infrastructures dans le développement régional," *Revue d'économie régional et urbaine*, no. 1 (1984): 5–22.

13 Harry W. Richardson and Peter M. Townroe, "Regional Policies in Developing Countries," in Peter Nijkamp ed., *Handbook of Regional and Urban Economics* 1 (Amsterdam: North-Holland, 1986), 1:663.

14 B. Drummond Ayres, Jr., "Virginia Coal Region's Progress Slow," *New York Times*, 28 December 1987, 9.

15 Niles Hansen, "Some Neglected Factors in American Regional Development Policy: The Case of Appalachia," *Land Economics* 42, no. 1 (February 1966): 1–9; and idem, *Rural Poverty and the Urban Crisis: A Strategy for Regional Development* (Bloomington: Indiana University Press, 1970).

16 Appalachian Regional Commission, "Appalachia: Twenty Years of Progress," special number of *Appalachia* 18, no. 3 (March 1985): 106.

17 Ayres, *Virginia Coal*.

18 Commissariat général du plan, *Rapport du groupe de travail disparités spatiales* (Paris: La Documentation Française, 1984), 97.

19 See, for example, Philippe Aydalot, "Crise économique, crise de l'espace, crise de la pensée spatiale," in Bernard Planque, ed., *Le développement décentralisé* (Paris: Presses universitaires de France, 1983), 87–105; and Jean-Claude Perrin, "La reconversion du bassin industriel d'Alès: Contribution à une théorie de la dynamique locale," *Revue d'économie régionale et urbaine*, no. 2, (1984): 237–56.

20 Savoie, *Regional Economic Development*, 22.

21 Ibid., 141.

22 Fernand Martin, "L'entrepreneurship et le développement local: Une évaluation," *Canadian Journal of Regional Science* 9, no. 1 (Spring 1986): 12.

23 Savoie, *Regional Economic Development*, 22.

24 Serge Christophe Kolm, "Public Economics," in John Eatwell, Murray Milgate, and Peter Newman, eds., *The New Palgrave: A Dictionary of Economics* (New York: Stockton Press, 1987), 3:1053.

9 Equity, Efficiency, and the Managerial Paradigm

ROBIN MARRIS

It comes as a surprise to neuro-scientists to discover that many psychologists, linguists in particular, have very little or no interest in the actual brain, or at least what goes on inside it. The brain, they feel, is far too complicated to understand. Far better to produce simple models which can do the job in an intelligible manner. That such models may have little resemblance to the way the brain actually behaves is not seen as a serious criticism. If it describes, in a succinct way, the psychological data, what can be wrong with that? Notice, however, that by using such arguments, one could easily make a good case for alchemy or for the existence of phlogiston.[1]

EQUITY, EFFICIENCY, AND BEN HIGGINS

I cannot forbear from beginning this essay with some remarks about its honorandum. I am supposedly an expert in the economic theory of the modern corporation. I have done some work in the "globalony" of development economics, but almost none in the field of the actual development process in actual Third World countries. Furthermore, the theory with which my name is associated is not at first sight very relevant to the problems of Third World countries. It is potentially more relevant to mid-range countries or newly industrialized countries (NICs), and also, probably to NDSs ("newly de-socialized countries"); it is relevant too as a base from which to discuss the future of industrial organization in a world where high technology may have reduced the minimum efficient scale for effective administrative units.

However, I lack the basic qualifications for a contributor to this book and properly should have declined the invitation. But that was quite impossible because Ben Higgins is one of my oldest friends; that I greatly admire him as an economist goes without saying. Our early meetings were quite intense; later they took on a cycle of about forty-eight hours every ten years, but the friendship has remained as strong.

We first met in the latter part of the Second World War when I was posted to Montreal as a Royal Air Force transatlantic delivery pilot. The stock of aircrew had become excessive relative to the flow of aircraft, so having time to spare and having done a year of economics at Cambridge (England) before joining up, I brashly looked up the first McGill economics professor I could find in the phone book (I was looking for Keirstead, but H for Higgins came first), and asked if I could sit in on classes. I was received with the greatest possible warmth and attended Ben's excellent course on pre- and post-Keynesian trade-cycle theory. I especially remember his devastating critique of Hayek.

From this relationship of pupilage there developed a friendship based on other interests, and I was always rather jealous of Ben's Renaissance qualities. One of the interests we shared was the cosmopolitan night life of Montreal, especially chasing the opposite sex, but Ben always seemed to win out. He had an excellent circle of friends, and I was welcomed warmly into his family, with whom I am still in touch down to the third generation.

Some subsequent spasmodic meetings were quite memorable. Once Ben came to dinner in a tiny two-room London flat. The phone was in the living-dining room, and at a certain point the guests had to retire to the bedroom while Ben phoned Australia and talked for twenty minutes, I believe attempting a marriage proposal to his present wife, Jean. On another occasion, when I was living in Grantchester, outside Cambridge, Ben called out of the blue from London airport to say he was between planes (and developing countries) – could he come down for the night? In fact he was seriously ill. The Indonesian amoeba had broken into his liver. A clutch of professors of tropical medicine gathered around and he was kept in a national health isolation hospital for some weeks.

HIGGINS IN THE ROLE OF HOST TO A NEAR STILL BIRTH

Another occasion was especially memorable for me, and actually relevant to this essay, for it saw the first public appearance of the theory on which the essay is based. After producing and privately circulating a first draft of *Managerial Capitalism*, around 1960, I decided to become a Marshall scholar and tout the work around the United States. I took it *inter alia* to Berkeley and to Harvard; in the latter place, Jim Duesenberry invited me to prepare the paper that subsequently became "Marris, *QJE*, 1963," the most that most people have read of my theory. Towards the end of the seminar, J.K. Galbraith came into the room and subsequently xeroxed my notes. As a result, in

The New Industrial Estate, only three economists get acknowledgments, Smith, Schumpeter, and Marris. And I won hands down over those others – three footnotes, no less, with the reference differently wrong in each.

But before visiting the great places of the United States, I had decided to have a trial run at the home of my old friend Higgins, now mysteriously transformed into economics chairman at the University of Texas. With my then wife, Jane, and six-months-old babe, we spent a hilarious sojourn in Austin through Christmas 1960–61. Among other adventures, we drove *a quâtre* (plus various children) to Acapulco and back.

The unveiling of *Managerial Capitalism* eventually occurred, sometime in the fall of 1960 at a University of Texas Economics Department seminar starting around 3:00 p.m. I didn't feel I was making much impression on the audience and was further mortified when, part way through the discussion period, a distinguished figure arose and said, "Well I guess it's time for us all to get home." It was the late Clarence Ayres. I did not understand that in Austin 5:30 p.m. was dinner time.

Since then, both Ben and I have had our academic vicissitudes. His development economics work has been gradually established as classic. My theory had a truly mixed reception, but because it is a very good theory, I am glad to report that twenty-five years later it remains basically unchanged, and its citations performance is moderately increasing rather than diminishing: a new edition is currently in process of publication (see note 8 below). I believe this will please Ben Higgins, who a few years after that fateful seminar, asked me rather plaintively what had happened to it!

The theory was developed during the time, 1955–60, when Oliver Williamson, ten years younger, was gestating *The Economics of Discretionary Behaviour* and thus laying the foundations for his subsequently great career as a rival contributor to this field – the field, that is, which tries to incorporate into economics proper the self-evident fact that the organization of real-life, modern, developed economies bears no resemblance whatsoever to the examplar that is implicit even to this day in almost every textbook on theoretical microeconomics: that is, the paradigm of a system of production agents who are owner-managed, single-product, small, numerous, subject to diminishing returns to scale, and more or less symmetrically size-distributed.

THE MANAGERIAL THEORY

The managerial theory is an integrated theory that sees the firm as a financially autonomous administrative organization subject to almost no constraints on its ultimate size, but subject to determinate constraints on its rate of growth. The institution is inherently set up to want to grow, to be able to grow, and often to be forced to grow. The firm's success in growing will of course be subject to all kinds of shocks and disturbances, so the size distribution that we actually see – in natural numbers grotesquely skewed, in logarithms roughly symmetrical – is inevitable. The size distribution is the result of a stochastic process whereby disturbances to the exogenous factors in the growth rates of firms generate a form of Markov chain in the logs of the sizes of firms, a process in which the variance of the logs of size will tend to be continuously increasing. The increasing variance of a logarithmic distribution, implies large and increasing skewness (= inequality = concentration) in the natural numbers.[2]

The peculiar feature of the corporate constitution – namely, the existence of a body of shareholders with no collective rights and with individual rights strictly confined to equitable voting and equitable shares in distributed profits – is an essential element in the theory. Notice we emphasize legal reality, rather than neoclassical ideal; the result is potent but "different," creating not only the stock market, not only the take-over raid, but also a special theoretical interaction between the policy of the firm (i.e., of the management) on the one hand and its stock market value on the other. The resulting market for corporate control is highly important but inherently imperfect.

F.M. Scherer, in flattering language, recently credited me with having "discovered" the corporate-control market before it had attracted the attention of economists. Unfortunately, no doubt quite innocently, he suggested that I had implied that this "third market" could be seen as "correcting" other market failures, notably in the market for goods. Scherer used some syntax that could be taken to mean that, rather than giving my own interpretation of my own theory, he was giving his. But all such ambiguity was subsequently firmly removed in an account printed in the *New York Times*. Neoclassicism thus dealt me a final punishment: I am depicted as its saviour![3] In fact, in the 1960s, I had not ventured into the field of take-over theory from the side of the acquiring firm; my interest was mainly confined to the role of take-over as a restraint or limitation on managerial power in acquirable firms. On the acquiring side of the subject, the crucial contribution came from Dennis Mueller. It is to his extremely important paper, written in the late 1960s,[4] that one must look for a true understanding of what we now see happening in the 1980s: that is to say, the manic behaviour of acquiring corporations is not to be explained by desires to benefit their own shareholders (who nearly always lose out) but by the acquiring management's desire for power and benefits, including unpoliceable opportunities for insider dealing by themselves or their "financial advisers."

When all the financial and physical aspects of the managerial theory are brought together, it turns out to be possible to represent the stock market value of the firm as an explicit function of the firm's expected physical growth rate. Although the original theory was often criticized for excessive complexity, here we have a fortunate simplicity: the two variables thus traded off, stock market value and growth rate, can be taken to summarize both the stockholders' interest and the managerial-constraint system – management benefits from growth on account of the prospective increase in privileges and earnings, but also suffers if stock market value is low because a low stock price increases the hazard of take-over, that is, increases the risk that at some future date the expected stream of managerial benefits will be terminated (the theory relates to high management, who, after a take-over, are almost always dismissed – a fact that explains why high management nearly always resist take-overs, irrespective of the interests of shareholders).

We can thus find a growth rate that maximizes shareholders' utility and we can find another that maximizes managerial utility, that is, represents the policy that will actually be pursued. The growth rate, in turn, controls many other variables that are strategic in the theory of the firm and of major importance to both macro- and microeconomics: investment, research and development, market promotion, diversification, and profit distribution.

The following material, based on a synthesis of my own ideas and of those, such as H. Odagiri,[5] who have contributed to the field, is currently used to instruct those interested in exploring these ideas. I think that this material is by and large self-explanatory.

ORIGINS OF THE MANAGERIAL ECONOMY

BUSINESS ENTERPRISE AFTER THE INDUSTRIAL REVOLUTION

(During the 19th century few industrial producer-organizations were listed as shareholder corporations; most were considered as bureaucratic hierarchies; they were typically still quite small.)
(Around 1900 only a small proportion of manufacturing industry was represented on the stock exchanges of the US and Europe.)
(In the UK only 15% and in the US 20% of total industrial assets were in the hands of the 100 largest industrial companies.)

After 1900

| Spread of Bureaucratic Hierarchies | Spread of the Quoted Company |

| Increasing Merger Activity | Increasing Diversification |

Increasing Profit Retention

The Organizational Revolution

THE ORGANIZATIONAL REVOLUTION 1900–1950

CONSTANT OR INCREASING RETURNS TO SCALE
LONG-TERM GROWTH OF FIRMS
OLIGOPOLY
Micro and Macro Industrial Concentration
Managerial Motivation in the Behaviour of the Firm
Growth Efforts of Firms =
R&D, Marketing, Diversification, Investment >
Growth Performance of the Macroeconomy
All Leading To
THE MANAGERIAL PARADIGM

Leading to:

I   A view of the firm as a managerial producer-organization
II   A view of the structure of the economy
III   A growth-oriented theory of the firm
IV   A firm-oriented theory of macro growth

THE MANAGERIAL VIEW OF THE FIRM

The firm is an operational team in which the agenda, information, and initiation procedure for decisions is mainly controlled by the same people who will carry the decisions out, i.e., the full-time high and high-middle management. The operations are decided by the operators.

Quite significantly, these people are also the initiators of proposals concerning monitoring and incentives, including the monitoring of their own performance and their own incentives (e.g. share options and profit-bonus schemes). The reason for this situation is that only these people have the time and resources to access and adequately to evaluate the required information.

In other words, the people in a society who are in a position to initiate schemes for controlling the "agency problem" are, in fact, professional agents.

Given this starting point, we then recognize numerous powerful influences, restraints, and constraints upon the decisions that are made and on the way they are executed.

Such influences include the mass of shareholders through their influence on the market price of the shares (which latter feeds back in various ways, onto the situation of the management), individual large shareholders, middle and lower employees, and, through imperfect competition, customers.

For example, in the managerial paradigm, rather than asking "How can shareholders control managers?" we ask, "What are the limits on managers' powers to pacify shareholders?" Although the two questions may seem similar, their effects on economic theory and research are in practice very different.

THE INDUSTRIAL STRUCTURE

"Firms"		"Industries" (= Products)		
(= Producer-orgs)		j	M	Row Total
1	v_1	etc.	etc.	x_1
.				
i	v_{i1}	v_{ij} (value-added)	$v_{i\alpha}$	x_i
.				
N	$v_{\alpha 1}$	etc.	etc.	
Column total y_1		y_j		$\Sigma y = \Sigma x =$ prod.-org. GDP

Competitive paradigm (also neoclassical oligopoly-IO paradigm): There is only one column entry per row but there are many row entries in each column.

Managerial Paradigm (also Institutionalists, ? Marxists): There is general scatter – although diversified firms do specialize in various ways, it is difficult, if not impossible, to create a method of calssifying and ordering the product list as in traditional industrial classifications, hence the bunching pattern is uncertain.

The entity operating in a single cell, whether part of a larger organization or not, is sometimes called a QUASI-FIRM.

"Entry," "Diversification," Conglomeration: The table is continually changing owing to different factors that are often confused in current theory and terminology. Mergers amalgamate rows. Genuine new firms add to the columns. Any organization may "diversify" by "entering" an existing column (thus potentially increasing competition in that "industry"), or by creating a new product (new column). The economic implications of all these are distinct.

Concentration: Micro or "industrial" concentration is measured down columns, macro or "business' concentration, down the row totals.

THE THEORY OF THE GROWTH OF THE FIRM

```
┌─────────────────────────────┐
│        STOCK MARKET         │
│       (Cash In–Out,         │
│        Take-Overs)          │
└─────────────────────────────┘

  ┌─────────────────────────┐
  │      HEADQUARTERS       │
  │      (Cash Pool)        │
  └─────────────────────────┘
```

```
┌──────────────────┐        ┌──────────────────┐
│   OPERATIONS     │        │      GROWTH      │
│  (Production,    │        │ (R&D, Investment,│
│   Pricing, etc.) │        │   Take-overs)    │
└──────────────────┘        └──────────────────┘
```

```
┌──────────────────────────────────┐
│     EXPECTED GROWTH RATE          │
│                                   │
│  Expected Path and Uncertainty of │
│             Dividends             │
│        > Stock Market Value       │
│       = SHAREHOLDER UTILITY       │
│                                   │
│  Expected Path and Uncertainty of │
│            Management             │
│             Earnings              │
│        + Hazard of Take-over      │
│       = MANAGEMENT UTILITY        │
└──────────────────────────────────┘
```

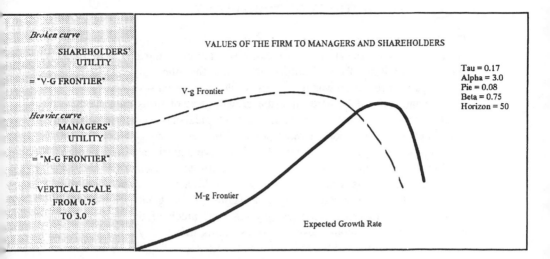

Broken curve

SHAREHOLDERS'
UTILITY

= "V-G FRONTIER"

Heavier curve
MANAGERS'
UTILITY

= "M-G FRONTIER"

VERTICAL SCALE
FROM 0.75
TO 3.0

VALUES OF THE FIRM TO MANAGERS AND SHAREHOLDERS

Tau = 0.17
Alpha = 3.0
Pie = 0.08
Beta = 0.75
Horizon = 50

V-g Frontier

M-g Frontier

Expected Growth Rate

EQUATIONS OF THE FRONTIERS

V = stock-market value of the firm, normalized by assets

V^* = value of V when maximized

π = shareholders and managers future consumption discount rate

M = normalized present value of expected future management emoluments, adjusted for take-over risk

τ = current operating profit normalized by

g = expected long-run growth rate of firm

a = coefficient (≥ 0) reflecting intensity of costs of growth if a = 0, growth costs = conventional investment; if a > 0, growth costs exceed conventional investment

B = coefficient (≥ 0) reflecting intensity of the take-over market; $B = \infty$ implies perfect market; B small implies imperfect market

h = time-horizon in years

$$V = [\tau - g - (ag)^2] \sum_{t=o}^{t=h} e^{(g-\pi)t} \qquad (1) - \text{``V-g Frontier''}$$

$$M = (1/10)[V/V^*]^B \sum_{t=o}^{t=h} e^{(g-\pi)t} \qquad (2) - \text{``M-g Frontier''}$$

Note: The model assumes all growth to be internally financed. Under managerial optimization, the selected growth-rate, g^*, is g [max M]. The profit retention ratio is g^*/τ.

PREDICTIONS OF THE THEORY

The foregoing theory has been accused of lacking "useful" predictions. What this usually means is it is lacking predictions lying inside the neo-classical paradigm. Robert Solow once said that the only qualitatively unambiguous prediction was that firms would grow faster – so what?[6]

So what, indeed! It is true that the growth rates of firms may not have much effect on variables of typical interest in typical classroom microeconomics,[7] but they are of considerable potential interest in areas which (unlike much classroom microeconomics) are of massive significance to economic welfare, for example, in the theory of macro growth. Essentially I see the managerial theory as a more realistic general description of the economic processes determining the strategic decisions of the giant firms that so influence our modern economies. By contrast, much of the neoclassical implicit theorizing about these questions seems naive. If you have a bad theory you can never tell when it is going to bite you.

More explicitly, looking back to the diagram above, the reason why the managerial optimum growth rate has to be greater or equal to the shareholders' optimum growth rate is that while managers benefit from growth (in time-discounted gains in material and other benefits), unlike shareholders they are not required to contribute from their own current consumption to the costs of growth. Rather the constraint is that if they do too much damage to the shareholders, there will be a take-over. In the model above, the risk of take-over increases, with an intensity reflected by the coefficient Beta, as and when the value to the shareholders (V-g Frontier) falls below its maximum. The discounted managerial benefits must be adjusted for this risk of take-over. Thus the "M-g Frontier" is derived from the "V-g Frontier."[8] If Beta is large, the effect is intense, and the optimum growth rate for management will be pulled towards equality with the shareholders' optimum (it could never fall below). Thus the Beta coefficient reflects all the various institutional factors in the stock market that see to it that in real life a take-over bidder must pay substantially more than the current market value.

But the theory is trying to do much more than conclude whether one growth rate will be higher than another. It claims to be a general description of the forces tending to encourage, or to discourage, as the case may be, the growth rates of firms. This is illustrated in the second graphic. Firms will grow less fast, for example, if Beta is larger; thus, societies with weak institutional barriers to take-over – meaning a less imperfect market for corporate control – will tend to have firms whose desired and actual micro-growth rates will be slower than would otherwise be the case: see left-moved curve. This means less investment, less research and development effort.

Similarly, firms will desire to and succeed in growing faster if the various costs and barriers to micro growth are relatively moderate (right-moved curve). Societies that develop socio/administrative techniques for smooth growth, with minimum "Penrose effect,"[9] will have faster-growing firms.

Finally, firms will grow faster if they can earn good profits (the coefficient Tau) relative to the real rate of interest (the coefficient Pie). The idea that high real interest rates discourage economic growth is hardly new, and yet it is an idea that is, in fact, quite elusive in neoclassical statics. In the latter type of economics, with embellishment or resort to particular models of risk and uncertainty, one is typically left in the intellectual situation that investment will occur if and when the real return (marginal productivity of capital) exceeds the real interest rate, and will continue until the real return has been reduced as a result of moving along a frontier. Such models are then typically dynamized by assuming that the frontier is moving out at a rate that is directly or indirectly (vintage models, learning by doing) exogenous. They have no capacity whatsoever to address the crucial links between the *strengths* of growth encouraging/discouraging forces (as reflected in the sort of coefficients I set out above) and the rates of growth; yet it is just such links, from micro dynamics to macro dynamics, that are the necessary key (as I know Ben Higgins agrees) to unlocking the mysteries of development.

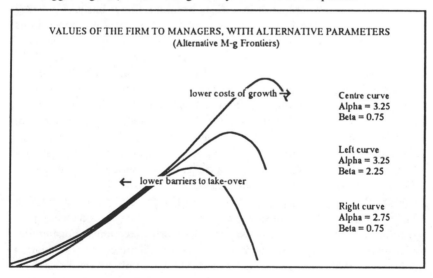

VALUES OF THE FIRM TO MANAGERS, WITH ALTERNATIVE PARAMETERS
(Alternative M-g Frontiers)

lower costs of growth →

Centre curve
Alpha = 3.25
Beta = 0.75

Left curve
Alpha = 3.25
Beta = 2.25

← lower barriers to take-over

Right curve
Alpha = 2.75
Beta = 0.75

THE MANAGERIAL PARADIGM AND MODERN CAPITALISM

The "managerialist" attitude to the form of capitalism we see around us is pragmatic, sceptical, admiring, non-idealistic. As a system for delivering benefits to disadvantaged groups, it is at least as successful as known and observed alternatives, such as the centrally planned socialism of the years

1950–80. Competition is generally beneficial, provided it is benignly medi-ated (absence of competition, we know, is bad, especially for X-Efficiency). But perfect competition is certainly impossible and probably undesirable. The reality, which is competition among giants (i.e., managerial capitalism), is probably, on balance, as good an economic system as one is likely to get. Given that fact, and given that this is in any case not only the system we have but also the system we are probably going to have for many centuries yet, the task of the economist is to analyse this system, not some alternative imagin-ary ideal-type. Furthermore, the methodology of attempting, for the sake of convenience (*pace* Francis Crick, above), to model the system *as if* it were otherwise, as if it were "competitive," is not merely inaccurate but mislead-ing.

I believe that the air of unrealism that pervades the neoclassical literature is at heart due to the profession's habit of taking itself too seriously. We are set up as a discipline for analysing markets. After listening (at McGill in 1944) to a devastating critique of the early work of Hayek by a brilliant lecturer named Benjamin Higgins, I have always been startled by the great baron's subsequent fame. The market is not a "marvel"; it is a convenience. When properly mediated, it is indeed an excellent thing, but it is patently obvious that in all the business of human life "non-market" transactions outnumber market transactions by several orders of magnitude. We humans live permanently in a welter of incomplete "contracts" and reasonably benign discretionary decision taking. How do we survive? We survive because although we have permanently conflicting interests (most especially within small organizations, like families), we have to cooperate. And co-operate we do. Why? Because we are playing a repeating non-zero-sum game. Formal theory tells us that in a repeating game among rational self-interested players, cooperative play is inevitable: if competitive play emerges, the players must be misguided. They are equally misguided if they spend too much of their time worrying about contracts.

When I graduated from Cambridge (England) after parting from Ben Higgins in the 1940s, I foresaw the science of economics as a steady pro-gression in elaborating the analysis of the imperfect economy. For familiar mathematical reasons (and lack of access to computers for simulation studies), the task was bound to be difficult, but one simply assumed that there was no other direction to go. The neoclassical revival was not only a com-plete surprise, like the recent so-called pro-life movement, it seemed a pure regression. But in the intervening years, the neoclassical movement moti-vated so much elegant work that I and many others wavered. Now, in retrospect, and with the greatest affection and respect for my many neo-classical friends, I, for one, revert to my original reaction of shocked disap-proval. I think that, as a profession, in our desire to be "scientific" we achieved the opposite. And as a final shaft, I conclude this polemical digression with another quotation from Crick: "I suspect that with most modellers a frustrated mathematician is trying to unfold its wings. It is not enough to make something that works. How much better if it can be shown to embody some powerful general principle ... if only to give an air of authority to an otherwise rather low-brow enterprise."[10] I think we should invite Francis to address the annual meeting of the AEA!

THE MANAGERIAL PARADIGM AND THE TCE[11] PARADIGM

Oliver Williamson[12] takes the normative view that "managerial discretion" is a fact of life and that the task of the economist is to discover ways of controlling it. This position implies of course that the exercise of managerial discretion is necessarily harmful to society. The corporation presents its "owners" with an agency problem: in possibly failing to maximize the shareholders interests, and thus failing to behave like a neoclassical firm, it (the corporation) Pareto-damages the economy in equal proportion. In the work of Oliver Williamson it is argued that market transactions require complete (i.e., clear-cut) contracts, but that in many cases these are unfeasible or undesirable. Within-firm activities, or non-market transactions, can successfully operate less formally, but may give rise to discretion. It can be seen that in a highly sophisticated and elegant way, all this remains squarely within the neoclassical paradigm: unless the corporation does exactly what a neoclassical owner-manager would do in comparable circumstances, it must violate Arrow-Debreu.

The differences between this type of approach and what I now modestly call the "Managerial" paradigm may explain some but not all of the difficulties the managerial theory has faced in the economics profession. The managerial approach is non-idealistic and consequently lacks an ideological constituency. It is no more popular among neo-Marxists than among neo-classicists. It agrees with Oliver Williamson only at the starting point, namely that managerial power (notice the semantic shift) is indeed a fact of life, on account of the pervasive and overriding reason that "them that do, decide." The full-time professionals at the top of any organization hold most of the initiative. Quite especially, as supposed "agents," they control the initiative concerning incentive structures. The "agency problem" is inherently insoluble because the only people available to devise and implement schemes for controlling it are those of the agent class themselves.[13] And even if the agency problem could be solved, there is absolutely no reason to pursue the solutions. Why? Because it is quite impossible to show, under the "inevitable" institutions of managerial capitalism, that to do so would be beneficial to society. As we shall see below, it is probably the case that the less the interests of shareholders dominate the decisions of corporations, the better!

MANAGERIALISM AND CYCLICAL MACROECONOMICS

Microfoundations

One "prediction" of the managerial theory is so obvious that its deeper significance is often missed. This is the prediction that in respect of almost any economic activity, there always exists some technical or administrative means by which the activity may be conducted under conditions that make diminishing returns to scale more or less impossible. Since the replication theorem[14] disposes of the technical side, only administrative factors remain to "explain" static diminishing returns (to scale); and they do not.[15] Exceptions exist where there is some combination of sociological and technical factors that prevents the transition from owner-management to manager-management.[16] As already emphasized, the essence of the managerial theory is that the crucial force in this area of economics is not a restraint on size, but on rate of change of size. This means that huge numbers of small and medium, wholly or partly owner-managed firms will always co-exist with the giants. Only a tiny minority will graduate to gianthood. And owing to the skewedness of the resulting size distribution, minnows, however valuable, produce only a relatively small proportion of total output. They are, however, *qualitatively* vital; without them, "managerial" capitalism would atrophy. And it is the system of dynamic restraint that ensures that although the system always appears as if it were converging to a state of total monopoly it not only never reaches this state, but never approaches it.[17]

It follows that a high degree of oligopoly throughout the goods-production-and-sale sector of the economy is inevitable. Again, few disagree with this proposition as a practical fact, but it is the conventional professional wisdom that the implications are confined to that special down-market branch of microeconomics known as "IO" (industrial organization). The proposition that it was undesirable to base conventional cyclical macroeconomics on patently impossible competitive micro foundations has, these twenty years past, cut little ice.

In the event, we have another outstanding example of devastating but unseen damage done by bad theory. Because, at the time, one could not see how it could matter, one decided that one might as well soldier on with perfect competition. Enormous harm to the subject, let alone thousands of wasted academic person-hours, resulted. Only relatively recently (1980s) has this chicken (but it is not a chicken, it is a monster) come home to roost.

The essential problem is that if we define "perfect competition" as *literally* meaning price taking, there is no general micro-foundation story that will permit a Keynesian slump. On price-taking assumptions, a fall in macro demand is experienced by micro sellers as a decline in the quantity that the macro goods-market can actually absorb, which means that micro sellers will find part of their current offerings unsold. But according to the rules of this game, unless or until there is a change in the ratio between nominal ruling price and nominal marginal costs, sellers must continue with the same offerings. If then, via some quasi-Walrasian process, the general price level does fall, it falls in all markets, including the labour market; hence the ratio of prices to costs is unchanged. Consequently, in the absence of special assumptions concerning relative adjustment rates, there is no change in profit-maximizing micro quantities-supplied; so if firms continue to profit-maximize, the whole effect of the fall in aggregate demand is taken on prices. The neo-Walrasian scenario ends, of course, with a real-balance effect restoring real demand and the aforementioned head scratching conclusion that slumps are impossible. And as we all know, the head scratching has involved an enormous industry, located across the world – Paris, Los Angeles, Chicago (I spare no one, including many good friends) – for producing weird and wonderful ways around the conundrum. Once, however, we import imperfect competition and suppose that the change in macro demand manifests itself as an income effect that shifts the demand curves (downward sloping, with any elasticity short of infinity) facing price-*setting* producers, the conundrum disappears. Without any significant difficulty, the Keynesian theory immediately "works" without the need for any special assumptions – sticky wages, dual decisions, disequilibrium, and so on.

But Keynes wrote those much-studied passages that seem to imply that he firmly believed that his theory did *not* depend on imperfect competition. At times I have thought he was playing a joke on us. I still have my copy of *General Theory*, heavily annotated with puzzlement, as from time to time I studied it while crossing the Atlantic (having set my aircraft to autopilot). I don't remember if we discussed the problem in Ben's class at McGill. I do remember that returning to take up my studies in Cambridge after the war, I eventually got to have weekly tutorials with Richard Kahn and he never raised the subject. In those days, most of us regarded the theory of perfect competition as dead as the Dodo, so the question of its macro implications simply never came up. In truth, as I have argued in a recent book, once one had imperfect competition, it was never necessary to "reconsider" Keynes.[18]

This story is distinctly relevant to the topic of equity, efficiency and managerialism, as may be seen via the following steps. First, the economics profession's state of disarray, evident since around 1970, concerning the micro foundations of Keynes has been responsible for the decline of influence of Keynesian policy economists. This in turn has deprived the world's governments of the coherent advice that might have substantially ameliorated the great world slowdown in economic growth after 1970. And finally, had our profession been more prepared with the facts of life of the modern corporation and the modern economy, its members would simply have been compelled, by intellectual *force majeure*, to finally abandon the clearly degenerating research program we call the "competitive model."

The Propensity to Save

As we all know, the original Keynesian theory discovered the break in the circulating flow in the dichotomy between the desires and intentions of investors (firms), on the one hand, and the behaviour of savers (households), on the other. Firms, whatever they were, did not save. Alternatively, if they did do so (e.g., were family businesses), they somehow separated their investment and savings decisions. It was generally recognized that societies where firms were mainly householdlike entities who saved in order to invest, or invested what they could currently save, could not be Keynesian: such societies, however, were seen as "primitive" or "pre-Keynesian" (best suited for study by down-market people like development economists). Later we had a flurry of intellectual activity, set off by one Nicholas Kaldor in the year 1977,[19] which ingeniously attempted to invert the Keynesian theory into a non-neoclassical theory of distribution. The fundamental idea was to assume full employment, steady economic growth and some form of differential savings behaviour with respect to income originating in wages and income originating in profits. Since the level of investment was "determined" by the rate of economic growth and the national-average propensity to save, given the assumption of full employment (similarly determined), only a unique distribution between profits and wages would produce the weights necessary for the necessary (weighted) national savings average.

The managerial theory generates some severe comments on both the original Keynesian and post-Keynesian theories. In both cases, the problems arise both from lack of goods-market micro foundations and from an additional disease, inadequate specification of *institutional* micro foundations. If the Keynesian economy was not "pre-Keynesian," what kind of an economy, institutionally speaking, was it? It could not easily be a corporate (managerial) economy, driven by a model such as set out above, because in all such models, including those examples where managerial behaviour comes close to shareholder-optimizing behaviour, a large part of total national savings takes the form of corporate profit retention, which (see above) in these models is truly endogenous to the growth-and-investment decision. So the original Keynesian economy must be some form of modern capitalism in which corporate retention rates are low, and the financing of investment mainly takes place either by new share issues or by debt. In their different ways, both of these latter possibilities are illogical. Widespread financing by new share issues inevitably makes the system managerial; heavy debt-financing creates heavy leverage and intolerable burdens of risk, especially borrowers' risk.[20] This of course explains the world we see, that is, the world where an overwhelming proportion of corporate investment is internally financed (if a firm is growing at a real rate of 10 percent per annum and earns a 20 percent real net internal return, it needs only a 50 percent retention ratio – quite typical – to be entirely independent of external finance).

The conclusion is not that the managerial theory denies Keynes, but rather that it states that in the corporate sector the investment multiplier will be close to one. Nothing is said about the multiplier in other sectors.

As regards the post-Keynesian distribution theory, I have never concealed my scepticism, first voiced in a rude passage about Kaldor in *The Economic Theory of Managerial Capitalism* in 1964 and pursued in different form in the *Economic Journal*[21] piece in 1972. Although the pistol was pointed mainly at Kaldor, the attack is relevant to much of the associated literature as well.[22] The first grievance is closely associated with the discussion of the previous section. As the original Keynesian theory lacked a micro-pricing theory to support its macro income-determination theory, so the post-Keynesian theory lacks the micro foundation for the distribution mechanism. Just how it was that market behaviour produced the necessary adjustments between nominal prices and nominal wages was rarely discussed. The contemporary imperfect-competition models, referred to above, that support the Keynesian theory of income determination also, inevitably, determine the price-cost ratio and hence the price-wage ratio. Therefore, they do indeed determine distribution. Some models even attempt to go further and postulate a process of entry that ends up with some kind of analogy to neoclassical normal profit.[23] If that is the case, if some other (e.g., post-Keynesian) distribution mechanism is posited to exist, in the absence of yet a third mechanism of reconciliation, the theory is overdetermined.

The other arm of this attack is similar to but more destructive than the above-explained attack on the institutional foundations (lack of them) of Keynes. It is essential to the post-Keynesian theory that there be a major difference between savings "from wages" and savings "from profits." If the society is supposed to be homogeneous, householders will be both wage-earners and dividend-receivers. In the latter capacity, given the highly skewed distribution of capital that inevitably exists, no doubt the households with the larger share of incomes in the form of dividends will also be the richer households. But we then depend on the presumption that richer households have higher savings propensities, a proposition that became both empirically and theoretically suspect. Faced with this criticism, Kaldor was wont to fall back on the argument that in practice a high proportion of the so-called capitalist savings – that is, savings from profits – represented the undistributed profits of corporations and that, compared to household savings ratios, corporate retention ratios were notoriously high. For the reasons already given, this was of course a catastrophic defence. With it, the separation of corporate savings decisions from investment decisions becomes inherently implausible. But unlike the Keynesian theory, the post-Keynesian literature cannot afford to lose that separation.

In my opinion a situation existed in the late 1960s for a brisk and purposeful development of the Keynesian theory consistent with modern (managerial) capitalism. In my book I offered a starting point, albeit not very succinctly. Be that as it may, it seems to me to have been a tragedy that whether from this starting point or some other, the post-Keynesians did not pursue a more rigorous course – the more so (from my point of view) as the managerialist shares with them a desire for realism (in contrast to neoclassical naïveté) concerning modern capitalism. A partial, but only partial, explanation lies in the Marxian aroma that lingers over much of the work of writers who actually joined the Society of Post-Keynesian Economists (founded in the late 1970s); persons under Marxian influences (not the same thing at all as official Marxian economists, who tend to be crypto neoclassicists) always appear fascinated by the idea of simultaneous determination of the level (or growth) and distribution of income. It ain't necessarily so!

ECONOMIC GROWTH AND DEVELOPMENT

It is a common observation that the branch of economics that may be classified as the formal theory of economic growth has been, over the past half century, largely separated from the branch we call "development economics." This is because, as noted above, the formal theory of economic growth has largely taken a form in which it is not a theory of growth at all; it is a theory of distribution, with growth exogenous. It is a theory of how an underlying natural growth rate, determined by (usually) demography and exogenous technical progress, affects, but is not affected by, the general macroeconomic model of cycles and growth.

To this situation, the managerial theory can contribute massively. If it is employed as a micro foundation for macro-growth economics, unlike in the case of formal growth theory, in the result the rate of growth is *en*dogenous. Furthermore, it is endogenous to the economic variables that are *ex*ogenous to the micro theory; more explicitly, the macro-growth rate of the outcome *results from* the micro theory of the growth of the firm.

In 1964 I saw this idea only dimly. It is approached in the final chapter of *Managerial Capitalism* but in an amateurish style, and during the next decades neither I nor anyone else attempted to follow up this hint. For that we had to wait for Hiro Odagiri.[24] Although Hiro is in no way to be held responsible for the remarks that now follow, they are totally inspired by his work.

Recollect that in the formal micro-managerial theory, as set out above, two forces are specified as affecting the managerially desired growth rate, the costs of growth and the costs of take-over. Moving to a less formal posture, we can envisage the costs-of-growth factor as representing all kinds of growth-restraining elements in the organizational environment: the supply of managers professionally equipped to manage growth; the educational factors affecting the productivity of R&D; and many factors already typically mentioned in development literature, such as the education, training, and adaptability of the non-managerial labour force. Notice also that throughout this essay, when we speak of the growth of firms, we speak of "internal" growth, that is, growth that is not the result of acquiring other firms. "External" (acquisition-led) growth clearly contributes nothing directly to the growth of the economy. The only available qualification to the general argument here, of course, would be the specific argument that in an economy with fewer barriers to take-over, apart from greater attention to the time preferences of shareholders, which is a negative factor in the macro equation, there could be a positive factor if one believed that more intensive take-over activity encouraged greater X-Efficiency.

Strictly interpreted, the "take-over factor" reflects the various stock-market institutional elements that tend to create barriers to take-over, that is, those things that make it expensive or impossible to launch successful take-over bids. This can be broadened to an interpretation that encompasses the sociology of management outlook, thus describing to what extent the type of person who will reach a position of corporate command is organizationally inward looking, that is to say, to what extent such a person is especially concerned with the welfare of the existing white- and blue-collar employees, and not so much concerned with shareholders. In this broadened conception, one is thinking not so much of the positive power of shareholders but rather of their role in the managerial superego. When the manager is taking strategic decisions, does he or she feel duty or guilt most strongly towards co-workers or towards stockholders? Clearly, this tendency may vary between societies.

Let us be clear about what we are saying. We are saying that in a society where objective or subjective factors tend to encourage managers to minimize their concern for shareholders, *ceteris paribus*, the *desired* growth rate of the representative large firm will be faster. The step from here to macroeconomics, as first properly taken by Hiro Odagiri, is a broad one, a dramatic one, for some people a startling one, but once one has taken it, it is difficult to go back; in retrospect the step looks natural and obvious. What, then, is it?

It is simply the observation that the micro-growth efforts of the firm are not ephemeral; they do not consist of nothing more than destroying other firms' markets and prospects. They consist of research and development, especially development, and analogous activities. They represent the acquisition of knowledge. They are, in fact, intrinsically learning processes.

Ergo the positive growth efforts of firms must affect positively the "natural" rate of growth of the economy. *Ceteris paribus* economies whose managers' micro-desired-growth rates are relatively fast will also be economies whose macro-growth rates are fast.

The conclusion that economies with growth-oriented managers will be growth-oriented economies is not controversial. But when this proposition is restated, according to the theory above, in words implying that countries should actively discourage the perfection of their capital markets, more specifically that they actively resist attempts to reduce barriers to take-overs on the stock market, 90 percent of conventional Western economists will be inclined to gulp. Most likely they will probably simply hear (or read) the opposite!

But here is food for thought. Crude of course, but meaty nevertheless. Among the developed market economies, over the past half century, the two slowest-growing, measured by income per capita, are the two countries that have had the most outstandingly active take-over markets.[25] Which countries are they? They are, of course, the United States and the United Kingdom. With more research one could probably establish that they are the English-speaking countries as opposed to the rest.

At the other end of the spectrum, one might ask which has been the fastest-growing country – Japan, of course. Japanese corporations are very large, very managerial. Tokyo is the world's second- or third-largest stock market. Nevertheless, in Japan, take-overs, at least to date, have been a rarity. For a variety of social, legal, and institutional reasons, take-overs are virtually barred – in fact, they are regarded as immoral. (Consequently, when Japanese firms expand abroad, they do not generally use this method.) Couple this with the notorious tendency of Japanese firms to accept low profit margins in return for long-term growth, manifested in low current dividends, and you have that side of the story in a nutshell.

On the other side, the costs-of-growth aspect, remember that many of these costs are administrative. Here we note the strong emerging literature demonstrating the link between Japanese management style and the needs of contemporary organizational technology. By encouraging low inter-firm mobility among managers, Japanese corporations not only *foster* but also *facilitate* the growth motive. All eyes in this field are currently focused on the longer planning horizons of Japanese firms as compared to North American or European. In addition, the Japanese appear to combine a superficially authoritarian, bureaucratic, hierarchical organizational style, with much hidden flexibility, lateralness, such as is essential for large organizations if their growth efforts are not to be stultified by rigidity.

In fact, there is much more to be said on the general theme that Japan, the great contemporary economic success story, is the managerial economy *par excellence*. Far more supporting detail may emerge when Hiro Odagiri publishes his already-mentioned book-in-progress. Of course, the correct story is more complex. I would be wrong to boast that in addition to "predicting" the current Anglo-American economists' interest in take-overs (see above), with my managerial theory I also "predicted" the Japanese economic miracle. But if only on account of the neoclassical taunts I have suffered, boast I will nevertheless. It all adds to the case for the philosophy "Do not be too obsessed with what this theory predicts; ask only if it is a good theory." To which one adds the more familiar warning that a bad theory is a bad theory, whatever it predicts. Notice that what we are saying here is (to a neoclassicist) quite remarkably shocking. We are saying that if in countries such as Japan the market for corporate control had been less imperfect, the whole society would by now have been worse off. In effect, your honest neoclassicist has to say that the Japanese people have suffered by growing "too fast." The cause of this intellectual confrontation is not myopia, but the fact that the development efforts of firms create externalities for the economy. And, in managerial capitalism, such externalities are pervasive.

MANAGERIAL CAPITALISM AND EQUITY

First I must define "equity." I shall employ a customized version of John Rawls's ideas.[26] I shall hypothesize a number of imaginary economies, each of which is identically endowed and ripe for transition from the "mid-range" state to some state that could be considered fully developed – from, say, a per capita income of one-fifth of the current (1990) level in Western Europe to that level itself. In all the societies the citizens are unequally endowed; there are classes. At present, however, the pattern of stratification, as between the societies, is the same. The societies are internally heterogeneous, externally homogeneous.

Each economy contains a mechanism that will both activate the development transition process and subsequently control its equity. I then imagine that I am a disembodied spirit who must become a member of one of these societies, without knowing who I will actually be – more precisely, without knowing my initial endowments – in short, without knowing to what socioeconomic class I will belong. This will eventually be decided by a lottery *after* I have made my choice of society. Once in a society, I cannot leave it; my children and my grandchildren will also be locked in; my and their progress will be probabilistic, with the life-chance probabilities determined by two things: first, the hidden mechanism (which is in effect a probability tree for the social classes, including intergenerational transition matrices) and second, my result in the lottery.

Now, knowing the probability trees for each society, and knowing also the probability distributions in the lotteries (chances of being assigned with various endowments), I must place the societies in an order of preference. I make the decision entirely on the basis of a risk-averse, time-related utility function defined with regard to the economic and moral welfare of myself, my children, and my grandchildren (and no other persons; no altruism, no patriotism, no utility, positive or negative, is attached to relative gains or deprivation) through present and future time. The cut-off date or time horizon is the birth date of my youngest grandchild plus the life expectancy of children born into their expected class.

Given risk aversion, there is no alternative to the maximin. I must inevitably choose the society which, through the transition process and after, maximizes my minimum expected outcome, that being the expected outcome if the dice assigns me to the least-advantaged class – more precisely, to that class that will gain least, and suffer worst, through the whole economic development process from now until the cut-off date.

It follows that both efficiency and equity must enter the evaluation. On the one hand, if growth is rapid (more precisely if it is rapid relative to the savings required, which will have to be borne by the population at large, including myself), I and my descendants will benefit through time from the average performance. On the other hand, if the spread of outcomes around the average is high (development is inegalitarian), the least-fortunate classes, to whom my sole attention is directed, will do less well relative to the average. This time-related evaluation is of course a form of social welfare function, in effect, an index of expected social welfare.

As is well known, given risk aversion, Rawls's Principle of Justice is inevitable: I join the society which, over time, maximizes the material welfare of the people who eventually draw the bad lottery tickets; this is what is meant by maximizing the welfare of the least advantaged. Without risk aversion, the Rawls's principle does not emerge. One feels that case may well have applied to the American founding fathers.

In the meantime, it seems to me that as compared to traditional capitalism on the one hand, or socialism as we have seen it in our time on the other, the performance of managerial capitalism, according to the criterion of expected social welfare, is quite good. There are several reasons for this. One is the inevitable tendency of managers to "accumulate, accumulate, accumulate," rather than consume luxury goods. The high corporate retention ratio implies a high "capitalist propensity to save," a benign distributional coefficient, it will be remembered, in post-Keynesian/neo-Marxian modelling. Another factor is that the professional managerial ethic tends to be employee oriented. While managerial capitalism is careerist and élitest and does not produce an egalitarian distribution, it nevertheless produces a reasonable one. Here again, see Japan. The top managers of those great companies that are terrorizing North America today, still, both absolutely and comparatively, pay themselves considerably less than their North American colleagues pay themselves. Futhermore, the general income distribution in Japan is one of the least unequal in the First World.

Of course, North America was the great managerial capitalist success story of its time. Today that mantle has fallen to Japan. Japan studies are for good reason currently very fashionable. Indeed, for such studies, the managerial paradigm is essential. She or he (Ben, Bob, or Irma) who tries to explain Japan entirely within the neoclassical paradigm is doomed to fail.

BROADER CONCLUSIONS

Despite the dubious origins of "stages" concepts in economic growth, they do make convenient discussion posts. Traditionally, we see the final stage as the transformation to industrial capitalism. Then we see two kinds of failure: countries that fail to make the grade and countries that, becoming patently capitalist and maybe efficient, seem seriously deficient in equity.

A subset of the second group especially interests me. These are typically mid-range countries with two further characteristics: (1) they have an obvious excuse for being originally behind, and (2) despite enormous wealth and luxury among the upper classes, on account of widespread poverty among other classes, average per capita income is still only moderate (e.g., Brazil, Mexico, Turkey). When professional economists from the First World visit these countries, they find that their opposite numbers are probably living at a higher standard than theirs.

We all know that a marked proportion of this subgroup are in fact countries that at one time had Catholic Christianity as a state religion (that religion is still very strong in these areas); generally, these are the ex-colonies of Spain or Portugal. Furthermore, the economic histories of the mother countries have been remarkably similar: Portugal, with a per capita income (PPP adjusted) less than half the OECD average, is the poorest country in Western Europe, with Spain and Ireland not far behind. We are all very solicitous of these countries, we are all proud of the political advances in Spain, but, in truth, all these countries, and especially well-endowed South American countries like Argentina, are a disgrace.

If my frankness is unusual, the thought is hardly so. But here is a suggestion. We need another stage in economic growth – the transformation to managerial capitalism. I merely put out the idea that for sociological reasons connected with the mysterious cultural effects of the Catholic tradition, it is that stage these countries have balked at. Max lives! And never forget that apart from discovering the link between Protestantism and capitalism, Weber also invented the theory of bureaucracy.

"What about Italy?" they cry. Well, Italy is two countries. The South fits perfectly; the North (whose per capita income is currently equal to the OECD average) – well, yes, the North is Catholic and permanently governed (from Rome) by a permanent party called Democratic Christian, meaning "Parliamentary Catholic." Furthermore, the industrial miracle of north Italy does not fit the managerial capitalist story well (perhaps this is why I have found as much interest in that country as in any!): the great success stories are family businesses. There are also large industrial organizations, some successful, but they are all directly or indirectly state owned! Some northern Italians, especially people from the very north of the country, near the Alps, attempt to explain these paradoxes by reminding one that for the first half of the nineteenth century, the country was run by Austrians. But here's the catch! Those Austrians were Hapsburgs, devout Catholics! In my opinion, northern Italy, a country I adore, is *sui generis*.

Finally, there is my own country, the United Kingdom. Superficially we seem like a managerial economy *par excellence*, but our economic performance in this century has not sparkled. There is, in fact, a fair amount of contemporary evidence that socially and professionally, almost certainly especially socially, England suffered from a comparative disadvantage in large organization against small organization. Honest bureaucracy, yes. Public bureaucracy, yes. But *enterprising* bureaucracy, not so good. And it was enterprising bureaucracy, at its height (1900–70) that made (North) America great then, and is making Japan great today.

Everybody knows that one reason for this is that we have a class system whose upper classes despise trade. And it's all true. Perhaps more interesting to the economist is the fact that this same phenomenon trapped Alfred Marshall into a really major failure, namely his failure to see the advent of managerial capitalism. Most of us know about the trees in the forest. Few of us know how Marshall rationalized his analogy: "They [successful firms] seem as though they would grow on for ever, and for ever become stronger as they grow. But they do not" (*Principles of Economics*, 1st ed. [London: Macmillan, 1890]). And there are other quotations – for example: "There are few exceptions to the rule that large firms ... are, in proportion to their size, inferior to businesses of more moderate size, in energy, resources ... and inventive power" (address to the British Association, 1902).

How did Marshall explain the first quotation, and why was he so wrong in the second? The answer to the first question was "Nursemaids." The original business was always a family business created by a dynamic traditional entrepreneur who became rich. Inevitably he handed over the upbringing of the sons who might succeed him to nursemaids, who inevitably brought them up soft – so they were no good for business. Unhappily this is not a parody of Marshall's level of argument. We could, however, make sense of it by noting that it is completely true that in the second half of the nineteenth century, when Marshall was forming his ideas, successful British industrialists had only one ambition for their children, to keep them out of trade. More significant is the implication that Marshall could conceive of no other form of economic organization. Yet at the time he was writing, modern corporation statutes had been passed in New York State as long previously as 1837, and similar laws had come into force in England before 1850. In the later editions of his book Marshall did two things: he removed the nursemaids and grudgingly admitted the existence of joint-stock companies, but he said that although these nasty entities could get quite big, they always eventually stagnated. In fact, Marshall quite explicitly asserted that joint-stock companies were very bad at growing! It is surely evident why the great man refused to see the obvious. His extremely strong economic intuition already told him that the success of joint-stock companies would be quite fatal to neoclassical economics. More precisely, they are quite fatal to the *validity* of neoclassical economics.

NOTES

1 From Francis Crick, "The Recent Excitement About Neural Networks," *Nature* (London), 12 January 1989. Crick, co-discover of the chemical structure of DNA, has for the past fifteen years worked at the Salk Institute on the neuroscience of the brain. The purpose of the quotation is to give a clue to this essay. I believe very similar words apply to neoclassical economics.

2 See R. Marris, *The Theory and Future of the Corporate Economy*, Hugo de Vries Lectures, 1977 (Amsterdam: North Holland, 1979).

3 F.M. Scherer, "Corporate Take-overs," *Journal of Economic Perspectives*, Winter 1988; and Leonard Silk, "The Merger Rise," *New York Times*, 18 March 1988, D2. To be fair, I certainly suggested that the take-over process could be seen as a kind of administrative restructuring of the corporate system, for which socialist systems had no easy substitute, but I constantly emphasized the imperfection of the process.

4 Dennis C. Mueller, "A Theory of Conglomerate Mergers," *Quarterly Journal of Economics*, November 1969.

5 H. Odagiri, *The Theory of Growth in a Corporate Economy* (Cambridge University Press, 1981).

6 See the exchange concerning J.K. Galbraith in the pages of *The Public Interest*, a journal published in New York during 1968.

7 In effect, neoclassical economics has no theory of the firm, only a theory of production. Ninety percent of neoclassical economics, including its ventures into imperfect competition, implicitly assumes that all firms are single-product, i.e., assumes that "firm" and "product" are *de facto* synonymous. Faced with the reality of corporate diversification, the "firm" becomes a corporate product division, sometimes known as a "quasi-firm." The resulting limitations are enormous. See "The Industrial Structure," 237, above.

8 This way of looking at the matter is vastly more elegant, as well as being considerably more logical, than the manner in which the V-g Frontier was first derived in R. Marris, *The Economic Theory of Managerial Capitalism* (London: Macmillan; New York: Free Press, 1964).

9 Of course, all this part of the managerial theory derives from Edith Penrose's *The Theory of the Growth of the Firm* (Oxford: Oxford University Press), 1959.

10 From Crick, "The Recent Excitement."

11 Transactions-cost economizing.

12 See O. Williamson, *The Economic Institutions of Capitalism* (New York: Free Press, 1985).

13 As these lines are written, a large British organization of the type known as a "Building Society" (something like a US Savings and Loan) has converted itself into a stockholder corporation. Building societies operate under a legal regime that makes them rather like co-ops. Superficially, the "members" (depositors) have quite considerable constitutional power, but in this case they were easily persuaded to vote themselves out of existence by the promise of a small bonus of new shares – the fact that they will have to pay for this out of diluted values passed virtually undiscussed. There was quite an amount of vague criticism in the national financial press, but no financial writer and certainly no British neo-classical economist explained what was (surely obviously) going on: within less than a week of counting the votes, the management granted themselves salary increases of around 70 percent! In the United States, there is also an extraordinary flavour of naïveté in typical economics teachers' beliefs about places like Wall Street: at least until recently they tended to believe that insider trading by professional managers was insignificant, and more recently, quite a few of one's academic friends seemed surprised to learn that people with inside knowledge of forthcoming take-overs, as well as buying the target stock, will also be found selling short the stock of the acquiring firm. They keep asking, If the bid is harmful to the stockholders of the acquiring firm, why is it occurring? Managerialists would never even pose such a question. They *know* the bid is motivated not by the interests of the stockholders of the acquiring firm, but by those of the acquiring management; the main question they (the managerialists) ask is, How far can this go without the acquiring management's laying themselves open to *counter* take-over? And here we have the advantage of possessing a theory, now a quarter century old, that continues to explain things that are happening with even greater intensity today than they did then.

14 If one is producing an output of X, one can also produce $2X$ at the same total cost by duplicating the technical equipment that created X.

15 For the case for this assertion, see Dennis Mueller and R. Marris, "The Corporation, Competition and the Invisible Hand," *Journal of Economic Literature*, March 1980.

16 In the past, the outstanding example lay in agriculture, but it is not at all clear that in areas such as Europe and the United States the same is true. The main cause of small scale in agriculture, it seems, is the inelasticity of supply of land; more precisely, there are institutional forces that make it artificially expensive for the most efficient farming enterprises to acquire all the land they could efficiently "manage."

17 Schumpeter's version of capitalism and the managerial version have much in common, but they are not the same.

18 R. Marris, *Reconstructing Keynesian Economics with Imperfect Competition – A Desk-Top Simulation* (Aldershot, England: Edward Elgar, 1991).

19 See N. Kaldor, "A Model of Economic Growth," *Economic Journal*, December 1957; for the complete subsequent literature, see F. Targetti, *Nicholas Kaldor* (Rome: Il. Molino, 1988).

20 Keynes was the first person to discuss the significance of borrowers' risk but never followed the idea up.

21 See Marris and idem, "Why Economics Needs a Theory of the Firm," *Economic Journal*, 1972.

22 Ibid.

23 See Blanchard and Kitotaki, "Monopolistic Competition."

24 Odagiri, *Theory of Growth*.

25 "U.K. Leads Field in European Takeovers," *The Times* (London), 13 February 1989. The story was presented like a sport's result.

26 John Rawls, *A Principle of Justice* (Harvard, 1973).

10 Hunger

PAUL STREETEN

INTRODUCTION

If we want to achieve equity, efficiency, and economic development, all people should at least have enough to eat. It is the fact that hunger today is unnecessary that makes its continued existence so shocking. The productive capacity of the world is now capable of feeding all the mouths in existence, yet it fails to do so.

The need for food is perhaps the most basic of all human needs. People must eat, even if they drink unsafe water, are illiterate, and are not inoculated or vaccinated against diseases. Not only does lack of adequate food make people hungry and less able to enjoy life, it also reduces their ability and, by causing apathy and in extreme cases lethargy, their willingness to work productively and, thereby, to raise the means to combat their hunger. In addition, it makes them more susceptible to disease by reducing their immunity to infection and making them more vulnerable to other environmental stresses. Prolonged malnutrition among babies and young children leads to reduced adult stature; severe malnutrition is associated with decreased brain size and cell number, as well as with altered brain chemistry. Malnutrition of pregnant women results in low birth weight of their children, a particularly important cause of infant mortality. Children who suffer from severe malnutrition show lags in motor activity, hearing, speech, social and personal behaviour, problem-solving ability, eye-hand coordination, and categorization behaviour, even after rehabilitation.

Among the world's chronically hungry people are the ultrapoor, the land-less and nearly landless labourers, young children of poor families, pregnant and lactating women, and the old. They live in Asia, on the Indian subcontinent, in Indonesia and the Philippines, and in Sub-Saharan Africa. They constitute about 10 to 15 percent of households, 15 to 20 percent of the population, and 17 to 25 percent of preschool children in these countries.

About a billion people consume less food than they would like; they spend between 70 and 80 percent of their total income on food and more than 50 percent of additional income. The poorest of the poor continue to spend the same proportion on food as their pitiful incomes rise until they reach the point when this proportion begins to decline. As their incomes rise further, they spend a smaller proportion on food, of that smaller proportion a smaller proportion on cereals, and of that smaller proportion a smaller proportion on the cheaper cereals.

Hundreds of millions are handicapped by undernutrition. According to a World Bank study, there are 340 million people in the developing countries suffering from nutritional deprivation (insufficient calories to prevent stunted growth and serious health risk), which represents about 16 percent of their populations. In low-income countries, this proportion rises to 23 percent. The same study suggests that 730 million people suffer from undernourishment by having ''not enough calories for an active working life.'' This amounts to 34 percent of the population of all developing countries and 51 percent of the low-income countries. A study by Reutlinger and Alderman[1] estimates the number of undernourished at over 800 million people.

Hunger and malnutrition today are not mainly the result of a global shortage of food. So far, over the long run, Malthusian predictions of population increasing faster than food have not come true. Current world production of grain alone could provide everyone with more than 3,000 calories and 65 grams of protein daily. It has been estimated that 2 percent of the world's grain output would be sufficient to eliminate malnutrition among the world's 500 million malnourished. Between 1950 and 1984, real cereal prices – the amount of manufactured goods that could be bought with a ton of cereal – fell by over a third, that is, by 1.3 percent per year per pound.

It is true that since 1984 world food production per head has fallen (between 1986 and 1988 by 14 percent) and is now (1989) where it was about two decades ago. The agricultural resource base has deteriorated, new technologies have not been forthcoming or have not been applied at the same rate as before, and depressed farm prices have discouraged production. And some observers argue that the rapid growth of grain production per head since 1973 was achieved by overploughing land and overpumping water, with the result that soils were eroded and water tables dropped – an unsustainable situation. Population growth has continued to be high. So, at least at the moment of writing, problems of supply are once again in the foreground. Yet the problem is not primarily one of food shortages (the productive capacity of the world is capable of feeding all the mouths in existence); it is also a matter of distribution – distribution between countries, between regions, and, in some groups, between the sexes and within households. Social and political arrangements at the international level are also responsible for the unprecedented amount of hunger and malnutrition, as can be seen from the distribution of cereals between the developing and the advanced countries.

The production of cereals by developing countries grew between 1961 and 1980 at an annual rate of 2.9 percent, while consumption grew at 3.2 percent per year. As a result, cereal imports in the developing countries grew from about 15 million metric tons to 64 million tons over these years. In the same period, cereal production in the advanced countries grew by 3.1 percent per year but consumption by only 2.5 percent. The difference was exported to the developing countries, whose share in world imports of cereals rose, as a result, from about 36 percent to 43 percent. Since the bulk of the increase in food production has occurred in the advanced countries, and since global redistribution through grants is ruled out for political reasons, developing countries must either grow substantially more food themselves or earn more foreign exchange to buy the food.

The other part of the solution is the generation of adequate income for the poor, which includes both what they produce for their own consumption and cash to buy food in the market. The entitlement approach to hunger and malnutrition, pioneered by A.K. Sen,[2] suggests that diversified employment and earning opportunities are as important as growing more food. It is true that this creates risks, such as the decline in markets or the rise in the price of food, but there are also risks in aiming at food self-sufficiency: harvests may fail or the soil may deteriorate. The need to consider such options is particularly important for Africa, where food production has fallen behind population increase. The best solution may be not to grow more food, but to create diverse, remunerative export industries.

More food does not necessarily meet the nutritional needs of poor people; it may simply meet the needs of the worms in their stomachs. Hunger and malnutrition are problems of the pathology of the environment, and raising food intake by itself may not help. It may be not more food that is needed, but education, safe water, medical services, reduced workloads, fewer unwanted pregnancies, shorter walks to workplaces, or better workplaces, counter-pressures to advertisements, or a land reform that would permit people to make better use of their higher incomes and the additional food supply. Food needs can sometimes be met more effectively by reducing requirements rather than by raising availabilities. Indeed, Sen has said that the danger today does not arise from Malthusian pessimism (the fear that food production does not rise with population), but from Malthusian optimism (the false belief that if we have solved the problem of food production, we have solved the problem of hunger).

Apart from the emergency of famine, nutrition policies for the chronically malnourished poor call for a long-term, sustained effort. Intervention can take the form of agricultural policy, supplementary feeding, food fortification programs, food subsidies and rationing, and complementary policies (such as employment creation) in non-food sectors. Particularly important are policies for foreign trade and the exchange rate, which determine how much the farmer gets for his crop.

The eradication of hunger is ultimately a question of the political power of the poor. It is sometimes said that free markets give everyone access to the labour force, and thereby to the opportunity to earn enough to meet all needs. But, as Partha Dasgupta has pointed out, "at systematically low levels of nutrition-intake a person's capacity for work is affected adversely. There is thus a possible vicious circle here. Those who have no title to non-wage income are vulnerable in the market for labour, their sole means of generating income."[3] Not until basic needs are met can the market mechanism be said to guarantee productive work.

While power structures and the alignment of interest groups are such that entitlements to adequate food supplies are denied to the poor, hunger will continue. In some conditions, the interest of the ruling group can be harnessed to alleviate poverty and hunger. Infectious diseases do not draw the line at class or income boundaries. The repeal of the Corn Laws in 1846 was in the interest of the industrial classes because it provided cheap food and low wages. A well-nourished, healthy, alert, and educated labour force is a more efficient labour force. But while such interests can be harnessed to hunger removal, in the last resort it is the access to political power of the poor themselves that alone can guarantee adequate food supplies to all. This does not mean that only one type of political system can guarantee hunger eradication. Historical evidence has shown that a wide variety of regimes have eliminated the worst types of hunger within a short period. But some types of regimes make this achievement impossible. Some form of participation of the poor in making the decisions that affect their life and work is helpful, though it is not a necessary condition. But ultimately, the problem of eradicating hunger is a political problem rather than a nutritional or economic one.

THE NEED FOR A MULTI-PRONGED ATTACK

To understand and combat hunger, malnutrition, and undernutrition, we must abandon the notion that these are simply the result of an imbalance between food production and population. We have seen that hunger is the result of the pathology of the environment. Many factors determine this environment. They can be roughly divided into those that work on the supply of food and those that work on the impact of available food on nutritional status. A principal objective of agricultural policies in developing countries is to raise the rate of growth of food production. A list dividing the factors on the food supply side into six "Ins" is useful in this regard:

1 Incentives (or prices)
2 Inputs (fertilizers, equipment, water, etc.)
3 Innovation (technology: new high-yielding varieties, irrigation, etc.)
4 Information (the diffusion of the technologies through extension services)
5 Infrastructure (roads, harbours, storage, education, health)
6 Institutions: credit (rural banks), marketing (institutions to buy, store, transport, ship, and process crops), and land reform

To these ''Ins'' we should add the need to change the composition of agricultural output in favour of higher-value crops, as long as the risks attached to growing and selling these do not exceed the extra benefits. Some of these ''Ins'' are best provided by a market, others by action in the public sector. It is the complementary and supplementary actions of the private and public sectors that produce the results (e.g., the combination of correct pricing policies for food and the provision of roads and vehicles).

Complex and difficult choices arise within each of the six ''Ins.'' Consider infrastructure, normally at least partly provided at public expense. There are choices between physical, legal, human, social, and producer-specific types of infrastructure to be made; choices between centralized and decentralized types of infrastructure, choices between infrastructure for small, deficit farmers and the landless and that for large farmers, producers, and consumers; choices between maintenance of existing and new projects; and choices between different methods of financing expenditure on infrastructure. The same is true for institutions and for information. Should, for example, extension workers concentrate on single lines of conveying information or should they combine several? All these activities compete for scarce resources with directly productive investment in food production.

Another set of choices arises in the phasing or sequencing of the six ''Ins.'' Where infrastructure, institutions, and innovation are already in place, it will suffice to emphasize price incentives. Alternatively, some of these ''Ins'' can be *in*duced by others. Prices can stimulate innovation, institutions, and even public action on infrastructure. In other cases, action on one front can be a substitute for action on others. Heavy public subsidies to well-chosen inputs can be a substitute for higher prices of outputs. Phasing and sequencing are of the utmost importance, since most countries are too poor to do everything at once.

COMPLEMENTARY MEASURES

The six ''Ins'' refer mainly to the supply side of food for the eradication of hunger. Complementary measures are also needed. Education, for example, can help people avoid diseases, such as diarrhoea, thereby raising absorption of food, and it can help them spend their money more wisely on nutritious food and prepare food more economically and hygienically. People can learn how to complement their diet with local food and how to plan their families; educated women tend to marry later and have fewer children. The battle against early weaning and against the use of baby formula has hit the headlines, but the desire of women to cease breast feeding is often part of the general process of modernization and urbanization, reflecting a wish to emulate the more-advanced groups in the country.

Measures are also needed for creating remunerative employment and incomes, for improving health care, for reducing food requirements through eliminating unnecessary work (e.g., land consolidation to eliminate long walks between plots), for food fortification, and for the distribution of food within households. Even with more than adequate food supplies and incomes, people starve either because parasites in their stomachs prevent proper food absorption, or because parasitic landlords-moneylenders or, in some societies, male heads of households deprive them of access to the nutritional benefits of food. The attack on hunger comprises reforms at the micro-micro level (what goes on within the family), at the meso-level (how macro-policies affect particular groups), at the macroeconomic level (what happens to the exchange rate), at the macro-policy level (the system of land distribution and money lending, and the power structure), and at all intermediate levels, both private and public, and at the global level. The eradication of hunger is much more than a problem of making the land more fertile and the women less fertile.

While some of the above approaches are slow and cumbersome, there are speedier and more direct ways to improve nutrition, such as food fortification. Iodine deficiency, which can cause goitre, apathy, and proneness to other diseases, is easily remedied by iodizing salt. More difficult to remedy are deficiencies in vitamin A, which can cause blindness and death in children, and deficiencies in iron, which lead to anaemia and reduced productive power. Protein-energy malnutrition, which may cause irreversible brain damage in children and apathy in adults, is the most difficult to remedy; yet it is the most serious problem in malnutrition, followed by deficiencies in iron and vitamin A.

Special foods and food fortification have been successful up to a point, though they meet with both technical and political difficulties; on the other hand, general food subsidies are very expensive, absorbing up to 20 percent of budgetary expenditure in some countries, and selective programs, such as food stamps, are difficult to administer. Programs are easier and cheaper to administer if the subsidies are for food that is eaten only by the poor. Rich countries tend to tax poor urban food consumers in order to subsidize relatively better-off farmers. Poor countries have tended, at least until recently, to tax (often indirectly and in a disguised form) poor farmers in order to subsidize food such as high-quality wheat and rice that is consumed by the better-off urban groups. But among the poorest are rural landless labourers and urban dwellers who have to buy food; these people are helped by such sub-sidies.

The dilemma is whether to target food subsidies on the most needy groups or to cover a wider group, possibly the whole population. There are bound to be leakages either way. It is very difficult to implement a program that covers *all* the poor, and *only* the poor. Wider coverage can become very costly, nar-rower coverage runs the danger of leaving out needy people. Wider coverage also taxes scarce administrative capacity. It is better to err on the side of ex-cess coverage, and recuperate some of the revenue through forms of taxes that do not hit the most vulnerable, at least directly, such as a tax on alcohol or cigarettes.

Food policy makers start from a related fundamental dilemma. Should they keep food prices high in order to encourage food production and raise the supply for all, including the poor, in the long run, at the risk of hunger and starvation of poor food buyers in the short run? Or should they keep food prices low in order to ensure affordable food for poor buyers at the risk of aggravating food shortages in the future? The dilemma is aggravated by the fact that many food producers are also poor. There are two ways of resolving the dilemma. First, the policy makers may set high prices and then take specific measures, such as rationing and subsidies, to protect poor buyers. Or they may set low prices and compensate producers by subsidies to inputs or to their crops. The third horn of the dilemma is that the capacity to raise tax revenue or to administer rationing or fair price shops is very scarce in developing countries.

The multi-pronged attack applies also to the agents. We normally think of government action as involving taxes, subsidies, employment programs, feeding programs, and so on. But non-governmental organizations (e.g., Oxfam) and private agents also play important roles. For example, Sen has shown the importance of a free press, both as an early warning system about impending famines and as a pressure group to encourage governments to respond quickly and adequately to threats of famine.

EXPORT CROPS VERSUS FOOD
FOR DOMESTIC CONSUMPTION

There has been a good deal of discussion of the respective merits of export crops and food for domestic consumption. Some have argued that if the com-parative advantage points to export crops, it is they that should be promoted and the foreign exchange earned should be used for inputs into agriculture or industry, or even for food imports. Others have argued that export crops im-poverish the poor, deprive the people of food, and lower nutritional standards. It has also been argued that export crops are ecologically destructive.

A parallel debate has gone on over the respective merits of marketing more food, whether for the domestic market or for exports, and growing more food for consumption within the farm household that grows it. Some of the arguments that apply to the debate on exports versus food for domestic consumption also apply to the debate on more marketing versus more production for own consumption.

Clearly much depends on the institutional arrangements. If export crops are grown on large plantations, perhaps owned by foreigners, which generate little employment, while food for domestic consumption is grown by small farmers, the impact on income distribution will be different according to which type of crop is promoted. If the foreign exchange earned by export crops accrues to the government and it spends it on arms or office buildings, while the receipts from food for domestic consumption go to the poor peasants, again the distributional impact will be different.

The interesting fact, at least in Africa, is that there is little evidence that there is a necessary conflict between the two forms of production. Where land and labour are not scarce, the movements in export crops go in the same direction as the movements in the production of food for domestic consumption. There is also little evidence that nutritional standards have suffered as a result of the growth of export crops, though sugar in Kenya may be an exception. There are several reasons for this. First, certain services can be in joint supply and help both export crops and food for domestic consumption. Among these are extension, marketing, and supplies of inputs. Similarly, equipment and fertilizer can be used to raise the production of both. It can also be the case that similar complementarities exist on the side of demand: the demand for food by the farmers who grow export crops creates a stable market for local food supplies and encourages their increase. For some export crops, such as cotton, a part of the export crop can be used as food, in the form of edible oil, or as feed in the form of cottonseed cake.

In spite of the positive relationship between export crops and food under some conditions, clearly, conflicts can arise. Where there has been in the past unwarranted discrimination against food crops, there is a case for removing that discrimination. Colonial governments have tended to favour export crops by improving infrastructure, such as transport, marketing, and distribution services, rather than facilities for domestic food consumption. Research activities and extension services also have been concentrated on export crops, particularly if they are linked to large firms with market power and the capacity to process the crops and make profits by raising prices in the face of an inelastic demand. On the other hand, export crops have frequently borne higher taxes than food crops and are more easily controlled by governments, since often they grow in specialized regions, they have to pass through ports, the buyers are more concentrated, and so on. But economists have a bias in favour of trade, whether international or intranational, and against locally consumed food. Such historical biases, where they exist, should be removed.

Some scholars have gone further and have criticized colonial governments for destroying the integrated farming-herding systems that in precolonial times protected the ecology while allowing substantial food production. In Africa, in precolonial days, farmers opened their fields in the dry season to pastoralists who brought their herds to graze on the harvested millet and sorghum stalks. The animals were fed through the grazing, they manured and fertilized the soil with their dung, and their hooves broke up the earth around the plant stalks, allowing oxygenation of the soil. The herdsmen traded their milk for the farmers' grain, and people, animals, and land were simultaneously maintained. The introduction of monocrop cash production (peanuts, cotton) by colonial governments destroyed this system. In addition, well digging concentrated animals around watering sites and their trampling turned these areas into small deserts. Postcolonial production further encouraged this erosion of land and, in the view of some, contributed to the present famines. It is, however, not clear how the traditional system could have been maintained in the face of a rapidly growing population.

In some cases export crops face an inelastic world demand. Here, production should be curtailed and total proceeds raised, unless current price rises reduce future demand, appropriately discounted, by more than present gains. Such reasoning underlies the attempts to design commodity agreements for tea, cocoa, coffee, sugar, spices, etc. Much current research is devoted to raising further the productivity and production of such export crops, not always to the benefit of the growers. The difficulty here is that, in the absence of effective commodity agreements, the national efforts of small countries are not coordinated with those of the growers and exporters in other competing countries.

A shift to export crops sometimes reduces the role of women in societies in which they traditionally produce, prepare, and distribute food. In spite of the higher family income earned, this can lead to a reduction in nutritional standards. Sometimes the men migrate to other areas and leave their families with less food. Women may increase their labour in food crop production to compensate for the reduced labour of men, sometimes producing surplus output for sale, thus raising both their income and their independence. A case is reported from Cameroon where men took up cocoa, coffee, and bananas, abandoning the food farms they had previously cultivated. Women took up the slack. But the women grew the food crops in an entirely different way from the men, using a system of cultivation involving small, daily outputs of labour throughout the growing season, in contrast to the men, who had cultivated a combination of crops that required occasional short peaks of concentrated labour. The result was an increase in total output, of export crops and of food crops, where the additional food was grown by fewer people (only women) who used more labour-intensive techniques than the average labour intensity of men and women combined in the past.

The impact of a shift to export crops on (1) expenditure patterns as a result of cash accruing to different members of the family, and in large, discontinuous lumps rather than as a steady flow, (2) the distribution of food to different members of the family, and (3) the allocation of time and effort by women to different types of work is an important area of study. On the other hand, a shift to export crops may raise employment opportunities and therefore offer more people access to food. Jute is produced more labour intensively than rice. A shift from rice to jute in Bangladesh, therefore, creates more jobs and contributes to better nutrition.

A good deal depends on the distribution of land and the mode of agricultural production. If export crops benefit large plantations or commercial farms, whereas food is mainly produced by small farmers or their wives, a switch to export crops can aggravate inequality in access to resources, income-earning power, and landownership. (Examples are sugar in Jamaica and cotton in El Salvador, but even in Africa the trade bias has favoured the large export-orientated farm and firm.) Export crops are often grown more efficiently in large farms, and the change-over can lead to an impoverishment of small farmers. In African countries, additional export earnings tend to increase the income of small farmers, and the extra foreign exchange contributes to reduced bottlenecks in transport and agricultural inputs, which are important for food production. This was certainly the case in Tanzania in the early 1980s.

How much should be devoted to export crops is also determined by trends in the cost of international transport, which, in turn, is affected by oil prices. The lower these costs, the stronger the case for international trade. Expectations of higher future transport costs, other things remaining equal, would justify a move towards reduced dependence on foreign trade.

Foreign exchange is often one of the scarcest resources, while its increase can make the fuller use of many domestic resources possible and contribute to greater food production, as well as to higher imports of food itself. It has already been mentioned that the production of export crops and food for domestic consumption can sometimes be increased, particularly if improved technologies are introduced. In some cases the opportunity costs of increasing exports are very small, and the choice does not arise. Land may be plentiful, and little labour and other inputs required. Where domestic food production does decline, it is possible to encourage home gardens simultaneously with the expansion of export cash crops to ensure continuing adequate nutrition. A Kenyan Ministry of Health study of 1979 showed little evidence that five export crops (coffee, tea, cotton, pyrethrum, and sugar cane) had been detrimental to nutritional status. We have seen that the only possible exception was sugar cane.

However, some qualifications are needed to the notion that resource allocation should be guided by comparative advantage, so that a comparative advantage in an export crop can buy more food from abroad than would be produced at home. The comparative advantage is not God-given but is itself determined by the direction of research, and research has been heavily biased in favour of export crops and the staple grains to the neglect of "inferior" food such as millet, sorghum, and cassava. With the growing importance of human capital, the direction of comparative advantage can be quite strongly influenced by research, extension services, education, and other forms of investment in human beings. It is no longer only or even mainly "endowments" that determine specialization in international trade, but conscious policy decisions.

Recently, there have been some successes in research on these "inferior" food crops. In Zimbabwe, hybrid varieties of maize, in the Sudan, high-yielding, drought-resistant strains of sorghum, and in Nigeria, a disease-resistant variety of cassava with three times the yield of native strains, have been developed. But a complete elimination of the bias in favour of export crops, combined with the provision of credit and delivery systems, would change the comparative advantage and convey benefits to poor people. There is also some evidence that poor people are more likely to produce the things they themselves consume and to consume the things they produce. There are several reasons for this. First, when households switch from semi-subsistence cropping for their own needs to monocropping for export, their incomes may rise but their nutritional status drop. Second, monocropping for export may raise the risk of crop failure, even though the average returns are higher. Third, export crops often take a long time to mature, and the outcome may turn out to be less profitable than expected. Fourth, there is a distributional consideration in favour of growing food.

There are two dangers in simply raising the productivity of the poor by switching to export crops. First, there may not be adequate demand for the things they produce, or export taxes may be levied, or marketing margins may be high. Second, the price of food, on which the poor will want to spend a large part of their income, may rise sharply, particularly if the change involves shortages of food in local markets. These two dangers are more likely to be avoided if the poor can meet their own needs in somewhat more self-sufficient units than would be indicated by a strict application of the theory of exchange and comparative advantage. This applies to families and households, to villages, to nations, and to groups of poor nations. There are distributional advantages in this mutual meeting of basic needs that have to be set against the conventional claims of the aggregate gains from trade, which may be greater but less well distributed, more uncertain, or longer delayed.

In some countries, such as Zambia, Mali, and Tanzania, a dilemma arises. The above arguments for encouraging smallholder production of food for local consumption are strong. At the same time, foreign-exchange scarcities constitute a bottleneck to expansion because they reduce the availability of consumer goods, fuel, transport equipment, and fertilizer. If productivity in food production is to be raised, growth of inputs is necessary, and this frequently depends on importing these inputs. Productivity growth depends crucially on moving towards machinery, fertilizer, and pesticides, which often have to be imported and cost foreign exchange. Imports have been scaled down to the minimum, so that, without extra aid, an increase in exports is the only solution. Local food production and consumption cannot be raised without raising exports, but exports can be raised only by curtailing food for local consumption. Non-project, untied foreign aid combined with the right policies can transform this vicious circle into a virtuous one.

Generalizations (e.g., that export crops are grown on large farms, food crops on small; export crops are grown as monocrops, food crops in diversified farming enterprises; or that food crops use more or less female labour) are quite impossible to make, though they are often made. Some progress has been made by combining output, sales, and methods of production in different ways. The best guideline is to avoid dogmatism on this issue and to promote policies that raise and stabilize the incomes of poor people, whether through exports or food for domestic consumption or both, and to make sure that they have access to the food.

To sum up the controversy: the passionate opponents of export crops, the value productivity of which is often higher than that of food production, have on the whole not provided good reasons for their attack, but there is a kernel of truth in their criticism of those who advocate comparative advantage as a guide to foreign trade. The issue can be summed up as follows:

1 Comparative advantage can change, particularly as a result of changes in the direction of research and human capital formation.
2 The institutional arrangements as to who benefits from foreign sales (government through export taxes, parastatals, foreign firms, plantations, large commercial farmers) and from domestic production of food (small farmers) make an important difference.
3 Local food production and local markets for food can be harmed or destroyed by foreign trade. In spite of higher earnings to the country, local food prices may rise or certain foodstuffs may cease to be available. But local self-sufficiency in food, like national self-sufficiency, may also harm the poor.
4 Higher incomes to the growers do not always mean that nutritional standards of all members of their families are improved.
5 Export crops sometimes carry higher risks in production: the costs of foreign transport and foreign demand.
6 The distribution of benefits (and power) between men and women, and between government and private agents, may be different.

7   Foreign trade contributes to a change in tastes that can both make the country more vulnerable and reduce nutritional standards.
8   Monocropping for export can be ecologically harmful.
9   In many situations, experience has shown that food and export production are not alternatives but complementary.

DISTRIBUTION OF FOOD WITHIN THE FAMILY

In the past, a common assumption was that if the head of a household earns enough income to feed all family members, they will be adequately fed. More recently, the distribution of food within the family has been more closely examined. The results are still controversial. According to some, women and children, especially girls under four years old, are discriminated against in favour of adult men and boys. According to others, reports of such discrimination are greatly exaggerated. Where children and women receive less food than adult men, this can be partly explained in terms of their lower requirements, their working less, or their lower productivity. It is generally agreed that in some cultures, such as Bangladesh and northern India, girls under four suffer from food discrimination. Of course, there is a disproportionately large number of small children in poor families, and they are among the most vulnerable groups. It may also be that poor families have to concentrate on feeding the member most likely to bring in earnings, and that is often the male adult. In Africa, female children are favoured compared with males. In many cultures, it is the women who distribute the food; they control grain stores and deplete them to feed themselves and their families. It is not likely that they will be entirely subservient to the selfish demands of their husbands.

If poor families suffer from hunger and undernutrition, it is not always best to raise their income, however desirable this may be on other grounds, if we are concerned with raising the nutritional status of their children. The GOBI package designed and propagated by UNICEF – growth charts, oral rehydration, breast feeding, and inoculation – may be a more effective and quicker way to improve children's nutrition when they have been suffering from diarrhoea.

Seasonal fluctuations in food consumption increase the damage both by making the shortfalls worse for the very poor and by increasing their number compared with a count taken on an average day. The range of benign adaptation for any given individual is likely to be exceeded, and more individuals will drop into the group of severely undernourished. In Gambia, for example, women's weight declined between pre-harvest and post-harvest seasons by 5 kilograms, and food intake per day was 60 calories lower. In Bangladesh the difference in calorie consumption per kilogram dropped from 62 to 50. Some of these variations may be planned. The variations may correspond to variations in required work or to the high cost and wastage of storing food. Temporarily raising body weight may be the best way to overcome these difficulties. In poor countries, people have adapted to mild cases of calorie deficiency by attaining a lower weight and height, by being less active, and, in the case of women, by ovulating less regularly. But for very poor people the shortfalls indicate serious stress, particularly since the periods of low intake coincide with increases in diseases and infections and higher prices of food bought.

Supplementary feeding may take place in schools, at work, or at clinics for pregnant or lactating women. With the receipt of extra institutional food, however, meals at home may be curtailed, so that the vulnerable groups do not get much additional food, and these programs do not reach the groups particularly at risk, such as children below school age. Here again, the ease of intervention (because schools already exist and delivery is cheap) is inversely related to its importance. Food supplementation at the workplace, if neither the food nor the extra energy is diverted to other activities, serves both a basic need and the goal of increased productivity.

INTERNATIONAL TRADE IN FOOD

Between 1960 and 1985, international trade in food increased both absolutely and as a ratio of total food supplies. In 1960 world imports of food were about 8 percent of production, in 1985, 12 percent. Food imports by developing countries doubled in terms of calories per head in the 1970s and then increased very little in the 1980s. By the mid-1980s, imports provided about 15 percent of their total food calories. This growing dependence gave rise to serious problems. Commercial food imports cost foreign exchange. Some developing countries were faced with serious debt-service problems. At the same time, the prices of their export commodities had fallen to all-time lows. Not only had domestic agriculture been discouraged by subsidized food imports, but tastes had been changed in the direction of wheat (of which imports by developing countries rose two and a half times in the 1970s), away from the commodities that could be produced economically in the developing countries.

As we have seen, by and large, the advanced and richer countries have taxed the majority of relatively less well off urban consumers to subsidize the better-off minority of food-growing farmers. In the poor developing countries, the relatively poorer rural population, including the food-growing farmers, have been exploited to subsidize the better-off urban communities. As a result, the world has produced large food surpluses in the advanced countries. Some of these surpluses have been used for food aid, others for commercial sales to socialist and developing countries.

But these policies have not been the only cause of the growth in food exports from the developed to the developing countries. There are more fundamental forces at work. In the advanced countries, higher incomes are not spent on food. The growth of agricultural output due to research combined with the difficulty of redeploying resources from agriculture to other sectors leads to a tendency to overproduce and export. In the developing countries, on the other hand, a large proportion of higher incomes is spent on food. Paradoxically, in those developing countries where domestic food production is growing fastest, the demand for imported food also grows rapidly. This is so because of the multiplier effects of agricultural growth on incomes and the demand for food, the autonomous growth of demand in other sectors, as well as the need to import feedstuffs for cattle. Demand for food and feed rises even more rapidly than the domestic supply of food. It is therefore the middle-income developing countries, where food production has grown rapidly but demand even more rapidly, that have been the booming markets for the food surpluses of the advanced countries.

FOOD AID

International food aid can play a useful part in alleviating hunger in low-income countries, although its beneficial role has been disputed. Most obviously in cases of disaster, whether natural or man-made, it can provide emergency relief. Its role as a more permanent instrument of policy is more controversial, particularly because it can reduce incentives to grow food domestically and can therefore aggravate the longer-term problems of hunger.

There are at least seven criticisms that have been made of food aid other than emergency famine relief. First, it reduces the pressure on recipient countries to carry out policy reforms, especially with respect to producer incentives and nutritional objectives. Second, it tends to depress domestic farm prices, to discourage domestic agricultural production, and to reduce the spread of production-increasing agricultural technology. Third, it is unreliable because it depends on donors' surpluses. When needs are greatest – that is, when prices are high – it tends to dry up. Thus, in the plentiful year 1970, annual food aid exceeded 12.5 million tons, whereas in the food crisis of 1973–74, when the price of wheat rose by 50 percent, annual shipments fell to below 6 million tons. Not only the amount and timing but also the country distribution serves the political, economic, and military interests of donor countries. Thus, in 1982 and 1983, Egypt received 18 percent of the food aid distributed by the Food Aid Convention. Moreover, since donors make their allocations in terms of money, higher prices buy a smaller amount of grain. Fourth, if the aid is administered through state agencies, it is said to reinforce state hegemony over people and does not reach the poor. Fifth, it promotes an undesirable shift in consumption patterns away from staples and towards wheat and wheat flour. Sixth, it disrupts international commercial channels.

Seventh, if the price of food contributions is overvalued, it leads to unfair burden sharing among donors.

The principal objection – that it discourages domestic agriculture by depressing prices – can be met if the counterpart funds from the sale of the food aid at market-clearing prices are used to make deficiency payments to the farmers who would otherwise be injured, so that supply prices are restored to the level at which they would be without the food aid. (Even food distributed free, say, in schools, frees budgetary revenue if the government would otherwise have paid for it.) In this way, the amount by which expenditure on food aid reduces demand for domestic food is channelled back to the farmers and incentives are fully restored. This obvious solution has been infrequently adopted because of the budgetary/political constraint. Financially straitened governments normally find uses of greater importance for the collected revenue and cannot, or do not wish to, collect additional revenue. The argument that counterpart funds should be used for deficiency payments to farmers applies also to subsidized food imports or to those admitted at an overvalued exchange rate.

Food aid can also be used to finance additional food consumed by construction workers on infrastructure projects for agriculture. Or food aid can be linked with other forms of agricultural assistance to avoid neglect of agriculture. Or additionality of demand can be ensured by distributing the food or its money equivalent to the poorest households, who could otherwise not afford it. But the importance of the charge has been greatly reduced, if not entirely eliminated, by the fact that many developing countries have become substantial food importers. (Only in low-income African countries is food aid increasing as a proportion of food imports.) In such a situation, the traditional roles of food aid and financial aid are reversed. Food aid, in so far as it replaces commercial purchases, becomes fully convertible foreign exchange, whereas financial aid often remains tied to procurement, commodities, or projects. It has, however, been argued that the free foreign exchange made available to governments presents an obstacle to fundamental reforms, such as devaluation of the exchange rate, or to investment and reforms in agriculture, which would raise food production. This is not, however, an argument against food aid, but against all forms of intergovernmental aid. Such aid can be used either to support or to delay reforms.

Food aid can be used either as balance-of-payments support or as budgetary support. The two extreme cases are as follows: (1) where the food aid is wholly additional to commercial purchases and is sold by the government in open markets at market-clearing prices, yielding government revenue in the form of counterpart funds of the maximum amount; and (2) where the food aid wholly replaces commercial imports and the foreign exchange saved is used to buy other imports or more food, or to repay debt.

Historically, there are many instances of food aid that did not harm domestic food production. Forty percent of Marshall aid consisted of food aid, yet European food production flourished excessively. Similarly, South Korea, Israel, and India received large amounts of food aid without apparent long-term harm to their agriculture.

The charge that food aid disrupts commercial sales is greatly reduced by the shrinking and now small role of food aid in total world food trade. If food aid wholly replaces commercial sales by the donor (the government pays the farmers what they otherwise would have earned), no disrupting effects on sales by other countries are suffered. Ensuring additionality (e.g., by linking it with job creation for poor people, who spend a large portion of their income on food) also reduces the damage to commercial sales.

Additionality of supply is also important in order to meet the charge that food aid creates a situation where advanced countries that are commercial food importers are faced with higher prices than if, in the absence of food aid, the food had to be sold through commercial channels, which would lower prices. The valuation of the food aid has to be done in a manner that ensures fair burden sharing between food-surplus donor countries and food-importing donor countries.

Another charge against food aid is that tastes depend, to some extent, on relative prices and food availabilities (and are not given exogenously, as is often assumed in economic analysis). A prolonged policy of finer-grain imports changes tastes away from domestically produced foodstuffs and, it is alleged, increases dependency on foreign supplies. The situation has been described as analogous to drug addiction, countries becoming "hooked" on grain. It should, however, be remembered that these changes in tastes have many causes, connected with development and urbanization, with commercial import policies, with the growing value of time as incomes grow, and with the reduced time available to women to prepare food as they join the labour force; food aid is only one, possibly small, contributory cause.

The volume of food aid has been greatly reduced in the last twenty years. Food aid has, however, increased since 1975. In the 1960s it had been as high as 16–17 million tons in some years. In 1973–74 the cereal tonnage had fallen to 5.5 million tons. In 1976–77 it was 9 million tons, and in 1984–85 it had risen to 10.4 million tons. The 1985–86 figure is higher because of emergency aid to Sub-Saharan Africa. There has been an increasing proportion of non-cereal food aid, not covered by these figures, especially European Community aid in dairy products. The aid component in food aid has also increased, and more has gone to the poorest countries. Africa has benefited at the expense of Asia, and within south Asia, Bangladesh at the expense of India. In addition, aid for projects and emergencies has replaced bilateral program aid.

At the same time, so-called subsistence crops (e.g., sorghum, millet, yams, cassava, and bananas) could be traded in local and even national markets if they were not discriminated against. Low prices for subsidized grain, the import of which is encouraged by overvalued exchange rates, or which is supplied by food aid, discourage the production of these "poor man's crops" for the market. Although devaluation would encourage the production of export crops, the demand for the subsistence crops would also rise, constituting an incentive to produce more. The precise amount would depend on the elasticities of substitution in supply and demand. Relatively little research is done on these crops, although there are some exceptions (sorghum in Maharashtra and the Sudan, maize in Zimbabwe). The International Institute for Tropical Agriculture in Ibadan (Nigeria), which is part of the system set up by the Consultative Group for International Agricultural Research, specializes in research on roots and tubers. However, more could be done for these crops, especially millet and sorghum. Even where research on food crops has been successful, African countries lack the indigenous research capacity to adopt the results of this research and adapt them to their particular situations, so that much expenditure on research has low yields.

There are a number of reasons why greater encouragement to research on subsistence crops should be given: they can be grown on marginal land, they do not require a sophisticated technology or complex skills, they are ecologically benign, and they frequently have great nutritional value. They can also be used to supplement the more preferred cereals when these are in short supply, through additions to wheat flour or maize meal. But even if research in this area were to yield good returns, there are limits to what can be expected. These crops, particularly roots and tubers, are bulky and expensive to transport. Storing and processing them is costly and often capital intensive.

The various criticisms advanced against food aid have led to the recommendation of better alternatives. Among these is a financial insurance scheme. Countries would then be able to buy food in commercial markets and would not be dependent on the political vagaries of donors. Unfortunately, such insurance schemes have not been very successful in the developing world, largely for the well-known reasons of adverse selection and moral hazard. The International Monetary Fund's Compensatory Financing Facility was extended in 1981 to apply to cereal imports. The criticism of unreliability of supplies can also be met by multi-year commitments of grain at flexible delivery. These can be bilateral or by groups of donor countries.

Food aid, properly designed and administered, is only one way in which the international community can help poor people in poor countries to be better fed. But its success depends on the ability to match the motivation and mobilization of food surpluses from advanced countries to the food needs of developing countries. A more sensible approach would be for the international community to support efforts by developing countries to eradicate hunger. Many domestic measures aiming at this entail difficulties. A land reform program, giving land to the tiller, may cause a temporary drop in food production. Tax reform may lead to capital flight. Redistribution of income through employment generation may lead to inflation, balance-of-payments difficulties, strikes, and capital flight. If the international community is serious in wishing to eradicate world hunger, it would provide resources to the reforming governments to tide them over such temporary crises and difficulties. These would be similar to the present structural adjustment loans of the World Bank, but they would be radical or reformist adjustment loans.

THE LIMITS OF FOOD SUPPLY

We have seen that for a long time people have expressed concern that population growth will outrun food supply, causing starvation. In fact, so far, food has increased more rapidly than population. In the last quarter century, 1,800 million additional people were born into this world. Agriculture has responded by producing enough food, and of a better quality, for these larger numbers. While certain regions, such as Africa, and certain groups have faced shortages, global quantities and qualities have not fallen short. Fears in the early 1970s of chronic global food shortages have proved wrong.

This does not mean that we can be complacent about food supplies. There are limits to raising food production. Environmental threats arise from the package of fertilizer, irrigation, pesticides, and mechanization. Water is becoming a very scarce resource. The chemical effects of fertilizers can be hazardous. Pesticides also threaten human health. Forest clearance, slash-and-burn agriculture, and cropping on hillsides in arid zones have led to soil erosion throughout South America, Africa, and south Asia. Desertification is spreading. There are ways of avoiding, or at least reducing, these threats without reducing food production. For example, chemical pesticides can be replaced by natural pest predators and resistant crop strains. Terracing, intercropping, and agroforestry can reduce soil erosion. Economies in the use of water can be achieved by raising the efficiency of irrigation systems. Pressures on available land can be relieved by more intensive cultivation. But this can lead to erosion, water shortages, and fertilizer and pesticide run-off. Erosion can be reduced by no-till farming, but this implies greater reliance on herbicides. Pest control can lead to resistant species. The high-yielding varieties make greater claims on water, fertilizer, and pesticides and reduce the genetic diversities of the wild varieties.

Sustainable food production calls for soil conservation and erosion control, more organic rather than artificial fertilizer (recycling of plant and animal wastes), conservation of water resources; more efficient irrigation (reuse of water and crops of less water demand), and promotion of diversity of biological strains in agriculture and of symbiotic relationships between cultivated and wild biota.

Many of these ecologically sound policies coincide with policies for greater equality. Ecologically sound techniques are particularly appropriate for small farmers. A land reform program that redistributes land to small farmers would also generate the demand for food crops.

CONCLUSION

The old New International Economic Order was concerned with various schemes, such as a common fund and an integrated commodity program, whose impact on poor people and on hunger was quite uncertain. A better new international economic order should be built from the bottom up. If a country is determined to attack hunger and malnutrition among all its citizens and if it is ready to incorporate these efforts in a strategy of environmentally sustainable development, the international community should support it by financial aid, technical assistance, and other concessions, such as opening its markets. Such an order would be an expression of human solidarity.

NOTES

1   Shlomo Reutlinger and H. Alderman, "The Prevalence of Calorie-Deficient Diets in Developing Countries," *World Development* 8 (1980).
2   See A.K. Sen, *Commodities and Capabilities* (Amsterdam: North Holland, 1985).
3   Partha Dasgupta, "Power and Control in the Good Polity," in Alan Hamlin and Phillip Pettit, eds., *The Good Polity* (Oxford: Basil Blackwell, 1989).

11 The Overexpansion of Higher Education in the Third World

MARK BLAUG

INTRODUCTION

The late 1950s witnessed the so-called human investment revolution in economic thought: the old view that education is a type of consumption, a way of spending income for the sake of current enjoyment, gave way to the new doctrine that education is a type of investment, more analogous to a capital good than a consumer good. Ever since, economists have been busy measuring the rate of return of education as a form of investment both for individuals and for society as a whole. In addition, an endless series of studies have correlated every conceivable measure of educational attainment with every possible indicator of economic performance in the effort to demonstrate that the observed association between education and economic growth around the world is causal and not just casual. From the present vantage point, however, it is extraordinary how little has been achieved by what is now an entire generation of economists of education.

We *cannot* say that education, however measured, is either a sufficient or even a necessary condition for economic growth and hence that any poor country is well advised to spend as much as possible on providing additional schooling for its people. From the standpoint of maximizing the rate of economic growth, it is all too easy to spend too much on education, judging at any rate by the history of such developing countries as Jordan, Egypt, Libya, and Zambia, countries that have long spent a larger than average proportion of their gross national product (GNP) on education and yet have below average records of economic growth. It is also all too easy to spend too much on one level of education as against another from the standpoint of either economic growth, economic efficiency, or social equity. And just as there are many countries that seem to have overspent on education without generating any discernible economic benefits, so there are also many countries that have had remarkable achievements in economic growth without having paid conspicuous attention to education. Thus, Korea, Taiwan, Singapore, and Hong Kong – the NICs (newly industrialized countries) – were laying the foundations of their subsequent high growth performance. Since then, they have emerged as high spenders on education, but that only says that rich countries spend more on education than poor ones, which suggests not that more education produces growth but that growth produces more education.

At one time, chiefly in the 1960s, there was the fond belief that it was possible to specify, more or less precisely, the manpower requirements of certain chosen targets of economic growth. Thus, once a country had decided to grow at a certain rate, the implications of that growth rate for upper secondary and tertiary education could be quantified, furnishing a definite foundation for technical and higher-education planning. However, this belief in the art of manpower forecasting died away in the 1970s as experience showed that long-term and even medium-term manpower forecasts were notoriously unreliable and not much better than pure guesswork.[1] In short, if education is indeed necessary for economic growth, it is not necessary in the technical sense that growth is absolutely impossible unless a country has the prerequisite of a certain stock of highly qualified workers.

Similarly, it has long been argued that education is a type of investment in economic growth because it makes certain individuals more productive in employment and generates "externalities" – that is, its effects spill over to the less-educated individuals who work alongside those who are more educated. However, the "screening hypothesis" argued that the educational process does little to make students more productive in later life; it merely selects those who are more able and more achievement motivated by virtue of birth or family upbringing. This hypothesis gained more and more adherents throughout the 1970s and has never been decisively refuted (although not for want of trying). In addition, thirty years of attempts to pin down the nature of the externalities of education and then to measure their magnitude have failed to produce many numbers and none that carry any conviction.[2] Here, too, the accomplishments of economists of education have been almost wholly negative.

Now, of course, we can make a case for more education by simply laying down the value judgment that everyone is entitled to education. Unfortunately, this does not get us very far. Everyone is also entitled to health care, to adequate housing, to sufficient nourishment – in short, to all the so-called basic needs. But when a country is poor, it is not possible to give everyone education until the age of sixteen, eighteen or twenty-two and, in addition, easily available health care, adequate housing, etc. However, the moment we have to choose between education, health, housing, and so forth, we need some other criterion besides the value judgment of universal entitlement to help us make the choice. It is precisely for that reason that economists had hoped to show that efficiency and growth provide the appropriate justifications for one or another educational policy.

In the same way, it is often argued that equity provides the touchstone for educational planning: since more education typically enhances an individual's lifetime income, it was thought that greater equality in the distribution of income in a country can always be secured by greater equality in the distribution of educational attainments. However, this optimism about the equalizing effects of greater access to educational opportunities has not stood the test of time and has in more recent years given way to a profound pessimism about ever achieving greater social and economic equality via the route of education.

THE GROWTH OF HIGHER EDUCATION

All this amounts to virtual nihilism in respect of the impact of education on social and economic development. Is there absolutely nothing we can say about educational policy in this context and particularly in the Third World? I believe there is, but what we can say is qualitative, judgmental, and subject to many ifs and buts. We can pronounce on matters of strategy even if we must perforce remain silent on questions of tactics. I wish now to show that one of the things we can say is that higher education in the Third World is probably, nay, almost certainly, overexpanded and that it must be cut back.

I begin by noting that we are in the midst of a worldwide financial crisis in education that is compounded in equal parts by global economic recession, a continued upward drift in the costs of education, and a tighter budgetary stance of governments almost everywhere. The nature of this financial crisis is admirably set out in Philip Coomb's *World Crisis in Education* (1985) or, for that matter, in dozens of other sources, and I shall take it as read. I shall also take it as read that there are essentially four ways in which educational systems can respond to this crisis: (1) by trimming enrolments by fiat; (2) by diluting the quality of education by spreading available resources more thinly over more and more students; (3) by reducing unit costs without diluting quality by improving the internal efficiency of schools; and (4) by tapping alternative and hitherto untried sources of funds for education. I do not intend to weigh the preponderance of probabilities among these four alternative solutions to the financial squeeze on education. I will focus attention instead on the fourth, tapping new funds for education, which I am convinced is going to play an increasing role, whatever the likelihood of cutting back enrolments or reducing unit costs.

If we take a broad historical glance at some of the most prominent advanced countries that were underdeveloped fifty or sixty years ago, say, Japan and the former Soviet Union, we discover the following pattern: The expansion of education was marked by a deliberate policy of attaining universal or nearly universal primary education before expanding secondary and higher education – this policy was pursued in Japan from about 1850 to 1912 and in Russia from 1917 to about 1930. Then, with the attainment of universal primary education, a more generous attitude was taken towards secondary education, but higher education was still kept tightly under control. Only when secondary education had become almost universal in these countries – about 1930 for Japan and about 1950 for the Soviet Union – was higher education allowed to expand. This classic pattern of allowing the educational pyramid to grow at the base, and of only allowing growth in the middle and at the apex when the base had expanded substantially, has been completely reversed in the Third World since the Second World War. Ever since 1952, in practically every one of the hundred or so developing countries in the world, secondary education and higher education have grown faster than primary education both in terms of enrolment and in terms of educational expenditure.

Not only has third-level education been the fastest-growing level of education in Africa, Asia, and Latin America since 1950, but the spread of unit costs between the first and third level of education varies from 1:2 in America and Europe to 1:50 in most of Latin America to 1:100 in Sub-Saharan Africa; in short, in most of the Third World one higher-education student costs as much as 50 to 100 primary-education students. So whatever the complex nature of the world financial crisis in education, the nub of the problem in the Third World is clearly the enormous expense of university education, which, paradoxically, falls almost wholly on the public purse. Many governments in Africa, Asia, and Latin America tolerate and even encourage fee-paying primary and secondary schools but virtually none tolerate private, fee-paying universities and colleges – the Philippines is a lonely, conspicuous exception to that rule. The third level of education in the Third World is at one and the same time the most expensive and the most subsidized of all levels of education. One may therefore conclude, without further ado, that if any progress is going to be made in tapping new funds for education, it must take the form of requiring families with children in higher education to pay a larger share of the costs of their children's schooling directly out of their own pockets.

We can sugar the pill by appropriate provisions for scholarships (grants and loans for poorer students), but unless we abandon the notion that university education must always be subsidized out of public funds, and indeed more generously subsidized than either primary or secondary education, we may as well call a halt to the discussion of new ways of financing education. Even if we were to commit ourselves to the value judgment that everyone in a poor country is entitled to higher education, that is not to say that they are entitled to it for free. When we consider the fact that higher education in most of the Third World is confined to 1 to 2 percent of the population and that the relatively affluent are grossly overrepresented among those who enter institutes of higher education, we strengthen the argument for raising fees in universities and colleges and, in the case of Africa, reducing or even abolishing the unbelievably generous maintenance allowances given to university students.[3]

To be sure, if higher education in the Third World were less generously subsidized, there is little doubt that somewhat less of it would be privately demanded. Thus, any case for shifting a larger part of the expenditure on higher education from public to private sources must rest on the demonstration that higher education is overexpanded in the Third World relative to the size of primary and secondary school enrolments. I have been arguing against the further expansion of higher education in the Third World for almost twenty years,[4] and it is with considerable satisfaction that I have witnessed some educational authorities coming round to this view in recent years.[5] Whatever criteria one adopts -manpower shortages and surpluses, rate-of-return calculations, qualitative judgments of the direct and indirect economic benefits of education – they all point to the overwhelming significance of primary education in the educational programs of developing countries.

The move to raise tuition fees must be accompanied by student loan schemes to avoid making the higher-education choice even more dependent upon parental income than it already is. But student loans commend themselves anyway on grounds both of equity and efficiency.[6] A modest scholarship program for particularly disadvantaged groups completes the policy package of increased private finance for higher education, a package whose appeal does *not*, I would insist, rest on the question of whether the public funds so released can be feasibly applied to lower levels of education. Obviously, if they could, the policy package becomes even more attractive. But it remains appealing even if it proves to be impossible to earmark the released funds for lower-level educational activities.

THE EVIDENCE

Let us now take a closer look at the empirical evidence for the contention that higher education is relatively overexpanded in the Third World. The signs of growing open unemployment among individuals with secondary and higher education throughout Asia and Africa in the 1960s and 1970s[7] have become even more pronounced in the 1980s, and the dubious practice of manpower forecasting is nowadays more likely to produce predictions of manpower surpluses than of shortages. However, unemployment statistics in developing countries are notoriously unreliable, and the technique of manpower forecasting has no scientific standing. Moreover, evidence of educated unemployment and forecasts of impending manpower surpluses are at best suggestive because they refer solely to the benefits (or lack of benefits) of education but are silent about its costs. The only appraisal technique that takes account of both the benefits and the costs of education is rate-of-return analysis. Now, as a matter of fact, there is overwhelming evidence that the social rate of return on investment in education throughout the Third World is invariably lower in secondary and higher education than in primary education (see Table 11.1).

There are two sorts of questions that may be raised about the meaning of rates of return: (1) Is it possible to explain the private demand of education in terms of the private rate of return on investments in education – that is, do individuals really choose to acquire additional education as an investment in future earning capacity? and (2) Is it possible to explain government spending on education in terms of the social rate of return on education spending, or at least to argue that governments *ought* to guide their spending on education by means of the social rate of return? It is much easier to say no to the second than to the first question. We cannot rely on monetary earnings as a measure of the total economic contribution of education, particularly for countries in which half of all secondary-educated and more than half of all higher-educated individuals work for the government at publicly determined pay scales. Given the crude methods employed by rate-of-return analysis to separate the contributions of genetic ability, family background, and years of schooling to an individual's earnings, we cannot be sure that we are in fact measuring the rate of return on schooling expenditures as such. Finally, considering that rates of return on education spending are in practice calculated from cross-section data on monetary earnings, it is doubtful that cross-section data accurately reflects the time-series evidence that we are actually after. These are only the most serious of the many objections that have been brought forward against rate-of-return analysis.[8]

Rightly or wrongly, it is widely believed that education generates significant externalities that are not captured by individual earnings. This would not matter from our point of view if each level of education generated exactly the same amount of externalities. However, it is difficult to believe that this is the case except by accident. Hence, it does matter whether, say, higher education generates greater external effects than secondary education. But as we noted earlier, all efforts to quantify the social as distinct from the individual benefits of education have so far failed, and *a priori* reasoning is of little help in placing upper or lower limits on the magnitude of the externalities of higher education.[9] For that reason alone, the evidence on *social* rates of return on education spending cannot seriously be taken to indicate anything about the appropriate size of the higher-education sector in Third World countries.

I would be inclined to pay more attention to the private rather than the social rate of return on education spending. I do believe that the strikingly high private yields of education in Africa, Asia, and Latin America, despite growing educated unemployment at the secondary and tertiary levels, are an important part of the explanation of the relentless growth of higher education

TABLE 11.1
The Private and Social Returns on Investment in Education, by Level, Region, and Country Type

Region/Country Type	N	Primary	Secondary	Higher	Primary	Secondary	Higher
Developing Countries							
Africa	9	45	26	32	28	17	13
Asia	8	31	15	18	27	15	13
Latin America	5	32	23	23	26	16	16
Intermediate Countries	8	17	13	13	13	10	8
Advanced Countries	14	–	12	12	–	11	11

Source: Psacharopoulos (1985, Table 1).
Note: N = number of countries in each group

in the Third World. Moreover, data on the private rate of return on education spending seem to suggest that the policy of squeezing earnings differentials in labour markets is yet another way of dealing with the pell-mell growth of higher education. Income policies, to use a widely accepted shorthand, are now a regular feature of economic policy in a number of Third World countries, and although they are rarely designed to deal expressly with the problem of depressing the relative earnings of university graduates, they all have the effect of doing precisely that. Nevertheless, even a general incomes policy that narrows earnings differentials in labour markets, and thus effectively saps the private incentive to acquire higher education, is inadequate unless it is accompanied by specific changes in public sector hiring practices. As a principal employer of the bulk of educated people, Asian and African governments in particular share a heavy responsibility for the excessive growth of the upper levels of the educational system. Throughout the two continents, they tie salary scales rigidly to educational qualifications; they promote by age almost automatically, with little use of performance rating; they fail to provide well-defined job titles and fail to practise job evaluation; and they invariably cap monetary earnings with generous fringe benefits and absolute tenure of employment. Even if they paid university graduates no more than secondary school leavers, such practices would be enough to create a large demand for university education. In short, the recruitment and promotion policies of the public sector in Asia and Africa have done much to promote the "diploma disease." Large salary differentials and free university education have done the rest.

There are those who regard figures on the private rate of return on education spending as having no more meaning than figures on the social rate; they argue that there is no rational private calculus with respect to education: individuals stay on in the educational system as much, if not more, for consumption than for investment reasons. But those who employ this line of argument have never satisfactorily explained the relative plausibility of almost all the rate-of-return figures that have so far been calculated. After all, would rate-of-return calculations ever have survived the light of day if they had produced figures of minus 10 percent or plus 300 percent for the private and social rates of return on education spending? In other words, the figures we actually get range from 54 to 75 percent and form a meaningful pattern, not just in one country but in some fifty countries for which rate-of-return figures have been calculated.

Having discarded social rates of return as decisive criteria for evaluating the relative size of higher education, what, then, is the basis of my contention that higher education in the Third World is overexpanded? To say that higher education is overexpanded is to say that primary education is underexpanded; it is to say that the achievement of universal primary education at the earliest possible date has greater priority in the educational programs of Third World countries than the further expansion of higher education. But why not both? Not both for the reason, as we said earlier, that Third World education is in the grip of a financial crisis. There is some scope for cost-saving measures in primary education itself, but these can finance only a small part of the expansion required to achieve universal primary education. The bulk of the resources will have to come from the contraction of secondary and higher education. And as long as a year of higher education costs eighty times as much as a year of primary education – a median figure for Africa and Asia – even a marginal shift of resources from tertiary to primary education could work wonders in increasing enrolments in the first level of education. It has been calculated that in six African countries primary enrolment ratios could be raised to 100 percent overnight merely by shifting 20 percent of current educational expenditure on secondary and higher education to primary education.[10] Similarly, even modest fees charged to higher-education students could generate surprisingly large sums for the expansion of primary education, large that is in terms of the expansion they would purchase.[11]

PRIMARY EDUCATION

What is the evidence that universal primary education has priority among the desirable objectives of educational planning in the Third World? It must be conceded that evidence of the direct economic benefits of the first four to six years of schooling is very thin on the ground. To many, it is simply obvious that rudimentary literacy and numeracy are absolute prerequisites to economic development, but if that were so, it would be difficult to explain the one-time industrialization of the First and Second World, which typically proceeded with an essentially illiterate workforce.[12] Even today, the cognitive requirements of semi-skilled factory work in Europe or America are no more demanding than what is involved in driving an automobile. The qualities that modern industry does require from its workforce are compliance, punctuality, attentiveness, drive, and so on – in short, a definite set of what social psychologists call "effective behavioural traits." These traits are willy-nilly inculcated by every schooling process as part of the "hidden curriculum."[13] However, they are also inculcated by parental rearing, and although it is plausible to argue that primary schools in developing countries bear a much larger burden of the socialization process than those in developed countries, the fact remains that little progress has yet been made in quantifying these relationships. Similarly, some studies show that primary schooling has a positive effect on the agricultural output of small farmers in Africa and on the propensity of youngsters to participate in the informal sector in urban areas,[14] but these studies are too few in number and too crudely executed to allow firm conclusions to be drawn.

There are also studies that demonstrate that primary schooling generates indirect economic benefit in the form of lower birth rates and improved standards of sanitation and health care.[15] One may also insist that some of the non-economic benefits of primary schooling, such as greater participation in political life via greater access to the mass media, are in fact economic benefits if one adopts a sufficiently long time horizon. After all, economic development is impossible without political stability, which in turn implies a measure of national solidarity and social cohesion, and all of these are encouraged by widespread primary education. So, without pretending that universal primary education is a sufficient condition for modernization, it is, surely, a necessary condition.

And yet at the end of the day what we are left with is not decisive evidence, but a qualitative judgment that the economic and social returns on investment in primary schooling in most developing countries are higher than the returns on investment in secondary and higher education.

EQUITY

The argument so far has been conducted entirely, or almost entirely, in terms of the objectives of static efficiency and dynamic growth. I wish now to turn to questions of equity, which I would insist (against Benjamin Higgins) are, at least in principle, separable from and additive to issues of efficiency and growth. The question is, Would user charges or tuition fees in Third World higher-education institutions promote equity? Or, alternatively expressed, do subsidies to higher education as implied by the present system of "free" higher education promote equality in some sense of that term such that any reduction in subsidies would reduce equality? There has been a long and inconclusive debate on the distributional effects of public subsidies for higher education in the United States that tests the contention that those subsidies actually have the perverse effect of transferring income from poor to rich taxpayers.[16] A few studies dealing with the Third World tend on balance to support that contention.[17] But all of these studies, whether for developed or developing countries, are based on cross-section observations of pre- and post-tax incomes. Programs of public finance for higher education, however, are motivated and justified by considerations of intergenerational transfers of income: the electorate agrees to be taxed now for the sake of subsidies their offspring may enjoy in the future. Since the benefits of higher education are not received by the same generation that pays taxes, public subsidies for higher education must be evaluated in the context of lifetime incomes.

In the absence of lifetime income data, we can only speculate about the possible effects of higher education subsidies in Third World circumstances. These effects depend in essence on the respective degrees of progression of both taxes and subsidies in the sense of the changing ratio of taxes/subsidies to income levels.

Higher education tends to raise lifetime incomes, and it is possible to imagine a tax system so steeply progressive that university graduates eventually repay the costs of their own subsidized higher education out of extra taxes paid on their education-augmented income. In that kind of world, higher education subsidies would be nothing more than society's peculiar way of lending to students the wherewithal to participate in higher education, the costs of which would be fully recouped in the course of the graduate's working life. But this is not the world we live in. No tax system in the world, and certainly no tax system in the Third World, is so progressive that graduates ever pay back to society the full costs of their higher education. It follows that higher-education subsidies always involve some transfer of income from the less to the more educated, from those who fail to receive higher education to those who do receive it. And since the unequal incidence of higher-education subsidies necessarily results in unequal effects on future incomes, we can hardly escape a life-cycle approach to the distributional effects of higher-education subsidies.

To gauge these life-cycle effects, we need to form a judgment on (1) the magnitude of the tendency of schooling to raise future incomes and (2) the degree to which opportunities to gain additional schooling are independent of parental incomes. The greater the impact of schooling on income and the greater the rate of intergenerational mobility, the greater is the chance that higher-education subsidies work to equalize lifetime incomes. If schooling raises incomes markedly, then the existence of a progressive system of income taxation maximizes the tendency of graduates to pay back the costs of their own schooling via taxation; if schooling acts as an avenue of upward mobility in the sense of educated children earning more than their parents ever did at the same age, then higher-education subsidies might well promote greater equality in the distribution of lifetime incomes. Given the low level of tax compliance in Third World countries, the first of these two considerations suggests that higher-education subsidies probably have perverse effects on lifetime income distribution in Asia, Africa, and Latin America. On the other hand, the second of the two considerations suggests exactly the opposite. It follows that there is no obviously correct answer to the question of whether higher-education subsidies in Third World countries are or are not equitable.

CONCLUSION

Such agnostic conclusions about the present system of subsidizing higher education should not affect our central argument about reforming the entire system of finance for higher education. There can be little doubt that if current subsidies to Third World higher education were increasingly directed towards poorer students through a combination of tuition fees and student loans repayable as a proportion of future income, the results in terms of equity would almost certainly represent an improvement over the present system. And if the funds thus released from higher education were reallocated to primary education, thereby expanding educational opportunities for poor people in rural areas, the equity case for the introduction of user charges in higher education would be complete. In other words, despite the fact that the economics of education has so far disappointed virtually all the great hopes that were held out for the subject twenty-five years ago, it is possible to draw one dramatic conclusion about educational policy in the Third World that runs diametrically counter to what is currently practised in just about every Third World country.

NOTES

1 B. Ahamad and M. Blaug, *The Practice of Manpower Forecasting* (Amsterdam: Elsevier, 1973); and R.J. Youdi and K. Hinchliffe, *Forecasting Skilled Manpower Needs* (Paris: UNESCO-IIEP, 1985).
2 M. Blaug, "The Economics of Education in Developing Countries: Current Trends and New Priorities," *Third World Quarterly*, January 1979, reprinted in M. Blaug, *The Economics of Education and the Education of an Economist* (Aldershot: Edward Elgar, 1987).
3 G. Psacharopoulos, J.P. Tan, and E. Jimenez, *Financing Education in Developing Countries: An Exploration of Policy Options* (Washington, DC: World Bank, 1986), box 1.3.
4 M. Blaug, "The Economics of Education in Developing Countries: Current Trends and New Priorities," *Third World Quarterly*, January 1979, reprinted in Blaug, *The Economics of Education*.

5 Psacharopoulos, Tan, and Jimenez, *Financing Education*; and World Bank, *Education in Sub-Saharan Africa: Policies for Adjustment Revitalization and Expansion* (Washington, DC: World Bank, 1988).
6 M. Woodhall, *Student Loans as a Means of Financing Higher Education: Lessons from International Experience* (Washington, DC: World Bank, 1983), Staff Working Papers no. 599; idem, *Lending for Learning: Designing a Student Loan Program for Developing Countries* (London: Commonwealth Secretariat, 1987); G. Psacharopoulos and M. Woodhall, *Education for Development: An Analysis of Investment Choices* (New York: Oxford University Press, 1985); A. Mingat and J.P. Tan, "Expanding Education through User Charges: What Can Be Achieved in Malawi and Other LDCs," *Economics of Education Review* 5, no. 3 (1986); and idem, "Financing Public Higher Education in Developing Countries: The Potential Role of Loan Schemes," *Higher Education* 15 (1986).
7 UN-ECAFE, *Economic Survey of Asia and the Far East 1973, Part 1 Education and Employment* (Bangkok: UN-ECAFE, 1973); and UN-ECA, *Economic Survey of Africa 1977, Part 1 Education and Employment* (Addis Ababa: UN-ECA, 1978).
8 M. Blaug, "The Empirical Status of Human Capital Theory: A Slightly Jaundiced Survey," *Journal of Economic Literature*, September 1976, reprinted in Blaug, *The Economics of Education*.
9 M. Blaug, "Declining Subsidies to Higher Education: An Economic Analysis," in H. Giersch, ed., *Reassessing the Role of Government in a Mixed Economy*, 228–30 (Kiel, Germany: Institute fur Weltwirtschaft, 1983), reprinted in Blaug, *The Economics of Education*.
10 A. Mingat and J.P. Tan, "Subsidization of Higher Education versus the Expansion of Primary Enrollments: What Can a Shift of Resources Achieve in Sub-Saharan Africa?" *International Journal of Educational Development* 5, no. 4 (1985); and Psacharopoulos and Woodhall, *Education for Development*, Table 2:1.
11 Mingat and Tan, "Financing Public Higher Education."
12 M. Blaug, *An Introduction to the Economics of Education* (London: Penguin Books, 1972), 247–64.
13 M. Blaug, "Where Are We Now in the Economics of Education?" *Economics of Education Review* 4, no. 1 (1985), reprinted in Blaug, *The Economics of Education*.
14 C. Colclough, "The Impact of Primary Schooling on Economic Development: A Review of the Evidence," *World Development* 10, no. 3 (1982); and C. Colclough, K. Lewin, and J. Oxemham, "Donor Agency Support for Primary Education: Strategies Considered," *International Journal of Educational Development* 5, no. 4 (1985).
15 Colclough, Lewin, and Oxemham, "Donor Agency Support."
16 M. Blaug, "The Distributional Effects of Higher Education Subsidies,"

Economics of Education Review 2, no. 3 (1982), reprinted in Blaug, *The Economics of Education*.

17   Psacharopoulos and Woodhall, *Education for Development*, 10–44; and Psacharopoulos, Tan, and Jimenez, *Financing Education*.

PART FOUR

International Aspects

12 New Directions in Canada's Foreign Aid? The Winegard Report and Beyond

IRVING BRECHER with the
assistance of David Gillies

INTRODUCTION

Perhaps no aspect of international development policy has generated more controversy than foreign aid. Development assistance is typically a very small percentage of national income for donor and recipient countries alike; yet there have been voluminous debates about its impact on both. Some have argued that aid retards the development of the recipient, others have insisted that aid accelerates donors' growth, and still others have maintained that aid is good for both or bad for both. A basic premise underpinning this essay is that there is now a preponderance of empirical evidence pointing to significant net economic gains for many aid recipients over the past four decades.[1] A second major premise is that while direct donor and recipient benefits are not necessarily incompatible, the most efficient, least-cost ways of achieving the former are generally to be found outside the aid program.

This essay is rooted in several other kinds of conviction. One has to do with the ubiquitous role of market forces in neoclassical economics. In recent years, to be sure, it has become increasingly clear that stunted growth in many of the less-developed countries (LDCs) stems partly – sometimes largely – from neglect or suppression of market signals reflected in real prices and costs. But gross market failure is no less a fact in much of the Third World, and so is the inappropriateness of the market to meet a variety of social goals. Foreign aid stands, above all, for the general proposition that substantial government intervention in the marketplace is a necessary condition for maximizing welfare.

Two of our working premises centre on the concept of equity. That it is not only a question of reducing extreme inequalities in the distribution of income has come to be universally accepted by development economists; in the aid context, equity also involves the desire to benefit the poorest people in the poorest countries, and to satisfy such basic needs as food, health, housing, and education. There is more, however. Equity embraces protecting and promoting socio-economic needs as a matter of right, and giving parallel recognition to equal treatment before the law in a free society. We believe that pursuing equity in this broadest sense unlocks enormous amounts of creative human energy and that, in the long run, the pursuit of equity is therefore likely to be in close harmony with the search for efficient aid-programming and for least-cost economic growth in recipient countries. We also believe that "development" entails the fullest possible realization of *all* basic human rights and that the equity objective of foreign aid therefore stands on its own, quite apart from any impact on economic efficiency or growth.

A final underlying premise of this essay involves its focus on Canada. Conceptually, there is no compelling reason here for singling out Canada's aid program. But Canadian experience does underscore the fact that highly complex policy issues confront even a middle-power donor relatively unconstrained by security and geopolitical factors. Perhaps more to the point, Canada has long provided a major venue for lively public debate on rethinking foreign aid. Needless to add, Ben Higgins has contributed much to the intellectual foundations of that debate; there is thus no more fitting way to honour him than with an essay on Canadian aid.

We turn, now, to *For Whose Benefit?* – a report produced in May 1987 by the Standing Committee of the House of Commons on External Affairs and International Trade, then chaired by William Winegard.[2] It represents the most comprehensive review of Canada's foreign-aid program since the ill-fated *Strategy for International Development Cooperation*.[3] Canadian official development assistance (ODA) had suffered from a combination of policy drift and inertia for a number of years, and the Winegard report was a welcome injection of new energy and ideas into that vacuum. It is, in fact, a landmark study, both in the breadth of issues considered and in the range of specific measures proposed.

The report addresses four fundamental themes: (1) the role of international development in foreign policy, (2) unease over expanded commercial objectives in aid giving, (3) a growing interest in linking human rights to the selection of aid recipients and the allocation of funding, and (4) the aid problems posed by bureaucratic centralization, inadequate personnel, and rudimentary evaluative mechanisms. There is an overarching emphasis on human-resource development for the poorest groups and regions in the Third World. Taken together, the recommendations of the Winegard committee are far-reaching and, if implemented, would produce a radical restructuring of the priorities and organization of Canada's aid program.

But change, even if long overdue, is by no means certain. Foreign aid, which accounts for a small fraction of federal spending (roughly 2 percent), is not a crucial item on the political agenda and will probably continue to be overshadowed by such pressing government concerns as free trade, tax reform, and constitutional revision.

One of the more disturbing features of a number of earlier policy reviews is their tendency to be ignored. The 1976 strategy provides a vivid illustration. Its key pledges remain largely unrealized. Will the Winegard report endure the same fate? Let us keep this question in mind while we take a closer look.

A STRONGER ROLE FOR INTERNATIONAL DEVELOPMENT

Although international development has long been rhetorically accorded a central place in Canada's international relations, it has rarely been given the real priority that it deserves. Foreign aid, to repeat, is not a prime political issue. The development thrust has been further constrained by a fragmented system of ODA delivery and by the absence of a clear legislative mandate for the Canadian International Development Agency (CIDA). Over the years, CIDA has struggled to maintain a precarious identity – its credibility continually under threat from unrelenting media criticism and from the encroachment of other government organizations on its policy-making turf. In these circumstances, it has been very difficult to raise a loud and influential development voice within the federal cabinet.

The Winegard report tackles this problem head-on by proposing a number of initiatives to strengthen ODA's legislative base within the broader foreign-policy framework. Surprisingly, for an agency that is responsible for the bulk of Canada's $2.5-billion aid program, CIDA continues to operate without a legislative mandate. Currently, all legislation concerning its portion of the ODA budget is implemented in an *ad hoc* way or by order-in-council. By contrast, the International Development Research Centre (IDRC), which accounts for only a fraction of the total ODA budget, was created by an act of Parliament and has considerable organizational autonomy by virtue of its status as a Crown corporation. The lack of a legislative basis for CIDA is a serious flaw that weakens performance and discourages public scrutiny through Parliament.

The Winegard report recommends the replacement of the minister for external relations, who is currently responsible for CIDA, by a "Minister for International Development." The new minister would be supported by an "International Development Advisory Council" containing academics, business people, and representatives from non-governmental organizations (NGOs). In effect, the present minister would be elevated from a junior position to equal status with the minister for international trade, as part of the senior hierarchy within the Department of External Affairs.

A second limb of the proposed legislative foundation for Canadian ODA is the proclamation, for the first time, of a "Development Assistance Charter." The charter would entrench the primacy of development priorities in ODA planning and implementation, while recognizing that other foreign-policy goals can be pursued through the ODA program where these do not conflict with development objectives. It would reiterate the established principle that ODA be concentrated on "the poorest countries and people"(*WR*, 12). Finally, it would emphasize the importance of strengthening "the human and institutional capacity" of recipient countries (ibid.).

The Winegard committee provides a broad new focus on the question of legislative mandate. Its recommendations have the potential to strengthen the role of development objectives in Canada's foreign-policy system, and this upgrading is likely to be increasingly necessary as ODA issues extend further into the trade, diplomatic, and political domains. Some caveats are in order, however. New legislative instruments do not, in themselves, guarantee greater influence or the protection of the development thrust of the ODA program. Particularly in the case of the minister for international development, much will depend on the commitment, skills, and experience of the incumbent. The record in recent years is not overly reassuring in this regard.

AID AND TRADE

A perennial debate in the field of foreign aid turns on the issue of compatibility among the multiple objectives of aid giving. This debate has been particularly heated over the use of ODA funds to promote the commercial interests of the donor. Some critics claim that the introduction of essentially self-interested commercial criteria is irreconcilable with the development objectives of ODA. We do not take this extreme position here; rather, we agree with the Winegard report that there is no logical reason why the Canadian business sector should not contribute to international development while deriving domestic benefits in terms of job creation and increased trade. In practice, however, complementarity has often failed to be achieved; in Canada, as in other donor countries, the twin objectives of development and commercial self-interest have rested uneasily alongside each other. The question *For Whose Benefit?* is highly pertinent here.

Perhaps the most widely criticized and enduring feature of Canadian ODA is its heavy reliance on tied aid.[4] Approximately 80 percent of Canadian bilateral aid and roughly 95 percent of Canadian food aid has had to consist of domestically produced materials and services. Such requirements are well known to be counterproductive in that they frequently force recipients to buy goods and services that are available more cheaply from other sources.[5] The practice of tying thus reduces the overall value of the aid dollar. It also constrains South-South trade by inhibiting recipients from tendering contracts with other LDCs.[6]

Over the years, the Development Assistance Committee (DAC) of the Organization for Economic Co-operation and Development (OECD) has worked to reduce the amount of aid tying. Canada has been remarkably recalcitrant, however; it still has one of the poorer records among the eighteen members of the DAC. This intransigence stems, in part, from the conviction of successive governments that since many Canadian exporting firms are uncompetitive internationally, they require state help to maintain productivity and employment. Persistent lobbying by Canadian exporters has strengthened this perception.[7] And there has been substantial bureaucratic resistance to change. The fact is, however, that the market-penetration and job-creation potential of the tied-aid program is small and certainly very costly in comparison with alternative mechanisms.[8]

In sum, aid tying is a mercantilist, trade-distorting practice that cannot easily be reconciled with claims that Canadian aid is overwhelmingly focused on economic development. Tied aid serves as an inefficient export subsidy that props up uncompetitive Canadian firms and retards the difficult but necessary process of domestic structural adjustment.

The Winegard report recommends a gradual increase in untied aid to a maximum of 50 percent of bilateral funding, as well as some additional food untying in relation to LDC suppliers. No target date is suggested for the 50 percent figure, and it is reasonable to ask why the ceiling is not higher. But this is certainly a welcome proposal as far as it goes. Also helpful is the committee's emphasis on the "import ... side of the aid-trade equation" (WR, 43). While voices are loud on export promotion through ODA, relatively little is heard about the impact of Canadian restrictions on imports from aid recipients in particular and the Third World in general. Such measures are a powerful brake on the economic growth of LDCs. Accordingly, the committee urges the government to make import promotion "a declared objective of ODA policy" and to "work out a realistic agenda for reducing protectionist barriers to developing country imports" (WR, 44).

The committee is more cautious when confronting the issue of concessional export financing. "Credit mixte" and other forms of "associated financing" have become increasingly popular in recent years. Now used by virtually all Western countries, they are devices for "blending" aid funds with commercial loans.[9] In this way, a lender can offer a foreign-exchange-starved developing country an export-credit package with interest rates well below prevailing market rates and generous repayment terms. France was the pioneer; its term "credit mixte" remains in widespread use.

The global economic recession of 1981–82 was the main reason for the increasing recourse to concessional export financing. Sluggish growth rates, balance-of-payments deficits, and fluctuating interest rates in the North were mirrored in the South by severe foreign-exchange constraints, debt rescheduling, and a reduced ability to import capital goods. In an atmosphere of intensified competition, Western nations felt compelled to consider this new approach in order to protect markets. Canada is a relative newcomer, and Canadian transactions remain modest in comparison to those of other lenders. Nonetheless, in the decade after 1977 CIDA aid funds were "blended" with the market-oriented loans of the Export Development Corporation (EDC) in twenty-three co-financed projects yielding a total value of $1.5 billion in Canadian goods and services.[10]

But rapid changes in the international economy were not the only important factor prompting a Canadian desire to use ODA for export promotion. Declining export competitiveness (particularly in the Third World, where Canada's market share has weakened) and a renewed interest in trade diversification also contributed to a more determined effort on mixed credits.

Proponents argue that such credits have a developmental impact by (1) stretching the aid dollar over a wider range of projects and (2) enabling LDCs to continue their national development programs despite foreign-exchange constraints and debt-repayment problems. Moreover, it is claimed that associated-financing packages can be instrumental in helping the lending country break into new markets and expand current ones by generating "follow-up" orders. United Kingdom experience is instructive here. A study of six projects financed in 1977–78 under the British line of mixed credit, the Aid/Trade Provision (ATP), found that by 1985 only one of those projects had generated follow-up orders.[11] On the basis of such comparative data, the study concludes that "the balance of evidence is against the proposition that aid can enable exporters to win *and retain* a foothold in a market previously unavailable to them" (p. 217).

Critics of associated financing point to its trade- and development-distorting tendencies. Export orders won through ODA are, in fact, likely to be "trade diverting" – that is, won at the expense of lower-cost exporters in other countries – rather than "trade creating"; to that extent, the commercial benefits that aid is able to generate are particular to a single donor. This is really a form of protectionism contrary to the spirit of the General Agreement on Tariffs and Trade (GATT).

From a development perspective, the major problem with combining ODA with commercial loans is that the package is fundamentally "trade-driven." Given the competitiveness of the capital-goods export sector, there is little time for the donor agency to assemble the information needed to appraise the developmental viability of a project. By the same token, there is less scope for meaningful policy dialogue between donor and recipient. "In such circumstances, any developmental benefit which does materialise will be a lucky by-product, and by no means a planned outcome of the decision to give aid."[12]

The prevailing ambivalence on concessional export financing is reflected in the Winegard report. The committee recognizes the trade-distorting problem and acknowledges that mixed credits are used to finance projects "for what are essentially trade, not development, reasons" (WR, 40). This is also deemed to be "a high-stakes game in which neither Canada nor the poor are likely to win many benefits" (ibid.). On the other hand, the committee downplays the finding of a major public-opinion poll that most Canadians view the ODA program principally as a form of humanitarianism rather than as an instrument for export promotion or job creation.[13] "There will be occasions when development can be exporter-led" (ibid.), and trade promotion, says the report, is a legitimate component of Canadian aid strategy as long as it does not compromise development objectives. True, but there is also the compelling fact that mixed credits tend to deepen the concentration on large-scale, infrastructural projects and divert ODA funds from the poorest countries to middle-income LDCs. Moreover, as with tied aid, the market and job-creation potential of such subsidies is not impressive.

UK experience is again worth noting. A 1982 UK government report found that the costs to the British economy of creating employment via export credits was £33,000 per job, as compared with £7,000 per job for both a "Community Enterprise Programme" and a "Young Workers Scheme."[14]

A major study sponsored by the Economic Council of Canada (ECC) examined the activities and costs of the EDC and found that the benefits of export subsidies to the Canadian economy were "by no means clear."[15] The same trade advantages could be achieved by removing tariff barriers; hence, "the public financing of exports in a protectionist environment is at best a compensatory measure and at worst a measure that adds more distortions to the efficiency losses caused by tariffs" (pp. 53, 59). The ECC study also found that the *net* results of subsidized intervention were nil in terms of job creation.

The Winegard committee does reiterate that Canadian aid policy should be driven primarily by recipient needs and development goals. "CIDA's responsibility ... is not to improve Canada's trade prospects as such; [there] are more appropriate instruments with which to tackle these" (WR, 42). However, the committee's recommendations on associated financing are less than fully consistent with these principles. First, the government is asked to continue using its voice in the Development Assistance Committee to discourage such financing "by increasing the costs to donors and by strengthening ... [the] transparency [of] reporting" (ibid.). But this route has yielded slender results beyond an increase in the grant element of aid-blended credits to 35 percent (with a 50 percent minimum vis-à-vis the least-developed countries). The voluntary basis of DAC and the absence of effective compliance mechanisms have so far prevented any agreement on the phasing-out of this essentially mercantilist practice.

The Winegard committee's bottom line is that concessional funds blended with commercial loans can be reported as ODA provided they meet "CIDA's development criteria as defined in the ODA charter" (ibid.). But "development priorities" in the proposed charter are pitched at too broad a level to offer much protection. At present, large infrastructural projects are considered to have a development component if they involve a sector that has priority in a recipient's current five-year or national development plan. This is hardly a rigorous definition; indeed, it encourages abuse. Similarly, the absence of more specific operational criteria undermines the credibility of the safeguards that the committee seeks to enshrine. Moreover, if the charter is to be the standard, then much of what Canada currently reports as "associated financing" negates objectives proclaimed in terms of the "poorest countries and people." Finally, the committee's tacit approval of associated financing is at odds with its pointed recommendations to cut tied aid and with its urgent plea that Canada lead the way in a global attack on "the debt problem that is strangling prospects for economic recovery in so many countries" (WR, 127).

We agree that export promotion is an important policy concern, particularly in the light of Canada's small and declining share of developing-country markets. We remain unconvinced, however, that mixed credits are an effective technique for promoting this objective. Indeed, given the slow progress on these credits in the OECD, their limited benefits, and their negative implications for development, it is time for Canada to begin phasing out this trade-and-development-distorting practice.

The government's abandonment of a planned "Trade and Development Facility" was certainly a step in the right direction. An even stronger signal would be sent by a graduated reduction in the proportion of ODA used for export promotion over the next five to ten years. Then, too, aid-trade funds should be substantially diverted to the enhancement of information services (including feasibility studies) that CIDA provides for domestic businesses seeking entry into LDC markets. The international financial institutions (IFIs) are especially relevant here. As has been long recognized, there is a marked imbalance between Canadian contributions to the multilateral development banks and the procurement levels of Canadian firms competing for bank tenders. A diversion of aid-trade funds from export credits to non-distortive trade promotion would not be in conflict with the Winegard committee's view that "the business community is the most underutilized resource in Canadian official development assistance," and that Canadian business should "become much more aggressive in meeting the needs and responding to the commercial opportunities within developing countries" (WR, 99, 103).

HUMAN RIGHTS: THE MISSING LINK

Perhaps the most innovative part of the Winegard report is its approach to human rights. The committee could not help but be impressed by the strength of conviction among Canadians that foreign aid should be linked to respect for basic human rights in recipient countries.[16] It is, says the committee, a sensitive and complex issue that "understandably makes a lot of governments, bureaucracies and businesses very uncomfortable. But it must be confronted squarely ... fear of controversy should not dictate policy"(*WR*, 23).

An interesting "classification grid" is put forward for CIDA's consideration. It ranges from "human rights negative" through "human rights watch" and "human rights satisfactory" to "human rights positive"(*WR*, 27–8). Eligibility for government-to-government aid would range, accordingly, from zero to the highest level of claims on increased resources. It would remain for CIDA to (1) set up a "Human Rights Unit" for training development officers and for coordinating policy with the Department of External Affairs ; (2) work out the specifics of a "Human Rights in Development Policy Framework"; (3) table annually in Parliament an "ODA-Human Rights Review" prepared in collaboration with External Affairs; and (4) include a human-rights-evaluation section in all country-program reviews, as well as in documents pertaining to project approval (*WR*, 29–30). In the multilateral sphere, Canada should seek to have human-rights concerns openly discussed by the IFIs and should "examine very critically multilateral loans to countries deemed 'human rights negative' or 'human rights watch'' ' (*WR*, 30).

The Winegard committee takes dead aim at CIDA's core-country programming system – largely on the grounds that it "betrays a confusion of objectives ... and that nothing is said specifically about human rights or about our capacity to reach the poorest people" (*WR*, 65). Core status, it is argued, should not be at all driven by diplomatic or commercial considerations. In this context, the committee recommends that the existing system be abolished and that core eligibility be determined by developmental factors, including absolute economic need in the recipient country and "respect ... for human rights in the broadest sense" (*WR*, 66).

Country selection is one thing, program selection quite another. But *both* provide scope for linkage with human rights. The challenge in the latter case is, in the committee's words, "to shape the aid program so as to promote strategies of development that enhance human rights" (*WR*, 15). Out of this recognition comes its overriding emphasis on human-resource development, through particular sectors like education and health care and through technical assistance built into virtually all ODA programs. The report speaks eloquently of "the struggle to liberate human potential ... Thinking 'Human Resource Development' in everything we do should become a trademark of Canadian aid" (*WR*, 13, 15).

There is yet another facet of aid linkage to human rights.[17] To the extent that Canadians care about civil and political freedoms abroad, it makes sense to enrich our ODA policy with a new mechanism for sharing our experience with interested Third World countries. The committee sees a compelling case for this view and commends the federal government for responding favourably to a 1986 parliamentary proposal that an "International Institute of Human Rights and Democratic Development" be established. So far so good. But we wish that the committee had said more – even while two "special rapporteurs" were preparing to advise the government on how best to proceed. (The rapporteurs' report was submitted in June 1987 and released in November; more on that report later.)

Socio-economic rights now enjoy almost universal acceptance. And civil-political rights are catching up; witness the ongoing human-rights revolution in Eastern Europe.

In a juridical sense, to be sure, there has been no time lag at all. The Universal Declaration of Human Rights, adopted without dissent by the United Nations General Assembly in 1948, stipulates that everyone has the right not only to a job, an education, and an adequate standard of living, but also to freedom of expression, assembly and political participation, and to a variety of freedoms proscribing arbitrary arrest, detention, and deprivation of life. In 1966 these and related principles assumed treaty status through two international covenants: one on economic, social, and cultural rights, and the other on civil and political rights. As of 1989, the covenants had been ratified by more than half the UN member-states.[18]

This kind of consensus is important, but it could not guarantee that all countries – or even the ratifying countries – would translate legal obligations into government policy. In fact, as the postwar focus on Third World development grew sharper, it became quite fashionable to act on the presumption that during the economic take-off, civil and political freedoms were a luxury that poor nations generally could not afford.

Massive poverty, starvation, and disease do have a unique way of capturing hearts and minds everywhere. Restrictions on freedom of speech and choice tend to produce a lesser sense of urgency, but they also have a propensity for outcomes that include arbitrary imprisonment, torture, and summary execution. Global revulsion has risen with the scale of such outcomes and with the spread of instant-communications technology. In addition, the international development community is now coming to recognize that there is no necessary incompatibility between socio-economic and civil-political rights, and that, on the contrary, the latter "are best calculated to release creative energies, to generate adaptability, and to advance the welfare of disadvantaged groups which do not share equitably in the fruits of economic growth."[19]

Canada has travelled a long way in this regard. But like most other countries in the West, it only recently began to acknowledge that protection against life-threatening denials of personal liberty rings hollow when it comes and goes with the whims of an authoritarian regime, and that the ultimate goal should be *enduring* protection under a system embracing pluralism, free dissent, the rule of law, and periodic free and fair elections whereby existing governments can be removed and new ones installed.[20]

Several types of spurious argument have created a lingering reluctance to legitimize "democratic development": first, for example, that "democracy" cannot be clearly defined; second, that it is nothing more than the hand-maiden of *status quo* capitalism; and third, that Western political institutions and concepts of rights are inherently unsuited to non-Western societies. As such hang-ups fade, civil-political rights *and* democratic change can logically be viewed as the third pillar of the conceptual structure housing Third World development. They become a central aim of foreign policy, quite apart from their impact on social and economic growth.

But civil-political rights are no more bound up with democracy than with socio-economic rights. Freedom, to repeat, militates against gross economic inequality. And focusing on freedom makes it difficult to forget that economic development is ultimately not about dams, roads, or factories, but about *individual* human beings and about achieving decent levels of material welfare. High rates of growth, on the other hand, are an antidote for fragility in regard to freedom and democratic advance.

For development theorists and practitioners alike, it has become conventional to speak of "basic human needs" – food, housing, health, and education in particular. From a UN perspective, these are simply socio-economic rights by another name. As such, they have the same linkages with civil-political freedom. What is more, those indivisibilities are pertinent to any assessment of foreign-aid programs. And yet there are cogent arguments for maintaining a policy distinction between socio-economic "needs" and civil-political "rights." For one thing, the aid community continues to dissociate basic needs from human rights.[21] For another, the civil-political covenant binds each country to directly honouring specific human rights, while much of the economic-social-cultural covenant is couched in terms of promised steps towards future implementation.[22] Perhaps most important, basic needs are an integral part of economic aid per se; they are *internal* to the complex process of judging socio-economic efficiency. By contrast, civil-political freedom is largely *external* to this process; it centres on the question of how to best condition economic aid on violation of, and respect for, non-economic human rights.[23] Here, indeed, is one of the newest challenges on the aid stage. In this context, it may well be appropriate to equate liberty with human rights.

If the Winegard report had made these points, it might have avoided some of its shortcomings on the issue of aid-rights linkage. In any event, the gaps are there.

Consider, first, the omission of human rights from the proposed "Development Assistance Charter." The most plausible explanation would seem to be that in drafting its statement of charter principles, the committee took absolute need and "human development" as a joint proxy for the totality of human rights. Operating at such levels of generality, however, opens the door to inconsistency and detracts from precise formulation of public policy.

We return, in this connection, to the committee's criteria for core-country eligibility. There, by contrast with the charter, "human rights in the broadest sense" are listed *in addition* to poverty and human skills. There also, by contrast with the latter specifics, "the broadest sense" is left undefined. Earlier references are made to civil-political and cultural rights. And there is the helpful "classification grid" for linking aid to abuse of human rights. But that is as far as the report goes. No attempt is made to itemize, assess, or rank these rights. It follows, of course, that one would look in vain for committee ideas on quantifying human-rights performance.

Constructing an index is a daunting task. Information is often sketchy and inaccurate, sometimes because of concealment by rights-violating countries. There are also cross-cultural differences in the interpretation of human rights. But concrete, reasonably reliable data have become increasingly available from a variety of sources. And all member-states of the United Nations do subscribe to a charter enshrining "universal respect for, and observance of, human rights and fundamental freedoms for all without distinction as to race, sex, language, or religion" (article 55[c]).

Indexing is, in fact, as feasible as it is desirable. Gastil, Humana, and Claude and Jabine provide particularly interesting proof on the civil-political front.[24] Such indexes could indirectly enrich the process of core-country selection in Canadian aid. More importantly, they plant the seeds for some broad principles.

First, adding in socio-economic rights produces a diluted index that invites distortions in policy judgment; even the poorest civil-political record might be ignored as a result of such dilution.[25] Second, precise measurement requires not only that the civil-political rights be specified, but also that they be weighted to reflect different degrees of repression.[26] Third, there is a dynamic element: the index should allow for up and down trends in human-rights protection, and it should include the development of institutions that make such protection less arbitrary and therefore longer lasting. Fourth, core status in Canadian economic aid should not be assigned to countries that show little respect for civil-political freedoms; that is to say, substantial respect – like strong absolute need and a clear capability in aid use – should be a necessary, though not sufficient, condition for core status. Fifth, aid giving in non-core countries will frequently reflect situations where absolute need is deemed to override human-rights performance; it is vital that Canadians be kept informed as to the rationale for such decisions.[27]

CIDA should move quickly to develop its own human-rights index. Such an index cannot be a substitute for qualitative judgment on aid-rights linkage, and it will take time, partly because index construction carries its own qualitative problems; but it would be a distinctive plus for Canadian aid policy. Meanwhile, there is plenty of quantitative material at hand. CIDA should be using it to sharpen Canada's human-rights thrust.[28] In addition, this country should be assessing the limits of its bilateral leverage and should be working with like-minded countries to achieve the greatest impact.[29]

One of the major challenges for concerted action involves the IFIs – in particular, the World Bank, the International Monetary Fund, and the regional development banks. The conventional wisdom is that these organizations are not mandated to promote civil and political freedoms and that their doing so would politicize them to the point of endangering their viability. But this is really argument by assertion. The truth is that the IFIs are not juridically precluded from using respect for human rights as a criterion for aid giving and that their doing so could "help entrench and reinforce international acceptance of a set of basic rights that are already almost universally acknowledged."[30]

Commendably, the Winegard report urges a stronger poverty orientation in IFI programs – a view that is starting to be taken up by some of these multilateral institutions. It also proposes, as already noted, that Canada look critically at multilateral development loans in the light of human-rights performance. But by the logic of the committee's own analysis, this is still not enough. Canada should be working to persuade like-minded donors to vote against multilateral lending to gross and systematic violators of basic civil and political rights. At the same time, and by way of example, Canada should oppose such aid – even if it means standing alone.[31]

Constraining abuse is one side of the human-rights coin. Rewarding progress is equally important. The Winegard committee is well aware of the need for flexibility in the country allocation of Canadian aid. Curiously, however, it seems quite comfortable with a "no change" strategy for the regional distribution of bilateral government-to-government funding – set at 84 percent (shared equally) for Asia and Africa and 16 percent for the Americas in 1987. A virtually complete focus on absolute need may well be the likeliest explanation. In any event, there can be little doubt that Latin America has become a most exciting region in terms of national breakthroughs on civil-political rights. Fragile freedoms join with stubborn poverty and massive external debt to dictate a substantial shift in aid allocation for political change.

THE ORGANIZATION AND DELIVERY
OF CANADIAN ODA

If tied aid is a major anachronism that continues to tarnish the generally good reputation of Canadian ODA, so are bureaucratic red tape and sluggish aid planning and delivery. The two phenomena are, of course, linked, since one of the more unfortunate side-effects of a high degree of tying is that it contributes to the excessive bureaucratization of aid.

As things stand, three interconnected elements of the organizational framework of Canadian ODA militate against the Winegard committee's long-term aim of reorienting the program towards human-resource development and the basic needs of the poorest groups and countries. These are (1) excessive centralization within CIDA, (2) personnel constraints and externally set rules, and (3) efficiency criteria that emphasize rapid disbursement. In turn, these characteristics reflect CIDA's emphasis on large-scale, capital-intensive infrastructural projects. Any sizable shift towards small-scale, labour-intensive projects that meet basic human needs will require a funda-mental rearrangement of ODA planning and delivery. In what follows, it will be argued that while the committee makes some important suggestions to bring this about, the road to change will not be smooth.

The Winegard report recognizes that in a climate of slow growth in the total aid budget, aid effectiveness and quality are of critical concern. Aid delivery, it affirms, can be improved by a radical decentralization of person-nel and decision-making authority from Ottawa to field officers working in recipient countries. The committee notes that while the main trend among DAC members is towards greater decentralization, CIDA remains one of the more centralized donor agencies, with only one-tenth of its staff in the field. Overcentralization is costly and ineffective because it leads to delays in the gestation and implementation of aid projects and because it tends to accentu-ate donor control at the expense of policy dialogue with the recipient. As a result, the latter is rarely involved in more than the earliest and most rudi-mentary stage of the planning cycle.

The report urges CIDA to abandon "a management philosophy that sees overseas posts as mailboxes for decision makers at headquarters"(*WR*, 86). It recommends a large-scale transfer of senior officials to field-based "Canada Partnership Centres" with a maximum project approval authority of $5 million. Estimated financial costs ($20 to $40 million) are put in clear perspective:

Decentralization is not a cost-free process – financially, administratively or political-ly. Financially, it entails spending a large proportion of the aid budget on administra-tion; administratively, it means losing some control at the centre; and politically, it means accepting the risks of an aid program truly responsive to the needs of our developing country partners. We strongly support decentralization only because we are convinced that its costs are far outweighed by its likely benefits. (*WR*, 90)

The committee approvingly quotes a 1987 study by CIDA maintaining that decentralization improves the quality of aid "through better monitoring, quick adjustments [and] prompt resolution of problems," and that it "allows for better project design in those areas where planning requires close familiarity with the environment and in-depth knowledge of local institutions" (*WR*, 85). Time and again, critics of the "control-oriented" style of development administration underscore the importance of "letting go" and of being sensitive to local conditions.[32]

The complexity of the development process and the absence of tried and tested formulae often require aid solutions that are both experimental and unconventional. Overcentralization works against this. While an aura of technical competence may provide an aid agency with insulation from external criticism, it is likely to do so at the considerable cost of stunted innovation.

But overcentralized decision making does not tell the whole story. The Winegard committee should also have called attention to the "money-moving syndrome" and to the related problem of insufficient desk officers. There are pressures on CIDA's country-desk staff to disburse their aid quickly. Large amounts are at stake, and each officer tends to be assessed by his or her ability to spend allocated funds within a one-year time-frame.

Given the limited person-years available to handle these large sums, desk officers opt pragmatically for large infrastructural projects, with the bulk of the work undertaken by private consultants and with minimal back-up work in terms of monitoring, evaluation, and maintenance. By contrast, basic-needs projects often require a long gestation period, a greater number of person-years, and considerable "after-care" in terms of monitoring and maintenance. As such, they represent an administrative burden to the embattled desk officer. In the words of a North-South Institute study of Canadian aid to Bangladesh, there is "no pay-off for innovation when progress is measured by the quantity of disbursements."[33]

While decentralization will go some way towards loosening the controls surrounding ODA management, it is difficult to believe that, of itself, this will alter the money-moving syndrome or contribute to a significant increase in the volume of projects promoting human-resource development. More person-years and more expertise are prerequisites for greater emphasis on labour-intensive projects. But there is still a freeze on the growth of personnel in CIDA. And there is the fact that decentralization, as such, will only marginally affect the formidable web of regulations that now surrounds the ODA program. CIDA has limited organizational autonomy. Many of the key rules under which it operates are imposed by outside departments with little understanding of the complexities of aid planning and delivery.[34]

Paradoxically, the imposition of rigid planning and financial controls on CIDA seems to have produced an effect opposite to that intended. Administrative delay is perhaps the single most consistently voiced complaint by recipients and Canadian private sector partners alike. It takes an estimated average of twenty-six to twenty-eight months to proceed from the project-proposal stage to final approval – and this before implementation even begins.[35] Be that as it may, persistent budgetary and manpower constraints and regulatory controls are bound to impede the innovative restructuring envisaged by the Winegard committee.

OTHER ISSUES

A few other issues are particularly worth noting. Complementing the Winegard report's focus on decentralization are a series of proposals to expand the role of the private sector in the planning and delivery of Canadian ODA. The committee speaks of "building partnerships" with NGOs, universities, and the business community; it recommends that these three groups receive up to 15 percent of total ODA by 1995–96 (WR, 105). Also proposed is the creation of "centres of excellence ... in development studies" at selected Canadian universities (WR, 113). Similarly, the report seeks to strengthen the links between the business community and the aid program by providing increased funding for the Industrial Cooperation Program (CIDA-INC) and by "establishing good lines of communication between the proposed regional offices, CIDA headquarters and the Canadian business community" (WR, 103).

Then, too, the committee recommends that the government entrench, in legislation, a 0.5 percent ODA/GNP target as the annual Canadian minimum, and that Ottawa move immediately (not in 1990–91 as planned) towards 0.6 percent by 1995–96. On the other hand, the committee declines to endorse the "less moderate," internationally recognized target of 0.7 percent. It also recommends against IDRC (unlike other development agencies) reporting to Parliament through the newly proposed "Minister for International Development" – in other words, the *status quo* for IDRC in relation to the secretary of state for external affairs.

The report gives blunt notice that the Third World's spiralling debt "has the potential to swallow up any gains in the aid field, or worse, to cancel out past achievements" (WR, 127). This, of course, raises a host of complex problems that go beyond the Winegard committee's terms of reference.[36] It nonetheless urges, in a general way, consideration of "additional steps such as partial debt forgiveness [and] interest rate reductions" (WR, 52). However, one could have reasonably expected some fresh, concrete thoughts on long-range solutions – for example, the idea that easing the debt burden should be linked not only to poverty levels and economic adjustment skills in the Third World, but to human-rights performance as well. The committee is silent in this regard. And silence is not golden when governments shy away from in-depth remedies – on whatever front.

PROSPECTS FOR REFORM

At the outset of this essay, we asked whether the Winegard report would suffer the same fate as earlier policy reviews of Canada's aid program. For several reasons, the prospects look brighter. In the first place, the report has not been produced in isolation but is part of a series of governmental reviews of Canada's international relations. The Hockin-Simard report, for one, led to a favourable government response on some issues concerning the aid program and on the linkage of human rights to development assistance.[37] In turn, a number of the recommendations of the Winegard report have implications for the orientation and conduct of other facets of Canadian foreign policy.

The growing complexity of most policy issues has undermined the ability of Parliament to influence Canadian public policy. More recently, however, there have been efforts to reform and enhance Parliament's role, particularly through its committee system. The quality of the Winegard report suggests that these attempts may be succeeding. This is a healthy trend that should strengthen the legislature as an open arena for the representation of private interest groups, and weaken their less-than-public networking with influential government departments and agencies.

The federal government responded to the recommendations of the Winegard committee in September 1987 with its *To Benefit a Better World*. A new "strategy" document appeared in March 1988: *Sharing Our Future*. The "response" will receive more attention here, because it provides fuller discussion and deeper insight into the likely direction of government policy in this field.

At first blush, the government appears to have endorsed the great bulk of the committee's recommendations, rejecting only three. Closer inspection reveals a less striking picture. The "accepted" recommendations are frequently hedged in with a variety of qualifications: accepted "in principle," "in part," "with modifications," or "in another form." The net impact of these qualifications is a dilution of the committee's more innovative views, particularly those concerning the legislative basis of Canadian ODA and various aid-trade and human-rights issues.

But even the clearest government response would not be the last word. The final outcome on each issue will depend on the relative strength of various forces in the aid-policy process. A range of government agencies claim jurisdiction over – or expertise on – portions of the aid budget, including the Department of Finance (multilateral ODA), the Department of Agriculture (food aid), and the Export Development Corporation (mixed credits). Other important organizations are the Treasury Board and the departments of External Affairs and Industry, Science and Technology. CIDA, of course, will have its own views and interests on specific issues. These public players are influenced, in turn, by business, the NGOs, and other private sector groups. The net result is a complex of pressures on the aid program and a form of "bureaucratic politics" that strongly affect final policy outcomes.[38] Let us look more closely at the government's response to Winegard and consider the prospects for basic reform.

Overall Mandate and Structure

Dealing first with the mandate of the aid program, the government endorses the Winegard proposal for a "Development Assistance Charter," adding a fourth principle that ODA should "foster a partnership between the people of Canada and the peoples of the Third World."[39] But while agreeing to a change in ministerial title – a "Minister for External Relations and International Development" – the government is not sympathetic to recommendations seeking a firm legislative basis for the charter. It also rejects the proposal to establish an "International Development Advisory Council," and it is not prepared to define the minister's role in legislative terms.

Avoiding legislation allows the government to maintain policy flexibility. But the absence of a clear mandate for CIDA, or for its minister, undercuts the urgent need to fit development issues into the broader context of Canadian foreign policy. This stance is certainly at odds with that of other Western donors – Norway, Sweden, the Netherlands, the United States – which have a legislative basis for ODA or for the linkage of development aid and human rights. Within Canada, the contrast between CIDA and IDRC is especially sharp. In any case, the government does not spell out a rationale on this issue.

The response is quite explicit on the advisory council, however: it "is not considered essential to ensure consultations with [interested] Canadians [;] ... the primary responsibility for advising the Government rests with Parliament" (*GR*, 78). Yet autonomous advisory bodies have become an increasingly familiar part of the policy landscape in Canada. They offer the advantage of providing specialized expertise, an independent voice, and an open channel for the views of interest groups. Moreover, questions pertaining to international development have not been well integrated in the work of the Commons Committee on External Affairs and International Trade. Thus, ODA is often dealt with separately from Third World debt and human rights. A broader view of international development would also require some integration with refugee and immigration issues – matters largely outside the purview of the committee. An advisory council on international development could provide more focus and would have the advantage of drawing its membership from people experienced in the field.

There are some risks, too. The aid-policy framework is already highly fragmented. The presence of yet another policy actor could confuse as well as clarify. It could also dilute the gains already made by Parliament in influencing the early stages of policy making. But the pluses would clearly seem to outweigh the minuses. Parliamentary committees, however strong, cannot escape the problems of membership turnover and partisan politics. A high-quality advisory council would almost certainly play a complementary, educative role. And it would help to sustain public support for an expanding, increasingly complex aid program. On balance, it would be a source of policy enrichment in terms of both process and outcome.

Not surprisingly, given the negligible costs of change, there is now a minister for external relations and international development – although one may wonder why the new title is not confined to international development. The proposed "Development Assistance Charter" has also been adopted.[40] Its broad principles are unobjectionable, and its language sufficiently vague to provide wide latitude for interpretation and practice. But the government is far more sensitive on the issues of legislative mandate and an advisory council. Particularly in the arena of foreign policy, *raison d'état* usually takes precedence over democratic impulses for "open" policy. This is clear in Ottawa's response to Winegard. Nor are these rejections likely to be soon reversed. Further, prospects for an advisory council have to be viewed from the perspective of a long history of government apathy and bureaucratic resistance. Even sustained pressure and the soundest analysis might prove futile.

On the other hand, it is worth noting that in its response the government accepts the Winegard committee's recommendation that "the results of major program evaluations and of core country reviews be made available ... to Parliament and exposed to independent public review" (*WR*, 119). A resistant bureaucracy has long been evident here, a point echoed by researchers and parliamentarians who have struggled to obtain reliable evaluations of individual projects. CIDA has had an understandable propensity to shield itself from criticism by the media and the auditor-general. Yet closer public scrutiny of development projects is imperative, not only because large amounts of taxpayers' money are involved, but also because poorly planned projects can have disastrous effects on the displaced or impoverished groups the aid program is committed to assist.[41] While the response is sketchy on this issue, it does nonetheless represent a step forward.

Aid and Trade

One of the strongest recommendations of the Winegard report was the proposal to reduce tied aid to a minimum of 50 percent of government-to-government ODA. Although still well short of the DAC average, the proposal, if implemented, would go a considerable way towards eliminating a serious flaw in Canada's program. But the government's response is equivocal on this issue. It agrees to untie up to 50 percent of bilateral aid to sub-Saharan Africa "and to LLDCs [least-developed countries] in other regions where needs are greatest" (*GR*, 58). This reflects a recognition of the importance of increasing local procurement of goods and services. "Other countries," however, are limited to a ceiling of one-third untied aid. The reasons for the distinction are not elaborated. One can surmise that a number of the more prosperous, middle-income LDCs are believed to have good trade potential for Canada. Maintaining a higher proportion of tied aid in these countries increases the exposure of Canadian goods and firms, whether competitive or not, that seek to expand their sales. The creation of two tiers for "Canadian content" underlines the government's continued inefficient promotion of commercial objectives through the aid program.

Also disconcerting is Ottawa's decision not to reduce the level of tied food aid below 95 percent so as to permit a recipient to purchase from another LDC with an exportable food surplus. Domestic economic considerations would again seem to underpin the government's rejection of the Winegard proposal that non-emergency food aid not exceed 10 percent of the ODA budget – this despite an admission "that food aid is not always the best form of development assistance, especially when it has the effect of discouraging local agricultural production" (GR, 70).

On the issue of mixed credits, the government accepts the Winegard recommendation that Canada focus on multilateral efforts to curb these devices, as well as the recommendation that development criteria take priority in decisions regarding concessionally financed projects. But this amounts to little change in current policy.

In the light of Ottawa's long-standing unwillingness to reduce tying levels, the government response on this problem can be considered a major victory for the development community over opposing forces – and over muddled economic thinking. What is more, there is every likelihood that action will follow intent – so glaringly poor has been Canada's comparative record, and so well made the case against tied assistance. There remains, however, the important question, how much action? One is entitled to be sanguine about the government honouring its commitments vis-à-vis the African and other LLDCs; they have become a key ingredient of Canadian aid policy. On the other hand, two-tier tying (as against other Third World countries) is likely to persist, given the ubiquitous commercial dimension; so too is virtually complete tying for food aid. One can also expect Canada's prairie farmers and the federal Department of Agriculture to lobby hard against attempts to reduce the food-aid budget. By the same token, it would be unrealistic to expect Ottawa to go beyond the 50 percent untying recommended by Winegard.[42]

The prognosis for untied aid is modestly positive nonetheless. No such comfort can be derived from mixed credits. The "Trade and Development Facility" has been scrapped, to be sure, but there is little evidence that Ottawa is persuaded by studies pointing to concessional-financing costs in excess of benefits. These devices are viewed by the EDC, by the Canadian business lobby, and by the departments of External Affairs and Finance as legitimate "defences" against the trade-distorting practices of other OECD countries. Even CIDA regards mixed credits as a normal part of the process of forging closer links with the business community. The government's search for more efficient, more development-oriented alternatives has been muted, to say the least. Nor is the Winegard report very helpful in this context. All things considered, the prospects for a phasing-out of Canada's mixed credits are not bright.

Human Rights

Ottawa's response to the Winegard report is effusive in its broad endorsement of respect for human rights:

Item: "The Government is committed to provide increased funds for development, to promote a strengthened, more stable economic order, and to emphasize the importance of human rights in Canada's relations with the Third World." (*GR*, 21)

Item: "Respect for human rights is one of the most important conditions for development. It is equally true that the existence of poverty and under-development is often due to the same conditions which gave rise to human rights abuses." (*GR*, 27)

Item: "Human rights concerns must be fully integrated in Canada's development policies ... Canada will continue to use a combination of public pressure and private persuasion to register our concerns and to make clear the importance of these issues in Canadian foreign and development policy." (*GR*, 52)

The fine print tells a different story, however. There are, admittedly, some concrete pluses. The government commits itself to setting up a special human-rights unit within CIDA. There is also an undertaking to consult with NGOs and other private sector institutions in evaluating human-rights situations for development-assistance purposes. Then, too, Ottawa is unequivocal in affirming that government-to-government aid will be denied or reduced when human rights are violated in a gross, systematic, and continuous manner. There is even a commitment to adopt a new eligibility system for aid recipients, with due regard for such Winegard criteria as "the respect shown for human rights in the broadest sense" (*GR*, 75). But not the slightest indication is given of how this will be done. Indeed, it is in essence ambiguity, not clarity, that carries the day with Ottawa's response on human rights.

The Winegard plea for universality, consistency, and transparency in developing human-rights criteria is "accepted in part." This turns out to mean several things: first, that the government is sceptical about the validity of "fixed and coherent rules in an area as controversial as human rights" (*GR*, 50); second, that it considers the Winegard country-classification grid for human-rights performance "too subjective ... [to] serve the overall interest of Canadian development assistance (*GR*, 52); third, that in the government's view, the relevant parliamentary committees "may wish to [meet] in camera" when being given human-rights information about aid-receiving countries (*GR*, 53); fourth, that annual ODA/human-rights reports to Parliament "would [not] serve the foreign policy interests of Canada" (*GR*, 54); and fifth, that the cabinet will be apprised of human-rights situations so that it may – presumably in secret – take them into account in making aid allocations by country and channel.

What, then, will become of the Winegard report's thrust on human rights? Very possibly, not much. The committee's basic message is that Canadian aid should be systematically linked "to the observance of specific human rights standards by recipient countries"(WR, 23), that such linkages should be developed in spite of inherent controversy and sensitivities, that the linking process should be open to public scrutiny, and that "a consistent, considered approach ... can be in Canada's long-term foreign policy interests" (ibid.). Rhetoric aside, the government has responded mainly by restating present policy – on the one hand, an *ad hoc* punitive approach to flagrant abuse of human rights, and on the other, continued development assistance whenever "effective programs ... can be delivered" (GR, 51). The specifics of flagrant abuse and effective delivery are not addressed, nor is the question of setting aid priorities among countries deemed to be in gross violation of human rights. How respect for such rights might bear on CIDA decisions about core-country status is hardly even mentioned.

The response speaks of combining public pressure and private persuasion. But it is difficult to escape the impression that, in the context of aid conditionality, Ottawa's overriding aim is to maximize the "private" and so forestall any awkward outcomes from an unquiet diplomacy. If the price of secrecy is vagueness and stunted conceptual growth, so be it.

There are, of course, those in Canada's foreign-aid bureaucracy who are more than comfortable with the *status quo* on human rights. And there are, indeed, Canadians in the human-rights community who oppose conditioning aid on respect for democratic values abroad. We submit, however, that the main obstacle to reform on this front is not self-serving resistance, but inadequate appreciation of human rights in the "development" scheme of things. The Winegard report has helped to clear the air, but much remains to be done.

An important step has, in fact, already been taken. In November 1987, the federal government made public the special rapporteurs' report on the Hockin-Simard proposal for a new "Human Rights Institute."[43] The government, to its credit, had already accepted that proposal in principle. What it sought from the two rapporteurs were "ideas and recommendations" on how to proceed with the creation of the proposed agency (RR, 37).

The rapporteurs were confronted with some highly contentious questions: for example, the meaning of "democratic development," the role of Western values and institutions in Third World protection and promotion of human rights, and the issue of linkage between the proposed organization and existing Canadian bodies concerned with human rights in the international sphere. It would be unrealistic to expect a perfect record in terms of cogent answers. And one can, for instance, justifiably quarrel with the report's recommendation that the words "Democratic Development" in the new agency's proposed title be replaced by the less sensitive (but more ambiguous) "Institutional Development," and also with the recommendation that formal working links with CIDA and IDRC should be built into the organization *before* it gains some experience of its own. On balance, though, there can be no doubt as to the rapporteurs' valuable contribution to the debate on human rights in Canadian foreign policy.

In particular, their conceptual approach to "democracy" speaks louder than their reticence on the matter of title. True, they are silent on multi-party politics, but they do stress "the notion of ... participation of citizens in decision-making which affects their lives ... [and] the related hypothesis ... that in the long term, an administration based on the participation of the administered is one of the best guarantees that a government will respect the rights of the governed" (*RR*, 25). One also finds the key feature of government accountability through the courts. And while acknowledging the risk of perceived paternalism, the report deems it "entirely appropriate for Canada, a trusted partner in international development, ... to respond ... [to countries that need] human or financial resources to ... strengthen [their] own institutions or to improve [their] own safeguards for human rights consistent with [their] international undertakings" (*RR*, 24).

From this perspective, the rapporteurs are able to appreciate the need to have "a focal point" for Canada's human-rights activities on the international front and for "a networking role" through shared knowledge and experience with like-minded organizations abroad (*RR*, 21). They are also able to be quite explicit about the public and private sector bodies – the judiciary, the electoral system, cooperatives, and trade unions, for example – that could benefit from Canadian informational, training, and research programs. "The ultimate objective, therefore, is to assist the population to develop the ability to intervene on its own behalf in the decision-making process ... and to assist the public powers to create institutions to safeguard the rights and liberties of citizens" (*RR*, 25).

In September 1988, fifteen months after receiving the special rapporteurs' report, the federal government secured parliamentary approval for "An Act to establish the International Centre for Human Rights and Democratic Development."[44] Another fifteen months later, in December 1989, the first president of the centre was appointed. It began operations in March 1990.

This is not the place for detailed discussion of the new centre or its mission.[45] A number of specific points seem worth making, however:

• After an excessive gestation period, the centre emerged as an autonomous body with a five-year, $15-million budget, and a forthright title free of the serious ambiguities that would have been generated by the phrase "institutional development."
• The centre's *raison d'être* is defined, in the act, in terms of promoting "the *International Bill of Human Rights*, including ... the rights of free-

dom of opinion and expression and ... the right to vote and be elected at periodic, genuine elections in pluralistic political systems'' (section 4[1]).

- The act explicitly links *democratic* institutions to the enjoyment of basic rights.
- In recognition of the *universality* of human rights, the centre is authorized to extend its activities beyond the Third World (though funds are not specifically appropriated for that purpose).
- The centre is broadly mandated to "foster and fund research," to "sponsor and support seminars, workshops and other meetings," and to "provide financial resources [as well as] technical assistance [and] training programs ... in response to [direct or indirect] requests from governments, public or private organizations, ... [and] individuals" (section 5[1]).
- The centre's thirteen-member board of directors must have both a majority of Canadians and three-person representation from the Third World. "The Board must [also] have knowledge of Canadian foreign policy and experience in international development, the development of democratic institutions, the promotion of human rights internationally and international law relating to individual and collective rights" (section 13[3]).

The centre is an important initiative. It can be a major force moving human rights to "front-centre" in Canadian foreign policy. By the same token, it can help to make Canada a world-class actor on the international stage. Much will depend on the courage and imagination with which it seeks to carve out a special niche in areas that may be too sensitive or too action-oriented for the government, as such, to be involved.

A final, sobering point. The rapporteurs on the centre were not asked to – and did not – address one of the main concerns of the Winegard report, namely, that Canada find new and better ways of making its economic aid conditional on human-rights performance in developing countries. Of course, the centre may well come to exert some influence in that regard as it builds up its expertise and reputation on human-rights issues. But the fact remains that its establishment can in no sense be viewed as a government reply to the Winegard appeal for expanded conditionality in Canadian aid giving.

Aid Delivery

A major part of the case for decentralized delivery of aid is that great success in accommodating basic needs and promoting human-resource development cannot be achieved without it. For the Winegard committee, aiming at such success should, indeed, be what Canada's aid program is all about. The government's response clearly affirms that "the progress that has been made in the last 35 years is increasingly threatened by the perpetuation of mass poverty" and that "[inadequate] investment in education (particularly for women), in sanitation, in health and nutrition, threatens to undermine what has been [accomplished]'' (*GR*, 17).

It does not necessarily follow that Ottawa's commitment to the "human-needs-resources" goal is a deep and enduring one. The "strategy" paper of 1976 had a similar thrust; yet the sectoral distribution of Canadian aid remains weighted towards capital-intensive projects. Nor have bureaucratic, organizational, and lobbying constraints become purely a thing of the past. However, the focus of donor countries on human development has never been so analytically sharp or so widely shared. It is reasonable to believe that Canadian governments will grow increasingly appreciative of the implications of this commitment and that there will be a parallel strengthening of the political will to make it prevail.

In any event, there are other signs pointing towards decentralized Canadian aid. The government's response to the Winegard report is unequivocally positive in terms of viewing decentralization to the field as "a means to improve the efficiency of management, and also to improve the quality and ... efficiency of [the] development assistance program" (*GR*, 82). More important, the government has already begun to take concrete steps in this direction. And still more important, the general "efficiency" and "responsiveness" arguments for decentralization are now regarded as compelling by Western policy makers throughout the international aid community. Canada's bureaucracy will no doubt continue to reflect some resistance to large-scale transfers out of Ottawa, but logic is not on the side of those who would treat such resistance as a match for the broadly held conviction that Canadian aid has long been seriously flawed by overcentralized administration.

There is more, however. Decentralization cannot, by itself, ensure a successful "human development" strategy. While the government has agreed to restore CIDA's authority to carry over unspent funds from year to year, a variety of constricting rules and regulations remain. But the most worrisome points are that *far-reaching* decentralization implies large-scale expenditure for additional, well-trained CIDA staff; that the Winegard report is sketchy, and the response completely silent, with respect to estimated costs; and that silence speaks loudly in the presence of budgetary cuts and a virtual freeze on new personnel.

In sum, the challenge ahead is not to secure decentralization per se, but to gain government acceptance for the argument that substantial, continuing increases in personnel are a prerequisite to efficiency in the delivery of Canadian aid. This will not be an easy task.

Other Issues

While somewhat less specific in dollar terms, the government's response is highly supportive of the Winegard report's theme on expanding the role of the private sector in Canada's development assistance. Ottawa's position on Canadian NGOs and universities is particularly encouraging. It agrees on the need to provide funding increases for the NGOs. Given their "grass-roots" basis and their now-vital place in the ODA scheme of things, this is likely to happen. Furthermore, "CIDA will ... support, at their request, organizations seeking to decentralize their operations to the field" (GR, 85). Given the momentum towards decentralized government aid, this too will probably happen. The response is nonetheless explicit – and wise, we believe – in sharing the Winegard concern over strained NGO "absorptive capacity" and in opting for *gradual* increases in funding levels.[46]

As for Canada's universities, the government response commits Ottawa "to increase the number of publicly funded students ... from Third World countries" and to "address [with the provinces] the problem of differential tuition fees for foreign students" (GR, 46–7). This is, of course, a plus, but hardly conspicuous for precision. What we find especially interesting is the government's undertaking to "open a dialogue" with the universities on the creation of world-class centres for the study of Third World development (GR, 94). There is a long, curious history of insensitivity on this issue – a consistent lack of governmental "willingness or ... ability to appreciate the fact that skilled Canadian human resources do not grow on trees; and that in the long run, they can be effectively tapped only if steps are taken to ensure their continuing regeneration."[47] The Winegard report has provided a fresh context and a reinforced credibility for university "centres of excellence." Given sustained pressure along such lines, this may well soon prove to be an idea whose time has come.

Some other special issues are less reassuring, however. Ottawa has accepted the Winegard proposal that IDRC continue, as an exceptional case, to report to Parliament through the secretary of state for external affairs. We are much impressed by IDRCs achievements (though we would welcome an independent review of its experience over the past two decades), but this argues in favour of enhancing shared benefits by investing responsibility for *all* development agencies in one cabinet office. The Winegard committee extols the virtues of a closer working relationship between CIDA and IDRC. Logic would appear to dictate that *both* report to an upgraded minister overseeing Canada's aid program. Yet given the dubious but strong perception of IDRC's autonomy being at risk under a new reporting system, it will be very difficult, if not impossible, to induce change.[48]

We are concerned, as well, about ODA targets. ODA as a proportion of GNP has become an important index of a donor country's commitment to international development. Canada continues to fall short on several counts. The government's response rejects the 0.5 percent legislated minimum proposed in the Winegard report. Also rejected is the Winegard recommendation that the government begin to move towards 0.6 percent in 1988–89; instead, there is the "intention" to begin in 1991–92, a year later than Ottawa itself had previously specified (*GR*, 103). Most revealing, perhaps, is the fact that the government response makes no reference at all to the widely accepted Pearson Commission target of 0.7 percent. But even a specific pledge on that score would have left us bearish about prospects for meeting Canadian ODA targets. Given the record of frequently postponed commitments and the ongoing preoccupation with budget cutting, it would be heroic to expect otherwise – despite the special urgency of sharply increased aid flows to help cope with the mounting burden of Third World debt.[49]

The debt crisis will not be quickly or easily resolved. It extends far beyond aid policy per se, and there are large constraints on what any single country like Canada can do. A few points seem worth noting here. First, both the Winegard committee and the government's response come up short on the debt issue. Second, while Canada has forgiven some soft loans to developing countries, little more than the surface has been scratched; we should, for example, join with other industrial nations to make drastic cuts in interest rates on export credits to poorer LDCs. Third, while Canada has contributed to multilateral initiatives on the debt problem, it is still a long way from assuming the major catalytic role it could play. Fourth, there is little evidence to suggest that Ottawa is now prepared to translate lofty rhetoric into a bold, coherent plan for debt management *and* reduction; nor will any such plan emerge unless our public *and* private creditors come to recognize that the ultimate cost of debt tinkering is likely to be large-scale default, economic stagnation, and political repression over much of the Third World.

"Sharing Our Future"

It remains for us to comment on the federal government's "aid strategy" document (*Sharing Our Future*) released early in 1988, some six months after the response to the Winegard report.[50] In one sense, it was indeed something special. An updating of the 1976 strategy was overdue. Canada and the world had changed a great deal over the previous dozen years. The new strategy signals a deeper commitment to human-resource development and to the principle that the "primary purpose of Canadian [ODA] is to help the poorest countries and people" (*SOF*, 23). There is also a first-time commitment to human rights as a factor in foreign-aid decisions on scale, eligibility, and channels. Then, too, there is a specific agenda for action on environmental concerns, on decentralizing aid, and on fostering "partnership" among Ottawa, Canadians, and Third World governments and peoples. The pertinent question here, however, is whether *Sharing Our Future* takes us significantly beyond the achievement level of the government's 1987 response.

The 1988 strategy reaffirms Ottawa's commitment to the 0.7 percent ODA/GNP target by the year 2000. It pledges to open four new regional field offices in the Third World and to establish up to one-quarter of CIDA staff in field postings. Scholarships for foreign students are slated to double over the subsequent five years, to a total of 12,000 students and trainees per year. The government "is prepared to support [Canadian university] centres of excellence by providing up to $10 million annually" (*SOF*, 71).

Many of the specifics generate difficult questions, however. How firm is the 0.7 percent commitment? Our scepticism is compounded by the fact that in 1989–90 a 12 percent budget cut in ODA reduced it from 0.49 to 0.43 as a percentage of GNP, that in early 1990 the federal government reaffirmed an ODA/GNP target of only 0.47 percent by 1994, and that ODA funding will be vulnerable to continuing pressures for economic assistance to Eastern Europe. As for aid decentralization, does a severely constrained hiring policy not continue to dampen the prospects for success? Could the "centres of excellence" program not be seriously weakened, or even derailed, by Ottawa's prior condition that "universities should agree among themselves on the sectors of activity and geographic regions overseas in which the centres would specialize" (*SOF*, 70)? And what about aid-allocation decisions like the 50-50 split between "National Initiatives" and the "Partnership Program"; an increased bilateral share for Africa (45 percent), with declines for Asia (39 percent) and no change for the Americas (16 percent); and a doubling of the ODA share (to 4 percent) for the Canadian business sector? Is there a convincing rationale for such numbers?

In any event, the new strategy document is no more notable for what it specifies than for some of the things it leaves unsaid. While the government's response gives a brief "accepted" to the Winegard report's call for comprehensive Canadian trade liberalization vis-à-vis the developing countries, the strategy gives only silence; bearing in mind the domestic adjustment problem and a strongly resistant business lobby, one can hardly be optimistic about rapid progress on the trade front. While the government response confronts (and rejects) the Winegard-proposed "International Development Advisory Council," the strategy does not even mention it; it is difficult to understand the logic of vigorously "reaching out to Canadians" (*SOF*, 81) by abandoning the advisory council approach in favour of such devices as a designated "Development Day" and "consultations with concerned groups" (*SOF*, 82). Finally, while the government response discusses (and rejects) the Winegard committee's country-classification grid for linking aid to human-rights performance, the proposal has disappeared by the time the new strategy unfolds; if the response fails to achieve precision in this regard, the strategy does not even try.

For the most part, though, both documents cover the same ground. And they provide the same setting for our assessment of "prospects for reform." The authors of the strategy would have done well to focus more on supportive analysis and less on catchy – often repetitive – graphics. Overall, we do not find the actual product particularly impressive.

CONCLUSIONS

It seems fair to characterize the past half-decade as a period of unprecedented public debate on Canadian foreign policy. Development assistance has been a central theme in that debate. And a newly reformed parliamentary committee system has been a major catalytic force on the aid front.

The Winegard report emerges as a landmark contribution in this context. It provides an eloquent restatement of the case for anchoring Canadian aid in "basic needs and human resources." It gives cogent reasons for linking aid to human-rights performance in the Third World. It calls convincingly for extensive decentralization in the delivery of aid, for a more effective system of partnership between the public and private sectors within Canada and vis-à-vis the developing countries, and for increased openness and public scrutiny throughout the aid program. It comes up with significant, often-imaginative proposals for program improvement.

The report does have its shortcomings, mostly in terms of omission. Constrained by the usual "pressures of time" (*WR*, xiii), committee members made only a single field trip – to Africa, and there only to Ethiopia, Senegal, and Tanzania. There is no explicit reference to human rights in the "Development Assistance Charter." The report provides no in-depth discussion of those rights or of the civil-political dimension in Third World development. It fails to attack the mixed-credits problem head-on. The aid implications of the Third World debt crisis are barely mentioned. And the important 0.7 percent ODA/GNP target is dropped, for reasons that are less than persuasive.

But if the Winegard report left gaps, it was also solid enough and concrete enough to clear a significant aid-reform path for the Canadian government. Perhaps the prime question is whether that path will be followed. Finding the answer would be easy on the basis of two assumptions: (1) that the government has responded to all the major Winegard recommendations in a straightforward yes-no manner *and* (2) that acceptance or rejection is the final word as far as government action is concerned. The reality, however, is that neither assumption is valid.

Ottawa has given some unequivocal replies, to be sure. One of the most compelling examples is the commitment to a decentralized aid-delivery system. Here, in fact, intent has merged with execution. But what remains unclear is whether the process of decentralization will go far enough and whether it will be accompanied by the personnel enrichment necessary for true effectiveness.

Thus, unequivocal response is not synonymous with simple outcome. What is more, in many respects Ottawa's reaction to the Winegard report is nothing if not equivocal. The issue of openness and transparency is an important case in point.

The government's response did undertake to have CIDA develop abstracts of program and project evaluations and to ensure that those abstracts are distributed to Parliament, CIDA's partners, and the general public. Basic decision making, however, is quite a different matter. Witness the pertinent language of the new country-eligibility framework promised in the response and spelled out in the 1988 strategy: "Decisions on levels of bilateral aid will be made each year by Cabinet. Ministers will establish confidential five-year bilateral planning figures" (*SOF*, 30). Witness, as well, the stipulation that "*Cabinet* will annually consider" the human-rights information relevant to determining channels and levels of bilateral assistance (*SOF*, 31); and that when government ministers give such information to parliamentary committees, the latter "may wish to hold such meetings *in camera*" (*SOF*, 32). These last two pronouncements – along with the strategy's total silence on annual ODA/human-rights reports to Parliament – are the net effect of "accepted in part" and "accepted with modifications" in the government's response.

Indeed, human rights have proved to be the most fertile ground for this kind of equivocation. Procedurally, it meant decision making rooted in secrecy. Substantively, it yielded a spotty action program. There are some promising initiatives – for instance, human-rights training for Canadian development officers, a CIDA unit responsible for ensuring that ODA programs are consistent with Canada's broader foreign-policy concerns on human rights, and the International Centre for Human Rights and Democratic Development.[51] But the government's bottom line on the Winegard report is "accepted in part" and "accepted in principle" – a restatement of the existing position against extreme violations of human rights and an unwillingness to adopt any specific criteria for conditioning aid on human-rights performance. A continuing knowledge gap joins with substantial bureaucratic reserve to dampen prospects for an early breakthrough on this front.

It does not, of course, follow that the government should have unequivocally accepted all of the Winegard committee's recommendations. To the extent that they were flawed, deviation could be sound and concurrence unwise. In the latter connection, going along with the Winegard views on mixed credits provides perhaps the most significant example. The government has tried to strengthen the development criteria for such credits. But like the committee, it skates around the basic issue – unwilling or unable to recognize that they should be phased out and replaced with more efficient measures that promote Canada's exports without compromising its development objectives.

Taking final stock, we are nonetheless comfortable about underscoring some of the pluses. As never before, the Canadian public has been drawn into the foreign-policy and foreign-aid review process. The Winegard report has raised the curtain on an ODA system attuned to the 1990s and beyond. That vision has been enriched by the report of the special rapporteurs on a new Canadian agency for promoting human rights and democratic development. The federal government, for its part, has endorsed the principle of comprehensive linkage between ODA and human rights, has given concrete expression to an overriding developmental concern with "basic needs and human resources," and has embarked on a substantial program of decentralization in the delivery of Canadian ODA.

We return, full circle, to our essay title. Do such pluses add up to "new directions in Canada's foreign aid?" Not yet, from our perspective. The gap between Winegard proposals and government "acceptance" turns out to have been a wide one – especially in terms of legislative mandate, human rights, and development-oriented trade policy.[52] There is, as well, a great deal of room for scepticism about the likelihood of early policy reversals that will significantly narrow this gap. And there is much uncertainty about how far Ottawa will go to carry out specific commitments in such fields as decentralization, tied aid, ODA/GNP targets, and development research.

In short, Canada's aid-policy future remains clouded. One can expect continuing resistance to basic reform – all the more so on issues, like mixed credits, that the Winegard committee itself did not sufficiently confront. The resistance will, of course, have its usual bureaucracy and lobby-group ingredients. But "the ignorance factor" will become increasingly evident as Canadians struggle to define a policy role better geared to the new realities of economic, social, *and political* development. Careful, sustained analysis of ODA issues and the development process is the sensible way of dealing with this problem. It will also reinforce the political will that is so vital for getting things done.

It is not only *Canadian* aid that is at stake. There is now growing evidence of major changes in outlook within the entire Western aid community. Strikingly illustrative are recent policy statements coming from the World Bank, the International Monetary Fund, and the Development Assistance Committee of OECD – in particular, their emphasis on the "vital connection, now more widely appreciated, between open, democratic and accountable political systems, individual rights and the effective and equitable operation of economic systems."[53] Such international advances may well have positive effects on Canada's aid program. But Canadians are entitled to believe that the direction of impact can run *both* ways.

The Winegard report deserves high marks as a focal point for national debate on Canadian development assistance. Hopefully, the debate is far from over.

POSTSCRIPT

As of December 1991, scarcely more than a year since the time of writing, events have been continuing to unfold at such a torrential pace on the human-rights front as to require posing, once again, this essay's central question, "New directions in Canada's foreign aid?"

Consider some of the facts of sea change on the global stage: the Helsinki-inspired Charter of Paris for a New Europe, proclaiming in November 1990 – on behalf of Canada, the United Stated, and thirty-four European countries – that "ours is a time for ... steadfast commitment to democracy based on ... inalienable ... human rights and fundamental freedoms ... guaranteed by law ... [to] all human beings" (p. 1); the follow-up Document of the Moscow Meeting of the Conference on the Human Dimension, declaring – only ten months later – that "human rights, fundamental freedoms, democracy and the rule of law are ... matters of direct and legitimate concern to all participating States and do not belong exclusively to the internal affairs of the State concerned" (p. 2); the demise of central authoritarian rule in the Soviet Union, followed by the disintegration of the Soviet state itself; the consolidation of democratic regimes over much of Latin America; the accelerating trend towards multi-party democracy in Africa; the increasingly harsh international censure of human-rights violations, as dramatically exemplified by Haiti, Yugoslavia, and Burma; and perhaps most pertinent here, the November 1991 suspension of foreign-aid pledges to Kenya by twelve donor countries (including Canada) convened under World Bank auspices – with full aid renewal made contingent on economic reforms, greater respect for human rights, and increased political pluralism.

The global human-rights picture remains deeply flawed, to be sure. Many of the steps forward are fragile at best. The human-rights consequences of the Soviet collapse and the Persian Gulf War are in serious doubt. And one can readily cite Tibet, East Timor, Tiananmen Square, and the Iraqi Kurds – and more. But the overall message is crystal clear: human rights and democratic development will be front-centre in the world in the 1990s, and by the end of the decade, it may well be universally unacceptable to use national sovereignty as a defence for human-rights abuse.

Over the past year, Canada has been a substantial player on this world stage. In a variety of international bodies – the United Nations, the Organization of American States, the Commonwealth, and La Francophonie – the Canadian government has campaigned vigorously for stronger mechanisms to protect and promote human rights and democratic pluralism. More specifically, the prime minister himself has been urging donor countries to link their foreign aid directly to human-rights performance in recipient nations. Canada also suspended all government-to-government assistance to Haiti shortly after the September 1991 military coup, and roughly 40 percent of such aid to Indonesia was halted in early December, in protest against a November massacre of unarmed civilians in East Timor.

It might be tempting, in this context, to infer that Canada's foreign-aid program has indeed been undergoing fundamental reform. The record, however, still speaks in terms of "not yet."

On reflection, this should come as no surprise. Rapid international advance on human rights and democratic development does not necessarily mean international support for conditioning foreign aid on recipient countries' performance with respect to those goals. In fact, the alleged "intrusiveness" of such linkage continues to be a focal point of considerable resistance among Third World and donor nations alike. There are, as already noted, some interesting positive signs – the Kenya case, for example.[54] But Canada's pleas for international acceptance of aid linkage to human rights have gone largely unheeded.

In any event, there is a world of difference between foreign-aid rhetoric abroad and foreign-aid performance at home. While Prime Minister Mulroney was eloquently making the human-rights case in Harare and Paris, Canadian officials in Ottawa were pointing out that this was not a new initiative, that Canada's aid policy was still rooted in *Sharing Our Future* and in the government's response to the Winegard report, and that there was no intention of opening up the aid program to public scrutiny in relation to the role of human rights. In other words, from the perspective of Canadian aid policy put in place some four years ago, it is essentially business as usual on human rights – with all of the pluses and minuses that were spelled out in the main text of this essay. Similarly, the suspensions of aid to Haiti and Indonesia emerge as an extension of earlier practice vis-à-vis countries in flagrant abuse of human-rights – Uganda, Guatemala, El Salvador, and (very briefly) China, for example.[55]

It remains for us only to make some "update" comments on other facets of Canadian aid. Repeated governmental commitments to meeting basic human needs have not been matched by actual spending. A recent United Nations study reports that in 1989 Canada ranked tenth among twelve industrialized countries in terms of its share of GNP allocated to aid expenditure on such "human development" items as primary health care, basic education, and clean water – far behind the Netherlands, Sweden, France, and Germany.[56] On the purely quantitative side, the story is one of continuing retreat from the ODA/GNP target of 0.7 percent – the minister of finance, in February 1991, having announced a further cut of $1.6 billion from aid budgets projected through to 1995–96.

The record on tied aid is more favourable, but mixed. A recent Canadian Council of Churches report found large increases in untying for some recipient countries between 1987 and 1990, but sharp reductions for others.[57] The limited available evidence suggests that Canada is still a long way from the untied-aid levels promised by the government during the months following the Winegard report.

Developments with regard to decentralized aid delivery are also mixed. In 1988 CIDA launched a five-year $250-million program of staff decentralization to twenty-two field offices. The 1990–91 budget included funding for 146 Canadian staff posted abroad. In November 1990, however, the government announced that the remaining plans for decentralization would not be implemented, and soon afterwards came a decision to repatriate up to 25 percent of Canadian field staff in 1991–92. Budget-cutting fever in Ottawa was taking its toll in many different ways. While there seems, nonetheless, to have been some increase in management efficiency, it also appears that "the early evidence does not demonstrate a significant improvement over CIDA's past performance."[58]

What is significant is the government's continuing emphasis on aid-blended commercial loans to finance Canadian exports. There is, of course, still the appropriate rhetoric about satisfying development objectives while promoting Canadian business. One keeps looking in vain, however, for official recognition of the high risk that neither goal will be efficiently achieved through trade-driven aid. What one finds, instead, is an expanding "lines of credit" system, along with increased funding for CIDA's Industrial Cooperation Program. In this context, perhaps the most useful government initiative would be to produce, for public debate, a policy paper that assesses the distortive effects of concessional export financing and explores ways and means of ensuring compatibility in the pursuit of trade and development goals. One thing seems certain: without such an initiative, the prospects for a phasing-out of mixed credits, and for a major dismantling of Canadian barriers against LDC exports, are bleak indeed.

Needless to say, public debate is no guarantee. Witness the pervasive problem of Third World indebtedness. In June 1990, the external affairs committee of Canada's House of Commons published a first-class report analysing the debt crisis, urging a governmental commitment to linkage between debt relief and human-rights performance, and recommending a variety of other measures designed to give Canada a leading role in this field.[59] The government responded in November 1990, underscoring its $1.2 billion worth of forgiveness on ODA debt and expressing broad agreement with the committee's call for global action.[60] What the government did not do, however, was to acknowledge the meagre real effects of its forgiveness programs and the need for drastic relief action on commercial, IMF, and World Bank debt. The committee's own "response to the response" put it more bluntly in March 1991:

The [government's] response is dispiriting in its approach, especially in what it has evaded or managed not to say. The response tries to convey the impression of rhetorical agreement with the Committee's report, when in fact in substantive terms the Committee's recommendations are mostly rejected without any alternative initiatives being proposed in their place. If the Government has a bold agenda for further action, it is well hidden. The response paints a large canvas but delivers only a minimal impact.[61]

There is, finally, little sign of boldness in yet another aid-policy sphere – what this essay has called "overall mandate and structure." In July 1991, the House of Commons established a "Subcommittee on International Development and Human Rights." Along with the subcommittee on international debt, it reports to the House external affairs committee. This is an institutional plus. But it is no substitute for two of the important Winegard recommendations rejected by the Canadian government in 1987: entrenching CIDA's mandate in an act of Parliament and creating an "International Development Advisory Council" to provide private sector expertise for the cabinet minister responsible for CIDA. Those relatively low-cost proposals, still dormant, should have great appeal for any government truly intent on upgrading the status of foreign aid and of development objectives in Canada's foreign-policy system.

Taking stock one more time, we are led inescapably to the conclusion that, as of December 1991, the policy advances made over the past four years do not add up to "new directions," or fundamental reform, in Canadian foreign aid – despite the tumultuous global events that have recently been pushing human rights forward and national sovereignty backward as never before. By the same token, the fast-shrinking new world of the 1990s – in which Canada is likely to play a larger role than ever before – will intensify the reform pressures already being felt in the international aid community. Sustained public debate in Canada would draw strength from those pressures, while also contributing substantially to their development. For Canadian aid, the end-result may still not be basic reform, but there are uniquely good grounds for hope.

NOTES

Author's Note: I wish to thank Michael Brecher, Clovis Demers, and Ben and Jean Higgins for their helpful comments on an earlier draft of this paper.
1 Robert Cassen and Associates, *Does Aid Work?* (Oxford: Clarendon, 1986).
2 Standing Committee of the House of Commons on External Affairs and International Trade, *For Whose Benefit?*, report on Canada's official development assistance policies and programs (Ottawa: House of Commons, 1987). Subsequently cited in text as *WR* (Winegard report).
3 Nearly three years in the making, the *Strategy for International Development Cooperation 1975–1980* was Canada's response to the "basic human needs" approach that became popular in the mid- and late 1970s. The document stated that the objective of Canadian aid was to contribute to a "wide distribution of

the benefits of development'' and to ''enhance the quality of life and improve the capacity of *all* sectors of recipient populations to participate in national development efforts'' (emphasis added) (Canadian International Development Agency [CIDA], *Strategy for International Development Cooperation 1975–1980* [Hull: CIDA, 1976], 9). See also CIDA, *Elements of Canada's Official Development Assistance Strategy* (Hull: CIDA, 1984); idem, *Study of the Policy and Organization of Canada's Official Development Aid*, report to the Minister for External Relations (Hull: CIDA, 1986); and idem, *Sharing Our Future: Canadian International Development Assistance* (Ottawa: Minister of Supply and Services, 1987).

4 See Keith A.J. Hay, *The Implications for the Canadian Economy of CIDA's Bilateral Tied Aid Programme*, discussion paper (Ottawa: Economic Council of Canada, 1978); and John Hendra, ''Only 'Fit to be Tied': A Comparison of the Canadian Tied Aid Policy with the Tied Aid Policies of Sweden, Norway and Denmark,'' *Canadian Journal of Development Studies* 8, no. 2 (1987): 261–81.

5 See Jagdish Bhagwati, ''The Tying of Aid,'' in J. Bhagwati and Richard S. Eckaus, eds., *Foreign Aid* (Harmondsworth: Penguin Books, 1970), 235–93; and Carl Hamilton, ''On the Mixed Blessing of Tied Aid,'' *Bangladesh Development Studies* 6, no. 4 (August 1978): 286–94.

6 It has been argued that most LDCs have become so proficient at negotiating their aid packages that they get what they want from each donor, whether aid is tied or not – in other words, that they get from each country what they would have bought there, in a free market, if there were no aid at all. This view is open to serious question. In any event, there can be no doubt that from an overall LDC perspective, untied aid is better than tied aid (always assuming that untying does not reduce the total flow of aid).

7 See David Gillies, ''Do Interest Groups Make a Difference? Domestic Influences on Canadian Development Aid Policies,'' in Irving Brecher, ed., *Human Rights, Development and Foreign Policy; Canadian Perspectives* (Halifax: Institute for Research on Public Policy, 1989), 435–65.

8 Hay, *The Implications for the Canadian Economy*; and Peter Wyse, *Canadian Foreign Aid in the 1970s: An Organizational Audit*, Occasional Monograph series, no. 16 (Montreal: Centre for Developing-Area Studies, McGill University, 1983), 6.

9 See David Gillies, ''Commerce over Conscience? Export Promotion in Canada's Development-Aid Program,'' *International Journal* 44 (winter 1988–89): 102–33.

10 Martin Rudner, ''Trade cum Aid in Canada's Official Development Assistance Program,'' in Brian W. Tomlin and Maureen Molot, eds., *Canada among Nations: 1986/Talking Trade* (Toronto: James Lorimer 1987), 136.

11 Paul Mosley, *Overseas Aid: Its Defence and Reform* (London: Wheatsheaf Books, 1987), 216.

12 Ibid., 213.

13 Decima Research Ltd., *The Canadian Public and Foreign Policy Issues*, prepared for the Department of External Affairs (Toronto: Decima Research Ltd.1985); see also CIDA, *Report to CIDA: Public Attitudes towards International Development Assistance* (Ottawa: Minister of Supply and Services, 1988).

14 HM Treasury, Department of Trade and Industry, and Overseas Development Administration, '' The Costs and Benefits of Support for Capital Goods Exports'' (London, England, 1982, Mimeographed).

15 A.R. Raynauld, J.M. Dufour, and D. Racette, *Government Assistance to Export Financing* (Ottawa: Economic Council of Canada, 1983), 53, 59.

16 See also Special Joint Committee of the Senate and the House of Commons on Canada's International Relations (Hockin-Simard committee), *Independence and Internationalism* (Ottawa: Minister of Supply and Services, 1986); Martin Rudner, "Human Rights Conditionality and International Development Cooperation" (CIDA, Hull, 1983, Mimeographed); and T.A. Keenleyside, "Canadian Aid and Human Rights: Forging a Link," in Brecher, ed., *Human Rights*, 329–53.

17 See Robert Miller, "Canada and Democratic Development" (Parliamentary Centre for Foreign Affairs and Foreign Trade, Ottawa, 1985, Mimeographed).

18 On 4 December 1986, the UN General Assembly adopted the Declaration on the Right to Development. Article 1(1) proclaims: "The right to development is an inalienable human right by virtue of which every human being and all peoples are entitled to participate in, contribute to, and enjoy economic, social and cultural development, in which all human rights and fundamental freedoms can be fully realized." Canada voted for the declaration, while eight Western countries abstained. The United States was the only country to record a negative vote. It has yet to ratify the two UN human-rights covenants of 1966.

19 Irving Brecher, "Rethinking Foreign Aid," *Policy Options* 8, no. 3 (April 1987): 25; see also Rhoda Howard, "The Full-Belly Thesis: Should Economic Rights Take Precedence over Civil and Political Rights? Examples from Sub-Saharan Africa," *Human Rights Quarterly* 5, no. 4 (1983): 467–80.

20 The conceptual case that human rights are most powerfully guaranteed in liberal, pluralistic democracies has been persuasively made in Rhoda Howard, and Jack Donnelly, "Human Dignity, Human Rights and Political Regimes," *American Political Science Review* 80, no. 3 (September 1987): 801–15. This, however, leaves open the empirical question of whether the *path* of political development tends to be democratic. There has been much controversy on this issue. And the optimism of early modernization theorists has been tempered by a recognition that many Third World polities have experienced an unpredictable cycle of regime change. Moreover, the modal political system in Africa is markedly authoritarian, with a constraining one-party rule, while functioning Third World democracies have been relatively few in number and mostly fragile in nature. These verities notwithstanding, there is now striking evidence

of an evolving democratic pluralism in Asia and Latin America. For a variety of reasons, Africa will probably continue to lag behind. But even there the winds of freedom blow, and one can already see "spread" effects from the East European revolutions of 1989.

21 See Paul Streeten, "Human Rights and Basic Needs," *World Development* 8 (1980): 107–11, for an interesting discussion of this relationship; see also Frances Stewart, "Basic Needs Strategies, Human Rights, and the Right to Development," *Human Rights Quarterly* 11, no. 3 (1989): 347–74.

22 A distinction is often drawn between "integrity rights ... which are absolute and unconditional, and other rights which are imperfectly realizable entitlements that depend in part on the development of a society's material and human resources" (Gerald J. Schmitz, *Human Rights: Canadian Policy toward Developing Countries* [Ottawa: North-South Institute, 1988], 4, 6). It is, however, "important to recognize that all human rights make fundamental *a priori* claims on the actions of states" (4).

23 The language of "violation" and "respect" is not exclusive to civil-political performance. One can, for example, conceive of an aid recipient deliberately engaging in discrimination that reduces the living standards of people already at subsistence level.

24 Raymond D. Gastil, *Freedom in the World: Political Rights and Civil Liberties* (New York: Freedom House, 1985); Charles Humana, *World Human Rights Guide* (London: Economist Publications, 1986); and Richard P. Claude and Thomas B. Jabine, "Editors' Introduction" (Symposium: Statistical Issues in the Field of Human Rights), *Human Rights Quarterly* 8, no. 3 (1986): 551–66. See David L. Banks, "Measuring Human Rights," in Brecher, ed., *Human Rights*, 539–62, for a useful assessment of alternative approaches to the measurement of human-rights performance.

25 This, of course, is not to rule out a socio-economic index incorporating both need and performance. Indeed, such indexing has long been part and parcel of aid programs around the world.

26 Robert O. Matthews and Cranford Pratt, in their "Conclusion: Questions and Prospects," in Robert O. Matthews and Cranford Pratt, eds., *Human Rights in Canadian Foreign Policy* (Kingston and Montreal: McGill-Queen's University Press, 1988), 285–311, identify freedom from detention without trial, from torture, from extra-judicial killing, and from starvation as "basic human rights." But for a number of reasons with which they "are not terribly comfortable," Matthews and Pratt "hesitate to suggest that emphasis on political participation [or] political liberties ... should be a paramount feature of Canadian foreign policy" (287–8).

27 The Winegard committee is justifiably at pains to underscore the imperative of "emergency humanitarian relief ... Human rights should never be used as a reason for turning our backs on human suffering" (*WR*, 25). The committee is also perceptive enough to note that "with respect to long-term development,

while Canadians have delivered a message that they do not want our aid to go to governments that violate the fundamental rights of their own citizens, they have not said to abandon people who may be in desperate need in part because they have been victimized by the policies of these governments'' (ibid). The latter point is a tricky one, however. It implies the exclusion of government-to-government aid. Furthermore, under these circumstances, there should be very solid evidence supporting the feasibility of assistance through private channels. And whenever meaningful country comparisons are possible, priority should go to the poorest people in countries that rank best within the ''severe'' category of human-rights violation.

28   T.A. Keenleyside and Nola Serkasevich, in their ''Canada's Aid and Human Rights Observance: Measuring the Relationship,'' *International Journal* 45 (Winter 1989–90): 138–69, have worked out a human-rights classification system that is particularly helpful in the Canadian context. But they base their rankings only on freedom from detention without trial, from torture, and from extra-judicial execution – even while acknowledging that ''the whole range of other basic political, civil, economic, and social rights defined in various United Nations declarations and conventions [cannot] be overlooked in the shaping of Canadian aid policy'' (168).

29   On Dutch and Swedish aid, for example, see Peter R. Baehr, ''Concern for Development Aid and Fundamental Human Rights: The Dilemma as Faced by the Netherlands,'' *Human Rights Quarterly* 4, no. 1 (1982): 39–52; and Ernst Michanek, ''Democracy As a Force for Development and the Role of Swedish Assistance,'' *Development Dialogue* 1 (1985): 56–85.

30   Cranford Pratt, ''Canadian Policy towards the International Monetary Fund: An Attempt to Define a Position,'' *Canadian Journal of Development Studies* 6, no. 1 (1985): 24.

31   This approach is not entirely without precedent. Witness Canada's abstaining vote on a World Bank loan to Chile in 1986.

32   See, for example, Dennis A. Rondinelli, ''The Dilemma of Development Administration: Uncertainty in Control Oriented Bureaucracies,'' *World Politics* 35, no. 1 (October 1981): 43–72; and idem, ''Development Administration and American Foreign Assistance: An Assessment of Theory and Practice in Aid,'' *Canadian Journal of Development Studies* 6, no. 2 (1985): 211–40.

33   Roger Ehrhardt, *Canadian Development Assistance to Bangladesh* (Ottawa: North-South Institute, 1983), 112.

34   The Treasury Board imposes financial controls and guidelines on project evaluation; the Public Service Commission provides the regulations on hiring; and the Department of Supply and Services establishes the procurement rules. In Ehrhardt's view, the pressure on CIDA to conform to general government regulations has become more intense since the late 1970s in the wake of highly critical reports on CIDA's financial operations by the auditor-general (see note

33, 110). The agency's authority to carry unspent funds from one year to the next was revoked in 1978, adding force to the "money-moving syndrome" and making even more difficult any reorientation towards smaller-scale projects.

35　Ehrhardt, *Canadian Development Assistance*, 120.

36　See, for example, Standing Senate Committee on Foreign Affairs, *The International Financial Institutions and the Debt Problem for Developing Countries* (Ottawa: Minister of Supply and Services, 1987); and Roy Culpeper, *The Debt Matrix* (Ottawa: North-South Institute, 1988).

37　Government of Canada, *Canada's International Relations*, response to the report of the Special Joint Committee of the Senate and the House of Commons (Ottawa: Minister of Supply and Services, 1986).

38　See Kim Richard Nossal, "Allison through the (Ottawa) Looking Glass: Bureaucratic Politics and Foreign Policy in a Parliamentary System," *Canadian Public Administration* 22, no. 4 (Winter 1979): 610–26; and Wyse, *Canadian Foreign Aid in the 1970s*, 12.

39　Government of Canada, *To Benefit a Better World*, response to the report by the Standing Committee on External Affairs and International Trade (Ottawa: Minister of Supply and Services, 1987), 41. Subsequently cited in text as *GR* (government response).

40　See CIDA, *Sharing Our Future: Canadian International Development Assistance* (Ottawa: Minister of Supply and Services, 1987). Subsequently cited in text as *SOF*.

41　See J.C.N. Paul, "International Development Agencies, Human Rights, and Humane Development Projects," in Brecher, ed., *Human Rights* , 275–327.

42　It is worth pointing out that the Canadian government never implemented the tied-aid-reduction pledge that it had made in the "strategy" paper of 1976.

43　Gisèle Côté-Harper and John C. Courtney, *International Cooperation for the Development of Human Rights and Democratic Institutions*, report to the Right Honourable Joe Clark and the Honourable Monique Landry (Ottawa: Department of External Affairs, 1987). Subsequently cited in text as *RR* (rapporteurs' report).

44　House of Commons, Bill C-147 (as amended), an Act to establish the International Centre for Human Rights and Democratic Development, 30 September 1988.

45　See Robert Miller, "The International Centre for Human Rights and Democratic Development: Notes on Its Mission," in Brecher, ed., *Human Rights*, 377–88; and David Gillies and Marie Cocking, "The Centre for Human Rights: A Distinctive Vision?" *International Perspectives*, March 1990, 36.

46　See Tim Brodhead and Brent Herbert-Copley, *Bridges of Hope? Canadian Voluntary Agencies and the Third World* (Ottawa: North-South Institute, 1988), 151, for concurrence on both counts.

47　Irving Brecher, "The Continuing Challenge of International Development: A Canadian Perspective," *Queen's Quarterly* 82, no. 3 (Autumn 1975): 342.

48 A cogent argument could be made for having the new International Centre for Human Rights and Democratic Development report to Canada's "aid minister," rather than (as is the case) to the secretary of state for external affairs. There is, on the other hand, the fact that the centre will be dealing with particularly sensitive foreign-policy issues and that its mandate extends beyond the Third World.

49 The ODA budget was actually cut by 12 percent in 1989 ($360 million) and by 4 percent in 1990 (116 million); more on these cuts later.

50 CIDA, *Sharing Our Future*.

51 As of November 1990 (the time of writing), however, CIDA's "human rights unit" consisted of a single individual.

52 Cranford Pratt, "Ethics and Foreign Policy: The Case of Canada's Development Assistance," *International Journal* 43 (Spring 1988): 264–301, provides an incisive concurring view.

53 Organization for Economic Cooperation and Development, Development Assistance Committee, *Development Cooperation in the 1990s: 1989 Report* (Paris: OECD, 1989), iii. See Katarina Tomasevski, *Development Aid and Human Rights* (New York: St. Martin's Press, 1989), for an instructive general update on this issue in the aid context. See also World Bank, *Sub-Saharan Africa: From Crisis to Sustainable Growth* (Washington, DC: World Bank, 1989).

54 In early December 1991, the president of Kenya – bending to both domestic and foreign pressures – decided to allow multi-party politics. That decision came less than one week after the meeting at which twelve Western donors had suspended their aid pledges. How (and whether) the president's decision is implemented has, of course, yet to be seen.

55 Interested Canadians, among them the president of the International Centre for Human Rights and Democratic Development, continue to press the government for bolder action on linking Canadian foreign aid to human-rights performance. See, for instance, Edward Broadbent, "Democracy and Human Rights: An International Obligation," speech delivered to the Canadian Institute of International Affairs (Montreal Chapter, 6 November 1991); and "Kenya: Tell the tyrants the future has arrived," *Globe and Mail*, 25 November 1991, A23. See also Gerald J. Schmitz, "Foreign Aid: Nice talk, but will there be action?" *Globe and Mail*, 24 October 1991, A19.

56 United Nations Development Programme, *Human Development Report 1991* (New York: Oxford University Press, 1991), 54. There may be a looming conflict between the Canadian government's commitment to basic needs and CIDA's increasing recent emphasis on the "macro" and "scructural adjustment" aspects of foreign aid. For a critical review of this emphasis, see Interchurch Fund for International Development and Churches' Committee on International Affairs, "Diminishing Our Future – CIDA: Four Years after Winegard" (Canadian Council of Churches, Ottawa, October 1991, Mimeographed), 17–36.

57   Interchurch Fund, "Diminishing Our Future," 40.

58   Ibid., 48.

59   Standing Committee on External Affairs and International Trade, *Securing Our Global Future: Canada's Stake in the Unfinished Business of Third World Debt* (Ottawa: House of Commons, 1990).

60   Government of Canada, *Government Response to the Report of the Standing Committee on External Affairs and International Trade entitled Securing Our Global Future: Canada's Stake in the Unfinished Business of Third World Debt* (Ottawa: Minister of Supply and Services, 1990).

61   Standing Committee on External Affairs and International Trade, *Unanswered Questions/Uncertain Hopes* (Ottawa: House of Commons, 1991), 105: 4–5.

13 The Static Welfare Economics of Foreign Aid: A Consolidation

MURRAY C. KEMP

INTRODUCTION

In the 1950s, when the profession of development economics was in its infancy, it was widely believed that chronically poor countries could be set on the path of self-sustaining growth only by means of an initial "big push," with substantial technical and financial support from abroad. Today's practitioners have greater confidence in the efficacy of small stimuli; for them, "haste makes waste." However, most of them would accord to foreign aid an important facilitating role in the growth process. They also emphasize its role in achieving more equitable intranational and international distributions of income. This being so, it is remarkable that nowhere in the vast literature on the economics of development can one find a systematic theoretical examination of questions relating to the incidence of aid or to the optimal level and timing of aid.

In the present essay, I seek to remedy this deficiency, at least in part. The exposition is systematic; that is, a large number of related questions are examined from a fixed point of view and by means of unified theoretical analysis. However, the treatment is far from comprehensive; important questions remain out of reach of the apparatus employed and, doubtless, others have simply not occurred to me. Thus, the entire discourse is static, with no provision for the passage of time: nothing is said about the optimal *timing* of aid, including its division into stock and flow components;[1] nothing is said about the important concept of "absorptive capacity";[2] and nothing is said about the role of aid in promoting research on the process of economic development and in gradually raising the quality of civil services in the recipient countries.[3] Moreover, the analysis rests on the traditional but unsatisfactory assumption of complete and competitive markets. Finally, aid is treated throughout as a parameter to be varied at the policy maker's will, not as a variable to be explained by the analysis. Nevertheless, it may be useful to have a consolidation of information; at a minimum, this would serve as a starting point for further, more policy-relevant analysis.

In a world economy in which everything depends on everything else, there are as many means of international aid as there are instruments of economic policy. However, to keep the discussion within reasonable bounds, attention is restricted to (1) transfers of goods or of command over goods and (2) transfers of information ("technical assistance").[4]

Transfers of goods have been much discussed by trade theorists as the raw material of the "transfer problem" and the "reparations problem." They are the archetypical instruments of aid, although in practice they are rarely used in isolation. Of course, access to valuable information is also a good; however, it is a public good, not a private good, and therefore merits our special attention.

If this essay has a theme, it is that some of the folklore of international aid – that is, the body of propositions treated as self-evident – must be given up. Consider the proposition that one country can always help another by a transfer of private goods. It will emerge that in a wide variety of contexts this proposition is invalid; indeed, it will be shown that a particular country may be unable to help *any* other country by that means. Moreover, even if one particular country can help another by a direct transfer of goods, it yet may be optimal (i.e., it may entail least utility cost to the donor) to give only part of the aid by direct transfer, the rest indirectly, by direct transfer to third countries. (However, it is never optimal to give all aid indirectly.) Finally, even if each direct transfer does good when viewed as an isolated act, one cannot be sure that the sum of all gifts by all donors does good.

Similarly, a country with a global absolute advantage over all other countries may be unable to help any other country by technical assistance. Moreover, even if one particular country can help another by direct technical assistance, it yet may be optimal (i.e., it may entail least utility cost or greatest utility gain to the donor) to give only part of the aid by direct transfer, the rest indirectly. Finally, even if each direct transfer hurts the donor when viewed as an isolated act, one cannot be sure that the aggregate of all gifts by all donors hurts any donor.

AID BY TRANSFER OF GOODS:
THE SIMPLEST CASE

It is easy to see that, in general, an international transfer of goods will bring about a change in world prices. Only in the singular situation in which marginal propensities are the same, commodity by commodity, in donor and recipient, will this not be so. The change in prices might favour the recipient, thus reinforcing the initial welfare impact of the transfer, or it might be to the advantage of the donor, thus offsetting, more or less, the initial impact. For a long time, it was unclear whether the change in prices might so favour the donor that, on balance, the donor would be better off after the transfer and the recipient worse off. Evidently, there could be no firmly based welfare economics of international aid until this question was answered.

Professional discussion of the question reached a local peak with the appearance in 1947 of Paul Samuelson's *Foundations*. Earlier, Leontief[5] had produced a two-by-two example in which a transfer worked to the net advantage of the donor and, therefore, to the net disadvantage of the recipient. Samuelson's contribution was to note that if the assumption of Walrasian stability is added to Leontief's specification, his conclusions are reversed. Much later, Balasko[6] showed that in quite general two-by-two contexts the donor benefits if and only if the system is stable.

It will be useful to have a proof of Samuelson's proposition to which we can later refer. There are two free-trading countries, α and β, and there are two commodities, 1 and 2. The population of each country is completely homogeneous, both in preferences and in asset holdings. Each commodity is a private consumption good. In an initial world trading equilibrium, α exports commodity 1 and β exports commodity 2; this assumption is for concreteness only. The initial equilibrium is disturbed when α extends aid to β. The following notation will be employed.

$T^{\alpha\beta}$ the amount of aid, in terms of commodity 2, from α (the donor) to β (the recipient); initially, $T^{\alpha\beta} = 0$

p the price of commodity 1 in terms of commodity 2

u^j the utility derived from consumption in country j ($j = \alpha, \beta$)

e^j the expenditure function of country j, expenditure in terms of commodity 2 ($j = \alpha, \beta$)

r^j the revenue function of country j, revenue in terms of commodity 2 ($j = \alpha, \beta$)

z^{ji} the excess demand by country j for commodity i ($i = 1,2; j = \alpha,\beta$)

The aid is financed in α and distributed in β by means of lump-sum taxes and subsidies. Hence the private budget constraint of α is

(1) $e^{\alpha}(p,u^{\alpha}) = r^{\alpha}(p) - T^{\alpha\beta}$

and that of β is

(2) $e^{\beta}(p,u^{\beta}) = r^{\beta}(p) + T^{\alpha\beta}$,

The description of world equilibrium is then completed by the market-clearing condition[7]

(3) $z^{\alpha 1}(p,u^\alpha) + z^{\beta 1}(p,u^\beta) = 0.$

Equations (1) to (3) contain the three variables p, u^α and u^β, as well as the parameter $T^{\alpha\beta}$. The system is assumed to possess a unique solution (p^*, u^{α^*}, u^{β^*}), with p^* positive and finite.

We wish to know how each of the three variables responds to a small change in $T^{\alpha\beta}$. Differentiating (1) to (3) with respect to $T^{\alpha\beta}$, we find that

(4)
$$\begin{bmatrix} e_p^\alpha - r_p^\alpha & e_u^\alpha & 0 \\ e_p^\beta - r_p^\beta & 0 & e_u^\beta \\ z_p^{\alpha 1} + z_p^{\beta 1} & z_u^{\alpha 1} & z_u^{\beta 1} \end{bmatrix} \begin{bmatrix} dp \\ du^\alpha \\ du^\beta \end{bmatrix} = \begin{bmatrix} -1 \\ 1 \\ 0 \end{bmatrix} dT^{\alpha\beta}$$

where subscripts indicate differentiation (e.g., $e_p^\alpha \equiv \partial e^\alpha/\partial p$ and $r_p^\alpha \equiv dr^\alpha/dp$). Recalling the envelope result that $e_p^j - r_p^j = z^{j1}$ ($j = \alpha,\beta$), choosing units of utility so that $e_u^j = 1$, defining $z_p^1 \equiv z_p^{\alpha 1} + z_p^{\beta 1}$, and noting that $T^{\alpha\beta} = 0$, we can rewrite (4) in the more streamlined form

(5)
$$\begin{bmatrix} z^{\alpha 1} & 1 & 0 \\ z^{\beta 1} & 0 & 1 \\ z_p^1 & z_u^{\alpha 1} & z_u^{\beta 1} \end{bmatrix} \begin{bmatrix} dp \\ du^\alpha \\ du^\beta \end{bmatrix} = \begin{bmatrix} -1 \\ 1 \\ 0 \end{bmatrix} dT^{\alpha\beta} .$$

Solving,

(6) $\Delta(dp/dT^{\alpha\beta}) = (pz_u^{\alpha 1} - pz_u^{\beta 1})/p$

   $\Delta(du^\alpha/dT^{\alpha\beta}) = -z_p^1 = -\Delta(du^\beta/dT^{\alpha\beta})$

where

(7) $\Delta \equiv z_p^1 + z^{\beta 1}(pz_u^{\alpha 1} - pz_u^{\beta 1})/p$

is the determinant of the matrix of coefficients in (5). We note that $pz_u^{j1}/e_u^j = pz_u^{j1}$ is the marginal propensity to consume commodity 1 in country j and may be of either sign, and that z_p^1 is the sum of two pure (or "compensated") price slopes, one for each country, and is necessarily negative. Moreover, it can be shown that, as a sufficient and almost necessary condition of Walrasian stability, $\Delta < 0.$[8] Applying this information to (6), we see that aid necessarily hurts the donor α and benefits the recipient β. Thus, it seems, common sense has been vindicated and a firm foundation provided for the welfare economics of international aid.

However, Samuelson's proposition is based on very strict assumptions. There are only two commodities. Moreover, only two countries, the donor and the recipient, are recognized; there are no bystanders. Finally, markets are not only competitive but free of all distortions. In particular, the aid is financed and disbursed by means of non-distorting lump-sum taxes and subsidies, and it is spent in a manner determined by the preferences of the recipient, unconstrained by tying conditions of any kind. Until recently, it was simply taken for granted that the proposition survives under more realistic assumptions.

The proposition can be generalized to a limited extent. Thus, it can be shown that the number of commodities is immaterial[9] and that in a world of many countries the proposition remains valid if the donor and recipient are small. However, we now know, principally from the work of Michihiro Ohyama[10] and David Gale,[11] that, in general, the proposition does not survive outside the context in which Samuelson proved it.

AID BY TRANSFER OF GOODS: TIED AID

Externalities, commodity taxes, factor-market distortions, aid tying, and elements of monopoly power (including the monopoly power of labour unions) can all generate outcomes that, in the light of Samuelson's result, appear to be paradoxical. Space does not allow me to consider in detail all types of distortions. Here, I perturb the basic model in just one respect, by allowing for the possibility that aid is tied.[12]

The provision of aid may be conditional on the recipient meeting conditions imposed by the donor. The recipient may be required to spend the aid in a particular way – on defence or on commodities exported by the donor, for example; or it may be required to modify its commercial policy – aid may then be viewed as compensation for foregone tariff revenue. In general, aid may be tied to any variable under the control of the recipient government. Here the focus is on just one of several possibilities.[13] It is assumed that the recipient β is required to spend a proportion m^β of the aid on the commodity exported by the donor α; as in the previous section, it is assumed that commodity 1 is exported by α.

As in the simple case studied by Samuelson, the aid is financed in α by means of lump-sum taxes. The private budget constraint of α is, therefore,

$$(1) \qquad e^\alpha(p,u^\alpha) = r^\alpha(p) - T^{\alpha\beta} .$$

The aid is spent by the government of β; it influences the welfare w^β of β but does not enter the private budget constraint

(8) $\qquad e^{\beta}(p,u^{\beta}) = r^{\alpha}(p)$

where u^{β} must now be interpreted as that part of β-well-being derived from private expenditure. The description of world equilibrium is completed by the condition of market clearance,

(9) $\qquad z^{\alpha1}(p,u^{\alpha}) + z^{\beta1}(p,u^{\beta}) + m^{\beta}T^{\alpha\beta}/p = 0 .$

Differentiating our new system [(1), (8), (9)] with respect to $T^{\alpha\beta}$, we find that

(4') $\qquad \begin{bmatrix} z^{\alpha1} & 1 & 0 \\ z^{\beta1} & 0 & 1 \\ z_p^{\alpha1} + z_p^{\beta1} & z_u^{\alpha1} & z_u^{\beta1} \end{bmatrix} \begin{bmatrix} dp \\ du^{\alpha} \\ du^{\beta} \end{bmatrix} = \begin{bmatrix} -1 \\ 0 \\ -m^{\beta}/p \end{bmatrix} dT^{\alpha\beta} .$

Solving,

$$\Delta(dp/dT^{\alpha\beta}) = -(m^{\beta} - pz_u^{\alpha1})/p$$

(11) $\quad \Delta(du^{\alpha}/dT) = -z_p^1 - z^{\beta1}(m^{\beta} - pz_u^{\beta1})/p$

$\qquad \Delta(du^{\beta}/dT) = z^{\beta1}(m^{\beta} - pz_u^{\alpha1})/p$

From (7) and (11) we see that for both $\Delta < 0$ and $du^{\alpha}/dT > 0$ it is necessary and sufficient that

(12) $\quad -z^{\beta1}(m^{\beta} - pz_u^{\beta1})/p < z_p^{\alpha1} + z_p^{\beta1} < -z^{\beta1}(z_u^{\alpha1} - z_u^{\beta1})$

Evidently, this condition can be satisfied without inferiority. However, it does imply that the recipient's offer curve is inelastic at the initial equilibrium. Consider the first inequality of (12). Making use of a well-known relationship between substitution terms

$$pz_p^{\beta1} + z_p^{\beta2} = 0$$

and of the identity between marginal propensities to consume

$$pz_u^{\beta1} + z_u^{\beta2} = 1 ,$$

that inequality can be rewritten as

(13) $\quad z_p^{\beta2} - z^{\beta1}z_u^{\beta2} < pz_p^{\alpha1} - (1-m^{\beta})z^{\beta1} < 0 .$

But the left-hand expression in (13) is the total derivative $dz^{\beta 2}/dp$; hence, $-dz^{\beta 1}/d(1/p) < 0$. Thus, the recipient's offer of its export commodity decreases when its terms of trade improve, implying that the recipient's offer curve is inelastic.

The fate of the recipient is easily determined. Since the initial equilibrium is Pareto-efficient, a small change in the real income of one country must be accompanied by an opposite change in the real income of the other country. Indeed, given the normalization $e^{\alpha}_u = e^{\beta}_u = 1$, we have

$$dw^{\beta}/dT^{\alpha\beta} = 1 + du^{\beta}/dT^{\alpha\beta} = -du^{\alpha}dT^{\alpha\beta}$$

where, it will be recalled, w^{β} is the total well-being of β.

Thus, we have established that, if and only if condition (12) is satisfied, the economy is locally stable but the donor benefits from aid and the recipient suffers. Let us try to construct the common sense of the proposition. Because the aid is marginal, it has the same direct welfare effect however it is spent by the government of β. But its indirect effects, through prices, do depend on how it is spent. If $m^{\beta} \neq pz^{\beta 1}_u$, that is, if the government's tied marginal propensity to spend on the first commodity differs from the corresponding marginal propensity to consume of individuals in β, then, in effect, the Engel curves of β contain kinks at the initial equilibrium point. The kinks serve to moderate or magnify the price effects of the transfer. In particular, if $m^{\beta} > pz^{\beta 1}_u$, that is, if the marginal propensity of the β-government is greater than that of β-individuals, then any aid-induced increase in p (improvement in α's terms of trade) must be exaggerated and it is this exaggeration of the price change that lies behind any perverse welfare outcomes.

It must be emphasized that, in the above formulation, aid is tied to *marginal* consumption. To verify that the tying requirement has been satisfied, the donor must know a great deal about the recipient's economy — often, more than can be known. Verification would be much easier if aid were tied to the recipient's *total* consumption, as in Schweinberger,[14] for then only post-aid consumption need be known. However, tying in that sense has little to do with real-world tying, which is typically of the marginal kind. Relevant information may be found in the Organization for Economic Co-operation and Development (OECD) document *Development Cooperation, 1986 Review* (December 1986). In particular, it is there shown that two-thirds of the "bilateral official development assistance" given by members of the Development Assistance Committee is directed to specific projects, while only 5 percent is program assistance.

It must be emphasized also that in a two-country formulation the tying of aid necessarily assumes a larger-than-life importance. In practice, there are many recipients and many potential donors. Each recipient does much preliminary shopping about, seeking to match its particular needs to donors with the appropriate comparative advantages. Thus, the formal tying of aid might disrupt world allocation hardly at all. More will be said about the tying of aid in the next section.

AID BY TRANSFER OF GOODS: BYSTANDERS

In Samuelson's world, there is a donor and there is a recipient, but there are no other countries. It was David Gale's great contribution to show that when aid is given in the presence of bystanders, it is no longer inevitable that the donor suffers and the recipient benefits – even if the world economy is stable and free of distortions, including tying.[15] Of course, the Samuelsonian outcome is still possible; indeed, that outcome is inevitable if donor and recipient are small or if they have the same marginal propensities to consume. But paradoxes can no longer be ruled out by appeal to stability alone.

Aid in the Absence of Distortions

Adding a bystander γ to system (1) to (3), we obtain

(1) $\quad e^{\alpha}(p,u^{\alpha}) = r^{\alpha}(p) - T^{\alpha\beta}$

(2) $\quad e^{\beta}(p,u^{\beta}) = r^{\beta}(p) + T^{\alpha\beta}$

(15) $\quad e^{\gamma}(p,u^{\gamma}) = r^{\gamma}(p)$

(16) $\quad \sum\limits_{j=\alpha,\beta,\gamma} z^{j1}(p,u^j) = 0 .$

Differentiating this system totally with respect to $T^{\alpha\beta}$, and redefining z_p^1 as $\sum\limits_{j=\alpha,\beta,\gamma} z_p^{j1}$, we obtain

(17) $\begin{bmatrix} z^{\alpha 1} & 1 & 0 & 0 \\ z^{\beta 1} & 0 & 1 & 0 \\ z^{\gamma 1} & 0 & 0 & 1 \\ z_p^1 & z_u^{\alpha 1} & z_u^{\beta 1} & z_u^{\gamma 1} \end{bmatrix} \begin{bmatrix} dp \\ du^{\alpha} \\ du^{\beta} \\ du^{\gamma} \end{bmatrix} = \begin{bmatrix} -1 \\ 1 \\ 0 \\ 0 \end{bmatrix} dT^{\alpha\beta}$.

Solving,

(18) $\quad \Delta''(dp/dT^{\alpha\beta}) = z_u^{\alpha 1} - z_u^{\beta 1}$

(19) $\quad \Delta''(du^{\alpha}/dT^{\alpha\beta}) = -z_p^1 - z^{\gamma 1}(z_u^{\beta 1} - z_u^{\gamma 1})$

(20) $\quad \Delta''(du^{\beta}/dT^{\alpha\beta}) = z_p^1 + z^{\gamma 1}(z_u^{\alpha 1} - z_u^{\gamma 1})$

(21) $\quad \Delta''(du^\gamma/dT^{\alpha\beta}) = -z^{\gamma 1}(z_u^{\alpha 1} - z_u^{\beta 1})$

where

(22) $\quad \Delta'' \equiv \sum_{j=\alpha,\beta,\gamma} (z_p^{j1} - z^{j1}z_u^{j1}) \equiv z_p^1 - \sum_{j=\alpha,\beta,\gamma} z^{j1}z_u^{j1}$

is negative as a sufficient condition of local stability.

We see at a glance that the donor might benefit and/or the recipient suffer. For the donor to benefit, it is necessary that the bystander be a net trader in the initial equilibrium, with marginal propensities to consume that differ from those of the recipient; if either condition fails to be satisfied, we are effectively back to Samuelson's two-country model. Similarly, for the recipient to suffer, it is necessary that the bystander be a net trader, with marginal propensities that differ from those of the donor; if either condition fails to hold, we again are back to the two-country model. Finally, we notice that the donor might benefit even when initially it does not trade, so that $z^{\alpha 1} = 0$, and that the recipient might suffer even when initially it does not trade, so that $z^{\beta 1} = 0$. Of course, it is not possible for both outcomes to occur simultaneously.

Alternative necessary conditions can be obtained by making use of the Slutzky decomposition of the uncompensated net demand function $\bar{z}^{j1}(p)$:

(23) $\quad \bar{z}_p^{j1} = z_p^{j1} - z^{j1}z_u^{j1} \qquad j = \alpha,\beta,\gamma.$

Thus, substituting for $z_p^{\gamma 1}$, equations (19) and (20) can be rewritten as

(24) $\quad \Delta''(du^\alpha/dT^{\alpha\beta}) = -(z_p^{\alpha 1} + z_p^{\beta 1}) - \bar{z}_p^{\gamma 1} - z^{\gamma 1}z_u^{\beta 1}$

and

(25) $\quad \Delta''(du^\beta/dT^{\alpha\beta}) = (z_p^{\alpha 1} + z_p^{\beta 1}) + \bar{z}_p^{\gamma 1} + z^{\gamma 1}z_u^{\alpha 1}.$

However, differentiating the jth country's budget constraint $p\bar{z}^{j1} + \bar{z}^{j2} = 0$, we obtain

(26) $\quad \bar{z}^{j1} + p\bar{z}_p^{j1} + \bar{z}_p^{j2} = 0 \qquad j = \alpha,\beta,\gamma.$

Applying (26) to (24) and (25), and recalling that the marginal propensities to consume pz_u^{j1} and z_u^{j2} add to one, we obtain, respectively,

(27) $\quad \Delta''(du^\alpha/dT^{\alpha\beta}) = -(z_p^{\alpha 1} + z_p^{\beta 1}) + (\bar{z}_p^{\gamma 2}/p) - z^{\gamma 1}z_u^{\beta 2}/p$

and

(28) $\Delta''(du^\beta/dT^{\alpha\beta}) = (z_p^{\alpha 1} + z_p^{\beta 1}) - (\tilde{z}_p^{\gamma 2}/p) - z^{\gamma 1}z_u^{\alpha 2}/p$.

Suppose that $z^{\gamma 1}$ is negative [positive], that is, that the bystander exports the first [second] commodity. Then, from (24) [from (27)], we can infer that if a transfer enriches the donor, then either the commodity exported by the bystander is inferior to the recipient, or the bystander's export supply is backward-bending, or both; and from (25) [from (28)], we can infer that if a transfer impoverishes the recipient, then either the commodity exported by the bystander is inferior to the donor, or the bystander's export supply is backward-bending, or both.

Gale's contribution was to show that, in the presence of bystanders, it is not always possible for one country to enrich another by means of a direct international transfer. This answer to one question suggests a further question: Given that α cannot help β by means of a direct transfer, can α help β in a round-about way, by directing the transfer to bystander γ? More generally, whether or not α can help β directly, is it possible that a given amount of aid (in terms of β-utility) can be given at less utility cost to α if it is given indirectly? It will be shown that each of the following outcomes is possible; necessary and sufficient conditions for each outcome will be provided.

(i)   Any transfer from α, whether to β or to γ or to both, impoverishes β. In this case, clearly, it is impossible for α to play Good Samaritan to β. (Negative transfers by α are ruled out.)

(ii)   A transfer from α to β impoverishes β, but a transfer from α to γ enriches β. In this case, α can aid β only indirectly, by making a grant to γ.

(iii)   A transfer from α to β enriches β, but a transfer from α to γ impoverishes β. In this case, α can aid β only directly, by making a grant to β.

(iv)   Any transfer from α, whether to β or to γ, enriches β. In some circumstances, a transfer of a given size will do most good to β if it is made directly; in other circumstances, the transfer will be most efficacious if made indirectly.

Of these possibilities, (i) and (iv) are of special interest: it is not always feasible for a potential donor to enrich another country by a direct transfer, and even if a direct transfer is efficacious, it yet may be less efficacious than an indirect transfer.

Equation (20) gives us the effect on β's welfare of a direct transfer from α; equation (21), with the superscripts β and γ permuted, describes the effect on β's welfare of an indirect transfer. Thus,

(29) $\Delta''(du^\beta/dT^{\alpha\beta}) = z_p^1 + z^{\gamma 1}(z_u^{\alpha 1} - z_u^{\gamma 1})$

$$\Delta''(du^\beta/dT^{\alpha\gamma}) = -z^{\beta 1}(z_u^{\alpha 1} - z_u^{\gamma 1})$$

where $T^{\alpha\gamma}$ is, of course, the amount transferred by α to γ. Inspection of (29) reveals that, even with Δ'' constrained to be negative, $du^\beta/dT^{\alpha\beta}$ and $du^\beta/dT^{\alpha\gamma}$ can be both negative, both positive, or (either) one positive, the other negative; that is, none of the outcomes from (i) to (iv) distinguished above can be ruled out.

We can look beyond the binary possibilities of (i) to (iv) and show that if α cannot help β [outcome (i)] then γ can do so, at least indirectly. In other words, β always has at least one potential friend. (Of course, the potential friend may be even poorer than β.) The plausibility of this proposition can be established by observing that indirect aid from γ to β reverses the direction of indirect aid from α to β; in effect, the former removes the natural sign restriction from $T^{\alpha\beta}$. Whether γ can also help β directly is another matter. It can be verified that if α and γ export the same commodity, then at least one of them can help β directly.[16] On the other hand, α may be able to help neither β nor γ, either by directing all aid to β or by directing all aid to γ or, therefore, by dividing aid between β and γ.[17] While each country has a potential friend, it is not always the case that each country can serve as a friend. This finding is of some theological and ethical interest; not every country can play the part of the Good Samaritan. Finally, we note that if $z^{\alpha 1} = 0$ and under other sufficient conditions, the donor's utility may increase, both when aid is given wholly to β or γ and, therefore, when it is divided in any manner between them. This possibility serves as a warning that the textbook practice of lumping together all countries but one as "the rest of the world" does not necessarily bring back the orthodox Samuelsonian conclusions.

To this point we have confined our attention to aid directed wholly to one country. It remains to consider the *optimal* mode of assistance, optimality defined in terms of the utility cost to α of a given small increase in the welfare of β.[18] Suppose that u^β has been raised to the required level by setting $T^{\alpha\beta} = \bar{T}^{\alpha\beta} > 0$ and $T^{\alpha\gamma} = \bar{T}^{\alpha\gamma} > 0$. Let $T^\alpha = T^{\alpha\beta} + T^{\alpha\gamma}$ and $\varepsilon \equiv T^{\alpha\beta}/T^\alpha$, so that (2) and (15) take the more general form

(30) $e^\beta(p,u^\beta) = r^\beta(p) + \varepsilon T^\alpha$

and

(31) $e^\gamma(p,u^\gamma) = r^\gamma(p) + (1-\varepsilon)T^\alpha$.

We are interested in the response of u^α to a small change in ε, with u^β held constant and T^α allowed to vary. Differentiating the system [(1), (30), (31), (16)] with respect to ε, we obtain

$$(32) \quad \begin{bmatrix} z^{\alpha 1} & 1 & 0 & 1 \\ z^{\beta 1} & 0 & 0 & -\varepsilon \\ z^{\gamma 1} & 0 & 1 & -(1-\varepsilon) \\ z_p^1 & z_u^{\alpha 1} & z_u^{\gamma 1} & 0 \end{bmatrix} \begin{bmatrix} dp \\ du^\alpha \\ du^\gamma \\ dT \end{bmatrix} = \begin{bmatrix} 0 \\ T \\ -T \\ 0 \end{bmatrix} d\varepsilon .$$

Solving,

(33a) $\Delta'''(dp/d\varepsilon) = -T^\alpha(z_u^{\alpha 1} - z_u^{\gamma 1})$

(33b) $\Delta'''(du^\alpha/d\varepsilon) = T^\alpha z_p^1 = -\Delta'''(du^\gamma/d\varepsilon)$

(33c) $\Delta'''(dT^\alpha/d\varepsilon) = -T^\alpha[z_p^1 - z^{\alpha 1}(z_u^{\alpha 1} - z_u^{\gamma 1})]$

where

(34) $\quad \Delta''' \equiv \varepsilon z_p^1 - z_u^{\alpha 1}[\varepsilon z^{\alpha 1} + z^{\beta 1}] - z_u^{\gamma 1}[\varepsilon z^{\gamma 1} - (1-\varepsilon)z^{\beta 1}]$

is negative as a sufficient condition of local stability.

Equation (33b) tells us that *for all permissible ε $du^\alpha/d\varepsilon$ is positive*. This implies that it is never optimal to give all aid indirectly, through γ. It is possible that the optimal value of ε is one. However, it is also possible that at some value of ε less than one, say $\varepsilon(u^\beta)$, T^α reaches its maximum feasible value; in that case, the optimal value of ε is $\varepsilon(u^\beta)$. Thus, we know that there are circumstances in which α can help β by giving all aid indirectly but cannot help β by giving all aid directly. In those circumstances, we can make use of (29) to write

$$z_p^1 + z^{\gamma 1}(z_u^{\alpha 1} - z_u^{\gamma 1}) > 0$$

$$-z^{\beta 1}(z_u^{\alpha 1} - z_u^{\gamma 1}) < 0$$

so that, subtracting the second inequality from the first, and appealing to (33c)

$$z_p^1 - z^{\alpha 1}(z_u^{\alpha 1} - z_u^{\gamma 1}) > 0$$

and $dT^\alpha/d\varepsilon > 0$; eventually, at $\varepsilon = \varepsilon(u^\beta) < 1$, the T^α required to maintain the given level of u^β is unfeasible. In general, the optimal ε must lie in the half-open interval (0,1].

Tied Aid Again

We have seen that it may be impossible for α to aid β, either directly or indirectly (or by a mixture of the two modes). However, that conclusion was derived from the assumption that aid is "clean" or untied. Now it is usually taken for granted that aid is most beneficial to the recipient when it is completely untied. In fact, this is not the case. In particular, even when it is impossible for α to help β by means of an untied transfer, it yet may be possible to help with a tied transfer. Thus, while tying can create paradoxes in a two-country setting, it can remove them when there are three or more countries.

To see this, let us suppose that $\varepsilon = 1$ and that α requires the government of β to spend a proportion m^β of the aid on the first commodity $(0 \le m^\beta \le 1)$. Then, the conditions of international equilibrium become

(1) $\quad e^\alpha(p,u^\alpha) - r^\alpha(p) = -T^{\alpha\beta}$

(8) $\quad e^\beta(p,u^\beta) - r^\beta(p) = 0$

(15) $\quad e^\gamma(p,u^\gamma) - r^\gamma(p) = 0$

(35) $\quad z^{\alpha 1}(p,u^\alpha) + z^{\beta 1}(p,u^\beta) + z^{\gamma 1}(p,u^\gamma) + m^\beta T^{\alpha\beta}/p = 0$

It should be recalled that (8) is the private budget constraint of β and u^β that part of β's welfare generated by that budget. The total welfare of β, w^β, is greater than u^β by the contributon of α's aid. Initially, $T^{\alpha\beta} = 0$.

Differentiating $[(1), (8), (15), (35)]$ with respect to $T^{\alpha\beta}$ and solving for $du^\alpha/dT^{\alpha\beta}$ and $du^\gamma/dT^{\alpha\beta}$, we find that

(36a) $\quad (du^\alpha/dT^{\alpha\beta}) = \frac{1}{\Delta''}[- z_p^1 + z^{\gamma 1}z_u^{\gamma 1} + z^{\beta 1}z_u^{\beta 1} + z^{\alpha 1}m^\beta/p]$

(36b) $\quad (du^\gamma/dT^{\alpha\beta}) = \frac{1}{\Delta''}[(z^{\gamma 1}/p)(m^\beta - pz_u^{\alpha 1})]$.

Since $T^{\alpha\beta} = 0$, the initial equilibrium is Pareto-efficient; hence an infinitesimal transfer has the same effect on the recipient's welfare *however it is spent* and

$$\Delta''(dw^\beta/dT^{\alpha\beta}) = - \Delta''(du^\alpha/dT^{\alpha\beta} + du^\gamma/dT^{\alpha\beta})$$

(37) $$= z_p^1 + z^{\gamma 1}(z_u^{\alpha 1} - z_u^{\gamma 1}) + (z^{\beta 1}/p)(m^\beta - pz_u^{\beta 1}) .$$

It is easy to verify that (36a) may be negative even when $du^\alpha/dT^{\alpha\beta}|_{\varepsilon=1}$ and $du^\alpha/dT^{\alpha\beta}|_{\varepsilon=0}$ are positive, and that (37) may be positive even when $du^\beta/dT^{\alpha\beta}|_{\varepsilon=1}$ and $du^\beta/dT^{\alpha\beta}|_{\varepsilon=0}$ are negative. For those comforting outcomes, it is necessary that $z^{\beta 1}(m^\beta - pz_u^{\beta 1})$ be negative, that is, that the government of β be required marginally to spend more on β's exported commodity than would β-individuals. This is a thoroughly plausible condition. If the aid had been tied both in the donor country and in the recipient country, the condition would have been even weaker.

Thus, by tying its aid, a donor can circumvent the impossibility results of this section. Notice, however, that if α and β export different commodities, then circumvention can be achieved only by unconventionally tying aid to the good *imported* by the donor.

Joint Donors and Joint Recipients

So far, I have concentrated on a few basic questions raised by the desire of a single country to aid another. However, the poorer countries typically receive aid from several quarters, and most wealthy countries spread their aid widely. These well-known facts suggest additional questions. If both α and γ help β and wish to extend their aid, cooperatively sharing the utility burden, equally or in any other fashion, how should the additional aid be shared among the donors? If α helps both β and γ and wishes to extend the aid, dividing the additional utility benefits equally or in some other fashion, how should the additional aid be shared by the recipients? Each question is grist for the mill constructed in this section.

Thus, suppose that in an initial equilibrium β receives $T^{\alpha\beta}$ from α and $T^{\gamma\beta}$ from γ, both $T^{\alpha\beta}$ and $T^{\gamma\beta}$ positive. The equilibrium is described by the equations

(38) $\quad e^{\alpha}(p,u^{\alpha}) - r^{\alpha}(p) = -T^{\alpha\beta}$

(39) $\quad e^{\beta}(p,u^{\beta}) - r^{\beta}(p) = T^{\alpha\beta} + T^{\gamma\beta}$

(40) $\quad e^{\gamma}(p,u^{\gamma}) - r^{\gamma}(p) = -T^{\gamma\beta}$

(21) $\quad z^{\alpha1}(p,u^{\alpha}) + z^{\beta1}(p,u^{\beta}) + z^{\gamma1}(p,u^{\gamma}) = 0$.

Treating u^{β} as a parameter and $T^{\alpha\beta}$, $T^{\gamma\beta}$ as variables, we can differentiate the system with respect to u^{β}, add the equality-of-sharing condition $du^{\alpha} = du^{\gamma}$, and solve for the additional contributions of the donors α and γ. Omitting the detailed calculations, we have

(41a) $\quad \Delta''''(dT^{\alpha\beta}/du^{\beta}) = -z^{\alpha1}(z_u^{\alpha1} - 2z_u^{\beta1} + z_u^{\gamma1}) + z_p^1$

(41b) $\quad\quad\quad\quad\quad\quad = \Delta'' - (z^{\alpha1} - z^{\gamma1})(z_u^{\gamma1} - z_u^{\beta1})$

(42a) $\quad \Delta''''(dT^{\gamma\beta}/du^{\beta}) = -z^{\gamma1}(z_u^{\alpha1} - 2z_u^{\beta1} + z_u^{\gamma1}) + z_p^1$

(42b) $\quad\quad\quad\quad\quad\quad = \Delta'' - (z^{\gamma1} - z^{\alpha1})(z_u^{\alpha1} - z_u^{\beta1})$

where $\Delta'''' \equiv 2z_p^1 < 0$. If $z^{\alpha1} = z^{\gamma1}$ or if $z_u^{\beta1}$ lies midway between $z_u^{\alpha1}$ and $z_u^{\gamma1}$, then $dT^{\alpha\beta}/du^{\beta} = dT^{\gamma\beta}/du^{\beta} > 0$. Otherwise, the vector $(dT^{\alpha\beta}, dT^{\gamma\beta})$ of incremental aid can have any pattern of signs. In particular, it is possible that the recipient β can be made better off with less aid from each donor. However, for that outcome, it is necessary that the recipient's offer curve be inelastic and/or that the commodity exported by the recipient be inferior in at least one of the donor countries,[19] and as (41b) and (42b) reveal, it is necessary also that the recipient's marginal propensity to buy any good fall between the donors' marginal propensities to buy the same good. Of course, whatever the manner in which aid changes, both donors find themselves worse off: $du^\alpha = du^\gamma = - du^\beta/2.$[20]

Suppose alternatively that in an initial equilibrium the single donor α gives $T^{\alpha\beta}$ to β and $T^{\alpha\gamma}$ to γ, both $T^{\alpha\beta}$ and $T^{\alpha\gamma}$ positive. The equilibrium is described by the equations

(43) $e^\alpha(p,u^\alpha) - r^\alpha(p) = - T^{\alpha\beta} - T^{\alpha\gamma}$

(44) $e^\beta(p,u^\beta) - r^\beta(p) = T^{\alpha\beta}$

(45) $e^\gamma(p,u^\gamma) - r^\gamma(p) = T^{\alpha\gamma}$

(16) $z^{\alpha 1}(p,u^\alpha) + z^{\beta 1}(p,u^\beta) + z^{\gamma 1}(p,u^\gamma) = 0$

Treating u^α as a parameter and $T^{\alpha\beta}$, $T^{\alpha\gamma}$ as variables, both positive, we can differentiate [(43) – (45), (16)] with respect to u^α, add the equality-of-benefit condition $du^\beta = du^\gamma$, and solve for the aid received by the recipients β and γ. Thus,

(46a) $- \Delta''''(dT^{\alpha\beta}/du^\alpha) = z^{\beta 1}(-2z_u^{\alpha 1} + z_u^{\beta 1} + z_u^{\gamma 1}) - z_p^1$

(46b) $\qquad\qquad = - \Delta'' + (z^{\beta 1} - z^{\gamma 1})(z_u^{\gamma 1} - z_u^{\alpha 1})$

(47a) $- \Delta''''(dT^{\alpha\gamma}/du^\alpha) = z^{\gamma 1}(-2z_u^{\alpha 1} + z_u^{\beta 1} + z_u^{\gamma 1}) - z_p^1$

(47b) $\qquad\qquad = - \Delta'' + (z^{\beta 1} - z^{\gamma 1})(z_u^{\alpha 1} - z_u^{\beta 1}) .$

If $z^{\beta 1} = z^{\gamma 1}$ or if $z_u^{\alpha 1} = z_u^{\beta 1} = z_u^{\gamma 1}$, then $dT^{\alpha\beta}/du^\alpha = dT^{\alpha\gamma}/du^\alpha < 0$.

Otherwise, the vector $(dT^{\alpha\beta}, dT^{\alpha\gamma})$ of incremental aid can have any pattern of signs. In particular, it is possible that both recipients can be made better off with a smaller total outlay by the donor. However, for that outcome, it is necessary that the donor's offer curve be inelastic and/or that the commodity exported by the donor be inferior in at least one of the recipient countries,[21] and as (46b) and (47b) reveal, it is necessary also that the donor's marginal propensity to buy any good fall between the recipients' marginal propensities to buy the same good. Of course, whatever the manner in which aid changes, the donor is left worse off:

$du^\alpha = - du^\beta/2 = - du^\gamma/2.$

Summary

In the traditional stable two-country setting, additional aid implies an additional transfer. What we have established in this section is that when there are more than two countries, there is no comparable result, even when donors and recipients share the burden or benefit equally. In particular, incremental binary aid may bring about paradoxical changes in the well-being of donor and/or recipient. However, this finding should not be taken quite literally. In the world about us, there are hundreds of countries; in that world, incremental binary aid almost always will bring about welfare changes of the Samuelsonian kind. Rather, the α, β, and γ of our models should be interpreted as aggregates of aid-giving countries, aid-receiving countries, and bystander countries. *Even if each gift of each donor does good when considered as an isolated act, one cannot be sure that the sum of all gifts by all donors does good.*

AID BY TRANSFER OF INFORMATION: THE SIMPLEST CASE

Let us turn now to the welfare implications of international technical assistance. Aid of this kind differs in at least one important respect from aid by the transfer of goods. By spreading useful information, it makes the world economy more efficient. This suggests that there are circumstances in which technical assistance improves the well-being of all countries simultaneously. On the other hand, the transfer of information improves the recipient's productive capacity, and as we know from the work of J.S. Mill and F.Y. Edgeworth, this may give rise to such an adverse change in the recipient's terms of trade that, on balance and paradoxically, the recipient is impoverished.

In the present section, these and related questions are considered in the familiar setting of two countries and two commodities. Now, however, it is specified that one country (α) is technically advanced, the other (β) technically backward, in the sense that, in each industry, α is more efficient than β. Thus, if v^{ij} denotes the vector of primary inputs used in the ith industry and jth country and $F^{ij}(v^{ij})$ the production function of that industry and country, then

$$\text{for all } v^{i\alpha} = v^{i\beta} = v^i > 0,\ F^{i\alpha}(v^i) = \mu(v^i)F^{i\beta}(v^i) \text{ and } \mu(v^i) > 1$$

Suppose now that α makes a free gift of part of its technology to β such that in each industry the new production function is a constant $\lambda > 1$ times the old production function and β's production set expands in uniform proportion. We wish to know how the gift affects the terms of trade and the well-being of each country.

Introducing the β-productivity parameter λ, we rewrite the model of section 2 as

(48) $e^{\alpha}(p,u^{\alpha}) - r^{\alpha}(p) = 0$

(49) $e^{\beta}(p,u^{\beta}) - \lambda r^{\beta}(p) = 0$

(50) $\quad z^{\alpha 1}(p,u^{\alpha}) + e_p^{\beta}(p,u^{\beta}) - \lambda r_p^{\beta}(p) = 0$

where λ is initially equal to one and increases when technical assistance takes place. Equation (50) is a less compact version of the market-clearing condition (3). Differentiating this system totally with respect to λ, and recalling that $\lambda = 1$ and that $e_p^j - r_p^j = z^{j1}$, we obtain

(51) $\quad \begin{bmatrix} z^{\alpha 1} & 1 & 0 \\ z^{\beta 1} & 0 & 1 \\ z_p^1 & z_u^{\alpha 1} & z_u^{\beta 1} \end{bmatrix} \begin{bmatrix} dp \\ du^{\alpha} \\ du^{\beta} \end{bmatrix} = \begin{bmatrix} 0 \\ r^{\beta} \\ r_p^{\beta} \end{bmatrix} d\lambda$.

Solving,

$$\Delta(dp/d\lambda) = r_p^{\beta} - r^{\beta}z_u^{\beta 1}$$
$$= [(px^{\beta 1}/r^{\beta}) - pz_u^{\beta 1}]r^{\beta}/p$$

(52a) $\qquad\qquad = (\theta^{\beta 1} - m^{\beta 1})(r^{\beta}/p)$

(52b) $\Delta(du^{\alpha}/d\lambda) = (m^{\beta 1} - \theta^{\beta 1})(z^{\alpha 1}r^{\beta}/p)$

(52c) $\Delta(du^{\beta}/d\lambda) = (m^{\beta 1} - \theta^{\beta 1})(z^{\beta 1}r^{\beta}/p) + r^{\beta}z_p^1$

where $x^{\beta 1} \equiv r_p^{\beta}$ is β's output of the first commodity, $\theta^{\beta 1} \equiv px^{\beta 1}/r^{\beta}$ is the share of the first industry in β's national product, and $m^{\beta 1} \equiv pz_u^{\beta 1}$ is β's marginal propensity to consume the first commodity.

We see at once that at least one of the countries benefits from the transfer of knowledge. Otherwise, the vector of welfare changes $(du^{\alpha}, du^{\beta})$ can have any pattern of signs. Either country can suffer; in particular, the recipient can suffer, confirming the Mill-Edgeworth discovery. However, it is possible also that both countries benefit; for that outcome it is necessary and sufficient that $pz_p^1 < - z^{\beta 1}(m^{\beta 1} - \theta^{\beta 1}) < 0$.

Suppose that preferences in β are homothetic. Then, $m^{\beta 1} = a^{\beta 1}$, where $a^{\beta 1}$ is β's average propensity to consume the first commodity, and $z^{\beta 1}(m^{\beta 1} - \theta^{\beta 1}) \geq 0$. Bearing in mind that Δ is negative, we see from (52b) that the donor is never impoverished and, if there is some initial trade, is necessarily enriched by its act of generosity. Moreover, the incentive to transfer information persists, both at the level of government and at the level of the individual firm, for as long as α is more efficient in each industry, that is, for as long as α has a global absolute advantage. This finding has destructive implications for textbook trade theory.[22] Whether economists interested in economic development should pay attention to it will depend on its robustness under less restrictive assumptions.

It is easy to see that the proposition is impervious to the addition of commodities. If preferences in β are homothetic, the transfer of information by α causes β to increase its demand for imports and increase its supply of exports. The upshot is an improvement in α's terms of trade and well-being.

In the following section, we shall check the robustness of the finding to the addition of countries.

AID BY TRANSFER OF INFORMATION: BYSTANDERS

Adding a third country γ, we arrive at the system

(1) $e^{\alpha}(p,u^{\alpha}) - r^{\alpha}(p) = 0$

(49) $e^{\beta}(p,u^{\beta}) - \lambda r^{\beta}(p) = 0$

(15) $e^{\gamma}(p,u^{\gamma}) - r^{\gamma}(p) = 0$

(53) $z^{\alpha 1}(p,u^{\alpha}) + e_p^{\beta}(p,u^{\beta}) - \lambda r_p^{\beta}(p) + z^{\gamma 1}(p,u^{\gamma}) = 0$.

Differentiating with respect to λ, we obtain

(54) $$\begin{bmatrix} z^{\alpha 1} & 1 & 0 & 0 \\ z^{\beta 1} & 0 & 1 & 0 \\ z^{\lambda 1} & 0 & 0 & 1 \\ z_p^1 & z_u^{\alpha 1} & z_u^{\beta 1} & z_u^{\gamma 1} \end{bmatrix} \begin{bmatrix} dp \\ du^{\alpha} \\ du^{\beta} \\ du^{\gamma} \end{bmatrix} = \begin{bmatrix} 0 \\ r^{\beta} \\ 0 \\ r_p^{\beta} \end{bmatrix} d\lambda \; .$$

Solving,

(55a) $\Delta''(dp/d\lambda) = - (m^{\beta 1} - \theta^{\beta 1})r^{\beta}/p$

(55b) $\Delta''(du^{\alpha}/d\lambda) = (m^{\beta 1} - \theta^{\beta 1})r^{\beta}z^{\alpha 1}/p$

(55c) $\Delta''(du^{\beta}/d\lambda) = - [\Delta'' - (m^{\beta 1} - \theta^{\beta 1})z^{\beta 1}/p]r^{\beta}$

(55d) $\Delta''(du^{\gamma}/d\lambda) = (m^{\beta 1} - \theta^{\beta 1})z^{\gamma 1}r^{\beta}/p$.

We notice the strong symmetry between $du^{\alpha}/d\lambda$ and $du^{\gamma}/d\lambda$; the identity of the donor is of no significance. We see also that, given homotheticity of the recipient's preferences, the donor benefits if and only if the donor and recipient export different commodities. When there are just two countries, that condition is necessarily satisfied, but when there are three or more countries, the condition need not be satisfied.

As a corollary of these propositions, both donor and bystander benefit if and only if they export the same commodity. To the extent that wealthy countries tend to export the same commodities and to the extent that aid flows from wealthy to poor countries, *the corollary gives some basis for believing that wealthy countries are individually enriched by their collective generosity.*

We now know that when there are just two countries and the recipient's preferences are homothetic, the donor is necessarily enriched, and that when there are three countries, technical assistance to one country may impoverish the donor even though the recipient's preferences are homothetic. Can we infer from these findings that if preferences are homothetic in both β and γ, then the transfer of information by α to both β and γ must enrich α? If the answer to that question were in the affirmative, then we would know that, the more widespread its generosity, the more likely is the donor to benefit from its generosity. Unfortunately, the inference is not generally valid; the inclusion of γ in α's program of technical assistance might or might not work to α's advantage. Thus, we find again that the practice of lumping together all other countries as "the rest of the world" does not bring back the orthodox two-country conclusions. However, if both recipients export the same commodity, then the inference can be made. To verify that this is so, we write the revised system

(56) $\quad e^{\alpha}(p,u^{\alpha}) - r^{\alpha}(p) = 0$

(57) $\quad e^{\beta}(p,u^{\beta}) - \lambda r^{\beta}(p) = 0$

(58) $\quad e^{\gamma}(p,u^{\gamma}) - \lambda r^{\gamma}(p) = 0$

(59) $\quad z^{\alpha 1}(p,u^{\alpha}) + e_p^{\beta}(p,u^{\beta}) - \lambda r_p^{\beta}(p) + e_p^{\gamma}(p,u^{\gamma}) - \lambda r_p^{\gamma}(p) = 0 .$

Differentiating with respect to λ, we obtain

(60) $\begin{bmatrix} z^{\alpha 1} & 1 & 0 & 0 \\ z^{\beta 1} & 0 & 1 & 0 \\ z^{\gamma 1} & 0 & 0 & 1 \\ z_p^1 & z_u^{\alpha 1} & z_u^{\beta 1} & z_u^{\gamma 1} \end{bmatrix} \begin{bmatrix} dp \\ du^{\alpha} \\ du^{\beta} \\ du^{\gamma} \end{bmatrix} = \begin{bmatrix} 0 \\ r^{\beta} \\ r^{\gamma} \\ r_p^{\beta} + r_p^{\gamma} \end{bmatrix} d\lambda .$

Solving,

(61a) $\quad \Delta''(dp/d\lambda) = - (r_p^{\beta} + r_p^{\gamma}) + (r^{\beta} z_u^{\beta 1} + r^{\gamma} z_u^{\gamma 1})$

(61b) $\quad \Delta''(du^{\alpha}/d\lambda) = (z^{\alpha 1}/p)[r^{\beta}(m^{\beta 1} - \theta^{\beta 1}) + r^{\gamma}(m^{\gamma 1} - \theta^{\gamma 1})]$

(61c) $\quad \Delta''(du^{\beta}/d\lambda) = r^{\beta} \Delta'' + [r^{\beta}(m^{\beta 1} - \theta^{\beta 1}) + r^{\gamma}(m^{\gamma 1} - \theta^{\gamma 1})](z^{\beta 1}/p)$

(61d) $\quad \Delta''(du^{\gamma}/d\lambda) = r^{\gamma} \Delta'' + [r^{\beta}(m^{\beta 1} - \theta^{\beta 1}) + r^{\gamma}(m^{\gamma 1} - \theta^{\gamma 1})](z^{\gamma 1}/p) .$

Evidently $du^{\alpha}/d\lambda$ may be negative, even if preferences are homothetic in both β and γ. However, for that outcome, it is necessary that β and γ export different commodities. In other words, for donor enrichment, it suffices that both recipients export the same commodity. On the other hand, even that condition does not ensure that both recipients gain; indeed, it does not ensure that one of them gains.

Many additional questions, most of them with counterparts in the "Aid by Transfers of Information: The Simplest Case" section above, might be addressed to the model of this section. To work through the details would be tedious. Here we simply note that, even if α has a global absolute advantage over both β and γ, it may be unable to help β directly (by technical assistance to β) or indirectly (by technical assistance to γ); indeed, α may be unable to help β or γ, either by extending technical assistance to one of them or by assisting both according to some sharing formula.[23] Thus, a country may be incapable of playing the Good Samaritan, either by gifts of private goods or by technical assistance.

THE RESOURCE-USING ADMINISTRATION OF FOREIGN AID

It is inevitable that some part of every program of foreign aid will be absorbed by administrative procedures or in downright waste. Indeed, there may have been historical instances in which the net aid received was negative.[24] In the present section, I briefly rework the two-country analysis of the "Aid by Transfers of Goods: The Simplest Case" section above to accommodate resource leakages of this sort. Several unexpected possibilities come to light. In particular, it emerges that if only a proportion ω, $\omega < 1$, of the aid reaches the recipient, then, it is possible that (a) the donor is enriched by its act of charity, the extent of the enrichment increasing with the extent of the leakage, and that (b) the recipient is impoverished by aid, the extent of the impoverishment increasing with the extent of the leakage. Indeed, it is possible that outcomes (a) and (b) are realized simultaneously. Of course, it is also possible that both donor and recipient are impoverished by a particular program of aid, but it is not possible that they are both enriched.

Suppose, for the sake of simplicity only, that the costs of administering aid are borne by the recipient and that the administration of aid is subject to the same laws of production as the numéraire. Then, the equilibrium of the world economy is described by equations (1) to (3), with one small change – the aid received by β is now $\omega T^{\alpha\beta}$, not $T^{\alpha\beta}$:

(1) $e^{\alpha}(p,u^{\alpha}) = r^{\alpha}(p) - T^{\alpha\beta}$

(62) $e^{\beta}(p,u^{\beta}) = r^{\beta}(p) + \omega T^{\alpha\beta}$

(3) $z^{\alpha 1}(p, u^{\alpha}) + z^{\beta 1}(p, u^{\beta}) = 0$.

Differentiating the system with respect to $T^{\alpha\beta}$, we obtain

(63) $\begin{bmatrix} z^{\alpha 1} & 1 & 0 \\ z^{\beta 1} & 0 & 1 \\ z^1_p & z^{\alpha 1}_u & z^{\beta 1}_u \end{bmatrix} \begin{bmatrix} dp \\ du^{\alpha} \\ du^{\beta} \end{bmatrix} = \begin{bmatrix} -1 \\ \omega \\ 0 \end{bmatrix} \quad dT^{\alpha\beta}$.

Solving,

(64a) $\Delta(dp/dT^{\alpha\beta}) = z^{\alpha 1}_u - \omega z^{\beta 1}_u$

(64b) $\Delta(du^{\alpha}/dT^{\alpha\beta}) = (1-\omega)z^{\beta 1}z^{\beta 1}_u - z^1_p$

(64c) $\Delta(du^{\beta}/dT^{\alpha\beta}) = (1-\omega)z^{\alpha 1}z^{\alpha 1}_u + \omega z^1_p$.

Inspection of (64b) reveals that if $z^{\beta 1}z^{\beta 1}_u < 0$, that is, if β imports (exports) the first or non-numéraire good and that good is inferior (normal) in β-consumption, then $du^{\alpha}/dT^{\alpha\beta}$ is a declining function of ω, with $du^{\alpha}/dT^{\alpha\beta}$ positive if $\omega < 1 - z^1_p/(z^{\beta 1}z^{\beta 1}_u) < 1$ and $du^{\alpha}/dT^{\alpha\beta}$ negative if $\omega > 1 - z^1_p/(z^{\beta 1}z^{\beta 1}_u)$. Equation (64c), on the other hand, reveals that if $z^{\alpha 1}z^{\alpha 1}_u > 0$, that is, if α imports (exports) the first good and if that good is normal (inferior) in α-consumption then $du^{\beta}/dT^{\alpha\beta}$ is an increasing function of ω, with $du^{\beta}/dT^{\alpha\beta}$ negative if $\omega < z^{\alpha 1}z^{\alpha 1}_u / (z^{\alpha 1}z^{\alpha 1}_u - z^1_p) < 1$ and positive if $z^{\alpha 1}z^{\alpha 1}_u/(z^{\alpha 1}z^{\alpha 1}_u - z^1_p) < \omega \leq 1$. Since not both countries can benefit from a program of aid, we can be sure that

$$[1 - z^1_p/(z^{\beta 1}z^{\beta 1}_u)] < z^{\alpha 1}z^{\alpha 1}_u/(z^{\alpha 1}z^{\alpha 1}_u - z^1_p) = [1 - z^1_p/(z^{\alpha 1}z^{\alpha 1}_u)]^{-1}$$

and, therefore, that if $\omega < 1 - z^1_p/(z^{\beta 1}z^{\beta 1}_u)$, then the conventional or Samuelsonian welfare responses are reversed. In the special case $z^1_p = 0$, if $z^{\beta 1}z^{\beta 1}_u < 0$ then, for Walrasian stability, it is necessary that $z^{\alpha 1}z^{\alpha 1}_u > 0$; from (64b) and (64c), therefore, for $du^{\alpha}/dT^{\alpha\beta} > 0$ and $du^{\beta}/dT^{\alpha\beta} < 0$ it suffices that $\omega < 1$ and $z^{\beta 1}z^{\beta 1}_u < 0$.

Thus, it has been verified that (a) and (b) are possible outcomes. Just as the Samuelsonian conclusions failed to survive the introduction of bystanders and of market distortions like aid tying, so they fail in a context of administrative costs and wastage.

The paradoxical flavour of (a) and (b) can be removed by reflecting that resource-absorbing administration represents a loss of β-income. Thus, superimposed on the Samuelsonian costs and benefits of aid are the costs and benefits associated with a Mill-Edgeworth country-specific loss of income. The latter can dominate the former, leaving the donor α better off and the recipient β worse off than in the absence of aid.[25]

NEXT STEPS

The welfare economics of international aid, as expounded in previous sections, is deficient on several counts. As noted in the introduction, the theory is static, with no time dimension; it is based on the assumption of well-functioning competitive markets, failing to accommodate the market aberrations characteristic of all countries; and it treats the level and worldwide allocation of aid as parameters, not as variables the equilibrium values of which are determined on a network of imperfectly competitive markets in which the usual prices (rates of interest) are replaced by vectors of broadly defined tying conditions. It must now be added that the theory is based on the assumption that aid is financed and distributed by lump-sum taxes and subsidies. The assumption is unrealistic; moreover, such devices create problems of incentives not recognized in the theory. Finally, the entire analysis makes sense only if all trading countries are solvent. It does not apply if, before or after aid, one or more of the countries finds itself in the disequilibrium condition of insolvency.

There is plenty of useful work to be done.

NOTES

Author's Note: To Ben Higgins I offer thanks for forty years of friendship, instruction, and fun; and for two hours of expert technical assistance in getting this paper into shape. Helpful conversations and correspondence with Horst Herberg and Albert Schweinberger are also gratefully acknowledged.

1 For a preliminary treatment of these matters, the reader may consult M.C. Kemp, N.V. Long and K. Shimomura, "On the Optimal Timing of Foreign Aid," *Kobe Economic and Business Review* 35 (1990): 31–49.

2 For an authoritative discussion of the concept, the reader is referred to B.H. Higgins, "Assistance étrangère et capacité d'absorption," *Développement et Civilisations*, October–December 1960, 28–43. See also *United Nations and U.S. Foreign Economic Policy* (Homewood, Ill.: Richard D. Irwin, 1962), chap. 2.

3 For a persuasive statement concerning the importance of this role, see B.H. Higgins, *The Road Less Travelled*, vol. 2 of *History of Development Studies* (Canberra: National Centre for Development Studies, Australian National University, 1989).

4 For a related welfare analysis of concessionary commercial policy, the reader may consult M.C. Kemp and K. Shimomura, " 'Trade' or 'Aid,' " in A. Takayama, M. Ohyama and H. Ohta, eds, *Trade, Policy, and International Adjustments* (San Diego: Academic Press, Inc., 1991).

5   W. Leontief, "On the Pure Theory of Capital Transfer," *Explorations in Economics: Notes and Essays Contributed in Honor of F.W. Taussig* (New York: McGraw-Hill, 1936), 84–92.

6   Y. Balasko, "The Transfer Problem and the Theory of Regular Econmomies," *International Economic Review* 19 (1978): 687–94.

7   Alternatively, we may make use of the market-clearing condition

$$(*)\ z^{\alpha 2}(p,u^{\alpha}) + z^{\beta 2}(p,u^{\beta}) = 0$$

However, (1) and (2) can be rewritten as

$$pz^{\alpha 1} + z^{\alpha 2} = -T^{\alpha\beta}$$

and

$$pz^{\beta 1} + z^{\beta 2} = T^{\alpha\beta}$$

respectively, so that, adding,

$$p(z^{\alpha 1} + z^{\beta 1}) + (z^{\alpha 2} + z^{\beta 2}) = 0$$

Hence (1) to (3) imply (*).

8   In the singular case in which $\Delta = 0$, the system may be locally stable or unstable; it all depends then on the non-linear terms in the expansion of the functions in (1) to (3) about the equilibrium point.

9   This proposition seems to be missing from the literature. For an unpublished statement and proof of the proposition, see A. Safra, "The Transfer Paradox: Stability, Uniqueness and Smooth Preferences" (Harvard University, 1983).

10 M. Ohyama, "Trade and Welfare in General Equilibirum," *Keio Economic Studies* 9 (1972): 37–73; and idem, "Tariffs and the Transfer Problem," in *Keio Economic Studies* 11 (1974): 29–45.

11 D. Gale, "Exchange Equilibrium and Coalitions: An Example," *Journal of Mathematical Economics* 1 (1974): 63–6.

12 The analysis of the *Foundations* has been extended in L.F.S. Wang, "Factor Market Distortions, the Transfer Problem, and Welfare," *Keio Economic Studies* 22 (1985): 57–64, to accommodate factor-market distortions, and by Samuelson ("The Transfer Problem and Transport Costs II: Analysis of Effects of Trade Impediments," *Economic Journal* 64: 246–89), Ohyama ("Trade and Welfare"), and J.N. Bhagwati et al. ("The Generalized Theory of Transfers and Welfare: Exogenous [policy-imposed] and Endogenous [transfer-induced] Distortions," *Quarterly Journal of Economics* 100 [1985]: 697–714) to allow for import duties. Recently, A.H. Turunen-Red and A.D. Woodland ("On the

Multilateral Transfer Problem: Existence of Pareto Improving International Transfers," *Journal of International Economics* 22 [1988]: 57–64) have shown that in a protectionist world it may be possible to find a Pareto-improving multilateral transfer.

13 For a more detailed treatment, see M.C. Kemp and S. Kojima, "The Welfare Economics of Foreign Aid," in G.R. Feiwel, ed., *Issues in Contemporary Microeconomics and Welfare* (London: Macmillan, 1985), 470–83; Kemp and Kojima, "Tied Aid and the Paradoxes of Donor-Enrichment and Recipient-Impoverishment," *International Economic Review* 26 (1985): 721–9; and idem, "More on the Welfare Economics of Foreign Aid," *Journal of the Japanese and International Economics* 1 (1987): 97–109. The reader may also consult, for a pioneering treatment of other forms of tying, Ohyama, "Trade and Welfare."

14 A.G. Schweinberger, "On the Welfare Effects of Tied Aid," *International Economic Review* 31 (1990): 457–62.

15 Gale's example involves pure exchange, two commodities and individual preferences of the fixed-proportions type. However, perverse outcomes are possible without those special features. Thus, D. Léonard and R. Manning ("Advantageous Reallocations: A Constructive Example," *Journal of International Economics* 15 [1983]: 291–5) have shown how to construct whole families of two-commodity examples characterized by smooth preferences, market stability, and perverse outcomes of Gale's type. The phenomenon of perversity in three-country economies is further discussed by M. Yano ("Welfare Aspects of the Transfer Problem," *Journal of International Economics* 15 [1983]: 277–89) and J.N. Bhagwati et al. ("The Generalized Theory of Transfers and Welfare: Bilateral Transfers in a Multilateral World," *American Economic Review* 83 [1983]: 606–18). The exposition of the next subsection follows that of Bhagwati et al.

16 Suppose that α cannot help β directly. Then, from (20),

$$(*) \ z^{\gamma 1}(z_u^{\alpha 1} - z_u^{\gamma 1}) > 0 \ .$$

Permuting the subscripts α and γ in (19), we see that a transfer from γ to β helps β if

$$(**) \ z^{\alpha 1}(z_u^{\alpha 1} - z_u^{\gamma 1}) > 0 \ .$$

But if α and β export the same commodity, (*) implies (**).

17 For α to be a friend to neither β nor γ, it is *necessary* that β and γ export different commodities and that, for each commodity, α's marginal propensity to consume be intermediate to those of β and γ. By way of proof, assume that (20) and (21) are positive with and without the superscripts β and γ interchanged and then note that the four inequalities imply the conditions for the proposition.

To establish beyond doubt that both β and γ might be made worse off, however the aid is divided between them, we offer the following example: $z_p^1 = 0 = z_u^{\alpha 1}$, $z^{\beta 1} > 0$, $z_u^{\gamma 1} < z_u^{\alpha 1} < z_u^{\beta 1}$.

18 This paragraph contains a corrected version of the analysis in Kemp and Kojima, "More on the Welfare Economics," 102–4.

19 If both $dT^{\alpha\beta}/du^\beta$ and $dT^{\gamma\beta}/du^\beta$ are negative, then, adding (41) and 42) and making use of (16),

$$- z^{\beta 1}(z_u^{\alpha 1} - 2z_u^{\beta 1} + z_u^{\gamma 1}) - 2z_p^1 < 0 .$$

Substituting from the Slutzky equation $z_p^{\beta 1} = \bar{z}_p^{\beta 1} + z^{\beta 1} z_u^{\beta 1}$,

$$(\dagger) - z^{\beta 1}(z_u^{\alpha 1} + z_u^{\gamma 1}) - 2\bar{z}_p^{\beta 1} - 2(z_p^{\alpha 1} + z_p^{\gamma 1}) < 0 .$$

If $z^{\beta 1} < 0$, the proposition follows immediately. Suppose then that $z^{\beta 1} > 0$. By Walras's law,

$$p\bar{z}^{\beta 1}(p) + \bar{z}^{\beta 2}(p) - T^{\alpha\beta} - T^{\gamma\beta} = 0 ,$$

so that, differentiating with respect to p,

$$(\dagger\dagger) \ z^{\beta 1} + p\bar{z}_p^{\beta 1} + \bar{z}_p^{\beta 2} = 0 .$$

Substituting from ($\dagger\dagger$) and recalling that for each country the two marginal propensities to consume add to one, ($\dagger$) becomes

$$(z^{\beta 1}/p)(z_u^{\alpha 2} + z_u^{\gamma 2}) + (2/p)\bar{z}_p^{\beta 2} - 2(z_p^{\alpha 1} + z_p^{\gamma 1}) < 0 .$$

The proposition then follows from the twin facts that $z^{\beta 1} > 0$ and $z_p^{\alpha 1} + z_p^{\gamma 1} < 0$.

20 In this paragraph we have answered the question, How does equal utility sharing translate into aid sharing (where aid is measured in terms of the numéraire). The question can be turned about: How does equal aid sharing translate into utility sharing? To answer the second question, one treats u^β as a parameter and u^α, u^γ, $T^{\alpha\beta}$ and $T^{\gamma\beta}$ as variables, with the revised equality-of-sharing condition $dT^{\alpha\beta} = dT^{\gamma\beta}$. Again omitting the detailed calculations, we have

$$\Delta''''(du^\alpha/du^\beta) = (z^{\alpha 1} - z^{\gamma 1})(z_u^{\beta 1} - z_u^{\gamma 1}) - z_p^1$$

$$\Delta''''(du^\gamma/du^\beta) = (z^{\gamma 1} - z^{\alpha 1})(z_u^{\beta 1} - z_u^{\alpha 1}) - z_p^1$$

$$\Delta''''(dT^{\alpha\beta}/du^\beta) = \Delta'''(dT^{\gamma\beta}/du^\beta) = \Delta''$$

where $\Delta'''' \equiv -(z_u^{\alpha 1} - z_u^{\gamma 1})(z^{\alpha 1} - z^{\gamma 1}) + 2z_p^1 < 0$. If $z^{\alpha 1} = z^{\gamma 1}$ or if $z_u^{\beta 1}$ lies midway between $z_u^{\alpha 1}$ and $z_u^{\gamma 1}$ then $du^\alpha/du^\beta = du^\gamma/du^\beta < 0$; otherwise, the vector $(du^\alpha/du^\beta$,

du^{γ}/du^{β}) may contain one positive term. In general, it is possible that the recipient β can be made better off with less aid from each donor.

21 The proof follows the general line of note 19.

22 See M.C. Kemp and K. Shimomura, "The Impossibility of Global Absolute Advantage in the Heckscher-Ohlin Model of Trade," *Oxford Economic Papers* 40 (1988): 575–6.

23 This assertion can be verified on the basis of (55) only.

24 See P.T. Bauer, *Dissent on Development* (London: Weidenfeld and Nicolson, 1971), 99–100.

25 For a more detailed reconciliation of (a) and (b) with Samuelson's findings, the reader may consult M.C. Kemp and K.Y. Wong, "Paradoxes Associated with the Administration of Foreign Aid"(University of New South Wales, 1990).

14 Trade Restrictions versus Foreign Aid As a Means of Improving a Country's Welfare

JOHN S. CHIPMAN

INTRODUCTION

One of the recurring themes in the literature on international trade and economic development is the contention that while free-trade policies will lead to efficient world allocation of resources and a Pareto-optimal distribution of goods and services among countries, they tend to have deleterious effects on the global *distribution* of welfare; rich countries get richer and poor countries poorer. This view has been expressed in various forms by Kindleberger,[1] Balogh,[2] Robinson,[3] Prebisch,[4] Singer,[5] Williams,[6] Hicks,[7] Robertson,[8] Lewis,[9] Myrdal,[10] Emmanuel,[11] Amin,[12] and others. The doctrine is usually expressed in the context of technological change and economic growth; it is maintained that the engines of growth are a few industrial countries (such as Great Britain in the nineteenth century and the United States in the 1950s) whose technical progress brings about a deterioration of the terms of trade of the "peripheral" countries and results in a chronic "dollar shortage." These peripheral countries thus fail to share in the increasing prosperity unless they take remedial measures. Such measures usually take the form of (a) borrowing or procuring aid from abroad or (b) protectionist policies of various kinds, although – as Haberler[13] notes with his usual perspicacity – such policies are generally described by euphemisms such as "import substitution."

In the 1980s, these doctrines have been revived,[14] with Japan as the new culprit replacing the United States, and the latter as the new victim replacing the periphery. The situation is described as "declining international competitiveness," and while the remedies proposed include policies to encourage saving and growth of productivity, most of the ones actually resorted to again come under the headings of (a) foreign borrowing to finance massive budget deficits or (b) protectionist policies, although the new euphemisms are "fair trade," "level playing fields," and so forth.[15]

In all these accounts one finds two interrelated analytic problems. First, if a country experiences unfavourable circumstances that lead to either a loss of welfare or a failure of welfare to achieve expected or target levels, is there a convenient and accurate way to measure this welfare loss as a monetary magnitude? Second, Can this welfare measure usefully provide a ranking of alternative policies to mitigate the welfare losses? In particular, can it evaluate the relative merits of protectionism and foreign financing as means to alleviate a welfare loss?

In this paper, my aim is to try and bring some precision to the welfare analysis of countries' adjustments to external events. In particular, following Hicks,[16] it is natural to look for a numerical monetary indicator of welfare loss consequent upon an external disturbance.[17] Let us suppose, for example, that a country experiences a deterioration in its terms of trade. This is analogous to the situation of an individual who experiences a rise in the market price of a commodity he or she consumes. In the latter case, we may consider (a) a hypothetical rise in the individual's income which, following the price increase, would exactly compensate him or her for the rise in price or (b) a hypothetical fall in income which, at the original prices, would have led to the same welfare loss as was brought about by the price increase with constant income. The first of these (with opposite sign) is Hicks's Compensating Variation, and the second is his Equivalent Variation. Can a similar analysis be applied to a country?

In the case of a country that is assumed to behave as a rational unit, an analogous procedure is possible provided that on the basis of some ethical postulates we can interpret the utility the country acts as if it maximizes as a measure of the country's "welfare." In place of a consumer's utility function that has amounts consumed as arguments, we may substitute, following Meade,[18] a trade-utility function whose arguments are the amounts traded – specifically the net imports – of the tradable commodities. Analogously to the Marshallian demand function, whose values are amounts consumed and whose arguments are prices and income, the trade-demand function has as its values the country's net imports of tradable commodities (imports and negatives of exports) and as its arguments the prices of tradables and the deficit in the country's balance of payments on goods and services (cf. Chipman[19]).[20] Thus, if a country faces a deterioration in its terms of trade, say a rise in the nominal prices of its imports, we may consider (a) the amounts of foreign aid it would have to receive (i.e., the necessary increase it would have to experience in its payments deficit) to compensate for the worsened terms of trade or (b) the hypothetical reduction in foreign aid it would have had to undergo or the increase in aid it would have had to provide to other countries (i.e., the necessary fall in its payments deficit or rise in its payments surplus), at the original external prices, in order to suffer exactly the same loss of welfare as caused by the rise in import prices. The first of these (with opposite sign) we might provisionally take as our measure of Compensating Trade-Variation and the second as the measure of Equivalent Trade-Variation. The negatives of either of these could be taken as a measure of "dollar shortage,"[21] or more generally, "shortage of foreign exchange."[22]

However, an important difference between the case of an individual and that of a country makes the above analogies unnatural. If a transfer of income is made to an individual, it is quite reasonable to assume that the prices faced by this individual remain constant; in the case of a country, however, it is in the nature of the case that a transfer generally changes its terms of trade. Of course, there are special assumptions under which a unilateral transfer from one country to another will leave the terms of trade unaffected,[23] but it would be quite limiting to have to restrict oneself to these assumptions. One could argue that, as in the case of an individual, if a country is very small compared to the rest of the world, a transfer (which, if it is a fraction of its national income, will be a very small fraction of that of the rest of the world) will have a negligible effect on its terms of trade; the analysis would then be of interest in the case of "small countries." However, the literature on dollar shortage is replete with illustrations of trade-offs between foreign aid and import restrictions, it being assumed that by restricting its imports a country can improve its terms of trade. Therefore, in order to find a precise concept of "dollar shortage" that can be usefully employed to analyse the issues dealt with in the literature, it is better to take explicit account of the transfer problem.

A simple example will illustrate the importance of this. Suppose it be granted that import-biased technical change takes place in an advanced country, leading to a deterioration in the terms of trade of a backward country; if the Mill-Taussig-Keynes "orthodox" presumption holds that a transfer will improve the receiving country's terms of trade, then the compensating trade-variation will exaggerate the amount of aid the backward country will need to compensate for its worsened terms of trade, since the aid will itself have the "secondary" effect of improving its terms of trade. In other words, the compensating trade-variation will overstate the amount of dollar shortage. Of course, if a transfer should on the contrary have the "anti-orthodox" effect of worsening the receiving country's terms of trade, the compensating trade-variation would understate the amount of dollar shortage.[24]

In this paper, analogues of the Hicksian concepts of compensating and equivalent variation are developed for application to countries, and the application of such measures to the evaluation of changing terms of trade is discussed. Then a self-contained treatment will be provided of the effect of technical change on a country's terms of trade in the case of two models: the standard two-commodity HOLS model and a model in which each of two countries specializes in an export good and a non-tradable, giving rise to what Samuelson called the "orthodox presumption" that a transfer will improve the terms of trade of the receiving country.

The final section of the paper takes up a topic that recurs in Balogh's writings but was first systematically analysed by Kahn:[25] the question whether a country is better off receiving foreign aid than imposing trade restrictions. This includes the particular problem posed by Kahn of whether the country is better off (in the short run only, of course) losing reserves or resorting to "distress borrowing" than imposing import restrictions.[26]

Of course, from a global point of view a unilateral lump-sum costless transfer from a rich to a poor country (if such a thing is possible) is preferable to restrictive measures imposed by the poor country, for it follows immediately from the so-called Fundamental Theorem of Welfare Economics that there exists a transfer from the rich country to the poor one that would make both of them better off than if a tariff were imposed by the poor one. Likewise, if the poor country imposes a tariff, there is some transfer from the poor country to the rich one that would make both countries worse off than under free trade. However, it is not obvious that a country imposing a tariff is worse off than it would be if it instead received an amount of foreign aid equal to the previous tariff revenues.

The problem is solved in the final section as follows: Since in both cases the poor country faces the same price of commodity 1 (its export good) and has the same deficit (denominated in its own prices) in its balance of payments on goods and services (equal to the tariff revenues in the one case and to the foreign aid in the other), the country is better off according as the policy chosen leads to a lower price on *domestic markets* of its import good (commodity 2). Now, if a unilateral transfer to country 1 improves its terms of trade (in accordance with the orthodox presumption), then foreign aid in the absence of any trade restrictions will lower this import price; a tariff, however, will normally raise it – unless the so-called "Metzler paradox" holds (cf. Metzler,[27] Chipman[28]). Under these conditions, therefore, the domestic price of the import good must be higher under the tariff with no foreign aid than under the foreign aid with no tariff; consequently, the country is better off accepting foreign aid than imposing a tariff yielding the same revenues. Thus, for the country to be better off with a tariff than with foreign aid, one of two anomalies must hold: either a transfer to the country must worsen its terms of trade, or imposition of a tariff must lower rather than raise the domestic price of the import good – that is, the tariff must be the opposite of protective. It is shown in Chipman[29] that it is impossible for both these anomalies to subsist simultaneously; thus, it is rather unlikely *a priori* that a country would be better off imposing a tariff rather than accepting an amount of foreign aid equal to the revenues it would receive from the tariff. Combining this with the Fundamental Theorem of Welfare Economics, we see that the choice of trade restriction as an alternative to foreign aid, when the latter is equal in amount to the revenues that would be earned from the trade restriction, would result in both countries being worse off, unless one of the above anomalies prevails.

MONETARY MEASUREMENT OF CHANGE IN A COUNTRY'S WELFARE

The simplest conceptual tool to use in evaluating the different circumstances a country may face is that of the trade-demand function, which expresses the dependence of a country's trade in a commodity (which I define as the net import of that commodity – a positive quantity for an import good and a negative one for an export good) on the prices (on domestic markets) of the traded commodities and the deficit in the country's balance of payments on goods and services (or "trade balance" for short). For analytic simplicity, I consider the case of two tradable goods; the derivation of a country's trade-demand function from its aggregate demand function and production relations is carried out in the next section for the cases in which (a) each country produces both commodities (but no non-tradables) with the aid of two factors of production, and (b) each country produces an export good and a non-tradable good (but no import-competing good) with two factors of production. (For other cases, see Chipman.)[30]

Denote country k's trade-demand for commodity j by $z_j^k = \hat{h}_j^k(p_1^k, p_2^k, D^k; l^k)$, where $z_j^k = x_j^k - y_j^k$ denotes the net import of commodity j and x_j^k and y_j^k denote consumption and production of this commodity; p_j^k denotes the price of commodity j on country k's markets; D^k denotes the deficit in country k's trade balance; and l^k denotes the vector of country k's factor endowments. For $j = 1,2$ these maximize country k's trade-utility function $\hat{U}^k(z_1^k, z_2^k; l^k)$ subject to the balance-of-payments constraint $p_1^k z_1^k + p_2^k z_2^k \leqq D^k$. Country k's indirect trade-utility function may be defined as[31]

(1) $\hat{V}^k(p_1^k, p_2^k, D^k; l^k) = \hat{U}^k(\hat{h}_1^k(p_1^k, p_2^k, D^k; l^k), h_2^k(p_1^k p_2^k, D^k; l^k); l^k)$.

This function satisfies the Antonelli-Allen-Roy partial differential equation[32]

(2) $\dfrac{\partial \hat{V}k}{\partial p_j^k} = -\hat{h}_j^k(p_1^k, p_2^k, D^k; l^k) \dfrac{\partial \hat{V}k}{\partial D^k} \ (j = 1,2)$.

Since by convention we assume that country k exports commodity k, it follows (assuming local non-satiation of trade-preferences, implying that $\partial \hat{V}^k/\partial D^k > 0$) that for country 1 $\partial \hat{V}^1/\partial p_2^1 < 0$ (since $h_2^1 > 0$), whereas for country 2 $\partial \hat{V}^2/\partial p_2^2 > 0$ (since $\hat{h}_2^2 < 0$). In words, country 1 gains, *ceteris paribus*, from a fall in the domestic price of its import good, while country 2 gains from a rise in the price of its export good (its terms of trade). This is illustrated for $k = 1$ in the three panels (*a*), (*b*), and (*c*) of Figure 14.1, where $D^1 = 0$, $D^1 < 0$, and $D^1 > 0$ respectively, it being assumed that country 1 initially exports commodity 1 and imports commodity 2.

Analogously to McKenzie's[33] minimum-income function and Hurwicz and Uzawa's[34] income-compensation function, we may define country k's *minimum-deficit function* as[35]

$$(3) \quad \hat{\mu}^k(p_1^k,p_2^k;p_1^{k*},p_2^{k*},D^{k*},l^{k*}) = \min \{D^k : V^k(p_1^k,p_2^k,D^k;l^{k*}) \geq V^k(p_1^{k*},p_2^{k*},D^{k*};l^{k*})\}$$

where p_1^k,p_2^k,D^k are the current prices of the tradables (on country k's home markets) and country k's trade deficit, and p_1^{k*},p_2^{k*},D^{k*} are the same variables in some base period; l^{k*} is country k's factor-endowment vector in the base period. Finally, by analogy with the definition in Chipman and Moore,[36] we may define the *compensating trade-variation* in going from $(p_1^{k*},p_2^{k*},D^{k*},l^{k*})$ to (p_1^k,p_2^k,D^k,l^{k*}) by

$$(4) \quad \hat{C}^k(p_1^k,p_2^k,D^k;p_1^{k*},p_2^{k*},D^{k*},l^{k*}) = D^k - \hat{\mu}^k(p_1^k,p_2^k;p_1^{k*},p_2^{k*},D^{k*},l^{k*})$$

and the *equivalent trade-variation* in going from $(p_1^{k*},p_2^{k*},D^{k*},l^{k*})$ to $(p_1^k,p_2^k, D^k,l^{k*})$ by

$$(5) \quad \hat{E}^k(p_1^k,p_2^k,D^k;p_1^{k*},D^{k*},l^{k*}) = \hat{\mu}^k(p_1^{k*},p_2^{k*};p_1^k,p_2^k,D^k,l^{k*}) - D^{k*}.$$

Assuming $p_1^1 = p_1^{1*} = 1$ and $D^1 = D^{1*}$ to be constant and $p_2^1 > p_2^{1*}$ (country 1's terms of trade to worsen),[37] the three panels of Figure 14.1 show for $k = 1$ the compensating and equivalent trade-variations corresponding to the three cases, where $M^1 = \hat{\mu}^1(1,p_2^1;1,p_2^{1*},D^1,l^{1*})$ is the minimum trade deficit (hence $-M^1$ is the maximum trade balance) at the new prices and old welfare level and $M^{1*} = \hat{\mu}^1(1,p_2^{1*};1,p_2^1,D^1,l^{1*})$ is the minimum trade deficit (hence $-M^1$ is the maximum trade balance) at the old prices and new welfare level.

Either one of these concepts would provide a reasonable measure of shortage of foreign exchange, not in the sense of a "shortage" that might result from foreign-exchange control, but in the programming sense of indicating the amount of foreign aid required to compensate for a terms-of-trade deterioration – or the loss of foreign aid that would be equivalent to a terms-of-trade deterioration – provided these compensating or equivalent transfers did not themselves affect the terms of trade. With this qualification it would be reasonable to use either concept as an indicator of what Machlup[38] called "a PROGRAMME BALANCE, i.e. a balance of hopes and desires," as opposed to the more usual accounting definitions of the balance of payments. However, it seems worthwhile to examine how the concept should best be altered when the qualification is removed.

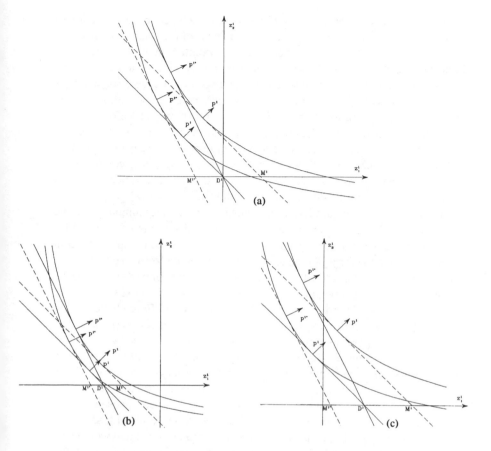

Note: In each panel the original and final budget lines are shown as the solid lines tangential to the two trade-indifference curves with normals (perpendiculars) p^{1*} and p^1 at the points of tangency respectively, and both going through the point $(D^1,0)$. With commodity 1 as numéraire, the equations of the budget lines are $z_1^1 + p_2^{1*}z_2^1 = D^1$ and $z_1^1 + p_2^1z_2^1 = D^1$ respectively. A rise in country 1's import price from p_2^1 to p_2^{1*} leads to a contraclockwise rotation of the budget line and a reduction in country 1's trade-utility. The dashed line parallel to the new (flatter) budget line and tangential to the original trade-utility curve goes through the point $(M^1,0)$; this corresponds to the maximum balance of trade (i.e., the minimum trade deficit) at the new prices subject to the old welfare level. The segment M^1D^1 measures (in absolute value) the compensating trade-variation in units of commodity 1, corresponding to equation (4) of the text. Likewise, the dashed line parallel to the old (steeper) budget line and tangential to the new trade-indifference curve goes through the point $(M^{1*},0)$; this corresponds to the maximum balance of trade at the old prices subject to the new welfare level. The segment D^1M^{1*} measures (in absolute value) the equivalent trade-variation in units of commodity 1, corresponding to equation (5) of the text.

It is of some interest to note that in panel (c), the point of maximum trade balance subject to the old welfare level is one in which country 1 imports both commodities.

Figure 14.1
Compensating and Equivalent Trade-Variations

Suppose we consider a case in which there is technical change in country 2 that worsens country 1's terms of trade. In terms of the traditional model in which there are no non-tradable goods, as first pointed out by Haberler[39] and later by Hicks[40] (see also Corden,[41] Findlay and Grubert,[42] and Johnson[43]), this would require that technical change in country 2 be *import-biased* (or "anti-trade-biased" in Johnson's terminology), that is, concentrated in its import-competing industry. In particular, the result would follow if there were factor-augmenting technical improvement in the factor used relatively intensively in country 2's import-competing industry (normally this would be its relatively scarce factor).[44] In this case, at the existing prices country 2, by virtue of the Rybczynski theorem, would shift its resources from exportables to importables. This would reduce the supply of country 2's export good (commodity 2) and increase its supply of its import good (commodity 1). The net result would be an improvement in country 2's terms of trade and a worsening of country 1's. By a similar argument, a technical improvement in country 2 taking the form of increasing efficiency of the factor used relatively intensively in its export industry would worsen its terms of trade and improve country 1's. (These propositions are proved in detail in the next section.)

Under these same circumstances, with identical and homothetic preferences between as well as within countries (hence identical marginal trade-propensities to spend as between countries on either of the two tradable commodities, a transfer from one country to the other will, according to Samuelson's criterion,[45] have no effect on the terms of trade. The above concepts of foreign-exchange shortage would then provide reasonable measures of the actual amount of foreign aid needed to compensate for (or the reduction in foreign aid equivalent to) the worsened terms of trade.

Suppose we consider, on the other hand, the kind of model that would lead to what Samuelson called the "orthodox presumption" that a transfer would improve the receiving country's terms of trade.[46] An example of such a model would be one in which each country produces an export good and a non-tradable good, but does not produce any import-competing good; this would be a likely result of each country having fewer than three factors of production – for definiteness I shall assume that each country has two factors. In these circumstances, assuming all goods to be superior goods in consumers' preferences, a transfer from country 2 to country 1 would reduce purchasing power in country 2 and increase it in country 1; the increased demand for the non-tradable in country 1 would require its resources to move into the non-tradables sector out of its export industry (since it does not produce import-competing goods), and likewise the reduced demand for non-tradables in country 2 would require its resources to move out of the non-tradables sector into its export industry. The net result would be a rise in the world output (equal to country 2's output) of commodity 2 and a fall in the world output (equal to country 1's output) of commodity 1. If the three goods are Hicksian substitutes this must result in an improvement in country 1's terms of trade.[47]

Now suppose a technical change in country 2 is concentrated largely in its non-tradables sector. In particular, suppose there is factor-augmenting technical improvement in the factor used relatively intensively in its non-tradables sector. In this case, at unchanged prices there would be an increased demand for imports; since, however, at unchanged prices of tradables the prices of non-tradables would fall, there would – assuming the three goods to be Hicksian substitutes – be a diversion of demand towards non-tradables away from imports that might be strong enough to counteract the original income effect. Thus, there could be, but need not be, a fall in demand for imports and a consequent improvement in country 2's, and worsening of country 1's, terms of trade. An unambiguous result can be obtained, however, in the case in which the technical improvement increases the efficiency of the factor employed relatively intensively in the export industry. As before, at unchanged prices there is an increased demand for imports; but at unchanged prices of tradables the technical change will increase the price of non-tradables and – again assuming the goods to be Hicksian substitutes – cause a diversion of consumer demand from non-tradables to importables. Since both effects go in the same direction, there is an increased demand for imports and a worsened terms of trade for country 2.

It is worth noting that if both countries produced import-competing goods as well as export and non-tradable goods (which would be more likely if they had a third factor of production), there would be no strong presumption that either a technical improvement in country 2's non-tradables sector or a transfer of funds from country 1 to country 2 would draw more resources out of country 2's export industry than out of its import-competing industry. Thus, there is no strong presumption that either the technical improvement or the transfer would affect the terms of trade. It follows that if country 2's technical change takes the form of factor-augmenting improvement in the factor used relatively intensively in its non-tradables sector, the circumstances that make it likely that this technical improvement will worsen country 1's terms of trade also make it probable that a compensating transfer from country 2 to country 1 will result in an offsetting improvement in country 1's terms of trade. Thus, there is a general presumption that the above measures of foreign-exchange shortage will overestimate the magnitude of the compensating or equivalent transfers needed to alleviate a worsening of a country's terms of trade.

TECHNICAL IMPROVEMENT AND
THE TERMS OF TRADE

This section will be devoted to deriving explicit conditions for factor-augmenting technical change to improve or worsen a country's terms of trade in a model of two countries endowed with two factors of production and trading in two commodities. Two cases will be considered: (a) the standard model in which these two commodities and no others are produced by both countries and (*b*) a model in which each country specializes in an export good and a non-tradable good. For the standard model a fairly general taxonomy has been developed in the literature using traditional geometrical techniques (Johnson,[48] Mishan,[49] Corden,[50] Findlay and Grubert[51]). The theoretical analysis of the second model is less well developed, though there have been pertinent contributions by Balassa,[52] Aukrust,[53] McKinnon,[54] Haberler,[55] Edgren, Faxen, and Odhner,[56] and Corden and Neary,[57] all of which have stressed that technical change tends to be more rapid in the tradables sector (both export and import-competing) than in the non-tradables sector.[58] In general, this carries important implications for the "real exchange rate" (considered as the ratio of prices of non-tradables to those of tradables) rather than the terms of trade, but in the special case in which no import-competing goods are produced it implies that one could generally expect technical improvement to worsen the progressive country's terms of trade.

In this section a uniform analytic treatment will be applied to both models. Assuming factors of production to be measured in efficiency units, increases in endowments will be interpreted as increases in their efficiency.[59] I shall consider technical improvements in each factor separately, as well as a uniform proportionate improvement in both. In the case of uniform improvement it is shown under fairly mild theoretical assumptions (basically, identical homothetic preferences) that in both models technical improvement, will worsen the terms of trade of the progressive country – a result that goes back to Mill.[60] A *fortiori*, improvement that takes the form of increased efficiency of the factor used relatively intensively in the export industry will have an even greater tendency to worsen the terms of trade of the expanding country. In the case of the first model, technical improvement in the form of increased efficiency of the factor used relatively intensively in the import-competing industry unambiguously improves the terms of trade of the expanding country. In the case of the second model, the results of increased efficiency of the factor employed relatively intensively in the non-tradables sector are less clear-cut. The income effect of the technical improvement will lead to increased demand for imports, tending to a worsening of the progressive country's terms of trade, but the substitution effect of the fall in the price of the non-tradable relative to that of the export good will lead consumers (at unchanged terms of trade) to switch from importables to non-tradables; only if this outweighs the income effect will there be a net fall in the demand for imports and therefore an improvement in the progressive country's terms of trade.[61]

World equilibrium is defined by the equation

$$(6) \quad h_2^1(p_1, p_2, A^1; l_1^1, l_2^1) + h_2^2(p_1, p_2, -A^1; l_1^2, l_2^2) = 0$$

where the $\hat{h}_2^k$ are the countries' trade-demand functions for commodity 2, A^1 is the amount of foreign aid country 1 is getting from country 2, and l_i^k is country k's endowment in factor i. Since the l_i^k are measured in efficiency units, a rise in l_i^k will be interpreted as a factor-i-augmenting technical improvement in country k. Fixing the price of commodity 1 as numéraire (i.e, setting $p_1 = \bar{p}_1$, equation (6) implicitly defines the function

(7)　　$p_2 = \bar{p}_2(A^1, l_1^1, l_2^1, l_1^2, l_2^2).$

Differentiating it with respect to l_i^2 we have from (6)

(8)　　$\dfrac{\partial \bar{p}_2}{\partial l_i^2} = -\dfrac{\dfrac{\partial \hat{h}_2^2}{\partial l_i^2}}{\dfrac{\partial \hat{h}_2^1}{\partial p_2} + \dfrac{\partial \hat{h}_2^2}{\partial p_2}}.$

The denominator of (8) is negative by the usual dynamic stability condition, hence

(9)　　$\dfrac{\partial \bar{p}_2}{\partial l_i^2} > 0 \leftrightarrow \dfrac{\partial \hat{h}_2^2}{\partial l_i^2} > 0 .$

In words: *A rise in country 2's endowment in factor* i *will improve its terms of trade if and only if, at unchanged world prices, it raises its trade-demand for its export good (commodity 2).* Since $\hat{h}_2^2$ is negative, what this means is that country 2's terms of trade will improve if and only if the increased endowment of factor i *lowers* country 2's supply of exports. It is in conformity with intuition that the increased world scarcity of commodity 2 will cause its price (country 2's terms of trade) to rise.

For the case of uniform technical improvement we may define the composed function

(10)　　$\hat{h}_2^2(p_1, p_2, D^2; l_1^2, l_2^2, \lambda) = \hat{h}_2^2(p_1, p_2, D^2; \lambda l_1^2, \lambda l_2^2) .$

Likewise, defining $\breve{p}_2(A^1, l_1^1, l_2^1, l_1^2, l_2^2, \lambda) = \bar{p}_2(A^1, l_1^1, l_2^1, \lambda l_1^2, \lambda l_2^2)$, formula (8) is replaced by

(11)　　$\dfrac{\partial \breve{p}_2}{\partial \lambda} = -\dfrac{\dfrac{\partial \hat{h}_2^2}{\partial \lambda}}{\dfrac{\partial \hat{h}_2^1}{\partial p_2} + \dfrac{\partial \hat{h}_2^2}{\partial p_2}} = -\dfrac{\dfrac{\partial \hat{h}_2^2}{\partial l_1^2} l_1^2 + \dfrac{\partial \hat{h}_2^2}{\partial l_2^2} l_2^2}{\dfrac{\partial \hat{h}_2^1}{\partial p_2} + \dfrac{\partial \hat{h}_2^2}{\partial p_2}}.$

THE STANDARD TWO-COMMODITY–
TWO-FACTOR CASE

Let us first consider the standard case in which each country produces and trades two commodities with two factors of production, factor i being used relatively intensively in the production of commodity i for $i = 1,2$. This is the model considered by Johnson,[62] Mishan,[63] Corden,[64] Findlay and Grubert,[65] and Johnson.[66] Country 2's trade-demand function is then given by

$$(12) \quad \hat{h}_2^2(p_1,p_2,D^2;l_1^2,l_2^2) = h_2^2(p_1,p_2,\Pi^2(p_1,p_2,l_1^2,l_2^2) + D^2) - \hat{y}_2^2(p_1,p_2,l_1^2,l_2^2),$$

where Π^2 is country 2's national-product function and $\hat{y}_j^2 = \partial\Pi^2/\partial p_j$ is its Rybczynski (supply) function for commodity j. Then

$$(13) \quad \frac{\partial\hat{h}_2^2}{\partial l_i^2} = \frac{\partial h_2^2}{\partial Y^2}\frac{\partial\Pi^2}{\partial l_i^2} - \frac{\partial\hat{y}_2^2}{\partial l_i^2} = c_2^2 w_i^2 - \frac{\partial\hat{w}_i^2}{\partial p_2} = \frac{w_i^2}{p_2}\left[p_2 c_2^2 - \frac{p_2}{w_i^2}\frac{\partial\hat{w}_i^2}{\partial p_2}\right],$$

where $c_j^2 = \partial h_j^2/\partial Y^2$ and use is made of Samuelson's[67] reciprocity condition $\partial\hat{y}_j^2/\partial l_i^2 = \partial\hat{w}_i^2/\partial p_j$, the $\hat{w}_i^2(p_1,p_2)$ being the Stolper-Samuelson functions. Since by the factor-intensity assumption the Stolper-Samuelson theorem gives

$$\frac{p_2}{w_1^2}\frac{\partial\hat{w}_1^2}{\partial p_2} < 0 \text{ and } \frac{p_2}{w_2^2}\frac{\partial\hat{w}_2^2}{\partial p_2} > 1,$$

it follows immediately (assuming both goods to be superior, i.e., $c_j^2 > 0$) that $\partial\hat{h}_2^2/\partial l_1^2 > 0$ and $\partial\hat{h}_2^2/\partial l_2^2 < 0$, hence from (9) $\partial\bar{p}_2/\partial l_1^2 > 0$ and $\partial\bar{p}_2/\partial l_2^2 < 0$. In words: *A rise in the efficiency of the factor used relatively intensively in country 2's import-competing industry will improve country 2's terms of trade, while a rise in the efficiency of the factor used relatively intensively in country 2's export industry will worsen country 2's terms of trade.*

Now consider the case of uniform factor-augmenting technical change. For this case we will need to assume homotheticity of preferences, implying that $\partial h_j^2/\partial Y^2 = h_j^2/Y^2$, where Y^2 is country 2's disposable national income (absorption) $\Pi^2 + D^2$. Differentiating (10) with respect to λ and using the homogeneity of degree 1 of Π^2 and $\hat{y}_2^2 = \partial\Pi^2/\partial p_2$ in l_1^2, l_2^2 and the budget equation $p_1 x_1^2 + p_2 x_2^2 = Y^2$ we obtain from (12)

$$(14) \quad \frac{\partial\hat{h}_2^2}{\partial\lambda} = \frac{\partial h_2^2}{\partial Y^2}\Pi^2 - y_2^2 = \frac{\Pi^2}{Y^2}x_2^2 - y_2^2 = \frac{x_2^2}{Y^2}(p_1 y_1^2 + p_2 y_2^2) - y_2^2$$

$$= \frac{p_1 x_1^2 y_1^2}{Y^2}\left[\frac{x_2^2}{x_1^2} - \frac{y_2^2}{y_1^2}\right] < 0,$$

the inequality following from the fact that country 2 by assumption exports commodity 2 and imports commodity 1, hence $x_1^2 > y_1^2$ and $x_2^2 < y_2^2$, so that

$$\frac{x_2^2}{y_2^2} < 1 < \frac{x_1^2}{y_1^2} .$$

Thus, a uniform technical improvement in both factors will worsen country 2's terms of trade. Note that these results are valid even if country 2's trade is unbalanced ($D^2 \neq 0$), but not so unbalanced as to prevent commodity 1 from being imported and commodity 2 from being exported.

THE CASE OF SPECIALIZATION ON EXPORTS AND NON-TRADABLES

Now let us consider a model of two countries specializing in exports and non-tradables with two factors of production. Let country 1 produce commodities 1 and 3 and country 2 produce commodities 2 and 3, the third commodity being non-tradable; let each country have two factors of production. I shall assume that in country 2 factor 2 is used relatively intensively in the export sector (industry 2), and thus factor 1 is used relatively intensively in the non-tradables sector (industry 3).

To obtain the expression for $\partial \hat{h}_2^2 / \partial l_2^2$ we need to derive country 2's trade-demand function. Let $\Pi^2(p_2, p_3^2, l_1^2, l_2^2)$ denote country 2's national-product function, equal to the maximum national product at prices p_2, p_3^2 and factor endowments l_1^2, l_2^2, and let

$$(15) \quad y_j^2 = y_j^2(p_2, p_3^2, l_1^2, l_2^2) = \frac{\partial}{\partial p_j^2} \Pi^2(p_2, p_3^2, l_1^2, l_2^2) \quad (p_2^2 = p_2)$$

denote country 2's Rybczynski function (supply function) for commodity $j = 2,3$ (see for instance Chipman).[68] Let the aggregate consumer demand function for commodity j in country 2 be denoted $x_j^2 = h_j^2(p_1, p_2, p_3^2, Y^2)$ where Y^2 is disposable national income. Equating the aggregate demand and supply of the non-tradable good implicitly defines the price of the non-tradable as a function of the remaining variables, that is,

$$(16) \quad h_3^2(p_1, p_2, \bar{p}_3^2(\bullet), \Pi^2(p_2, \bar{p}_3^2(\bullet), l_1^2, l_2^2) + D^2) = \hat{y}_3^2(p_2, \bar{p}_3^2(\bullet), l_1^2, l_2^2)$$

where

$$(17) \quad p_3^2 = \bar{p}_3^2(p_1, p_2, l_1^2, l_2^2, D^2) .$$

Country 2's trade-demand function for its export good (commodity 2) is then defined as

(18) $\hat{h}_2^2(p_1,p_2,D^2;l_1^2,l_2^2) = h_2^2(p_1,p_2,\bar{p}_3^2(p_1,p_2,l_1^2,l_2^2),\Pi^2(p_2,\bar{p}_3^2(p_1,p_2,l_1^2,l_2^2),l_1^2,l_2^2) + D^2)$

$\qquad -\bar{y}_2^2(p_2,\bar{p}_3^2(p_1,p_2,l_1^2,l_2^2),l_1^2,l_2^2).$

Differentiating (17) implicitly in (16) we obtain, using the usual duality relationships (cf., e.g., Chipman)[69]

(19) $\dfrac{\partial \bar{p}_3^2}{\partial l_i^2} = \dfrac{-1}{s_{33}^2 - t_{33}^2}\left[\dfrac{\partial h_3^2}{\partial Y^2} w_i^2 - \dfrac{\partial \bar{y}_3^2}{\partial l_i^2}\right]$

where w_i^2 is the rental of factor i in country 2 and

(20) $s_{ij}^2 = \dfrac{\partial h_i^2}{\partial p_j^2} + \dfrac{\partial h_i^2}{\partial Y^2} h_j^2$ and $t_{ij}^2 = \dfrac{\partial \bar{y}_i^2}{\partial p_j^2}$

define country 2's Slutsky and transformation terms. Defining also $c_j^2 = \partial h_j^2/\partial Y^2$, these terms satisfy

(21) $p_1 c_1^2 + p_2 c_2^2 + p_3^2 c_3^2 = 1$
$\qquad p_1 s_{13}^2 + p_2 s_{23}^2 + p_3^2 s_{33}^2 = 0$.
$\qquad\qquad p_2 t_{23}^2 + p_3^2 t_{33}^2 = 0$

We are now able to compute from (18) [using (19) and the fact that $\partial \Pi^2/\partial p_3^2 = y_3^2 = x_3^2$]

(22) $\dfrac{\partial \hat{h}_2^2}{\partial l_i^2} = \left[\dfrac{\partial h_2^2}{\partial Y^2} w_i^2 - \dfrac{\partial \bar{y}_2^2}{\partial l_i^2}\right] - \dfrac{s_{23}^2 - t_{23}^2}{s_{33}^2 - t_{33}^2}\left[\dfrac{\partial h_3^2}{\partial Y^2} w_i^2 - \dfrac{\partial \bar{y}_3^2}{\partial l_i^2}\right]$.

Using Samuelson's[70] reciprocity conditions (cf., e.g., Chipman[71]), the bracketed terms in (22) may be written

(23) $\dfrac{\partial h_j^2}{\partial Y^2} w_i^2 - \dfrac{\partial \bar{y}_j^2}{\partial l_i^2} = \dfrac{w_i^2}{p_j^2}\left[p_j^2 c_j^2 - \dfrac{p_j^2}{w_i^2}\dfrac{\partial \hat{w}_i^2}{\partial p_j^2}\right]$.

Thus, (22) becomes

(24) $\dfrac{\partial \hat{h}_2^2}{\partial l_i^2} = \dfrac{w_i^2}{p_2}\left\{ \left[p_2 c_2^2 - \dfrac{p_2}{w_i^2}\dfrac{\partial \hat{w}_i^2}{\partial p_2}\right] - \dfrac{p_2(s_{23}^2 - t_{23}^2)}{p_3^2(s_{33}^2 - t_{33}^2)}\left[p_3^2 c_3^2 - \dfrac{p_3^2}{w_i^2}\dfrac{\partial \hat{w}_i^2}{\partial p_3}\right]\right\}$.

The first bracketed term in (24) gives the effect the technical change would have if the price, p_3^2, of the non-tradable good were fixed. This is the same as the bracketed term in (13). The second term gives the effect of the change in the price of the non-tradable. From (19) and (23) we have

$$(25) \quad \frac{\partial \bar{p}_3^2}{\partial l_i^2} = \frac{-1}{s_{33}^2 - t_{33}^2} \frac{w_i^2}{p_3^2} \left[p_3^2 c_3^2 - \frac{p_3^2}{w_i^2} \frac{\partial \hat{w}_i^2}{\partial p_3^2} \right]$$

where, from the Stolper-Samuelson theorem and the assumption that all goods are superior,

$$p_3^2 c_3^2 - \frac{p_3^2}{w_1^2} \frac{\partial w_1^2}{\partial p_3^2} < p_3^2 c_3^2 - 1 < 0 \text{ and } p_3^2 c_3^2 - \frac{p_3^2}{w_2^2} \frac{\partial \hat{w}_2^2}{\partial p_3^2} > p_3^2 c_3^2 > 0 .$$

Thus, as is to be expected, $\partial \bar{p}_3^2 / \partial l_1^2 < 0$ and $\partial \bar{p}_3^2 / \partial l_2^2 > 0$, that is, the price of the non-tradable falls when the factor used relatively intensively in the non-tradables sector becomes more efficient and rises when the factor used relatively intensively in the export sector becomes more efficient. Owing to the factor-intensity situation, the bracketed terms in (24) necessarily have opposite sign; hence if (as I shall assume) goods 2 and 3 are substitutes in the sense that $s_{23}^2 - t_{23}^2 > 0$, since necessarily $s_{33}^2 - t_{33}^2 < 0$, formula (24) does not allow for an unambiguous sign.

The solution to this problem is to study country 2's demand for imports rather than its supply of exports. Since

$$p_1 \frac{\partial \hat{h}_1^2}{\partial l_i^2} + p_2 \frac{\partial \hat{h}_2^2}{\partial l_i^2} = 0 ,$$

these derivatives of course have opposite sign; further, since $y_1^2 = 0$, we have $\partial \hat{y}_1^2 / \partial l_i^2 = \partial \hat{w}_i^2 / \partial p_1 = 0$. Thus,

$$(26) \quad \frac{\partial \hat{h}_1^2}{\partial l_i^2} = \frac{w_i^2}{p_1} \left\{ p_1 c_1^2 - \frac{p_1 s_{13}^2}{p_3^2 (s_{33}^2 - t_{33}^2)} \left[p_3^2 c_3^2 - \frac{p_3^2}{w_i^2} \frac{\partial \hat{w}_i^2}{\partial p_3^2} \right] \right\} .$$

In the case $i = 2$, the bracketed term in (26) is unambiguously positive, by virtue of the Stolper-Samuelson theorem and the assumption that all goods are superior. Assuming commodities 1 and 3 to be Hicksian substitutes (i.e., $s_{13}^2 > 0$), the term preceding the bracketed expression in (26) is negative; consequently, we can conclude that $\partial \hat{h}_1^2 / \partial l_2^2 > 0$ and hence $\partial \hat{h}_2^2 / \partial l_2^2 < 0$. The intuitive explanation is straightforward: The term $p_1 c_1^2$ corresponds to the increased demand for imports at unchanged prices – there being of course no change in the (zero) supply of importables. Now an increase in the efficiency of the factor used relatively intensively in the export industry causes the price of the non-tradable to rise; the import good by hypothesis being a Hicksian substitute of the non-tradable, this price rise causes consumers to switch from non-tradables to imports. Therefore, both effects lead to an increase in the demand for imports, resulting in a worsening of country 2's terms of trade. This is fully in accord with the results of the standard model with no non-tradables, except that the negative effect on country 2's terms of trade is stronger in this case.

In the case $i = 1$, the bracketed term in (26) is negative, as is the term preceding it (assuming substitutability between commodities 1 and 3); thus, the term within braces is the difference between two positive terms, an income effect and a substitution effect. Thus, while the technical change with unchanged relative prices will as before lead to an increase in the demand for imports, it will cause the price of the non-tradable to drop, causing consumers to switch from importables to non-tradables. If this substitution effect is sufficiently strong, it will outweigh the income effect and the demand for imports will fall. Thus, it is possible but by no means certain that the technical change will improve country 2's terms of trade.

Now we consider the case of uniform factor-augmenting technical progress. Assuming preferences to be homothetic we find readily that

$$(27) \quad \frac{\partial \hat{h}_2^2}{\partial \lambda} = \left[\frac{\Pi^2}{Y^2} \, x_2^2 - y_2^2 \right] - \frac{s_{23}^2 - t_{23}^2}{s_{33}^2 - t_{33}^2} \left[\frac{\Pi^2}{Y^2} \, x_3^2 - y_3^2 \right].$$

If trade is balanced, $\Pi^2 = Y^2$ (national product equals absorption) and the second term vanishes; the whole expression reduces to country 2's export, z_2^2, of commodity 2 (a negative quantity). Thus, under these circumstances a uniform factor-augmenting technical improvement in country 2 must worsen country 2's terms of trade. If trade is unbalanced a small amount either way, then by continuity the qualitative result still holds.

To summarize, as in the case of the standard model, either a uniform improvement in factor efficiency or an improvement in efficiency of the factor employed relatively intensively in country 2's export industry will worsen country 2's terms of trade. In the standard model an improvement in efficiency of the factor used relatively intensively in country 2's import-competing industry will improve its terms of trade, while in the model in which country 2 produces only export and non-tradable goods an improvement in efficiency of the factor used relatively intensively in the non-tradables sector may, but need not, improve country 2's terms of trade. Thus, in the second model it is less likely for technical progress in country 2 to worsen country 1's terms of trade; and even if it does have this effect, a smaller transfer payment from country 2 to country 1 will be needed than in the first model to compensate country 1 for its welfare loss.

IMPORT RESTRICTIONS VERSUS FOREIGN AID

I shall assume that country 1 is in the process of receiving a certain amount A^1 of foreign aid from country 2, and/or tariff revenues from country 2 resulting from its imposition of a tariff of $100\tau_2^1$ percent on its imports of commodity 2 from country 2. For convenience I work with the tariff factor $T_2^1 = 1 + \tau_2^1$ in place of the tariff rate τ_2^1. As is customary, the price of country 1's export good (commodity 1), which will be the same in both countries (i.e., $p_1^1 = p_1^2 = \bar{p}_1^2$), will be taken as numéraire.

Country 1's excess demand for its own import good (commodity 2), expressed as a function of the external (country-2) prices of the two tradable goods, is defined as the solution of the functional equation

(28) $\hat{z}_2^1(p_1^2,p_2^2,A^1,T_2^1,l^1) = \hat{h}_2^1(p_1^2,T_2^1p_2^2,A^1 + (T_2^1 - 1)p_2^2\hat{z}_2^1(p_1^2,p_2^2,A^1,T_2^1,l^1);l^1)$.

Country 2's excess demand for commodity 2 (its export good) is defined simply by

(29) $\hat{z}_2^2(p_1^2,p_2^2,A^1,T_2^1,l^2) = \hat{h}_2^2(p_1^2,p_2^2, - A^1;l^2)$.

World equilibrium is then defined by the equation

(30) $\hat{z}_2^1(p_1^2,p_2^2,A^1,T_2^1,l^1) + \hat{z}_2^2(p_1^2,p_2^2,A^1,T_2^1,l^2) = 0$.

Recalling that $p_1^2 = \bar{p}_1^2$ = constant, and assuming the countries' factor endowments l^1, l^2 also to be constant, equation (30), which holds for all values of the parameters A^1, T_2^1, implicitly defines the functions

(31) $p_2^2 = \bar{p}_2^2(A^1,T_2^1)$ and $p_2^1 = \bar{p}_2^1(A^1,T_2^1) \equiv T_2^1\bar{p}_2^2 (A^1,T_2^1)$.

Now let us consider the question at issue. Suppose country 1 initially receives no foreign aid but imposes a tariff of $\tau_2^1 = T_2^1 - 1 > 0$ on its imports of commodity 2 from country 2. Its tariff revenues, which are equal to its trade deficit (denominated in its own prices), are then equal to

(32) $R^1(T_2^1) = (T_2^1 - 1)\bar{p}_2^2(0,T_2^1)$,

Now, suppose country 1 is offered an amount A^1 of foreign aid by country 2 equal to these tariff revenues (32), on condition that it remove its tariff; then its trade deficit (denominated in its own prices) remains equal to the quantity (32). Is country 1 better or worse off than before? The question can also be put in the converse form. Suppose country 1 was initially receiving an amount A^1 of foreign aid from country 2 and imposed no tariffs. Now country 2 withdraws the foreign aid; if country 1 in these circumstances imposes a tariff at a level such as to yield tariff revenues equal to the previous level of foreign aid (i.e., a T_2^1 satisfying $R^1(T_2^1) = A^1$), will it be better or worse off?

This question may be answered by considering each country's indirect trade-utility function. For example, we may take this to be the equivalent trade-variation (5) for some fixed base prices of tradables and factor endowments.

With the tariff, country 1's potential welfare is

$$(33) \quad u_T^1 = \dot{V}^1(\bar{p}_1^2, T_2^1\bar{p}_2^2(0,T_2^1),(T_2^1 - 1)\bar{p}_2^2(0,T_2^1);l^1) ,$$

whereas with foreign aid it is equal to

$$(34) \quad u_A^1 = \dot{V}^1(\bar{p}_1^2,\bar{p}_2^2(A^1,1),A^1;l^1) \text{ where } A^1 = (T_2^1 - 1)\bar{p}_2^2(0,T_2^1) .$$

Since (33) and (34) have identical first and third (as well as fourth) arguments, and country 1 must be better off, *ceteris paribus*, with a lower domestic price of its import good, we have the simple criterion

$$(35) \quad u_A^1 \gtreqless u_T^1 \text{ according as } \bar{p}_2^1(A^1,1) = \bar{p}_2^2(A^1,1) \lesseqgtr T_2^1\bar{p}_2^2(0,T_2^1) = \bar{p}_2^1(0,T_2^1) .$$

In words: *In order for country 1 to be better off with foreign aid than with a tariff that will yield the same revenue as the foreign aid, it is necessary and sufficient that the internal price of its import good be lower (relative to the price of its export good) with the foreign aid than with the tariff.*

A sufficient condition for this result is readily established. Suppose that the following two conditions hold:

(*a*) A transfer from country 2 to country 1 has the "orthodox" effect of improving (or at least not worsening) country 1's terms of trade in the absence of tariffs, that is,

$$\bar{p}_2^2(A^1,1) \leqq \bar{p}_2^2(0,1) ;$$

(*b*) A tariff imposed by country 1 does not lead to the "Metzler paradox," that is, does not lower the domestic price of its import good:

$$\bar{p}_2^1(0,T_2^1) \geqq \bar{p}_2^1(0,1) .$$

Then

(36) $\bar{p}_2^2(A^1,1) \leqq \bar{p}_2^2(0,1) = \bar{p}_2^1(0,1) \leqq \bar{p}_2^1(0,T_2^1) = T_2^1 \bar{p}_2^2(0,T_2^1)$.

From (35) and (36) we may conclude that $u_T^1 \leqq u_A^1$, with strict inequality holding if either of the inequalities (a) or (b) is strict. In words: *Under conditions (a) and (b) country 1 can never be better off with a tariff than it would be with an amount of foreign aid equal to the tariff revenues; and if either (a) a transfer to country 1 strictly improves the latter's terms of trade or (b) a tariff imposed by country 1 strictly raises the domestic price of its import good, then country 1 must be better off with foreign aid than with a tariff yielding the same amount of revenues.*

A simple alternative sufficient condition can be stated for this result. Suppose that

(37) $\bar{p}_2^2(0,T_2^1) \geqq \bar{p}_2^2(A^1,1)$, where $A^1 = (T_2^1 - 1)\bar{p}_2^2(0,T_2^1)$ and $T_2^1 > 1$;

then

(38) $\bar{p}_2^1(0,T_2^1) = T_2^1 \bar{p}_2^2(0,T_2^1) > \bar{p}_2^2(A^1,1) = \bar{p}_2^1(A^1,1)$,

hence $u_T^1 < u_A^1$ by (35). In words: *If foreign aid leads to at least as great an improvement in country 1's terms of trade as a tariff that yields the same amount in revenues, then the domestic price of imports is greater under the tariff and consequently country 1 is better off with the foreign aid than with the tariff.*

It might be thought that by reversing the two inequalities in (a) and (b) one could reverse the conclusion; that is, that by assuming (a') that a transfer has the "anti-orthodox" effect of worsening the receiving country's terms of trade and (b') that the Metzler paradox holds, one could conclude that country 1 would be better off under a tariff than with an equal amount of foreign aid. However, it has been shown in Chipman[72] that the Metzler paradox can occur only if the orthodox presumption of the transfer problem holds. Thus, (a') and (b') cannot both be true and we cannot therefore obtain the converse result.

To understand the situation, it is instructive also to investigate *necessary* conditions. Suppose we assume that country 1 will be better off with the tariff and that the Metzler paradox does not hold. Then, using the corresponding two inequalities (35) and (b) in succession, we obtain

$$\bar{p}_2^2(A^1,1) > T_2^1 \bar{p}_2^2(0,T_2^1) = \bar{p}_2^1(0,T_2^1) \geqq \bar{p}_2^1(0,1) = \bar{p}_2^2(0,1) .$$

This shows that a transfer must have the anti-orthodox effect of worsening the receiving country's terms of trade. Likewise, suppose that country 1 will be better off under the tariff and that the orthodox presumption holds that foreign aid will improve or at least not worsen its terms of trade. Then, using the corresponding inequalities (35) and (a) in succession, we obtain

$$\bar{p}_2^1(0,T_2^1) = T_2^1\bar{p}_2^2(0,T_2^1) < \bar{p}_2^2(A^1,1) \leqq \bar{p}_2^2(0,1) = \bar{p}_2^1(0,1) \ .$$

This implies that the Metzler paradox must hold. Thus we may conclude: *In order for country 1 to be better off under a tariff than with foreign aid equal to the amount of the tariff revenues, it is necessary either that the tariff give rise to the Metzler paradox, that is, cause a lowering of the post-tariff internal import price, or that the foreign aid have the anti-orthodox effect of worsening its terms of trade.* Thus, one of two anomalies must hold if it is to be the case that country 1 is better off with the tariff. As pointed out above, it is logically impossible for both these anomalies to hold simultaneously.

NOTES

Author's Note: Work supported in part by NSF grant SES-8607652. I wish to thank Irving Brecher for his comments on the initial draft.

1   C.P. Kindleberger, "International Monetary Stabilization," in Seymour E. Harris, ed., *Postwar Economic Problems* (New York: McGraw-Hill 1943), 375–95.

2   Thomas Balogh, "The United States and the World Economy," *Bulletin of the Oxford University Institute of Statistics* 8 (October 1946): 309–23; idem, "The United States and International Economic Equilibrium," in Seymour E. Harris, ed., *Foreign Economic Policy for the United States* (Cambridge, Mass.: Harvard University Press, 1948), 446–83; idem, "The Concept of a Dollar Shortage," *Manchester School of Economic and Social Studies* 17 (May 1949): 186–201; idem, *The Dollar Crisis* (Oxford: Basil Blackwell, 1949); and idem, "The Crisis of the Marshall Plan," *Economia Internazionale* 3 (February 1950): 18–51.

3   Joan Robinson, "The Pure Theory of International Trade," *Review of Economic Studies* 14 (1947): 98–112.

4   Raúl Prebisch, *The Economic Development of Latin America and its Principal Problems* (Lake Success, NY: United Nations, 1950); and idem, "Commercial Policy in the Underdeveloped Countries," *American Economic Review, Papers and Proceedings* 49 (May 1959): 251–73.

5   H.W. Singer, "The Distribution of Gains between Investing and Borrowing Countries," *American Economic Review, Papers and Proceedings* 40 (May 1950): 473–85.

6   John H. Williams, *Economic Stability in the Modern World* (London: Athlone Press, 1952); published as *Trade Not Aid: A Program for World Stability* (Cambridge, Mass.: Harvard University Press, 1953).

7   J.R. Hicks, "An Inaugural Lecture. II. The Long-Run Dollar Problem," *Oxford Economic Papers*, n.s., 5 (June 1953): 121–35.

8   Dennis H. Robertson, *Britain in the World Economy* (London: George Allen & Unwin, 1954).

9   W.A. Lewis, "Economic Development with Unlimited Supplies of Labour," *Manchester School of Economic and Social Studies* 22 (May 1954): 139–91.

10 Gunnar Myrdal, *Development and Underdevelopment* (Cairo: National Bank of Egypt, 1956); and idem, *Economic Theory and Underdeveloped Regions* (London: Duckworth, 1957).

11 Arghiri Emmanuel, *Unequal Exchange* (New York: Monthly Review Press, 1972).

12 Samir Amin, *Unequal Development* (New York: Monthly Review Press, 1976).

13 Gottfried Haberler, *International Trade and Economic Development* (Cairo: National Bank of Egypt, 1959; expanded edition [with a new introduction], San Francisco and Panama: International Centre for Economic Growth, 1988), 11–12.

14 George N. Hatsopoulos, Paul R. Krugman, and Lawrence H. Summers, "U.S. Competitiveness: Beyond the Trade Deficit," *Science* 241 (15 July 1988): 299–307.

15 For a fuller discussion of these doctrines and their historical development, see John S. Chipman, *On the Concept of International Competitiveness*, Essays in International Finance (Princeton, NJ: International Finance Section, Department of Economics, Princeton University, forthcoming.

16 J.R. Hicks, J.R., "Consumers' Surplus and Index-Numbers," *Review of Economic Studies* 9 (Summer 1942): 126–37.

17 Hicks, in his "An Inaugural Lecture" (p. 122), himself, rather curiously, did not pursue this approach to explaining why deterioration in a country's terms of trade would lead to a "dollar shortage"; rather, he regarded a balance-of-payments deficit as the first but temporary step in a dynamic adjustment to the worsening terms of trade. This could not explain an alleged *chronic* "dollar shortage." Other writers (e.g., Ragnar Nurkse, *Problems of Capital Formation in Underdeveloped Countries* [Oxford: Basil Blackwell, 1953]) have resorted to the explanation that poor countries, via an alleged "demonstration effect," decide to ape the living standards of prosperous ones and therefore dissave. The psychological basis for this effect seems to be quite flimsy, but even if it could be accepted, it fails to explain why this demonstration effect would occur precisely when the country experiences a deterioration in its terms of trade. A more reasonable explanation is surely that the country's inhabitants will put pressure on their government to take measures to preserve their previous standard of living either by (*a*) dissaving or borrowing and thus (in the phrase used by Gottfried Haberler in his "Dollar Shortage?" in Seymour E. Harris, ed., *Foreign Economic Policy for the United States* [Cambridge, Mass.: Harvard University Press, 1948]) living beyond their means or by (*b*) adopting restrictive trade policies that will reverse the deterioration in the terms of trade and, in effect, increase their means. This provides the positive counterpart to the normative criterion considered in the text.

18 James Edward Meade, *A Geometry of International Trade* (London: George Allen & Unwin, 1952).

19 John S. Chipman, "The Theory and Application of Trade Utility Functions," in Jerry R. Green and Jose Alexandre Scheinkman, eds., *General Equilibrium, Growth, and Trade: Essays in Honor of Lionel McKenzie* (New York: Academic Press, 1979), 277–96.

20 The trade-demand function is also affected by the shape of the country's production-possibility set, which in the context of the usual Heckscher-Ohlin-Lerner-Samuelson (HOLS) model means that it is a function of the country's factor endowments (as well as of any parameters of the production functions representing technical change).

21 According to Raúl Prebisch (*Economic Development of Latin America*, 19), "the dollar shortage means that the United States does not purchase merchandise and services, or lend money, in an amount sufficient to cover the needs, justified or not, of other countries." This definition is substantially the same as in Kindleberger, "International Monetary Stabilization," 375. It, of course, begs the question of what is meant by "needs," since presumably these could be unlimited. For example, according to this definition the total amount of dollar shortage could easily exceed the entire US gross national product.

22 A somewhat similar concept is that of a "trade gap" in the "two-gap model" developed by Chenery and his associates. See, for instance, the interchange between Henry J. Bruton ("The Two-Gap Approach to Aid and Development: Comment," *American Economic Review* 59 [June 1969]: 439–46), and Hollis B. Chenery ("The Two-Gap Approach to Aid and Development: A Reply to Bruton," *American Economic Review* 59 [June 1969]: 446–9).

23 Paul A. Samuelson, "The Transfer Problem and Transport Costs: The Terms of Trade When Impediments Are Absent," *Economic Journal* 62 (June 1952): 278–304.

24 There is a further problem to which attention has been drawn in John S. Chipman and James C. Moore, "Compensating Variation, Consumer's Surplus, and Welfare," *American Economic Review* 70 (December 1980): 933–49. If one is comparing two hypothetical price changes faced by an individual, and if the compensating variations are both negative, then while in both cases we can conclude that the individual is made worse off by the price changes, we are not in general entitled to conclude that the price change that leads to the larger (absolute) compensating variation is worse than the price change that leads to the smaller (absolute) compensating variation. Such a conclusion could be drawn only if special assumptions are made about the individual's preferences, unless only one price varies (cf. Chipman and Moore, 1980, p. 947n). The equivalent variation, however, does not suffer from this deficiency, because it is a true indirect utility function.

25 R.F. Kahn, "The Dollar Shortage and Devaluation," *Economia Internazionale* 3 (February 1950): 89–113.

26 Kahn's formulation was somewhat confusing in that it assumed that both import restrictions and foreign aid were alternatives to currency devaluation.

This entails the implicit assumption that the nominal and real exchange rate are proportional to each other and to the terms of trade; this could be true in certain circumstances (cf. John S. Chipman, "The Classical Transfer Problem and the Theory of Foreign Exchanges," in George R. Feiwel, ed., *Joan Robinson and Modern Economics* [New York: New York University Press, 1989]: 739–73), but is not true in general. Trade restrictions will in general improve a country's terms of trade; a transfer to a country may (but need not) strengthen its real exchange rate (and if so, may strengthen its currency), but even if it does, it need not improve its terms of trade.

27 Lloyd A. Metzler, "Tariffs, the Terms of Trade, and the Distribution of National Income," *Journal of Political Economy* 57 (February 1949): 1–29.

28 John S. Chipman, "Metzler's Tariff Paradox and the Transfer Problem," in A. Asimakopulos, R. Cairns, and C. Green, eds., *Economic Theory, Welfare and the State: Essays in Memory of J.C. Weldon* (London: Macmillan Press, 1990), 130–42.

29 Ibid.

30 John S. Chipman, "A General-Equilibrium Framework for Analyzing the Responses of Imports and Exports to External Price Changes: An Aggregation Theorem," in Gottfried Bamberg and Otto Opitz, eds., *Methods of Operations Research*, vol. 44, Königstein: Verlag Anton Hain, Meisenheim, 1981), 43–56; idem, "International Trade," in John Eatwell, Murray Milgate, and Peter Newman, eds., *The New Palgrave: A Dictionary of Economics* (London: Macmillan Press, 1987), 2: 922–55; and idem, "The Classical Transfer Problem," 739–73.

31 A more general definition is possible without requiring the existence of a direct trade-utility function, but this need not be pursued here. A definition alternative to (1) is given in A.D. Woodland, "Direct and Indirect Trade Utility Functions," *Review of Economic Studies* 47 (October 1980): 909, but it is applicable only to the case in which all goods are traded; this assumption was also made in Chipman, "The Theory and Application of Trade Utility Functions," 277–96. For derivations of trade-demand and trade-utility functions in the presence of non-traded goods, see Chipman, "A General-Equilibrium Framework," 43–56; idem, "International Trade," 934, 944; and idem, "The Classical Transfer Problem," 739–73.

32 I use this terminology in place of the more customary but inaccurate expression "Roy's identity." Cf. John S. Chipman and James C. Moore, "Compensating Variation, Consumer's Surplus, and Welfare," *American Economic Review* 70 (December 1980): 934n.

33 Lionel W. McKenzie, "Demand Theory without a Utility Index," *Review of Economic Studies* 24 (June 1957): 185–9.

34 Leonid Hurwicz and Hirofumi Uzawa, "On the Integrability of Demand Functions," in John S. Chipman et al., eds., *Preferences, Utility, and Demand* (New York: Harcourt Brace Jovanovich, 1971), 114–48.

35 Note that the negative of this function has the interesting mercantilist interpretation as the function that maximizes the country's balance of trade; cf. Chipman, *On the Concept of International Competitiveness*.

36 Chipman and Moore, "Compensating Variation," 933–49.

37 In the absence of trade restrictions $p_j^1 = p_j^2$, hence p_1^1/p_2^1 corresponds to country 1's terms of trade p_1^2/p_2^2. The case of trade restrictions is taken up in the final section.

38 Fritz Machlup, "Three Concepts of the Balance of Payments and the So-Called Dollar Shortage," *Economic Journal* 60 (March 1950): 46–68.

39 Gottfried Haberler, "Dollar Shortage?" in Seymour E. Harris, ed., *Foreign Economic Policy for the United States* (Cambridge, Mass.: Harvard University Press, 1948), 438.

40 Hicks, "An Inaugural Lecture," 121–35. Hicks adopted the Ricardian assumption of constant costs and argued that if there was technical progress in country A that was limited to its import-competing industry, this would lower the relative price of its imports and improve its terms of trade. This argument can only make sense, as E.J. Mishan pointed out ("The Long-Run Dollar Problem: A Comment," *Oxford Economic Papers*, n.s., 7 [June 1955]: 217 n) if country A is so large that its cost ratio determines the world price ratio, as in Frank D. Graham's model (*The Theory of International Values* [Princeton, NJ: Princeton University Press, 1948]). On the other hand, if increasing cost is allowed, then Hicks's analysis is inadequate, since it neglects consumption effects, as Mishan also showed. This is of importance when analysing Hicks-neutral change in production functions, but not when analysing technical change that takes the form of uniform enhancement to a factor's productivity, which automatically gives rise to what Harry G. Johnson called the required "ultra-anti-trade-biased" technical change ("Economic Development and International Trade," *Nationaløkonomisk Tidsskrift* 97 [1959]: 253–72).

41 W.M. Corden, "Economic Expansion and International Trade: A Geometric Approach," *Oxford Economic Papers*, n.s., 8 (September 1956): 223–8.

42 Ronald Findlay and Harry Grubert, "Factor Intensities, Technological Progress, and the Terms of Trade," *Oxford Economic Papers*, n.s., 11 (February 1959): 111–21.

43 Johnson, "Economic Development and International Trade."

44 Thomas Balogh, stated: "Technical progress is not unlikely to be haphazard both in timing and industrial incidence. If any bias can be detected it is towards the economizing of that productive factor which in relation to others is scarce and expensive in the dominant country" ("The Dollar Crisis Revisited," *Oxford Economic Papers*, n.s., 6 [September 1954]: 278). One could perhaps justify this on the basis of the theory of induced innovation, but only if factor rentals were not equalized among countries. Balogh apparently overlooked the fact that this suggestion did not square with his rejection of Hicks's hypothesis that technical change would be import-biased.

45 Samuelson, "The Transfer Problem and Transport Costs."
46 Ibid.
47 For details see Chipman "International Trade," 945–6. Treatment of the one-factor case is dealt with in Chipman, "The Classical Transfer Problem."
48 Harry G. Johnson, "Economic Expansion and International Trade," *Manchester School of Economic and Social Studies* 23 (May 1955): 95–112; and idem, "Economic Development and International Trade."
49 Mishan, "The Long-Run Dollar Problem," 215–20.
50 Corden, "Economic Expansion and International Trade."
51 Findlay and Grubert, "Factor Intensities."
52 Bela Balassa, "The Purchasing-Power Parity Doctrine: A Reappraisal," *Journal of Political Economy* 72 (December 1964): 584–96.
53 Odd Aukrust, "PRIM I: A Model of the Price and Income Distribution Mechanism of an Open Economy," *Review of Income and Wealth* 16 (March 1970): 51–78.
54 Ronald I. McKinnon, *Monetary Theory and Controlled Flexibility in the Foreign Exchanges*, Essays in International Finance no. 84 (Princeton, NJ: Princeton University, Department of Economics, International Finance Section, 1971).
55 Gottfried Haberler, "International Aspects of U.S. Inflation," in Philip Cagan et al., *a New Look at Inflation* (Washington, DC: American Enterprise Institute for Public Policy Research, 1973), 79–105.
56 Gösta Edgren, Karl-Olof Faxen, and Clas-Erik Odhner, *Wage Formation in the Economy* (London: George Allen & Unwin 1973).
57 W. Max Corden and J. Peter Neary, "Booming Sector and De-Industrialization in a Small Open Economy," *Economic Journal* 92 (December 1982): 825–48.
58 For a general formulation, see John S. Chipman, "Relative Prices, Capital Movements, and Sectoral Technical Change: Theory and an Empirical Test," in Karl Jungenfelt and Douglas Hague, eds., *Structural Adjustment in Developed Open Economies* (London: Macmillan Press, 1985), 395–454. The thesis that technical progress is more rapid in the "exposed" or tradables sector than in the "sheltered" or non-tradables sector is found to be well supported by the data.
59 Because of its possible confusion with the concept of productive efficiency, "efficiency" is not the best word to describe the intrinsic productive capacity of a factor of production, but it is employed here for convenience because of its common use in the phrase "efficiency units."
60 John Stuart Mill, *Principles of Political Economy, With Some of Their Applications to Social Philosophy*, 3rd ed. (London: John W. Parker, 1852), 2: 148.
61 The strong *a priori* presumption is thus that technical improvement in one country will improve rather than worsen the terms of trade of other countries, contrary to the Balogh-Prebisch-Singer thesis. The empirical evidence likewise does not support that thesis; cf. Haberler, *International Trade and Economic*

Development; idem "Terms of Trade and Economic Development," in Howard S. Ellis, ed., *Economic Development for Latin America* (London: Macmillan, 1961), 275–97; Fritz Machlup, "Dollar Shortage and Disparities in the Growth of Productiviy," *Scottish Journal of Political Economy* 1 (October 1954): 250–67; Robert E. Lipsey, *Price and Quantity Trends in the Foreign Trade of the United States* (Princeton, NJ: Princeton University Press for the National Bureau of Economic Research, 1963); Benjamin Higgins and N.T. Dung, "Dualism and Dependency in Continuing Underdevelopment,' in R.P. Misra and M. Honjo, eds., *Changing Perception of Development Problems* (Nagoya, Japan: Maruzen Asia, for and on behalf of the United Nations Centre for Regional Development; Hong Kong: Maruzen Investment [Hong Kong]; and Singapore: Maruzen Asia Pte. 1981), 123–76; and Deepak Lal, *The Poverty of "Development Economics"* (London: Institute of Economic Affairs, 1983). Higgins and Dung ("Dualism and Dependency," 138) could hardly be more emphatic: "Considering the thoroughness with which the 'deteriorating terms of trade' thesis has been disproved on both theoretical and empirical grounds, it may seem astonishing that the radicals continue to repeat it." They go on in a footnote to say, "the case is so clear that informed men of reason cannot help but be in agreement."

62   Johnson, "Economic Expansion and International Trade."
63   Mishan, "The Long-Run Dollar Problem."
64   Corden, "Economic Expansion and International Trade."
65   Findlay and Grubert, 'Factor Intensities."
66   Johnson, "Economic Development and International Trade."
67   Paul A. Samuelson, 'Prices of Factors and Goods in General Equilibrium," *Review of Economic Studies* 21 (1953): 1–20.
68   John S. Chipman, "The Theory of Exploitative Trade and Investment Policies: A Reformulation and Synthesis," in Luis Eugenio Di Marco, ed., *International Economics and Development: Essays in Honor of Raúl Prebisch* (New York: Academic Press, 1972), 209–44.
69   Ibid.; and idem, "International Trade."
70   Samuelson, "Prices of Factors and Goods."
71   John S. Chipman, "The Theory of Exploitative Trade and Investment Policies," and "International Trade."
72   Chipman, "Metzler's Tariff Paradox."

15 The Underdevelopment of Development[*]

ANDRE GUNDER FRANK and MARTA FUENTES FRANK

How can Gunder Frank and Higgins like the same book?[**]

And even like each other? The answer is: *Easy.*

Ben Higgins and Gunder Frank so demonstrate in their essays in this volume.

FROM A PERSONAL PREFACE TO THE AUTHORS' INTENTIONS

Economics and development economics thinking have often been roughly divided into (right) neoclassical, (centre) Keynesian, and (left) Marxist. More colloquially and usefully, we may distinguish conservative, reformist, and radical variants, as in the recent *Economic Development: The History of an Idea* by H.W. Arndt.[1] Most authors in the present volume (as elsewhere) probably regard themselves as too heterodox to be classified in any of these orthodox categories. Or they regard themselves as technician-scientists, with no political colour. If obliged to choose, however, they probably would feel themselves least uncomfortable, like President Eisenhower, in the extreme middle of the road.

Moreover, the *methodenstreit* has often been more severe without each of these categories than between them. Indeed, the first of these categories almost never, and the second only rarely, even take explicit account of the third. For instance, a decade ago Ben Higgins observed with chagrin that when development economics was reviewed for the American Economic Association in 1971, one of its reviewers, Robert Solow, said "we neglected

---

[*] A more extensive version along with a bibliography of A.G. Frank publications 1955–1990 may be found in *Scandinavian Journal of Development Alternatives* 10, no. 3 (1991).

[**] B. White, "Agriculture Involution and Its Critics: Twenty Years After," *Bulletin of Concerned Asian Scholars* 40, no. 2 (April–June 1983).

radical economics because it is negligible.''[2] Even now, *The State of Development Economics: Progress and Perspectives*, edited by Gustav Ranis and T. Paul Schultz,[3] out of eighteen chapters, devotes only one to dependence, written by Raúl Prebisch. He makes little mention, and the other authors and chapters of the book none at all, of more radical or Marxist writings.

All of these three varieties of development economics are, however, represented in the present volume in honour of Ben Higgins. His own introductory chapter, as well as other evidence, suggests that he would himself like to have a foot, or at least a toe, in each major camp and several of their subdivisions. For instance, in the above-cited essay, Higgins noted that "once one is immersed in the problems of less developed countries one cannot help but become something of a Marxist."[4] Therefore, the request for a contribution from Andre Gunder Frank is to assure at least one full-blown representation from the last category – no matter that neither co-author has ever laid any claim to being an orthodox, neo- or any other kind of Marxist. Indeed, I have argued the contrary.[5]

Nonetheless, we welcome and accept this invitation by Dr Savoie to write "a philosophical and contemplative essay ... [which] need not be 'scientific' ... [but instead] an occasion for reflection and summing up of a sort that 'learned journals' would not publish." We do so for the following reasons, and therefore we intend to comply in the following ways: (1) Gunder's thirty-year friendship and Marta's twenty-five-year acquaintance with Ben; (2) the receipt by Gunder of more and more invitations (especially by anthropologists!) to lecture on something like "the rise and decline of dependence and Gunder Frank"; (3) our co-author Paul Streeten's proposal to Gunder to write down an autobiographical account of the same, and the enthusiastic encouragement by Ben to do so here and now; (4) the encouragement by others to write a full-blown autobiography, of which the present might become a draft chapter or two; (5) the agonizing reappraisal by Gunder and Marta, like so many others, of our experience with "development"; (6) Marta's long-time intention and growing desire to work on if not out *another* concept of *development*; and last but not least, (7) the call for responses to the increasingly generalized (consciousness of) crisis in development and development thinking.

We, therefore, intend to make a political-sociology-of-knowledge review of "The Birth, Life and Death of Development Economics"[6] or "The Rise and Decline of Development Economics"[7] based on our own experience and perspective. Thus, we will pass review on the three varieties of development economics – and autobiographically, on our own participation in all of them – nearly as unequally as others have done. However, we will devote respective shares of emphasis and space to them in reverse order: the least to the conservative, if not reactionary, orthodox neoclassical variety preponderantly treated elsewhere; more to the right- and left-centre Keynesian and other structural/reformist theory and policy, which is most the perspective represented by our co-authors; and most to the supposedly radical left (and mostly left out) dependency and "neo-Marxist" writings – and their battles with the former, especially in Latin America – with which Gunder Frank is generally associated. Thus, we will also be able to show how we have had, perhaps more sequentially than Ben, a foot or toe in each of these camps and several of their subdivisions.

Perhaps we can also clarify how, on further "reflection and summing up," our multiple choice is now none of the above. Nor would we wish to find ourselves in any of these camps when H.W. Arndt can write: "Are we then to conclude that Adam Smith, Karl Marx, Gunnar Myrdal and Peter Bauer, all proponents of material progress, must be regarded as "Right" and A.G. Frank, Dudley Seers, the Ayatollah Khomeini, and the pope as "Left"? Or is it the other way around? Clearly there is something wrong, certainly in relation to economic development as a policy objective, with these labels."[8]

FROM THE DEVELOPMENT CRISIS TOWARDS A CONCEPTUAL INTRODUCTION

In 1988, the New Delhi 1,000-delegate strong congress of the International Society for Development was dominated by the theme of crisis. There was a sensation of total bankruptcy in development policy, thinking, theory and ideology, indeed in development *tout court*: "There emerged a strong and recurrent theme: We are at the end of an era and need to look beyond development to the survival strategies of the people if we want to understand what is really happening in the Third World" (Development Forum, July–August 1988, p. 1). Little wonder, as Latin Americans were lamenting their 1980s "lost decade of development." The per capita income and/or product, which is still their main official measure of development, had fallen by 10 to 15 percent and was lower than that of a decade before. In Africa, per capita national income had fallen over 25 percent to a level below that at the time of independence, over two decades before. In both continents as elsewhere, these average declines of course hide their also worsening distribution, as "the poor pay more" of this decline than the rich. Thus, export-led growth had failed in Latin America and self-reliance and "African Socialism" in Africa.

The socialist countries first seemed to do well, but then they too were caught in the vice of crisis. Socialist national product and income had also fallen 25 percent in a four-year period in Poland. Economic and political crisis went from bad to worse in Stalinist Rumania (lights out), worker-management Yugoslavia (threat of army intervention), not to mention liberated Vietnam (chaos and reprivatization). Even in reformist showcase Hungary, the average real wages in 1989 returned to the 1970 level. According to recent revelations, 25 percent of Hungarians live in poverty. In the Soviet Union, the Brezhnev period has been re-baptized as one of "stagnation." In reality many economic sectors (heavy industry) and social indices (infant mortality rates) have in fact deteriorated.

In the short run, not development, but crisis management has become the order of the day in much of the South and East (with significant partial exceptions in India, China, and the East Asian NICs [newly industrialized countries]). In the West Reaganomic military Keynesianism was keeping the economy (temporarily?) afloat on borrowed time and money. No one anywhere – left, right, or centre – any longer has any practical solutions to offer. Neither advocates of neoclassical capitalist stabilization and adjustment in their neo-liberal guises, nor neo-structuralist advocates of reformist structural change, or even of radical socialist *perestroika* and *glasnost*, can promise a credible solution to the crisis, much less for development. Even so, many of the former still, and some of the latter newly, prefer to masquerade their own ideological, theoretical, and policy bankruptcy behind the newly fashonable neo-liberal phrases of promoting economic growth (= development?) by letting "the magic of the market" "get the prices right."

For the longer run, the environmental costs of past and present development styles have become increasingly ominous. The need for ecologically "sustainable development"[9] has become more urgent and obvious than when the Club of Rome referred to "the limits of growth" two decades ago. Similarly, there is greater consciousness of how in the long run economic "development is bad for women" and largely at their expense.

Moreover, as we will observe below, it turns out that there is more in common between capitalist and socialist development orthodoxies on all these and other scores than there are differences – differences their right and left advocates have so long fought about. Both have come up against their respective or common dead end(s). Therefore, both orthodoxies (or their commonality) are also subject to refutation, rejection, and replacement by an ever-changing kaleidoscope of alternative ideological views and by practical implementation of another development.

Furthermore, each of these alternatives is representative of and carried or promoted by one or more social movements. Some are reactionary against, and others progressive beyond, the postwar development orthodoxy/ies. Islamic and various indigenous revivalists and other ethnic groups combat Western (including Marxist socialist) modernization and promote a variety of cultures instead. Environmentalists try to reverse or at least to avoid further ecological degradation. Countless community and small-is-beautiful groups seek to protect their members' livelihood and identity. To do so, they pursue and organize productive, distributional, political, and cultural self-development through self-mobilization. Feminists and other women, who often express *de facto* feminist prose on the stage of social oppression, fight to change the gender structure of society. Thereby, they also improve the *de facto* conception and *de jure* definition of development. Their conceptions of equity, efficiency, and economy in development are altogether different from those measured by growth rates of GNP.

FROM EQUITY TO EFFICIENCY IN ECONOMIC DEVELOPMENT

After this preface and introduction, the reader and the authors themselves might like to have us get down to the brass tacks of at least our own version of this volume's title and concern: equity and efficiency in economic development. Donald Savoie, the co-editor, and Ben Higgins, the honoured man himself, wrote that this should be easy to do – almost automatic – in anything we write on the subject. But is it? Equity and efficiency, not to mention economic development, for whom?

Equity ... for whom? What is it (or its measure) in an unequal world? Should unequals receive equal or (what?) unequal treatment, as the old but still unresolved adage goes? The policy of affirmative action acknowledges that it is only equitable to provide, even to assure, unequal treatment to unequals. Of course, this new inequality is intended to counteract or balance the original inequality and inequity a bit. But then the very little affirmative action that there is, is in turn rejected (e.g., recently by the United States Supreme Court) as too much, because it is also inequitable. And equal-competitive-market treatment of unequals, not to mention monopolistic treatment of those who have neither property nor power, further increases both inequality and inequity.

Efficiency ... for whom? That is a measure of the relation of means to (whose?) ends. What if, as Ben suggests in his introduction, the end is or even includes equity? Then neither market "efficiency," nor planning "efficiency," nor perhaps not even participatory democracy, is efficient. The market is not, because it accepts and enlarges inequity and inequality. Planning is not, because it gives the planners or their political bosses inequitable and unequal power to serve their own interests at the expense of others. Moreover, planning produces more red tape than economic welfare. Participatory democracy may also not be efficient because it is often unworkable. And when it works, it institutionalizes endless discussion or dispute. What is more, what if we reject means-end-efficiency altogether as a male (imposed) and otherwise unacceptable Aristotelian schema? For it may operate at women's and others' expense and counter to their spiritual or (other) intellectual dispositions.

Economic development ... for whom? What if it turns out that development is bad for women (that's already half the population)? And what if it is bad for quite a few others as well, inasmuch as much development occurs at their expense and omits or even marginalizes them from its benefits? *A fortiori* for *economic* development. Perhaps *social* development would be a more equitable and better end. But then what is the measure of equity, let alone of efficiency?

For whom? Our above-mentioned Chinese and Russian (and ex-Georgian) emperors and the postwar right, left, and centre development ideologies all referred to development for the "country." *De facto*, of course, it was never for everybody in the country. Moreover, everybody claimed explicitly or implicitly that someone did or might have a development "policy" for the country. Frankly, we have long since and all along doubted the verity and even the plausibility of this last proposition, at least under capitalism. Moreover, as we will argue below after retracing our tortuous road, it appears that if "development" has any operational sense at all, it is not in reference to a country or (often non) nation-state; rather, the only meaningful development is of the world economy and society at one level and for much smaller social groups or individuals at another level. For the latter, development policy is very different from that implied by development policy writers and planners. Efficiency may be individual or group means to their respective ends, but equity between individuals or groups is hardly considered. World development still seems to follow a macro historical course, which is largely beyond intentional human micro controls. Therefore, policy (making) is hardly even relevant for world development at all.

In a word, dealing with equity and efficiency in economic development is really not as easy as suggested by the letters of invitation we received. Below we will show that when it all began for us in the 1950s, we were driven by our passion for justice and equity, and thus saw more difficulties than others in combining equity and efficiency under capitalism. But since then, experience and reflection have obliged us to make (shades of John Foster Dulles) agonizing reappraisals of some "socialist" illusions about equity and efficiency in economic development. We shared these illusions with many in the 1960s, agonized over them in the 1970s, and had to leave them by the wayside of our long and not yet ending road in the 1980s. Alas moreover, we do not have the comfort of replacing our old illusions with the new ones about the "magic of the market," which are now so popular west, east, and south. We may now retrace some of the steps and major bends, as well as the changing scenery, along the way of development thinking and praxis for others and for us to indicate where we stand now. Who knows for how long.

The recipes for the establishment main course and even the proof of the pudding in the eating of the development of development thinking are well known and have recently been oft reviewed, as noted above. Even the rise and decline of dependent underdevelopment (supposed) alternatives have been widely reviewed. Therefore, we can here confine ourselves to doing the same once over lightly and devote more attention instead to how our own nuisance-value flea-bite participation in this unfolding story has changed our own perceptions.

FROM DEVELOPMENT OF DEVELOPMENT THINKING TO ITS UNDERDEVELOPMENT (WITH APOLOGIES TO MY SOME-TIME COLLEAGUE IAN LIVINGSTON)

The idea if not always the name of economic development started long ago, like the idea of progress with which it is largely synonymous. Where and when it started is hard to tell. However, it may be well to recall some famous "developers": the Chinese emperor Qin Shi Huang-di who had all wheels cut to the same size to promote standardization and exchangeability of parts (like Colt and Ford millennia later), Peter the Great who wanted to "develop" Russia, and Stalin who sought the same and by many of the same means.

Closer to home, development was also the first and foremost concern of all classical political economists from Petty and Hume, via Smith and Ricardo, to Mills and Marx. These same economists were also concerned with equity distribution and efficiency allocation in development. Indeed, this concern with equity and efficiency in development long dominated economics. Then the neoclassical marginalist (counter) revolution of the 1870s subtracted both distributional equity and economic development to leave only allocational efficiency in economics. This was just as the world economy was going into a long Kondratieff B-phase crisis and its British hegemonic centre was beginning its decline in the face of growing competition from its German and American rivals. One result was the growth of more monopoly capitalism (while marginalists focused on the efficiency of competition). Another result was renewed colonialism and the drain of resources and capital from South to North (while marginalists deleted development from the economists' menu). Before this "marginal" counter-revolution, our present above-cited subtle distinctions among varieties of (development) economics would have been hard to make. Indeed, Marx had written that England showed India the "developed" mirror of its future and that the Mexican-American war was progressive because (Texans and New Mexicans will be glad to know) it promoted the development of the annexed territories and perhaps even of the remainder of Mexico as well. Since the advent of neoclassical marginalism, economists would have none of that! *Marginalist microeconomists* preferred to sit out on a side track while the world economic development was passing by on the main track.

It took another Kondratieff B-phase crisis in the world economy and the Keynesian revolution response to put economists back on track. Even then, they only did so for particular western countries, where they put macroeconomic problems, some considerations of macro equity and development by another name (stagnation à la Hansen) back on the agenda. Any other development elsewhere was only of interest insofar as it might pose a competitive threat to the west. Thus, Folke Hilgerdt studied *Industrialization and Foreign Trade* in *The Network of World Trade* for the League of Nations.[10] The also non-marginalist Schumpeter[11] remained marginal with his emphasis on technological growth in the *Theory of Economic Development*, and even his immediately relevant *Business Cycles*, not to mention his macro political economic *Capitalism, Socialism, and Democracy. De facto*, the Keynesians (though perhaps not Keynes himself) continued to accept the neoclassical tenets of (non)equity through perfect competition at the micro level and to exclude world and Third World development from the agenda.

Another Kondratieff B-phase world economic crisis today has now led to another crisis and the total bankruptcy of all neoclassical micro theory and (post) Keynesian macro theory as well as of their policies. This new crisis has therefore put the remarriage of (reformed) macro- and microeconomics in a world political economic development union on the economists' agenda. However, their now congenital short-sightedness and self-imposed blinkers prevent most (development) economists from seeing either the crisis or how to resolve it. Demand-side macroeconomics must divert itself from the unrealistic assumption of a supply curve, which is infinitely elastic until it becomes totally inelastic at a mythical full-employment level. (So interpreted, the supply-siders on the Reaganite right and the Marxist left have a valid point). Supply-side microeconomics must divert itself from the unreal assumption of perfect competition and foresight. (The monopolistic and imperfect competition economists like Robinson and Chamberlain had a point in the previous crisis).

Macro- and microeconomics must then be married into a union that takes account of the macroeconomic effects of individual (firm) microeconomic decisions – and vice versa, the macroeconomic influences on these same microeconomic decisions. Both must devote special attention to supply-side technological change decisions and policies and the demand-side conditions under which they are made. Moreover, perhaps following Pasinetti,[12] we must reinsert the classical political economists' distributional equity, sectoral imbalance and dynamic developmental considerations into this new demand- and supply-side union. Finally, all these must be united in face of a single world economy, whose political economic development is the final arbiter of all this economic theory and policy, although it is itself hardly subject to either. But this is getting ahead of our story, and we may leave it to return to this matter at the end. But not before a brief glance at the Marxist supposed alternative.

Marxism and then Marxist socialism as well have not always turned out quite as their proponents since Lenin and Stalin hoped, or as their marginalist and then cold warrior antagonists feared. As it turned out, the development of socialism everywhere has become, or rather remained, the existing "social-ism" of development, often without even the sometimes dubious virtues of capitalist development but with most of its vices of inequity/inequality – therefore also with inefficiency, environmental degradation, and the alien-ation of man, not to mention woman, against which Marx inveighed. (An old joke in the socialist countries: Capitalism is the exploitation of man by man; socialism is just the opposite. A new even more cruel joke there: Commu-nism/socialism is the most painful road from capitalism to capitalism). Let us now take up our story again at the end of the Second World War.

If anthropology was the child of imperialism and colonialism,[13] then the new development thinking was the child of neo-imperialism and neocolonial-ism. It developed (not the least at MIT) as a part and parcel instrument of the new postwar American hegemony. American ambitions extended over the ex-colonial world in the South and against both the real old Western colonialism and the perceived threat of new Eastern colonialism and imperialism. At the end of the Second World War, the "newly emerging" "young nations" – like millenarian China and India! – came of post-semi-colonial age. Simulta-neously and not independently, the First New Nation (Lipset's title), the United States, ascended to neo-imperial hegemony. That is when develop-ment studies came into their own and the new development ideology swept the world. The Chinese Communist peasant victory among one-quarter of the world's population in 1949 put the fear of God in many minds. They feared its extension or indigenous repetition in newly independent India, self-liberated Korea, and elsewhere. A decade later, the Cuban revolution would revive this same fear again. Developing a more harmless alternative became a matter of the greatest urgency, especially in the newly hegemonic United States.

These circumstances, and the new American need, help explain the significant changes in the development of development thinking and termi-nology in the 1950s and since. They followed the enunciation of the Truman Doctrine and his Point Four Technical Aid Program. The wartime and early postwar major writings on development issues had been mostly by Euro-peans, like Rosenstein-Rodan, Nurkse, Myrdal, and Singer, and then by the Latin American Prebisch. These writers soon found themselves embattled and overcome by the more conservative and more neoclassical theses from American pens. For the general public at the same time, new euphemisms for the subject peoples and countries were launched to replace previous ones as each became unpalatable or impolitic: "colonial" and "backward" were replaced by "undeveloped" and then by "underdeveloped." More recently the latter was replaced again by "less developed" (LDCs) or the better sounding but less accurate "developing" countries. Their models are now "new(ly) industrializing countries" (NICs).

Of course, the new American development of development theory also partook of American pragmatism and empiricism. "Science Is Measurement" was engraved on the cornerstone of the University of Chicago building where I (Gunder) studied for my economics PhD. Development became increasingly equated with economic development, and that became equated *de facto* if not *de jure* with economic growth. It in turn was measured by the growth of gross national product (GNP) per capita. The remaining "social" aspects of *growth = development* were called "modernization," and the political ones, "freedom."

The new United Nations commissioned five wise men to write out the American way of development.[14] Americans with no previous Third World experience, like the neoclassical Jacob Viner, pontificated about development. Ben Higgins was at MIT's Center for International Studies (CENIS) when Rostow[15] wrote his *Process of Economic Growth* and later his *Stages of Growth: A Non-Communism Manifesto*, not to mention the CIA stuff he wrote with Millikan.[16] Although Rostow and Co. dealt with Keynesian-type macroeconomic and even social problems, they did so to pursue the neoclassical, explicitly counter-revolutionary, and even counter-reformist Cold War ends, which were newly in vogue.

The quintessential modernization book, Lerner's *Passing of Traditional Society: The Modernization of the Middle East*, appeared at MIT's CENIS in 1958, while I was there. At the same time, Everett Hagen wrote his *On the Theory of Social Change*[17] and David McClelland his *Achieving Society*[18] there, and Ithiel de Sola Pool his Right Libertarian/Authoritarian Political works. All argued that development meant following step by step in America's (idealized) footsteps from tradition to modernity. The measure of it all was how fast the modern sector replaced the traditional one in each dual economy and society – that is, as long as, God and America forbid, there were no far-reaching structural reforms, let alone political revolutions. Of course, American-instigated and -supported counter-revolution and even invasion in Guatemala in 1954, Lebanon in 1958, etc., were okay. That is where we demurred.

FROM AUTOBIOGRAPHICAL BACKGROUND TO CHICAGO ECONOMICS (WITH APOLOGIES TO THE READER, WHO MAY SKIP AHEAD)

To explain why and how we demurred and sought to do otherwise, we must insert some autobiography into the unfolding of this development story. Our autobiographical reflections, however, may be of some interest and use to the reader also insofar as they will include when, where, and how along the winding road we bumped into and rubbed shoulders or exchanged snubs with various personalities in the "development field" and how we debated with their thinking.

We may get the most personal parts of this autobiography out of the way first. However, they may help explain our parts in the political sociology of knowledge that follows. My (Gunder's) pacifist novelist father had taken me out of Nazi Germany when I was four years old in 1933. In the 1950s, he wrote his autobiography under the title *Links wo das Herz Ist* (Heart on the Left). I went to Ann Arbor High School and then to Swarthmore College. There, in part under his influence, I studied economics and became a Keynesian. In 1950, not knowing what I was letting myself in for, I started a PhD in economics at the University of Chicago. I took Milton Friedman's economic theory course and passed my doctoral exams in economic theory and public finance with flying colours. Despite that, I received a letter from the Chicago Economics Department advising me to leave, because of my unsuitability or our incompatibility.

I went on to the University of Michigan and studied for a semester with our now co-authors Kenneth Boulding and Richard Musgrave. I wrote a paper on welfare economics for Boulding, which proved that it is impossible to separate efficiency in resource allocation from equity in income distribution. (Later Ian Little would become famous for doing the same thing. Now Little[19] also pontificates on economic development and dismisses my writings on the same as unpersuasive.) I took the paper, for which Boulding had given me an A+, back to Chicago to get at least an MA out of them. First they made me cut the heart of the argument out of my paper, and then they gave me a C for it. Then I dropped out altogether. I became a hippie at the Vesuvius cafe in San Francisco's North Beach before Jack Kerouac arrived there *On the Road*.

I, Gunder, was introduced to "development" and at the same time re-entered the University of Chicago through the back door by accident. This was the availability of a research assistantship in Bert Hoselitz's Research Center in Economic Development and Cultural Change at the University of Chicago. In Bert's absence on leave, the planner and active director Harvey Perloff hired me only to tell me to his dismay that I am "the most philosophical person" he had ever met. He put me to work evaluating the early World Bank reports. I gave their reports on Ceylon, Nicaragua, and Turkey barely passing marks in my earliest publications.[20]

For reasons of financial circumstance, I then spent an interval at Chicago working on the Soviet economy (in a research project whose final client was the US Army Psychological Welfare Division!). As a result, I subsequently wrote my Chicago economics PhD dissertation on a comparison between the productivity growth of agriculture and of industry in the Soviet Ukraine. In this thesis, I independently worked out the concepts and measures of general productivity, later to be known as total productivity, and the contribution of human capital and organization to economic growth. In journals edited and published at the University of Chicago, I published "General Productivity in

Soviet Agriculture and Industry"[21] and "Human Capital and Economic Growth."[22] According to H.W. Arndt,[23] the idea of human capital was "almost single-handedly introduced into economics" by the then chairman of the Chicago Economics Department, T.W. Schultz, who subsequently was awarded the Nobel Prize.

It was this work of mine to which John Toye[24] refers when he writes "the archetypical Western radicalized intellectual, who at that time [1970s] dominated development thinking was Andre Gunder Frank, the orthodox Chicago economist who abruptly became a Latin American revolutionary figure."[25] My ex-colleague and (ex?) friend at Michigan State, Paul Strassman[26] would later call me a "renegade" from Chicago economics.

Yet already at the University of Chicago, I spent more and more of my time studying and associating with the anthropologists. This helped me come to the same conclusion as my friend Bert Hoselitz had (but I thought, independently of him) – that the determinant factors in economic development were really *social*. Social change, therefore, seemed the key to both social and economic development. I wrote about social conflict and favourably reviewed (in Bert Hoselitz's journal) Albert Hirschman's *Strategy of Economic Development*.[27] I conferred with Hirschman and Bob Lindblom about our convergent conflict studies. In his own autobiographical reflections, published in *Pioneers in Development*,[29] Hirschman would later recall that this agreement was also about *unbalanced* growth. More recently, he suggested to me that I should do a similar autobiographical account myself.

FROM MIT'S CENIS POLITICS TO OURS

In 1958, I (Gunder) turned up as visiting researcher at MIT's Center for International Studies (CENIS) and met Ben Higgins, W.W. Rostow, and the others there. Meantime, I (Marta) had worked with the Catholic Church as a volunteer, distributing CARE/Caritas packages and ideas to the shantytown poor in Santiago, Chile. Then the parish priest enlightened my naiveté by telling me that the real purpose of this mission was not to fight poverty but to combat communism. That ended my development volunteer work. In reaction, the first time that I went to vote, I did so (but never again) for a local Communist candidate.

At CENIS, Rostow was working with Max Millikan for the CIA. Ben Higgins (when he was not wining and dining me [Gunder] at his home near Walden Pond) was directing the Indonesia project. He now assures us that he was not involved in the CIA work (which apparently took place behind closed doors) at CENIS, where I (Gunder) was innocently on a three-month visit in the lion's den. Walt Whitman Rostow "confided" to me (Gunder) that since the age of eighteen he had made it his life mission to offer the world a better alternative to Karl Marx. At the time, I did not understand what that meant.

After reflecting on the fate of really existing Marxism and socialism, we may now be permitted to wonder why Rostow wanted to dedicate his life to offering an alternative to them. Moreover, in case that were not enough, he proposed bombing Vietnam back into the Stone Age. We have often wondered since then what Rostow's parents would have felt about the ideological and political development of the children they named after Walt Whitnam and Eugene Debs. The first ideologist went on to plan his nuclear development policies in the Kennedy-Johnson White House basement, and the second super-hawk represented the Reagan White House in the pre-Gorbachev era arms-"control" talks. However, we may also ask how we came to propose an alternative "paradigm change from Rostow to Gunder Frank," as Aidan Foster-Carter called it.[29]

We may pursue the answer. In 1959, I (Gunder) visited Ben in Austin, Texas, on the way to the American Anthropological Association meetings in Mexico. There, I co-chaired the anthropological theory sessions with Maggie Mead and gave a paper on social change and reform through social conflict. At another anthropology conference, Maggie especially congratulated me on my delivery of a paper later published as "Goal Ambiguity and Conflicting Standards: An Approach to the Study of Organization" and "Administrative Role Definition and Social Change,"[30] the latter subsequently reprinted in the business management text *Studies in Managerial Process and Organizational Behaviour*.[31] I offered the same idea and more at a State Department training seminar for visiting Third World technicians. From this idea about social change it was but a short step (for me, Gunder, if not for others) to jump to the political conclusion that the really important real factors in development are political. Since political change seemed difficult if not impossible to achieve through reform, the obvious answer seemed to be political revolution. It became increasingly clear to me that all American – including my own – development studies and thinking were not at all part of the solution to development problems. Instead they were themselves part of the problem, since they sought to deny and obscure both the real problem and the real solution, which lay in politics.

To find out more about that, I went to Cuba in 1960, soon after the revolution. Then I briefly looked at political change in Kwame Nukrumah's Ghana (where I was disappointed to find little) and in Seku Toure's Guinea (where I mistakenly thought that I had found more and better). Then, I decided to be consequential: I quit my assistant professorship at Michigan State University (where I had led an interdisciplinary development seminar and had already complained about MSU training police forces in South Vietnam – many years before this CIA project would become a public scandal), and decided to find out for myself, from the "inside" in the "underdeveloped" "Third" World. Since I felt I would never become an African, I went to Latin America, where acculturation seemed less daunting.

FROM REFORM TO REVOLUTION IN LATIN AMERICA

In 1962, I left the United States and went to Mexico. I wrote about the "Janus faces" of Mexican inequality, for I saw internal colonialism there instead of separate sectors in a "dual" economy or society. In Venezuela, my friend Hector Silva Michelena told me I had written a Hamlet without the Prince of Denmark of American imperialism. Then, via Peru and Bolivia, I arrived in Chile. In Venezuela, the sociologist Julio Cotler (later at the Institute of Peruvian Studies in Lima) sent me to see his brother-in-law, Jose Matos Mar, in Peru, and he in turn to Aníbal Quijano, (later our friend and neighbour in Santiago, during the time he wrote on marginalization and other matters at the CEPAL/ECLA Division of Social Affairs). But first Aníbal gave me a letter to a friend in Santiago with instructions to introduce me to a lady there. He did, to Marta Fuentes.

We (Marta and Gunder) met and shared our concern for social justice, which would guide our concern for development with equity before efficiency. We married and had two children with whom, as with each other, we still speak Spanish. Together, but without consulting our children and at their cost, we embarked on the long – and as it turned out tortuous – road "to change the world." At least we sought to change some of its thinking in the name of equitable justice.

To begin with, I wrote a critique of an article on land reform by Jacques Chonchol. (Later he would direct agricultural development for the Christian Democratic Chilean President Frei and then become minister of agriculture for the Socialist Party President Allende). Chonchol had counselled, and later practised, slow land reform. I argued for the necessity of fast agrarian and other revolution, to forestall counter-reform. This was probably my first explicit critique of reformism from a more radical perspective. Marta had serious reservations about my thesis then and completely rejects it now. I also foretold that any economic integration of Latin America would help foreign investors more than local ones. All three articles were published in *Monthly Review* in the United States and the first and second respectively in *Politica* in Mexico and *Panorama Economico* in Chile. I started to direct myself first and foremost to a Latin American audience.

Upon marriage, we set off into the unknown. I wangled an invitation to a major reformist structuralist versus monetarist conservatism conference in Rio de Janeiro in January 1963. Albert Hirschman was there, but we arrived late because of visa problems and a bus stuck in the mud between the Brazilian-Uruguayan border and Puerto Alegre. By then, we wanted a curse on both their conservative and reformist houses. We increasingly saw the reformist house as no more than a remodelled capitalist one. We thought it was necessary to replace this reformist house with a different socialist house.

Just how much tearing down and rebuilding this change of houses might involve was less than clear.

This was the time of the Cuban revolution and of President Kennedy's response through the reformist Alliance for Progress. At its Punta del Este meeting, Che Guevara called the American initiative "the latrinization" of Latin America. These political issues of development put ECLA/CEPAL-type structuralism on the political economic agenda. They called for some land, tax, administrative, educational, health (including latrines), and other reforms and/or social development. However, this agenda was more theoretical than practical. It was not designed to overcome the political obstacles to reform, but to maintain them. Imputing the terms of this book backwards, we might say that the development policy, not to mention praxis, remained too inequitable and inefficient. Nor did its North and Latin American political sponsors have much confidence in their own announced policies: they offered reforms with one hand, and with the other they trained the Latin American armed forces to fight against guerrillas and the police forces to repress popular demonstrations and to torture civilians.

We still welcomed any proposed reforms, but considered them insufficient if not altogether unworkable. We regarded this social development to be inadequately attractive, we condemned the military and police repression of popular demands, and we put our confidence instead in the Cuban way. Of course, Cuba *was developing socially*, visibly improving education and health, reducing race and gender discrimination, etc. It was not yet clear that this social development was not being matched by or grounded on a concomitant development of its economic base. The inadequate or incorrect Cuban development of this economic base would ultimately make the continued social development dependent on massive foreign subsidy.

In a sense, the Cuban experience has been a test of the Ted Schultz et al. (and earlier Gunder Frank) thesis that the prior development of human capital through education, health, and improved social relations would then lead to social *and* economic development. The often-noted social development success in Cuba and to a lesser extent in other socialist countries has not proven to be enough for viable economic development. On the contrary, Cuba and other socialist countries now have to rein in their social welfare states because their insufficiently developed economies cannot afford them. Ironically, that is what Ronald Reagan and Margaret Thatcher argue at home as well. Indeed, they now argue that *less* social development is necessary for *more* economic development!

But to return to our story, after the 1962–63 Sino-Soviet split and their lengthy document debates, we also accepted the Chinese line, since it appeared more revolutionary. The line and praxis of the Soviet and Soviet-aligned Latin American Communist parties were too reformist. Indeed, in praxis they were hardly distinguishable from "national bourgeois" and

ECLA/CEPAL reformism. The only big difference was that the former did, and the latter did not, refer to American imperialism as an obstacle to development in Latin America and elsewhere in the Third World.

Gunder wrote, but Marta discussed and typed, an article on "Aid or Exploitation?" It countered the conservative claim of Lincoln Gordon, the American ambassador to Brazil (who was later implicated in and supportive of the 1964 military coup) that foreign aid helped Brazil much. The article also rebutted the more reformist reply that aid only helped a little, as Roberto Campos, the Brazilian ambassador to the United States (whom I met at lunch in Rio and who subsequently became minister of Planning for the military government), had suggested in a response to Gordon. Our article contained the then radical proposition and figures to show that Brazil and Latin America in fact were net capital exporters to the United States, which far from aiding them, thereby exploited them. At the same time, Hamza Alavi published a similar article about aid to Pakistan; we began exchanging our writings and corresponding about them. The leading Rio daily *Jornal do Brasil* gave my article a whole page, and it was republished about a dozen times. The article created a political storm and led to our invitation to the Brazilian Congress by Leonel Brizola and to the homes of other progressive parliamentarians.

We had moved to Brasilia for jobs (Gunder in anthropology and Marta in the library) in the new university there. These positions were offered to us by the university's anthropologist founder-president Darcy Ribeiro before he became Goulart's interior minister (Jefe da Casa Civil). (Later, after the military coup, I visited both Brizola and Darcy in their Uruguayan exile. Our relations with Darcy became closer in Venezuela and Chile, where he advised Allende before he became lieutenant governor and Brizola governor of Rio de Janeiro upon Brazil's return to democracy. However, we always found their pragmatic political reformism insufficiently revolutionary).

In Brasil, I, Gunder, also wrote an article on the foreign investment "Mechanisms of Imperialism" to counter the gospel according to which the Third World needed foreign investment and capital aid because the principal obstacle to its development was its shortage of capital. I countered this universally accepted supply-side theory with the essentially Keynesian demand-side argument that the real economic obstacle was insufficient market demand for productive national investment. The same kind of Keynesian and structuralist argument also underlay the policies of Brazilian and other nationalists, like Celso Furtado. However, I criticized Furtado, the founder of SUDENE, who was then minister of planning before the military replaced him with Campos. I argued that his and others' policies of structural reform were insufficient to expand the internal market and generate development.

At the University of Brasilia, Ruy Mauro Marini, Theotonio dos Santos, and his wife, Vania Bambirra, were my students, and Marta was Vania's.

None of us had yet thought of what would become of our dependence theory. Of course, neither could we then know how Latin American and our own political developments would later entangle our personal, intellectual, and political paths. We met again in their exile in Mexico and Chile and after the coup in the latter; we even met Marini in Germany. All three of them are now back at the University of Brasilia.

FROM DUALISM TO DEPENDENCE (WITH APOLOGIES TO BEN HIGGINS ET AL.)

I wrote my first three theoretical works in Brasilia and later in Rio, where our first son was born in 1963. They were directed at once against development theory and policy derived from (or camouflaged by) neoclassical and monetarist development theory; against Keynesian and structuralist explanations; and against CEPAL/ECLA Alliance for Progress, and orthodox Marxist and Communist Party theory, policy, and praxis. I put them all in the same sack. The reason was that, whatever their differences, the proponents of these ideas all shared the view that underdevelopment was original or traditional. They all posited that development would result from gradual reforms in dual economies/societies, in which the modern sector would expand and eliminate the traditional one. In a word, we quarrelled with them more about their vision of underdevelopment than about their vision of development itself. We did not then find it remarkable that all also shared the essentially similar vision that capital accumulation through industrial growth equals development. Because so did we! One of the subsequent critiques of our dependence paradigm change from Rostow to Gunder Frank was that I only turned orthodoxy on its head. Doing so evaded and rendered impossible any other fundamental *sideways* critique and reformulation, which we now regard as necessary.

The first of the three works argued against dualism. It went into battle especially against the then left-right-and-centre dominant version according to which Brazilian and Latin American (traditional) agriculture is feudal and that therefore capitalist reform was the order of the day. Half the Portuguese version was published by Caio Prado Jr. in his *Revista Brasiliense* before the 1964 military coup closed it down. The English version was then included in my *Capitalism and Underdevelopment in Latin America*.[32] I also wrote a book review critique and auto-critique entitled "Destroy Capitalism – Not Feudalism."[33]

The second theoretical work in 1963 was a much farther ranging critique of received theories. It was revised in 1965–66. After a dozen rejections, it was finally published in 1967 in the student magazine *Catalyst* under the title "The Sociology of Development and the Underdevelopment." The critique targeted the theories of all my former friends at Chicago, like Bert Hoselitz and Manning Nash, as well as acquaintances or not at MIT, like Rostow and

McClelland. In particular, I rejected the notion of "original" underdevelopment, "traditional" society, and subsequent "stages of growth," as well as development through non-Parsonian social pattern variables and neo-Weberian cultural and psychological change. I found this new sociology of development to be "empirically invalid when confronted with reality, theoretically inadequate in terms of its own classical social scientific standards, and policy-wise ineffective for underdeveloped countries."[34] In the late 1960s and I suppose independently, Suzanne Johas-Bodenheimer[35] wrote a similar critique. Since I was rejecting all dualism (also in another essay under the title "Dialectical, Not Dual Society,")[36] I threw Ben Higgins's technological dualism in for good measure, although I confess that I never understood it well then and still don't now. In his answer to the Ben White essay quoted in the epigraph, Ben Higgins argues (almost persuasively) that his version of dualism should never have been included in what I was trying to reject.

The third work in 1963 was an extension from the second in the same manuscript. I sought to develop an *alternative* reading, interpretation, and theory of *the development of underdevelopment*. I saw it as the result of *dependence* and as the opposite side of the coin (turning things on their head) of development within a *single world capitalist system*. All of these ideas and terms were in the original 1963 manuscript, which was not published until 1975 by Oxford University Press in India under the title *On Capitalist Underdevelopment*.[37] The 1963 manuscript began: "Underdevelopment is not just the lack of development. Before there was development there was no underdevelopment ... [They] are also related, both through the common historical process that they have shared during the past several centuries and through their mutual, that is reciprocal, influence that they have had, still have, and will continue to have, on each other throughout history."[38]

The second chapter went on to examine "The History and Sociology of Underdevelopment" in Asia, Africa, and Latin America (and even in the South of North America) after arguing: "Though it may be predicting if not prejudging our results a little, we may conveniently begin our inquiry with a historical experience which all, or certainly almost all, of today's underdeveloped areas have in common: their incorporation into and subsequent participation in the worldwide expansion of the mercantilist and/or capitalist system."[39]

The third and main chapter "On Capitalist Underdevelopment" began:

The central thesis of this essay may now be discussed in greater detail. My thesis is that underdevelopment as we know it today, and economic development as well, are the simultaneous and related products of the development on a world-wide scale and over a history of over more than four centuries at least of a single integrated economic system: capitalism ... The interpretation of underdevelopment and development as the related mechanisms and products of the development of the single capitalist system over the centuries raises a host of theoretical, empirical, and terminological problems.

Some of these are examined in the theoretical section of this essay below under the following titles: (a) Capitalism and Feudalism – one does not universally follow the other; (b) Capitalism and Mercantilism – their unity is more important than their differences; (c) Capitalism and Colonialism/Imperialism – capitalism inevitably takes some colonial/imperial form, but the form changes with the circumstances; (d) Capitalism and Internal Colonialism – essentials of the colonial relation inevitably occur within states as well as between them; (e) Capitalism and Exploitation/Diffusion ...; (f) Capitalism and Class vs Stratification ...; (g) Capitalism and Development/Underdevelopment [setting out my main thesis]...; (h) Capitalism and Socialism – socialism is the escape from the exploitation and underdevelopment ...; (i) Capitalism and Liberation – escape from underdevelopment and subsequent development is no longer possible for them as part of the capitalist system, and only liberation through socialist revolution offers that possibility.[40]

Today, I would have to significantly revise only the last two of these theses, and then only the half of them referring to what socialism *can* do.

Much of the historical material and many of the ideas in this manuscript were copied, albeit in reformulated form, from other Latin American writers, like the Argentinean Sergio Bagu and the Brazilian Caio Prado Jr., who recognized and appreciated my formulations. I similarly used and cited the writings of Celso Furtado and the Chilean Anibal Pinto (both of whom I met in Brazil), but both always rejected my writings and me personally (especially the latter who spent years deriding and combatting what he called my "catastrophism").

In short, it was quite a task for us at the time first to pose these questions, then to rethink the answers, and finally to persuade others to rethink both. Yet a decade and a half later in England, our by then more or less fifteen-year-old sons were able to cut through to the heart of the matter in one fell swoop. Both had the good judgment never to read any of my stuff or anything similar. Yet one day out of the blue, Paulo made his own discourse on imperialism and underdevelopment (which sounded to me like Marx, Hobson, Luxemburg, Lenin, Baran, and even Frank, none of whom he had ever read, rolled into one). And Paulo concluded with "if Latin America was a colony, it *could* not have been feudal!" It took me years to figure this out, and I never arrived at so clear and convincing a statement of it. About the same time in 1979, soon after we had arrived in England from Germany, our younger son Miguel observed "England is an *underdeveloping* country." I ran to my class to tell my British students, and their responses sounded stupefied or incredulous. After several years of British *deindustrialization* under the government of Mrs Thatcher, which took office in 1979, I repeated Miguel's earlier observation to a later generation of students, who then reacted "of course."

Returning to our story in 1963, I also wrote a long (still available) letter to Rodolfo Stavenhagen, who would later become famous for his "Seven Erroneous Theses." In my letter to him, I criticized his work prior to these and set out the alternative dependency analyses I wanted to develop. At the Brazilian Anthropological Society meetings in Sao Paulo in 1963, I criticized my fellow round table participants Fernando Henrique Cardoso, Octavio Ianni, Mauricio Vinhas, and others for their views on dual society and development. I argued for an analysis of the *relations* among these dependence socio-economic sectors and of their dependence on the outside. On 1 July 1964, by then already back in Chile, I wrote an also still-available, twelve-page, single-space mimeographed letter to a dozen friends in the United States recounting my political change of heart and my theoretical change of mind up to that time. I also set out a program of research and writing for the future, some but not all of which came to pass. (This private letter along with the published article on mechanism of imperialism was subsequently cited in a letter to me by the United States government as the ideological reasons and supposedly legal grounds for which I was then, and for fifteen years more after that, inadmissible to the United States.)

In 1964, also in Chile, I was given a one-month contract as a consultant to the Social Affairs Division of CEPAL/ECLA to write something for an upcoming conference on "popular participation." I wrote a long manuscript, part in English and part in Spanish. But the United Nations insisted on deleting its name from all of this "excessively radical" essay before distributing some copies to the conference participants. My contract, of course, was not renewed. Yet the essay quoted all sorts of UN declarations and documents to support my argument that governments should introduce a few reforms to permit and encourage people, including supposedly marginal but really participatory people, to work for their communities' self-development through politically self-empowering popular participation.

Since the United Nations then would have none this, I subsequently published much of this essay in separate parts. One was on "The Indian Problem," saying that it was created by the economy and society as a whole.[41] Another was on "Rural Economic Structure and Peasant Political Power."[42] The third was on "Urban Poverty in Latin America," also reprinted in *Latin America* as "Instability and Integration in Urban Latin America."[43] In this essay, my "excessively radical" thesis was that

it is possible to exaggerate the economic and socio-cultural importance of the urban-rural distinction. It may be useful, instead, to consider the distinction between what might be called the "stable" or well-structured and the "unstable" sectors of the economy; and the corresponding distinction between the "permanent" and the "floating" populations that are economically active or inactive in them ... [Both] exist in both the urban and rural environments ... [and] probably share a fairly similar economic structure and cause. Possibly more alike still are the rural and urban incumbents in these relatively "unstructured" and "unstable" roles. Certainly, they come from substantially the same socio-cultural group, especially if the society is a multi-racial or multi-ethnic one; and often they are the same individuals displaced from one environment to the other (and sometimes back again). Moreover, they occupy a large variety of these roles simultaneously or in quick succession, shifting rapidly and easily among the "unstructured" roles, but not between these and the more "structured" ones.[44]

What bitter irony that this same unstructured and unstable "informal" sector was discovered in Kenya a decade later by the United Nations International Labour Organization, five years after it too had fired me as excessively radical. After that, the informal sector became formally established at the ILO and even at the World Bank, as we will observe below. My office mates during my brief stay at CEPAL/ECLA had been Gert Rosenthal and Adolfo Gurrieri, now its executive secretary and its director of the same division of social affairs, respectively.

For us, the upshot of all these theoretical and political reflections – and maybe of the unpleasant experiences in and with reformist institutions – was that continued participation in the same world capitalist system could only mean continued development of underdevelopment: that is, there would be neither equity, nor efficiency, nor economic development. The political conclusions, therefore, were to de-link from the system externally and to transit to self-reliant socialism internally (or some undefined international socialist cooperation) in order to make in- or non-dependent economic development possible. We hardly considered how such postrevolutionary economic and social development would then be promoted and organized, not to mention guaranteed. We left that for crossing-that-bridge-when-we-come-to-it. We also gave short shrift to how the necessarily not so democratic (pre)-revolutionary means might or might not promote or even preclude the desirable postrevolutionary end.

These early general ideas on dependent underdevelopment in the world as a whole then were my guides; the more specific analyses – "The Development of Underdevelopment in Chile" – was written there in 1964 at the invitation of Hugo Zemmelman for a special pre-election issue of the socialist party magazine Aurauco, of which he was editor. The issue was then devoted to a collection of Salvador Allende's speeches instead, and my essay remained unpublished for several more years. It had also been solicited by Jim O'Conner for Studies on the Left, but its publication there was vetoed by his co-editors, especially Eugene Genovese. He regarded the essay as far too radical. Later as colleagues in Canada, he regarded me personally as far too radical, vide his comments on me in his book In Red and Black, not to mention an even more uncomradely article in our university newspaper.[45]

The following "the personal is political" anecdotes from 1964 in Santiago, Chile, perhaps reveal a different side. I wrote a letter to the editor of the progressive daily *La Ultima Hora* defending Cassius Clay for changing his name, for black nationalist and religious reasons, to Mohammed Ali. I submitted an article to the same paper predicting an imminent military coup in Brazil, but they instead published one by their own editor-owner, Clodomiro Almeyda (later to become Allende's foreign minister), saying that all was well in Brazil. The coup came three weeks later. When it did, I recommended to the socialist-Communist FRAP alliance that it should engage the Brazilian Paulo Freyre, whom I had met in Brazil when he was only known in its northeast, to work in the 1964 FRAP presidential campaign in Chile. FRAP paid no attention, but the Christian democratic election winner, Eduardo Frei, subsequently engaged the co-religious Freyre to work for him. Since then, Freyre has probably done more to promote self-development than anyone else in the world. In the meantime, I went to the Santiago airport to pick up Fernando Henrique Cardoso when he arrived as a Brazilian exile. On several occasions since, he told me appreciatively that he still regards this as more important and unifying than our supposed differences.

In 1964 we went to Mexico and in 1965 I wrote "The Development of Underdevelopment in Brazil" there. In 1966 I wrote the more general "The Development of Underdevelopment," whose original title continued "... and the Underdevelopment of Development." The essays on Chile and Brazil, along with some others, became my first book, *Capitalism and Underdevelopment in Latin America.*[46] However, I had to pass literally untold trials and tribulations before I was finally able to get it published in English in 1967, French in 1968, and Spanish only in 1970. The preface argued that "it will be necessary instead scientifically to study the real process of world capitalist development and underdevelopment" and that "*social* science must be *political* science."[47] The emphasis was in the original, which was dated (commemorating the Cuban revolution) on 26 July 1965. However, someone at the United States publisher changed the date of the preface from 1965 to 1966 to make it less distant from the long-delayed date of publication at the end of 1967.

FROM GENERALIZATION TO CRITIQUE AND APPLICATION

In Mexico, I initiated three new departures. I was the first professor at the National School of Economics of the National Autonomous University of Mexico to dream up and teach a course on economic (under)development of Latin America. I was the first person (after persuading the editors of *Comercio Exterior*, who had first rejected my "unorthodox" accounting procedures) to publish an accounting of Latin America's external payments and receipts, which distinguished between services and goods. That way, I clearly demonstrated that the Latin American current account deficit was due to a large deficit on service account, especially from financial service payments. These payments exceeded Latin America's surplus on commercial account of excess exports over imports of goods.[48] My "unorthodox" novelty itself subsequently became a new orthodoxy, which became particularly important in the now standard calculations of the ratio of debt service to export earnings. My third initiative was to organize prominent progressive Latin American economists to sign a statement on "The Need for New Teaching and Research of Economics in Latin America," based on its dependence.[49] I had drafted this statement with my colleague Arturo Bonilla and the Columbian Jose Consuegra, who later published it and dozens of my articles in his journal *Desarrollo Indoamericano*. As I recall, Celso Furtado refused to sign the statement.

In Mexico, I engaged in a number of debates about theoretical and political issues of development. At the School of Political and Social Science, whose director then was Pablo Gonzalez Casanova, I roundly criticized his recently published book *La Democracia en Mexico*[50] for being scientifically and politically unacceptable. We only made up again years later. I also debated about capitalism or feudalism (my title was "With What Mode of Production Does the Hen Lay Its Golden Eggs") in the Sunday supplement of a national newspaper with my Argentinean colleague, Rodolfo Puiggros. At the same time, Luis Vitale was making the same argument against the thesis of Latin American feudalism in Chile. Then, I began work on a "History of Mexican Agriculture from Conquest to Revolution." However, I eventually (in 1966 in Canada) wrote only on the first century of the same. My then still very controversial thesis was that Mexican agriculture (under)development was commercially driven from the beginning. I used the data of important previous analyses by the French writer François Chevalier[51] and the American historical geographer Woodrow Borah[52] to turn their own theses upside down. I sent the manuscript to Borah, and he wrote me that, because I did not use primary sources, my history was not worth publishing. So I did not publish it until over a decade later.[53] Borah wrote a review of the book, saying that it should not have been published because it was old hat. Indeed, as Leal and Huacuja[54] had demonstrated, in the meantime, further historical research and analysis had converted my far-out unorthodoxy of the 1960s into the orthodoxy of the 1980s. Before leaving Mexico, I also did some practical community development work in the field.

In Mexico, on our way to Cuba, which would never accept us, our second son was born. Gerrit Huizer was the first to appear at the hospital. Since then, he worked with and wrote about peasants all over Latin America and other parts of the world.[55] He is still helping us, with comments on this essay as well as on our other ones on social movements. Alonso Aguilar and Fernando

Carmona befriended us professionally, politically, and personally. We also saw Harry and Beatie Magdoff in Mexico before they joined our editor, friend, and helper Paul Sweezy at *Monthly Review*. Magdoff then arranged for a financial grant from the Rabinowitz Foundation to keep our bodies and souls together and to permit my writing these things in Mexico, where the university paid me too little and too late.

We visited Ben Higgins in Cuernavaca in 1964 and again in 1967 in Montreal, where we went in 1966 for lack of another job in Mexico. Bert Hoselitz came to visit us in Montreal after reading and declining to publish the still-unpublished "The Sociology of Development and the Underdevelopment of Sociology," which criticized Bert, Ben, and others so much. (Someone once said that I had really wanted to kill my father figure, Bert. But then it was also said that Fidel Castro made a revolution against the Yankees because they would not accept him as a major league baseball pitcher.)

In 1967, we returned for a vacation to Santiago, Chile. There we found our exiled Brazilian friends Theotonio dos Santos, Vania Bambirra, and Fernando Henrique Cardoso, and the latter's co-author Enzo Faletto. Faletto had been Marta's friend since the 1950s, and in 1964 he commented on my Chile manuscript as duly acknowledged in my preface. The Peruvian Aníbal Quijano (who had brought us together in 1962) also arrived in Santiago. All were now critically reading and discussing Regis Debray's recently published guerrilla focus pamphlet *Revolution in the Revolution*. His and my French publisher, François Maspero, claimed that my book provided the "scientific" basis for Debray's. Our friends in Chile were writing their own dependence books at this time. Cardoso and Faletto wrote their *Dependence and Development in Latin America*,[56] and Theotonio dos Santos wrote various articles on dependence. However, Theotonio always maintained rather reformist leanings. Nonetheless, others called his writings and mine, and later also those of our other Brasilia friend Ruy Mauro Marini, "new" dependence writings, since they supposedly led to more "revolutionary" conclusions than Cardoso and Faletto's version of dependence. Cardoso, Faletto, and Quijano were working in departments of ECLA/CEPAL (and ILPES), whose inward-looking Latin American industrialization program was running out of steam. Therefore, Prebisch himself now recommended more radical reforms, and his younger co-workers all the more so. Still, in my *Lumpenbourgeoisie: Lumpendevelopment* (which was written and published in Spanish in eight different country editions before the English)[57] I argued that they did not go far enough. In this regard, I remember my argument with Oswaldo Sinkel, another CEPAL stalwart with first structuralist and then dependence positions. Oswaldo insisted that his and my positions were the same, and I insisted that they were not. The irony is that two decades later, after repeated meetings between us, Oswaldo now claims that we no longer share our by now changed views, while I think that we do.

However that may be, on the return trip from Santiago to Montreal in 1967, we finally got our first opportunity to visit Cuba. I went as *Monthly Review* correspondent to the first conference of the stillborn OLAS (Organization of Latin American Solidarity). In January 1968, I went again, this time as invited delegate to the International Congress of Intellectuals in Havana. I would go once again in 1972 as a member of the jury for the literary prize (in my case in the essay category) awarded annually by the Casa de las Americas, Cuba's premier cultural organization. We had a falling out, first because they blamed me for the prize being declared vacant that year and second because I criticized them for taking insufficiently revolutionary positions regarding political literature. Later, my fellow jury member, the Catholic priest and poet Ernesto Cardinal (who would still later become revolutionary Nicaragua's minister of culture), published part of our private conversation in the memoirs of his Cuba trip. He quoted me as saying that our host organization, the Casa de las Americas, "was shitty before, and is more so now." I was never invited back to Cuba and only went again in 1981 as a member of the Chilean delegation to the Second Congress of Third World Economists (because I had been a member at the first one in Algiers in 1976, where I told Celso Furtado to his visible dismay that by then we both had nothing useful left to say).

However revolutionary any of us may or may not have been (or thought him/herself to be) then, it is evident looking back now that none of us, of course, was sufficiently "revolutionary" to incorporate the special dependence of women in patriachal society into our general dependence theory. That is a matter to which we will have to pay more attention below.

FROM PRODUCTION TO CONSUMPTION OF DEPENDENCE (WITH APOLOGIES TO OUR FRIEND FERNANDO HENRIQUE CARDOSO)

So far we have reviewed some of the economic, socio-political, and personal context of some of the conflicting, cooperating, and compounding *production* of dependence theory. Cardoso said we should not use the term "theory" but only "approach." However, Cardoso[58] then also talked and wrote about the consumption of dependence theory. Dependence theory prospered, despite early and continued rejection, resistance, and attacks. This alternative approach found little favour with the orthodox right, some of the structuralist reformist left, the Soviet aligned Communists, Trotskyists, and soon also the Maoists. Nonetheless, dependence was "consumed" in Latin America and elsewhere.

In Latin America, dependence (and I) were enshrined at the Latin American Congress of Sociology in Mexico in 1969 under the presidency of Pablo Gonzalez Casanova. He was the same person whose book I had criticized four years earlier in Mexico and who in between had been rector of the National University there. At the Congress of Latin American Economists in Maracaibo, Venezuela, resistance was much fiercer. Indeed, we were run out of town. In 1965 we had already sent the above-mentioned letter to about a hundred economists about the need for new (read dependence) economics teaching and research in Latin America. However, students, political groups, and parties, and eventually some of the press, all over the continent took up and fought about the battle cry of dependence. Of course, the reason for all this was Cuba and the progress of its revolution and the attempts to copy it elsewhere. Dependence theory and writing, including mine, also made a notable impact on and through "liberation theology," which was and still is spread through Catholic Church groups in Latin America. The Canadian theologian Christopher Lind claims that the Canadian Conference of Catholic Bishops "appropriated the analysis of Andre Gunder Frank on the basis of his ethics, not his Marxism."[59]

Moreover, dependence theory was also consumed elsewhere – in North America, Western Europe, and by slower and lesser degrees in Africa and Asia, but hardly in the socialist countries. There was also a reason for that consumption: Vietnam. The war and Vietnamese resistance and successes after the 1968 Tet offensive against the United States and its client government in the South mobilized people everywhere. Interest was especially great among potential draftee students and other young people in the United States itself. An (perhaps any) alternative to orthodoxy about the Third World could only be welcome, and it was soon consumed by social scientists as well.

As thirdworldism prospered in the West and in the South as well, my writings on dependence et al. were published in over twenty languages. These publications now include well over 100 different editions of my books, chapters in over 100 edited volumes, and some 600 versions of articles, many reprinted a dozen and more times. We refer to only a small portion of these publications here. There were also objections to and critiques of my writings. For instance, one writer complained about "Gunder Frank being exalted to authoritative status in [Bipan Chandra's] presidential address ... at the Indian History Congress" and another sought "to fire a red warning flare [against] importing Gunder Frank into Africa." We will return to critiques below.

In the meantime, modernization theory was also increasingly self-destructing. It did so with a little help from us, more from its friends, and most from the supposedly modernizing people themselves, who responded by revolting against their changing conditions in the course of world accumulation and development. Even Henry Kissinger pronounced modernization bankrupt after the Ayatollah Khomeini defeated the super-modernizing and super-armed Shah of Iran in 1979. Khomeini used nary a bullet and renounced the goals of Western-style modernization and "development."

FROM SOME MORE ANTHROPOLOGY AND DEPENDENCE TO A WORLD SYSTEM

Still keeping a finger in the anthropological pie, I also wrote to the founder-editor of *Current Anthropology*, Sol Tax, and other anthropologist friends to initiate the "Responsibility in Anthropology" debate, whose opening gun was the above-cited.[60] Some of us wanted to use anthropology to support instead of combat guerrillas in Indochina and other "developing" regions. I argued against liberal anthropology and for liberation anthropology.[61] The debate took on some significance, with Maggie Mead now on the other side. The scope of the debate extended from anthropologist advisers in Indochina and Thailand to the annual meetings and mushrooming teach-ins in the United States, which were originally invented for that purpose by the anthropologist Eric Wolf and his colleagues and students at the University of Michigan.

In another debate, I put a curse on both the formalist (microeconomic) and substantivist (institutionalist) houses in economic anthropology. I argued that neither took proper account of the effects of colonialism and imperialism on underdevelopment and on the people they studied. The journal printed a "reply" by George Dalton saying that there is no use replying to someone "as full of anger and ideology." Later, I returned to the theme of "liberation anthropology" in an article entitled "Anthropology = Ideology, Applied Anthropology = Politics" written for the 1973 International Congress of Anthropological and Ethnological Sciences in Chicago, for which the US government denied me an entry visa.[62]

In the meantime, still in Montreal, Said Shah and I put together, like a jigsaw puzzle, an anthology/reader constructing a dependence theory and analysis for all of the Third World. The reader was to have two or three volumes dealing with the past, present, and future. The first volume was finished. It began with a critique of received development theory using, among others, selections from Alexander Hamilton and Friedrich List. The next part on *theory = history* traced the development of a single capitalist world system. Then came parts which analysed within that same system the development of underdevelopment in each of Latin America, Africa, the middle east-north Africa, and Asia, with separate sections for India, China, southeast Asia, and Japan.

The last two sections drew heavily on Cliff Geertz's *Agricultural Involution: The Process of Ecological Change in Indonesia*.[63] Geertz countered Boeke's version of dualism and instead demonstrated how stage by stage Indonesia became underdeveloped through its colonialized participation in the world capitalist system. We also used Geertz's chapter contrasting Java and Japan. This contrast supported our argument (also based on Lockwood and Norman) that Japan was never *underdeveloped*, precisely because it was never economically or politically colonialized. So it is easy to explain how I could like Geertz's book, to which Ben had written the foreword. However, I failed to be adequately impressed by its reference to *ecological* change, or anti-development as Ben would now call it.

In the preface to our reader, we had expressed our hope that our book would soon make itself unnecessary and out of date. We hoped that its dependence message would soon be accepted and improved upon by others. I have always regarded this reader as my magnum opus. Alas, our book never saw the light of day. Mainstream publishers refused to publish it because, as some admitted, it was too radical for them, and smaller progressive publishers could not do it because it was too expensive for them and/or because they could not yet see the coming wave of dependence consumption and new production, which indeed outdated our book without us. Nonetheless, in the mid-1970s I noted that this kind of analysis was only just beginning to be made in Asia. Therefore, I again tried to get at least the sections' introduction and table of contents published as an article. However, even that failed. I finally placed the latter in an appendix of my essays collected as *Critique and Anti-Critique*.[64]

In 1968 we returned to Chile via "May 1968" in Paris, etc. Marta and the children went first, and I followed after signing on for an ILO project there. On arrival at the airport, I was detained and taken into town to see the head of the political police and his almost foot-high file on me. He sent me back out to the airport to be put on the next plane out. None left, however, before Pedro Vuscovic from CEPAL/ECLA (and later the controversial economics minister of Allende) brought the latter out to the airport to bring me back in under his authority as president of the Senate and therefore second in command in the country. The ILO then made a deal with the minister of the interior to withdraw me again. I refused to go, was fired after a month by the ILO, and got a job at the University of Chile. After repeated additional interventions by Allende, I received permission to remain in Chile.

I sat down in 1968–69 to write the theoretical introduction to the ill-fated "Reader on Underdevelopment." It addressed various inside and outside, friendly and unfriendly, critiques of dependence. I recast the whole question in terms of the historical development of the world system as a whole. In my 1963 manuscript, in my 1964 mimeographed letter, and in my 1965 preface to my first book, I had already written that underdevelopment through dependence was only a part of this whole capitalist world economic system. So now, in 1969–73, in ever-longer draft after draft, this "introduction" became my history and analysis of this capitalist world system as a whole. One publisher after another had refused the reader (though Cambridge University Press offered to do the first volume on the condition, among others, that we put "a Marxist view" in the title, which we refused to do).

Therefore, I decided to convert the theoretical introduction into a separate book. I rewrote it several times (while simultaneously also discussing and writing about current economic and political policy in Chile) until the military coup there put an end to my endeavours. However, no one was willing to publish this world system book manuscript until 1978, although Penguin Books had signed and then reneged on a contract to do so much earlier. The manuscript was finally divided into two parts, published separately as *World Accumulation 1492–1789* and *Dependent Accumulation and Underdevelopment.*[65] The former laid great stress on the role of long world economic cycles and crises of capital accumulation in shaping world development and underdevelopment.

As I completed my writing in Chile, I received a draft of the first volume of Wallerstein's *Modern World System.*[66] The publisher asked me to write a blurb for its dust jacket. I did and said the book would become an instant classic. It did. Dos Santos also said that we (in the Third World) have to study the whole system ourselves and proceeded to write on contemporary American imperialism. Samir Amin published his *Accumulation on a World Scale,*[67] of which he had written a draft for his PhD fifteen years before. These studies on *accumulation in the world system* reflected the ongoing changes in world development. They were one of the strands of new development thinking responses.

FROM CRITIQUES OF DEPENDENCE AND GUNDER FRANK ...

More academic and policy debates on equity and efficiency in economic development were going on elsewhere since the mid-1970s. On the left, dependence theory succumbed to the coup in Chile, as we will see below. Right, centre, and left (social democratic, Communist, Maoist, Trotskyist, and other) critiques abounded. I reviewed some one hundred of them dedicated totally or partially to my own writings in 1972. The list of critiques was updated in 1977 (but has grown to well over two hundred since), and my reply was reprinted as "Answer to Critics."[68] A sample of some of these "critiques" hold that I am a "theorist of an anarchic left," "provocateur," "diversionist," "confusionist," "divisionist" ... "pseudo-marxist." For one side, I am the principal "ideologist of terrorism in Latin America," and for the other, a "cat's paw of the CIA." One of my honourable academic critics went so far as to say in a public lecture in Poland that I had been in charge of exterminating Jews in a Nazi concentration camp there during the Second World War. (We may recall that at war's end, I was sixteen and still in high school in the United States.) Recurrent more-academic critiques were that my analysis was supposedly "circulationist" (demand side?) instead of "productivist" (supply side?) and therefore insufficiently – or altogether un-Marxist.

Very few of the often extremely esoteric academic and/or very interested political critiques have hit the real marks and weaknesses of dependence theory. The latter have, however, become (part of) my/our own later auto-critique:

1   Real dependence exists, of course, and more than ever despite denials to the contrary. However, dependence theory and policy never answered the question of how to eliminate real dependence and pursue the chimera of non- or independent growth.
2   Dependence heterodoxy nonetheless maintained the "obvious" orthodoxy that (under)development must refer to and be organized by and through (nation-state) societies, countries, or regions. However, this orthodox tenet turns out to be wrong.
3   We turned orthodoxy on its head, but we maintained the essence of the thesis that economic-growth-through-capital-accumulation equals development. Thereby, the socialist and dependence heterodoxies locked themselves into the same traps as the development orthodoxy. Therefore, we precluded any real alternative definitions, policy, and praxis of "development."
4   In particular, this orthodoxy incorporated the patriarchal gender structure of society as a matter of course. However much we may personally have been against male chauvinism, we therefore prevented examination of this dimension of dependence.

... TO DEPENDENCY ALTERNATIVES FROM THE LEFT

Supposedly progressive critiques of dependence and more-of-the same replacements came from the left. Some came in the form of inward-looking involution, which proposed to study all kinds of micro problems and regions and their "modes of production." The hope was to better analyse the local class structure, and thereby learn how to change it. Other alternatives were outward-looking extensions of dependence, which sought instead to analyse the whole world system. The former were largely stillborn as the world economic and political crisis itself changed the nature and direction of the struggle (of which more below). The latter generated little practical policy, as analysts of the world system lagged behind its rapid transformation which was generated by the crisis. Even so, I sought to predict it (of which also more below, e.g., "Let's Not Wait for 1984!").[69] Another variant, or combination of the above, involved making comparative studies of the internal and external conditions in some European and overseas settler economies. These studies sought to explain how these economies *avoided* dependent peripheralization and underdevelopment.[70]

FROM SOME LESSONS OF THE CHILEAN
EXPERIMENT VERSUS DEPENDENCE ...

In Chile in the meantime, Allende's attempt to introduce socialist reform and reformist socialism came and went between 1970 and 1973. It had our active but altogether undistinguished small-time participation. But it was an exciting time in which everybody debated every kind of economic, social, and political issue of equity and efficiency in economic development. All of these issues arose daily in a concrete way and took on political form. The Allende government drew substantially on dependence thinking and tried to introduce anti-dependence measures. Allende also sought, but failed to receive, Soviet socialist support for the same.

Achieving equity and efficiency in economic development praxis was more difficult than in theory. To begin with, as President Allende never tired of pointing out, he was in government but not in power. That is why we thought the peaceful reformist way would not do. Even to capture and re-direct the "potential surplus" was not so easy. It also turned out that improving equity by redistributing income was not so easy. The resulting change in the structure of consumer demand did not translate into a new structure of production. Thus, efficiency did not increase, except through lower unemployment. However, equity and social development took leaps and bounds as the people gained dignity and popular education. Political participation and democracy mushroomed like never before in Chile and perhaps elsewhere.

However, microeconomic neoclassical "efficiency" considerations did operate to keep the macroeconomy going: Sergio Ramos, the Communist Party economist representative on the interministerial economic committee, and our colleague, friend, and neighbour, came over to explain why prices had to rise (to get them right?). He also explained why the now nationalized banks had to continue lending credit to the self-same enterprises: they had to prevent them from going out of business. If they did, they would create more shortages, renewed unemployment, and greater political problems. In 1972–73, we saw success as increasingly difficult and doubtful. Domestic problems were growing and international ones were insufficiently appreciated. Kissinger and Nixon had just gone to Beijing and Moscow, making a detente pact with Brezhnev, who abandoned Chile as part of the bargain.

At CESO, our institute at the University of Chile (where Gunder was researcher and Marta librarian), dos Santos, Marini, Pio Garcia, Marta Harneker, and many others debated the ins and outs of the transition to the transition to socialism. I (Gunder) made myself unpopular by warning that we should rather worry about the coming reaction and the possible transition to fascism.

In 1972, at the UNCTAD III meetings in Santiago, I heard "development of underdevelopment" sloganized by establishment Third World delegates from afar. So we decided it was time for us to move on. In the same "UNCTAD" building a few months later, I gave a paper at the Latin American Congress of Sociology. It was entitled "Dependence Is Dead, Long Live Dependence and the Class Struggle." The message was that dependence itself was alive and kicking, but that the usefulness of dependence theory for political action had come and gone. That was true at least in Latin America. More/better class struggle was supposed to be on the agenda. Of course, more class struggle certainly would come. But it hardly became better, since it came in the form of military coups and repression in Chile and elsewhere.

A few months later, still in 1972, I went to Rome via Dakar. I stopped off in Dakar for a conference at which Samir Amin, who had also visited us in Santiago, wanted to introduce dependence theory to Africans. Then in Rome in September 1972, I announced that the world had entered a new Kondratieff B-period of crisis. I said that the socialist countries were starting to reintegrate in the capitalist world economy. I also repeated that not dependence theory but the analysis of the world crisis of capital accumulation was then on the analytical and theoretical agenda.[71] I, Gunder, would spend the next sixteen years full time on this agenda, writing several crisis books.[72] Alas, all that was to no avail. However, I, Marta, was moved by this same crisis *and other considerations and movements* (to be reviewed below) to revise my thinking – to better purpose.

... TO THE REACTION AND CHICAGO BOYS IN CHILE

The Chilean experimental laboratory (already in Christian Democratic President Frei's centre-right and Allende's centre-left times) has also been exemplary in more recent times. Chile was again important in development theory, praxis, our own experience and thinking, and the connection among all of these. Dependence theory and policy was dead indeed. General Pinochet decapitated it with his sword on 11 September 1973. Then he instituted an ultra-right counter-revolution and reform. Still confined at home by the twenty-four-hour post-coup curfew before we left for Germany, Gunder made several predictions to Marta. (1) Politically, the coup would be very bloody – inequitable, in the terms of this volume. However, the reality of 30,000 dead and countless disappeared and tortured to this day exceeded even my worst expectations. (2) Economically, Chilean agriculture would become another California – if that is efficiency. Now we have seen Chilean fruit in supermarkets not only here in Amsterdam, but also in Tokyo, Hawaii, and, yes, in California itself. In terms of development theory and praxis, Chile became a major example of export-led growth (albeit not much in manufactures, except for cluster bombs and other arms sold to Iraq and elsewhere).

The midwife for this transformation was Milton Friedman's monetarism carried to Chile by himself, Arnold Harberger, and the Chicago Boys (Chile's version of the Berkeley mafia in Indonesia, which Ben Higgins will remember). The new policies were imposed by General Pinochet as "equilibrium on the point of a bayonet" – that was the subtitle of my *Economic Genocide in Chile*, which started as two open letters to my former professors at Chicago, Milton Friedman and Arnold Harberger.[73] My open letters also recalled the arrival of the first Chilean students under Harberger's direction at Chicago while I was trying (and failed) to write a dissertation under his direction in the mid-1950s. I recalled that the Chicago line had argued in the mid-1950s, in the name of the efficiency of resource allocation, that Chile should abandon its relatively equitable social welfare system. Meeting Al Harberger again in Chile itself in 1964, I had argued against his contention that subsidizing urban bus fares was inefficiently misallocating resources. I claimed that lowered bus fares only helped a bit to redress other inequities and other inefficiencies of resource allocation, whose marginal cost did not equal either marginal revenue or price. In his militarized Chile, General Pinochet gave the Chicago Boys free reign over economic policy. Therefore, it was only natural for Friedman and Harberger to come down and recommend their shock treatment therapy. Free-to-choose Friedman argued that the magic of the market (efficiency?) comes first and (equity?) freedom later, and he was awarded the Nobel Prize (only for economics, not for peace, thank God). However, Harvard refused to accept Harberger for his part in the whole sordid story. Yet, the World Bank still gives Chile the first pride of place for its model. For us, it has cost the assassination of literally countless personal friends, some still very recently.

Monetarist and neoclassical supply-side reactionary theory and the magic of the market policy, of course, swept around the world. They were enshrined in Reaganomics (which was actually started by Jimmy Carter in 1977) and Thatcherism (which was actually started by James Callaghan in 1976), and so forth. They also went on to get pride of place in Chile, Argentina, Uruguay, Israel, and to proceed into China, the Soviet Union, etc. The Four Tigers or Dragons in East Asia became the export-led growth model. However, the economic and political importance of the state in South Korea, and its political repression, go largely unmentioned, except when Korea made world headlines because of the 1988 Olympics. If export-led growth has been efficient there and in Taiwan, it is also thanks to the prior increase in the equity of the distribution of income and the domestic market. These were due in turn to the land reforms forcibly imposed by the United States as also in Japan. Unlike the World Bank and others, we took account of these exceptional political and strategic factors, which make these NICs experience a more unique than copyable model. We were also unable to recommend their hardly equitable political repression as a model. However, we perhaps underestimated their capacity for technological upgrading and new participation in the international division of labour.[74]

In 1974, I said and wrote that the Third World response to the new world economic crisis would be the economic (efficient?) world market export model.[75] I also predicted how and why this model would be ushered in and supported by military coups, martial law, emergency rule, etc. That is the economic model's (inequitable) political other side of the coin. It requires the physical and political repression not only of workers and their unions, but also of industrialists and others working for the internal market. Alas, events in South Korea, the Philippines, Thailand, Bangladesh, Pakistan, Chile, Uruguay, Argentina, and too many countries to name in between proved me sadly right. For documentation, see my *Crisis in the Third World* chapter 6 on the state and chapter 7 on political economic repression.[76] In many cases the political repression worked, but the export-led growth led to the Third World debt crisis (foretold in chapter 4) and to a depression worse than in the 1930s.

In 1972, I predicted,[77] and in 1976 I analyzed, the reincorporation of the socialist countries in the capitalist world economy.[78] However, it was still not clear that the "import-led growth" in the East European socialist NICs was essentially the same as export led growth in the East Asian NICs. The former export to import and the latter import to export. The difference has been that NIC growth in Eastern Europe has been less successful than in East Asia. Now the East Asian NICs outcompete the East Europeans in the world market and want to invade their domestic markets too. Export-led growth has been about equally unsuccessful in South America. But all things considered, the East European model is still politically less repressive and inequitable (except partially in Rumania) than in both capitalist NIC areas. Looking ahead, proposals to resolve the Third World debt crisis abound. However, hardly anyone ever asks how the South American and East European NICs can be competitive against the East Asian ones and others after the debt service of the first two made them fall behind in technological and other competition on the world market.

FROM BASIC NEEDS AND NIEO TO THE ECONOMIC AND DEVELOPMENT CRISIS

However, the ever-deepening world economic crisis also undid some new progressive theoretical and policy thinking by the more-of-the-same establishment, thinking evidenced by, for example, *Growth with Distribution* and "basic needs" (BN), which began at the Institute for Development Studies (IDS) at Sussex, England. BN was adopted or adapted by the International Labour Organisation of the United Nations. It was also taken up by the World Bank under Robert McNamara. After his 1973 speech in Nairobi, the bank began directing more funding to agriculture and ostensibly to the poor. In fact, most of its farm support went to middle peasants. Both the ILO and the UN also discovered the "informal" sector. So now it appeared better to put thumbs up at people who have to fend for themselves informally than to try to reduce their need for doing so.

The evidence has mounted (and was documented by Adelman and Morris)[79] that even fast growth had increasingly skewed the domestic distribution of income in one country after another. This pattern of growth bypassed to some degree or even impoverished absolutely the growing masses of very poor and hungry. At the time, the ILO estimated their numbers at 600 million worldwide. Therefore, the new basic-needs strategy for the Third World was to guarantee everyone a basic minimum livelihood of food, shelter, clothing, as well as in some versions health, education, etc. This had long since been the policy, if not always the practice, in socialist countries. The ever-deepening world economic crisis, however, soon left the practice of this BN policy increasingly in the breach in both South and East. By the early 1980s, the ILO estimate of the very poor had risen to 800 million, and by now it is probably about 1,000 million.

The other new "development" of the 1970s was the call for a New International Economic Order (NIEO). This was decided by the non-aligned countries at their meeting in Algiers in 1973. Then the group of 77 (soon 125 "developing" countries) pushed it through the United Nations as resolutions in 1974. The argument was (shades of dependence) that since the old international economic order hinders development, a new one is needed. This NIEO should offer the developing world better prices for their commodity exports, greater access to northern markets for their manufacturing exports (which according to the Lima target should reach 25 percent of the world total by the year 2000), more finance such as the link between world reserve creation and its distribution to the South (already demanded and negated at UNCTAD III in 1972), and greater group-of-77 participation in United Nations and world decision making.

NIEO was the subject of countless international negotiating conferences to which the North only came, as a French minister astutely observed, because OPEC (Organization of Petroleum Exporting Countries) had (temporarily) given the South enough bargaining power to get the North to sit down at the negotiating table. However, this new Third World bargaining power was still insufficient to make the North say yes, let alone to give anything away. On the contrary, the West always, and the East much of the time, voted no at all UN and other conferences. In the real world in the meantime, the growing world economic crisis made the old international economic order go from bad to worse, instead of better.[80]

For a while, there were arguments about whether NIEO demands were a clever diversionary tactic. Were the rich in the poor countries using NIEO finger pointing at international relations to avoid the domestic reforms necessary to guarantee BN? Or was it the reverse? Was BN a clever diversionary tactic by northern interests like the World Bank to avoid confronting the real need for NIEO? A few people, like Paul Streeten, pointed out that far from being alternatives, BN and NIEO were really necessary complements. I, Gunder, argued that they were neither, but only hot air pie in the sky.[81]

The onset of the Third World debt crisis since 1982, especially in Latin America and Africa, in fact resolved the issues. If there was anything new in the economic order, it was that it became far worse in praxis than the old order of the 1950s–1960s. For the South, the new order of the 1980s became worse even than that of the 1970s. As for BN, the relative distribution of income and the number and depth of absolute poor became far worse than before.

Unlike many of our friends, we had never regarded the multinational corporations and their foreign investment as the bugaboos. Those who hoped that the replacement of the multinationals' direct foreign investment by foreign loans by, and debt to, banks did or would reduce, let alone eliminate, dependence were certainly proven wrong. Now the debt crisis has vastly increased the foreign dependence, even of "sovereign" national states. Their trade, monetary, fiscal, and social or "development" policies are even more constrained now by foreign debt than they were before by foreign investment.

The debt is an instrument of neocolonization and drains "surplus" from part of the South. By our calculations, this flow of capital from South to North was over $500 billion US from 1983 through 1986. $200 billion through debt service, over $100 billion through capital flight, $100 billion through the 40 percent decline in the South's terms of trade, and $100 billion through normal remission of profits and royalty payments. Since then, this South to North capital flow has been another $300 billion or so.

Through much of the 1980s, the annual Third World debt service has been about 6.5 percent of its GNP. This percentage may be compared to perhaps 1 percent of GNP spent by the US on the Marshall plan or by the West on higher oil prices in the 1970s.

Even German war reparations in the 1920s only averaged 2 percent and rose to 3.5 percent in 1929–31, before they contributed to the rise of Hitler, who abrogated them.[82] In our reading of history, this drain is not new, but has always increased *somewhere* in the South during each (Kondratieff B-phase) economic crisis in the North.[83] As already observed in our opening paragraphs above, this time the drain has led to an economic depression more severe than that of the 1930s in Latin America and Africa. The result is not development, but the development of underdevelopment, this time with *disinvestment* in productive infrastructure and human capital and loss of competitiveness. As we also observed above, another result, therefore, is that the concept that economic growth equals development has practically disappeared from all but the most academic discussions. From the earlier crises of liberal, Keynesian, and structural development theories, we have gone to the total irrelevance and bankruptcy of neo-liberalism, post-Keynesianism, and neo-structuralism for development policy. In the real world, the order of the day has become only economic or debt-crisis management instead.

... AND THE CRISIS OF SOCIALISM
AND DE-LINKING TOO

In the meantime, other momentous events were taking place with still more far-reaching implications and consequences for development and development thinking. One was the crisis in socialist development, and the other was the related failure of Third World de-linking and self-reliance in practice. Momentous changes occurred in the largest country of the Third, socialist, and entire world. In China the cultural revolution proved a failure sometime between 1971 and 1976 (although its human costs did not become clear abroad until later). Mao and Chou En Lai died in 1976. After three years interregnum and the unmasking of the Gang of Four, a new period of anti-Maoist reforms began in late 1978. Then followed the de-collectivization of agriculture, effective privatization first of agricultural production and then of some trade and industry. First some special economic zones and then much of the coastline were opened up to the West. After twenty years of stagnation and even decline in agricultural incomes, the 1980s have witnessed enormous increases in agricultural production and consumption. However, these changes have also brought on some seemingly typical capitalist inequities: more unemployment, serious inflation, growing regional and functional inequalities in income distribution, and threatening ecological degradation, all of which benefit some at the expense of others. China now participates in a *de facto* Beijing-Tokyo-Washington economic-political-strategic axis. China also went to war with Vietnam "to teach it a lesson."

All these and other developments obliged all the world, and even development thinkers, to rethink. In 1980, I began an article with this statement: "The events of 1979 in and between Kampuchea, Vietnam, and China oblige socialists to undertake an agonizing reappraisal."[84] They certainly obliged us to revise our own thinking about socialism, development, and democracy (of which more below).

Economic crisis, stagnation, recession, and even depression also visited some socialist countries of Eastern Europe. In part, these were home-grown problems inherent in the transition from extensive to intensive growth. In part, they reflected a conjuncture in the built-in political investment cycle. In part, they were the result of the importation of economic crisis, inflation, and debt from the West through the import-led growth of the 1970s. All these strands became entangled in the early 1980s, demonstrating that these socialist economies were not or no longer immune to the vagaries and costs of economic development in the world capitalist economy. We now know that the socialist economies are also subject to cycles and inflation, and will soon be subject to unemployment, not to mention inefficiency and inequity.

The decade following 1974 witnessed the "liberation" or "enslavement" (depending on the point of view) of fourteen countries in Indochina, the Gulf-Horn region of Africa, its ex-Portuguese colonies, and the Central American-Caribbean region. Gradual de-linking and self-reliance along the "non-capitalist road" of the 1950s and 1960s had previously led Indonesia, Syria, Egypt, Ghana, Guinea, Ujiama-model Tanzania, and so many others (excepting perhaps Algeria and until a few years later Burma) to a dead end before or by the 1970s. Now their new "socialism" or "socialist orientation" would lead these fourteen countries into another blind alley. Halfway down, several have already made a U-turn. Now Mozambique and others, and even socialist Vietnam, are attempting to get onto another development track or at least tack, but with little success so far.

After all these backs and forths in economic development theory and praxis, it increasingly appears that the real economic development problem or insufficiency is not human and other capital or social structure, values or ideology, but foreign exchange! The master key to the economic development door is the all mighty dollar. This is what all Third, Second, and not a few First World countries most need – and least have – to permit their acquisition of development capital and technology abroad and even at home. The debt-ridden economies of the South and East are all becoming "dollar-ized." The scarce US dollar increasingly replaces their excessively plentiful and devalued domestic currency as the medium of exchange, store of value, and unit of account. Curiously, of course, this dollarization spreads around the South and East just as the dollar and the US economy is faltering in the West – ironic that this should be the time the dollar is most revered and enshrined as king in all the "socialist" countries! Every alternative is rejected and no sacrifice is too great to worship at the golden dollar altar.

The lack of other socialist or capitalist development alternatives in the real world of these countries calls into question the superpowers' ideological battles and military confrontations over their respective models and clients.[85] What is all the political fuss about, if these – and other – countries really have no economic alternatives? And are there any *other* alternatives?

FROM SEPARATE NATIONAL AND SYSTEM DEVELOPMENT TO ONE-WORLD DEVELOPMENT ...

Before we hazard our own answers, if any, perhaps we would do well to return to Ben's review in this volume of his and others' answers. To begin with, Ben distinguishes between "is" and "ought" definitions of development. Gunder now leans to the former, and Marta did and does insist on the latter (like Ben). Gunder is prepared to (con)cede to them. Therefore, I (Gunder) will present my thesis that *only "world development"* as the "evolutionary" (to use Ben's terminology) constraint on the development there "ought" to be. Thus, my one-world development conception can perhaps be subsumed under Ben's classification of development views number 5 (no goals of society but only of particular groups or classes) and especially of number 6 (long process of development with periods of stagnation interrupted by rapid change, etc.), described on pages 00–00.

If this is so we can heartily agree to Ben's "simplest terms [definition of development] as a process of economic, social, and technological change by which human welfare is improved. Thus, development is 'good' by definition."

Anything that raises the level of human welfare contributes to development; anything that reduces welfare is anti-development, a subtraction from development. Thus, damage to the environment, exhaustion of non-renewable resources, deterioration of the quality of life, destruction of traditional cultural values, increasing inequalities, loss of freedom that may appear as side-effects of certain strategies to promote development reduce the amount of development that is actually achieved.

· · · · · ·

By definition – my definition – there can be no conflict between efficiency [including some concept of social justice, which Ben adds below] and development. They are one and the same thing, and so are improvements in the level of welfare.[86]

By this definition, *development is a process*, and not a state or stage. By analogy, socialism would at best also still be a process, as it was for Marx and Lenin, and not an already-reached happy state, as Stalin redefined it. Has someone also redefined development in the same way? Moreover, to Ben's economic, social, and technological development, we should add political, cultural, and perhaps spiritual and other dimensions of development. Presumably this would have his agreement, since he suggests about the same in his own discussion of anti-development. As Ben argues, therefore, the increase in some of these dimensions at the expense of others does not necessarily spell a process of development. Furthermore, by this definition, no country, nation-state, economy, or people would be developed. The industrial(ly) "developed" countries of the West would at best be *developing* if they are not *underdeveloping*. The same would then be true for the countries, regions, or peoples in the socialist East and the Third World South. In many of the latter, however, the underdeveloping process is proceeding apace and has recently even been accelerating; that is, to coin a phrase, they are now suffering from an even more rapid process of development of underdevelopment. Of course, the latter is also to be read to refer to a process, as we always intended.

The idea of one-world development ("as is") received an unexpected helping hand from the Soviet leader Mikhail Gorbachev at the United Nations on 7 December 1988:

The existence of any "closed" societies is hardly possible today. That is why we need a radical revision of views on the sum total of the problems of international cooperation as the most essential component of universal security. The world economy is becoming a single organism, outside which no state can develop normally, regardless of the social system it might belong to or the economic level it has reached ...

Further global progress is now possible only through quest for universal consensus in the movement toward a new world order ...

Freedom of choice is a universal principle. It knows no exceptions ... So what we need is unity through variety ... This new stage demand [s] that international relations be freed from ideology.[87]

Though we may wish to regard some of these as high-sounding words, we cannot deny or evade the verity and importance of the central thrust of what Gorbachev says. Moreover, it has direct relevance to our present concern with *development*, if we use this word as he spoke of "progress" and "security."

However, we and especially Gunder would argue that this verity is nothing new. World development – sorry, evolution – has been a fact of life for many centuries.[88] For a while, we thought that it started with the birth of the world capitalist system five centuries ago. However, we now believe in applying the rule of the American historian of China John King Fairbank,[89] that is, to study historical problems by pursuing them *backwards*. Therefore, we now suspect the *same continuing world system*, including its cyclical ups and downs, has been evolving (developing?) for five thousand years at least.[90] Never mind the mixtures and variations of different "modes" of production or social systems, as Gorbachev calls them only to dismiss their relevance to this new "development."[91] In this world system, sectors, regions, and peoples *temporarily and cyclically* assume leading and hegemonic central (core) positions of social and technological "development."[92] They then have to cede their pride of place to new ones. Usually, this happens after a long interregnum of crisis in the system, in which there is intense competition for leadership and hegemony. Thus, the central core has moved around the globe in a predominantly westerly direction. With some zigzags, the central core has passed through Asia, East (China), Central (Mongolia), South (India), and West (Iran, Mesopotamia, Egypt, Turkey), which are now called the "Middle East" in Eurocentric terminology. Then, the core passed on to southern and western Europe and Britain, via the Atlantic to North America, and now across the latter and the Pacific towards Japan. Who knows, perhaps one day it will pass back all the way around the world to China again.[93]

In the social evolution (to use Ben's terminology) of this world system in recent centuries, there has, of course, also been "as is" development *of* the capitalist and patriarchal system *in* the world. All positivist "as is" or even normative "ought to be" "development" at the lower orders of subsystem levels (like countries, regions, or sectors) occurred thanks to their (temporarily) more privileged position in the inter"national" division of labour and power. The recently prevalent notion about "as is" or "ought to be" "*national* development" is the result of a myopic optical illusion. It is derived from a self-interested selective tunnel-vision perception, instead of an objective global assessment of real-world development, either as is or as ought. The development ideology reviewed here was based on and is now doomed by this same self-illusory perception, which is less and less sustainable in the face of hard reality. Instead, as suggested above, we now need to replace it, as well as micro-supply and macro-demand-side economic theories, with a more rounded, dynamic, and all-encompassing supply- and demand-side economics to analyse, if not to guide, *world* economic and technological development.

Global world-system evolution has never been guided by or responsive to any global, or even to much local, "development" thinking or policy. However, each temporarily leading group probably considered itself as the "developed" civilization and the others as "barbarians." Global evolution (or "as is" development) has taken place for a long time. However, it has never been uniform but has always been centred in one or a few places. Leading peoples temporarily enjoyed privileged cultural, social, economic, technological, including military, and political positions relative to other "dependent" peoples. Clearly, general (much less uniform) global development (as ought instead of is) was and remains impossible because Gorbachev's (and Ben's) conditions were and remain unfulfilled and unfulfillable. Lower-order national/regional/sectoral/group/individual development policy can only marginally affect but not transform the stage of global evolution. Moreover, such policy can only have effect within the possibilities and constraints of that global evolutionary process, which it only helps to shape.

Therefore, any development "policy" for a particular country, region, sector, group, or individual must identify and promote some selected "comparative" advantage within the world economy. The "policy" is to find one or more niches in which it is possible to carry out a temporary position of "comparative" monopoly advantage in the international division of labour and to derive some temporary monopoly rent from the same. Some specialization is necessary because it is impossible today to have an advantageous or even loss-avoiding presence on all industrial and technological fronts simultaneously. Specialization is advantageous in a newly leading industry or sector, which can command temporary monopoly rents. However, each such sector, and even more each such region or group operating within it, must count on soon losing its advantage as it is displaced by competition from others on the world market. The element of classical "comparative advantage" in this strategy might be named after the snowmobile. Some Canadians developed the technologically new snowmobile in response to regional conditions, resources, and market possibilities. However, they then used the same locally developed snowmobile to carve out a temporary niche on the world market for themselves.

On the other hand, what Gorbachev observes correctly is that any discrete national or other subglobal development is now even less possible than before. No independent national state development (contrary to the unspoken assumption of *all* postwar development thinking) is possible at all. Moreover, Gorbachev also points out that a "development" policy of de-linking is now unrealistic. We now believe that is correct, contrary to our own previous view and that still held by Samir Amin.[94]

... AND TOWARDS MARGINALIZING DUALISM?

What *is* a realistic prospect, however, is the growing threat to countries, regions, and peoples of marginalization; that is, they may be involuntarily de-linked from the world process of evolution or development. However, they would then be de-linked on terms not of their own choosing. The most obvious case in point is much of Sub-Saharan Africa. There is a decreasing world market in the international division of labour for both its natural and human resources. Having been squeezed dry like a lemon in the course of world capitalist "development," much of Africa may now be abandoned to its fate. However, the same fate increasingly threatens other regions and peoples. Moreover, such threatened areas may be found everywhere: in the South (i.e., Bangladesh, the Brazilian northeast, Central America, etc.); in the ex-industrial rustbelt, south Bronx, and other regions and peoples in the West; and in whole interior regions and peoples in the "socialist" East (i.e., on both sides of the Sino-Soviet border).

People in all these and other places may now be sacrificed on the altar of growth-pole "development" policy and to efficient competitive participation the international division of labour in the world capitalist market and contemporary social evolution. However, North America and (for now Western but soon maybe also Eastern) Europe may well receive much more migration of the few who can, among the many who wish to, escape this marginal existence in Central America and Africa. They prefer to survive exploited by the division of labour in the North than to suffer death by war and starvation or endure a marginalized life without hope in the South.

In other words, a *dual economy and society* may now indeed be in the process of formation in the course of this stage of social evolution *in the world system*. However, this new dualism is different from the old dualism we rejected. The similarity between the two "dualisms" is only apparent. According to the old dualism, sectors or regions were supposedly separate (i.e., without past or present exploitation between them) *before* "modernization" would join them happily ever after. Moreover, this separate dual existence was seen within countries. We denied all these propositions. In the new dualism, the separation comes *after* the contact and often *after* exploitation (discarding the lemon after squeezing it dry) and *as a result of* the process of social and technological evolution, which others call "development." Moreover, this new dualism is between those who participate in and those who cannot participate in a worldwide division of labour. To the extent that the ins and outs of this world division of labour are in part technologically determined, this new dualism may partake of Ben's old technological dualism. Perhaps, we should never have lumped it in with the old socio-economic kind.

To summarize crudely, lower-order (country and regional) development can only carve out a usually temporary privileged (monopoly power) niche at the expense of others within the process of social, as well as technological, evolution. That process may be a positive-sum game, although the threats of nuclear war and environmental degradation render this possibility increasingly doubtful. However, even in a positive-sum game, most development for one group still comes at the expense of anti-development for others, who are condemned to dualistic marginalization and/or to underdevelopment of development. That is what real-world development really means. Therefore, Ben's definition of ought – development as raising *all human welfare* – turns out to be hardly operational. I, Gunder, seem to have long since come full circle from determinant economic, to social, to political, then back to the determinant economic factors in development. However, now I, Gunder, see these factors in terms of world economic development. Meantime, I, Marta, find that economic problems *cannot* be solved by economic means. The mistake has been to try that route. Solutions to economic problems must be sought in other ways.

TOWARDS DEMOCRACY

All these developments have elevated another consideration to the top of the agenda: *democracy* and especially *participatory democracy*. Of course, the word "democracy" has been a fellow-traveller along these roads all along. But the likes of Rostow, Pye, Pool, and Huntington wrote *and acted* to impose "democracy" under the military boot. Even the Quaker Benoit claimed to have statistically demonstrated that more military equals more development. Political modernizers like Apter, Almond, and Coleman at the very least condoned Third World right-wing authoritarian regimes in the name of political "democracy" and economic "development." Even before the US ambassador to the United Nations, Jeanne Kirkpatrick, popularized the subtle distinction, the long-standing practice in the name of "democratic freedom" was to defend right-wing authoritarianism as a necessary instrumental defence against left-wing totalitarianism. On the other side, the line was "economic democracy" in the country and "democratic centralism" in the party. The total lack of democracy today (and for all too many yesteryears before) was defended as instrumentally necessary to assure more democracy and development tomorrow. In the name of a top-down "mass line," *mea culpa, mea maxima culpa*, we too sometimes fell victim to or at least closed a blind eye to this short shrift for democracy on the left. Today, development must include more democracy, and (more) democracy must include (more) respect for human rights, and these must include (more) political freedom of speech, organization, and choice, as well as access to the economic and social basic human needs necessary to exercise such political choice.

The political crisis of military and authoritarian rule in the Third World and the crisis of socialism (and Marxism) in the East increasingly opened people's eyes. Even social "scientific" development thinkers followed. Military rule in Latin America and incessant coups d'état in Africa popularized the study of the state and of some other way to run it. The conversion of some socialist dreams into nightmares gave interest in democracy a new lease on life to people in the socialist countries themselves and to those outside who were sympathetic to them. Among socialists in the West, it became obvious (why so late?) that as an absolute minimum any socialist progress and any progress of socialism would have to safeguard and improve upon the advances and benefits of "bourgeois" democracy, rather than negating them as heretofore. Moreover, to sum up the matter from a worm's-eye view, if the economic crisis precludes present and foreseeable progress in economic development or welfare, we the people demand at least the political possibility to express our gripes about it democratically. We the people demand at least the possibility to pursue any alternatives we can find or forge ourselves – in participatory democracy – through our own popular social movements and with a minimum respect for everybody's human rights.

For by now it is sadly clear that, however they may differ, none of the now available "models" of development are adequate for the present, let alone for the future. This inadequacy is true of the magic of the world and domestic market, Western top-down political democracy, Eastern top-down economic democracy, attempts at self-reliant national state de-linking, any hoped-for capitalist new international economic order, and the non-existent and probably never-to-be-available alternative socialist division of labour/international economic order. Nor does anything else on the horizon offer most of the population in much of this Third World any chance or hope for equity or efficiency in economic development as long as we, and especially they, define it in any of the orthodox or even heterodox more-or-less-of-the-same ways so far reviewed above. As a result by the 1980s, for instance, the grand old men Gunnar Myrdal and Rául Prebisch, whom we had criticized as excessively conservative reformists in the 1960s, significantly radicalized their views and public statements shortly before they died. So what and where are the real alternatives and the more participatory democratic ways to forge and pursue them?

... TOWARDS SELF-DEVELOPMENT ALTERNATIVES

Armed with these alternative positivist ''as is'' and normative ''as ought'' definitions and goals of development, we can now pursue some other development alternatives. First, like the disadvantaged peoples themselves, we can do battle with anti-development or underdevelopment of development as it affects all sorts of ''minority'' peoples. However, on further inspection these disadvantaged minorities turn out to be in the majority. Minorities would not demand and merit their own and others' special attention *qua* minorities if they did not suffer from discrimination and worse at the hands of ''the majority.'' Ethnic, national, linguistic, racial, social, sectoral, age, vocational, and other minorities are all subject to the inequity and inefficiency of economic development. Adding them all up, they surely constitute a numerical majority both globally and nationally.

The biggest ''minority'' (which admittedly overlaps with these others) is women. They assuredly constitute a statistical majority of the world's and probably all countries' population. Moreover, it has belatedly been statistically confirmed (as women knew all along in their bones if not in their minds) that women do most of the work in the world. They do all the unpaid and much of the low-paid reproductive work. They also do much of the productive work. Women do most of the agricultural work in Africa and in many other parts of the world, including the socialist countries. Women also do much low-paid industrial and service work everywhere. Adding in the other minorities, probably almost all of the work, and especially the hard part of it, is done by ''minorities.''

Then, what is the ''majority,'' and what does it do? It is the élite that has and uses power and it uses power to define and promote (its own) ''development.'' For if ''development'' were largely the result of work by and for (the welfare of) the majority, then why don't the *majority* of these ''minority'' people benefit from (equity and efficiency in) economic development? There must be *something wrong*, both in the real world and in our ''majority'' thinking about it!

Some thinking and praxis has changed, but not much. Marx (!) wanted the greater incorporation of women in the labour force to be a vehicle of their liberation, but he also expressed fears about the resultant damage to the family. Stalin (!) was perhaps the greatest proponent of women's lib and did the most to incorporate women in the labour force. However, perhaps he wanted to further Soviet economic development more than to liberate women. Their work in the Soviet Union is still unquestioned, but their liberation less so. Their welfare benefit from "development" is certainly questionable. Elsewhere women also entered the productive labour force to replace men who went to war or migrated to spur production in other regions or countries. Or they simply entered for other practical reasons. Even so, much female work has failed to register in social norms or cultural thinking. Despite the above-noted work of women in agriculture, land-"to those who work it" reforms or technical extension and credit to "agricultural producers" nowhere has been directed at women instead of men! (Why did neither we nor the land reformers see this in Chile, when the ownership in land was distributed to men even where and when it was worked by women in female-headed households?) Nor have women in the informal sector in Africa, Asia, and Latin America fared much better when it comes to credit or institutional support. The (still small) recent redirection of development policy and extension work towards women in the Third World must be ascribed to the force of the (re)new(ed) worldwide women's (lib?) movement and its influence on perceptions and equity.

Academia in the West also discovered women and initiated affirmative action towards them. "Home economics" was transformed and vastly expanded into "women's studies," and courses or even entire programs taught by women mushroomed on "women's history," "women in society," "women and politics," etc. Logically, "women and development" had to follow. Of course, nobody ever said "men's history and development," and so forth, even if, like Molière's famous character, they were speaking male prose about men's history and male society and development. Nor does women's lib in the North automatically change women's views of their sisters in the South. At a women's history conference in Amsterdam, Third World women were excluded and told they had no history. They protested with signs reading "*history, herstory, and the real story.*" However, putting just some (mostly upper/middle-class white) women back into the picture, as we saw in a slide show about women's history in Peru, only inverts the matter, since this only means a focus on the history (or development) *of women* instead of, or in addition to, that of men.

Nor does looking at women and development necessarily tell the real development story. I, Marta, got an MA in "Women and Development" and learned nothing new about development but much about women and anti-development. The place of women *and* men in the patriarchal gender structure of society has not penetrated development theory and cannot be described simply by relating the story of one or/and the other. The real story to be (re)told is of the structure and development of society itself.

The personal is (also) political, as the feminist refrain has it; that is, the meaning of relational terms are transformed. Therefore, women and development should not be seen as only more-of-the-same-old women's development of women instead of or in addition to men. *Man-made development* must be transformed to encompass progressive change in the whole gender structure of society itself. In a word, we must reconceptualize and redefine development itself to refer to such social transformation of societal relations (and perceptions). Therefore, it is only a small step in the right direction to change the emphasis from *social factors in or for economic development* to *social and economic development*, especially for women and their children. Some additional feeble steps were taken, or perhaps more accurately recorded, at the UN-sponsored world women's congresses in Mexico in 1975, Copenhagen in 1980, and Nairobi in 1985. Women were encouraged to advance by their own efforts from their backstage work to at least visible stage performance, if not yet to centre stage. However, the present stage or moment of social evolution (if we may not say of world development) generates the feminization of poverty. On our topsy-turvy real-world wonderland, these women are only taking modest steps on a gigantic treadmill that is moving in the opposite direction under their very feet. Like the Red Queen in Alice's Wonderland, they would have to run a lot faster just to stay in the same place.

Therefore, this particular development issue calls for not only women but everybody to stop or reverse the treadmill. To do this, we would have to rewrite the whole gender play and reconstruct the social stage altogether. That would be development! It would be at once more equitable and more efficient, if we still wished to use these terms. By these new standards, Switzerland and Japan could no longer be called *developed societies*, no matter how financially or technologically "developed" their economies were. For in Switzerland, until recently, women could not even vote. In Japan, women are treated as geishas not only in men's clubs but also in their homes, offices, factories, and fields.

Many racial, ethnic, national, religious, and other minorities also suffer from anti-development; they too are on real-world wonderland treadmills. The real economic losses they suffer often more than counteract the sometimes legal and other steps taken by themselves or on their behalf. *Pro forma* or even *de jure* recognition of discrimination against these "minorities" hardly counteracts, much less undoes, the *de facto* plights they suffer. As a result, people resort to many self-empowering slogans and movements to at least enhance their own culture and dignity: small-is-beautiful, black-is-beautiful, (this) indigenous-is-noble, (our) nation-is-glorious, (true) religion-is-blessed, (our) community-is-ours, and other defensive (and sometimes, in more senses than one, offensive) slogans and movements. They may be an important element of and contribution to cultural reassertion and self-development. They may even increase the number and velocity of steps on the treadmill. However, they do not necessarily stop or reverse the treadmill or significantly affect the evolutionary process itself.

Other costs of anti-development and underdevelopment of development even substract from the welfare of the vast majority. Such costs can be combatted only by real numerical minority social movements. Ever-developing threats to peace and the environment are cases in point. The Scandinavian-headed Palme Commission and Brundtland Report, among others, including the report of the United Nations special session on development and disarmament, have drawn worldwide attention and sought to mobilize action on these problems and their connections. Although strong peace movements are more visible in the North, the problem of hot war is, of course, particularly important in and for the South. During the past four decades of accelerated Third World "development," every war in the world has taken place in the South, and every year several wars have gone on there simultaneously. Any outbreak of peace in the South, such as in 1988, is therefore a real (contribution to) development. Growing peace and human-rights movements in the South itself, with notable leadership and participation of women, are now making increasing contributions to this development.

Similarly, although environmental degradation may be more (locally) visible in the North (including the East), the globally most serious environmental anti-development is now probably taking place in the South. Important instances are the deforestation of Amazonia, Indonesia, the Himalayan slopes, and so on, and the desertification in Africa and Asia. Therefore, all around the globe, regional, local, peasant, native, tribal, and other environmental movements are mobilizing to protect their own sources of livelihood. However, they are thereby also protecting ecological survival for all of us through another and a sustainable development.[95]

To end on a positive upbeat note, we applaud and participate in these social movements of participatory civil democracy. They do all they can to mobilize their participants for real – that is self – development for themselves and often also for others in their respective spheres of influence. Indeed, they express and exercise their participants' freedom of choice for their own variety of civil democracy and development within the unity and diversity of our one world.[96]

NOTES

1   H.W. Arndt, *Economic Development: The History of an Idea* (Chicago and London: University of Chicago Press, 1987).

2   Benjamin Higgins, "Economic Development and Cultural Change: Seamless Web or Patchwork Quilt?" in M. Nash, ed., *Essays on Economic Development and Cultural Change in Honor of Bert F. Hoselitz. Economic Development and Cultural Change* (Supplement) 25 (1977): 117–18.

3   Gustav Ranis and T.P. Schultz, eds., *The State of Economic Development: Progress and Perspectives* (New York and Oxford: Basil Blackwell, 1988).

4   Benjamin Higgins, "Economic Development and Cultural Change," 118.

5   A.G. Frank, *Critique and Anti-Critique* (New York: Praeger Publishers; London: Macmillan Press 1984).

6   Dudley Seers, "The Birth, Life and Death of Development Economics," *Development and Change* 10, no. 4 (October 1979).

7   A.O. Hirschman, "The Rise and Decline of Development Economics," in A.O. Hirschman, *Essays in Trespassing: Economics to Politics and Beyond* (Cambridge: Cambridge University Press, 1982).

8   Arndt, *Economic Development,* 162–3.

9   M. Redclift, *Sustainable Development: Exploring the Contradictions* (London and New York: Methuen, 1987).

10 League of Nations, *The Network of World Trade* (Geneva: League of Nations, 1942); *Industrialization and Foreign Trade* (Geneva: League of Nations, 1945).

11 J. Schumpeter, *The Theory of Economic Development* (New York: Oxford University Press, 1934); *Business Cycles,* 2 vols (New York: McGraw-Hill, 1939); *Capitalism, Socialism, and Democracy* (New York: Harper & Brothers, 1942).

12 L.L. Pasinetti, *Structural Change and Economic Growth* (Cambridge: Cambridge University Press, 1981).

13 K. Gough, "New Proposals for Anthropologists," *Current Anthropology,* May 1968, revised as "Anthropology: Child of Imperialism," *Monthly Review,* 1968; and T. Asad, *Anthropology and the Colonial Encounter* (London: Ithaca Press, 1975).

14 United Nations, *Measures for the Economic Development of Underdeveloped Countries* (New York: United Nations, 1951).

15 W.W. Rostow, *The Process of Economic Growth* (New York: Norton, 1952).

16 M. Millikan and W.W. Rostow, *A Proposal: Key to an Effective Foreign Policy* (Cambridge: MIT Press, 1957).

17 E.E. Hagen, *On the Theory of Social Change: Economic Growth Begins* (Homewood: Irvin Press, 1962).

18 D. McClelland, *The Achieving Society* (Princeton: Van Nostrand, 1961).

19 I.M.D. Little, *Economic Development, Theory, Policy, and International Relations* (New York: Basic Books, 1982).

20 A.G. Frank, "The Economic Development of Nicaragua," *Inter American Economic Affairs* 8, no. 4 (Spring 1955); "Policy Decisions and the Economic Development of Ceylon," *Economia Internazionale* 8, no. 4 (November 1955).

21 A.G. Frank, "General Productivity in Soviet Agriculture and Industry: The Ukraine 1928–53," *Journal of Political Economy* 66 (December 1958).

22 A.G. Frank, "Human Capital and Economic Growth," *Economic Development and Cultural Change* 8, no. 2 (1960).

23 Arndt, *Economic Development*, 62.

24 John Toye, *Dilemmas of Development* (Oxford: Basil Blackwell, 1987), 104.

25 Cf. Frank, "General Productivity in Soviet Agriculture and Industry," and A.G. Frank, *Lumpenbourgeoisie: Lumpendevelopment* (New York: Monthly Review Press, 1972).

26 Paul Strassmann, "Development Economics from a Chicago Perspective," *Journal of Social Issues*, March 1976, 63–80.

27 Frank, "Human Capital."

28 G.M. Meier and D. Seers, eds., *Pioneers in Development* (Oxford and New York: Oxford University Press, 1981).

29 A. Foster-Carter, "From Rostow to Gunder Frank: Conflicting Paradigms in the Analysis of Underdevelopment," *World Development* 4, no. 3 (March 1976).

30 A.G. Frank, "Goal Ambiguity and Conflicting Standards: An Approach to the Study of Organization," *Human Organization* 17, no. 1 (Winter 1958–59); "Administrative Role Definition and Social Change," *Human Organization* 22, no. 1 (Winter 1963).

31 J.H. Turner et al., *Studies in Managerial Process and Organizational Behavior* (Glenview, Ill.: Scott, Foresman, 1972).

32 A.G. Frank, *Capitalism and Underdevelopment in Latin America* (New York: Monthly Review Press, 1967).

33 First published in 1963 and reprinted in A.G. Frank, *Latin America: Underdevelopment or Revolution* (New York: Monthly Review Press, 1969).

34 Reprinted in Frank, *Latin America*, 21.

35 Suzanne Jonas-Bodenheimer, "Dependency and Imperialism: The Roots of Latin American Underdevelopment," in K.T. Fann and D.C. Hodges, eds., *Readings in U.S. Imperialism* (Boston: Porter Sargent, 1971).

36 Also in Frank, *Latin America*.

37 A.G. Frank, *On Capitalist Underdevelopment* (Bombay: Oxford University Press, 1975).

38 Ibid., 1.

39 Ibid., 21.

40 Ibid., 43–4.

41 Frank, *Capitalism and Underdevelopment*.

42 Frank, *Latin America*.

43 Ibid.

44 Ibid., 277–8.

45 E.D. Geneovese, *In Red and Black* (New York: Random House Pantheon Books, 1968).

46 Frank, *Capitalism and Underdevelopment.*

47 Ibid., xii, xiv.

48 Frank, *Latin America.*

49 Ibid., chap. 4.

50 P. Gonzalez Casanova, *La Democracia en Mexico* (Mexico: Era, 1965).

51 François Chevalier, *Land and Society in Colonial Mexico: The Great Hacienda* (1952; Berkeley: University of California Press, 1970).

52 Woodrow Borah, "New Spain's Century of Depression," *Ibero-Americana* 35 (1951).

53 A.G. Frank, *Mexican Agriculture 1521–1630: Transformation of the Mode of Production* (Cambridge: Cambridge University Press, 1979).

54 J.F. Leal and M. Huacuja R., *Economia y sistema de haciendas en Mexico* (Mexico: Era, 1982).

55 G. Huizer, *The Revolutionary Potential of Peasants in Latin America* (Lexington, Mass.: D.C. Heath Lexington Books, 1972).

56 F.H. Cardoso and E. Faletto, *Development and Dependence in Latin America* (Berkeley: University of California Press, 1979).

57 Frank, *Lumpenbourgeoisie.*

58 F.H. Cardoso, "The Consumption of Dependency Theory in the United States," *Latin American Research Review* 12, no. 3 (1977).

59 Christopher Lind, "Ethics, Economics and Canada's Catholic Bishops," *Canadian Journal of Political and Social Theory* 7, no. 3 (Fall 1983).

60 Gough, "New Proposals for Anthropologists."

61 Reprinted in Frank, *Latin America.*

62 The last two are reprinted in Frank, *Critique and Anti-Critique.*

63 Cliff Geertz, *Agricultural Involution: The Process of Ecological Change in Indonesia* (Berkeley: University of California Press, 1966).

64 Frank, *Critique and Anti-Critique.*

65 A.G. Frank, *World Accumulation 1492–1789* (New York: Monthly Review Press; London: Macmillan Press, 1978); and idem, *Dependent Accumulation and Underdevelopment* (New York: Monthly Review Press; London: Macmillan Press, 1978).

66 I. Wallerstein, *The Modern World System* (New York: Academic Press, 1974).

67 Samir Amin, *Accumulation on a World Scale* (New York: Monthly Review Press, 1974).

68 Frank, *Critique and Anti-Critique,* chap. 24.

69 Amin, *Accumulation on a World Scale.*

70 Dieter Senghaas, *The European Experience: A Historical Critique of Development Theory* (Dover, NH: Berg Publishers, 1985).

71 A.G. Frank, *Reflections on the Economic Crisis* (New York: Monthly Review Press; London: Hutchinson, 1981).

72 A.G. Frank, *Crisis: In the World Economy* (New York: Holmes & Meier; London: Heinemann, 1980); *Crisis: In the Third World* (New York: Holmes &

Meier; London: Heinemann, 1981); *Dynamics of Global Crisis* (with S. Amin, G. Arrighi & I. Wallerstein) (New York: Monthly Review Press; London: Macmillan Press, 1982); *The European Challenge* (Nottingham, UK: Spokesman Press; Westbury, Conn.: Lawrence Hill Publishers, 1983–84); *El Desafio de la Crisis* (Madrid: IEPALA Editorial and Caracas: Editorial Nueva Sociedad, 1988a); and countless articles.

73   A.G. Frank, *Economic Genocide in Chile: Equilibrium on the Point of a Bayonet* (Nottingham, UK: Spokesman Books, 1976).

74   Frank, *Crisis: In the Third World.*

75   Reprinted in Frank, *Reflections on the Economic Crisis.*

76   Frank, *Crisis: In the Third World*, chaps. 6, 7.

77   Reprinted in Frank, *Crisis: In the Third World.*

78   A.G. Frank, "Long Live Transideological Enterprise! The Socialist Economies in the Capitalist International Division of Labor," *Review* 1, no. 1 (Summer 1977); and idem, *Crisis: In the World Economy*, chap. 4.

79   I. Adelman and C.T. Morris, *Economic Growth and Social Equity in Developing Countries* (Stanford: Stanford University Press, 1973).

80   Frank, *Crisis: In the World Economy*, chap. 5.

81   Ibid.

82   A.G. Frank, *El Desafio de la Crisis*; "The Socialist Countries in the World Economy: The East-South Dimension, in Lelio Basso Foundation, ed., *Theory and Practice of Liberation at the End of the XXth Century* (Brussels: Bruylant, 1988).

83   For some evidence, see Frank, *World Accumulation 1492–1789*; and idem, *Dependent Accumulation and Underdevelopment.*

84   Reprinted in Frank, *Critique and Anti-Critique*, chap. 20.

85   As is argued more extensively in A.G. Frank, "Debt Where Credit is Due," *Journal fur Entwicklungspolitik* 3, no. 3 (1987).

86   Benjamin Higgins, at the conference which was the source of this volume.

87   M. Gorbachev, "Speech by Mikhail Gorbachev at the UN General Assembly," *Moscow News*, supplement no. 51 (3351).

88   According to Higgins's aforementioned definitions.

89   John King Fairbank, *Trade and Diplomacy on the China Coast* (Stanford: Stanford University Presss, 1969).

90   A.G. Frank, "A Theoretical Introduction to 5,000 Years of World System History," *Review* XIII, no. 2 (Spring 1990): 155–248; and "A Plea for World History," *Journal of World History* II, no. 1 (Spring 1991): 1–28.

91   A.G. Frank, "Transitional Ideological Modes: Feudalism, Capitalism, Socialism," *Critique of Anthropology* 11, no. 2 (Summer 1991): 171–88.

92   B.K. Gills and A.G. Frank, "The Cumulation of Accumulation: Theses and Research Agenda for 5000 Years of World System History," *Dialectical Anthropology* (New York/Amsterdam) 15, no. 1 (July 1990): 19–42; and "5000 years of World System History: The Cumulation of Accumulation," in

C. Chase-Dunn & T. Hall, eds., *Precapitalist Core-Periphery Relations* (Boulder: Westview Press, 1991): 67–111; and B.K. Gills and A.G. Frank, "World System Cycles, Crises, and Hegemonial Shifts 1700 BC to 1700 AD," *Review*, 1992 forthcoming.

93 A.G. Frank, "1492 and Latin America at the Margin of World System History: 492 – 992 – 1492 – 1992 East ≥ West Hegemonial Shifts," *Latin American Perspectives*, 1992 forthcoming.

94 Samir Amin, *La déconnexion: Pour sortir du système mondial* (Paris: La découverte, 1986).

95 M. Redclift, *Sustainable Development, Exploring the Contradictions* (London and New York: Methuen, 1987).

96 Marta Fuentes and A.G. Frank, "Ten Theses on Social Movements," *World Development* 17, no. 2 (February 1989); A.G. Frank and M. Fuentes, "Social Movements in World History," in S. Amin, G. Arrighi, A.G. Frank, and I. Wallerstein, *Transforming the Revolution: Social Movements and the World System* (New York: Monthly Review Press, 1990).

16 Towards a New Paradigm? Two Views

DONALD J. SAVOIE and BENJAMIN HIGGINS

At the end of the introductory chapter of this volume, the editors suggested that the current mood of economists to question the validity of their own analyses as a basis for policy, as well as those of their colleagues, may presage a breakthrough to a new paradigm. In this final chapter, Donald Savoie and Benjamin Higgins speculate on what the new paradigm might look like. As a political scientist, Savoie addresses this issue in terms of the "government management *versus* the market" debate, using regional development as a test case. He argues that the Canadian experience with regional development does not demonstrate that government should not have intervened, but rather that the intervention should have been better designed and better implemented. He makes a crucial distinction between "government wrongly intervening" and "government intervening wrongly," and goes on to suggest some fundamental government reforms. As an economist, Higgins discusses policy trends implied by various contributors to the book, proposes a new methodology for economics as a whole, and makes suggestions responding to Savoie's call for government reform.

DONALD SAVOIE

What have we learned about regional development in the past thirty years or so? A great deal and nothing at all. Governments have tried this and that and we now have somewhat of a sense of what works and what does not. We know little else. The literature continues to offer essentially two competing approaches to regional development, the same two basic approaches we have had since regional development first surfaced as a field of study and government activity. We either support government intervention or we do not. The debate has raged for the past thirty years and it still does in the pages of this book.

What is different today? Those supporting government intervention are now (and have been for much of the 1980s) on the defensive. Somehow, they have had to explain the lack of success of costly government programs for regional development over the past thirty years. Neoclassicists, meanwhile, have been able to sit back and declare "we were right then and we are still right." Governments should not intervene to prop up the region, or the "patch."[1] It is disconcerting to have to report that after thirty years we have not made much progress beyond continuing a rather sterile debate about whether governments should intervene or not to promote regional development.

It is a sterile debate because governments continue to intervene, whatever we may report in learned journals. Albert Breton sums up the problem well in his essay in this book by asking a simple but straightforward question, "Why does virtually every government in the world pursue regional development policies when economists keep telling them that they should be encouraging mobility of people and non-sunk capital instead?" A noted Canadian neoclassicist, Thomas Courchene, made a similar observation when he reported that he had no illusion that governments would "stand idly by and allow the unfettered market to call the adjustment tune."[2] Governments will intervene, of that we can be certain. It takes only a moment's reflection to understand why. As long as we elect politicians to represent slower-growth regions, we will see governments "pushed" and "pulled" to do things for these regions. Indeed, politicians from whatever political party have great difficulty subscribing to the neoclassical approach. Even assuming for a moment that the theory holds the most promise to alleviate regional problems over the long term, it does not follow that politicians would wish to be identified with it. Imagine, if you will, a politician from a slow-growth region in the House of Commons or in the US Congress declaring that the solution to his or her region's economic woes is to unleash market forces and encourage out-migration. It is unlikely that this politician would be standing in the House of Commons or in Congress for very long, and most politicians do enjoy getting re-elected!

There is no indication that governments are losing their interest in intervening in the name of regional development. This is even true in the case of new and emerging governments. The European Community (EC), for example, has made it clear that regional development enjoys a priority standing in planning for a "market without frontiers" to be in place by the end of 1992. It explained why:

From an economic point of view the whole community, and not just the less-favoured groups and regions, has an interest in reducing the present disparities and strengthening economic and social cohesion as the large market is brought into being. This cohesion is actually a condition for the harmonious development of any society. Faced with international competition, Europe cannot allow itself the luxury of such a waste as the underdevelopment or decline of so many regions or the under-use of so many talents. Development of less-favoured regions also stimulates trade and provides more industrialized regions with new markets for capital goods and consumer goods. A wider spread of prosperity, industry and major infrastructure can also help to limit the dangers of congestion and ecological damage faced by the most prosperous regions, many of which are among the most densely populated in the world.[3]

The European commissioner for regional policies, Bruce Williams, was more blunt. He declared: "If we do not ensure a balanced regional development and a reduction of the disparities between our regions, then the creation of the single market and the furtherance of economic and monetary union cannot succeed."[4]

The European Community now has three funds from which member countries can draw resources to promote regional development. The community sought to strengthen its commitment to regional and rural development in February 1988 by increasing substantially the level of resources of the three funds. In 1987 the three funds represented about 19 percent of the community's budget. It is envisaged that the funds will account for one-quarter of the budget by 1993.[5]

This is not, however, to suggest for a moment that all is well with government measures to promote regional development. There are valid reasons why those of us who favour government intervention to promote regional development are now on the defensive. Though governments have committed large sums of public funds to the policy field, they have not been particularly adroit at promoting regional development. They have planned, programmed, and spent but they have not been very successful in telling us whether or not they have been successful. At the risk of making too sweeping a statement, evaluations of past government efforts to promote regional development have very often been incomplete, self-serving, and of limited use either in planning new efforts or in reporting accurately on past efforts.

Governments have also raised expectations unduly, no doubt, for purely political reasons. New concepts and approaches are introduced in rapid succession with great fanfare and with the promise that "this time" they will solve a region's economic woes. A closer look often reveals that the new approach has a striking similarity to the one it just replaced. Bureaucracies often take over the new approach and reshape it to look very much like the former one. This is why, for example, cash grants to private firms remain a central feature of so many regional development efforts. Governments have been told time and again that they ought to commit more of their regional development funding to human-resources development. They have hardly listened, or if they have, they have not followed through in the implementation phase.

All of this suggests that we may well have focused too much of our research efforts on the merits of government intervention and not enough on what governments have actually sought to accomplish and on the capacity of governments to be creative, to respond quickly to changing circumstances, to change direction quickly, and to operate effectively at the "regional" level. The argument here is that perhaps the idea of government intervention in the name of regional development has not failed, but that governments have.

We have – and I quickly add myself to the "we" – too often overlooked the "how" governments operate in studying regional development. Regional development programming has become the preserve of government bureaucracies in that it is public bureaucracies that plan, implement, and evaluate the programs.

We now know that public bureaucracies stand accused of many things: of being bloated, cumbersome, uncreative, lethargic, and insensitive.[6] This widely negative perception can be found in many countries. A keen and respected observer of American politics recently observed that "two thirds of the public believe that the federal government employs too many people and that they do not work as hard as those who hold private sector jobs. These attitudes are not held only by the uninformed; opinion polls consistently show that respect for government servants steadily dwindles as one moves up the scale of education and income. Indeed, among the more affluent and better educated, one of the few things that unites the left and the right is their common disdain for bureaucrats."[7] In Britain, a number of journalists and observers have begun to write about the scale, cost, and efficiency of the state and "what was thought to be the privilege of officialdom."[8] Canadians, meanwhile, told public opinion surveys throughout the 1980s that "they had less confidence in the public service than in any other institution, save for the trade union movement, politicians and more recently the tobacco industry."[9] A royal commission on the country's economic future warned in 1985 that "the reach of the state has in many ways outrun both our administrative and technical capacities, and our capacity to ensure democratic accountability.[10] Alan Cairns summed it up well when he observed that "the binge of post World War II state worship ... has ended, and a reassessment of state, market and state society is under way."[11]

It would be wrong, however, to assume that only the right has expressed strong reservations about public bureaucracies. John K. Galbraith, himself a leading twentieth-century proponent for a greater role for government in society, recently observed that bureaucracy has given government a bad name.[12] Galbraith argues that "it's more than the liberal task to defend the system. It is far more important now to improve the operation than enlarge and increase its scope. This must be the direction of our major effort."[13]

It is hardly possible, in my view, to overstate the importance of government organization to the success of regional development efforts. Indeed, one senses, as a former Canadian minister responsible for regional development once observed, that this is as crucial to the success of the regional development efforts as the policy itself. There have been a number of efforts in recent years to deal with the problem, particularly in Great Britain and Canada. In Canada, a major government department responsible for regional development was disbanded in 1987 and new regional development agencies, including the Atlantic Canada Opportunities Agency (ACOA), were established in various regions of the country. A 1990 review of ACOA called "for a major change in the *culture* of the agency – that is, from a pseudo-entrepreneurial organization to one which actively pursues its entrepreneurship. It will be important for ACOA personnel to practice what they preach."[14] The agency, it was felt, had after only three years of existence become too "bureaucratic." On this point, the review called on ACOA's senior management "to ensure that agency staff are encouraged to take up new challenges, to not stay in one position, in one office perhaps, or for that matter, with ACOA itself for too long ... if there is one group of people in Atlantic Canada that should be dynamic, at the forefront of new knowledge and outward looking it is ACOA personnel."[15]

Operating in every government department responsible for regional development is the constraint imposed by "creativity" shackles. The creativity shackles are, in my view, rooted in the way government is organized. With the aid of hindsight, I now suspect that the problem is not a recent one, but one that began in the late 1960s and 1970s when governments in all Western industrialized countries took in a lot of bright recent university graduates and policy analysts but failed to give them the kind of access, flexibility, and tools they needed to do their work properly.

We now see signs everywhere that the passing industrial society will leave in its wake many of the government organizational models it engendered. We have organizational models that were structured and designed for the industrial era and for military purposes in a time when wars were fought on the battle field with what have now become unsophisticated equipment. The models of organization, line, and staff, the way subjects are studied, the hierarchical nature of government departments and agencies are pure nineteenth-century administrative techniques.

The current structure of government was probably particularly well suited to the delivery of large-scale services – like the mail and transportation services – in a consistent, objective, and effective fashion. The delivery of large-scale and routine services were the main challenges for governments virtually into the 1960s. The 1960s, however, saw the advent of a host of highly "flexible" programs designed to spur economic development at the national, regional, and community levels, to promote adjustment in selected sectors, and to assist disadvantaged groups. Policy advice and program evaluation capacities were required to develop and assess these initiatives, but they were simply added on to the existing machinery of government. Meanwhile, central agencies put in place measures designed to keep all these new developments under control, with line departments responding with still more administrative units to keep up with new centrally prescribed procedures and controls.

In addition, many units, old and new, are organized along the same lines, all are integrated into the departmental structure, and all report through the same channels – through directors, director generals, and assistant deputy ministers to the deputy minister. This is even true of new government departments and agencies such as ACOA. Yet it may well be that the delivery of large-scale and routine services and the development and delivery of flexible or open-ended programs (not to mention the requirements for creative thinking about policy and the evaluation of ongoing programs) require quite different organizational structures. The first may best be served by a traditional hierarchical organization and the latter by a new form of government organization capable of encouraging thought-provoking ideas, and even quick access to political authority for decisions.

It is worth quoting at length Gerald Caiden's views on the problems of modern public bureaucracies:

Anyone familiar with the workings of the modern administrative state knows why administrative reform is necessary. Public administrators – indeed, high-level administrators of any large-scale organization – are so caught up in the rush of everyday business that they rarely have time to sit back and review their organizations to see if and where they are falling down (often they do not even know that their organizations are not performing as they believe they should), what has long needed overhauling but no one has yet gotten around to doing something about, and what could be improved without too much dislocation, expense, and anxiety. Instead they go on doing more of the same, compounding correctable errors. Worse still, they try to suppress problems in the hope that eventually things will right themselves. They get so used to not getting around to what should be done that they learn to live with both good and bad and forget that something different could be done. They consider themselves fortunate to accomplish, much less keep up with the state of the art.[16]

Notwithstanding the changes introduced by the Thatcher, Reagan, and Mulroney governments, bureaucracies remain overadministered and it is still often a trial for government officials simply to get things done.

Regional development policy, more than any other public policy field, needs a capacity to be creative, to adjust quickly to changing circumstances, to challenge the *status quo* and often conventional thinking both inside government and in the regions, to deliver initiatives quickly with a minimum of red tape, and to be in the field working with key economic actors and having the authority to plan and make decisions. One hardly thinks of government bureaucracies when one thinks of these requirements. We need to think of different organizational models to get the job done.

My plea, then, is for the next generation of scholars interested in regional development to focus their research efforts in areas that have thus far held limited interest. We know that governments will intervene to promote regional development no matter what we tell them. The challenge, then, is to see to it that public funds committed to this purpose are spent wisely and on programs showing the most promising prospects. One area that has thus far been largely overlooked but that holds promise for new solutions concerns how governments organize themselves to promote regional development. It is only fitting that this would be one conclusion in a book in honour of Benjamin Higgins. As I noted in the preface of the book, Ben has never been content to walk away from the fray and only write books and scholarly papers. He has been involved in development planning in over forty developed and less-developed countries.

BENJAMIN HIGGINS

Where do we stand at the end of this volume? Have we reached clear-cut conclusions regarding relations among equity, efficiency, and development?

In chapter 1, I argued that the classical school identified "efficiency" with "development," in the sense of general improvement of social welfare, and maintained that any acceptable concept of efficiency or social welfare must include some consideration of equity. Walt Rostow points out in his chapter that the classical school's concept of "the good society" also includes a foundation of "Sympathy." Thus, in the classical system there is no conflict among development, efficiency, and equity. There is also no need for "heart-rending soul-searching" about possible conflict between rigour and relevance of the sort that disturbs the equilibrium of the economics profession today. These are big advantages. Could we then return to the classical paradigm and bring it up to date? Would a modernized classical paradigm guide us to the right mix of market and management, tailored to the conditions of particular countries, so as to achieve development, efficiency, and equity in all of them? In chapter 1, I asked, "How efficient is the market?" Now that we are nearing the end of this volume, let us raise the question again and endeavour to answer it in the light of views expressed by contributors to this volume.

EFFICIENCY OF THE MARKET

More than a decade ago, Robert Solow, in his presidential address to the American Economics Association, pointed out that after two hundred years of studying *how* the market works, economists were not yet in agreement as to *how well* it works. This book provides evidence that the range of disagreement on this question among professional economists has narrowed in recent years. A major factor, of course, is the cataclysmic collapse of the socialist economies, bringing to an end (at least for a long time to come) the twentieth century's major economic, political, and social experiment. None of the contributors was prepared to argue that a centrally planned economy would work better than a market economy, even if the market is not totally free and is flawed with imperfections. Not even – or perhaps especially – André Gunder Frank, whom most people would put at the left end of the spectrum among contributors, takes that view. And none insisted that the market works perfectly, or even that it would work perfectly if it were free from government intervention. The essays by Albert Breton, John Chipman, Murray Kemp, and Richard Musgrave are perhaps closest to the neoclassical mould, but even they admit that the performance of the market can be improved by a few judiciously placed patches. The majority of contributors, moreover, do not embrace the concept of *wertfreiheit* with undiluted ardour, but imply the need for value judgments as a basis for designing development strategies and formulating policies.

To be sure, there are still some differences of opinion. Walt Rostow, on the basis of historical experience, thinks market economies have worked pretty well, but far from perfectly. Irma Adelman, treating history in a different way, thinks they have not done nearly well enough and are unlikely to do much better unless policy is improved. Robin Marris comes to the paradoxical (although Schumpeterian) conclusion that market economies do as well as they do, at least in terms of development, because of their *imperfections*.

It is my own view that, on balance, markets have performed better than governments. The role of government has certainly increased through time, and almost certainly the degree of government failure has increased as well. The degree of monopoly power has probably increased too, especially in terms of access to advanced technology and information. It is less certain, however, that the extent of market failure has increased proportionately. If we replace traditional neoclassical theory with Robin Marris's managerial theory of the firm, we are led to the conclusion that the degree of market failure is almost certainly declining.

It is not really surprising that economists should hold different views on a subject so central to their discipline. How well any particular market works at any point of time is a matter of facts, not of pure theory or logic. There is little disagreement about the facts of market performance. *Evaluations* of this performance differ because of varying preconceptions of how well economies *ought to work*. The major disagreements, however, relate to the question, Where do we go from here? Should some kinds of government intervention be scrapped, and if so, which ones? Should some new kinds of intervention be introduced, and if so, which ones?

Over recent years, there has been a distinct, but not clearly successful, swing away from government intervention towards greater reliance on the market, on the part of both academicians and politicians. Russia, China, and Eastern Europe are struggling painfully towards market economies. In North America, Reagan, Bush, and Mulroney have tried to dismantle parts of their welfare states inherited from earlier administrations, but have run into fierce opposition. Few of their goals have been met, and monstrous budgets and budget deficits continue to plague both the United States and Canada. In the United Kingdom, Margaret Thatcher was perhaps more successful in reaching similar goals; but unemployment, inflation, and other hardships, such as the hated poll tax, led to her overthrow. The New Zealand electorate has rebelled against the Labour government's efforts to move from a highly regulated and protected welfare state to something more closely approaching a free-market economy. In Australia another Labor government, described as out-Thatchering Thatcher, faces dwindling popular support as unemployment and inflation rise together, living standards fall, and crushing balance-of-trade deficits lead to soaring debt.

Why is returning to or creating a free market economy so difficult? Obviously, opposition comes from those who are aware of market imperfections and want the government to combat them or offset them. They lose sight of the fact that the market is much the most convenient instrument for allocation of resources among various fields of production, and that, for the most part, the market does not function badly enough to warrant the tremendous risks and complexities involved in tampering with it. Obviously again, the kind of intervention needed – getting rid of regulations, controls, discriminatory taxes and subsidies, bloated government departments, costly public enterprises, and monopoly power – is often a good deal more difficult politically, and basically more revolutionary, than simply adding a few more government activities to the list. In addition, in most real-world economies, government failure and market failure interact and reinforce each other in a tangled feedback system, so that it is an extremely difficult task to isolate causes of malperformance and determine what must be changed, and even more important, *how* it can be changed.

This particular difficulty is most clearly seen, perhaps, in the field of foreign trade. No country in the world has removed all barriers to trade and then watched "the market" adjust quickly, smoothly, and painlessly to free trade. Moves in the direction of free trade lead to screams of anguish from those hurt by them, rather than to "adjustment." Through political pressure and various dodges, "inefficient" enterprises whose protection is removed often manage to go on producing the same old products, rather than shifting into brand-new fields where "efficiency" and productivity are higher. Moreover, in the case of New Zealand, where a century or more of government failure has produced an economy where most people are engaged in activities in which they are at a comparative *dis*advantage, a suddenly freed market has not only destroyed inefficient industries, as in the case of the automobile industry, but has also led to soaring unemployment, accelerated inflation, and a balance-of-payments crisis. Instead of creating new and more competitive enterprises, New Zealand's most able people, especially among the young, are seeking employment in other countries. A free market alone can bring no quick and easy solutions.

Sydney Afriat argues that protection – diabolically opposed to the magical market – may not be a bad thing in *affluent* societies. I recall a meeting of philosophers and economists in Sydney, Australia, decades ago, assembled to define Australia's "economic philosophy" for a distinguished American philosopher, Yale's Professor Northrup. After days of somewhat embarrassed discussion (Australians do not like searching their hearts and souls in public), the group came up with "protection" and the "fair go": protection of all Australians against all foreigners and of every Australian individual and group against other Australian individuals and groups; and a basic egalitarianism expressed particularly through insistence on equality of opportunity. As mentioned in chapter 1, the philosophy was given concrete form in such institutions as the second-highest wall of protection against imports in the world, the Immigration Restriction Act, the Commonwealth Grants Commission, the Loans Council, and the Commonwealth Arbitration Court, with its nationwide basic wage and hours of work. Thus, protection as a goal in affluent societies was substantially implemented in Australia. Australians were well aware of the costs of protection and of a basic wage bearing little relation to productivity, but they put up with it out of a sense of "fairness," as Albert Breton would have it, or the "Sympathy" called for by Adam Smith and Walt Rostow. There was, in fact, an unwritten but highly effective "social contract" in operation. Today, with increasing Americanization in politics, management style, and trade union style, this social contract is breaking down. The market-oriented government pursues a callous monetarism, and Australian society is becoming increasingly aggressive. Can we be sure that this change is an improvement, given the precarious state of the Australian economy today? This question points to the fundamental difficulty in freeing the market: if we are to modernize the classical paradigm, we must explore ways to find the right balance between "Classical Sympathy" and the market.

SYMPATHY AND THE MARKET

While the various contributors to this volume have evaluated the performance of the market differently, there was a certain unanimity concerning the search for equity. In harmony with Rostow's call for Classical Sympathy to solve world problems, the authors justified equity *on solid grounds of efficiency,*

404 D.J. Savoie and B. Higgins

just as the classicists did. For example, Niles Hansen defends efforts to reduce regional disparities on grounds of efficiency as well as equity. Murray Kemp argues that intervention to reduce international disparities need not be a zero-sum game: both donor and recipient can gain. Kenneth Boulding emphasizes the value of "Liberation," "Learning," and investment in human capital. Paul Streeten stresses the sheer shamefulness of allowing people to starve, and also quotes others to the effect that efficiency requires a healthy, well-fed labour force. Irma Adelman suggests efficient ways of counteracting the harsher aspects of economic growth, especially in its earlier phases. Mark Blaug discusses the most efficient, and at the same time most equitable, expenditure on education. These economists are neither Marxists eager to squeeze the Bosses in order to improve the lot of the Workers, nor bleeding hearts willing to sacrifice a lot of efficiency to gain a little more equity. They are all mainstream economists, well versed in standard economic analysis and interested in using it to isolate measures that can make market economies more efficient.

But how does a society find its way between allowing the magic of the market to take effect and assuring that Sympathy is an integral element of the market economy? Mere hand-outs to people – in particular to social groups, occupations, or regions – are not enough; as Donald Savoie's essay in this chapter shows, they may undermine efficiency. The vast sums spent in Canada to reduce regional disparities have been justified by politicians, and by some economists and other social scientists, in terms of equity. But the problem of regional inequity remains, and much of the money spent has been wasted. Economists of neoclassical bent have argued that Canada would be better off if, instead, the market had been left free to do its job.

One thing is certain. No country is going to have an efficient, centrally planned economy in the near future, and no country is going to have a pure, totally free market economy either. To achieve efficiency, many, if not most, governments must make big government less big, shrinking or scrapping bloated and inefficient government departments and privatizing badly managed public enterprises. But all countries are going to have some sort of blend of market and management, a mix of decisions based on market signals and decisions based on considerations of equity and Sympathy. So, we had better make up our minds to spend as much time and energy finding out how to achieve an optimal blend as we have spent in the past trying to find out how to achieve a Pareto optimum or an optimal central planning system. The century-long debate on "Plan or No Plan" has been very largely a waste of time because it was not concerned with realistic alternatives, although some understanding has emerged from it. Developing a rigorous and relevant "Theory of the Optimal Blend" is the major task confronting the social sciences over the next couple of decades.

TOWARDS A THEORY OF THE OPTIMAL BLEND

I cannot pretend to have a ready-made, rigorous, and relevant Theory of the Optimal Blend to present in this volume. I *can* do three things: I can sketch a new methodology for economics that will, in my view, make the discipline more useful in the search for such a theory; I can suggest one type of reform of public administration that would contribute to the reorganization called for by Donald Savoie; and I can give a few examples from events in Australia which, by illustrating how *not* to manage an economy, may provide some clues as to how to do things right, and how to improve the blend.

A Cautionary Tale

When I began this synthesis in Australia in late 1990, the Australian economy was in crisis. The wool industry, still the source of Australia's major export, was on the verge of collapse. Australian graziers were shooting and burying a targeted 20 million sheep because the bottom had fallen out of the wool market, and at least 14,000 graziers were expected to go bankrupt and lose their land. Meanwhile, thousands of other enterprises were collapsing, including major banks and other financial institutions; these failures were being attributed to freewheeling deregulation by the Labor government as it strove to free the market.

In one sense, the wool crisis reflected the efficient operation of the market. The graziers were responding to falling prices in the way that both classical and neoclassical theory say they should, by reducing supply. In another sense, however, the story illustrates the cobweb theorem, the particular form of market failure caused by imperfect foresight of producers regarding supplies and prices. Two years earlier the price of wool was high, while American and European subsidies to their own cattle producers limited exports of Australian beef. The graziers responded by increasing their output of wool. The result was an oversupply of wool, with five million bales in storage, and plunging prices.

There is a third sense, however, in which the wool crisis can be regarded as the result of mishandled Sympathy. Seventeen years ago, the Whitlam Labor government established the Australian Wool Corporation as a statutory body to handle wool sales and protect graziers from the vagaries of the market. It set a floor under wool prices and had authority to tax graziers to finance the scheme. For some years the system worked reasonably well, but in recent years the floor was maintained despite falling world market prices, and the corporation borrowed billions of dollars to help finance the gap between the floor and the world market price. The government underwrote the loans. At the time of writing, the government has removed this support of the floor and has paid the graziers $1.80 a head for killing sheep instead, leaving the farmers with a $3-billion debt.

So what do we have here, market failure or government failure? Obviously, it is a particularly evil combination of both. At the root of the evil is excessive government intervention by the United States and Europe to protect their own farmers. The action by the Australian government in defence of Australian farmers might be justified in the name of Sympathy, although such stabilization schemes have seldom worked for long. What is not justified is enabling the Wool Corporation to prevent marginal adjustments in the market for so long that now the required adjustment is far from marginal and too vast for the market alone to handle quickly, smoothly, and painlessly. This experience provides a warning against inept intervention in the market.

On the other hand, Australia's experience with its financial system highlights the perils inherent in too hasty and inadequately monitored deregulation. The field of banking and finance was one of the first to be deregulated by the Hawke administration. One quick result was that foreign banks, with their basic reserves in other countries, flooded into Australia. In addition, many non-banking financial institutions, like building societies, assumed banking functions. Consequently, the Reserve (central) Bank of Australia virtually lost control of bank lending and of the money supply. Thus, since monetary policy is practically the only instrument used by the government to manage the economy, the emasculation of monetary policy means losing control of the whole economy. Interest rates are maintained at a high level to restrain inflation, but the high rates also attract short-term capital from abroad, so that the whole financial system retains a high degree of liquidity, and inflation is accelerating nonetheless. Meanwhile, the high-interest rates discourage long-term investment that expands the economy and creates jobs. So unemployment in Australia is increasing, too, and the GNP is falling.

Deregulation and lack of expert supervision also result in dubious banking practices. There are reports of leading banks literally pressing large loans on clients, especially farmers, which with today's depressed prices the borrowers cannot repay. Some of the country's private banks have encouraged clients to borrow abroad, to take advantage of lower interest rates abroad. The clients thus acquired debts in foreign currencies, exposing themselves to all the risks of the foreign exchange market. With the depreciation of the Australian dollar, many of the clients were unable to meet their obligations for repayment and were forced into bankruptcy. As part of the deregulation process, the State Banks of two states with Labor governments were instructed to conduct themselves like private enterprises. They interpreted this instruction to mean that instead of filling gaps in the credit structure, such as small businesses and low-cost housing, they should compete for the "high fliers," risky enterprises with the *chance* of high returns mainly by buying and selling other enterprises rather than producing goods and services themselves. This was a type of banking for which management obviously had neither the experience nor the skills. As a result, they lost billions of dollars and had to be bailed out by the state government. Deregulation is not a cure-all. Edna Carew, speaking of recent events in Australia, writes: "The picture has been clouded by a tendency to confuse a deregulated financial market with an unregulated market."[17]

Fundamentally, the Australian debacle reflects a dearth of Learning and Sympathy, and a serious lack of experience, skills, and perception. One also gets the impression that at times some policy makers lost sight of their goals. They want to make their entrepreneurs competitive internationally, yet they maintain such excessively high interest rates and taxes remain so high that entrepreneurship is effectively throttled. Less competitive enterprises have been bankrupted; more efficient enterprises are moving overseas where conditions are more favourable. Some Australians also seem to have forgotten that the ultimate goal of development is improved social welfare. *The* Australian dream is still to own one's home; over many decades the percentage of Australian families who did so hovered around 70 percent. After years of soaring mortgage rates, the percentage of home-owners shows signs of declining. Moreover, one encounters with increasing frequency the argument that too much capital is being diverted to home-ownership and that Australians should rent their accommodation so that more capital is available for "productive" investment. A deliberate policy of converting Australians from a nation of home-owners into one of renters would be the very antithesis of Boulding's "Liberation." The goal is not accelerated capital accumulation and growth as such, but development: that is, improved social welfare. Moreover, the argument is false. Somebody has to own and finance the housing. What the pro-renters are really proposing is that Australians accept a lower standard of housing to provide more capital for other things. They think that they are rallying to the cause of the market, but what they are advocating comes closer to what was actually done in the Soviet Union: crowding families into small apartments so that more capital would be available for building up heavy industry.

Australia may learn the hard way that the market can not only eliminate inefficient industries, but complete the undermining of an inefficient economy. During a debate on the Australian economy, it was pointed out that the New Zealand experience showed that after decades of protection of inefficient industries, too rapid deregulation narrows the options for what New Zealanders can still do; Australia must act before its own options have declined too far. Increasingly the forlorn question is asked, What can Australia make that the outside world will want to buy?

What happens to an inefficient national economy? Albert Breton points out above that a provincial government unable to meet competition cannot simply declare bankruptcy as an enterprise can. Still less can an entire nation declare itself bankrupt and disappear. Australia has an enormous foreign debt as a consequence of balance-of-trade deficits created, in part, by the extinction of local industry as the market was freed. Australia has been meeting this debt service by allowing Japanese investment on an enormous scale. Following Breton's line of reasoning, does Australia eventually come virtually under the control of a richer, more efficient country?

The international business community is neither blinded nor particularly pleased by the outcome of the Australian government's gestures in the direction of deregulation, privatization, and liberalization. In its annual Business Confidence Survey, conducted in early 1991, the Swiss-based World Economic Forum, together with the International Institute for Management Development, ranked Australia among the top-five "falling stars" (the other four were the United States, the United Kingdom, Poland, and Brazil). The 1,500 international business leaders polled found Australia to be one of the least competitive countries in the world and the one most vulnerable to recession over the next two years.[18]

Countries wishing to free their markets should make sure in advance that the requisite expertise for adjustment is already in place or that the system of education, training, and research can produce it in short order. They should also be sure that venture capital is available, and that the elusive quality of entrepreneurial capacity for rapid adjustment is already present in the required amount and in the right places, or that it can be quickly generated and applied. They should also be aware of *what their economic actors are likely to do in response to policies and what they are capable of doing in a given situation*. To assure that these conditions are put in place, a small team of experts may need to be recruited, as recommended in chapter 1. As well, governments should have the capacity to protect the required team of experts from being swamped and stifled by their own bureaucracies, as Donald Savoie has warned.

The truth is that freeing a socialist or over-regulated economy is a very complicated process. Getting rid of harmful controls, regulations, taxes, and subsidies and making markets more competitive – these measures must be managed with a great deal of skill if serious disruption is to be avoided, as the experience of the socialist countries, along with Australia and New Zealand, amply demonstrates. This kind of management must be based on thorough analysis by a team with the right kind of expertise to determine the optimal timing and sequence of various measures of liberalization, a team that can design instruments to help enterprises "adjust" to sudden exposure to competition and achieve smooth transitions.

Here the experience with "development planning" under the aegis of the various bilateral and multilateral aid programs can provide useful lessons. When former colonies became independent after the Second World War, most of them inherited from their former imperial masters highly regulated economies, often combined with large public sectors as well. Few of the ex-colonies were enamoured of capitalism, liberalism, and the free market, so they often made things worse by heaping new regulations of their own on the already large pile of old ones. Accordingly, much of the so-called development planning then undertaken by teams provided by foreign-aid programs was really a matter of persuading inexperienced governments to liberalize, deregulate, and privatize, while finding ways of doing all that without totally disrupting the existing economy. This sort of "planning" has been highly successful in a good many countries and may provide models for meeting today's similar problems.

A Glimpse of an Unregulated Market

As I was finishing this synthesis, I went on a mission to Southeast Asia for CIDA, and glimpsed what was happening in the international market. In Kuala Lumpur, I met a group of airline pilots from New Zealand at a cocktail party. They told me that when their government sold a large chunk of New Zealand Airways to a foreign consortium, many pilots lost their jobs, and fifty-one of them were now working for Malaysian Airlines. In both Kuala Lumpur and Bangkok, I learned that with the labour shortages and rising wages in Malaysia and Thailand, investors in Japan, South Korea, Taiwan, and other Asian countries were looking at Burma, Bangladesh, and Vietnam, where labour was still cheap, as potential sites for new enterprises. Thus, the international market (relatively unregulated) was working just as both classical and neoclassical theory said it should, moving labour and capital to countries where opportunities are better.

The probable flow of capital to Burma, Bangladesh, and Vietnam brightens prospects for these desperately poor countries. Why, then, should we not rejoice when Australian enterprises abandon Australia for Taiwan, Thailand, Malaysia, and Mexico? The answer is simple. The Asian movement of capital is a consequence of successful development, but the emigration of industry from Australia is a response to failure rather than success. For over a century, we have seen a positive "dominoes effect" in Asia. From the late nineteenth century onwards, Japan began borrowing technology from Europe, especially Germany, and the foundations of the Japanese Miracle were laid. After the Second World War, with US assistance and further transfers of technology, Japanese growth accelerated and Japan became a high-tech industrial giant. As Japanese wages rose, Japanese entrepreneurs began transferring capital to Taiwan, South Korea, and Hong Kong, where labour costs were lower. These countries then experienced rapid growth in their turn, labour costs rose there, and skilled labour became scarce. Consequently, investors in those countries, and in North America and Europe as well, turned to Malaysia, Thailand, and

Indonesia. More recently still, as we have seen above, they are now considering such seriously retarded countries as Bangladesh, Burma, and Vietnam.

Unfortunately, in Australia's case, the movement of industry abroad does not resemble the Asian case of industrial expansion and technological progress leading to a high rate of increase in productivity and wage rates. Instead, money wages have been stagnant, real wages have fallen, and unemployment is high and rising. The reasons for quitting Australia lie in dissatisfaction with the mismanagement of the economy, high interest rates, high taxes, uncertainties regarding future industrial relations, and Australia's obvious inability to compete in the world markets for services and manufactured goods. Thus, Australia must counter with vigour the *black* magic of the market, and Southeast Asia must counter the harsh side-effects of economic growth as the market works in its favour.

Two Successful Experiments: Third World Development Efforts and Foreign Aid

If indeed capital flows into Burma, Bangladesh, and Vietnam, leading to rapid industrialization, the harshness of the early years of the process can be alleviated by measures of the sort suggested by Adelman and Blaug, through domestic action and appropriate foreign aid. After forty years of experimentation, the foreign-aid agencies have learned a good deal. Indeed, if we look at the extraordinary economic experiments of this century, referred to in the introduction, laurels go to the international development effort, involving both industrialized and developing countries in joint programs, and to the Third World countries themselves, for programs and policies carried out on their own.

There have been many mistakes and failures; but on balance, Sympathy at the international level, well laced with expertise, has been a success. Certainly everyone engaged in that effort has learned a lot. When we consider the procession of "approaches" through the successive development decades, they form an interesting learning curve: the Big Push, Balanced Growth, Unbalanced Growth, the Unified Approach, the Basic Needs Approach, Another Development – a progression from Marxist or neoclassical approaches to "the Market with a Human Face." There remains much to be done on the international level. The new global financial market needs global rules for its management. We need Richard Musgrave's international tax system. The General Agreement on Tariffs and Trade (GATT) has far to go, especially where agricultural protection and subsidies are concerned. Shooting and burying millions of sheep in a world where famine still exists is an illustration at the international level of that inertia which so enrages Paul Streeten. Nevertheless, as Irving Brecher notes, international aid can take a share of the credit for Third World performance since the Second World War.

On the usual criteria of economic performance, the Third World countries are doing better than the First (industrialized capitalist) and much better than the Second (socialist) World countries: growth rates, unemployment and inflation, savings and investment ratios, incremental capital:output ratios, balance of trade, terms of trade, income distribution, all adding up to improved development, efficiency, and equity. There are, of course, big differences in the performance of different developing countries, including many tragic failures. Those that are doing best at the moment are the NICs (newly industrializing countries) and the ASEAN (Association of South East Asian Nations) countries. Is there any ideology or paradigm that unites these success stories? It is not easy to track one down. There is a generally expressed faith in private enterprise and the market, but there remains a good deal of regulation, and the public sectors, including public enterprises, are substantial. Private enterprises are left comparatively free to make profits, and do; but national and regional planning – the injection of expertise – plays an important role in the development process. These countries are in general "outward looking," their economies are open, foreign trade is comparatively free, and export promotion outweighs import replacement, but protection for import replacement does exist. The exact mix of all these aspects of development policy varies a good deal from country to country. Perhaps the unifying characteristic is a healthy pragmatism, identifying strengths and weaknesses, problems and potential, and devising tailor-made policies to fit, cutting the coat according to the cloth.

In sum, I believe that one of the main reasons for the emergence of these successful countries is that they did not unquestioningly embrace either of the two main paradigms inherited from the past century. Rather, they sought to learn from both, taking from each elements that seemed to serve their needs, and shaping them to fit their own culture, customs, and values (often high on Sympathy). They recognized that their economic men (and women) could differ in some respects from those of Adam Smith or Karl Marx, and that their development strategies and policies must differ accordingly. With this pragmatic approach, their vision not blinded by any one ideology, they could reach more realistic conclusions than those which elevated one or other of the earlier paradigms almost into a religion. These considerations have informed my own suggestions for a new approach to development theory.

Towards a Semi-anthropological Approach

I think that economics has gone as far as it can go on the basis of behaviourial assumptions that are supposed to apply universally and be true always and everywhere. Human behaviour is *not* the same always and everywhere, and the assumption that it is has led to serious error. In this regard, I am in accord with Brecher in his preference for designing policy at the local level. As a consequence of my regional planning missions, I have become increasingly convinced that intensive, on-the-spot observation of human behaviour – seeing societies steadily and seeing them whole – is not only the best way to design policy, but the best way to construct *theory* as well. So I am writing a book that calls for and illustrates a semi-anthropological approach to economic analysis, with behavioural assumptions for each type of society and economy derived from prolonged on-the-spot observation. I show how familiar tools of economic analysis can be adapted to construct micro-models for types of behaviour that do not conform to the usual assumptions, once one knows what the behaviour patterns really are – who the economic actors are, what they are trying to do, and what the results are. I then show how the models of micro-behaviour can be aggregated into macro-models for each type of society and economy.

This approach has major implications for economic policy. In the first place, *what kind* of macropolicy, and what kind of micropolicy, can be expected to work depends on *what kind* of behaviour is found to exist, and where, and on how widespread each type of behaviour is. In the second place, when a national economy comprises societies and regions that differ drastically in their economic behaviour (have totally different kinds of economic man), *no* macroeconomic policy can, by itself, take care of all the economic problems of all of them. Policy must be tailor-made for each *distinct* society and region.

Thus far I have identified seven major types of society, economy, and behaviour patterns. Each has its own set of leading actors, who determine the pace and pattern of development.

1 The managerial societies of the industrialized capitalist countries (ICCs). The leading actors whose behaviour must be observed on-the-spot are management teams, trade union leaders, government (politicians and bureaucrats who together determine policy), and foreigners (exporters, importers, investors, borrowers, foreign exchange speculators, migrants)
2 Societies dominated by owner-managers, in ICCs
3 The modern sectors of newly industrializing countries (NICs)
4 The modern sectors of other less-developed countries (LDCs)
5 Capitalist landlords in LDCs
6 Village capitalists in some LDCs
7 Peasant societies. These break down into four distinct types:
    a) Societies with scarce land and low productivity per hectare
    b) Societies with scarce land but high productivity per hectare
    c) Societies with abundant land but low productivity per hectare
    d) Societies with abundant land and high productivity per hectare

As we study the actors and their behaviour in each of these types of society, we find that the assumption of simple, straightforward profit-maximization, which still underlies most of neoclassical and Marxist theory, in fact explains economic behaviour fully and satisfactorily for very few of them. Most of the real-life actors are maximizing, minimizing, or optimalizing something different – in some cases, very different.

Category "1" is essentially Robin Marris–style managerial capitalism. The management teams are not essentially owners of means of production, but highly trained and skilled people *maximizing their own rate of advancement*, often in competition with others in the same team, but together *maximizing the rate of growth of the enterprise* within constraints imposed by the necessity of avoiding both stockholders' revolts and excessive indebtedness. The trade union leaders are interested in *staying in power*, share with other people in the management team the interest in the growth of the firm, and within these constraints strive to promote the interests of their membership. Governments (politicians and bureaucrats) are, of course, interested in *staying in power*. Beyond that, the governments of the ICCs want to curtail inflation, to avoid balance-of-payments crises, and in some cases, to limit unemployment. Foreigners have a host of aims, often conflicting. The result is a horrendously complicated game, the results of which are as indeterminate at the outset as that of a championship chess match. Government, however, plays the major role because the strategy of the other players depends mainly on "rational expectations" of what government is going to do. Conflict resolution plays a major role in the game process. It is of interest to note that this case is the one that mainstream economists are least able to handle and for which they are least able to design applicable policy, which may be one reason why, apart from the socialist countries and a few least-developed countries, the ICCs are performing worse in the economic sphere than in any other category. Mainstream economics is based on actors and behaviour patterns that were more typical of nineteenth-century Europe and North America than of today's ICCs. By the same token, it is more applicable to some categories of developing countries than it is to the ICCs.

Category "2" was based initially on comparative studies of francophone and anglophone entrepreneurs in Quebec undertaken for the Royal Commission on Bilingualism and Biculturalism, but similar situations were later found in Malaysia and East Africa. By and large, the anglophone Quebec entrepreneurs conformed to the behaviour patterns of Category "1." The francophone entrepreneurs (owner-managers) behaved in a strikingly different fashion. They felt that business was on the whole conducted in a manner opposed to the interests of society and was justified only as a means to fulfil one's obligations to family and church. They wanted to keep their enterprises small enough to keep complete control in their own hands. They wanted to *minimize risk, conflict, and effort* and to *maximize security, peace, and leisure*. They found it very difficult to save money for investment purposes. Their relations with their labour force were semi-feudal, in both the pejorative and laudatory senses of the term. Needless to say, with such attitudes and values, their behaviour, including their responses to policy, was very different from that of their anglophone neighbours. It should be noted that today, one generation later, this kind of entrepreneurial behaviour is rapidly disappearing in Quebec, being replaced by francophones who quite clearly belong to Category "1." Part of a semi-anthropological approach to economic analysis is the recognition of the need for "revisits," to see whether the society, its actors, and their behaviour have changed since the last field trip.

When we consider Category "3," we see that the behaviour of managers and entrepreneurs in the modern sectors of the NICs is very similar to that of their counterparts in the ICCs, but not identical. The divorce of management from ownership has gone a long way in these countries. In Kuala Lumpur, recently, the chief executive officer of a very large bank told me, with considerable pride, "I run this bank but I do not hold a single share in it." Still, the role of individual and family enterprises and partnerships remains higher in these countries than in the ICCs, so mainstream neoclassical economics is probably more applicable in these countries than in the ICCs. The same can be said for the operations of the modern enterprises in Category "4" and for the capitalist landlords (or employers) of Category "5," except that Yong Sam Cho's "w-1 curve," relating weekly hours of work to the level of nutrition, must be taken into account.

In Category "6," the "village capitalist" is of a different ethnic origin from the majority of villagers, such as the Chinese in Indonesia and the Indians in East Africa. Here, the small-scale capitalist – a batik manufacturer, say – starts with a social contract between himself and the village council. The capitalist, not being really a member of the society, is not bound by its values, morals, and rules, but the sanctions that can be brought to bear if he ignores his contract are powerful, including, as Indonesian experience shows, having his throat slit. This capitalist would be *maximizing profits within the constraints of the contract, and minimizing bodily risk*.

Within the peasant societies of Category "7a," such as those of the African Sahel and Haiti, *risk minimization*, with risk estimated in terms of the danger of starvation, is the dominant consideration. This pattern of behaviour leads to growing several different crops on postage-stamp holdings to minimize risks that all of them will fail. The risks entailed in raising and selling a single crop, and *buying* food, are too great to be considered. Where land is scarce but productivity per hectare high, as in irrigated and terraced rice culture in Southeast Asia, the result is monoculture or close to it. The crop provides food for subsistence, and thus *risk aversion* still plays a major role; but the peasants are highly sensitive to market prices and the proportion marketed varies with price. Where land is abundant but productivity per hectare low, the result is often slash-and-burn, shifting, subsistence agriculture; again risk aversion is high. Finally, when land is abundant and productivity high, we may have the case of the "subsistence affluence" societies of the South Pacific; the society has open to it a genuine choice between more income or more leisure and optimalizes a combination of the two.

Analysis of these widely varying cases involves some complex diagrams. Some tools are familiar: demand and supply curves, indifference curves, production functions – although in some cases the analysis leads to unfamiliar forms of these, such as vertical or backward-sloping supply curves. Other tools, such as the "w-1 curve," are less familiar. The main conclusions that emerge from the analysis are two: the impact of such widely differing behaviour patterns on the economic behaviour of different societies *can be analysed*; and the analysis leads to widely differing results, including different reactions to particular kinds of policy intervention. To be effective, policy must differ from one society to another.

I should like to make it clear that at this stage I am not trying to sell particular policies to particular societies. What I *am* trying to sell is a new methodology. Few economists would deny that if this methodology were universally adopted, economics would become a different discipline. For that very reason I do not expect the economics profession to follow my lead like a band of children lured by a Pied Piper, although there are already a few, such as C.J. Bliss and N.H. Stern, who are moving in the same direction.[19] The innovation I am suggesting is not the only way in which the discipline of economics can be made more effective, but we need *something* radically new, or perhaps several things, and my proposal is one possible means of strengthening our discipline.

Towards Government Reform

Under the heading of government reform, Donald Savoie's remark about regional development policy might be extended to the national economy: governments may not have wrongly intervened, but they may have intervened wrongly. In other words, government intervention as a principle may not have been proven a failure, but governments may have chosen ineffective policies, or implemented them inefficiently, or both.

Most countries need to replace their Brobdingnagian bureaucracies with astute minimal management of their economies. I have suggested that when problems arise as special and complex as trying to move towards a free market, a team of experts should be assembled to provide guidance in determining the optimal sequence and pace of removal of government controls, regulations, and protection; and to suggest measures to assist "adjustment" and assure a smooth transition to a free market economy. Similarly, tailor-made teams could deal with the special problems of particular sectors and regions, and grapple with unresolved problems in the environment, the balance of payments, intergovernmental relations, and last, but certainly not least, the problem of overgrown government itself.

In his book *The Politics of Public Spending in Canada*, Savoie has highlighted the enormous obstacles that are encountered in any attempt to shrink government from *within*.[20] Given these obstacles, what is needed, once again, is a small team of experts recruited from *outside* of government, who, in consultation with senior government officials and cabinet ministers, can hammer out a program to reduce government to a reasonable and efficient scale. In sum, rather than having a gigantic public service equipped to cover every eventuality, relatively small teams, hired for specific tasks and for specific time spans, working alongside a streamlined civil service, could permit the discharge of at least half the bureaucracy and enhance the overall efficiency of the government as a whole.

When we turn to the private sector, we find that there, too, injection of the requisite expertise must be assured if efficient and equitable development is to be achieved. Sometimes the required expertise may be available, at the right times and in the right places, within the private sector itself. But usually, the private sector cannot deliver all of the needed expertise when and where it is required; then government has the responsibility to assemble it in another way. Sometimes, teams of the right complexion can be assembled from existing government departments. More often they must be tailor-made, and the government's task is to recruit the team and pay for it in the way that development planning teams are assembled under the aegis of international and bilateral aid programs. Perhaps Donald Savoie can design the needed insulation from permanent bureaucracy.

It interests me that the suggestions for ACOA's personnel referred to by Savoie above closely resemble aspects of the teams of experts I endorsed in chapter 1: that staff members be "encouraged to take up new challenges, to not stay in one position, in one office perhaps, or for that matter, perhaps, with ACOA itself for too long ... [to] be dynamic, at the forefront of new knowledge and [be] outward looking," seems to me to describe the situation of a member of an international aid team, whether drawn from a private consulting firm, academia, the business world, or even government! A government servant on a foreign-aid mission may be the same bureaucrat as he or she was in the department back home, but will *behave* differently because the institutional framework is different. For one thing, where government departments often comprise thousands of people organized in a hierarchical fashion, foreign-aid teams seldom exceed fifty people, organized as partners in a joint effort. A similar structure appears in Douglas Hartt's team at Public Works Canada; as I pointed out in chapter 1, it consisted of some staff members, some academics, other independent consultants, and a small private consulting firm, acting with adequate insulation provided by the deputy minister and the minister.

A study published by the Canadian Institute for Research on Regional Development, comparing the effectiveness of regional development planning exercises undertaken by Canadian teams at home and in the Third World (some of the same individuals and private consulting firms were involved in both), found that the operations were much more successful in the less-developed countries than in Canada, largely because

- regional development in LDCs is less ensnared in central-intermediate government relations;
- in LDCs the plans are prepared by tailor-made teams outside of government rather than by central and provincial government bureaucrats;
- the experts in LDCs are more independent of the funding agency than in Canada;
- regional development in LDCs is more detached from government revenue sharing and implementation is more divorced from intermediate governments;
- the private sector is more involved in the planning phase in LDCs; and
- evaluation in LDCs can be made in terms of concrete, clear-cut goals.[21]

The book concludes by stating that "regional development policy in Canada" would be improved by a move in the direction of "an internal CIDA."[22] What I am proposing now is an extension of this same principle to the entire government.

CONCLUSIONS

An "optimal blend" of my own convictions (admittedly derived more from experience than from scientific analysis) and of views expressed by other authors of this book and by Adam Smith leads me to five conclusions:

1 To begin with, we should leave everything possible to individual choice – to the market, to the polls, and to other avenues of individual choice.
2 Bloated public bureaucracies should be reduced to small, streamlined, efficient organizations responsible for minimal management of the economy: for taking care of routine large-scale operations such as the post and transportation, and for national needs such as defence, foreign affairs, foreign trade, and monetary policy. Special problems should be dealt with by small semi-autonomous teams of experts, carefully selected for solving particular problems. A separate team should be appointed to prepare a program for shrinking and reorganizing the bureaucracy itself.
3 The pursuit of efficiency, equity, and development will be easier if conducted within a framework of pragmatism, rather than within one of ideological commitment to either of the two main paradigms inherited from the nineteenth century. Blind acceptance of either can lead a society into deep trouble. Their pragmatism has saved the NICs and the ASEAN countries

from opting for centralized planning, but has also induced them to "plan" in the sense of injecting badly needed expertise into the decision-making process. Like Japan before them, they have achieved rapid growth (development, efficiency, and considerable equity) by doing things right. Case histories, such as those recounted above, underline the benefits of applying the expertise needed to get things right, and the dire costs of not applying it and so getting things wrong. Applying only general theories like Marxism or neoclassical economics does not lead to getting things right.

4   Pragmatism in this context does not mean having no analytical framework as a basis for development strategy and policy. It would be self-destructive for the economics profession to forget the lessons of economic history or to throw away what is valid and useful in the knowledge accumulated over more than two centuries, whether its origins are classical or neoclassical, Marxist or neomarxist, Keynesian or institutionalist. But pragmatism does mean *adding* to this heritage the more directly relevant knowledge that can be gained by on-the-spot observation of actual behaviour in different societies, so that policy decisions can be based on accurate predictions of probable reactions to various policy options.

5   Nowhere is expertise more essential than in striving for the optimal blend of efficient operation of the free market and the exercise of "Sympathy." The most common form of Sympathy is well illustrated by Australia's social philosophy of "Protection and the Fair Go" and the institutions associated with it. But support for disadvantaged or defenceless social groups is not all that is implied by Sympathy.

   Sympathy has many facets; I would include among them the bank manager who chooses to devote attention and credit to small business and low-cost housing as well as to high fliers. While strictly business considerations might have indicated concentration on the latter, rather than devoting the time required to service many small accounts, I have no doubt that Australia would be in much better shape today if there had been more Sympathetic bankers in the past decade. Of crucial importance is seeking ways to achieve equity on solid grounds of efficiency, an endeavour pursued by contributors to this volume. A case in point is Blaug's recommendations for education expenditures that would be at once more efficient *and* more equitable. It is also obvious that vigorous action to create *productive* jobs that would reduce welfare payments is at once more efficient *and* more equitable. An integral and essential element in policy design is *understanding* – knowing as much as possible about the society for which policy is being designed, particularly knowing and understanding what the economic actors are likely to do in response to a proposed policy. The concept also encompasses an element of empathy for and understanding of the target groups, their problems, aspirations, and capabilities, so that decision makers can provide the people with what they *really* want. As pointed out in chapter 1, neither votes with dollars in the marketplace nor votes with ballots at the polls provide all the guidance decision makers need in order to make the right choices.

The whole debate about equity and efficiency in economic development boils down to this: neither imposition of new forms of intervention in the market nor removal of old ones should be undertaken without thorough analysis of their impact on the performance of the economy as a whole, and on the welfare of the various groups of which the society is composed. The impact of various changes in policy should be carefully monitored as time goes by so that the policy can be reversed if it turns out to have been misguided. Compact expert teams are the best vehicle that I know for ensuring the optimal balance between Sympathy and the market.

Would these recommendations, if implemented, lead to a new paradigm? In my view they would. I also believe this approach will prove timely, and consonant with the new swing in the West's continuing search for the Optimal Blend. At the time of writing, in countries like Australia, Canada, New Zealand, and the United States, whose governments have displayed profound faith in market-plus-legislature in recent years, disillusionment is setting in. The political pendulum is beginning to swing.

But a swing to what? The toppling of Margaret Thatcher's poll tax and its subsequent more *equitable* design may prove to be a harbinger of a more equitable approach. Yet at this time, there continues to be an aversion to big government, and at the same time disillusionment abounds with the results of the freeing of the market and also with insufficient freeing of the market. I have suggested a streamlined form of government organization for minimal, efficient management of the economy, leaving as much as possible to the market. I have also suggested how to achieve it. I maintain that the market has not been wrongly freed, but freed wrongly. I have suggested a way in which the market might be efficiently freed. Finally, I have drawn a philosophical precept from Adam Smith: any economic policy should be expertly scrutinized to see that its design is at once the most efficient and the most equitable; any policy aiming at equity should be scrutinized with equal severity for its efficiency. Efficiently implemented, these proposals could lead to true development.

NOTES

1   Benjamin Higgins and Donald J. Savoie, "Conclusions," in Benjamin Higgins and Donald J. Savoie, eds., *Regional Economic Development: Essays in Honour of François Perroux* (Boston: Unwin-Hyman, 1988), 381.
2   Thomas J. Courchene, "Avenues of Regional Adjustment: The Transfer

System and Regional Disparities," in M. Walker, ed., *Canadian Confederation at the Crossroads* (Vancouver: Fraser Institute, 1978), 148.

3   Commission of the European Communities, *The New Structural Policies of the European Community* (Brussels, June–July 1990), 3.

4   Commission of the European Communities, "Regional Policy Is at the Heart of the Development of the European Community," report prepared by Bruce Williams (Brussels, 24 November 1989).

5   Ibid., 7.

6   It was this largely negative perception that led Charles Goodsell to write a book in defence of public bureaucracies, a book, as the author readily acknowledged, that was a polemic in response to widespread bureaucrat-bashing. See Charles T. Goodsell, *The Case for Bureaucracy: A Public Administration Polemic* (Chatham, NJ: Chatham House Publishers, 1983).

7   Quoted in Derek Bok, "A Daring and Complicated Strategy," *Harvard Magazine*, May–June 1989, 49.

8   Quoted in Peter Hennessy, *Whitehall* (London: Seeker and Warburg, 1988), 590.

9   Quoted in Sheldon Ehrenworth, "A Better Public Service Needs Freedom to Manage Its People," *Globe and Mail*, 15 April 1989, B21.

10   Royal Commission on the Economic Union and Development Prospects for Canada, *Report* (Ottawa: Minister of Supply and Services, 1985), 3:148.

11   Alan Cairns, "The Nature of the Administrative State," *University of Toronto Law Journal* 40 (1990): 319–59.

12   Quoted in *Dimension*, winter 1986, 13.

13   Ibid.

14   See Donald J. Savoie, *ACOA: Transition to Maturity* (Moncton: Canadian Institute for Research on Regional Development, February 1991).

15   Ibid.

16   Gerald E. Caiden, "Reform or Revitalization?," in Gerald E. Caiden and Heinrich Siedentoff, eds., *Strategies for Administrative Reform* (Lexington, Mass.: Lexington Books, 1982), 85.

17   Edna Crew, *Fast Money 3* (London: Allen & Unwin, 1991), 31.

18   *Business Australian*, 5 April 1991, 15, 25.

19   See C.J. Bliss and N.H. Stern, *Palanpur: The Economy of an Indian Village* (Oxford: Clarendon, 1982).

20   Donald Savoie, *The Politics of Public Spending in Canada* (Toronto: University of Toronto Press, 1990).

21   Higgins and Savoie, eds., *Regional Economic Development*.

22   Ibid., 326.

Selected Works of
Benjamin Higgins

BOOKS

1946 *Public Investment and Full Employment*. Montreal: International Labour Office.

1952 *What Do Economists Know: Six Lectures on Economics in the Crisis of Democracy*. Melbourne: Melbourne University Press.

1957 *Indonesia's Economic Stabilization and Development*. New York: Institute of Pacific Relations.

1959 *Economic Development: Problems, Principles and Policies*. New York: W.W. Norton.

1962 *United Nations and U.S. Foreign Economic Policy*. Homewood, Ill.: Richard D. Irwin.

1963 *Social Aspects of Economic Development of Latin America* (with José Medina Echavarria). Paris: UNESCO.

1963 *Indonesia: The Crisis of the Millstones* (with Jean Downing Higgins). Princeton, NJ: D. Van Nostrand.

1965 *Technical Assistance and the Economic Development of Greece* (with Angus Maddison). Paris: OECD.

1967 (editor) *Investment in Education*. Bangkok: UNESCO.

1968 *Japan and Southeast Asia* (with Jean Downing Higgins). New York: Harcourt Brace.

1969 *The Economic Impact of Alternative Sites for the Proposed Montreal International Airport*. Ottawa: Department of Regional Economic Expansion.

1969 *Les Disparités Régionales au Canada et au Québec*. Québec: Office de Planification du Québec.

1970 *What Do Economists Know?* Shann Memorial Lecture. Perth: University of Western Australia Press.

1970 *Les Orientations de Développement Economiques Régional dans la Province du Québec.* Ottawa: Department of Regional Economic Expansion.

1976 *The Process of Economic Development.* Study Paper No. 64. Ottawa: Economic Council of Canada.

1979 *Economic Development of a Small Planet* (with Jean Downing Higgins). New York: W.W. Norton.

1986 *The Rise – and Fall? – of Montreal.* Moncton, NB: Canadian Institute for Research on Regional Development.

1989 *The Road Less Travelled: A Development Economist's Quest.* Canberra: Australian National University. A revised version of this work is forthcoming as *All the Difference: A Development Economist's Quest.* Montreal: McGill-Queen's University Press.

1990 *Regional Policy in a Changing World* (with N. Hansen and D.J. Savoie). New York: Plenum.

1991 *Anthropology: Social Science, Regional Science, Development Theory – or Literature?* Research Report no. 8. Moncton: Canadian Institute for Research on Regional Development.

1991 *The Frontier as an Element in National and Regional Development.* Research Report no. 10. Moncton: Canadian Institute for Research on Regional Development.

ARTICLES AND CHAPTERS

1935 "The Relationship between Psychology and Economics." *Manchester School,* Spring.

1935 "W.S. Jevons: A Centennary Estimate." *Manchester School,* Fall.

1943 "Problems of Planning Public Work." In S.E. Harris, ed., *Postwar Economic Problems.* New York: McGraw-Hill.

1947 "Keynesian Economics and Public Investment Policy." In S.E. Harris, ed., *The New Economics.* New York: Alfred A. Knopf.

1947 "The Economic Man and Economic Science." *Canadian Journal of Economics and Political Science,* November.

1949 "Towards a Science of Community Planning." *Journal of the American Institute of Planners,* Fall.

1950 "Savings and Welfare in the World Economy." *Economia Internazionale,* November.

1950 "The Theory of Increasing Underemployment." *Economic Journal,* June.

1951 "Economic Aspects of the Asian-African Conference and Its Aftermath" (with Guy Pauker). *Economics and Finance in Indonesia,* May–June.

1953 "The Rationale of Import Surcharges." *Economic and Finance in Indonesia,* May.

1954 "Central Bank Reserve Systems and Indonesia's Foreign Exchange Problem." *Economics and Finance in Indonesia*, November.

1955 "Economic Development of Underdeveloped Areas: Past and Present." *Economics and Finance in Indonesia*, January; reprinted in *Land Economics*, August.

1955 "The Dualistic Theory of Underdeveloped Areas." *Economics and Finance in Indonesia*, February; reprinted in *Economic Development and Cultural Change*, January 1956, and in Gerald Meier, ed., *Economic Development*, various editions.

1955 "Interactions of Cycles and Trends." *Economic Journal*, December.

1957 "Prospects for an International Economy." *World Politics*, April.

1958 "Hatta and Co-operatives: The Middle Way for Indonesia?" *Annals of the American Academy of Political Science*, July.

1959 "Políticas de establisación en los paises subdesarrolados." *Trimestro Económico* (Mexico), February–March.

1960 "Assistance étrangère et capacité d'absorption." *Développement et Civilisations*, no. 4, October–December.

1961 "Conditiónes necesarias para un rapido desarollo económico en America Latina." *Económica* (Chile) 19, no. 2.

1963 "Latin American Economic Development." *Economic Development and Cultural Change*, July.

1964 "Southeast Asian Society: Dual or Multiple?" *Journal of Asian Studies*.

1965 "Financing Accelerated Growth." In OECD, *Government Finance and Economic Development*. Paris: OECD.

1965 "Einige Bermerkungen zur Regional Plannung" and "Sektorale und Regional Aspekte des Entwicklungs Plannung." In Kruse-Rodenacker, ed., *Grundfragen des Entwicklungs Plannung*, Berlin.

1969 "Foreign Economic Policy and Economic Development." In Richard Butwell, ed., *Foreign Policy and the Developing Nation*. Lexington: University of Kentucky.

1971 "Planning Allocations for Social Development." *International Social Development Review*, November.

1971 "Pôles de croissance et pôles de développement comme concepts opérationnels." *Revue Européene des Sciences Sociales*, no. 24.

1972 "Regional Interactions, the Frontier, and Economic Growth." In A. Kuklinski, ed., *Growth Poles and Growth Centres in Regional Planning*. The Hague: Mouton; and in O.J. Firestone, ed., *Economic Growth Reassessed*. Ottawa: University of Ottawa Press.

1972 "The Employment Problem in Development." In Eliezer Ayal, ed., *Micro-Aspects of Development*, New York.

1973 "Trade-off Curves and Regional Gaps." In R. Eckaus and J. Bhagwati, eds., *Economic Development and Planning: Essays in Honour of Paul Rosenstein-Rodan*. London: Allen & Unwin.

1974 "The Unified Approach to Development Planning at the Regional Level: The Case of Pahang Tenggara." In A. Kuklinski, ed., *Regional Development and Planning: International Perspectives*. The Hague: Mouton.

1976 "Welfare Economics and the Unified Approach to Development Planning." In A. Kuklinski, ed., *Regional, Urban, and Environmental Policies in Comparative Perspective*. The Hague: Mouton.

1977 "Social Aspects of Regional Planning." In A. Kuklinski, ed., *Social Issues in Regional Policy and Regional Planning*. The Hague: Mouton.

1977 "Economic Development and Cultural Change: Seamless Web or Patchwork Quilt?" In Manning Nash, ed., *Essays on Economic Development and Cultural Change in Honor of Bert Hoselitz*. Chicago: University of Chicago Press.

1978 "Is 'Development' A Dirty Word?" In Antonio Milani, ed., *Studi in Honore di G. Demaria*. Padova.

1978 "Economics and Ethics in the New Approach to Development." In Stuart Armour, ed., *Philosophy in Context*, vol. 7. Cleveland: University of Cleveland Press.

1980 "The Disenthronement of Basic Needs Twenty Questions." *Regional Development Dialogue* 1, no. 1 (Spring).

1981 "The Reluctant Planner: An Overview" (with Jean Downing Higgins). In W.D. Cook and T.E. Kuhn, eds., *Planning and Development Processes in the Third World*. Amsterdam: North Holland (TIMS).

1981 "Dualism and Dependency in Continuing Underdevelopment" (with N.T. Dung). In R.P. Misra and M. Honjo, eds., *Changing Perceptions of Development Problems*. Nagoya: UNCRD.

1981 "Development Poles: Do They Exist." In A. Kuklinski, ed., *Polarized Development and Regional Policies: Tribute to Jacques Boudeville*. The Hague: Mouton (originally published in *Economie Appliquée* 2 [1977]).

1981 "Economic Development and Regional Disparities: A Comparative Study of Four Federations." In Russell Mathews, ed., *Regional Development and Economic Development*. Canberra: Australian National University, Centre for Research in Federal Financial Relations.

1982 "Appropriate Technology: Does It Exist?" *Regional Development Dialogue* 3, no. 1 (Spring).

1982 "Subnational Regions in Subregional Nations." In Benjamin Higgins, ed., *Regional Development in Small Island Nations, Regional Development Dialogue*, special issue, Fall.

1982 "Development Planning." In E.K. Fisk and H. Osman-Rani, eds., *The Political Economy of Malaysia*. Kuala Lumpur and New York: Oxford.

1982 "From Growth Poles to Systems of Interactions in Space." *Growth and Change*, October.

1984 "Jan Boeke and the Doctrine of 'The Little Push.'" *Bulletin of Indonesian Economic Studies*, December, special issue in honour of Heinz Arndt.

1988 "Australian Regional Development in International Perspective" and "Summary and Policy Conclusions." In B. Higgins and K. Zagorsky, eds., *Australian Regional Development*. Canberra: Australian Government Publishing Service.

1988 Chapter 1, "Introduction: The Economics and Politics of Regional Development"; chapter 2, "François Perroux"; chapter 9, "Regional and National Economic Development: Trade-off or Complementarity"; chapter 16, "Conclusions." In B. Higgins and D. Savoie, eds., *Regional Revelopment: Essays in Honour of François Perroux*. London and Boston: Unwin-Hyman.

1991 "Subsidies, Regional Development and the Canada-U.S. Free Trade Agreement." *Canadian Journal of Regional Science*, special issue.

Contributors

IRMA ADELMAN professor of economics, University of California, Berkeley

MARK BLAUG professor emeritus, University of London, and visiting professor, University of Exeter

KENNETH BOULDING emeritus distinguished professor of economcs, University of Colorado

IRVING BRECHER emeritus professor of economics, McGill University

ALBERT BRETON professor of economics, University of Toronto

JOHN S. CHIPMAN regents professor of economics, University of Minnesota

ANDRE GUNDER FRANK professor of economics, University of Amsterdam

MARTA FUENTES FRANK MacArthur Foundation grantee

NILES HANSEN regents professor of economics, University of Texas

BENJAMIN HIGGINS visiting fellow, Australian National University

MURRAY C. KEMP research professor of economics, University of New South Wales

ROBIN MARRIS professor of economics, University of London

RICHARD MUSGRAVE emeritus professor of political economy, Harvard University, and adjunct professor of economics, University of California

W.W. ROSTOW professor of economics, University of Texas

DONALD J. SAVOIE Clément-Cormier chair in economic development, Université de Moncton

NICOLAS SPULBER distinguished professor of economics, Indiana University

PAUL STREETEN professor of economics, Boston University